MILTON: POET OF EXILE

William Blake, "Expulsion from Paradise," Museum of Fine Arts, Boston.

Louis L. Martz

Milton: Poet of Exile

Second Edition
With a new Introduction

Yale University Press
New Haven and London

Originally titled *Poet of Exile: A Study of Milton's Poetry*, this book is now issued in paperback for the first time, with a new Introduction by the author.

Designed by Sally Harris and set in Baskerville type.
Printed in the United States of America by Murray Printing Company, Westford, Mass.

Library of Congress Cataloging-in-Publication Data

Martz, Louis Lohr.
    Milton, poet of exile.

    Rev. ed. of: Poet of exile, 1980.
    Includes index.
    1. Milton, John, 1608–1674—Criticism and interpretation.   I. Martz, Louis Lohr. Poet of exile.   II. Title.
PR3588.M376   1986   821'.4   86–7772
ISBN 0–300–03736–8 (pbk. : alk. paper)

The paper in this book meets the guidelines for permanence and durability of the Committee on Production Guidelines for Book Longevity of the Council on Library Resources.

10   9   8   7   6   5   4   3   2   1

For Edwine

Contents

Introduction (1986)

The myth of exile, says Leszek Kolakowski in a recent essay, "lies at the core of all religions," for "the fundamental message embedded in religious worship is: our home is elsewhere." Pondering this point, he adds, "Suppose that the theologians are right and that our progenitors in Eden would have acquired the knowledge of carnal love and produced offspring, even if they had resisted the temptation and remained blissfully unaware of Good and Evil." Still, under such conditions, he argues, they would never have begun "a race capable of creating" in a larger sense: "Creativity arose from insecurity, from an exile of a sort, from the experience of homelessness." He sees the condition of exile everywhere today: "we live in an age of refugees, of migrants, vagrants, nomads roaming about the continents and warming their souls with the memory of their—spiritual or ethnic, divine or geographical, real or imaginary—home. A total homelessness is unbearable. . . ."[1] Much the same might be said of the Europe of Milton's century, with its wars and religious refugees such as the Huguenots, from whom the very name refugee is derived. Amid such disruption the human response is often a demonstration of sustained creative power, building a home within the self and the foreign society.

This is what St.-John Perse found to be true when in his exile he discovered his creative powers welling forth in praise of the "Princes of exile": "And it is no error, O Peregrine, / To desire the barest place for assembling on the wastes of exile a great poem born of nothing, a great poem made from nothing" (see below, p. 80). And so too Milton in his darkest hours found that his love of that creative Light remained undiminished, was indeed more intense than before his disasters struck.

1. Leszek Kolakowski, "In Praise of Exile," *Times Literary Supplement*, Oct. 11, 1985, pp. 1133–34.

Milton, everyone would agree, is thus a "poet of exile" because he wrote of mankind's exile from Paradise; but beyond this the phrase could also apply to the writer of *Paradise Regain'd,* with the figure of the Son of God wandering solitary in the wilderness, preparing for his great creative mission. It could also apply to the poet who wrote of Samson, "Eyeless in *Gaza* at the Mill with slaves," but gradually displaying a recovery of his inward power to match the recovery of his physical strength. And when we consider Milton's fondness for the pastoral mode in his early poetry, it is possible to think that the phrase applies even to Milton's early years. The situation of the pastoral poet may indeed be seen as wryly indicated in that frontispiece of 1645 which Milton so disliked (see below, p. 31), where the background presents a pastoral scene with a shepherd piping and a shepherd and shepherdess dancing, while in the foreground we have the dour visage of the author, exiled, we might say, by the faulty engraver from the pastoral joys of his imagination. But then all pastoral poetry is in some sense the poetry of exile from that world of imagination where man and woman, despite the sorrows of love, live in a close relationship with nature and with the gods: hence the motifs of pastoral poetry enter so easily into Milton's account of the Garden in Eden.

At the same time the phrase "poet of exile" may suggest an allusion to Ovid, whose relation to Milton plays a large part in this book. One thinks first of Ovid in his literal exile at Tomis on the shores of the Black Sea, banished from all the pleasures of the Rome he loved. As a new translation from the *Tristia* says:

> If anyone *there* still remembers exiled Ovid, if my
>   Name survives in the City now I'm gone,
> Let him know that beneath those stars that never dip in Ocean
>   I live now in mid-barbary, hemmed about
> By savage Sarmatians, Bessi, Getae, names unworthy
>   Of my talent! . . .
>   No sweet grapes here beneath thick shady vine-leaves,
>   No frothing must to top up the deep vats;
> No orchards, no fruit-trees, no apple on which Acontius
>   Could cut the message for his love to read;
> Nothing to meet the eye here but bare plain, leafless, treeless—
>   Not the habitat any luckier man would choose.

> *This*, with the whole wide world's expanse to choose from,
>   Is the region selected for my punishment![2]

But not long before his exile Ovid had completed the *Metamorphoses*, with those ringing final lines (one would like to think—it has been suggested—that the final passage may have been added after his exile): "And now my work is done, which neither the wrath of Jove, nor fire, nor sword, nor the gnawing tooth of time shall ever be able to undo. . . ." That is indeed a solemn and lofty conclusion for a poem often now remembered chiefly for its wit and for the endless fascination of its tales of passion. Or perhaps it is considered as a handy encyclopedia of ancient myth, frequently consulted but seldom read entire, seldom realized as the *carmen perpetuum*, the unbroken song, whose hexameters everywhere announce the author's design to rival Vergil's *Aeneid*. Certainly for the Renaissance the *Metamorphoses* held deeper meanings. We look with astonishment at the effort of the Renaissance commentators to allegorize Ovid, but the best of them, such as George Sandys, present their case reasonably. They are not simply justifying an illicit enjoyment; they are finding something in Ovid that is really there, according to their general view of the meaning of all ancient fables. Thus Sandys in the preface to his translation finds "Some [fables] under Allegories expressing the wonderfull workes of nature; Some administring comfort in calamitie; others expelling the terrors and perturbations of the mind; Some inflaming by noble examples with an honest emulation . . . For the Poet not onely renders things as they are; but what are not, as if they were, or rather as they should bee, agreeable to the high affections of the Soule." The poets, he declares, "among the Heathen preserved that truth of the immortalitie of the Soule."[3]

The Renaissance commentators were right, I think, to feel that Ovid's concern with ancient myth, both here and in the *Fasti*, went deeper than a mere delight in the witty narration of amusing or horrifying stories. Ovid searches in these tales for the roots of

2. *Tristia*, III.x.1–6, 71–78, trans. Peter Green, *TLS*, Oct. 11, 1985, p. 1143. This issue of *TLS* has for its theme "Exiles and Refugees."

3. George Sandys, *Ovids Metamorphosis Englished, Mythologiz'd, and Represented in Figures* (Oxford, 1632), "To the Reader." See Deborah Rubin, *Ovid's Metamorphoses Englished: George Sandys as Translator and Mythographer* (New York and London: Garland, 1985), chap. 2.

human passion and its consequences; his gods and goddesses become the emanations of forces eternally present in his universe of constant change. He can do all this because he views the myths from a skeptical distance: he has for them the affection of a nonbeliever not very far removed from an age of belief. He preserves these myths as memorials of a past when people could believe that men and women and the gods lived together—often tragically and unhappily—but at least the divine and the human in that past seemed to share one undivided world—a single home.

In this sense, then, Ovid in the *Metamorphoses* is a poet of exile, writing, like Milton in *Paradise Lost,* of an age that no longer exists, but which he hopes to preserve in his affectionate memory. One can see that there was, for this reason, a deep affinity between the two poets of exile, and hence we have the manifold evidence of Milton's lifelong love of Ovid, evidence presented at various points throughout this book. By the concentration of Ovidian motifs in chapters 1 and 4 (see especially pages 6–7, 17–19, and 90–92), along with brief allusions to Ovid elsewhere, I hoped to prepare the way for a sort of Ovidian epiphany in Part III, where the presence of Ovid in *Paradise Lost* is developed at length. I would like to take this opportunity to add some further thoughts on this relationship, arising from the preparation of several lectures since the first publication of this book.

Milton's admiration for Ovid and his saturation in Ovidian rhetoric and themes are thoroughly demonstrated in one of his very earliest poems: Elegy I, the Latin poem written when he had been rusticated after a quarrel with his tutor during his second year at Cambridge. The poem's opening prepares the way for a remarkable tribute to Ovid. "At present," he says, writing his poem as an epistle from London,

> I feel no concern about returning to the sedgy Cam and I am troubled by no nostalgia for my forbidden quarters there. The bare fields, so niggardly of pleasant shade, have no charm for me. How wretchedly suited that place is to the worshippers of Phoebus! It is disgusting to be constantly subjected to the threats of a rough tutor and to other indignities which my spirit cannot endure [Caeteraque ingenio non subeunda meo]. But if this be exile [Si sit hoc exilium], to have returned to the paternal home and to be carefree to enjoy

a delightful leisure, then I have no objection to the name or to the lot of a fugitive and I am glad to take advantage of my banishment [Laetus et exilii conditione fruor].[4]

The pleasant conditions of his "exile," contrasted with the "nuda arva" and the rough inhabitants of Cambridge, suggest how different this poet's situation is from that of the other poet who suffered banishment to Tomis, the poet whose words he has already echoed (and will continue to echo plentifully throughout the poem):[5]

> O utinam vates nunquam graviora tulisset
> Ille Tomitano flebilis exul agro;
> Non tunc Ionio quicquam cessisset Homero
> Neve foret victo laus tibi prima, Maro.

Ah! Would that the bard who was a pitiful exile in the land of Tomis had never had to bear anything worse! Then he would have yielded nothing to Ionian Homer and you, O Maro, would have been conquered and stripped of your prime honors.   [21–24]

As one scholar has said, "his ranking of Ovid as potentially equal to Homer and above Virgil indicates the degree of his youthful admiration."[6] It was a degree of admiration, or rather affection, that continued throughout his life.

Milton's absorption into the world of Ovid is indicated here by the dozens of Ovidian allusions and turns of style: it is indeed an Ovidian epistle from exile, done in the verse form of Ovid's own epistles. The echoes here are drawn from virtually all of Ovid's writings. There is an overt reference to Ovid's *Heroides* (1.63) and another to Ovid as "Tarpeia Musa" (1.69), Ovid's home being near the Tarpeian rock. Above all there is the continuous parallel explored by Ralph Condee—the implicit, reverse, and ironic parallel

---

4. Lines 11–20. Texts and translations for Milton's Latin poetry are taken from *John Milton: Complete Poems and Major Prose*, ed. Merritt Y. Hughes (New York: Odyssey Press, 1957).

5. See the many parallels cited by Douglas Bush in *A Variorum Commentary on the Poems of John Milton*, I (New York: Columbia University Press, 1970), especially the notes to lines 9, 11, 12, 19, 21–22: "Ovid often begins a line with *O utinam*" (p. 50). Compare the passages just quoted from the *Tristia* (III.x): barbaric inhabitants, bleak landscape, unsuitability to the creation of poetry: "quam non ingenio nomina digna meo" (l. 6). Ovid at the close of this poem (l. 75) describes the scene as "nudos sine fronde, sine arbore, campos."

6. *Variorum Commentary*, I, 50. ·

between Ovid's exile from Rome and Milton's exile from Cambridge.[7] Ovid's exile, as he constantly laments in his epistles, deprived him of all the urban delights that Milton says he now enjoys in London: the theater and the beautiful young women. The really barbaric place is the Cambridge from which Milton has been so fortunately exiled! This irony may help to explain why Milton's account of the dramas he is "watching" in London seems to describe, not English plays, but Roman comedy and Greek or Senecan tragedy, which he is reading; these were the plays that banished Ovid once enjoyed at Rome in a theater that Milton describes in terms reminiscent of Ovid himself.

Here in this very first elegy we thus meet the theme of exile, and we might predict from this elegy the state of symbolical exile that lay ahead for Milton: "ingenio non subeunda meo"; my *ingenium*,[8] my natural capacity, my genius, the very essence of my being, cannot endure such indignities. So, later on, the threat of censorship brought forth the *Areopagitica,* and still later, "though fall'n on evil dayes, / On evil dayes though fall'n, and evil tongues," he sings his great poem "In darkness, and with dangers compast round, / And solitude," hoping defiantly to find fit audience, though few. As the chorus says at the close of *Samson Agonistes*:

> he though blind of sight,
> Despis'd and thought extinguish't quite,
> With inward eyes illuminated
> His fierie vertue rouz'd
> From under ashes into sudden flame. . . .

What I am suggesting, then, is that Ovid and Milton, with all their vast differences, nevertheless shared a quality of independent vision, a stubborn, even reckless independence based essentially upon their belief in the immortal power of the poet as *vates*. *Ille ego Romanus vates*: Ovid asserts his claim even as he apologizes for having to use the Sarmatian language and for perhaps allowing some of its corruptions to slip into his poetry:

Yet for fear of losing the use of the Ausonian tongue and lest my

7. Ralph Condee, *Structure in Milton's Poetry* (University Park and London: Pennsylvania State University Press, 1974), pp. 21–27.
8. Compare Ovid's similar use of *ingenium* (note 5 above).

own voice grow dumb in its native sound, I talk to myself, dealing again with disused words and seeking again the ill-omened currency of my art. Thus do I drag out my life and my time, thus do I withdraw myself from the contemplation of my woes. Through song I seek oblivion from my wretchedness. If such be the rewards I win by my pursuit, it is enough.[9]

Sat est: fit audience, though I speak to myself alone; Ovid relies upon his poetry to save him, if not from exile, then from despair. It is such a quality that made both Ovid and Milton, inevitably, exiles from the society in which they lived.

The full complex of Milton's independent vision is brought together very early in his career in three poems from his twentieth or twenty-first year, 1629: Elegy V, "On the Coming of Spring;" the ode "On the Morning of Christs Nativity;" and Elegy VI, the epistle to Diodati written during the Christmas festivities of that same December or in early January.

Elegy V, in theme, style, and allusion, is the most consummately Ovidian of all Milton's poems. The theme of Time's movement in its perpetual cycle is announced in the opening line: "In se perpetuo Tempus revolubile gyro." We are plunged at once into Ovid's perpetually metamorphosing universe; then soon the Ovidian devices of style appear:

> Fallor? an et nobis redeunt in carmina vires,
>   Ingeniumque mihi munere veris adest?
> Munere veris adest, iterumque vigescit ab illo
>   (Quis putet?) atque aliquod iam sibi poscit opus.

Am I deluded? Or are my powers of song returning? And is my inspiration with me again by grace of the spring? By the spring's grace it is with me and—who would guess such a thing?—it is already clamoring for some employment.   [5–8]

Fallor? an is "an especially Ovidian mannerism,"[10] while the parenthetical query and the verbal repetition are hallmarks of the Ovidian mode. Then follows a variety of Ovidian terms and qualities; all these, coming at the outset of the poem, serve to set our minds firmly in an Ovidian mould, despite the many other authors

9. *Tristia*, trans. Arthur Leslie Wheeler, Loeb Classical Library (London: Heinemann, 1924), V.vii.55–68.
10. *Variorum Commentary*, I, 97.

echoed here. "I am driven on by the madness [furor] and the divine sounds within me. Apollo himself [comes]—I see the locks that are braided with Daphne's laurel—Apollo himself comes." Thus the translator, but Milton does not say *Apollo* and *Daphne*. He uses the Ovidian epithets:

> Delius ipse venit—video Peneide lauro
> Implicatos crines—Delius ipse venit.   [13–14]

These are the first of many such epithets in the poem: *Lycaonius, Luciferas, Aeolides, Tartesside, Semeleia, Phaetonteo*—such terms, all in the *Metamorphoses*, constantly remind us of that work.[11] Then we have the repeated use of the word *furor* (lines 12 and 22), a word peculiarly associated with the wild inspiration of Bacchus in the *Metamorphoses* (see below, Appendix 2). All these things move us into the heart of an Ovidian universe where love and Ovidian rhetoric reign, as in the witty line, "Semicaperque Deus, semideusque caper": "the god who is half goat and the goat who is half god" (122). This line, like certain other phrases, may have reached Milton through a Renaissance or a late Latin imitator of Ovid, but the ultimate rhetorical model is undoubtedly Ovid himself.[12]

So we move into the pagan finale, where satyrs and dryads lurk in every bush, a passage that culminates in the poem's most resounding Ovidian repetition: "The gods do not hesitate to prefer our woods to their heaven and every grove possesses its own deities. And long may every grove possess its deities! And my prayer to you, O gods, is not to desert your forest home." That splendid repetition shows the slight variation typical of Ovid:

> Et sua quisque sibi numina lucus habet.
> Et sua quisque diu sibi numina lucus habeto.   [132–33]

The words *numen* and *lucus* belong to Ovid himself.[13]

But soon after this springtime revel of 1629, in the Nativity Ode of that year, we find Milton saying farewell to Apollo, who "Can no more divine, / With hollow shreik the steep of *Delphos* leaving."

---

11. See the detailed analysis of these and other Ovidian echoes by Davis Harding, *The Club of Hercules* (Urbana: University of Illinois Press, 1962), pp. 11–17.
12. In the *Ars Amatoria*, 2.24: "semibovemque virum semivirumque bovem."
13. See *Metamorphoses*, 7.95: "lucoque foret quod numen in illo."

And the whole world of Ovid's god-populated forests is purged of pagan deities, with a sense of sadness and loneliness, as the pagan spirits depart:

> From haunted spring, and dale
> Edg'd with poplar pale,
>   The parting Genius is with sighing sent,
> With flowre-inwov'n tresses torn
> The Nimphs in twilight shade of tangled thickets mourn.
>   [184–88]

Yet their absence is brief. Elegy VI, which announces the composition of the Nativity Ode at the end, begins by resurrecting Ovid and his world in the style and tone of Ovidian wit:

> Song loves Bacchus and Bacchus loves songs. Phoebus was not ashamed to wear the green garland of ivy and to prefer its leaves to his own laurel. On the Aonian hills the chorus of the Nine has often mingled with the rout of Thyoneus and raised the cry, *Euoe*. Ovid sent bad verses from the Corallian fields because there were no banquets in that land and the vine had not been planted.   [14–20]

Milton then turns to other authors and to epic themes, but the opening allusions to exiled Ovid and his world of myth remind us that figurations of Ovid can appear in Milton's poetry when least expected.

Thus the first extended Ovidian allusion in *Paradise Lost*, the use of the myth of Scylla in Satan's encounter with Sin and Death, strikes the reader with surprise, as it strikes Satan, for the preceding book and a half of the poem has led the mind in quite another direction: toward the heroic models of Homer and Vergil, and especially Vergil. Milton's use of this particular heritage has been explored so often and so well that there is no need to develop the issue here.[14] But a few remarks on the Vergilian aspects of Milton's opening books may serve to stress the effect of surprise that bursts upon us (and Satan) in the middle of book 2.

With the many allusions to Homer and the lesser allusions to

---

14. See Harding, *The Club of Hercules*; Mario Di Cesare, "Paradise Lost and Epic Tradition," *Milton Studies*, 1(1969): 31–50; Francis C. Blessington, *Paradise Lost and the Classical Epic* (London: Routledge, 1979); George K. Hunter, *Paradise Lost* (London: Allen and Unwin, 1980), chap. 2; Georgia B. Christopher, *Milton and the Science of the Saints* (Princeton: Princeton University Press, 1982), chap. 3.

Ovid in book 1, the prime exemplar that springs to mind at the outset must be the *Aeneid*, for what other epic opens *in medias res* with the hero attempting to encourage his shattered followers after encountering a fearful assault from the elements—an assault inspired by an angry deity? Aeneas, like Satan, represses his own anguish when he speaks to his afflicted followers, saying:

> "Now call back
> Your courage, and have done with fear and sorrow.
> Some day, perhaps, remembering even this
> Will be a pleasure. Through diversities
> Of luck, and through so many challenges,
> We hold our course for Latium, where the Fates
> Hold out a settlement and rest for us.
> Troy's kingdom there shall rise again. Be patient:
> Save yourselves for more auspicious days."
> So ran the speech. Burdened and sick at heart,
> He feigned hope in his look, and inwardly
> Contained his anguish.[15]

Later, as he views the paintings of the Trojan war in Dido's temple, he sheds tears, as Satan later does. Just as we are privileged to watch the building of the palace of Pandaemonium in Hell, so Aeneas watches the building of Carthage. And as he does so, Vergil brings in from Homer and passes on to Milton that famous simile of the bees:

> There the Teucrians
> Were hard at work: laying courses for walls,
> Rolling up stones to build the citadel,
> While others picked out building sites and plowed
> A boundary furrow. . . .
>   as bees in early summer
> In sunlight in the flowering fields
> Hum at their work, and bring along the young
> Full-grown to beehood; as they cram their combs
> With honey, brimming all the cells with nectar,
> Or take newcomers' plunder, or like troops
> Alerted, drive away the lazy drones,
> And labor thrives and sweet thyme scents the honey.
> Aeneas said: "How fortunate these are

15. *Aeneid,* trans. Robert Fitzgerald (New York: Random House, 1983), 1.202–09. Subsequent quotations in verse are also from this translation.

> Whose city walls are rising here and now!"
> He looked up at the roofs, for he had entered,
> Swathed in cloud—strange to relate. . . .   [1.423–39]

Mirabile dictu—a phrase that Milton seems to echo only two lines after his own simile of the bees, near the end of book 1:

> So thick the aerie crowd
> Swarm'd and were straitn'd; till the Signal giv'n,
> Behold a wonder! they but now who seemd
> In bigness to surpass Earths Giant Sons
> Now less then smallest Dwarfs, in narrow room
> Throng numberless. . . .   [1.775–80]

And then the simile immediately following includes the allusion to one of Vergil's best-known similes, the comparison of Dido's shade to the clouded moon, with the words "aut videt aut vidisse putat per nubila lunam." "Phoenician Dido was wandering in the great forest, and soon as the Trojan hero stood nigh and knew her, a dim form amid the shadows—even as, in the early month, one sees or fancies he has seen the moon rise amid the clouds— he shed tears, and spoke to her in tender love."[16] So in Milton the transformed angels

> Throng numberless, like that Pigmean Race
> Beyond the *Indian* Mount, or Faerie Elves,
> Whose midnight Revels, by a Forrest side
> Or Fountain some belated Peasant sees,
> Or dreams he sees, while over head the Moon
> Sits Arbitress, and neerer to the Earth
> Wheels her pale course. . . .   [1.780–86]

Thus from beginning to end of his opening book Milton stresses his emulation and transformation of Vergilian motifs, an effect of course reinforced by the sinuous style, "the sense variously drawn out from one Verse into another," as Milton explains in his famous note on "The Verse" of *Paradise Lost*.

In book 2 the opening council seems primarily Homeric, like the roll call of pagan gods in book 1; but after Satan leaves on his

---

16. *Aeneid*, trans. H. Rushton Fairclough, in *Virgil*, Loeb Classical Library, rev. ed., 2 vols. (London: Heinemann, 1935), 6.450–55. A later passage is also taken from this translation.

mission to earth and the fallen angels disperse to engage in their
various games, songs, debates, and explorations, we return to the
Vergilian model, with a terrible irony, for the closest analogy to
these activities in Milton's Hell is found in Vergil's account of the
activities of the shades whom Aeneas sees in the "happy seats of
the Blissful Groves" (6.637–59) just before he is greeted by the
shade of his father, Anchises. "And he, as he saw Aeneas coming
towards him over the sward, eagerly stretched forth both hands,
while tears streamed from his eyes and a cry fell from his lips:
'Art thou come at last, and hath the love thy father looked for
vanquished the toilsome way? Is it given me to see thy face, my
son, and hear and utter familiar tones?'" Satan's meeting with his
son and daughter in Milton's next scene is hardly one of paternal
and filial joy. Milton enforces his movement away from the Ver-
gilian (and Homeric) model by shifting to the mode of the alle-
gorized Ovid in Satan's meeting with Sin and Death; this scene is
immediately followed by Satan's immersion in an Ovidian Chaos,
a bath from which he emerges changed, utterly changed.

At this point, then, at the close of book 2, the impression that
Milton is going to write an heroic poem after the manner of Vergil
and Homer is dispersed, and a different kind of action begins
with the prologue to book 3. It is worth pausing a moment to
ponder this bold and I think unprecedented creation of an epic
with two beginnings. If we try hard, it is almost possible to imagine
Paradise Lost as a successful poem without the first two books. We
do know the story. But what, then, is the function of books 1 and
2, those books so justly and so universally admired? They seem to
represent a brief epic, a sub-epic, a pseudo-epic, an epyllion, dem-
onstrating Milton's great capacity to write in this heroic vein when
he so chooses, while at the same time demonstrating the essential
weakness of evil in the midst of an illusion of great power, yes,
even an illusion of creative power rivalling God's. For Satan has
succeeded in arousing his troops from their stupefied condition
on the burning lake; they build a capitol; they hold a parliament
(themselves the Rump of Heaven).

Milton's development of this powerful illusion is handled with
his utmost subtlety. The technique might be described as cine-
matic. The scene opens with a blur, formless, shapeless, in that

darkness visible. Then as Satan speaks out of the blur, "With Head up-lift above the wave," verbal order begins to emerge, as Satan's language, at first jagged and hesitant, appalled, gradually takes oratorical form. Then "One by one objects are defined" (in Williams's words): first Satan and then Beelzebub fly above the waves and stand upon the burning shore; then Milton's huge cluster of similes allows the substance of earthly actuality to penetrate the blur, with the famous comparisons that include "the *Tuscan* Artist," the pine "Hewn on *Norwegian* hills," the "Autumnal Leaves that strow the Brooks / In *Vallombrosa*," and the "scattered sedge" of the Red Sea, along with the memory of those "floating Carkases / And broken Chariot Wheels" that marked the Egyptian disaster there. Now, as the fallen angels take on the names and functions of the pagan gods, the history of the Old Testament gives further focus and definition to the scene; and finally, after further oratory and similes, the building of the palace of Pandaemonium develops the full and clear illusion of order and organized power—an illusion that begins to show its weak foundations even as the hellish council meets in heroic session. Milton closes this unified heroic movement toward clarity and definition with a simile that firmly moves the lens from Hell to earth:

> Thus they thir doubtful consultations dark
> Ended rejoycing in thir matchless Chief:
> As when from mountain tops the dusky clouds
> Ascending, while the North wind sleeps, o'respread
> Heavn's chearful face, the lowring Element
> Scowls ore the dark'nd lantskip Snow, or showre;
> If chance the radiant Sun with farewell sweet
> Extend his ev'ning beam, the fields revive,
> The birds thir notes renew, and bleating herds
> Attest thir joy, that hill and valley rings.   [2.486–95]

The pastoral scene, with its suggestions of the Lord's promise in Ezekiel 34, is so clear and joyful that we forget its alleged application to the fallen angels and instead rejoice in an earth that is all our own. But Milton at once steps in to remind us that the warlike threats and panoply that we have witnessed in Hell are parables of earthly actions:

> O shame to men! Devil with Devil damn'd
> Firm concord holds, men onely disagree
> Of Creatures rational, though under hope
> Of heavenly Grace: and God proclaiming peace,
> Yet live in hatred, enmitie, and strife
> Among themselves, and levie cruel warres,
> Wasting the Earth, each other to destroy. . . .   [2.496–502]

After this the illusion of form and order in Hell fades away, and chaos comes again: "the ranged powers / Disband, and wandring, each his several way / Pursues" (2.522–24); some "In confus'd march forlorn . . . With shuddring horror pale" explore their "Universe of death" (2.615–22); Satan himself meets with Sin and Death and makes his troubled, erratic voyage through Chaos to sight the world ahead. Thus the brief epic ends appropriately with the hero's achievement of his immediate goal.

Now, as Milton's poem begins anew, our already changed Satan begins a series of further changes. In book 3 he appears to Uriel in the guise of a stripling cherub; then at the outset of book 4 that guise itself is transformed:

> Thus while he spake, each passion dimm'd his face
> Thrice chang'd with pale, ire, envie and despair,
> Which marrd his borrow'd visage, and betraid
> Him counterfet, if any eye beheld.   [4.114–17]

And soon we see him assuming the forms

> Of those fourfooted kindes, himself now one,
> Now other, as thir shape servd best his end
> Neerer to view his prey, and unespi'd
> To mark what of thir state he more might learn
> By word or action markt: about them round
> A Lion now he stalkes with fierie glare,
> Then as a Tiger, who by chance hath spi'd
> In some Purlieu two gentle Fawnes at play,
> Strait couches close, then rising changes oft
> His couchant watch. . . .   [4.397–406]

It is a series of changes that reaches its lowest point in the image of Satan "Squat like a Toad, close at the eare of *Eve,*" an image that explodes at the touch of Ithuriel's spear into the gigantic figure of the "grieslie King" (4.800–21). Satan now represents, in

books 3 and 4, not the epic or pseudo-epic hero, but the very
principle of change entering into the world of permanence, a prin-
ciple emphasized by the structure of book 4 with its alternating
panels: Satan's utterances of envy and hate alternating with scenes
of pristine innocence and love.

Meanwhile, at our first hearing of Adam and Eve in conversa-
tion, we meet the most detailed imitation of Ovid thus far in the
poem: Milton's echoes of the myth of Narcissus in Eve's tale of
her earliest memories. I have dealt with this briefly in the body of
this book,[17] but now I wish to explore it in closer detail, in the
light of the rhetorical patterns just described in Milton's elegies.
"As I bent down to look" in the lake, Eve says,

> just opposite,
> A Shape within the watry gleam appeerd
> Bending to look on me, I started back,
> It started back, but pleasd I soon returnd,
> Pleas'd it returnd as soon with answering looks
> Of sympathie and love. . . .   [4.460–65]

The technique of repetition we have seen before; here is an op-
portunity for Ovid to use the technique with a special function
that Milton has not missed:

> cunctaque miratur, quibus est mirabilis ipse:
> se cupit inprudens et, qui probat, ipse probatur,
> dumque petit, petitur. . . .

He admires for which he is himself admired. Unwittingly he desires
himself; he praises, and is himself what he praises; and while he
seeks, is sought. . . .   [3.424–26]

Now, in both accounts, a voice of warning intervenes:[18]

> there I had fixt
> Mine eyes till now, and pin'd with vain desire,
> Had not a voice thus warnd me, What thou seest,
> What there thou seest fair Creature is thy self,
> With thee it came and goes: but follow me,
> And I will bring thee where no shadow staies

17. See below, pp. 219–20 and p. 333, note 1.
18. I owe this suggestion to one of my students, Ronald Kopnicki.

Thy coming, and thy soft imbraces, hee
Whose image thou art. . . .   [4.466–72]

In Ovid the warning voice is that of the narrator, who so often
intervenes in Ovid's intimate way:

credule, quid frustra simulacra fugacia captas?
quod petis, est nusquam; quod amas, avertere, perdes!
ista repercussae, quam cernis, imaginis umbra est:
nil habet ista sui; tecum venitque manetque;
tecum discedet, si tu discedere possis.

O fondly foolish boy, why vainly seek to clasp a fleeting image? What
you seek is nowhere; but turn yourself away, and the object of your
love will be no more. That which you behold is but the shadow of a
reflected form and has no substance of its own. With you it comes,
with you it stays, and it will go with you—if you can go.   [3.432–36]

But Adam is not the shadow of an image: he is made in the image
of God, and he will not vanish. "What could I doe," Eve continues,

But follow strait, invisibly thus led?
Till I espi'd thee, fair indeed and tall,
Under a Platan, yet methought less faire,
Less winning soft, less amiablie milde,
Then that smooth watry image; back I turnd,
Thou following cryd'st aloud, Return fair *Eve*,
Whom fli'st thou? whom thou fli'st, of him thou art,
His flesh, his bone; to give thee being I lent
Out of my side to thee, neerest my heart
Substantial Life, to have thee by my side
Henceforth an individual solace dear;
Part of my Soul I seek thee, and thee claim
My other half . . .   [4.475–88]

In Ovid's tale we see also a disturbance and a threatened disap-
pearance of the fair image, followed by a cry for that lovely image
to return. Narcissus becomes distraught by the elusive nature of
the image:

et lacrimis turbavit aquas, obscuraque moto
reddita forma lacu est; quam cum vidisset abire,
"quo refugis? remane nec me, crudelis, amantem
desere!" clamavit; "liceat, quod tangere non est,
adspicere et misero praebere alimenta furori!"

His tears ruffled the water, and dimly the image came back from
the troubled pool. As he saw it thus depart, he cried: "Oh, whither
do you flee? Stay here, and desert not him who loves thee, cruel one!
Still may it be mine to gaze on what I may not touch, and by that
gaze feed my unhappy passion."   [3.475–79]

But Adam's love is not Ovidian *furor*; it is composed of body and
soul; it asks for a response to human touch; and it receives a
different reply:

> with that thy gentle hand
> Seisd mine, I yeilded, and from that time see
> How beauty is excelld by manly grace
> And wisdom, which alone is truly fair.   [4.488–91]

What is the effect of this Miltonic recreation of the Ovidian
myth, almost exactly in the middle of his book of the Garden?[19]
It is not, I think, primarily to stress the vulnerability of Eve,
though it does this; the main effect, I think, is to stress the con-
ditional quality of life in Paradise ("If ye be found obedient"), by
strongly evoking the world of the *Metamorphoses*: to show, under-
lying paradisal life, the possibility of the fallen world to come, that
world of flux and change represented so poignantly by Ovid and
recalled by all the other Ovidian allusions in the poem.

As these chapters on *Paradise Lost* will show, Ovidian myths enter
the poem forcefully at crucial points: at Satan's departure from
Hell; in the first description of the paradisal landscape (the myth
of Proserpine); in the prologue to book 7, where Milton recalls
the fate of Orpheus at the hands of "Bacchus and his Revellers";
in book 9, at the crucial point before the Fall, when Eve insists on
leaving Adam to work separately, and as she leaves Milton sur-
rounds her with a cluster of Ovidian myths; and in book 10, as
Satan returns in triumph to Hell, and Milton disperses his exul-
tation by a scene modelled on Ovid's story of the transformation
of Cadmus into a serpent, with echoes of other Ovidian tales.

19. See the acute analysis of the Eve-Narcissus episode and other aspects of Ovidian
presence in *Paradise Lost* in the recent book by Richard J. DuRocher, *Milton and Ovid* (Ithaca
and London: Cornell University Press, 1985), esp. pp. 85–93. I should like to note also the
recent book by Anthony Low, *The Georgic Revolution* (Princeton: Princeton University Press,
1985); see chap. 7, which tends to support the view of *Paradise Regain'd* set forth below in
Appendix 1.

Ovid, then, along with Homer and Vergil, is a creative force in the imagery, movement, and structure of Milton's epic, as he has been throughout Milton's previous poetical career. Exile has once again brought forth a demonstration of creative power within the heart of a poet who longs for home.

L. L. M.

Acknowledgments

Major portions of this book have received previous publication in earlier versions; these materials have been carefully, sometimes extensively revised, and they have been combined with about a hundred pages of new writing. Details concerning previous publication and extent of revision are given in the headnote to each of the chapters concerned.

I am greatly indebted to the National Endowment for the Humanities for a fellowship that enabled me to complete this work. I also wish to thank the following for permission to include here materials previously published: Yale University Press, University of California Press, Columbia University Press, The Johns Hopkins University Press (*ELH*), University of Pittsburgh Press (*Milton Studies*), *English Literary Renaissance, Ocidente, Yale French Studies,* and *Ventures.* I am deeply grateful to Maynard Mack, Bernard Schilling, Douglas Bush, Ellen Graham, and Isabel MacCaffrey for their warm encouragement of this study, and also to Gordon Williams for advice concerning pastoral poetry and Ovid's poetry. I wish also to thank Sally Serafim for her scrupulous styling of the manuscript, and Sally Harris for her deep interest in the book's physical design. I wish to express my appreciation to the anonymous reader of this manuscript for the Yale University Press, whose wise and tactful suggestions have greatly improved several parts of this book. Finally, I am very grateful to Andrea Snell for assistance in research and for many creative suggestions, especially with regard to the illustrations, and to Alice Kaplan for assistance in research and for indispensable help in the preparation of the manuscript and index.

L. L. M.

Saybrook College
Yale University

PART I

The Shepherd's Trade:
Poems of Mr. John Milton, Both English and Latin
London, 1645

What leaf-fring'd legend haunts about thy shape
Of deities or mortals, or of both,
In Tempe or the dales of Arcady?

Keats

The Pastoral Music:
A Maske Presented
at Ludlow Castle

At the close of the seventh idyll of Theocritus, the poet Simichidas and his companions arrive at the scene of the harvest festival of Demeter, after Lycidas has gone another way, giving his stick to Simichidas "to pledge our friendship in the Muse." Their friendly exchange of songs in the earlier part of the idyll has prepared the way for the harmonious scene at the end where nature and man and the Muses mingle in a happy concord:

> Tall elms and poplars murmured in profusion overhead;
> near by, the sacred water from the Nymphs' own cave
> bubbled up and sparkled; among the shady branches,
> inky crickets chattered busily; far away,
> the tree-frog's croak was muffled in deep thistledown.
> Larks and linnets made their song, the dove his moan,
> bees hummed and hovered round the springs.
> The harvest's richest smells were everywhere;
> the air was filled with fruit-time's fragrance.
> Pears lay round our feet, apples by our side,

3

> rolling in abundance; wild plums in bunches
> weighed the boughs right down to the ground.
> We broke the wine-jars' four-year seals.

But there is more than wine to drink here. Amid the rich vital-
ity, the murmuring, chattering, humming, and singing of nature
in its harmonious fulfillment, the nymphs have graciously served
from their spring a drink to mix with the wine, a drink that for
Milton and the Renaissance could only mean poetical in-
spiration—the gift that has created the pastoral music of this en-
tire Theocritean idyll. Gratitude to Demeter for her gift of food
combines with gratitude to the Muses for their gift of song: both
are mingled here as nature and man join in grateful appreciation
of the gods' bounty:

> Nymphs of Castalia, high on Parnassus' slopes,
> was it quite such a vintage as this
> old Chiron poured for Heracles in Pholus' rocky cave?
> Was it quite such nectar had Polyphemus dancing
> around his folds by the Anapus? Polyphemus the shepherd,
> the mighty man who heaved mountains at ships?

In this context the allusion to Chiron reminds one of his skill in
music, healing, and other arts, while the allusion to Polyphemus
suggests his pastoral role as singer and piper;[1] the two allusions
thus lead into the closing account of the "drink" served by the
nymphs to Simichidas and his companions:

> Say, Nymphs, was either quite such a drink
> as you served for us from your spring that day
> by the shrine of Demeter of the Threshing-Floor?

Then the idyll ends with a prayer for the continuation of all these
gifts, addressed to the mother-goddess who presides over the
fruits of the earth:

> I pray that I may one day plant again
> the great winnowing fork in her heap of corn
> as the goddess smiles her blessing on us,
> with wheatsheaves and poppies in either hand.
>   [7.135–end; trans. Holden][2]

Such is the pastoral music that, in Milton's *Maske,* will answer

the parody of nature's bounty that Comus pours forth in such
cloying abundance:

> Wherefore did Nature powre her bounties forth
> With such a full and unwithdrawing hand,
> Covering the earth with odours, fruits and flocks,
> Thronging the Seas with spawn innumerable,
> But all to please, and sate the curious taste?   [710–14]

In Theocritus this bounty is full and unwithdrawn, but it never
overwhelms, for eating is accompanied with prayer, drinking is
accompanied with song. The "all-giver" is thanked by man's pro-
found appreciation, not only by the act of consumption.

Milton had already provided a glimpse of his answer to Comus's
temptation when, a year or so before his *Maske,* he wrote the
pastoral entertainment *Arcades* to honor the mother-in-law of the
Earl of Bridgewater for whom the *Maske* was presented at Ludlow
Castle. *Arcades* is "Part of an entertainment presented to the
Countess Dowager of *Darby* at *Harefield,* by som Noble persons of
her Family, who appear on the Scene in pastoral habit, moving
toward the seat of State with this Song"—"Look Nymphs, and
Shepherds look." After this opening song has presented its tribute
to the Countess as reigning deity, "the genius of the Wood ap-
pears" in a role almost certainly enacted by Henry Lawes—
foreshadowing his appearance as the Attendant Spirit in the
Maske. But here the Genius represents a fostering and healing
power within nature, not above it, a power related to the healing
and the fostering power of words and music:

> For know by lot from *Jove* I am the powr
> Of this fair Wood, and live in Oak'n bowr,
> To nurse the Saplings tall, and curl the grove
> With Ringlets quaint, and wanton windings wove.
> And all my Plants I save from nightly ill,
> Of noisom winds, and blasting vapours chill.
>
> . . . .
>
> And early ere the odorous breath of morn
> Awakes the slumbring leaves, or tasseld horn
> Shakes the high thicket, haste I all about,
> Number my ranks, and visit every sprout
> With puissant words, and murmurs made to bless . . .
>   [44–49,56–60]

Then from these fostering words and murmurs on earth the Genius moves on to describe how at night he listens

> To the celestial *Sirens* harmony,
> That sit upon the nine enfolded Sphears,
> And sing to those that hold the vital shears,
> And turn the Adamantine spindle round,
> On which the fate of gods and men is wound.
> Such sweet compulsion doth in musick ly,
> To lull the daughters of *Necessity,*
> And keep unsteddy nature to her law,
> And the low world in measur'd motion draw
> After the heavenly tune, which none can hear
> Of human mould with grosse unpurged ear . . .   [63–73]

One cannot miss the implications of the Orphic theory of music so widely held throughout the Renaissance: a theory traced to Orpheus, whose disciples, tradition said, passed this knowledge on to Pythagoras, from whom it passed to Plato and his followers.[3] Thus the neoplatonic "Daemon," the name given to the Attendant Spirit in the manuscripts of Milton's *Maske,* is associated with the Orphic theory of music as the principle that fosters harmony throughout the universe.

Arcades then closes with two songs, apparently sung by the Genius, demonstrating the power of music by voice and string.[4] The final song ties the whole entertainment together: it echoes the opening address of the first song ("Nymphs and Shepherds") and repeats the last two lines of the second song; and it brings together a cluster of Arcadian myths, evoked by the opening and closing allusions to the musical myth of Syrinx:

> Nymphs and Shepherds dance no more
>   By sandy *Ladons* Lillied banks.
> On old *Lycaeus* or *Cyllene* hoar,
>   Trip no more in twilight ranks,
> Though *Erymanth* your loss deplore,
>   A better soyl shall give ye thanks.
> From the stony *Maenalus,*
> Bring your Flocks, and live with us,
> Here ye shall have greater grace,
> To serve the Lady of this place.
>   Though *Syrinx* your *Pans* Mistres were,

> Yet *Syrinx* well might wait on her.
>   Such a rural Queen
> All *Arcadia* hath not seen.   [96–109]

The Arcadian place-names tie the song to the opening lines of the
speech of the Genius:

> Of famous *Arcady* ye are, and sprung
> Of that renowned flood, so often sung,
> Divine *Alpheus,* who by secret sluse,
> Stole under Seas to meet his *Arethuse* . . .   [28–31]

for three of the place-names in the song, Cyllene, Erymanth, and
Maenalus, occur together in Arethusa's account of her flight from
Alpheus: "Right on past Orchomenus and Psophis, past Cyllene
and the ridges of Maenalus, past chill Erymanthus and Elis, I kept
on running" (*Metamorphoses,* 5.607–09, trans. Innes).[5] The moun-
tain Maenalus, one may recall, was the scene of the Arcadian myth
in which the nymph Callisto is seduced by Jove (*Met.* 2.405–65).
The other place-names are directly associated with the myth of
Syrinx: in Ovid's tale, this wood nymph was living in "the chill
mountains of Arcadia" when one day Pan saw her "as she was
returning from Mount Lycaeus"; she refused his proposals and
fled "through the pathless forest till she came to the still waters of
sandy Ladon"—"donec harenosi placidum Ladonis ad amnem /
venerit" (*Met.* 1.689,699,702–03, trans. Innes). There occurred
her transformation into marsh reeds in the arms of Pan: "and
while he sighed in disappointment, the soft air stirring in the
reeds gave forth a low and complaining sound. Touched by this
wonder and charmed by the sweet tones, the god exclaimed: 'This
union, at least, shall I have with thee.' " Then he created the
reed-pipe that bears her name. (*Met.* 1.690–712, trans. Miller).[6]

So too in Milton's masque at Ludlow Ovid's myths of transfor-
mation mingle with the Orphic music as the Attendant Spirit (or
Daemon) becomes a presiding musical presence, healing or caus-
ing to be healed, by his pastoral harmonies, all nature's harms,
and especially those caused by the wiles of Comus. But we do not
realize for quite some time that the masque being presented is a
pastoral, since the first half of the work is almost entirely given
over to anti-pastoral or un-pastoral elements.

First comes the long prologue, like the prologue of a god in Euripides, foretelling trouble in the world of men, and at the very close revealing the promise of the pastoral music to come:

> But first I must put off
> These my skie robes spun out of *Iris* Wooff,
> And take the Weeds and likenes of a Swain,
> That to the service of this house belongs,
> Who with his soft Pipe, and smooth-dittied Song,
> Well knows to still the wilde winds when they roar,
> And hush the waving Woods . . . [82–88]

The wit of the passage depends upon the sort of recognitions peculiar to the masque-genre, for the audience knows that the Spirit is describing the musician enacting the role, thus paying a compliment to his own musical abilities and also a compliment to the poet who wrote the ditties, that is, the words, for his song—the poet who indeed wrote this compliment itself! But I do not think the Spirit changes his garb here: he leaves the scene to change his gorgeous heavenly costume for that of a shepherd, and he is at once replaced by Comus and his crew, "their Apparel glistring," with Comus himself clad in some sort of "quaint habits," strange and exquisite clothing, which he fears will astonish the Lady (157) and cause her to flee. So he throws the "Magick dust" in her eyes which causes him to appear as "som harmless Villager / Whom thrift keeps up about his Country gear" (165–67).

In actual performance[7] a brilliant effect is created if Comus does not change his garb here—and indeed the lines require no change. As he hurls his "dazling Spells" into the air, "Of power to cheat the eye with blear illusion," (154–55) the Lady sees Comus as a shepherd, while the audience continues to see him in his original "quaint" attire. Her illusion is then stressed by the way in which she repeatedly addresses this figure in glistering garb with the words "gentle Shepherd," "Gentle villager," "good Shepherd," "Shepherd I take thy word, / And trust thy honest offer'd courtesie,"—and finally, "Shepherd lead on." Meanwhile Comus in his own words supports the "blear illusion" by addressing her as a goddess with Orphic powers of pastoral song:

Hail forren wonder
Whom certain these rough shades did never breed
Unlesse the Goddes that in rurall shrine
Dwell'st here with *Pan*, or *Silvan*, by blest Song
Forbidding every bleak unkindly Fog
To touch the prosperous growth of this tall Wood.   [265–70]

And he creates for himself a pastoral persona by his vital imagery
of natural growth:

I saw them under a green mantling vine
That crawls along the side of yon small hill,
Plucking ripe clusters from the tender shoots . . .
I know each lane, and every alley green
Dingle, or bushy dell of this wilde Wood,
And every bosky bourn from side to side . . . [294–96,311–13]

Yet the stichomythic dialogue at the outset of their interview
(277–90) creates a touch of "ill-beseeming" artifice that stresses
the illusory quality of the scene; such dialogue belongs to a genre
widely differing from pastoral.

Moreover, at her entrance the Lady has spoken anti-pastoral
words, describing the harvest festivals of the local swains as a
turbulent wassail quite unlike the harvest festival of Theocritus
and even more significantly unlike the pious, harmonious festivals
offered by these same swains in honor of Sabrina, as we are to
hear near the close of the masque:

For which the Shepherds at their festivals
Carrol her goodnes lowd in rustick layes,
And throw sweet garland wreaths into her stream
Of pancies, pinks, and gaudy Daffadils.   [848–51]

But here the Lady fears a different scene, evoked by the "riotous
and unruly noise" of Comus and his crew:

This way the noise was, if mine ear be true,
My best guide now, me thought it was the sound
Of Riot, and ill manag'd Merriment,
Such as the jocond Flute, or gamesom Pipe
Stirs up among the loose unleter'd Hinds,
When for their teeming Flocks, and granges full
In wanton dance they praise the bounteous *Pan*,
And thank the gods amiss. I should be loath

> To meet the rudenesse, and swill'd insolence
> Of such late Wassailers . . .   [170–79]

The contrast between these two versions of pastoral measures the
distance that the Lady and the masque must travel to reach the
meaning and the motive of true pastoral music.

As the Lady leaves with her false shepherd, the Elder Brother
breaks even the slight illusion of pastoral as he unbuckles his
schoolboy rhetoric:[8]

> Unmuffle ye faint stars, and thou fair Moon
> That wontst to love the travailers benizon,
> Stoop thy pale·visage through an amber cloud,
> And disinherit *Chaos,* that raigns here
> In double night of darknes, and of shades;
> Or if your influence be quite damm'd up
> With black usurping mists, som gentle taper
> Though a rush Candle from the wicker hole
> Of som clay habitation visit us
> With thy long levell'd rule of streaming light,
> And thou shalt be our star of *Arcady,*
> Or *Tyrian* Cynosure.   [331–42]

The Younger Brother, in his own more forthright way, also
stresses their distance from pastoral as, in his simpler language, he
longs for simple things:

> Or if our eyes
> Be barr'd that happines, might we but hear
> The folded flocks pen'd in their watled cotes,
> Or sound of pastoral reed with oaten stops,
> Or whistle from the Lodge, or village cock
> Count the night watches to his feathery Dames,
> 'Twould be som solace yet, som little chearing
> In this close dungeon of innumerous bowes.   [342–49]

Then Elder Brother, in his long-winded way, retails the lessons he
has learned from "vertues book," recalling legends that show the
power of chastity, and summoning up evidence from "the old
schools of Greece." Well-schooled he surely is—but we see his lack
of experience when he declares:

> So dear to Heav'n is Saintly chastity,
> That when a soul is found sincerely so,

> A thousand liveried Angels lacky her,
> Driving far off each thing of sin and guilt . . .   [453–56]

He knows his Plato well and overawes the younger brother—but
we have just seen their sister leaving the stage with Comus.

Amid all this deception, naiveté, schoolboy learning, and am-
bitious rhetoric, we have nevertheless had one moment of the true
pastoral music, in the Lady's song to Echo, where she creates a
natural setting for the nymph, a *locus amoenus* such as Ovid so
often provides for his metamorphoses, while she sings of the
stories of Echo, Narcissus, and Philomela; and then, like the
Genius in *Arcades,* she closes by associating earthly music with the
music of the heavens:

> Sweet Echo, sweetest Nymph that liv'st unseen
>   Within thy airy shell
>   By slow *Meander's* margent green,
> And in the violet-imbroider'd vale
>   Where the love-lorn Nightingale
> Nightly to thee her sad Song mourneth well.
> Canst thou not tell me of a gentle Pair
>   That likest thy *Narcissus* are?
>   O if thou have
>   Hid them in som flowry Cave,
>   Tell me but where
> Sweet Queen of Parly, Daughter of the Sphear,
> So maist thou be translated to the skies,
> And give resounding grace to all Heav'ns Harmonies.
>
> [230–43]

But the last line in the song that Lawes has set to music reads
differently and in some ways more effectively in the musical manu-
scripts: "And hold a Counterpoint to All Heavn's Harmonies."[9]
Milton's revision has the advantage of adding the overtones of
heavenly "grace," but it lacks the power of the word "Counter-
point," which indeed represents the central principle of the
masque: the attempt to create, by earthly sounds and words, a
melody that will work in counterpoint with heaven's harmonies—
the music of the spheres and the music of the higher Heaven.

Such is the music that the Attendant Spirit recalls in the first of
the three great pastoral arias (as we might call them) by which he
brings the imagery of music to bear upon the riot and disorder of

Comus. At line 489 the Spirit at last appears "habited like a Shepherd," and his musical function is at once indicated by the name bestowed upon him by the Elder Brother—*Thyrsis,* the name of the skillful singer of the elegy to Daphnis in the first Idyll of Theocritus, a performance that gives the name Thyrsis an archetypal significance in the Orphic tradition, as the Elder Brother makes clear in his compliment of greeting:

> *Thyrsis?* Whose artful strains have oft delaid
> The huddling brook to hear his madrigal,
> And sweetn'd every muskrose of the dale . . .   [494–96]

Then both he and Thyrsis combine to build a strong pastoral setting as they converse, creating thus a verbal antidote to the actual scene in this dark "dungeon of innumerous bowes":

> How cam'st thou here good swain? hath any ram
> Slip't from the fold, or young Kid lost his dam,
> Or straggling weather the pen't flock forsook?   [497–99]

And the Spirit answers:

> I came not here on such a trivial toy
> As a stray'd Ewe, or to pursue the stealth
> Of pilfering Woolf, not all the fleecy wealth
> That doth enrich these Downs, is worth a thought
> To this my errand, and the care it brought.   [502–06]

Then he tells the brothers the story of Comus, developing a contrast between an harmonious pastoral setting and the riot of Comus and his crew:

> this I have learn't
> Tending my flocks hard by i'th hilly crofts,
> That brow this Bottom glade, whence night by night
> He and his monstrous rout are heard to howl
> Like stabl'd wolves, or tigers at their prey . . .   [530–34]

Against this story he now proceeds to build a much stronger abode for the pastoral music, as he describes the vitality of nature amid which, like the shepherd of Vergil's *Eclogues,* he "meditates" his song:[10]

> This evening late by then the chewing flocks
> Had ta'n their supper on the savoury Herb

> Of Knot-grass dew-besprent, and were in fold,
> I sate me down to watch upon a bank
> With Ivy canopied, and interwove
> With flaunting Hony-suckle, and began
> Wrapt in a pleasing fit of melancholy
> To meditate my rural minstrelsie . . .   [540–47]

The echo of the "bank where the wild thyme blows . . . Quite over-canopied with luscious woodbine" (*Midsummer Night's Dream*, II.i.249–51), has often been noted, but not so often hints of another "bank" in Shakespeare, famous for its musical atmosphere: the scene with Jessica and Lorenzo in the *Merchant of Venice* (V.i):[11]

> How sweet the moonlight sleeps upon this bank!
> Here will we sit, and let the sounds of music
> Creep in our ears. Soft stillness and the night
> Become the touches of sweet harmony.   [V.i.54–57]

Any similarities between this scene and the words of Thyrsis are no doubt mainly due to the power of the general Orphic tradition, and yet the additional Shakespearean echoes that accompany the Spirit's account of hearing the Lady's song enforce the echo of Lorenzo's scene; for in these lines we hear echoes of *Romeo and Juliet, Macbeth,* and *Antony and Cleopatra,*[12] and also perhaps an echo of Nerissa's answer to Portia's remark that the music of Lorenzo's scene "sounds much sweeter than by day": "Silence bestows that virtue on it, madam" (V.i.100–01).

"But ere a close," the Spirit continues, before he could finish even one cadence of his meditated song,

> The wonted roar was up amidst the Woods,
> And fill'd the Air with barbarous dissonance,
> At which I ceas't, and listen'd them a while,
> Till an unusuall stop of sudden silence
> Gave respit to the drowsie frighted steeds
> That draw the litter of close-curtain'd sleep.
> At last a soft and solemn breathing sound
> Rose like a steam of rich distill'd Perfumes,
> And stole upon the Air, that even Silence
> Was took e're she was ware, and wish't she might
> Deny her nature, and be never more
> Still to be so displac't. I was all eare,

And took in strains that might create a soul
Under the ribs of Death . . .   [548–62]

A distant suggestion of the strains of Orpheus in Pluto's realm
may evoke the passage in Lorenzo's scene where he explains to
Jessica the power of music over wild beasts:

For do but note a wild and wanton herd,
Or race of youthful and unhandled colts,
Fetching mad bounds, bellowing and neighing loud,
Which is the hot condition of their blood;
If they but hear perchance a trumpet sound,
Or any air of music touch their ears,
You shall perceive them make a mutual stand,
Their savage eyes turn'd to a modest gaze
By the sweet power of music: therefore the poet
Did feign that Orpheus drew trees, stones, and floods;
Since nought so stockish, hard, and full of rage,
But music for the time doth change his nature.   [V.i.71–82]

"But O ere long," the Spirit says,

Too well I did perceive it was the voice
Of my most honour'd Lady, your dear sister.
Amaz'd I stood, harrow'd with grief and fear,
And O poor hapless Nightingale thought I,
How sweet thou sing'st, how neer the deadly snare!
                                                           [562–67]

Thus he picks up the imagery of Philomela in the Lady's song and
reminds us of the temporary quietening effect that her pastoral
music has had upon the "rout" of Comus:

Then down the Lawns I ran with headlong hast
Through paths, and turnings oft'n trod by day,
Till guided by mine ear I found the place
Where that damn'd wisard hid in sly disguise
(For so by certain signes I knew) had met
Already, ere my best speed could praevent,
The aidless innocent Lady his wish't prey . . .   [568–74]

One need not take this to indicate that Comus has actually donned
a disguise here, for the Spirit, as usual, is telling the story in
keeping with his own disguise. What we should notice here is the
emphasis upon the "air" and the "eare",[13] for, in conjunction with

all the other reminiscences of renaissance musical theory, these words summon up a well-known passage where Ficino is explaining why the sense of hearing affects the human spirit more than any other of the senses. It is, he says, because sound is motion transmitted through the air:

> Although visual impressions are in a way pure, yet they lack the effectiveness of motion, and are usually perceived only as an image, without reality; normally therefore, they move the soul only slightly. Smell, taste and touch are entirely material, and rather titillate the sense-organs than penetrate the depths of the soul. But musical sound by the movement of the air moves the body: by purified air it excites the aerial spirit which is the bond of body and soul: by emotion it affects the senses and at the same time the soul: by meaning it works on the mind [Ficino is clearly thinking here of the words that live within a song]: finally, by the very movement of the subtle air it penetrates strongly: by its contemperation it flows smoothly: by the conformity of its quality it floods us with a wonderful pleasure: by its nature, both spiritual and material, it at once seizes, and claims as its own, man in his entirety.[14]

"I was all eare"—"Guided by mine ear"—thus music begins to play its role in the rescue.

But other pastoral properties are needed to complete the mission, and these Thyrsis explains in his second pastoral aria, where he tells of the rare herb *Haemony* that he received from a "certain Shepherd Lad." (619) The recent definitive article by Charlotte Otten[15] makes it plain that Milton is here describing a real plant belonging to the genus called in Milton's day *Hypericum,* a genus which "includes a number of species with an array of vernacular and scientific names such as St. John's Wort, Fuga Daemonum, Perforata (Porosa), and Androsaemon." All the plants of this genus bear a yellow flower, but it is from the last, Otten argues, that Milton has taken his name: *Andros-haemon,* a name derived from the Greek genitive for *man,* plus the Greek *haima, blood*—the latter part of the name indicating "the blood-red juice (a characteristic of the entire genus *hypericum*)." The leaf of this plant is "deep green," with "prickles" in the sense of perforations (not thorns); and it is a plant that, according to Lyte's popular *Herball,* "groweth not in this country, except in gardens where as it is sowen and planted." It was a plant for which "no pharmaceutical

uses" had been established, and therefore, as Lyte's *Herball* re-
ports, it is "unknowen to the Apothecaries." But it was everywhere
known for its powers of putting evil demons to flight (as one of its
names indicates), and thus it was regarded as a cure for all kinds
of "harms" caused by malicious spirits. In short, nearly every de-
tail of Milton's description of *Haemony* finds a parallel in the her-
bals of Milton's day:

> Amongst the rest a small unsightly root,
> But of divine effect, he cull'd me out;
> The leaf was darkish, and had prickles on it,
> But in another Countrey, as he said,
> Bore a bright golden flowre, but not in this soyl:
> Unknown, and like esteem'd, and the dull swayn
> Treads on it daily with his clouted shoon,
> And yet more med'cinal is it then that *Moly*
> That *Hermes* once to wise *Ulysses* gave;
> He call'd it *Haemony,* and gave it me,
> And bad me keep it as of sov'ran use
> 'Gainst all inchantments, mildew blast, or damp
> Or gastly furies apparition . . .   [629–41]

Otten suggests that Milton's description of the "bright golden
flowre" (which, it seems, does not appear in English soil) may
allude to the variety described by a German herbalist as bearing
"Goldfarben blümen," not simply yellow. But other varieties of
the genus, especially St. John's Wort, grow throughout the En-
glish landscape.

Milton, then, is describing the qualities of an actual plant popu-
larly regarded as an antidote to enchantments caused by evil
powers—an aspect of the plant well known to Henry Lawes, ac-
cording to an amusing anecdote told by Aubrey and quoted by
Otten in her article. According to Aubrey, Lawes had a musical
friend whose house was haunted by some spirit by which "the
Curtains would be rashed at Night, and awake the Gentleman that
lay there" (*rashed* means "torn or drawn violently").[16] "*Henry Laws*
to be satisfied did lie with him; and the curtains were rashed so
then: The Gentleman grew lean and pale with the frights, One
Dr. ——— Cured the House of this disturbance, and Mr. *Laws*
said, that the principal Ingredient was *Hypericon* put under his
Pillow."[17] It seems quite possible that Lawes may have told this

story to Milton, and that the description of *Haemony* is yet another
of those witty personal recognitions characteristic of the masque-
genre.

At the same time, through the allegorical nature of the
masque-genre, the plant is bound to take on "mysterious" qual-
ities. Its blood-red juice and its ambiguous "prickles" may accord
with the interpretation of those who find in the plant's "divine
effect" some indications of the redemption accomplished by the
blood of Christ.[18] Meanwhile those may also be right who feel in
the name *Haemony* an allusion to Thessaly, frequently called
Haemonia by Ovid, and so called by Milton in his second elegy,
when he refers to the rejuvenation of Jason's father by Medea,
using a concoction of herbs and roots gathered in a valley of
Haemonia:

> O dignus tamen Haemonio juvenescere succo,
> Dignus in Aesonios vivere posse dies . . .   [7–8]

Certainly the magical implications of Thessaly are appropriate,
but much more significant, in this context, are the other implica-
tions of Haemonia as a region dedicated to poetry. It was in
Haemonia that Apollo fell in love with Daphne, daughter of the
river-god Peneus; it was here that Apollo wooed her with words
describing his powers of prophecy, poetry, and medicine: espe-
cially his power of curing through the use of herbs:

> per me, quod eritque fuitque
> estque, patet; per me concordant carmina nervis . . .
> inventum medicina meum est, opiferque per orbem
> dicor, et herbarum subiecta potentia nobis.
> ei mihi, quod nullis amor est sanabilis herbis
> nec prosunt domino, quae prosunt omnibus, artes!

> By me what shall be, has been, and what is are all revealed; by me
> the lyre responds in harmony to song. . . . The art of medicine is
> my discovery. I am called Help–Bringer throughout the world, and
> all the potency of herbs is given unto me. Alas, that love is curable
> by no herbs, and the arts which heal all others cannot heal their
> lord!
>   [*Met.* 1.517–18,521–24, trans. Miller]

And it is here, on the banks of the river Peneus, that Daphne calls
upon her father for help, and she is changed into the laurel tree,

sacred to Apollo (*Met.* 1.545–67). Immediately after this comes Ovid's description of the vale of Tempe in Haemonia:

> Est nemus Haemoniae, praerupta quod undique claudit
> silva: vocant Tempe; per quae Peneus ab imo
> effusus Pindo spumosis volvitur undis
>
> . . . .
>
> haec domus, haec sedes, haec sunt penetralia magni
> amnis, in his residens facto de cautibus antro,
> undis iura dabat nymphisque colentibus undas.

There is a grove in Haemonia, shut in on every side by steep wooded slopes. Men call it Tempe. Through this grove flow the foaming waters of Peneus, gushing out from the bottom of Pindus' range. . . . This was the home, the dwelling, the most secret haunt of the great river. Sitting here, in a cave hewn out of the cliffs, he was dispensing justice to the waves and to the nymphs who inhabited his stream.   [1.568–70,574–76, trans. Innes]

This is a passage that Milton seems to have remembered when he created his compliment to Manso, weaving together various motifs concerned with the region of Haemonia:

Men will say that, of his own free will, Apollo dwelt in your house, and that the Muses came like servants to your doors. Yet that same Apollo, when he was a fugitive from heaven, came unwillingly to King Admetus' farm, although Admetus had been host to mighty Hercules. When he wanted to get away from the bawling ploughmen Apollo could, at any rate, retreat to gentle Chiron's famous cave, among the moist woodland pastures and leafy shades beside the river Peneus. There often, beneath a dark oak tree, he would yield to his friend's flattering persuasion and, singing to the music of his lute, would sooth the hardships of exile. Then neither the river banks, nor the boulders lodged in the quarry's depths stayed in their places: the Trachinian cliff nodded to the tune, and no longer felt its huge and familiar burden of forest trees; the mountain ashes were moved and came hurrying down their slopes, and spotted lynxes grew tame as they listened to the strange music.   [*Mansus* 54–69, trans. Carey][19]

After the renaissance fashion, one is expected to admire the wit of this very free commingling of Thessalian and Thracian themes. The Orphean incident where the trees of Thrace gathered round the singer (*Met.* 10.86–105) is here transferred to Haemonia, scene of Apollo's exile from heaven while he served as herdsman

to Admetus, while the allusion to Hercules recalls the story of the
Alcestis (where of course Hercules came to the house of Admetus
after, not before Apollo) and especially the great chorus of
Euripides:

> Apollo of the beautiful lyre
> Deigned to dwell in you
> And to live a shepherd in your lands!
> On the slope of the hillsides
> He played melodies of mating
> On the Pipes of Pan to his herds.
>
> And the dappled lynxes fed with them
> In joy at your singing;
> From the wooded vale of Orthrys
> Came a yellow troop of lions;
> To the sound of your lyre, O Phoebus,
> Danced the dappled fawn
> Moving on light feet
> Beyond the high-crested pines
> Charmed by your sweet singing.   [570–87, trans. Aldington][20]

Having thus mingled the singing of Orpheus and Apollo, Mil-
ton merges the cave of Chiron with the cave of Peneus: for Chi-
ron's cave was on mount Pelion, not beside the river Peneus.[21] The
stories easily blend, for after the death of that Haemonian girl
Coronis, Apollo had taken the child Aesculapius to the cave of
Chiron for upbringing (*Met.* 2.630), and therefore might often
have visited that cave.

All these associations, then, show how the name *Haemony* would
recall *Haemonia,* how that region would in turn suggest the powers
of music, and how that in turn would suggest a recognition of the
shepherd lad who gave his virtuous plants to Thyrsis and would
often beg him to sing:

> a certain Shepherd Lad
> Of small regard to see to, yet well skill'd
> In every vertuous plant and healing herb
> That spreds her verdant leaf to th'morning ray,
> He lov'd me well, and oft would beg me sing,
> Which when I did, he on the tender grass
> Would sit, and hearken even to extasie,
> And in requitall ope his leather'n scrip,
> And shew me simples of a thousand names

Telling their strange and vigorous faculties;
Amongst the rest a small unsightly root,
But of divine effect, he cull'd me out;
The leaf was darkish, and had prickles on it . . .   [619–31]

And indeed the leaf of the genus *Hypericum,* in color and in shape,
bears a strong resemblance to the laurel leaf (as we may see in part
from the illustration of St. John's Wort in Otten's article). Can one
avoid the implication that Haemony has something to do with
poetry, that it represents the power of poetry and song (as united
in the word *carmen*), and that here is a pastoral account of the close
relation between Milton and the music and voice of Henry Lawes?
Is the "divine effect" of Haemony a tribute to the doctrine of the
Orphic powers of music? Such a meaning may emerge if we look
more closely at the presence of music throughout the masque.[22]

II

In this exploration I shall use the word "music" in all the senses
held by the word *carmen:* "tune, song; poem, verse; an oracular
response, a prophecy; a form of incantation", or in a broader
sense also implied in the Latin, "every kind of poetical produc-
tion."[23] I shall move from the musical scores that actually exist to
hints of further music that may have existed, and from there to
the fabric of musical allusions and analogies that bring the entire
work into harmony.

The five songs for which the music exists include (as the second,
third, and fourth in the musical manuscripts) three of the verses
noted as "Song" in the work itself: the Lady's Song, beginning,
"Sweet Echo," the Spirit's invocation, "Sabrina Fair," and the dou-
ble song of the Spirit, "Back Shepherds, back," followed by the
address, "Noble Lord, and Lady Bright." The fifth song consists
of the last twelve lines of the Spirit's epilogue, beginning, "Now
my task is smoothly don."[24]

The last four of these appear in the acting version, that is, in the
Bridgewater manuscript,[25] at the points where they occur in the
other texts. But the first song in the musical manuscripts has a
special interest, for the Bridgewater version shows that it was
designed to be sung at the very beginning of the performance.

For this purpose Lawes has set to music fourteen lines that, in all
other versions of the masque, occur with some variations at the
opening of the Spirit's epilogue. Lawes·clearly wished to open the
production with song rather than with the spoken prologue in
blank verse which immediately follows in the acting version. To
accomplish this, the opening line of Milton's epilogue, "To the
Ocean now I fly," has been changed to read: "From the Heavn's
now I fly," while the rest of the song follows closely the lines of the
Spirit's epilogue:

> From the Heavn's now I fly,
> And those happy Climes that lie
> Where day never shuts his eye,
> Up in the broad Fields of the Sky,
> There I suck the liquid Air
> All amidst the Garden fair
> Of Hesperus and his daughters three
> That Sing about the golden Tree:
> Iris there with humid Bow
> Waters the od'rous Banks that blow
> Flowers of more mingled Hew
> Than her purfled scarfe can shew,
> Beds of Hyacinths and Roses
> Where many a Cherub soft reposes.[26]

In Milton's published epilogue the equivalent of the last line
reads, "Where young *Adonis* oft reposes," and the poem then con-
tinues with the allusions to Venus, Cupid, and Psyche. There is an
important advantage in opening the poem with a song, particu-
larly with a song that includes a reference to the singing of the
daughters of Hesperus, for in this way Lawes can prepare us to
grasp the significance of musical imagery and theme throughout
the masque. From the outset the Spirit is thus identified as a
musical presence: a neoplatonic "daemon" who helps to create a
universal harmony.[27] It is an effect that should always be retained
in any actual performance of the work.

In addition to these five songs, the manuscripts and the printed
version[28] of the poem contain a great deal of evidence that further
music of some kind was at least planned. Sabrina's answer, "By the
rushy-fringed bank," is preceded by the direction, "Sabrina rises,
attended by water-Nymphes, and sings."[29] At the same time, the

last words of Sabrina's song, "I am here," form a rhyme with the
Spirit's answer, "Goddess dear" (901–02). As Haun says, "To
carry over the rhyme without carrying over the music would have
been an error in taste which Milton with his sensitivity and Lawes
with his knowledge of masque-technique would not have been
likely to have committed."[30] Then thirty-five lines after this, im-
mediately following the line, "With Groves of myrrhe and cinna-
mon," we find in the manuscripts the significant direction: "Songe
ends," a direction that may be taken to imply that the intervening
thirty-five lines have all been designed for music.

In a similar way, immediately after the Spirit's song of invoca-
tion, "Sabrina fair," the succeeding lines are introduced in the
Bridgewater manuscript with the direction: "The verse to singe or
not,"[31] and then the following twenty-three lines of the poem are
divided in this manuscript among three speakers: the elder
brother, the younger brother, and the "Daemon":

> listen and appeare to vs
> in name of greate Oceanus,
> by th'earth-shakinge Neptunes mace,
> and Tethis grave maiestick pace,
> *El bro:* by hoarie Nereus wrincled looke,
> and the Carpathian wizards hooke,
> *2 bro:* by scalie Tritons windinge shell,
> and ould sooth-sayinge Glaucus spell,
> *El br:* by Lewcotheas lovely hands,
> and her sonne that rules the strands,
> *2 bro:* by Thetis tinsel-slipperd feete,
> and the songs of sirens sweete,
> *El br:* by dead Parthenopes deare tombe,
> and fayer Ligeas golden Combe,
> wherewith she sitts on diamond rocks,
> sleekinge her soft alluringe locks,
> *De:* By all the Nimphes of nightly daunce,
> vpon thy streames with wilie glaunce,
> rise, rise, and heave thy rosie head,
> from thy Corall paven bed,
> and bridle in thy headlonge wave,
> till thou our summons answered have,
>   Listen & save.   [Bridgewater MS. 788–810]

It seems then that this section was designed to be sung, provided
that the boys could do the singing. This division of parts is highly

effective in performance, and should be retained, for thus we
hear the brothers' voices enclosed by and inspired by the voice of
the guardian spirit. We have powerful evidence, then, that the
concluding portion of the masque, from the invocation of Sabrina
to the end (128 lines in the acting version), was dominated by
music and perhaps very largely set to music, with the result that
Haun describes when he says, "If this does not make *Comus* an
opera, at least it makes it operatic."[32]

Meanwhile there are clear indications of instrumental music at
three points: the dances at the very close; the scene of Comus's
temptation of the Lady, where the stage direction of the published
version requires "soft Musick" at the outset; and the dance of
Comus and his monsters near the beginning of the work, where
some kind of wild "noise"—perhaps with the pipe and flute
suggested by the Lady—would seem to be required, for after the
entering speech of Comus, the manuscripts have the stage direc-
tion: "The measure in a wild, rude, & wanton Antick."[33] (The
published version spoils the effect by giving simply "The Mea-
sure.") In connection with the last point, one should note that the
entering words of Comus are written mainly in the same swift
tetrameter that is elsewhere set to or associated with music; and
indeed the opening speech of Comus suggests poetry very close to
the lyric form of the Anacreontic:

> Mean while welcom Joy, and Feast,
> Midnight shout, and revelry,
> Tipsie dance, and Jollity.
> Braid your Locks with rosie Twine
> Dropping odours, dropping Wine.
> Rigor now is gon to bed,
> And Advice with scrupulous head,
> Strict Age, and sowre Severity
> With their grave Saws in slumber ly.   [102–10]

But shortly after this, in keeping with the loss of rigor and
scrupulosity here urged, the tetrameter begins to expand into
pentameter, with significant variations that ebb and flow through-
out the remainder of Comus's speech, as the imagery serves to
suggest:

> The Sounds, and Seas with all their finny drove
> Now to the Moon in wavering Morrice move,

> And on the Tawny Sands and Shelves,
> Trip the pert Fairies and the dapper Elves.   [115–18]

It is a wavering morris dance, indeed; these irregularities form a striking contrast with the strict tetrameter form that dominates the end of the masque, a regularity symbolizing the return of order to the scene, as indicated also by the dancers at the conclusion.[34] In the original performance, this contrast would have been reinforced by opening the masque with Lawes's song in strict tetrameter form, binding together beginning and end.

In addition to actual music, a great many allusions to and descriptions of music help to develop this theme of disorder versus harmony, as we have seen. The theme is stressed at the end of the "Antick" dance by Comus and his crew when Comus breaks off the "measure" with a metrical pun: "Break off, break off, I feel the different pace / Of som chast footing neer about this ground" (145–46). As Comus thus shifts his "footing" from tetrameter couplets to blank verse, he alerts us to the way in which music and dance merge into the music of poetry.

The Lady then enters and at once reinforces the theme by the harmonies of her song to Echo. Some readers have felt, perhaps rightly, that her isolation is stressed by the fact that no echo here responds,[35] yet the Lady's words to Comus may indicate some kind of echo:

> Not any boast of skill, but extreme shift
> How to regain my sever'd company
> Compell'd me to awake the courteous Echo
> To give me answer from her mossie Couch.   [273–76]

Would she refer to "courteous Echo" if Echo had not already in some way answered her? It is hard to believe that Lawes would have passed up a chance to perform this song with echoes, which the pauses in the musical phrasing would allow. Perhaps he himself sang the echoes.

In any case, there is counterpoint, as Comus receives the song within himself and responds, adding another melody:

> Can any mortal mixture of Earths mould
> Breath such Divine inchanting ravishment?
> Sure somthing holy lodges in that brest,

> And with these raptures moves the vocal air
> To testifie his hidd'n residence . . .   [244–48]

Comus here is forced to recognize the truth of the pythagorean-platonic view of music as the emanation of the soul. Then, echoing Juliet's passionate wish for Romeo's presence,[36] he moves toward another kind of music, with his characteristic mutation into sensuous imagery, as of someone's hair being stroked:

> How sweetly did they float upon the wings
> Of silence, through the empty-vaulted night
> At every fall smoothing the Raven doune
> Of darkness till it smil'd . . .   [249–52]

And from here we move quickly into the world of Ovidian metamorphosis, where Circe and her crew put on an operatic performance all their own:

> I have oft heard
> My mother *Circe* with the Sirens three,
> Amid'st the flowry-kirtl'd *Naiades*
> Culling their Potent hearbs, and balefull drugs,
> Who as they sung, would take the prison'd soul,
> And lap it in *Elysium, Scylla* wept,
> And chid her barking waves into attention,
> And fell *Charybdis* murmur'd soft applause:
> Yet they in pleasing slumber lull'd the sense,
> And in sweet madnes rob'd it of it self,
> But such a sacred, and home-felt delight,
> Such sober certainty of waking bliss
> I never heard till now. Ile speak to her
> And she shall be my Queen.   [252–65]

Thus Comus is impelled to pay powerful tribute to the harmonizing effect of song that is holy, sacred, or blessed, in contrast to the "balefull" kind of song that Comus remembers.

Soon the two brothers enter, aged nine and eleven at the original performance; and they proceed to hold their schoolboy conversation about their sister and the power of chastity. Here is a good example of Milton's way of creating an operatic effect through poetry. When we watch an early opera by Monteverdi, such as his *Orfeo,* we are aware that the interest cannot reside in what we ordinarily call dramatic tension. The interest often resides in watching two performers work their skillful ways through contrasting parts, each part a set piece, a show piece, designed to draw forth the utmost power of the performer's vocal skill, while evoking the essence of the character or the dilemma represented. So here, each brother is characterized by his poetry. The nine-year-old is closer to earth and natural fears; the eleven-year-old is full of superior knowledge, all out of books, able to quote Ovid and Plato to excess in order to quell his brother's fears. Thus the younger brother cries out:

> But O that haples virgin our lost sister
> Where may she wander now, whether betake her
> From the chill dew, amongst rude burrs and thistles?
> Perhaps som cold bank is her boulster now
> Or 'gainst the rugged bark of som broad Elm
> Leans her unpillow'd head fraught with sad fears.
> What if in wild amazement, and affright,
> Or while we speak within the direfull grasp
> Of Savage hunger, or of Savage heat?   [350–58]

And the elder brother replies with a highly condescending tone:

> Peace brother, be not over-exquisite
> To cast the fashion of uncertain evils;
> For grant they be so, while they rest unknown,
> What need a man forestall his date of grief,
> And run to meet what he would most avoid?   [359–63]

But when the younger brother has the temerity to continue with his fear that some "ill greeting touch" may harm his sister, the elder brother answers with an even more supercilious tone in the following interchange:

> My sister is not so defenceless left
> As you imagine, she has a hidden strength
> Which you remember not.
> 2 Bro. What hidden strength,
> Unless the strength of Heav'n, if you mean that?
> Eld. Bro. I mean that too, but yet a hidden strength
> Which if Heav'n gave it, may be term'd her own:
> 'Tis chastity, my brother, chastity.   [414–20]

I do not see how any audience, particularly the original audience, could do anything but smile at this encounter: the whole scene

could, and should, I think, be acted or imagined in such a way as
to create something of the effect of a school play on Parents' Day.

Then, when the brothers fail to rescue the Lady, through their
inexperience, the Attendant Spirit himself moves to the rescue
through poetical (musical) means described in his third pastoral
aria:

> Som other means I have which may be us'd,
> Which once of *Melibaeus* old I learnt
> The soothest Shepherd that ere pip't on plains.

(The heavy alliteration serves to identify the shepherd as Edmund
Spenser.)

> There is a gentle Nymph not farr from hence,
> That with moist curb sways the smooth Severn stream,
> *Sabrina* is her name, a Virgin pure . . .
> . . . .
> And, as the old Swain said, she can unlock
> The clasping charm, and thaw the numming spell,
> If she be right invok't in warbled Song,
> For maid'nhood she loves, and will be swift
> To aid a Virgin, such as was her self
> In hard besetting need, this will I try
> And adde the power of som adjuring verse.   [821–26,852–58]

Then follows the operatic conclusion to the poem in which song,
dance, and orchestral music serve to create a harmony in which
the oppositions of life are reconciled, and nature and spirit are
brought into a rich union represented by Sabrina's song:

> By the rushy-fringed bank,
> Where grows the Willow and the Osier dank,
> My sliding Chariot stayes,
> Thick set with Agat, and the azurn sheen
> Of Turkis blew, and Emerauld green
> That in the channell strayes,
> Whilst from off the waters fleet
> Thus I set my printless feet
> O're the Cowslips Velvet head,
> That bends not as I tread,
> Gentle swain at thy request
> I am here.   [890–91]

Indeed, the more we ponder the work, the sounder Gretchen

Finney's basic argument appears to be: that the masque, as Milton
developed it, resembles the form that opera was beginning to take
in the early part of the seventeenth century.[37] To see the work as
thus related to opera may help to resolve some of our critical
problems. The operatic analogy seems to be the best way of an-
swering the usual criticism of the work, as put by Samuel Johnson,
who complained that the speeches "have not the spriteliness of a
dialogue animated by reciprocal contention, but seem rather dec-
lamations deliberately composed and formally repeated on a
moral question. The auditor therefore listens as to a lecture, with-
out passion, without anxiety." From this point of view, Johnson
contends: "The dispute between the Lady and Comus is the most
animated and affecting scene of the drama, and wants nothing
but a brisker reciprocation of objections and replies, to invite at-
tention and detain it."[38]

But if we listen operatically, we will not seek a brisker reciproca-
tion, which would prevent the greatest delight of opera: the listen-
ing, with passion, to an aria deliberately composed and formally
repeated by a skillfull performer. From this standpoint Comus's
great aria of temptation is a showpiece designed to outdo all pre-
vious exhortations of the *carpe diem* kind, including Thomas Ran-
dolph's recent Cavalier piece:[39] while the Lady's answer,
strengthened by Milton's addition in the published version (778–
805), provides her with a worthy response, as she utters her own
operatic climax:

> Thou art not fit to hear thy self convinc't;
> Yet should I try, the uncontrouled worth
> Of this pure cause would kindle my rap't spirits
> To such a flame of sacred vehemence,
> That dumb things would be mov'd to sympathize,
> And the brute Earth would lend her nerves, and shake,
> Till all thy magick structures rear'd so high,
> Were shatter'd into heaps o're thy false head.   [792–99]

Thus the Lady proves to have a power of eloquence that defeats
the sensual music of Comus.[40] "She fables not," Comus admits to
himself; "I feel that I do fear / Her words set off by som superior
power" (800–01).

For us today Milton's masque must have its value, I believe, in

its demonstration of Milton's vital belief in the civilizing power of
poetry and music. I do not mean to say that we should ignore the
many studies that have shown the importance of Milton's moral
and religious themes in the masque. But we should not lose sight
of the fact that Milton's simple plot, like his whole volume of 1645,
is designed to show a progress toward maturity.[41] Perhaps that is
why he has allowed his young lady of fifteen to utter that famous
substitution of chastity for charity:

> O welcome pure-ey'd Faith, white-handed Hope,
> Thou hovering Angel girt with golden wings,
> And thou unblemish't form of Chastity . . .   [213–15]

The full power of chastity is represented, not in the Lady, but in
Sabrina, who combines the spirit of music with the spirit of charity
and evokes throughout the countryside, not the riotous noise that
the Lady has feared to meet in her earlier speech, but rather the
music of a Theocritean festival:

>   still she retains
> Her maid'n gentlenes, and oft at Eeve
> Visits the herds along the twilight meadows,
> Helping all urchin blasts, and ill luck signes
> That the shrewd medling Elfe delights to make,
> Which she with pretious viold liquors heals.
> For which the Shepherds at their festivals
> Carrol her goodnes lowd in rustick layes,
> And throw sweet garland wreaths into her stream
> Of pancies, pinks, and gaudy Daffadils.   [842–51]

The spirit of music which the Lady has revealed in her opening
song shows that she has within herself a richer nature than her
philosophic speeches to Comus can reveal. Like Sabrina, she will
live to fulfill that promise, until her own shepherds, at their festi-
vals, will "Carrol her goodnes lowd in rustick layes."

Milton's masque, then, is a recital, "musical as is Apollo's lute,"
performed with all the arts that Milton has now mastered from
various models.[42] It is a poem that displays a mastery of the blank
verse of Shakespeare and the Jacobean drama. It displays a mas-
tery of the art of madrigal and air. It displays to perfection the
Jonsonian mode of couplet-rhetoric, especially in the form of the

tetrameter. It echoes the whole range of Elizabethan and Jaco-
bean dramatic productions, from the *Old Wives' Tale* to the latest
masques by Thomas Carew and Aurelian Townshend.[43] It dis-
plays the prologue of the supernatural agent derived from
Euripides, along with the stichomythic dialogue of the Greek
drama. It can draw upon the whole range of pastoral poetry from
Theocritus to Spenser, along with the myths of Ovid. It is indeed
a mannerist display of poetical mastery, with the young Milton, at
the age of twenty-five, showing himself now almost ready to em-
bark upon the great baroque work for which he has been so care-
fully preparing his powers.[44]

CHAPTER 2

The
Rising
Poet

It is hard to maintain a clear view of Milton's volume of 1645, since the editions that we are most likely to be using have broken up Milton's groupings and have rearranged the poems in chronological order, interspersed with other poems that Milton did not choose to publish here. I do not mean to quarrel with these rearrangements, which have the advantage of allowing one to trace the development of Milton's early poetical career. And indeed Milton himself has taken the lead in making such a view of his career possible, since his volume of 1645 takes care to date many of the poems and arranges them in rough chronological order, within various groups.[1] At the same time Milton's original arrangement creates the growing awareness of a guiding, central purpose that in turn gives the volume an impressive and peculiar sense of wholeness. In order to regain the significant integrity of the volume one must, now and then, go back to the original.

Perhaps the best way into the volume is to follow Milton's own description of it, in the Latin ode that he sent in January, 1646–47, to John Rouse, Bodley's librarian, with a copy of the book. This is a mock-heroic poem of remarkably high spirits, written in an unprecedented form that MacKellar calls a "metrical experiment or jest."[2] The manner is one of learned wit that makes translation almost impossible; I give here a composite version of the first strophe, with intermittent comments:[3]

> Gemelle cultu simplici gaudens liber,
> Fronde licet geminâ,
> Munditiéque nitens non operosâ,
> Quam manus attulit
> Juvenilis olim,
> Sedula tamen haud nimii Poetae;
> Dum vagus Ausonias nunc per umbras
> Nunc Britannica per vireta lusit
> Insons populi, barbitóque devius
> Indulsit patrio, mox itidem pectine Daunio
> Longinquum intonuit melos
> Vicinis, & humum vix tetigit pede . . .

"Book in twin parts, rejoicing in a single cover, yet with a double leaf" [these are "Poems of Mr. John Milton, both English and Latin," with a separate title page for the Latin poems and separate pagination for the English and the Latin parts; the "double leaf," however, may allude not only to the two title pages, or the two parts, but at the same time may suggest the double wreath of laurel that the poet has won for his performance in two languages], "and shining with unlabored elegance which a hand once young imparted—a careful hand, but hardly that of one who was too much a poet—" [that is, not yet a master-poet] "while he played, wandering, now in the forest-shades of Ausonia and now on the lawns of England" [*Ausonias umbras:* the phrase may be taken to include a reference to his own Italian journey, to the poems in the Italian language, to the Latin poems, and to the pervasive atmosphere of Greek and Roman pastoral that plays throughout the volume: Ausonia includes Magna Graecia]; "aloof from the people, and forsaking the common paths, he indulged his native lute, and presently in like fashion with Daunian quill called forth for his neighbors a melody from far away, his foot scarcely touching the ground" [*pectine Daunio:* the song and instrument of ancient Italy].

Here is the picture of a youthful poet, free from adult cares, sometimes wandering alone, amusing himself, sometimes making music for his friends or acquaintances, sometimes writing in his

native vein, sometimes evoking a strain from idealized an-
tiquity—but with a light and dancing posture that we do not
usually associate with John Milton: *et humum vix tetigit pede.* It is
clear, from many indications, that Milton has designed his book
with great care to create this impression.

The entire volume strives to create a tribute to a youthful era
now past—not only the poet's own youth, but a state of mind, a
point of view, ways of writing, ways of living, an old culture and
outlook now shattered by the pressures of maturity and by the
actions of political man. Even the frontispiece, by William Mar-
shall, attempts to set this theme. The aim of the engraving is
clearly to present the youthful poet surrounded by the Muses,
with a curtain in the background lifted to reveal a pastoral land-
scape of meadow and trees, where a shepherd is piping in the
shade, while a shepherd and a shepherdess are dancing on the
lawn. The legend around the portrait identifies it as a picture of
the poet in his twenty-first year—but in fact the portrait presents
the harsh and crabbed image of a man who might be forty or fifty!
Marshall could do better than this, as his engraving of the youth-
ful Donne testifies; one almost suspects deliberate sabotage here.[4]
If so, Milton performed slyly an appropriate revenge. For under
the portrait, neatly engraved in Greek—engraved no doubt by
Marshall himself—we have the following comment by Milton:

> That an unskilful hand had carved this print
> You'd say at once, seeing the living face;
> But, finding here no jot of me, my friends,
> Laugh at the botching artist's mis-attempt.

With this learned practical joke, the volume begins in high spirits;
how can we doubt, after this, that Milton had a considerable sense
of humor?

Meanwhile, the facing title page prepares us for a volume that
will contain songs of unlabored elegance, in the recent courtly
style: "The Songs were set in Musick by Mr. Henry Lawes Gen-
tleman of the Kings Chappel, and one of His Maiesties Private
Musick"—a notice quite in line with Moseley's preface, which as-
sociates Milton's volume with the poems of Waller that Moseley
had published a year before. Waller, as everyone knew, had been

exiled for his plot against the Parliament on the King's behalf;
nevertheless Moseley insists on saying: "that incouragement I
have already received from the most ingenious men in their clear
and courteous entertainment of Mr. *Wallers* late choice Peeces,
hath once more made me adventure into the World, presenting it
with these ever-green, and not to be blasted Laurels." This bland
ignoring, or bold confronting, of the political situation, with its
emphasis upon the transcendent values of art, is maintained by
reprinting here, from the 1637 edition, Henry Lawes's eloquent
dedication of Milton's *Maske* to a young nobleman with strong
royalist associations; by the Latin poems in memory of the bishops
of Winchester and Ely; by the complimentary writings prefixed to
the Latin poems, showing the high regard that Milton had won in
Catholic Italy; and by the sonnet beginning: "Captain or Colonel,
or Knight in Arms, / Whose chance on these defenceless dores
may sease."

> Lift not thy spear against the Muses Bowre,
>   The great *Emathian* Conqueror bid spare
>   The house of *Pindarus,* when Temple and Towre
> Went to the ground: And the repeated air
>   Of sad *Electra's* Poet had the power
>   To save th' *Athenian* Walls from ruine bare.

But will the King's Captain do the same for one who is not yet "too
much a poet"? There is room for doubt, and hence the plea, with
its undertone of self-irony;[5] but there is no doubt at all about the
power of poetry and this poet's hopes to achieve the immortality
of Fame. He has told us this through the motto on the title page,
there identified as coming from Vergil's seventh eclogue:

> ————Baccare frontem
> Cingite, ne vati noceat mala lingua futuro.

The whole context is essential: the lines are spoken by Thyrsis as
he opens his answer in the singing match with Corydon, *Arcades
ambo:*

> Pastores, hedera crescentem[6] ornate poetam,
> Arcades, invidia rumpantur ut ilia Codro;
> aut, si ultra placitum laudarit, baccare frontem
> cingite, ne vati noceat mala lingua futuro.

POEMS

OF
Mr. *John Milton*,
BOTH
ENGLISH and LATIN,
Compos'd at several times.

Printed by his true Copies.

The SONGS were set in Musick by
Mr. HENRY LAWES Gentleman of
the KINGS Chappel, and one
of His MAIESTIES
Private Musick.

——— *Baccare frontem*
Cingite, ne vati noceat mala lingua futuro,
Virgil, Eclog. 7.

Printed and publish'd according to
ORDER.

LONDON,
Printed by *Ruth Raworth* for *Humphrey Moseley*,
and are to be sold at the signe of the Princes
Arms in S. *Pauls* Church-yard. 1645.

Bring ivy-leaves to decorate your rising poet, shepherds of Arcady, and so make Codrus burst his sides with envy. Or, if he tries to harm me with excessive praise, twine foxglove round my brows, to stop his evil tongue from hurting your predestined bard.
[7.25–29, trans. Rieu][7]

Thyrsis loses the match, but other contests no doubt lie ahead; he ends by sending his love to his friend Lycidas.

That epigraph, summoning up the world of Vergil's *Eclogues*, prepares the way for the many Vergilian characters and scenes to be encountered in the English poems here: Corydon and Thyrsis, Phillis and Thestylis, in *L'Allegro;* Thyrsis and Meliboeus in the *Maske; Lycidas,* with Amaryllis, and Damoetas, and the setting of Vergil's seventh eclogue, "where the Mincius embroiders his banks with a green fringe of bending rushes";[8] and the shepherds of *Arcades*—the entertainment at Harefield. The epigraph prepares us too for the echoes of Vergil's Messianic eclogue that occur in the volume's opening poem, the Nativity Ode; and, above all, it prepares us to watch, as we read the Latin poems, the poet's growth away from the light elegy toward the Vergilian mode in which Milton wrote the most mature and the finest of all the Latin verses in this volume: *Ad Patrem, Mansus,* and *Epitaphium Damonis,* all three of which confirm the "rising poet's" place as a "predestined bard."

The *Epitaphium Damonis,* spoken by Thyrsis, becomes appropriately the final poem of the entire volume, for with all its echoes of Greek pastoral it is the most deliberately Vergilian poem in the book. Here, clustered together, are those pastoral names that Vergil drew together in his *Eclogues:* Thyrsis and Damon, Daphnis, Tityrus, Alphesiboeus, Aegon, Amyntas, Mopsus, Aegle, and Menalcas; the use of the refrain recalls Vergil's eighth eclogue, the singing match between Damon and Alphesiboeus, while the words of Milton's refrain are modeled upon a line from the seventh eclogue (7.44) and also upon the final line of the last eclogue; the account of the two cups which Manso gave the poet is bound to recall the pairs of cups carved by Alcimedon, as described in Vergil's third eclogue; and verbal echoes of Vergil are so frequent that the poem seems to grow within a Vergilian matrix.[9]

The unity of Milton's volume, from title page to final poem, is further suggested by the fact that the *Epitaphium Damonis* laments the death of the very friend to whom the first Latin poem in the book had been written—*Elegia prima*, that playful and thoroughly Ovidian elegy composed by the arrogantly clever and quite unrepentant sophomore during his rustication. At the same time, the reader is bound to recall that *Elegia sexta* and the fourth sonnet have also been explicitly addressed to this same friend, Charles Diodati. The final poem, then, in paying tribute to a friend of youth, becomes a farewell to the pleasures and attitudes of youth, including the pleasures of pastoral poetry and the imitative pleasures of writing such Latin verse—a farewell that Milton appropriately gives with unmistakable echoes of Vergil's *Eclogues:*

> Ipse etiam, nam nescio quid mihi grande sonabat
> Fistula, ab undecimâ jam lux est altera nocte,
> Et tum forte novis admôram labra cicutis,
> Dissiluere tamen rupta compage, nec ultra
> Ferre graves potuere sonos, dubito quoque ne sim
> Turgidulus, tamen & referam, vos cedite silvae.

> And I—for I know not what my pipe was grandly sounding—it is now eleven nights and a day—and then perhaps I had put my lips to new pipes, but they burst asunder, broken at the fastening, and could no more bear the deep tones—I hesitate too lest I seem puffed up, yet I will tell the tale—give place then, O forests.
>
> [155–60, trans. MacKellar]

Milton's *vos cedite silvae* is a clear echo of the *concedite silvae* with which Gallus bids farewell to Arcadian pleasures in Vergil's last eclogue (10.63); while Milton's following farewell to Latin poetry and Latin themes is based explicitly on the wording of Vergil's seventh eclogue:

> aut, si non possumus omnes,
> hic arguta sacra pendebit fistula pinu.   [7.23–24]

Thus, after the famous passage in which Milton tells of his resolve to write an epic on British themes, he cries:

> O mihi tum si vita supersit,
> Tu procul annosa pendebis fistula pinu
> Multum oblita mihi, aut patriis mutata camoenis

Brittonicum strides, quid enim? omnia non licet uni
Non sperâsse uni licet omnia . . .

Ah! then if life remain, you, my pipe, shall hang on some aged pine
far off and forgotten, unless forsaking your native songs you shrilly
sound a British theme. Why not a British theme? One man cannot
do all things, cannot hope to do all things.

[168–72, trans. MacKellar]

MacKellar's version of these lines helps to bring out the complex-
ity of the state of mind here expressed. The poet is resolved to
leave behind the *fistula,* the reed pipe of his pastoral muse, and he
will turn instead to write of those deeper themes which have al-
ready on one occasion proved to be stronger than that youthful
pipe could bear. At the same time the *fistula* may represent Latin
poetry, and the words *patriis camoenis* may thus suggest the Latin
language itself.[10] That is to say, the poet is contemplating deeper
themes, British themes, and themes composed in English. The
power of poetry represented by these early compositions on the
fistula will not be developed unless the poet can commit himself to
English. Perhaps he has already tried those deeper themes in
Latin, but without success: the rising poet knows, as Vergil says in
the eighth eclogue, *non omnia possumus omnes* (63); and he foresees
that his future fame must be entrusted to his native tongue.

His maturing prowess in that tongue has already been demon-
strated in the other pastoral monody that, with beautiful sym-
metry, closes the series of his shorter English poems in the first
part of his double book. *Lycidas,* like the *Epitaphium Damonis,* rep-
resents the climax of its part; each monody is the culmination of
the many strands of experimentation that have been growing
throughout each part. The Ludlow *Maske* is printed after *Lycidas,*
as a work distinctly separate from the preceding groups; it is
provided with elaborate introductory matter and a separate half-
title—almost a full title-page, for it bears the imprint "Anno Dom.
1645." The pagination, however, is continuous throughout the
English part. The whole book, then, displays particular care for
balance and harmony in all its proportions, while the poems
themselves have been arranged to convey a sense of the predes-
tined bard's rising powers.

II

The theme of poetical development is particularly clear in the Latin poems, most of which, as the Latin title page points out, were written *intra Annum aetatis Vigesimum:* that is, before his twentieth year had ended. In keeping with this emphasis, Milton has taken unusual care in dating his Latin poems, so as to make clear their youthfulness and the rising poet's precociousness. This atmosphere is borne out, in the elegies, by their heading *Liber primus*—a first book, a primer, for which no second book follows; and also by the retractation which ends the sequence of the seven numbered elegies. There is no need to suspect a misprint in the dating of the seventh, which comes out of chronological order,[11] for the placing of this elegy seems to be dictated by the presence of the retractation, evidently written for the seventh elegy alone, and not for this whole set of elegies; yet placed here as it is, the retractation covers any similar materials in the preceding poems and puts last the latest piece of composition, the retractation itself. This palinode creates the impression of having been composed for some special occasion (such as, perhaps, a recitation of the seventh elegy before one of those "privat Academies in *Italy*," where Milton tells us that he presented "some trifles . . . compos'd at under twenty or thereabout"),[12] when it was appropriate for the poet to speak of this youthful love poem with a tone of humorous exaggeration and a touch of mock-heroic banter:

> Haec ego mente olim laevâ, studioque supino
> Nequitiae posui vana trophaea meae.
> Scilicet abreptum sic me malus impulit error,
> Indocilisque aetas prava magistra fuit.
> Donec Socraticos umbrosa Academia rivos
> Praebuit, admissum dedocuitque jugum.
> Protinus extinctis ex illo tempore flammis,
> Cincta rigent multo pectora nostra gelu.
> Unde suis frigus metuit puer ipse Sagittis,
> Et Diomedéam vim timet ipse Venus.

These are the monuments to my wantonness that with a perverse spirit and a trifling purpose I once erected. Obviously, mischievous error led me astray and my undisciplined youth was a vicious teacher until the shady Academy offered its Socratic streams and

taught me how to escape from the yoke to which I had submitted.
From that hour those flames were extinct and thenceforward my
breast has been rigid under a thick case of ice, of which the boy
himself fears the frost for his arrows, and Venus herself is afraid of
my Diomedean strength.   [trans. Hughes]

After this coda to the formal elegies Milton adds his epigrams
written in the same verse form: first, a group of five pieces related
to the Gunpowder Plot, which we assume must be early, because
of their relation to *In quintum Novembris, Anno aetatis 17;* and lastly,
three epigrams that we know to be late, since they deal with the
singer Leonora Baroni, whom Milton heard during his visits to
Rome in 1638–39.[13] By this method of grouping Milton has man-
aged to end his section devoted to elegiac verse with poems that
give exalted praise to the Orphic powers of voice and verse, mar-
ried in song:

> Altera Torquatum cepit Leonora Poëtam,
>   Cujus ab insano cessit amore furens.
> Ah miser ille tuo quantò feliciùs aevo
>   Perditus, & propter te Leonora foret!
> Et te Pieriâ sensisset voce canentem
>   Aurea maternae fila movere lyrae,
> Quamvis Dircaeo torsisset lumina Pentheo
>   Saevior, aut totus desipuisset iners,
> Tu tamen errantes caecâ vertigine sensus
>   Voce eadem poteras composuisse tuâ;
> Et poteras aegro spirans sub corde quietem
>   Flexamino cantu restituisse sibi.

> Another Leonora captivated the poet Torquato, who for fren-
> zied love of her went mad. Ah, poor unfortunate! How much more
> happily had he been lost in your times and for love of you, Leonora!
> He would have heard you singing with Pierian voice as the golden
> strings of your mother's lyre moved in harmony. Though he had
> rolled his eyes more fiercely than Dircean Pentheus, or all insensible
> had raved, yet you by your voice could have composed his senses
> wandering in their blind whirl; and, inspiring his distempered
> heart with peace, you could have restored him to himself with your
> soul-moving song.   [trans. MacKellar]

The same Orphic theme dominates the conclusion to the sec-
ond, much longer grouping here, the *Sylvarum Liber,* poems in
various meters, where the growth toward maturity of poetic
power is marked by the poet's growing appreciation of the

philosophic and religious meaning of music's power in the universe. The first poem in this section is headed *Anno aetatis 16. In obitum Procancellarii medici,* with the date given special prominence by thus forming part of the title; and the same is true of the two following poems dated *Anno aetatis 17.* Thereafter the poems are not dated, but the first three headings have served to suggest a chronological movement while implicitly apologizing for the immaturity (and by the way implying perhaps the precocity?) of these opening pieces. After the two academic exercises that follow, the remaining poems are drawn together by interlocking themes, above all by the theme of poetical dedication set forth in *Ad Patrem*—still, as he says, one of his youthful works (*iuvenilia carmina*)—but nevertheless a poem that by its fervor and wit and firm command of hexameter marks the beginning of this poet's mature strength:

> Nec tu vatis opus divinum despice carmen,
> Quo nihil aethereos ortus, & semina caeli,
> Nil magis humanam commendat origine mentem,
> Sancta Prométhéae retinens vestigia flammae.
> Carmen amant superi, tremebundaque Tartara carmen
> Ima ciere valet, divosque ligare profundos,
> Et triplici duros Manes adamante coercet.

Scorn not the poet's song, a work divine, which more than aught else reveals our ethereal origin and heavenly race. Nothing so much as its origin does grace to the human mind, possessing yet some sacred traces of Promethean fire. The gods love song, song that has power to move the trembling depths of Tartarus, to bind the nether gods, and restrain the cruel shades with triple adamant.

[17–23, trans. MacKellar]

The implicit allusion to Orpheus is made explicit a few lines later, after Milton has imagined "the bard, seated at the festal board," singing of "the feats of heroes" and of "chaos and the broadly-laid foundations of the world."

> Denique quid vocis modulamen inane juvabit,
> Verborum sensusque vacans, numerique loquacis?
> Silvestres decet iste choros, non Orphea cantus,
> Qui tenuit fluvios & quercubus addidit aures
> Carmine, non citharâ, simulachraque functa canendo
> Compulit in lacrymas; habet has à carmine laudes.

> And finally, what will the empty modulation of the voice avail, void
> of words and sense, and of eloquent numbers? That song will do for
> the sylvan choirs, but not for Orpheus, who with song and not with
> lute held back the rivers, and gave ears to the oaks, and moved the
> shades of the dead to tears; these praises he has from song.
>
> [50–55, trans. MacKellar]

This passage prepares the way for the Orphic allusion at the close
of the poem written to the Roman poet Salzilli, where Milton
hopes that this poet's illness may be cured so that he may resume
his writing, with the result that "Swollen Tiber himself, charmed
by the song, will favor the annual hope of the husbandmen" (36–
37, trans. MacKellar).

But what shall we make of the two poems in Greek that lie
between *Ad Patrem* and *Ad Salsillum?* The first of these, the Greek
version of Psalm 114, can be securely dated in November 1634, as
we know from Milton's letter to Alexander Gill, in which he de-
scribes how he was inspired to adapt this work of the "truly divine
poet . . . to the rules of Greek Heroic song."[14] The poem thus
follows chronologically after *Ad Patrem,* if we believe, as I do, that
Ad Patrem dates from 1631–32, or, as Parker has argued, from the
earlier part of 1634.[15] But more important, the Greek version of
the psalm follows naturally after the gratitude that the poet has
just expressed to his father for encouraging him to learn, not only
Latin, but also Greek, French, Italian, and Hebrew. By his skill
in adapting and expanding the Hebrew original into Greek
hexameters we may see how far this poet has travelled intellectu-
ally since that time when, "at fifteen yeers old,"[16] he had made an
English paraphrase of the same psalm in the style of Sylvester's
Dubartas, using the current English versions as his guides. The
brief Greek epigram that follows is easily brought in here
(whenever it was written) as further evidence of linguistic com-
mand.

Then the whole volume closes with the two latest and most
complex of his Latin poems, *Mansus* and the *Epitaphium Damonis,*
bound together by Milton's elaborate description in the *Epi-
taphium* (181–97) of the two "cups" (*pocula*) that Manso gave to
Milton—gifts that Milton had hoped to show to Diodati—books,
perhaps, that they might have discussed together, as in their

younger days.[17] But above all, these two closing poems are linked
by their revelation of this poet's hopes to write a British epic:

> O mihi si mea sors talem concedat amicum
> Phoebaeos decorâsse viros qui tam bene norit,
> Si quando indigenas revocabo in carmina reges,
> Arturumque etiam sub terris bella moventem;
> Aut dicam invictae sociali foedere mensae,
> Magnanimos Heroas, & (O modo spiritus ad sit)
> Frangam Saxonicas Britonum sub Marte phalanges.

O, if my lot might but bestow such a friend upon me, a friend who
understands how to honor the devotees of Phoebus—if ever I shall
summon back our native kings into our songs, and Arthur, waging
his wars beneath the earth, or if ever I shall proclaim the mag-
nanimous heroes of the table which their mutual fidelity made in-
vincible, and (if only the spirit be with me) shall shatter the Saxon
phalanxes under the British Mars!

[Mansus, 78–84, trans. Hughes]

> Ipse ego Dardanias Rutupina per aequora puppes
> Dicam, & Pandrasidos regnum vetus Inogeniae,
> Brennúmque Arviragúmque duces, priscúmque Belinum,
> Et tandem Armoricos Britonum sub lege colonos;
> Tum gravidam Arturo fatali fraude Jögernen
> Mendaces vultus, assumptáque Gorlöis arma,
> Merlini dolus.

I would tell of Dardanian ships along the Rutupian Sea, and of the
ancient realm of Imogen, Pandrasus' daughter, of the leaders
Brennus and Arviragus, and old Belinus, and of colonists in Ar-
morica under British laws; then I would tell of Igraine pregnant
with Arthur by a fatal fraud, of the seeming face and counterfeit
arms of Gorlois, Merlin's artifice.

[Epitaphium, 162–68, trans. MacKellar]

"Quid enim?" Milton asks—"Why not a British theme?"

III

The dating of the English poems is less explicit in most cases,
but the mode of arrangement is clear. As with the Latin poems,
the over-arching structure runs from poems of early youth to
poems that enact a movement toward the broader visions of
maturity. Within this larger movement the poems are then sorted

into subordinate groupings: devotional poems, secular poems in the Jonsonian mode, sonnets, and pastoral poems; and within each of these a rough chronological arrangement can be discerned.[18]

The group headed "Sonnets," for example, opens with the English love sonnet that echoes Italian addresses to the Nightingale, but basically follows the medieval and pseudo–Chaucerian tradition of the Cuckoo and the Nightingale. Then follow the five sonnets in Italian, with their *Canzone,* paying tribute to the Petrarchans by using, as Milton says, "the language of which Love makes his boast" ("Questa e lingua di cui si vanta Amore").[19] These are all poems written in the atmosphere of the "young, unassuming and artless lover" suggested by the opening line of Sonnet 6 ("Giovane piano, e semplicetto amante"), and dramatized in the *Canzone,* where the poet shows himself surrounded by "Amorous young men and maidens . . . jesting."[20] After these playful exercises in a fading, once-popular mode, the stern lines of Sonnet 7, on the flight of his three-and-twentieth year, come with the shock of a sudden recognition, setting a severe Calvinist view of life against these early trifles:

> All is, if I have grace to use it so,
> As ever in my great task Masters eye.

The meaning of these lines, I think, is clarified if we take the word "grace" in a strict Calvinist sense: the speaker's future lies completely in the hands of God.[21] Though Time has stolen away his youth, all his hopes remain as valid as they ever were; nothing has really changed, for the use of his life depends upon the timeless will and eye and grace of God. Nothing could form a sharper contrast with the preceding sonnets; and yet the sternness of the doctrine itself may suggest a veering from one youthful extreme to another—especially since the movement of the sonnet still maintains a conventional, end-stopped, balanced manner. The succeeding sonnet on the military threat to London shows (as the earlier discussion has implied) a greater maturity, reflected in its ironic posture and in the graceful sentence that winds its sinewy length over the last five lines.

Then the group closes with two more sonnets addressed to

women, both sonnets forming a tacit contrast with the Petrarchan mode, in theme and in technique. Recalling the "Donna" of Milton's Italian sonnets, we are alert to appreciate the growth and change represented in the suspended opening of Sonnet 9:

> Lady that in the prime of earliest youth,
>> Wisely hast shun'd the broad way and the green,
>> And with those few art eminently seen,
>> That labour up the Hill of heav'nly Truth,
> The better part with *Mary,* and [with] *Ruth,*
>> Chosen thou hast . . .

Lastly, Sonnet 10, with an even greater suspension and involution,[22] addresses a married lady who in herself maintains the virtues that once ruled in England, before the turmoil of the present age began:

> Daughter to that good Earl, once President
>> Of *Englands* Counsel, and her Treasury,
>> Who liv'd in both, unstain'd with gold or fee,
>> And left them both, more in himself content,
> Till the sad breaking of that Parlament
>> Broke him, as that dishonest victory
>> At *Chaeronèa,* fatal to liberty
>> Kil'd with report that Old man eloquent,
> Though later born, then to have known the dayes
>> Wherin your Father flourisht, yet by you
>> Madam, me thinks I see him living yet;
> So well your words his noble vertues praise,
>> That all both judge you to relate them true,
>> And to possess them, Honour'd *Margaret.*

Thus the syntax involves the troubled, more inclusive vision of maturity, while the *disio amoroso* of the Italian sonnets lies far in the past.

Similarly, it is helpful to read *L'Allegro* and *Il Penseroso* in the context of Milton's chosen arrangement; for these two poems come at the end of a group that might best be described as Jonsonian: poems in the mode of the "terse" couplet characteristic of Jonson and his Sons. First, the "witty" *Epitaph on the Marchioness of Winchester;* next, that perfect distillation of the Elizabethan madrigal, the *Song On May morning;* then the rather labored epigram on Shakespeare, dated 1630, and marked as early by the archaic

"Star-ypointing"; and then the two jocular epitaphs for the University Carrier. Out of these experiments arise the two great companion poems, or twin poems, or the double poem, as we have come to call them. Reading these two poems in their original context may guide us toward a slight modification or qualification of these descriptive phrases. They are companion poems, certainly, but they are not of equal strength and stature.[23] Their relation is rather that of Younger Brother to Elder Brother. The parallels between them, so familiar to everyone, should not lead us to read the poems in parallel, as though they were two sides of a coin, or two sides of an academic debate. For the poems develop a linear, sequential effect, moving from youthful hedonism toward the philosophic, contemplative mind.[24]

It has often been noted that *L'Allegro* is looser in its handling of versification and syntax than *Il Penseroso*. According to Sprott, for example, the basic iambic tetrameter is varied with trochaic lines thirty-two percent of the time in *L'Allegro,* but only sixteen percent of the time in *Il Penseroso*.[25] Hence the subtle effect of "uncertainty" that Weismiller finds in reading the rhythms is much greater in *L'Allegro* than in *Il Penseroso*.[26] As for syntax, its occasional looseness in *L'Allegro* may be indicated by the sharp debate[27] that has arisen over these lines:

> To hear the Lark begin his flight,
> And singing startle the dull night,
> From his watch-towre in the skies,
> Till the dappled dawn doth rise;
> Then to com in spight of sorrow,
> And at my window bid good morrow,
> Through the Sweet-Briar, or the Vine,
> Or the twisted Eglantine.   [41–48]

Is it the lark or is it L'Allegro who comes to the window to greet the speaker in his bed? At first "to com" may seem to be in parallel with "to hear". Yet consideration of the context indicates that this cannot be so, for the lines immediately following, and all the rest of the poem, present L'Allegro as the receiver of impressions from without—"list'ning," "walking," measuring the landscape with his eye, hearing tales about the "lubbar Fend," and so on. No, "to com" is rather in rough parallel with "begin." It is the lark who

greets L'Allegro with his song, just as in the next lines "the Cock
with lively din, / Scatters the rear of darknes thin."

A greater freedom of syntax occurs in the speaker's memory of
the tales about the goblin:

> She was pincht, and pull'd she sed,
> And he by Friars Lanthorn led
> Tells how the drudging *Goblin* swet,
> To ern his Cream-bowle duly set . . .   [103–06]

In the edition of 1673 the second line is altered to read "And by
the Friars Lanthorn led"—but this change does not affect the
colloquial looseness of the phrasing.

Such syntactical looseness is hardly a defect in the poem, any
more than the striking variations in meter: these are all part of a
poem designed with "wanton heed, and giddy cunning," the
poem of "fancies child," warbling "his native Wood-notes wilde," a
poem that moves with "light fantastick toe" to celebrate "The
Mountain Nymph, sweet Liberty." Freedom of movement, with-
out concentration of mind, is implicit in those floating participles:
"list'ning" (53) and "walking" (57), which relate to the wish of the
"I" and "me" (34–35) some twenty lines before. Indeed the pro-
nouns "I" and "me" occur only four times in *L'Allegro,* as com-
pared with eleven times in *Il Penseroso.* Instead it is "mine eye"—
an "it"—that measures the lawn and sees the towers; and when the
"upland Hamlets . . . invite," they invite no particular person,
but everyman; and later on "Towred Cities please *us.*" In every
possible way a generalized receiver of shifting impressions is
created, so that at the close even Orpheus becomes, not a singer,
but a listener! For the speaker wishes

> That *Orpheus* self may heave his head
> From golden slumber on a bed
> Of heapt *Elysian* flowres, and hear
> Such streins as would have won the ear
> Of *Pluto,* to have quite set free
> His half-regain'd *Eurydice.*   [145–50]

All this presents a sharp contrast with the poem of "the fixed
mind" whose presiding goddess, "Sober, stedfast, and demure," is
urged to keep her "wonted state, / With eev'n step, and musing
gate." The "Cherub Contemplation" here works within a personal

presence whose mind not only receives impressions from without, but also actively addresses and "woos" their action:

> Sweet Bird that shunn'st the noise of folly,
> Most musicall, most melancholy!
> Thee Chauntress oft the Woods among,
> I woo to hear thy eevn-Song . . .   [61–64]

This speaker does not float with loose participles; his stance is precise, active, personal: "I walk," "I hear". He hopes to set his lamp in the lonely tower in order to spend the night in deep study of Hermes, Plato, and the great tragedians, while his mind longs to behold Orpheus in vital action:

> But, O sad Virgin, that thy power
> Might raise *Musaeus* from his bower,
> Or bid the soul of *Orpheus* sing
> Such notes as warbled to the string,
> Drew Iron tears down *Pluto's* cheek,
> And made Hell grant what Love did seek.   [103–08]

And after his dreams, set in an harmonious Theocritean landscape, he hopes to hear the music represented in *Arcades* and the Ludlow *Maske:*

> And as I wake, sweet musick breath
> Above, about, or underneath,
> Sent by som spirit to mortals good,
> Or th'unseen Genius of the Wood.   [151–54]

But even such listening is too passive for this speaker: he soon directs himself "To walk the studious Cloysters pale," and to "love" the beauties of Gothic architecture, while "the pealing Organ" and "the full voic'd Quire" will, he hopes, inspire the contemplative mind to its highest reaches, and

>   through mine ear
> Dissolve me into extasies,
> And bring all Heav'n before mine eyes.   [164–66]

Looking back now, we can see that the first poem has summed up a youthful world of Elizabethan poetry now past; the tone has been set in the opening archaism, "In Heav'n ycleap'd *Euphrosyne.*" It is full of all the maying and the pastoral joys celebrated in hundreds of Elizabethan airs and madrigals, including the famous "Come live with me," strongly echoed near the beginning (39) and at the very end; and it remembers too those popular legends about Mab and the drudging goblin, celebrated by Shakespeare and Drayton. Then there are the allusions to the "high triumphs" of archaic chivalry, to the courtly "Ladies, whose bright eies / Rain influence" in Petrarchan fashion, to "mask, and antique Pageantry," to Jonson's comedies, and to Shakespeare in his comic and pastoral vein.[28] It is a joyous celebration and re-creation of an era, a state of mind, now past; but we note that it ends with hints that suggest this is not the highest mode of harmony. As every Platonist knew, Plato had condemned the "soft *Lydian* Aires," and Milton subtly recalls the condemnation, while seeming to ignore it:

> With wanton heed, and giddy cunning,
> The melting voice through mazes running . . .   [141–42]

But the words "wanton," "giddy," and "melting" recall the implications of the *Republic:*

> Again, drunkenness, effeminacy, and inactivity are most un-suitable in Guardians. Which are the modes expressing softness and the ones used at drinking-parties?
> There are the Ionian and certain Lydian modes which are called "slack."
> You will not use them in the training of your warriors?
> Certainly not.   [III.398c–400c, trans. Cornford][29]

The final picture of Orpheus heaving up his head "From golden slumber on a bed / Of heapt *Elysian* flowres" carries on, however beautifully, the "softness" of the Lydian mode, in contrast to the potent, active Orpheus of *Il Penseroso.* Furthermore, this second reference to Orpheus is subsumed within the middle of *Il Penseroso,* where he is only one of many great poets and thinkers. The spirit of Plato's "shady Academy"[30] (derived traditionally from Orpheus and Pythagoras) dominates *Il Penseroso,* from the opening salutation of the Goddess "sage and holy" to the grand musical close which extends this poem two dozen lines beyond the length of *L'Allegro.* All is, however, subtly qualified at the very end, as the poem presents a picture that is too obviously archaic and senti-

mental to be taken solemnly: its excess tells us that Melancholy too
needs tempering:

> And may at last my weary age
> Find out the peacefull hermitage,
> The Hairy Gown and Mossy Cell,
> Where I may sit and rightly spell,
> Of every Star that Heav'n doth shew,
> And every Herb that sips the dew;
> Till old experience do attain
> To somthing like Prophetic strain.
> These pleasures *Melancholy* give,
> And I with thee will choose to live.

That echo of "Come live with me" is phrased more positively than
the closing couplet of *L'Allegro:*

> These delights, if thou canst give,
> Mirth with thee, I mean to live.

Yet the echo reminds us that either choice involves a limitation.

Thus the two poems move from youth to age—the word
"youthfull" is invoked twice in *L'Allegro,* and not at all in *Il
Penseroso*—while in their movement these two unequal but com-
patible companions suggest the growth toward maturity that con-
stitutes this volume's dominant theme.

IV

Turning now, finally, to the devotional group that begins Mil-
ton's book, we note that he has carefully stressed the youthfulness
of the four opening poems. First, out of strict chronological order,
we have the poem headed: *On the morning of Christs Nativity. Com-
pos'd 1629.*—with the date thus given prominence as part of the
title.[31] Then come the two psalms, "don by the Author at fifteen
yeers old," as the headnote tells us. Then the unfinished poem on
the Passion, with the famous note at the end: "This Subject the
Author finding to be above the yeers he had, when he wrote it,
and nothing satisfi'd with what was begun, left it unfinisht." One may
wonder why Milton bothered to include this acknowledged failure
and fragment, when he did not include the more interesting and
at least completed English poems that he added in 1673: the poem

On the Death of a fair Infant, and the lines from the *Vacation Exercise.*
But the inclusion of the fragment has a clear function: to stress
the immaturity of these opening pieces, to suggest the ambitious
young man outreaching his powers, and achieving poetical success
only when he can subject his muse to some deliberate limitation.
What he can accomplish is then demonstrated in the three short
pieces that follow: *On Time, Upon the Circumcision,* and *At a solemn
Musick;* these are undated, and thus, we assume, not quite so
youthful. *Upon the Circumcision,* in particular, suggests a new be-
ginning, in a less venturous mode, after the false start of *The
Passion;* here the poet, by skillfully imitating the stanza-form of
Petrarch's canzone to the Virgin, creates a carefully controlled
meditation on the love of the suffering Infant.[32] The other two
lyrics are experiments in the handling of the canzone, anticipating
the flexible verse-form of *Lycidas. At a solemn Musick* bears a special
significance as the final poem in this group, for its transcendent
praise of the wedded powers of voice and verse links with the view
of music's power to be found in *Arcades,* the Ludlow *Maske,* the
epigrams to Leonora, *Ad Patrem,* and *Mansus.* It is thus a poem
that helps to tie the entire volume together, as well as this small
opening group, where the final lyric recalls the heavenly music
heard by the shepherds in the long youthful poem on the Nativity
that Milton has wisely chosen to open his book, as prologue to the
rising poet's achievement.

The dating, "Compos'd 1629," accords with the Nativity poem's
relation to an age and mode of English poetry now outgrown,
both by the nation and by the poet. In understanding this poetical
mode, one may gain important clues from Milton's description of
the Nativity Ode in his sixth Latin elegy—especially when we read
this elegy in Milton's chosen context, between the Ovidian celebra-
tion of Spring in *Elegia quinta* and the mildly Ovidian eroticism of
Elegia septima. Read thus, *Elegia sexta* does not lend itself easily to
the widely held view that the Ode "teaches us to read the contrast
of the elegiac and the heroic vein as a repudiation of the former,
to transliterate the description of the heroic poet into Christian
terms as the account of a dedicated spirit divinely inspired."[33] This
elegy begins with a broad joke about Diodati's feasting at the
Christmas season:

Mitto tibi sanam non pleno ventre salutem,
    Quâ tu distento forte carere potes.

With a stomach anything but full, I send you a prayer for sound
health, of which, perhaps, you, with your stomach stretched to its
uttermost, may be in sore need.   [trans. Knapp][34]

Then follows lively praise of festive poetry and the "light elegy,"
in a passage twice as long as the subsequent praise of epic: wine,
feasting, maidens, and dancing inspire, says Milton, an excellent
kind of poetry, blessed by many gods. Of course, he adds, if a poet
wants to write on grand epic themes, then he must live quite
differently; and Milton proceeds to write a hyperbolical account
of the ascetic life required for such a bard:

Ille quidem parcè Samii pro more magistri
    Vivat, & innocuos praebeat herba cibos;
Stet prope fagineo pellucida lympha catillo,
    Sobriaque è puro pocula fonte bibat.

let him live sparingly, like the Samian teacher [Pythagoras] and let
herbs furnish his innocent diet. Let the purest water stand beside
him in a bowl of beech and let him drink sober draughts from the
pure spring.   [59–62, trans. Hughes]

He goes on to express his belief in the exalted power of this kind
of bard, but he does not wholly lay aside the tone of "Ovidian
banter" that Rand has found in the earlier part.[35] Milton no doubt
hopes to reach that higher vein himself; but he does not appear to
be saying so here. When he turns to discuss himself at the end of
the poem, he makes a clean break with the previous discussion of
elegy and epic; both are excellent in their kinds, the poet implies,
but he is not writing in either vein at the moment:

At tu siquid agam, scitabere (si modò saltem
    Esse putas tanti noscere siquid agam)
Paciferum canimus caelesti semine regem,
    Faustaque sacratis saecula pacta libris,
Vagitumque Dei, & stabulantem paupere tecto
    Qui suprema suo cum patre regna colit.
Stelliparumque polum, modulantesque aethere turmas,
    Et subitò elisos ad sua fana Deos.
Dona quidem dedimus Christi natalibus illa,
    Illa sub auroram lux mihi prima tulit.   [79–88]

One must stress the *At tu siquid agam, scitabere:* "But if you will know what I am doing (if only you think it of any importance to know whether I am doing anything)"—note how he maintains the familiar tone with which the poem has opened—"I am singing the heaven-descended King, the bringer of peace, and the blessed times promised in the sacred books—the infant cries of our God" [which in fact are not mentioned in the Nativity poem as we have it; but Milton is emphasizing the poem's allegiance to the naïve tradition of the Christmas carol, as his next words further indicate] "and his stabling under a mean roof who, with his Father, governs the realms above. I am singing the starry sky and the hosts that sang high in air, and the gods that were suddenly destroyed in their own shrines. These are my gifts for the birthday of Christ—gifts which the first light of its dawn brought to me" (trans. Hughes). In that last clause Milton seems to be saying only that the writing of the poem began at dawn; there seems to be no indication of a special experience of religious dedication.

In this elegy's final couplet the opening *Te quoque* has allowed various interpretations:[36]

> Te quoque pressa manent patriis meditata cicutis,
> Tu mihi, cui recitem, judicis instar eris.

In some versions it appears that Milton is referring to certain *other* English poems that he has also written; but the *quoque* modifies *te;* or, rather, it is pleonastic and is best omitted, as in the revised translation of Hughes, which makes it plain that the passage is still alluding to the Nativity poem: "For you these simple strains that have been meditated on my native pipes are waiting; and you, when I recite them to you, shall be my judge." *Patriis meditata cicutis:* meditated on the native hemlock pipes of the humble shepherd. Milton has suggested here the Nativity poem's basic decorum.

It is, first of all, a poem that declares, in many ways, this poet's indebtedness to his predecessors in the line of English poetry. The four prefatory stanzas, written in a variation of rhyme royal, suggest the use of this ancient stanza-form by Chaucer and the Chaucerians, by Spenser, in *The Ruines of Time* and the *Fowre Hymnes,* and by Shakespeare, in *Lucrece;* while the modification

into hexameter in the final line declares a further allegiance to
Spenser and the Spenserians. The stanza of the Hymn proper is
even more significant, for its first six lines suggest the movement
of a popular song or carol:

> It was the Winter wilde,
> While the Heav'n-born-childe,
>   All meanly wrapt in the rude manger lies;
> Nature in aw to him
> Had doff't her gawdy trim,
>   With her great Master so to sympathize.

The use of three-foot and five-foot lines, in various combinations,
is found in many Elizabethan songs: thus among Thomas Mor-
ley's canzonets we find this stanza running 335335335, though the
rhyme differs from Milton's:[37]

> I follow, lo, the footing
> Still of my lovely cruel,
> Proud of herself that she is beauty's jewel.
>   And fast away she flieth,
>   Love's sweet delight deriding,
> In woods and groves sweet Nature's treasure hiding.
>   Yet cease I not pursuing,
>   But since I thus have sought her,
> Will run me out of breath till I have caught her.

But the first six lines of Milton's stanza also suggest another pat-
tern: the combination of two- and three-foot lines, with Milton's
rhyme scheme, found in some of the ancient Christmas carols:

> The God Almyght
> And Kyng of Lyght,
>   Whose powr is ouer all,
> Gyue vs of grace
> For to purchas
>   Hys realme celestyall.

> Wher hys aungels
> And archangels
>   Do syng incessantly,
> Hys princypates
> And potestates
>   Maketh gret armony.

> The cherubyns

And seraphyns
　　With ther tvnykes mery,
The trones al,
Most musycall,
　　Syng the heuenly Kery.[38]

Then, by allowing his last line to swell out into a Spenserian
alexandrine, Milton draws his poem out of the realm of the popu-
lar song into the larger area of this poet's predestined goals. In
stanza after stanza we may feel this change from the simple lan-
guage and steady beat of the ballad into the realms of a more
ambitious art:

But wisest Fate sayes no,
This must not yet be so,
　　The Babe lies yet in smiling Infancy,
That on the bitter cross
Must redeem our loss;
　　So both himself and us to glorifie:
Yet first to those ychain'd in sleep,
The wakefull trump of doom must thunder through the deep.
　　　　　　　　　　　　　　　　　　　　[149–56]

With all the poem's lofty expansions in rhythm, in language,
and in rich allusion, the poet's chosen method of control never
falters: he clings to the central mode of the ancient naïve, the
mode of the Nativity ballad, the mode that Milton points to in his
prologue when he calls his poem a "humble ode" that he seeks to
lay "lowly at his blessed feet." The touches of archaic, Spenserian
language sprinkled throughout, very lightly, are all adjusted to
maintain this effect, as in the "ychain'd" of the stanza just quoted,
the "lusty Paramour" of the Hymn's opening stanza, the "silly
thoughts" of the shepherds, or the "dusky eyn" of the doomed
god Osiris. At the same time touches of old-fashioned heavy allit-
eration recall the style, not only of Spenser, but of all those lesser
writers whom Sidney mocked for their "rimes, running in ratling
rowes."

This decorum of an ancient and traditional simplicity pervades
every aspect of the poem, versification, language, scene painting,
imagery, and theme.[39] The scenes and images are given in broad
and simplified terms, as in some old tapestry or pageant. The

original line (143) in which Truth and Justice wear "Th'enameld
Arras of the Rainbow" is more closely in accord with the poem
than Milton's more sophisticated revision: "Orb'd in a Rain-bow."
Thus Nature seeks to hide her "guilty front" with "The Saintly
Vail of Maiden white"; and "the meek-eyd Peace . . . crown'd
with Olive green, came softly sliding / Down through the turning
sphear" (39,42,46–48). "The Shepherds on the Lawn . . . Sate
simply chatting in a rustick row"; then

> At last surrounds their sight
> A Globe of circular light,
>   That with long beams the shame-fac't night array'd,
> The helmed Cherubim
> And sworded Seraphim,
>   Are seen in glittering ranks with wings displaid.
>   [85,87,109–14]

One should note, too, in these quotations, the curious mixture
of past and present tense, which Lowry Nelson has ably inter-
preted to indicate the poem's sense of a timeless world;[40] this is so,
yet Milton's manner of thus mixing past and present also adds to
the effect of the naïve, as though the poet were artlessly following
the instinct of a momentary mood or were using past and present
tense as the needs of rhythm and rhyme might, for a moment,
require.

Then, in the latter half of the poem, this effect is strongly
heightened by Milton's treatment of the various characters that
here are shown in action. The Dragon of Revelation is presented
in the guise of a dragon out of folklore:

> And wrath to see his Kingdom fail,
> Swindges the scaly Horrour of his foulded tail.   [171–72]

And his antagonist, the blessèd Babe, is likewise shown in the
manner of some ancient folk-hero, some infant Hercules:

> Our Babe to shew his Godhead true,
> Can in his swadling bands controul the damned crew. [227–29]

Meanwhile, in the superb rendition of the fall of the pagan deities,
it is helpful, while we recognize the foreshadowing of *Paradise
Lost,* to notice also how utterly lacking in sophistication this ac-

count is, when compared with Milton's later roll call of the fallen
angels. In *Paradise Lost* it is made plain that these are devils adored
as deities, and the horror of the deception is brought home by
showing in detail the effect of these devils upon mankind:

> First *Moloch,* horrid King besmear'd with blood
> Of human sacrifice, and parents tears,
> Though for the noyse of Drums and Timbrels loud
> Their childrens cries unheard, that past through fire
> To his grim Idol. Him the *Ammonite*
> Worshipt in *Rabba* and her watry Plain . . .   [1.392–97]

and so on for eight more lines of particular detail, showing the
ravages wrought by Moloch on the earth.

But here in the Nativity poem Moloch is simply mentioned as a
totally defeated character, while the scene of his idolatry is repre-
sented in elementary colors and sounds:

> And sullen *Moloch* fled,
> Hath left in shadows dred,
>   His burning Idol all of blackest hue,
> In vain with Cymbals ring,
> They call the grisly king,
>   In dismall dance about the furnace blue.   [205–10]

These vanquished gods are not devils in disguise; they are the
supernatural beings of antique folklore, who exist in their own
right as a part of nature, a part of man's primitive consciousness
of forces that lie beyond his control:

> The lonely mountains o're,
> And the resounding shore,
>   A voice of weeping heard, and loud lament;
> From haunted spring, and dale
> Edg'd with poplar pale,
>   The parting Genius is with sighing sent,
> With flowre-inwov'n tresses torn
> The Nimphs in twilight shade of tangled thickets mourn.
>   [181–88]

Finally, bringing to a brilliant close this basic effect of the simple
and naïve, Milton ends with two stanzas that sum up the basic
techniques and attitudes of the poem. First we have the poem's
most extravagantly naïve image—one that would have offended at

the outset—but, now, with our minds attuned to the poem's pecu-
liar decorum, we can perhaps accept it as a youthful excess:

> So when the Sun in bed,
> Curtain'd with cloudy red,
>   Pillows his chin upon an Orient wave . . .   [229–31]

Then come the ghosts and fairies of folklore, treated with sym-
pathy and even affection:

> The flocking shadows pale,
> Troop to th'infernall jail,
>   Each fetter'd Ghost slips to his severall grave,
> And the yellow-skirted *Fayes,*
> Fly after the Night-steeds, leaving their Moon-lov'd maze.
>   [232–36]

And lastly, we return to the traditional scene, ten thousand times
represented in ancient poetry and painting: the manger scene
upon which this technique of the naïve has been based:

> But see the Virgin blest,
> Hath laid her Babe to rest.
>   Time is our tedious Song should here have ending.

Here, still, is the simple, humble singer, who is well aware of his
defects, but nevertheless has been led by gratitude to sing this
song of praise:

> Heav'ns youngest teemed Star,
> Hath fixt her polisht Car,
>   Her sleeping Lord with Handmaid Lamp attending:

All Heaven, whether physical or spiritual, stands fixed in a service
of unlabored elegance:

> And all about the Courtly Stable,
> Bright-harnest Angels sit in order serviceable.

The last rhyme seems to call attention to the way in which
Milton has contrived, within his chosen mode, to make even the
poem's defects appear as virtues, contributing to the total effect of
the youthful singer writing as well as he can in an ancient, tra-
ditional manner of tribute. The poem is a total success because
Milton has chosen and maintained a mode of writing that does not
tempt him beyond the range of his precocious powers.

That is not to say that the poem is simple-minded in the range of its implications, but that the chosen mode of simplicity creates a world in which theological problems are pushed beyond the fringe of our vision; there is no sense of struggling with theological issues, no sense that we need to consult the church fathers, no sense of attempting to enforce anything but the most easily grasped and broadly acceptable truths. This, says the poet, is the happy morn when, as everyone knows,

> the Son of Heav'ns eternal King,
> Of wedded Maid, and Virgin Mother born,
> Our great redemption from above did bring.   [2–4]

Everyone shares the story, how the Son laid aside the majesty that was his due as part of Trinal Unity,

> and here with us to be,
> Forsook the Courts of everlasting Day,
> And chose with us a darksom House of mortal Clay.   [12–14]

How can we express our gratitude for this gift of the Almighty? By a song of praise for the peace and harmony that the divine child has brought to earth, not only on the day of his birth, and in the long-range future, but, in some measure, now: it "now begins," as this poet can best testify by writing a song that in itself represents a simple and unworried harmony.

But—"Compos'd 1629." More difficult and much more complex harmonies lie ahead for the rising poet, the predestined bard.

CHAPTER 3

Lycidas: Building the Lofty Rhyme

Nothing could pay a higher tribute to Milton's sense of significant balance and contrast than the placement of the Nativity Ode and *Lycidas* in his volume of 1645: at the beginning and the end of his shorter English poems. Both poems have a personal prologue and an objective conclusion in one stanza, while the body of each poem displays a movement that modulates into three sequences.[1] But there the similarity ends. The Nativity poem shows its origins in English poetry and popular song by the stanza that ends the opening sequence of the Hymn:

> The Shepherds on the Lawn,
> Or ere the point of dawn,
>   Sate simply chatting in a rustick row;
> Full little thought they than,
> That the mighty *Pan*
>   Was kindly com to live with them below;
> Perhaps their loves, or els their sheep,
> Was all that did their silly thoughts so busie keep.   [viii]

But *Lycidas,* moving far beyond such deliberate naiveté, recalls within its intricate measure the entire range of European pastoral, ancient and modern.[2]

A figure named Lycidas plays an important role in the seventh idyll of Theocritus and the ninth eclogue of Vergil. In Theocritus the character named Lycidas is a goatherd: "nor could one that saw him have mistaken him, for beyond all he looked the goatherd. On his shoulders he wore the tawny skin of a thick-haired, shaggy goat reeking of fresh curd, and round his breast an aged tunic was girt with a broad belt; in his right hand he grasped a crooked club of wild olive."[3] There is not much resemblance, it would seem, to the young Cambridge graduate whose death has provided the occasion for Milton's poem. But if we read on in this idyll some relationships will emerge. The idyll is told in the first person by the poet Simichidas, who seems to represent a persona of Theocritus; on the way to a harvest festival, this poet meets with Lycidas and greets him thus:

> Friend Lycidas, all tell me you are
> a piper without all peer among herdsmen or reapers.
> And happy I am to hear it—yet I've a lurking
> hope I may prove your equal . . . .
> let's sing
> country-style: the pleasure may well be mutual.
> I too am a sounding reed of the Muses, and called by all
> an excellent poet—though Zeus knows, I'm no gull!
> I am not, in my own conceit, a match as yet
> for the noble Samian Sicelidas, nor Philetas.
> I should rival their song as a frog vies with cicadas!
> [27–31,36–41, trans. Rist]

Lycidas, with a hearty laugh, offers to give Simichidas his olive stick because of the younger poet's lack of pretensions. "But let us begin the singing," he continues, "See here, friend, if you like / a trifling thing I laboured over lately on the hillside." Lycidas proceeds to sing a song in which he wishes fair voyage to Mitylene for his friend Ageanax, hoping he may "find all weather to his turn and reach his haven"—a fate quite the opposite of that which overtakes Milton's Lycidas. Now Simichidas answers:

> Lycidas, friend, I too
> have herding on the mountains learned from the nymphs
> many a noble theme—it may be fame
> has borne them even to the throne of Zeus! But this

I shall regale you with is by far the foremost.
Hear me, then, for dear you prove to the Muses.
[91–95, trans. Rist]

Then after Simichidas sings a rather comic love-song, the idyll
quickly concludes as Lycidas takes another road, giving
Simichidas his olive stick "as a token of our friendship from the
Muses," while Simichidas and his friends turn "toward
Phrasidamus' farm" to celebrate the harvest festival of Demeter
described in my opening chapter.

This is, then, an idyll which represents man and nature in per-
fect harmony, fulfilling at the close the harmony promised by the
two songs that we have just heard; and above all it is an idyll about
poets and poetry. The figure of Lycidas here has been interpreted
by Gilbert Lawall as a "goatherd-satyr" who "embodies the pas-
toral hillside world and is by nature a consummate musician or
piper." "The hillside is a world of poetry, where Lycidas com-
posed his song and where Simichidas learned his from the
nymphs." Lycidas, in short, is a symbol of the "perfect poet," while
the poem's frame of the harvest festival may be interpreted as "an
allegory of poetic inspiration."[4] Whether or not one wholly agrees
with this interpretation, the mere fact that such a view is possible
and plausible suggests a powerful reason for Milton's choice of
this name out of all the pastoral names available.

When the figure Lycidas[5] reappears in Vergil's Eclogue Nine,
he is still a poet who appreciates other poets, and especially he
appreciates the poems of one Menalcas, often regarded as a per-
sona for Vergil himself. In Eclogue Nine we find that the life of
the absent Menalcas has been endangered by disputes over the
expropriation of property, as Lycidas exclaims:

To think, Menalcas, how near we came to losing you and, with you,
all you did to cheer our lives! Who would have sung to us about the
Nymphs? Who would have strewn wild flowers on the ground or
given our springs green cover from the sun? Who else could have
written the lines I overheard you sing the other day, quite unaware
of me, as you were on your way to see our darling Amaryllis?
[17–22, trans. Rieu]

This seems to be the Amaryllis celebrated in Eclogue One, and
mentioned in two other eclogues; a girl derived from that Amaryl-
lis who is comically serenaded in the third idyll of Theocritus:

Charming Amaryllis, why no more dost thou peep out of this thy
cave and call me in—me, thy sweetheart? Dost hate me? Am I, then,
snub-nosed to thy eye on closer view, maiden? And does my beard
stick out? Thou'lt make me hang myself.   [6–9, trans. Gow]

In Vergil's ninth eclogue, however, a sad note of imminent
destruction is eroding the pastoral harmony in which the Lycidas
of Theocritus had flourished. Nevertheless, Vergil's Lycidas is
optimistic and still trusts in the power of song, saying, "I too am a
poet who has found some favour with the Muse. I too have written
songs. I too have heard the shepherds call me bard." And then he
adds an echo of a passage that I have quoted from Theocritus:
"But I take it from them with a grain of salt: I have the feeling that
I cannot yet compare with Varius or Cinna, but cackle like a goose
among melodious swans" (32–36). His friend Moeris, however, is
quite despondent, saying, "Time carries everything away, even
our memories. How often as a boy I sang through the long sum-
mer day and put the sun to bed! So many songs forgotten! And
now my very voice is failing me" (51–54). But Lycidas encourages
him, finding still a harmony in nature and finding still a time for
song: "Now is the moment—look around! Through all its length
the lake lies calm and hushed for you; the blustering wind has
fallen: not a murmur left . . . here, Moeris, let us sing. Rest your
kids now, and we shall still reach town. Or, if it looks as though the
night might turn to rain before we are in, why not go forward
singing all the way?" (57–65; trans. Rieu).[6]
     Among the followers of Vergil, singers named Lycidas play
important roles in the third and sixth eclogues of Calpurnius
Siculus (first century A.D.) and in the fourth eclogue of
Nemesianus (third century A.D.); these poems were well known in
the Renaissance (see below, chapter 13). But for Milton perhaps
the most important of the later appearances of the singer Lycidas
in Latin poetry occurs in the first "Piscatorial Eclogue" of Sanna-
zaro, which seems to have exerted an influence upon the latter part
of Milton's poem.[7] In Sannazaro Lycidas is again a poet, who, in a
setting among the fishermen by the Bay of Naples, sings a lament
for his beloved Phyllis, buried on the shore. "Sweet are the sounds
of your singing, Lycidas," says the fisherman Mycon, as he urges
Lycidas to repeat the song. But Lycidas, overcome by sorrow,
declines, adding:

Yet these and many others besides shall I sing for you, and better perhaps, if the Muse will be with me as I sing. But these too I shall some day inscribe to be seen by the sailing ships, whether under the spreading cliff of Procida or Miseno, and shall trace in rust great letters which the passing sailor may scan from the open sea and say: "Lycidas, Lycidas made these songs."   [119–25; trans. Nash][8]

It is clear that the creative powers of Lycidas have been in no way weakened by his loss of Phyllis; his songs will dominate the scene, while man and sea and land survive in pastoral harmony.

But now in Milton's poem it appears that the destruction feared by Moeris in Vergil has in fact overtaken both Lycidas and his pastoral harmony: a loss that Milton's opening stanza evokes in every possible way, by imagery, by statement, by faltering verse and rhymes (for one line is short and two of the lines are un-rhymed). Milton's prologue suggests a sonnet, for it consists of fourteen lines containing echoes of the familiar Petrarchan rhyme-scheme;[9] but the form is eroded and disrupted by sorrow and fear:

> Yet once more, O ye Laurels, and once more
> Ye Myrtles brown, with Ivy never-sear,
> I com to pluck your Berries harsh and crude,
> And with forc'd fingers rude,
> Shatter your leaves before the mellowing year.
> Bitter constraint, and sad occasion dear,
> Compels me to disturb your season due . . .   [1–7]

Thus in faltering form the prologue speaks of the disruption of the order of seasonal growth, the disruption of that "mellowing year" celebrated by Theocritus in his imagery of the harvest festival.

Meanwhile the repetition of the words "once more" in Milton's opening unrhymed line evokes echoes of language that lies far beyond the realm of Theocritus and Vergil; for the line echoes a passage from the Epistle to the Hebrews (12:25–27):[10]

See that ye refuse not him that speaketh. For if they escaped not who refused him that spake on earth, much more shall not we escape, if we turn away from him that speaketh from heaven: Whose voice then shook the earth [at Mt. Sinai]: but now he hath promised, saying, Yet once more I shake not the earth only, but also heaven. And this word, Yet once more, signifieth the removing of those things that are shaken, as of things that are made, that those things which cannot be shaken may remain.

The modern translation of the Jerusalem Bible[11] makes the point for Milton's *Lycidas* as clear as possible: "The words *once more* show that since the things being shaken are created things [i.e., laurels, myrtle, ivy, poetry, men], they are going to be changed, so that the unshakeable things will be left."

Thus even within the sad and shaken opening of Milton's poem, there seems to lie a secret promise of redemption, for the passage from the Epistle to the Hebrews contains a promise that the things of earth will be shaken, in order that certain immortal things may be revealed. But we cannot see this promise now, so deep is the speaker's sorrow:

> For *Lycidas* is dead, dead ere his prime
> Young *Lycidas,* and hath not left his peer:
> Who would not sing for *Lycidas*? he knew
> Himself to sing, and build the lofty rhyme.
> He must not flote upon his watry bear
> Unwept, and welter to the parching wind,
> Without the meed of som melodious tear.   [8–14]

A heavy emphasis falls upon that word *welter,* occurring as it does in an unrhymed line, and linked by sound to "watry," "wept," and "wind." What does it mean—*welter*? "To rise and fall tumultuously, or roll, toss, or tumble, as if by the motion of waves; hence, figuratively, to be agitated or disturbed; to be in a turmoil; as, the people's passions *weltered* in revolution; a vessel *weltering* in the trough of the sea."[12]

The poem indeed begins and for a long time continues in what might be called a *weltering* motion, with the lines rocking and repeating, as if in some directionless agony:

> For *Lycidas* is dead, dead ere his prime
> Young *Lycidas,* and hath not left his peer:
> Who would not sing for *Lycidas*?

This sort of repetition, inherited from previous pastoral elegists,[13] becomes by Milton's accentuation a very theme of the poem, a sign of the poem's anguish:

> Begin then, Sisters of the sacred well,
> That from beneath the seat of *Jove* doth spring,
> Begin, and somwhat loudly sweep the string.   [15–17]

Yet the repeated "Begin" contains the stabilizing power of tradition, as it echoes the refrains from the first idyll of Theocritus and the *Lament for Bion*: "Begin, dear Muses, begin the pastoral song"; "Begin, Sicilian Muses, begin the dirge" (trans. Gow). The repetition thus prepares the way for the living poet's hope that at his own death some fellow-singer will pay him tribute, even as he is now paying tribute to his own poetical friend and to the whole line of poets who sang under the name Lycidas:

> Hence with denial vain, and coy excuse,
> So may som gentle Muse
> With lucky words favour my destin'd Urn,
> And as he passes turn,
> And bid fair peace be to my sable shrowd.   [18–22]

It is a pagan consolation, in which the succession of poets passes by the funeral bier and preserves in poetry the memory of the singer, as Bion's pupil had once done with a floral tribute:

> Now orchards, sorrow with me; sigh, groves;
> flowers, breathe grief from your tight clusters;
> now roses, deepen your red in mourning; and yours,
> anemones; now hyacinth, let your lettering speak,
> your leaves chatter their grief.
> The beautiful flute-player is dead.
> . . . .
> Thrice-beloved, who now will play your pipe?
> Who will put your flute to his mouth?
> What man would dare? For your lips and your breath
> live on; the sound of your music still echoes
> in those reeds.   [3–7,51–54; trans. Holden]

Nevertheless, toward the end of this dirge for Bion a belief in the power of poetry provides a consolation in the sense of poetical succession:

> For I am no stranger
> to pastoral song, but a pupil of yours,
> an heir to your Dorian style,
> honoured, when others inherited
> your wealth, to be left your music.   [93–97]

The poem concludes with a memory of the visit of Orpheus to the realm of Hades, and a hope that Bion may be singing there:

> Let it be some song of Sicily,
> for Persephone, some sweet country song,
> for she too is Sicilian, she once played
> on Etna's shores; she knows Dorian music;
> your singing would not go unrewarded.
> As once she granted Orpheus, for the rhythms
> of his harp, the return of his Eurydice,
> so shall she return you, Bion, to the hills.
> Could my pipe ever match the magic of his harp,
> I would myself have sung for you to Hades.   [119–26]

In Milton's poem this pagan view of the succession of poets leads into a pagan vision of the succession of hours, days, and seasons in the cyclic year that grants an immortality to *kinds,* but not to individual beings. At first this long passage of traditional pastoral imagery takes us back to the hillside world of Theocritus, where the happy life of man is found to be in tune with nature. It is the landscape of the seventh idyll, which Lawall describes in words that will aptly apply to Milton:

> The world inhabited by Lycidas is not wholly equivalent to the actual geography of Cos; he lives in a mental landscape of his creator, Theocritus. Just as Lycidas is Theocritus' fictional poetic exemplar, so this world of the mind is an inner realm of poetic imagination. Peopled by nymphs and Muses in addition to wondrous goatherd-satyrs, it is a world into which the pastoral poet retires (by a process of psychological introspection, as it were) to shepherd his flock and compose his poetry.   [p. 85]

> For we were nurst upon the self-same hill,
> Fed the same flock, by fountain, shade, and rill.
>   Together both, ere the high Lawns appear'd
> Under the opening eye-lids of the morn,
> We drove a field, and both together heard
> What time the Gray-fly winds her sultry horn,
> Batt'ning our flocks with the fresh dews of night,
> Oft till the Star that rose, at Ev'ning, bright
> Toward Heav'ns descent had slop'd his westering wheel.
> Mean while the Rural ditties were not mute,
> Temper'd to th'Oaten Flute;
> Rough *Satyrs* danc'd, and *Fauns* with clov'n heel,

From the glad sound would not be absent long,
And old *Damaetas* lov'd to hear our song. [23–36]

But now, as in the *Lament for Bion,* this happy landscape seems utterly shattered, in a passage that begins by weltering in heavy repetitions:

But O the heavy change, now thou art gon,
Now thou art gon, and never must return!
Thee Shepherd, thee the Woods, and desert Caves,
With wilde Thyme and the gadding Vine o'regrown,
And all their echoes mourn.
The Willows, and the Hazle Copses green,
Shall now no more be seen,
Fanning their joyous Leaves to thy soft layes.
As killing as the Canker to the Rose,
Or Taint-worm to the weanling Herds that graze,
Or Frost to Flowers, that their gay wardrop wear,
When first the White thorn blows;
Such, *Lycidas,* thy loss to Shepherds ear. [37–49]

It is the loss of the whole harmonious world of pastoral in which Lycidas, that ancient figure of the poet, once sang. No one could help to save the poet. Milton's Lycidas was as helpless as Bion—or Vergil's Menalcas before the soldiers of the State, as Moeris says to Vergil's Lycidas in Eclogue Nine, "But this poetry of ours, Lycidas, can do no more against a man in arms than the doves we have heard of at Dodona, when an eagle comes their way" (11–13; trans. Rieu).

Now Milton's poem becomes even more deeply troubled in its measure, as the poet addresses the Nymphs, but breaks off abruptly, shattering the rhythm of his lines with words that are harsh and crude:

Where were ye Nymphs when the remorseless deep
Clos'd o're the head of your lov'd *Lycidas?*
For neither were ye playing on the steep,
Where your old *Bards,* the famous *Druids* ly,
Nor on the shaggy top of *Mona* high,
Nor yet where *Deva* spreads her wisard stream:
Ay me, I fondly dream!
Had ye bin there—for what could that have don? [50–57]

Yet even within this despairing cry, we can feel the singer reso-
lutely and skillfully maintaining his place in the poetic succession,
for this passage gives the most explicit imitation of Theocritus and
Vergil in the whole poem. In his first idyll, Theocritus has Thyrsis
begin his lament for Daphnis with the question:

> Where were you, nymphs, when Daphnis lay dying? Where
> were you, nymphs? In Peneus' precincts or about Pindus?
> You surely held not to the great River Anapus,
> nor the summit of Etna, and holy waters of Acis.
>
> [66–69; trans. Rist]

Then Vergil begins the lament for Gallus in his tenth eclogue with
the imitative question:

> Where were you, gentle Naiads, in what high woods or in what
> glades, while Gallus lay dying of unrequited love? Nothing de-
> tained you on Parnassus; nothing on any ridge of Pindus; and
> nothing at Aonian Aganippe's spring.   [9–12; trans. Rieu]

Thus even as the living poet laments the death of Orpheus, with
anguished repetitions, we may feel that the ending on Sappho's
island carries more than a hint of poetic succession:

> What could the Muse her self that *Orpheus* bore,
> The Muse her self, for her inchanting son
> Whom Universal nature did lament,
> When by the rout that made the hideous roar,
> His goary visage down the stream was sent,
> Down the swift *Hebrus* to the *Lesbian* shore.
>   Alas! What boots it with uncessant care
> To tend the homely slighted Shepherds trade,
> And strictly meditate the thankles Muse . . .   [58–66]

Even in the depth of this despair, however, he is echoing the
words of Vergil's *Eclogues: musam meditaris* (1.2) and *meditabor . . .
musam* (6.8). Perhaps the shepherd's trade is not so slighted, after
all.

Now, from that cry "Alas!" the poem moves toward its first
great crest, the first of three great crests (or crescendos, as Arthur
Barker has called them)[14] in this weltering of poetical waves. Now
we have the great meditation on the possible futility of striving to

achieve great poetry—but again, with significant echoes of names
immortalized by other poets:[15]

> Were it not better don as others use,
> To sport with *Amaryllis* in the shade,
> Or with the tangles of *Neaera's* hair?
> *Fame* is the spur that the clear spirit doth raise
> (That last infirmity of Noble mind)
> To scorn delights, and live laborious dayes;
> But the fair Guerdon when we hope to find,
> And think to burst out into sudden blaze,
> Comes the blind *Fury* with th'abhorred shears,
> And slits the thin spun life.   [67–76]

It seems that we have reached here a crest of anguish, but then the
line is suddenly capped by an unexpectedly higher movement, as
the poet hears the words of a power beyond this crest—words that
begin with an echo of Vergil's Eclogue Six (3–5):

> But not the praise,
> *Phoebus* repli'd, and touch'd my trembling ears;
> *Fame* is no plant that grows on mortal soil,
> Nor in the glistering foil
> Set off to th'world, nor in broad rumour lies,
> But lives and spreds aloft by those pure-eyes,
> And perfet witnes of all judging *Jove;*
> As he pronounces lastly on each deed,
> Of so much fame in Heav'n expect thy meed.   [76–84]

There is then something that remains; there is a meed beyond the
meed of a melodious tear, though the promise exists here only as
assertion, not as a full poetic action.

The first wave of grief is thus expended, and the poem sinks
back to the pastoral mode of Theocritus and Vergil, in which the
poet rests for a time, pondering further issues and gaining
strength for a new cresting of poetic and redemptive power:

> O Fountain *Arethuse,* and thou honour'd floud,
> Smooth-sliding *Mincius,* crown'd with vocall reeds,
> That strain I heard was of a higher mood:
> But now my Oate proceeds . . .   [85–88]

In this pastoral mode the poet now listens to a procession of
mythological figures, inquiring into and lamenting the disaster—

a passage that clearly echoes similar processions in the first idyll
of Theocritus and in Vergil's tenth eclogue. But Triton and Hip-
potades suggest no answer except an ugly superstition that ex-
plains nothing:

> It was that fatall and perfidious Bark
> Built in th'eclipse, and rigg'd with curses dark,
> That sunk so low that sacred head of thine.   [100–02]

Next comes the world of learning, but the reverend Camus has
only a cry for an answer, "Ah; Who hath reft (quoth he) my
dearest pledge?"—"Last came, and last did go / The Pilot of the
Galilean lake . . ." (107–09). The Pilot, of course, is generally
identified as St. Peter, but there are strong overtones of Christ in
the passage.[16] Thus the line, "The Pilot of the *Galilean* lake,"
seems designed to evoke the vision and voice of Christ speaking
through the figure of his earthly representative and denouncing
the latest generation of money-changers in the temple. This whole
anti-clerical polemic gathers power as it goes; the satirist's fierce
indignation has a purifying, strengthening effect, with the result
that the ending of the denunciation takes the stable form of a
passage in *ottava rima:*

> What recks it them? What need they? They are sped;
> And when they list, their lean and flashy songs
> Grate on their scrannel Pipes of wretched straw,
> The hungry Sheep look up, and are not fed,
> But swoln with wind, and the rank mist they draw,
> Rot inwardly, and foul contagion spread:
> Besides what the grim Woolf with privy paw
> Daily devours apace, and nothing sed,
> But that two-handed engine at the door,
> Stands ready to smite once, and smite no more.   [122–31]

I take my stand with those who interpret the famous "engine" as
an allusion to the "sharp two-edged sword" that comes forth from
the mouth of God in the first chapter of the book of Revelation
(verse 16), a sword that in the nineteenth chapter of Revelation
(verse 15) is associated with the "Word of God" and is promised as
an instrument that God will use to "smite the nations."[17] It is an
image of Divine Justice, an image of the Day of Judgment. Thus

the whole speech helps to confirm the promise of the poem's opening words, "Yet once more," for the Pilot's final words signify "the removing of those things that are shaken, as of things that are made, that those things which cannot be shaken may remain."

From that fearsome crest of prophetic vision (worthy of Amos or Ezekiel), the poem yet once more drops back to the mode of pastoral:

> Return *Alpheus,* the dread voice is past,
> That shrunk thy streams; Return *Sicilian* Muse,
> And call the Vales, and bid them hither cast
> Their Bels, and Flourets of a thousand hues.   [132–35]

The power of this long floral offering arises from its revelation of the poet's love of natural beauty. Despite the hints of sorrow and death, created nature is a place of comfort and rest,[18] when properly appreciated, but alas, it is one of the things that are made, and nature's consolation can be no more than temporary:

> Bid *Amaranthus* all his beauty shed,
> And Daffadillies fill their cups with tears,
> To strew the Laureat Herse where *Lycid* lies.
> For so to interpose a little ease,
> Let our frail thoughts dally with false surmise.
> Ay me!   [149–54]

With this echo of the earlier "Alas!" that began the meditation on poetic fame, the poem now begins its third great movement from depths to crest, as the poet faces clearly the destruction of the body that was made:

> Ay me! Whilst thee the shores, and sounding Seas
> Wash far away, where ere thy bones are hurld,
> Whether beyond the stormy *Hebrides,*
> Where thou perhaps under the whelming tide
> Visit'st the bottom of the monstrous world . . .   [154–58]

As in the earlier passage on fame, this depth of despair is answered by the voice of faith, although here the transition toward the redemptive moment is more gradual:

> Or whether thou to our moist vows deny'd,
> Sleep'st by the fable of *Bellerus* old,
> Where the great vision of the guarded Mount

> Looks toward *Namancos* and *Bayona's* hold;
> Look homeward Angel now, and melt with ruth.
> And, O ye *Dolphins,* waft the haples youth. [159–64]

The poet's vision has shifted from depth to height, from a vision
of the world of sea-monsters in the ocean depths to a vision of the
Archangel Michael, guardian of England's southern shore. With
that vision the "moist vows" are answered, as the poet appeals
directly to the Angel and receives within his mind a consoling
answer:[19]

> Weep no more, woful Shepherds weep no more,
> For *Lycidas* your sorrow is not dead,
> Sunk though he be beneath the watry floar . . . [165–67]

It is an answer that forms a striking contrast with the ending of
Bion's lament for Adonis, which concludes with an allusion to the
annual feast of Adonis: "Cease thy laments today, Cytherea; stay
thy dirges. Again must thou lament, again must thou weep
another year" (trans. Gow). But now the cycles of the day and of
the seasons and the fluctuations of the poet's grief are all trans-
muted into the imagery of Christian death and resurrection, in a
movement toward a crest that fulfills the secret promise of the
poem's opening line and reveals, through allusions to the Book of
Revelation,[20] the faith that cannot be shaken:

> So sinks the day-star in the Ocean bed,
> And yet anon repairs his drooping head,
> And tricks his beams, and with new spangled Ore,
> Flames in the forehead of the morning sky:
> So *Lycidas* sunk low, but mounted high,
> Through the dear might of him that walk'd the waves
> Where other groves, and other streams along,
> With *Nectar* pure his oozy Lock's he laves,
> And hears the unexpressive nuptiall Song,
> In the blest Kingdoms meek of joy and love.
> There entertain him all the Saints above,
> In solemn troops, and sweet Societies
> That sing, and singing in their glory move,
> And wipe the tears for ever from his eyes. [168–81]

Finally, with that third cresting of poetic power, Milton's poem
can end securely within the pastoral setting. First the poem re-
turns, in two serene couplets, to the poem's classical basis:

Now *Lycidas* the Shepherds weep no more;
Hence forth thou art the Genius of the shore,
In thy large recompense, and shalt be good
To all that wander in that perilous flood.   [182–85]

And then the poet can replace that eroded sonnet of prologue with a perfect concluding stanza of *ottava rima,* a stanza that accepts the daily movements of time and reaches out with hope toward another day. The modern shepherd-poet is seen once more in harmony with nature, prepared to build the lofty rhyme:

Thus sang the uncouth Swain to th'Okes and rills,
While the still morn went out with Sandals gray,
He touch'd the tender stops of various Quills,
With eager thought warbling his *Dorick* lay:
And now the Sun had stretch'd out all the hills,
And now was dropt into the Western bay;
At last he rose, and twitch'd his Mantle blew:
To morrow to fresh Woods, and Pastures new.   [186–93]

There is a special decorum in this concluding metrical form; whereas the sonnet is dedicated to intimate, personal utterance, this traditional eight-line stanza is best known as a form used for objective narration. Appropriately, as the stanza builds its perfect rhyme, the mode of the poem shifts to the third person, and Milton brings a new figure into his poem: a detached observer, whose poise and serenity give a new vitality to the shepherd-singer, as we see him move away into the sunset.[21] Or rather, it might be better to say that Milton at the close reveals the presence of the mature consciousness that has guided the words of his "uncouth Swain" throughout the poem.

Who, then, is Lycidas? He is a composite figure to be seen simultaneously in several aspects. He is the robust, smiling goatherd-satyr of Theocritus, who sings in joyful harmony with nature. He is the troubled singer of Vergil, whose friend makes him aware of worldly power, time, and death, but who has not yet lost his faith in the possibility of singing happy songs in an harmonious landscape. The name Lycidas therefore prepares us from the outset for the poem's movement beyond the limitations of the pastoral elegy into the broader reaches of the pastoral eclogue, with its awareness of the world of history.[22] He is also the sorrowful singer of Sannazaro's eclogue, whose songs transcend and dominate the seaside. He is the dead singer of Milton's poem, who at first seems to have no home except the whelming tide, but who is at last reborn within a supernatural landscape, through the faith and imaginative power of his fellow-poet. And finally, through the theme of poetical succession, the name Lycidas is related to the detached observer who sings that final stanza: the mature consciousness whose underlying presence in the poem has provided, from the opening line, the unrecognized or dimly apprehended signs of religious and poetical faith.

PART II

Paradise Lost:
Poem of Exile

Me voici restitué à ma rive natale . . . Il n'est d'histoire que de l'âme, il n'est d'aisance que de l'âme.

St.-John Perse, Exil

CHAPTER 4

Princes
of Exile

Summing up his situation, Milton wrote with bitter wit in a letter of 1666: "For what you call *Politica,* but I would rather have you call *loyalty to one's country,*—this particular girl, after enticing me with her fair name, has almost expatriated me, so to speak." But he adds: "one's country is wherever it is well with one"[1]—for Milton, the country of the soul. Doubly exiled from the community of men, first by his loss of eyesight, and then by political isolation, Milton at last found the freedom to write his poem of exile, the last great poem of the European Renaissance, a poem that combines the cool objectivity of Homer, the delicate sensitivity of Vergil, and the strong personal presence of Ovid and the renaissance poets.[2] Standing as it does on the very latest verge of the Renaissance—indeed beyond that verge—the poem looks backward toward the traditional examples of epic narrative; but it also represents a motion forward to the time when the figure of the poet, representing the individual consciousness of man, will become the only organizing center for the long poem, as in Wordsworth's *Prelude,* Whitman's *Song of Myself,* or Pound's *Cantos.*

79

Without ignoring ancient analogies, I would like for a time to explore the poem's reliance on the individual consciousness by reading it in the context suggested by a modern analogy, the poetry of St.-John Perse. The analogy arises in part from the similarity in the conditions under which the poetry was composed. Perse too had for many years left poetry for political work, rising to become secretary general of foreign affairs in the French government. Then in 1940, with the German conquest, all his years of political effort fell into ruin. He fled into exile in America; impoverished, defeated, on the seacoast of New Jersey Perse faced his dismal situation, and in his poem *Exil,* composed in 1941, he found to his surprise and comfort that the inner resources of his poetic power remained (I will quote from the translation by Denis Devlin):

And it is no error, O Peregrine,
    To desire the barest place for assembling on the wastes of exile a great poem born of nothing, a great poem made from nothing. . . .
    I have built upon the abyss and the spindrift and the sand-smoke. I shall lie down in cistern and hollow vessel,
    In all stale and empty places where lies the taste of greatness. . . .
    "Where the sands go to their song, there go the Princes of exile,
    Where there were high taut sails, there goes the wreck more silken than a lute-maker's dream,
    Where there were great military actions, there lies whitening now the jawbone of an ass,
    And the rounding sea rolls her noise of skulls on the shores,
    And all things in the world to her are in vain, so we heard
        one night at the world's edge
From the wind's militias in the sands of exile."
. . . .
    And morning, for our sake, moves her prophetic finger through sacred writings. . . .
    "O vestiges, O premises,"
Says the Stranger on the sands, "the whole world is new to me."[3]

One may think of the opening book of *Paradise Lost,* where another exile arises from the "fiery waves" with his "expanded wings" and stands upon a "dreary plain" to face his fate with words that win our admiration:

> Is this the Region, this the Soil, the Clime,
> Said then the lost Arch Angel, this the seat
> That we must change for Heav'n, this mournful gloom
> For that celestial light? Be it so, since hee
> Who now is Sovran can dispose and bid
> What shall be right: fardest from him is best
> Whom reason hath equald, force hath made supream
> Above his equals.   [1.242–49]

This is one response to exile: defiance, hatred of the conqueror, courageous, fierce, and resourceful determination never to submit or yield, however great the cost and pain. But there is another response, and we hear it at the opening of Milton's third book, as the poet intervenes to sing his hymn to light:

> Hail holy light, ofspring of Heav'n first-born . . .
> Thee I re-visit now with bolder wing,
> Escap't the *Stygian* Pool, though long detain'd
> In that obscure sojourn, while in my flight
> Through utter and through middle darkness borne
> With other notes then to th' *Orphean* Lyre
> I sung of *Chaos* and *Eternal Night*,
> Taught by the heav'nly Muse to venture down
> The dark descent, and up to reascend,
> Though hard and rare . . .   [3.1,13–21]

From this standpoint the first two books of Milton's poem come to represent an experience which the poet has endured, and understood, and transcended. Certainly it is true that Satan and his host are permeated with the poet's sympathy, for the poet knows what exile is, and he knows too that the first, spontaneous, inevitable response to defeat is bitterness, dismay, desperation, frustrated anger, hatred of the victor, and emotional refusal to submit or yield; he has dramatized these feelings and attitudes in Satan and Satan's followers, recognizing everywhere the power and the sombre beauty of these figures with all the strength of his immense capacity for imaginative projection:

> All in a moment through the gloom were seen
> Ten thousand Banners rise into the Air
> With Orient Colours waving: with them rose
> A Forrest huge of Spears: and thronging Helms
> Appear'd, and serried Shields in thick array

> Of depth immeasurable: Anon they move
> In perfect *Phalanx* to the *Dorian* mood
> Of Flutes and soft Recorders; such as rais'd
> To highth of noblest temper Hero's old
> Arming to Battel, and in stead of rage
> Deliberate valour breath'd, firm and unmov'd
> With dread of death to flight or foul retreat . . .   [1.544–55]

It wins our admiration, as it should, for we are witnessing here the remnants of a power that derives from the divine creativity. In Milton's view nothing created by God is ever quite destroyed: the remnants of the divine energy still work even in those cast out from light. And so we see the fallen angels rising from that chaos on the burning lake, forming this phalanx, making this music, building a palace, observing a form of government, and engaging in formal parliamentary debate under impressive leadership: thus we see Beelzebub:

> deep on his Front engraven
> Deliberation sat and publick care;
> And Princely counsel in his face yet shon,
> Majestick though in ruin: sage he stood
> With *Atlantean* shoulders fit to bear
> The weight of mightiest Monarchies; his look
> Drew audience and attention still as Night
> Or Summers Noon-tide air, while thus he spake.   [2.302–09]

So Milton encourages our admiration and our pity to play upon the scene; he admits, he insists upon the fading presence of beauty and nobility in Hell. This is particularly clear as the fallen angels disperse to await the results of Satan's mission to earth, and Milton shows us how, while some "with vast *Typhoean* rage" create a "wilde uproar," others sing

> With notes Angelical to many a Harp
> Thir own Heroic deeds and hapless fall
> By doom of Battel; and complain that Fate
> Free Vertue should enthrall to Force or Chance.   [2.548–51]

"Thir song was partial," Milton adds—partial to their own point of view—

> but the harmony
> (What could it less when Spirits immortal sing?)
> Suspended Hell, and took with ravishment

> The thronging audience. In discourse more sweet
> (For Eloquence the Soul, Song charms the Sense,)
> Others apart sat on a Hill retir'd,
> In thoughts more elevate, and reason'd high
> Of Providence, Foreknowledge, Will, and Fate,
> Fixt Fate, free will, foreknowledge absolute,
> And found no end, in wandring mazes lost.   [2.552–61]

All this, however "pleasing," Milton adds, is nevertheless "vain," "false," and "fallacious," as Milton then proceeds to show by revealing the full shape of the first two books, which are designed to have the unity of an arch—an arc of insurrection, rising out of that chaos on the burning lake, gradually assuming form and focus, as the legions move in phalanx, and stand before their leader. Then, topping the arch, they build their great palace, where, at the opening of book 2, Satan exalted sits. But after they have engaged in their "great consult" within that palace, the forces of evil fall toward chaos again, in ways that Milton skillfully devises. First Satan departs alone, by his own choice—"this enterprize / None shall partake with me" (2.464–65); and then the fallen angels "disband" their gathered ranks

> and wandring, each his several way
> Pursues, as inclination or sad choice
> Leads him perplext, where he may likeliest find
> Truce to his restless thoughts, and entertain
> The irksome hours, till his great Chief return.   [2.523–27]

While some choose games or song or philosophical debate, others, in groups of varying size, move out "On bold adventure to discover wide / That dismal World" (2.571–72). And what they find are the rivers of hate, sorrow, lamentation, rage, and oblivion, along with the tortures of heat and cold that await the damned:

> Thus roving on
> In confus'd march forlorn, th'adventrous Bands
> With shuddring horror pale, and eyes agast
> View'd first thir lamentable lot, and found
> No rest . . .   [2.614–18]

Even their leader, now moving toward the gates of Hell, is forced to recognize with horror his monstrous offspring, Sin and Death, in that allegorical scene where Satan makes his peace with

Death and flatters his daughter Sin, in order to gain his way out of Hell into Chaos. This allegory is an overt step in Satan's degradation in our eyes, a degradation that continues as he moves out into Chaos, where Milton gives a parody of the traditional heroic voyage. Satan, we ought to note, gets through partly by chance, not only by his own efforts:

> all unawares
> Fluttring his pennons vain plumb down he drops
> Ten thousand fadom deep, and to this hour
> Down had been falling, had not by ill chance
> The strong rebuff of som tumultuous cloud
> Instinct with Fire and Nitre hurried him
> As many miles aloft . . .   [2.932–38]

So on he slogs: "behoves him now both Oare and Saile," says the poet sarcastically:

> Ore bog or steep, through strait, rough, dense, or rare,
> With head, hands, wings, or feet pursues his way,
> And swims or sinks, or wades, or creeps, or flyes . . . [2.948–50]

At length he blunders into "a universal hubbub wilde" which represents the storm-center of Chaos, and there from the faltering Anarch manages to find directions toward the newly created world, where Satan at last arrives at the very close of the second book, "like a weather-beaten Vessel"—with "Shrouds and Tackle torn."

Thus Milton's first two books display a self-enclosed form, from Chaos back to Chaos, from stupefaction on the burning lake to floundering through this region of eternal anarchy. Satan's escape is an illusion, as the rest of the poem shows.

II

Satan's sort of insurrection, then, is one way of dealing with the pain of exile. But now, in the prologue to book 3, Milton continues to suggest a better way, despite his blindness:

> Yet not the more
> Cease I to wander where the Muses haunt
> Cleer Spring, or shadie Grove, or Sunnie Hill,
> Smit with the love of sacred song . . .   [3.26–29]

The spring of Helicon, or of Castalia, the grove of the muses, the hill of Parnassus: all this refers to ancient pagan poetry—and yet he calls it sacred; though of course there is more sacred song:

> but chief
> Thee *Sion* and the flowrie Brooks beneath
> That wash thy hallowd feet, and warbling flow,
> Nightly I visit . . . [3.29–32]

This motif of the singer in darkness returns a few lines later, as the poet compares himself to the nightingale tuning "her nocturnal Note,"[4] and it returns again in the prologues to two later books, where he calls upon the heavenly muse who visits his "slumbers Nightly" (7.29) or "who deignes / Her nightly visitation unimplor'd / And dictates to me slumbring" (9.21–23). He literally composes at night, while he is also living in the night of his blindness; yet, like David the psalmist in Zion, he knows that "the Lord will command his loving-kindness in the daytime, and in the night his song shall be with me" (Ps. 42:8). "Thou hast proved mine heart", says the psalmist, "thou hast visited me in the night" (Ps. 17:3). "I have remembered thy name, O Lord, in the night, and have kept thy law" (Ps. 119:55).

> If I ascend up into heaven, thou art there: if I make
>   my bed in hell, behold, thou art there.
> If I take the wings of the morning, and dwell in the
>   uttermost parts of the sea;
> Even there shall thy hand lead me, and thy right hand shall
>   hold me.
> If I say, Surely the darkness shall cover me; even the night
>   shall be light about me.
> Yea, the darkness hideth not from thee; but the night shineth
>   as the day . . . [Ps. 139:8–12]

It is this abiding confidence in the presence of God that creates a kind of happiness even within the bounds of his sorrow and lamentation:

> Thus with the Year
> Seasons return, but not to me returns
> Day, or the sweet approach of Ev'n or Morn,
> Or sight of vernal bloom, or Summers Rose,
> Or flocks, or herds, or human face divine;

But cloud in stead, and ever-during dark
Surrounds me, from the chearful waies of men
Cut off . . .   [3.40–47]

As his love of poetry remains undiminished, so his love of natural
beauty remains, even increased by the fact that he now can find
that beauty only in his memory. But most important, his love of
mankind continues, in exalted terms: he speaks of the *human face
divine,* as he remembers it, for he knows that man was made in the
image of God, and that in this image the vestiges of divinity are
still discernible, vestiges of the spiritual beauty that Milton is soon
to show us in his Adam and Eve:

in thir looks Divine
The image of thir glorious Maker shon,
Truth, Wisdome, Sanctitude severe and pure . . .   [4.291–93]

We ought to notice the trinitarian way in which that image is
described, in words that seem to echo Augustine: through the
human countenance shines the Truth of God the Father, the Wis-
dom of the Son, Word of the Father, and the Sanctity of the Holy
Spirit.[5] But more surprising, perhaps, is the phrase "chearful
waies of men." For the first two books have hardly presented an
altogether cheerful picture of the ways of men. We remember
that long catalogue of the pagan gods in book 1, showing how, as
Milton plainly says:

By falsities and lyes the greatest part
Of Mankind they corrupted to forsake
God their Creator . . .   [1.367–69]

Furthermore, the poet's outbursts of indignation have through-
out the first two books cast considerable doubt upon the ways of
men. Thus in book 2, at the end of the satanic parliament, he
cries:

O shame to men! Devil with Devil damn'd
Firm concord holds, men onely disagree
Of Creatures rational, though under hope
Of heavenly Grace; and God proclaiming peace,
Yet live in hatred, enmitie, and strife
Among themselves, and levie cruel warres,
Wasting the Earth, each other to destroy . . .   [2.496–502]

How can we reconcile these harsh utterances with his poignant regret for his loss of the sight of the human face divine and the cheerful ways of men? The contrast may alert us to the vast range of moods and attitudes that the poem represents. Those scenes in Hell have been carefully designed to represent some of the most discouraging ways of men, since it is clear that the fallen angels are being treated as the representatives of human error. Nevertheless the poem includes, even in Hell, some recognition of more cheerful ways. I am not thinking only of the ways in which the fallen angels show that they still retain some rays of their original brightness; but rather of certain subtle ways by which the poem manages to suggest that Satan and his crew are not the only princes of exile. Let us return to see exactly what St.-John Perse meant by that enigmatic phrase. Perse, it appears, is not alluding to anything satanic, when he cries out, "Honour thine exile, O Prince! / And all at once all is power and presence for me, here where the theme of nothingness rises still in smoke" (p. 17). What arises gradually in Perse's poem is a vision of the true princes of exile. Here are some of them, among four brilliant pages of examples, set forth in a Whitmanesque catalogue:

. . . He who, in the midnight hours, ranges the stone galleries assessing the title-deeds of a beautiful comet; he who, between two wars, watches over the purity of great crystal lenses; he who rises before daylight to clean out the fountains, and the great epidemics are at an end;

. . . . .

he who has the job of consigning incoming ships; and he, too, who discovers one day the very perfume of his soul in the planking of a new sailboat; he who takes over the equinoctial watch on the ramparts of the docks, on the high, sonorous comb of great dams in the mountains and on the great ocean sluices;

. . . . .

He who opens an account in the bank for the researches of the mind; he who enters the arena of his new creation, uplifted in his whole being and, for three days, no one may look upon his silence save his mother, no one may have access to his room save the oldest of the servants;

. . . . .

he who deals, in the town, in such great books as almagesta, portulans and bestiaries; whose solicitude is for the accidents of phonetics, the alteration of signs and the great erosions of language; who takes part in the great debates on semantics; who is an authority on the lower mathematics . . .   [pp. 25–33]

"Those are the princes of exile," he concludes, "they have no need of my song." The true princes of exile, then, are those who find a zest in the act of living, those who do their work, out of love for the job, or out of a sense that what they do is significant, although the job may seem menial or trivial, to the great ones of the world. They are the guardians of mankind's past and future. These are the cheerful ways of men which Milton also includes in his poem, through many different devices. Most important is the figure of the poet himself, whose constant presence in the poem provides the most eloquent demonstration that Satan has not succeeded in his efforts to destroy mankind. But there are many others. Some are tucked away in parts of Milton's heroic similes, extraneous, often, to the strict logic of the comparison, but essential as a tacit reassurance that the human face divine has not been utterly lost. We find one in the famous simile of book 1 comparing Satan's shield to the moon:

> whose Orb
> Through Optic Glass the *Tuscan* Artist views
> At Ev'ning from the top of *Fesole,*
> Or in *Valdarno,* to descry new Lands,
> Rivers or Mountains in her spotty Globe.   [1.287–91]

This has sometimes been taken as a premonition of man's search for illegitimate knowledge, but I do not think this is the prime effect. There is here no hint of blame for the astronomer, who is an Artist, a master of his art or science, skilled in his profession; what we feel, rather, is the superiority of his whole situation and effort to that of Satan, though no doubt such artistry might be misused. In another famous simile (1.203–08) one may even feel a certain friendly concern for the pilot of that "small night-founder'd Skiff" who, as seamen tell, mistakes the whale for an island, and in his distress fixes his anchor in the monster's scaly rind and so "Moors by his side under the Lee, while Night / Invests the Sea, and wished Morn delayes." A deceptive anchorage, to be sure, but then Milton does not say that the whale submerged.

Or, as Satan flies toward the gates of Hell, in book 2, we are treated to a glimpse of the faithful voyagers of the earth, in a simile that reminds one of the Portuguese sailors of Camoens:

> As when farr off at Sea a Fleet descri'd
> Hangs in the Clouds, by *Aequinoctial* Winds
> Close sailing from *Bengala,* or the Iles
> Of *Ternate* and *Tidore,* whence Merchants bring
> Thir spicie Drugs: they on the trading Flood
> Through the wide *Ethiopian* to the Cape
> Ply stemming nightly toward the Pole.   [2.636–42]

Here again the mention of drugs may seem to suggest a harmful possibility: but whatever drug-taking may suggest nowadays, the basic meaning of the word "drug" was and still is: a medicinal substance, essential to the healing arts of man, a word "formerly used more widely to include all ingredients used in chemistry, pharmacy, dyeing, and the arts generally."[6] As for "spicie," the word alludes to the fragrant, pleasant aroma of those spices that were much in demand to preserve or make palatable the dreadful food of Milton's day. The implications of the phrase "spicie Drugs" are primarily beneficent and agreeable, though with an undercurrent of possible misuse. So the whole simile provides a . rich contrast with Satan's mission, along with a possible parallel.

Best of all, perhaps, is the frequently examined simile at the close of book 4, where, as Satan and the guardian angels are threatening to engage in a combat that might have turned Paradise into ruin, we read that the spears of the good angels ("sharpening in mooned horns / Their phalanx") seemed

> as thick as when a field
> Of *Ceres* ripe for harvest waving bends
> Her bearded Grove of ears, which way the wind
> Swayes them; the careful Plowman doubting stands
> Least on the threshing floore his hopeful sheaves
> Prove chaff.   [4.980–85]

The phrase "careful Plowman doubting" is a little richer in Milton's English than in ours, for "careful" has not only its modern implications of one who is attentive to his work, who takes good care of things, but it also implies a person who is anxious and troubled, full of care; and the word "doubting" implies both a state of uncertainty and also a state of fear lest some disaster happen. The sharpened "horns" of the phalanx, like a sickle, threaten both Satan and earth.[7] It is a superb image of the human condition, again displayed as superior to that of Satan, who, for all his appearance of power, flees abjectly before the sign that God hangs in the heavens. These glimpses of the cheerful ways of the true princes of exile are more frequent than we might think, for sometimes they flash upon us in only a line, or two, or three. Thus in book 9, before the Fall, Satan "works his way"

> As when a Ship by skilful Stearsman wrought
> Nigh Rivers mouth or Foreland, where the Wind
> Veres oft, as oft so steers, and shifts her Saile;
> So varied hee, and of his tortuous Traine
> Curld many a wanton wreath in sight of *Eve*,
> To lure her Eye . . .   [9.513–18]

Similarly, in book 9, Milton somewhat alleviates the effect of the Fall by bringing in his account of the fig tree from which Adam and Eve take those fig leaves:

> not that kind for Fruit renown'd
> But such as at this day to *Indians* known
> In *Malabar* or *Decan* spreds her Armes
> Braunching so broad and long, that in the ground
> The bended Twigs take root, and Daughters grow
> About the Mother Tree, a Pillard shade
> High overarch't, and echoing Walks between;
> There oft the *Indian* Herdsman shunning heate
> Shelters in coole, and tends his pasturing Herds
> At Loopholes cut through thickest shade . . .   [9.1101–10]

It is, no doubt, a barren and grotesque tree, and yet it can be used for man's pleasure and benefit.

Still another way of bringing in these more cheerful glimpses may be found in Milton's use of classical legends and classical history, allusions which are not always treated with some such derogatory tag as "feigned" or "thus they relate, Erring." As Satan is moving in the Serpent's body toward Eve, in book 9, we read this remarkable cluster of the beneficent things of earth:

> pleasing was his shape,
> And lovely, never since of Serpent kind
> Lovelier, not those that in *Illyria* chang'd

Hermione and *Cadmus,* or the God
In *Epidaurus;* nor to which transformd
Ammonian Jove, or *Capitoline* was seen,
Hee with *Olympias,* this with her who bore
Scipio the highth of *Rome.*   [9.503–10]

The story of the changing of Hermione and Cadmus into ser-
pents may seem an ominous and ugly one: Milton uses it thus later
on when he tells how Satan and his host in Hell, glorying in the
fall of man, are changed to serpents. But the story itself is a
curious mixture of implications; it may look ugly, and yet the gods
may here be beneficent after all; it is predominantly a story of
deep human love and ultimate gentleness. Here is the end of it, as
Cadmus feels himself changing into a serpent:

> his cheeks were human,
> And tears ran down them, as he cried: "Come nearer,
> My poor dear wife, while there is something left
> For you to come to; come and touch my hand
> Before I have no hand, am wholly serpent."
>
> . . . .
>
> She beat her breast. "O Cadmus,
> Unhappy man," she cried, "remain, put off
> This horrible appearance! What is this?
> Where are your feet, your shoulders, hands, complexion,
> Your—all of you? Why not transform me also,
> Gods of the Heaven, into another serpent?"
> He licked her face, glided between her breasts
> As if he knew them, twined around her neck,
> While all who stood there watching shook in horror.
> But the queen only stroked the serpent neck,
> Crested but smooth, and suddenly there were only
> Two serpents there, entwined about each other,
> And gliding, after a while, to hiding-places
> In the dark woods. Now as before, they never
> Hurt men, nor fear them, for they both remember
> What once they were; they are most gentle serpents.
> [Ovid, *Metamorphoses* 4.582–603, trans. Humphries][8]

What looks bad may indeed be good—or the reverse; but certainly
the reference to the god Aesculapius, the god of healing, and to
his vast sanatorium at Epidaurus—this reference is beneficent,
especially when we recall Ovid's story of how Aesculapius ap-

peared to the Romans who sought his help at Epidaurus in order
to stop the pestilence at Rome:

> the god, all crested
> With gold, in serpent-form, uttered a warning,
> Hissed terribly, a sign that he was coming,
> And all the altars, all the doors, the pavement,
> The roof of gold, the statue, shook and trembled.
> Reared high, he stood there, and he gazed about him
> With fiery eyes, and as the people shuddered,
> The priest, in ceremonial headdress, knew him,
> Calling: "The god! Behold the god! Bow down
> To him in word and spirit, all who stand here!
> That we may see his beauty as our blessing,
> Here at his shrine!"   [15.669–79; trans. Humphries]

And as for the tales that Jove, taking the form of a serpent,
seduced two women: legends say that one son thus produced was
Alexander the Great, who might be dismissed as a mere military
hero—but the other was the man whom Milton here calls the
greatest of all Romans, Scipio Africanus, who conquered Car-
thage, and yet was also a mystic and a lover of the arts of peace.

Lastly, to sum up this matter of the princes, we should recall the
short introduction to book 11, Milton's preface to his long tale of
human sin and suffering; for it is a passage in which Milton brings
home the redemption of man by comparing Adam and Eve in
prayer with a less ancient pair who, as Ovid tells, had prayed for
the restoration of the human race:

> yet thir port
> Not of mean suiters, nor important less
> Seem'd thir Petition, then when th' ancient Pair
> In Fables old, less ancient yet then these,
> *Deucalion* and chaste *Pyrrha* to restore
> The Race of Mankind drownd, before the Shrine
> Of *Themis* stood devout.   [11.8–14]

"There was no better man than this Deucalion," says Ovid, "No
one more fond of right; there was no woman / More scrupulously
reverent than Pyrrha" (1.322–23; trans. Humphries). So these
reminders of the possibility and the actuality of human restora-
tion grow everywhere in the poem, sometimes arising unexpec-
tedly out of the most appalling context. This poem represents a

shifting, incalculable mixture in which the poet stands ready not
only to castigate evil, but also to recognize and celebrate, however
briefly, the signs of excellence in the human story. It is this vari-
able, flexible, enigmatic union of opposites that St.-John Perse
seems to suggest in several appropriate passages of his own poem
of exile:

> And when this day's pale substance had dried into the sands,
> Fragments of beautiful stories adrift in spirals, in the sky full of
> errors and erring premises, went turning around to the scholiast's
> delight.   [p. 21]
>
> . . . . .
>
> And I, from all winged things for which you have no use, com-
> posing a language free of usage and pure,
> Now I have once more the design for a great, delible poem.
>   [p. 23]

Voici que j'ai dessein encore d'un grand poème délébile . . . But how can
a poem be both *great* and *delible*—that is, *erasable?*

In Perse that strange and rare word *délébile* implies the poet's
sense of the precarious nature of all great literary undertakings,
the difficulty, indeed the impossibility of fixing human utterance
in any form that might be called *in*delible; the poet faces the
constantly shifting, evasive, and elusive nature of the human ex-
perience that underlies all efforts to set down words, along with
the doubt whether, after all the effort, the work can survive "the
great erosions of language."

But there is another sense in which a poem may be both great
and delible—great because it is delible, great because it is com-
posed in such a way that one aspect of the poem is constantly
erasing, or replacing, or altering, or imposing itself upon another
part of the poem. *Paradise Lost* is such a poem, with constantly
shifting scenes and perspectives and moods and attitudes: it is a
poem subject to constant alteration, and even self-contradiction.

This strangely shifting, "delible" quality extends down to the
very roots of the poem's style. It is hard to believe that Milton's
style could ever have been viewed as a "Chinese Wall,"[9] as though
its most remarkable quality were stiffness and rigidity. The style is
strange, like that of Perse, remote in many ways from ordinary
speech, but it is strange because it is so utterly original in its

shifting, altering, flexible action, its way of breaking down all our normal expectations of what the English language can do. It defies grammar, chops out connectives, alters the parts of speech at will, lays bare the sources of the language; and in short, deals with the English language in a constantly bold, inventive, unpredictable and unprecedented way. Its syntax has the quality that Perse calls "syntax of lightning": a flashing mode of utterance, "pure speech of exile," full of surprise and reverberation.[10] It has something of the quality that Perse describes in the linguistic passage of "Snows," the last of the poems in his volume *Exile:*

> it is my design, now, to wander among the oldest layers of speech, among the farthest phonetic strata: as far as the most far-off languages, as far as the most whole and most parsimonious languages,
>
> like those Dravidian languages which had no distinct words for "yesterday" and "tomorrow" . . . Come and follow us, who have no words to say: ascending that pure unwritten delight where runs the ancient human phrase, we move about among clear elisions, the residues of old prefixes that have lost their initial, and, preceding the master works in linguistics, we clear our new ways to those unheard-of locutions where the aspiration withdraws behind its vowels and the modulation of the breath spreads out, under the sway of certain half-voiced labials, in search of pure vocalic finals.
>
> And it was at morning, beneath the purest of word-forms, a beautiful country without hatred or meanness, a place of grace and of mercy for the ascension of the unfailing presages of the mind; and like a great *Ave* of grace on our path, the great white rose-garden of all the snows all around . . .   [pp. 91–92]

Such a quest through linguistic means for "un beau pays sans haine ni lésine, un lieu de grace et de merci," is also the design that lives within the mind of Milton's exiled bard.

The Realms of Light

Paradise Lost begins with a heavy emphasis upon the last word of its title, for the words *lost* and *loss,* along with kindred words such as *ruin,* resound like a hideous dirge throughout books 1 and 2. This theme is set in the first words of Satan, as he and his mate lie "weltring" on the burning lake of Hell, and Satan speaks in the broken, hesitant, veering phrases of torment:

> If thou beest he; But O how fall'n! how chang'd
> From him, who in the happy Realms of Light
> Cloth'd with transcendent brightness didst outshine
> Myriads though bright: If he whom mutual league,
> United thoughts and counsels, equal hope,
> And hazard in the Glorious Enterprize,
> Joynd with me once, now misery hath joynd
> In equal ruin.   [1.84–91]

It is a loss so immense that Satan's mind cannot really grasp the horror; and so, only a few lines later, we find him asking and declaring:

> What though the field be lost?
> All is not lost; the unconquerable Will,
> And study of revenge, immortal hate,
> And courage never to submit or yield:
> And what is else not to be overcome?   [1.105–09]

95

And soon we find "the lost Arch Angel" calling upon "Th' associates and copartners of our loss" to arouse themselves; and at once they arise and come flocking to Satan:

> but with looks
> Down cast and damp, yet such wherein appear'd
> Obscure som glimps of joy, to have found thir chief
> Not in despair, to have found themselves not lost
> In loss it self.   [1.522–26]

Yet even in these passages Milton is not presenting simply a lament for loss: the appeal that these opening books have always exerted lies in the fact that they deal with the tenacious effort of these fallen spirits to retain consciousness and hope—to struggle toward the light even when the cause is hopeless and the effort a delusion. Satan cannot become truly wicked in our eyes, cannot become wholly lost, until he is seen to have lost hope, until it is plain that his cause can have no future except in meaningless destruction. There are degrees of Hell, as Satan says in his bitter soliloquy in book 4:

> Which way I flie is Hell; my self am Hell;
> And in the lowest deep a lower deep
> Still threatning to devour me opens wide,
> To which the Hell I suffer seems a Heav'n.   [4.75–78]

There are also, in Milton's poem, degrees of Heaven: for there is a Paradise that seems "a Heaven on Earth" and there is also within the poem a bard who can see within his mind glimpses of Heaven. Milton's poem is written to sustain true hope amid a sense of loss, and it is therefore a supremely complex poem with a double plot such as Shakespeare himself never surpassed. One action, begun in books 1 and 2, is the destructive movement that reaches a climax in the ninth book when Eve eats the forbidden fruit and Adam cries, "How art thou lost, how on a sudden lost" (9.900). The second action is a movement of redemption, the action that sustains hope and leads toward man's recovery of the "Realms of Light."

The first action, in books 1 and 2, begins with all the heroic equipment of epic poetry; but at the beginning of book 3 the second action begins quite differently. Or rather, the second action becomes overt here. It has been implicit throughout the first two books, but we have not really been able to see it, so powerful is

Milton's presentation of "heroic" Satan and his peers. This second
action now emerges from its "obscure sojourn" as Milton presents
the great prologue of book 3, the utterance of a man who suffers
blindness but who nevertheless still, in his fashion, sees the light:

> Hail holy light, ofspring of Heav'n first-born,
> Or of th' Eternal Coeternal beam
> May I express thee unblam'd? since God is light,
> And never but in unapproached light
> Dwelt from Eternitie, dwelt then in thee,
> Bright effluence of bright essence increate.
> Or hear'st thou rather pure Ethereal stream,
> Whose Fountain who shall tell?   [3.1–8]

One is struck here by the modesty and humility of this bard's
approach to the divine; he is uncertain how to address this holy
light and he does not insist upon any one view. He knows only that
it is a divine principle which he feels physically now shining upon
him, and feels also within himself, mentally and spiritually, in his
"love of sacred song," in his love of "the sweet approach of Ev'n or
Morn" and of all nature's beauties which he can no longer see; he
feels it also in his love of the "human face divine" and of "the
chearful waies of men" from whose society his blindness cuts him
off, but not without hope and not without the aid of prayer and
meditation:

> So much the rather thou Celestial light
> Shine inward, and the mind through all her powers
> Irradiate, there plant eyes, all mist from thence
> Purge and disperse, that I may see and tell
> Of things invisible to mortal sight.   [3.51–55]

At once, as though in answer to that prayer, the poem makes in
effect a new start, as we move to the scene in Heaven. The effect
of a new beginning is reinforced by the echoes of the heavenly
conferences that occur in the opening book of the *Odyssey* between
Zeus and Athena, in the opening book of the *Aeneid* between
Jupiter and Venus, and also in the opening book of the
Metamorphoses, as angry Zeus consults with all the gods about the
destruction of the human race and its regeneration. Here Milton
presents the theological principles from which the redemptive
action of his poem proceeds.[1] And here we meet the most puz-
zling and disconcerting passage in the entire poem, a passage that

has annoyed a good many readers, the speech where the Almighty
Father views all his works and, seeing Satan now emerged from
Hell, declares that man will succumb to Satan's "glozing lyes"

> And easily transgress the sole Command,
> Sole pledge of his obedience: So will fall
> Hee and his faithless Progenie: whose fault?
> Whose but his own? ingrate, he had of mee
> All he could have; I made him just and right,
> Sufficient to have stood, though free to fall.   [3.94–99]

Whose fault? Milton has composed the speech in a way that tends to
set our teeth on edge and to make us cry out rebelliously, "Whose
but your own? You made us insufficient to have stood, decreed to
fall." Perhaps the speech is designed to have a neutral quality, but
it seems impossible to read this passage aloud without creating
either a harsh defensive tone or a tone of grieved lament.[2] But
now, as though realizing the problems that his words have raised,
Milton's God goes on to argue patiently the reasonableness of his
procedure:

> Such I created all th' Ethereal Powers
> And Spirits, both them who stood & them who faild;
> Freely they stood who stood, and fell who fell.
> Not free, what proof could they have givn sincere
> Of true allegiance, constant Faith or Love,
> Where onely what they needs must do, appeard,
> Not what they would? what praise could they receive?
> What pleasure I from such obedience paid,
> When Will and Reason (Reason also is choice)
> Useless and vain, of freedom both despoild,
> Made passive both, had servd necessitie,
> Not mee.   [3.100–11]

The tone is better here. Milton's God is pleading with mankind,
perhaps a little too anxiously, to understand the gift of freedom.
God's apparent lack of control over Satan, we can now begin to
see, represents part of God's view of every creature's freedom to
break the bounds that are prescribed, not forced upon us. The
same problem is soon to be presented when Satan overleaps the
walls of Paradise and lands on his feet within those guarded pre-
cincts. Why bother to set up the walls and provide that angelic

guard, we may well ask? But again, these arrangements indicate
the ideal, the desired order of being, somewhat as human laws
attempt to indicate the desired limits of human self-will.

Milton is wrestling here, and allowing us to wrestle, with a prob-
lem of almost intolerable tension. Milton believes, with all the
force of his religious being, that there is an omnipotent God who
rules the universe with perfect justice; and he also believes, with
all the force of his humanistic self, that human beings have free-
dom of the will: the freedom to choose. So, as the divine plan of
redemption is now unfolded, the main point lies in the recovery
and sustaining of man's freedom of the will. God says that after
the Fall he will renew man's "lapsed powers" so that "once more
he shall stand / On even ground against his mortal foe" (3.178–
79). *On even ground:* the whole poem depends upon this promise.
Milton here solves the controversial problem of grace in a very
delicate way.[3] At first Milton may sound Calvinistic when he has
God say, "Some I have chosen of peculiar grace / Elect above the
rest; so is my will" (3.183–84). That is to say, some individuals will
be given special grace which makes them preeminent in virtue
and especially chosen for salvation: individuals such as St. Paul, St.
Augustine, or, perhaps, John Milton—but this does not mean,
Milton adds, that the rest of mankind will be damned, as the strict
Calvinists were asserting. Milton will have none of this doctrine,
for his God says, "I will cleer thir senses dark, / What may suffice"
(3.188–89); man will have what may suffice to achieve his salva-
tion. And God promises that he will "soft'n stonie hearts / To pray,
repent, and bring obedience due" (3.189–90). To stress the be-
neficent nature of this promise, he repeats the wording: "To
prayer, repentance, and obedience due, / Though but endevord
with sincere intent, / Mine eare shall not be slow, mine eye not
shut" (3.191–93). If we will only *try* to pray, repent, and be obe-
dient, even though we cannot in ourselves achieve these aims, the
effort in itself will be sufficient for salvation. He also promises that
he

> will place within them as a guide
> My Umpire *Conscience,* whom if they will hear,
> Light after light well us'd they shall attain,
> And to the end persisting, safe arrive.   [3.194–97]

The opportunity to regain the realms of light, then, is open to *all*, and only those who neglect or scorn the opportunity will be excluded from mercy. The Son offers to sacrifice himself in order to insure that God's grace will remain available to *all* mankind:

> And shall grace not find means, that finds her way,
> The speediest of thy winged messengers,
> To visit all thy creatures, and to all
> Comes unprevented, unimplor'd, unsought,
> Happie for man, so coming . . .   [3.228–32]

Then God goes on to explain the workings of his mercy in a subtly challenging way:

> Be thou in *Adams* room
> The Head of all mankind, though *Adams* Son.
> As in him perish all men, so in thee
> As from a second root shall be restor'd,
> As many as are restor'd, without thee none.   [3.285–89]

That guarded phrase, "As many as are restor'd," stands as both a warning and a promise; not all mankind will be restored to happiness, but the number of the restored remains within the choice of man. Milton, in this crucial part of his poem, where he is taking every possible care to make his theology absolutely clear, will not predict (as he does so strongly in books 11 and 12) that only a few shall be restored. Instead, he insists that the possibility of restoration lies open for every man to choose.

At the outset of the scene, Milton has deliberately evoked the full weight of every ultimate question about God's justice; then he has clearly and patiently offered the answers to those doubts; and now, at the very close, the voice of the poet, mankind's representative, seems to join in the angelic chorus of praise:

> Hail Son of God, Saviour of Men, thy Name
> Shall be the copious matter of my Song
> Henceforth, and never shall my Harp thy praise
> Forget, nor from thy Fathers praise disjoine.   [3.412–15]

That phrase, "Hail Son of God," may recall the opening line of the book: "Hail holy light, ofspring of Heav'n first-born."[4] For the Son of God said, in the Gospel of John: "I am the light of the world: he that followeth me shall not walk in darkness, but shall

have the light of life" (8:12). In this way the prologue and the
scene in Heaven tend to become inseparably one.

Thus far, then, a burst of light out of the darkness; but now,
exactly in the middle of book 3, the scene shifts back into darkness
as Satan is presented walking on the outward shell of the round
universe, in a place "Dark, waste, and wild, under the frown of
Night / Starless expos'd" (3.424–25). As though realizing a human
need to descend from abstract light to concrete earth, Milton now
gives one of the most detailed of all his epic similes, a simile filled
to overflowing with the varied activities of animals and of human
beings, activities set in landscapes that range from snowy ridge to
fertile springs to barren plains:

> As when a Vultur on *Imaus* bred,
> Whose snowie ridge the roving *Tartar* bounds,
> Dislodging from a Region scarce of prey
> To gorge the flesh of Lambs or yeanling Kids
> On Hills where Flocks are fed, flies toward the Springs
> Of *Ganges* or *Hydaspes, Indian* streams;
> But in his way lights on the barren plaines
> Of *Sericana,* where *Chineses* drive
> With Sails and Wind thir canie Waggons light.   [3.431–39]

It is a glimpse of a broad range of human possibilities: predatory,
with "the roving *Tartar*"; pastoral, on those "Hills where Flocks
are fed"; or ingeniously mechanical, as with those delightful sail-
driven wagons. Then, abruptly and savagely, Milton reminds us
that many men will turn these possibilities to folly as he presents
his surprising version of Limbo, reminiscent of Ariosto's Paradise
of Fools on the moon. By thus so obviously bringing in a motif
derived from a poet of the Italian Renaissance, Milton illustrates
pointedly how far he will range from the epic examples set by
Homer and Vergil. Already, by bringing in that Spenserian and
Ovidian allegory of Sin and Death near the end of book 2, and by
his unusually personal and intimate prologue to book 3, Milton
has shown that this poem will never abide by any ancient example,
or any modern example, as we now see from his treatment of
Limbo. Milton brings the poem down to earth by reminding us of
the violent religious quarrels of the Reformation, and by bringing

in the harsh voice of controversy which Milton so often uses in his prose treatises:

> then might ye see
> Cowles, Hoods and Habits with thir wearers tost
> And flutterd into Raggs, then Reliques, Beads,
> Indulgences, Dispenses, Pardons, Bulls,
> The sport of Winds: all these upwhirld aloft
> Fly o're the backside of the World farr off
> Into a *Limbo* large and broad, since calld
> The Paradise of Fools, to few unknown
> Long after . . .   [3.489–97]

Milton views this comical catastrophe of his opponents with a fierce revolutionary relish, while in his mention of the "few" we have more than a hint that most of mankind may perish. But there is something more important here than the satire in itself. The passage serves to bring back intimately the voice of the bard, to develop the personality of the singer within whose mind the poem's action from now on will clearly be performed.[5] Not only is he a blind and devout man, as we have learned from his prologue to book 3; he is also a political activist, a man deeply concerned with the immediate ecclesiastical issues in his own world.

Meanwhile, a new mode of construction is being introduced into the poem, in accord with this vast enlargement of the poet's voice and personality. The old epic mode of narration pursued superbly in books 1 and 2, with Satan as the apparent epic hero, is now dropped; and a quite different mode of operation is adopted, a mode that I should like to describe by the phrase "panels of action."[6] Book 3 seems to be composed of four panels: first, the prologue, bringing us to the center of the poet's mind; secondly, the objective consultation in Heaven; thirdly, the return of the intimate voice, with a different tone, in the darkness of Limbo; and fourthly, a panel that returns us to the realms of light. These panels, with harsh colloquial satire set sharply against the abstract theological language of the heavenly conclave, and set also against the devotional intimacy of the prologue, may suggest the many ways in which Milton includes within the major form of the classical epic certain examples of what Kenneth Burke calls minor form.[7] For the poem seems to contain at least one example of almost every literary kind known to man. The first two books provide examples of the oration and of formal allegory. Book 4 presents examples of the dramatic soliloquy in Satan's self-addresses, along with scenes of pastoral and a love-song, sung by Eve to Adam. In book 5 we have a psalm, sung by Adam and Eve to their Creator. Book 7 gives a meditation on the first chapter of Genesis. The opening portion of book 9 offers a short scene of domestic comedy, as Adam attempts to persuade Eve not to go off by herself, while the elements of a Greek tragedy will be found in the whole treatment of the Fall in this book.[8] In book 10 we have the formal "complaint" of Adam along with another tale of Ovidian metamorphosis, as Satan and his host are turned into serpents. And lastly, in books 11 and 12, we have a long, long example of the popular, didactic poem of biblical paraphrase. All this within a poem that constantly maintains its touch with the heroic mode of Homer and Vergil, along with reminiscences of Ovid, Tasso, Ariosto, Camoens, and Spenser. It is indeed an immense baroque edifice—a unique construction made by the technique of arranging adjacent and contrasting panels.

II

After the panel of Limbo, the poem again undergoes a metamorphosis, from dark to light, as Satan views the stairs that lead to heaven—stairs that symbolize the promise of God's everpresent grace, as Milton goes on to suggest by several beneficent comparisons:

> The Stairs were such as whereon *Jacob* saw
> Angels ascending and descending, bands
> Of Guardians bright, when he from *Esau* fled
> To *Padan-Aram* in the field of *Luz,*
> Dreaming by night under the open Skie,
> And waking cri'd, This is the Gate of Heav'n.   [3.510–15]

A few lines later, Satan looks down into the bright interior of the universe and sees

> A passage down to th' Earth, a passage wide,
> Wider by farr then that of after-times
> Over Mount *Sion,* and, though that were large,

> Over the *Promis'd Land* to God so dear,
> By which, to visit oft those happy Tribes
> On high behests his Angels to and fro
> Pass'd frequent, and his eye with choice regard
> From *Paneas* the fount of *Jordans* flood
> To *Bëersaba*, where the *Holy Land*
> Borders on *Aegypt* and the *Arabian* shoare . . .   [3.528–37]

It is an image of the promised action of grace within the fallen world. And with such intimations of God's future favor toward mankind, we should not be surprised to find Satan's "wonder" at the beauty of the world, a few lines later, recorded through a most benign simile:

> As when a Scout
> Through dark and desart wayes with peril gone
> All night; at last by break of chearful dawne
> Obtains the brow of some high-climbing Hill,
> Which to his eye discovers unaware
> The goodly prospect of some forein land
> First seen, or some renownd Metropolis
> With glistering Spires and Pinnacles adornd,
> Which now the Rising Sun guilds with his beams.   [3.543–51]

Some things of the fallen world, then, are cheerful and goodly; and the Scout, while perhaps the forerunner of a military force, may, on the other hand, be another of the princes of exile: a good man doing his job on a journey of exploration. His response to the scene is clearly distinguished from Satan's:

> Such wonder seis'd, though after Heaven seen,
> The Spirit maligne, but much more envy seis'd
> At sight of all this World beheld so faire.   [3.552–54]

The Scout may still be one of those who choose to be restored.

Even those who fail, it seems, are not always to be blamed quite as harshly as we might expect from Milton's outburst against the follies of Limbo. As Satan flies to the sun, and in that place "beyond expression bright" (3.591) adopts the disguise of a stripling cherub, it proves to be a disguise which all the light of the sun itself cannot reveal, and which all the brilliant vision of Uriel, angel of the sun, cannot penetrate. This the poet explains in one of his most familiar asides, a familiarity which is now growing

rapidly in the poem, stressing and sustaining the presence of the
bard in all its action:

> For neither Man nor Angel can discern
> Hypocrisie, the only evil that walks
> Invisible, except to God alone,
> By his permissive will, through Heav'n and Earth:
> And oft though wisdom wake, suspicion sleeps
> At wisdoms Gate, and to simplicitie
> Resigns her charge, while goodness thinks no ill
> Where no ill seems: Which now for once beguil'd
> *Uriel,* though Regent of the Sun, and held
> The sharpest sighted Spirit of all in Heav'n.   [3.682–91]

How, then, can we be expected to blame Eve very harshly when
she fails to penetrate Satan's disguise?

   Indeed, pity for mankind is soon to become the dominant feel-
ing of book 4, following naturally from the divine charity and pity
that the Son of God has just expressed in Heaven. We may grasp
this change very clearly if we set books 1 and 2 against books 3 and
4 and see them paired in an essential contrast. Books 1 and 2 are
books of loss that turn to books of hate; books 3 and 4 are books of
recovery that turn to books of love. Books 1 and 2 are inseparably
paired, as book 1 moves into book 2 with hardly a break, while at
the center of the junction Satan sits exalted on his throne:

> and from despair
> Thus high uplifted beyond hope, aspires
> Beyond thus high, insatiate to pursue
> Vain Warr with Heav'n, and by success untaught
> His proud imaginations thus displaid.   [2.6–10]

Book 3 discards these "proud imaginations" and begins the new
movement of the poem into the realms of light; at the end of book
3, we stand on the radiance of the Sun itself. And then book 3
flows on almost without a break into book 4, while at the center of
this junction, at the opening of book 4, we find the bard speaking
in an attitude of deepest pity and concern for all mankind:

> O for that warning voice, which he who saw
> Th' *Apocalyps,* heard cry in Heav'n aloud,
> Then when the Dragon, put to second rout,
> Cam furious down to be reveng'd on men,

Wo to the inhabitants on Earth! that now,
While time was, our first Parents had bin warnd
The coming of thir secret foe, and scap'd
Haply so scap'd his mortal snare; for now
Satan, now first inflam'd with rage came down,
The Tempter ere th' Accuser of man-kind,
To wreck on innocent frail man his loss
Of that first Battel, and his flight to Hell.   [4.1–12]

This cry will of course be answered in part when God sends the angel Raphael down to inform Adam and Eve of their danger. Yet the poet seems to have become so deeply immersed in the present action that he is unaware of that plan. He speaks in the human voice of one who does not wholly know what lies ahead and who waits for the muse to prompt his "unpremeditated verse." In the act of creation he discovers the nature of his own response, as he explores the way toward Eden. But what shall we make of the bard's sympathy for the plight of *innocent frail man* before the Fall? Are we really to regard man as "ill secur'd" in his happiness, as Satan says (4.370), unable to penetrate hypocrisy, *frail,* yet somehow made sufficient by God to have stood? The voice of pity here seems to draw out all the implications of that word *frail:* not simply the basic meaning, "liable to break or to be broken" ("free to fall"), but all the weight of all the other meanings of the word: "easily crushed or destroyed," "weak, subject to infirmities; wanting in power, easily overcome," or worse yet, "morally weak; unable to resist temptation; habitually falling into transgression."[9] We may well ask: how can a man be made sufficient to have stood, though frail? But the prime impact here is not theological, and the paradox may well pass unnoticed, for the main effect of the outcry is to stress the singer's presence, to tell us of his love and pity, so different from Satan's hate and envy.

Another contradiction immediately follows, as the poet describes the Hell that rages now within the breast of Satan: "Now conscience wakes despair / That slumberd, wakes the bitter memorie / Of what he was" (4.23–25). Satan with a conscience? This seems not quite in accord with the theology that has just been explained, for Milton has given in book 3 the traditional view that

Satan will never be granted grace, and thus, presumably, could never have a conscience. For conscience, we have been told, is the umpire that God will place within man's breast after the Fall, as a divinely given guide that may lead man from light to light toward his salvation. Then Milton goes on to create a more striking unorthodoxy[10] as he reveals a Satan who still seems to possess the power of choice, a Satan who starts to curse God and then turns to curse himself, "since against his thy will / Chose freely what it now so justly rues" (4.71–72). It even seems to Satan that a way out might still remain in repentance: "O then at last relent," he cries, that is, repent, give up your obstinate course: "is there no place / Left for Repentance, none for Pardon left?" (4.79–80). Milton is boldly raising here another of his ultimate questions: would not a just God prefer to see Satan repent, and give him the chance to repent? Milton seems to leave the question open by showing that Satan's pride would never have accepted the chance, and that therefore God has not offered it: "This knows my punisher," says Satan, "therefore as farr / From granting hee, as I from begging peace" (4.103–04). The effect of Satan's whole soliloquy at the outset of book 4 is this: Satan, like any mortal man, seals his own doom by making a deliberate choice of evil. Milton leaves us with the feeling that Satan somehow has the power, if he had only used it, to make a better choice.

Something very important is accomplished by this humanization of Satan, this treatment of his psychology as resembling that of fallen man. The effect is to place him on the same plane, "on even ground," with man. Satan constantly boasts that he is God's adversary, but it seems he is really fighting only man, whom God has placed on equal terms with Satan, giving man *what may suffice* even after the Fall. Though the poet, in his distress, has called man *frail,* man does not appear quite as frail as Satan appears in this soliloquy. For Milton has designed Satan's hymn to light, Satan's address to the sun, Satan's prologue to his life on earth, in such a way that we are bound to compare it, point by point, with the feelings and attitudes expressed by the poet in his great prologue to book 3. Satan's soliloquy begins as a poem of loss, quickly turns to a hymn of hate, and then to an expression of despair. Satan at the outset addresses not the Eternal nor the abstract

essence that is God, but simply addresses the physical planet in
terms that convey an implicit paganism, sun-worship:

> O thou that with surpassing Glory crownd,
> Look'st from thy sole Dominion like the God
> Of this new World; at whose sight all the Starrs
> Hide thir diminisht heads; to thee I call,
> But with no friendly voice, and add thy name
> O Sun, to tell thee how I hate thy beams
> That bring to my remembrance from what state
> I fell, how glorious once above thy Spheare . . .   [4.32–39]

We cannot fail to recall how the warmth of the sun shining on the
blind poet had brought to his remembrance his continuing love of
poetry, of nature, and of the human face divine.

Thus a contrast is set that will continue throughout the fourth
book; and then, after the interlude of the middle books, will re-
turn with redoubled intensity in book 9. Constantly, this fourth
book works through a contrast of what I have called panels of
action: the poet's love, the devil's hate. It is sometimes said that
books 4 and 9 represent the action of three main characters,
Adam and Eve and Satan; but there is a fourth character, in some
ways more important than any of these: the poet, whose tacit
presence and open intervention remind us that the freedom of
the human will is not all lost, but indeed remains in a voice of the
most remarkable beauty and power.

Thus as Satan fares on toward Eden, we gain our view of
Paradise through a moving camera-eye; but it is not wholly true to
say that we see Paradise through Satan's eyes.[11] Alongside Satan,
or behind him, or looking over his shoulder, we have the broader
vision of the poet, who includes Satan within his view, counteracts
Satan's envy, and promises Satan's defeat in the very fact that this
one fallen man, at least, can still love God's goodness to mankind.
We have at first the illusion of moving in with Satan's eyes:

> And of pure now purer aire
> Meets his approach, and to the heart inspires
> Vernal delight and joy, able to drive
> All sadness but despair.   [4.153–56]

It is not Satan whose heart feels vernal delight and joy in the scene, but the poet, or any normal human being, as Milton goes on to make clear in one of his most effective similes:

> As when to them who sail
> Beyond the *Cape of Hope,* and now are past
> *Mozambic,* off at Sea North-East windes blow
> *Sabean* Odours from the spicie shoare
> Of *Arabie* the blest, with such delay
> Well pleas'd they slack thir course, and many a League
> Cheard with the grateful smell old Ocean smiles.   [4.159–65]

Satan has truly sailed beyond the Cape of Hope into the despair of his soliloquy; but such a choice is not the only way, as the rest of the simile implies. Here again is Milton's reminder of the true princes of exile: those who appreciate the beauties of the creation, express their love of God's bounty, and carry on their work in cheerful ways.

So, in alternating scenes, we have the poet's admiring presentation of Adam and Eve, in passages clearly distinguished from Satan's view by the poet's commentary, while Satan, mouthing his bitter soliloquies, can only cry out, "O Hell! what doe mine eyes with grief behold" (4.358). It is essential to stress the many ways in which the poet's panels of delighted vision are distinguished from Satan's panels of hate. For here, "where the Fiend / Saw undelighted all delight" (4.285–86), Milton presents his views of Paradise and of Adam and Eve with continuous inclusion of us as audience, to whom the poet addresses a continuous commentary on the scene. Thus as Satan first approaches this "delicious Paradise" (an echo of the Vulgate's *in paradiso voluptatis*)[12] Adam is called "our general Sire" and the Tree of Knowledge is called "our Death."[13] From this kind of *our* the whole manner of the poet's address proceeds, including us within his many comparisons, his allusions to the world we know, whether in myth and legend or by contrast and analogy with daily life. Thus when the poet describes our first view of Adam and Eve, his commentary includes the beauty as well as the shame of our world: "Then was not guiltie shame, dishonest shame / Of natures works," he says, and his voice rises, while the direction of the sentence changes:

> honor dishonorable,
> Sin-bred, how have ye troubl'd all mankind
> With shews instead, meer shews of seeming pure,

> And banisht from mans life his happiest life,
> Simplicitie and spotless innocence.
> So passd they naked on, nor shund the sight
> Of God or Angel, for they thought no ill:
> So hand in hand they passd, the lovliest pair
> That ever since in loves imbraces met,
> *Adam* the goodliest man of men since born
> His Sons, the fairest of her Daughters *Eve*.   [4.313–24]

In the last two lines, through the peculiarities of Milton's syntax, the shame of man is in some measure ameliorated by the fact that goodly men and fair daughters are still derived from Adam and Eve.

All these comments and familiar interventions of the bard prepare the way for his longest internal intervention (internal as distinguished from the great prologues, but indeed it is as long as some of the prologues) which occurs about three-quarters of the way through book 4 (736–75). It is Milton's famous celebration of wedded love in Paradise, uttered as the poet watches Adam and Eve enter their bower for the night. Milton proceeds to tell us plainly what he thinks about the facts of married life,[14] both before the Fall and after:

>   nor turnd I weene
> *Adam* from his fair Spouse, nor *Eve* the Rites
> Mysterious of connubial Love refus'd:
> Whatever Hypocrites austerely talk
> Of purity and place and innocence,
> Defaming as impure what God declares
> Pure, and commands to som, leaves free to all.   [4.741–47]

For God commanded in Genesis: "Be fruitful and multiply." And with this thought Milton takes issue with St. Paul's advice concerning marriage and celibacy in I Corinthians, where St. Paul regards marriage as second best, though not sinful (7:38). Milton would have noticed that St. Paul offers this as his own opinion, saying that he has "no commandment of the Lord: yet I give my judgment, as one that hath obtained mercy of the Lord to be faithful" (7:25). Milton, following the Protestant tradition, thinks that St. Paul was simply mistaken here; the judgment of John Milton, as one who also has, he hopes, obtained mercy of the Lord, says quite otherwise:

> Our Maker bids increase, who bids abstain
> But our Destroyer, foe to God and Man?
> Haile wedded Love, mysterious Law, true sourse
> Of human ofspring, sole proprietie,
> In Paradise of all things common else.   [4.748–52]

Wedded Love, he goes on to say, still stands as an island of purity in the fallen life of exile:

> By thee adulterous lust was driv'n from men
> Among the bestial herds to raunge, by thee
> Founded in Reason, Loyal, Just, and Pure,
> Relations dear, and all the Charities
> Of Father, Son, and Brother first were known.
> Farr be it, that I should write thee sin or blame,
> Or think thee unbefitting holiest place,
> Perpetual Fountain of Domestic sweets,
> Whose Bed is undefil'd and chast pronounc't,
> Present or past, as Saints and Patriarchs us'd.   [4.753–62]

Here indeed, he adds, is the place where the god of love truly reigns, and he transfers to this place the attributes of the pagan Cupid: "Here Love his golden shafts imploies, here lights / His constant Lamp, and waves his purple wings, / Reigns here and revels" (4.763–65). *Revels:* a dangerous word, but for Milton not inappropriate in a garden which the Latin Bible calls the *Paradise of Delight.* Other kinds of "love" and "revelry" surround and threaten the married state, as he continues:

> Reigns here and revels; not in the bought smile
> Of Harlots, loveless, joyless, unindeard,
> Casual fruition, nor in Court Amours
> Mixt Dance, or wanton Mask, or Midnight Bal,
> Or Serenate, which the starv'd Lover sings
> To his proud fair, best quitted with disdain.   [4.765–70]

So much for those Petrarchan sonneteers; Adam and Eve had better music than Astrophel and Stella: "These lulld by Nightingales imbraceing slept, / And on thir naked limbs the flourie roof / Showrd Roses, which the Morn repair'd" (4.771–73).

Then the poet concludes the first view of Paradise by pronouncing a benediction upon the wedded pair, a conclusion that forms, in its rhetorical construction, an implicit contrast with the ending of Satan's last soliloquy of hate, where he snarled, "Live while ye

may, / Yet happie pair; enjoy, till I return, / Short pleasures, for
long woes are to succeed" (4.533–35). But now the bard blesses
and implores, "Sleep on, / Blest pair; and O yet happiest if ye seek
/ No happier state, and know to know no more" (4.773–75).

Milton's frank discussions of paradisal sexuality have embar-
rassed some people, including C. S. Lewis[15] and the angel
Raphael, but these discussions lie at the very center of his view of
human nature. It seems that Adam and Eve, before the Fall, are
not so utterly different from fallen man as might at first be
thought. For Milton, life in Paradise is not without its problems,
nor is life for fallen man without its joys. We have not only the
heritage of that original sin; there is also a continuity of grace
between us and our Grand Parents.

In all these ways, books 3 and 4 are designed as a unit to coun-
teract the thrust of Hell in the first two books. The unified action
of the two opening books, as I have said in the preceding chapter,
may be described as an arc, an arch, moving upward from Chaos
and then downward, back to Chaos. How should one describe the
utterly different action that grows from the introduction of light
in book 3? It is an action of illumination that continues with hardly
a pause throughout most of book 4; and then, after a strongly
shaded contrast at the close of book 4, resumes its action of light in
the first, pastoral half of book 5; then runs again into heavy
shadow through the war in Heaven, but emerges in triumphant
light at the close of book 6 as the Son of God goes forth to win his
victory:

> And the third sacred Morn began to shine
> Dawning through Heav'n: forth rush'd with whirl-wind sound
> The Chariot of Paternal Deitie,
> Flashing thick flames . . .   [6.748–51]

That victory of light is an image of the Resurrection on the morn-
ing of Easter Day, and also an image of the fearful light of the Last
Judgment. Thus the varied action of books 3, 4, 5, and 6 is bound
together into one enormous panel, composed of many subpanels,
moving from the merciful promise of the Son of God in book 3 to
the merciful and terrifying judgment by the same Son of God at
the close of book 6. Considering all this, we might speak, using

Milton's own term, of an *irradiated* action, an action of light and shade, as in some painting by Poussin, moving over a vast and peopled landscape,[16] spreading out from the poet's prayer for the gift of inner light, and accompanied by the light of his presence.

In the first two books the poet has allowed his presence to remain relatively minor, while we watch the arc of insurrection soar and fade. In book 3 the poet emerges into prominence, and the light of God floods the scene, illuminating Satan's blackness, his inner torment, his fading strength; then revealing his flight before the sign of power that God hangs in the heavens, and later telling of Satan's defeat in the heavenly war. Meanwhile, although the presence of Satan so frequently shadows the scene, we are encouraged to appreciate the goodness of the gifts given to Adam and Eve, gifts that still, in sufficient measure, remain to man in his exile from Eden. Man has what will suffice to enable him to choose his own salvation.

This, I think, is the meaning of the way in which Milton has framed this sequence of four books (3, 4, 5, 6) between two of his great prologues. In the prologue to book 3 the poet emerges from the darkness of Hell into the light of Heaven; and in the prologue to book 7 he prays that he may be allowed to return now to his native earth, even though life there for him has become a painful life of exile, "In darkness, and with dangers compast round" (7.27). The poem's basically baroque structure could not be more clearly defined than by the placement of these prologues. It is under firm control, while allowing room for the most elaborate variations, an inner plenitude of panels in "various style."

We should note, finally, one of the benefits of Milton's original ten-book division: for the long seventh book of 1667, devoted to the story of the Creation, is the only book framed (or guarded) between two of Milton's great prologues; and it is a book in which Satan does not set his foot. It is as though the poet had at last made his way out of Hell and Chaos into some bright and gracious sanctuary at the center of the mind. Like the blind Orion of Poussin's famous painting, he has penetrated to the farthest East, where his sight is miraculously restored.

The Diffusion of Good

Milton's conception of an expanding universe, motivated by the ever-creative goodness of God, is clearly represented in the movement from destruction to creation that occurs in books 6 and 7. As the numerological critics have pointed out, the manifestation of the chariot of the Son covers the exact center of the poem, which occurs in the sixth book of 1667 between lines 761 and 762, or at line 766 in the second edition.[1] Whichever version one is reading, everyone is bound to sense that this triumphal appearance is presented in the very middle of the poem, a fact especially evident in the twelve-book division of 1674. Yet it would be wrong, I think, to feel that after this manifestation of the Son's triumphant power the poem moves "downward", except in a physical sense.[2] The poem moves to earth, a movement enforced by Milton's great prologue to book 7; but, as the angels tell us in their hymn at the close of that book, the Son's act of creation is greater than his conquest of the rebellious angels:

> Creation and the Six dayes acts they sung,
> Great are thy works, *Jehovah,* infinite
> Thy power; what thought can measure thee or tongue
> Relate thee; greater now in thy return
> Then from the Giant Angels; thee that day
> Thy Thunders magnifi'd; but to create
> Is greater then created to destroy. [7.601–07]

114

If we compare this long hymn with the briefly reported praise
sung by the same angels at the Son of God's return from victory
over the "Giant Angels," we can sense how subtly Milton is prepar-
ing the way for the great vision of creative power soon to appear:

> Sole Victor from th' expulsion of his Foes
> *Messiah* his triumphal Chariot turnd:
> To meet him all his Saints, who silent stood
> Eye witnesses of his Almightie Acts,
> With Jubilie advanc'd; and as they went,
> Shaded with branching Palme, each order bright,
> Sung Triumph, and him sung Victorious King,
> Son, Heire, and Lord, to him Dominion giv'n,
> Worthiest to Reign: he celebrated rode
> Triumphant through mid Heav'n, into the Courts
> And Temple of his mightie Father Thron'd
> On high; who into Glorie him receav'd,
> Where now he sits at the right hand of bliss.   [6.880–92]

We do not hear the song itself; Milton is waiting for a greater
occasion to recite the angels' hymn of praise. For the present, the
reported celebration serves to complete the symbolism that has
marked his ending of the war in Heaven, which has mingled
suggestions of the victory of Christ at the Resurrection with
suggestions of his victory at the Day of Judgment. Thus the allu-
sion in the closing line above ("Where now he sits at the right hand
of bliss") evokes the Ascension of Christ as related in Hebrews
(1:3) and fulfills the implications of God's stress upon the fact that
the Son will come forth to win his victory at the dawning of the
third day:

> two dayes are past,
> Two dayes, as we compute the dayes of Heav'n
> . . . .
> Two dayes are therefore past, the third is thine
> . . . .
> And the third sacred Morn began to shine
> Dawning through Heav'n: forth rush'd with whirl-wind sound
> The Chariot of Paternal Deitie . . .   [6.684–85,699,748–50]

Meanwhile the constant use of the word "saints" to describe the
good angels as they battle in book 6 suggests the triumph of more

earthly "saints," that is, the just, in the common puritan usage. Thus the Son appears in his chariot:

> Attended with ten thousand thousand Saints,
> He onward came, farr off his coming shon,
> And twentie thousand (I thir number heard)
> Chariots of God, half on each hand were seen:
> Hee on the wings of Cherub rode sublime
> On the crystallin Skie, in Saphir Thron'd.
> Illustrious farr and wide, but by his own
> First seen, them unexpected joy surpriz'd,
> When the great Ensign of *Messiah* blaz'd
> Aloft by Angels born, his Sign in Heav'n:
> Under whose Conduct *Michael* soon reduc'd
> His Armie, circumfus'd on either Wing,
> Under thir Head imbodied all in one.　　　　[6.767–79]

The allusion here to "the sign of the Son of man" in Matthew (24:27–30) combines with a later allusion to Christ's prediction of the separation of the sheep from the goats (6.856–57; Matthew 25:31–33) to carry on the apocalyptic implications of the prophecy in Jude (14–15): "Behold, the Lord cometh with ten thousands of his saints, To execute judgment upon all." But most important here is the clear indication of God's immense reserves of power: he has held back a half of his angels to accompany the Son (though not to fight) in his victory; this is clear from the way in which Michael and his army see the "ten thousand thousand Saints" approaching from afar. This allocation of forces (half of the good angels equalling the third that has fallen) has been set forth from the outset of the battle; it is hard to see why some readers do not accept what seems to be the clear sense of what God is saying:[3]

> *Gabriel,* lead forth to Battel these my Sons
> Invincible, lead forth my armed Saints
> By Thousands and by Millions rang'd for fight;
> Equal in number to that Godless crew
> Rebellious . . .　　　　[6.46–50]

Equal in number they must be, for if the loyal angels were *twice* as numerous as Satan's host, how could we ever explain the remarkable strength of the rebellious angels in holding the fight to a destructive draw? In accordance with his theology Milton has the angels, like man, placed "on even ground" with the forces of evil, as a test of faith. God makes the point a second time when, addressing the Son, he describes the "Equal" strength of the two forces:

> sore hath been thir fight,
> As likeliest was, when two such Foes met arm'd;
> For to themselves I left them, and thou knowest,
> Equal in their Creation they were form'd. [6.687–90]

In this way Milton has created an allegory of the spiritual combat fought by God's "saints" on earth: a "sore" combat in which the just are rescued, first, by the atonement of the Crucifixion, and last, by the judgment of the Son at the Day of Doom. The vast reserve forces are of course not needed for these victories, which the Son performs alone, while the "saints," as Milton says at the close of the war in Heaven, "silent stood / Eye witnesses of his Almightie Acts," and only after his return sing jubilee.

But in the acts to follow in book 7 the angels begin to celebrate the Creation as soon as they hear the command given to the Son; they sing here a version of the Gloria sung by the angels at the birth of Jesus; here is the first incarnation:

> Glorie they sung to the most High, good will
> To future men, and in thir dwellings peace:
> Glorie to him whose just avenging ire
> Had driven out th' ungodly from his sight
> And th' habitations of the just; to him
> Glorie and praise, whose wisdom had ordain'd
> Good out of evil to create, in stead
> Of Spirits maligne a better Race to bring
> Into thir vacant room, and thence diffuse
> His good to Worlds and Ages infinite. [7.182–91]

The diffusion of good may be disturbed, as in the war in Heaven, but its onward impulse cannot be stopped, as Milton now proceeds to show, beginning with a brilliant contrast with the scene in book 2 where Hell's gates open upon Chaos "With impetuous recoile and jarring sound . . . and on thir hinges grate / Harsh Thunder," while "like a Furnace mouth" they "Cast forth redounding smoak and ruddy flame"(2.880–81,888–89).

Now in book 7 the Son of God again goes forth in all his majesty, to perform the greater act of diffusing good:

> About his Chariot numberless were pour'd
> Cherub and Seraph, Potentates and Thrones,
> And Vertues, winged Spirits, and Chariots wing'd,
> From the Armoury of God . . .
>   Heav'n op'nd wide
> Her ever during Gates, Harmonious sound
> On golden Hinges moving, to let forth
> The King of Glorie in his powerful Word
> And Spirit coming to create new Worlds.   [7.197–200,205–09]

The contrast with Satan's voyage in book 2 is stressed by a glimpse of "the vast immeasurable Abyss / Outrageous as a Sea, dark, wasteful, wilde" (7.211–12). But the Son of God rides out over the "surging waves" with absolute command in word and act:

> Silence, ye troubl'd waves, and thou Deep, peace,
> Said then th' Omnific Word, your discord end:
>   Nor staid, but on the Wings of Cherubim
> Uplifted, in Paternal Glorie rode
> Farr into *Chaos*, and the World unborn;
> . . . .
>   and in his hand
> He took the golden Compasses, prepar'd
> In Gods Eternal store, to circumscribe
> This Universe, and all created things:
> One foot he center'd, and the other turn'd
> Round through the vast profunditie obscure,
> And said, thus farr extend, thus farr thy bounds,
> This be thy just Circumference, O World.   [7.216–20,224–31]

Then after earth has been hung "self-ballanc't on her Center," and after light "Ethereal, first of things, quintessence pure" has been created, the angelic hosts again burst into song:

>   with joy and shout
> The hollow Universal Orb they fill'd,
> And touch't thir Golden Harps, & hymning prais'd
> God and his works, Creatour him they sung,
> Both when first Eevning was, and when first Morn.   [7.256–60]

It seems that they thus celebrate the action of each day of Creation, for after the second day we hear: "So Eev'n / And Morning *Chorus* sung the second Day" (7.274–75). But it is not clear

whether the angels or evening and morning form that chorus: the
two are fused. Thereafter only "Eev'n and Morn" record, or
crown, or solemnize, the days, until the sixth day is "accomplish't"
and the Creator returns to the Heaven of Heavens:

> Followd with acclamation and the sound
> Symphonious of ten thousand Harpes that tun'd
> Angelic harmonies :
> . . . .
> Open, ye everlasting Gates, they sung,
> Open, ye Heav'ns, your living dores; let in
> The great Creator from his work returnd
> Magnificent, his Six days work, a World;
> Open, and henceforth oft; for God will deigne
> To visit oft the dwellings of just Men
> Delighted, and with frequent intercourse
> Thither will send his winged Messengers
> On errands of supernal Grace.   [7.558–60,565–73]

And the echo of Psalm 24 shows that the prophecy of grace will be
fulfilled on earth.

Then, as the "Filial Power" rejoins the Father (from whom he
has never been separated) the angels celebrate the seventh day
with a service filled with pomp and gold, appropriate to Heaven,
if not to earth:

> the Harp
> Had work and rested not, the solemn Pipe,
> And Dulcimer, all Organs of sweet stop,
> All sounds on Fret by String or Golden Wire
> Temper'd soft Tunings, intermixt with Voice
> Choral or Unison; of incense Clouds
> Fuming from Golden Censers hid the Mount.   [7.594–600]

And the celebration concludes with the thirty-line hymn to God's
creative power, beginning with the lines that I have quoted at the
outset of this chapter, and continuing on with triumphant praise
of God's creative bounty diffused to worlds and multitudes as yet
unknown:

> Who seekes
> To lessen thee, against his purpose serves
> To manifest the more thy might: his evil
> Thou usest, and from thence creat'st more good.

> Witness this new-made World, another Heav'n
> From Heaven Gate not farr . . .   [7.613–18]

Here, then, at the close of book 7, or, in the first edition, in the middle of book 7, is the climax of one strand in the poem's twofold plot: the strand of redemption, showing the irresistible flowing forth of God's creative goodness,[4] which man's fall, like the war in Heaven, may disturb, but never stop. There is a continuity between this Creation and the creative light that still can work within the vision of the redeemed man. Milton's vision of Creation proves that the apprehension of God's goodness can still be recovered, with love and gratitude, by fallen man. Here is the paradise within.

II

The climactic nature of this vision is stressed in the first edition by the length of the original seventh book, with its 1290 lines forming the longest book thus far in the poem. It is all one book of Creation, for Adam has still to tell his memories of his first "up-springing" and the story of the creation of Eve. Yet, despite the advantage of this emphasis, Milton's division of the latter half of this long book into a new book 8 is highly effective and appropriate. For this eighth book of the second edition has essentially a different theme from the preceding account of the six days of Creation. Book 7 in the new division is one sustained hymn of praise to God's creative bounty. The new book 8 reveals the presence of what Milton here calls "doubt." The word "doubt" here performs in exactly the ambiguous way that the words "frail," "wanton," or "error" have performed in the scenes before the Fall:[5] they are words wholly innocent, not "noxious" in this paradisal context—but they imply the presence of certain qualities inherent in the Creation that will lead to man's fall, qualities inherent in the gift of freedom and the gift of reason.

This shift of basic theme is made plain at the outset of book 8 as Adam thanks the angel for allaying his desire to know "Of things above his World," to learn what Raphael calls "the secrets of another world, perhaps / Not lawful to reveal"—though for man's good, the angel adds, "This is dispenc't"(5.455,569–71). But

Adam's thirst for knowledge is not yet satisfied, despite his gratitude:

> What thanks sufficient, or what recompence
> Equal have I to render thee, Divine
> Hystorian, who thus largely hast allayd
> The thirst I had of knowledge, and voutsaf't
> This friendly condescention to relate
> Things else by me unsearchable, now heard
> With wonder, but delight, and, as is due,
> With glorie attributed to the high
> Creator; some thing yet of doubt remaines,
> Which only thy solution can resolve.   [8.5–14]

There is of course no doubt of God's goodness; the doubt is only uncertainty about how to interpret God's ways. Adam proceeds to ask, in larger terms, much the same question that Eve had asked in book 4, when, after her echoing love-song, she so abruptly changed her tone to ask why the stars shine while the two of them are sleeping: "But wherfore all night long shine these, for whom, / This glorious sight, when sleep hath shut all eyes?"(4.657–58). Adam beautifully explains that the stars have their duty "to Nations yet unborn," that their influence helps to temper or nourish all things that grow on earth, and that even if mankind did not exist, "Millions of spiritual Creatures walk the Earth / Unseen, both when we wake, and when we sleep" (4.677–79).

Nevertheless, as he looks upon the entire universe, Adam is led to wonder why such an immense and intricate creation of stars should have been designed only to provide light for the earth, "in all thir vast survey / Useless besides;"

>   reasoning I oft admire,
> How Nature wise and frugal could commit
> Such disproportions, with superfluous hand
> So many nobler Bodies to create,
> Greater so manifold to this one use . . .   [8.24–29]

Reasoning, we see, is not infallible in its conclusions, for, although Raphael says, "To ask or search I blame thee not," (66) he makes it clear that Adam's question has carried man beyond the range of legitimate searching; and the angel predicts the "quaint opinions" that Adam's descendants will put forth as a result of just this kind

of "reasoning." He concludes by urging Adam not to pursue this
kind of study, but to concentrate his thoughts on "what he gives to
thee, this Paradise / And thy fair *Eve*":

> Heav'n is for thee too high
> To know what passes there; be lowlie wise:
> Think onely what concernes thee and thy being . . . [8.171–74]

Then Adam, "cleerd of doubt," declares himself fully satisfied,
once again, and says that he now understands that man should
live without "perplexing thoughts" and "anxious cares"—which
he says will "not molest us, unless we our selves / Seek them with
wandring thoughts, and notions vaine"(8.179–87). But there is
the problem, as Adam realizes when he contemplates his own and
Eve's interior motions:

> But apte the Mind or Fancie is to roave
> Uncheckt, and of her roaving is no end;
> Till warn'd, or by experience taught, she learn
> That not to know at large of things remote
> From use, obscure and suttle, but to know
> That which before us lies in daily life,
> Is the prime Wisdom . . .   [8.188–94]

Adam is recognizing here the inherent, created tendency of the
"Fancie" which he has described to Eve at the outset of book 5,
while reassuring her that her disturbing dream, though containing
evil thoughts, has left "No spot or blame behind." When Reason is
asleep or at rest, he has explained,

> Oft in her absence mimic Fansie wakes
> To imitate her; but misjoyning shapes,
> Wilde work produces oft, and most in dreams,
> Ill matching words and deeds long past or late.   [5.110–13]

Adam is not limiting the "wilde work" of fancy to the state of
dreaming; the tendency toward such roving or wildness is a part
of man's created perfection. Only warning or experience will
teach mankind how to control such roving of his "unexperienc't
thought."

But even when abstruse studies are given up and the mind is
devoted to the problems of daily life in Paradise, the doubts arise,
"yet sinless." Adam now goes on to tell the story of the workings of

his reason upon his first upspringing, when he rightly understood
that he could not have been self-created:

> Not of my self; by some great Maker then,
> In goodness and in power praeeminent;
> Tell me, how may I know him, how adore,
> From whom I have that thus I move and live,
> And feel that I am happier then I know.   [8.278–82]

Then he shows his dignity and his boldness as he tells how he has
reasoned with God over man's need for a mate, winning the di-
vine approbation for his request:

> Thus farr to try thee *Adam,* I was pleas'd,
> And finde thee knowing not of Beasts alone,
> Which thou hast rightly nam'd, but of thy self,
> Expressing well the spirit within thee free,
> My Image, not imparted to the Brute,
> Whose fellowship therefore unmeet for thee
> Good reason was thou freely shouldst dislike,
> And be so minded still; I, ere thou spak'st,
> Knew it not good for Man to be alone,   ⤶
> And no such companie as then thou saw'st
> Intended thee, for trial onely brought,
> To see how thou could'st judge of fit and meet:
> What next I bring shall please thee, be assur'd,
> Thy likeness, thy fit help, thy other self,
> Thy wish, exactly to thy hearts desire.   [8.437–51]

Well and good; but, Adam goes on to say, a problem has arisen
from this so desirable gift of God, for Adam admits that he feels a
"Commotion strange" whenever he looks at Eve—*Commotion
strange,* a charming euphemism that perfectly suggests the combi-
nation of dignity and innocence in our grand parents. Milton
insists on bringing out the whole difficult problem: Adam himself
asks the embarrassing question, since he finds himself "here onely
weake / Against the charm of Beauties powerful glance":

> Or Nature faild in mee, and left some part
> Not proof enough such Object to sustain
> Or from my side subducting, took perhaps
> More then enough; at least on her bestow'd
> Too much of Ornament . . .

"For well I understand," Adam says, that she is supposed to be inferior to me intellectually,

> yet when I approach
> Her loveliness, so absolute she seems
> And in her self compleat, so well to know
> Her own, that what she wills to do or say,
> Seems wisest, vertuousest, discreetest, best;

(Adam's confusion here seems to have produced Milton's worst line!)

> All higher knowledge in her presence falls
> Degraded, Wisdom in discourse with her
> Looses discount'nanc't, and like folly shewes;
> Authoritie and Reason on her waite,
> As one intended first, not after made
> Occasionally . . .
>
> [8.532–56]

All this questioning of "nature" amounts to saying that perhaps God has made a mistake in creating Adam and Eve in this fashion. Thus the angel rebukes Adam sharply, "with contracted brow," pointing out at length that man was made for higher purposes than "carnal pleasure." But Adam is only "half abash't" at this stern rebuke, and he defends himself by saying that what most attracts him about Eve are the "decencies" that he finds in her— "decencies" in the old sense of qualities of fitness and harmony:

> those graceful acts,
> Those thousand decencies that daily flow
> From all her words and actions, mixt with Love
> And sweet compliance, which declare unfeign'd
> Union of Mind, or in us both one Soule:
> Harmonie to behold in wedded pair
> More grateful then harmonious sound to the eare.   [8.600–06]

The link with Milton's earlier praise of wedded love in book 4 makes Adam's defense here very strong. And after all, Adam cleverly asks, don't the angels in heaven also love? Here the angel gives his famous blush, "Celestial rosie red, Loves proper hue," and answers, in effect, yes, we are happy, and yes, we do love, but I've got to be getting on home now, for it's sunset, and remember,

> take heed least Passion sway
> Thy Judgement to do aught, which else free Will
> Would not admit; thine and of all thy Sons
> The weal or woe in thee is plac't; beware.
> I in thy persevering shall rejoyce,
> And all the Blest: stand fast; to stand or fall
> Free in thine own Arbitrement it lies.
> Perfect within, no outward aid require;
> And all temptation to transgress repel.   [8.635–43]

Perfect within—all the preceding doubts have been allowed and caused by the nature and conditions of man's perfection. Sexuality, under reason's control, is justified by the example of the angels, and attractive reluctance, modesty, and blushing in Eve (as in the angel) are all part of that perfection before the Fall:

> She heard me thus, and though divinely brought,
> Yet Innocence and Virgin Modestie,
> Her vertue and the conscience of her worth,
> That would be woo'd, and not unsought be won,
> Not obvious, not obtrusive, but retir'd,
> The more desirable, or to say all,
> Nature her self, though pure of sinful thought,
> Wrought in her so, that seeing me, she turn'd;
> I follow'd her, she what was Honour knew,
> And with obsequious Majestie approv'd
> My pleaded reason. To the Nuptial Bowre
> I led her blushing like the Morn . . .   [8.500–11]

It is passages such as this that have led some readers, perhaps most readers, to feel that Milton is having difficulty in distinguishing between fallen and unfallen sexuality and that indeed, as Tillyard has put it, Milton is constantly "faking" in his account of paradisal life by "attributing to Eve and Adam feelings which though nominally felt in the state of innocence are actually not compatible with it." Both, he says, "are virtually fallen before the official temptation has begun." Poetically and dramatically, he argues, Milton could not have done otherwise.[6]

But the issue should be put another way, as J. M. Evans has shown in his demonstration that in Milton's view "Man's innocence was not 'effortless,' " was not "a condition of stability." "The perfection of Adam and Eve no less than the perfection of the garden they inhabit is nothing if not conditional, for it requires their constant vigilance to preserve the balance of forces on which it depends."[7] The poem, then, means exactly what it seems to say: that Adam and Eve, before the Fall, were very much like their descendants, that the difference between the fallen and the un-fallen state does not reside in any change of the essential human qualities: free will, and the power of choice. The change is only in the non-essential conditions of life: in the presence of pain, sor-row, and temporal death (for ultimate immortality is not denied), and in the outward conditions of life: harshness of climate, sweat of the brow to provide food and shelter—all non-essential to man's happiness in Milton's view. For happiness resides in the love of God: in gratitude and praise for the gifts that God still showers upon fallen man through the vestiges of God remaining in the Creation and in the bounty of his grace.

CHAPTER 7

The Power
of Choice

Adam and Eve, before the Fall, have all our basic psychological qualities: they are "frail" in the sense that their power of choice may wrongly choose; choice is difficult because "wandring thoughts" and passions and the wild work of fancy are all part of the broad field in which human choice must operate. Adam and Eve find it difficult to choose rightly because they are so "unexperienc't"; their descendants find it difficult to choose because they have so much experience, see so many possibilities, dangers, and advantages. Yet in Milton's universe the power of choice is essential to man's perfection and man's happiness, whether fallen or unfallen. That is why the words "choice" and "choose" ring throughout *Paradise Lost*, from the opening words of Satan, "and in my choyce / To reign is worth ambition though in Hell . . ." (1.261–62) through the words of God declaring "Reason also is choice," on to the famous closing lines where Adam and Eve must learn "where to choose / Thir place of rest" (12.646–47).[1]

As in these instances, so in book 8 these crucial words are placed in an emphatic position, at the end of a line, when Adam recalls the divine prohibition in the very phrase that Satan has used in book 1:

127

> Sternly he pronounc'd
> The rigid interdiction, which resounds
> Yet dreadful in mine eare, though in my choice
> Not to incur . . .   [8.333–36]

The power of choice, then, is essential to Milton's view of the
dynamic, progressive, eternal expansion of God's goodness; by
warning and experience man must learn to manage the gift of
freedom, and seek his happiness beyond the limitations of the
flesh.

Nothing could stress the essential humanity of Adam and Eve
more strongly than the scene that opens book 9, after Satan has
uttered his Euripidean, or Senecan prologue to the tragedy of the
Fall (99–178). Here Milton brings our grand parents closer to us
than we have thus far seen them. This is not done suddenly: it has
been a gradual process from their first appearance in book 4. The
more we see of them and the more we hear them talk, the more
they seem like us. In book 5, for example, Adam and Eve have
already begun to drop the formal modes of address that marked
their speeches in book 4. When Adam sees the angel approaching
his door he calls to Eve, who is within "due at her hour" preparing
dinner,

> Haste hither *Eve*, and worth thy sight behold
> Eastward among those Trees, what glorious shape
> Comes this way moving . . .
>   But goe with speed,
> And what thy stores contain, bring forth and poure
> Abundance, fit to honour and receive
> Our Heav'nly stranger . . .   [5.308–10,313–16]

Eve is amused at Adam's abrupt and excited concern for her
"stores" and she answers in a leisurely and stately way (one can
imagine her quiet smile):

> *Adam*, earths hallowd mould,
> Of God inspir'd, small store will serve, where store,
> All seasons, ripe for use hangs on the stalk;
> Save what by frugal storing firmness gains
> To nourish, and superfluous moist consumes:
> But I will haste and from each bough and break,
> Each Plant & juiciest Gourd will pluck such choice
> To entertain our Angel guest, as hee

> Beholding shall confess that here on Earth
> God hath dispenst his bounties as in Heav'n.
>   So saying, with dispatchful looks in haste
> She turns, on hospitable thoughts intent
> What choice to chuse for delicacie best . . .   [5.321–33]

Thus Eve shows her command of the household affairs, using her reason wittily to pun before going forth to exercise her power of choice in the preparation of that elegant vegetarian meal.[2]

The sense of comedy here, enforced by Milton's own quiet wit in regarding this pastoral feast—"No fear lest Dinner coole"—is carried on in the early part of book 9, where, though Milton has said that he must now change his notes to tragic, the first act of his tragedy might well be described as a domestic comedy. Here at the outset the grand titles of address are completely dropped, and Adam and Eve are introduced simply as the "human pair." "And *Eve* first to her Husband thus began," without any of those words about "My Author and Disposer," "Unargu'd I obey," and so on, such as we heard in book 4. Eve opens her speech here in what might be called a normal wifely fashion: "*Adam*," she says, quite informally—

> *Adam*, well may we labour still to dress
> This Garden, still to tend Plant, Herb and Flour.
> Our pleasant task enjoyn'd, but till more hands
> Aid us, the work under our labour grows,
> Luxurious by restraint; what we by day
> Lop overgrown, or prune, or prop, or bind,
> One night or two with wanton growth derides
> Tending to wilde.   [9.205–212]

We must believe that Eve is truly concerned about her work here, and not simply fishing for a compliment, for Milton's whole account of life in Paradise has stressed the importance of this element of labor.[3] Milton is placing a special stress upon the words of Genesis where God says to Adam and Eve: "Be fruitful and multiply, and replenish the earth, and subdue it," along with the later statement that "the Lord God took the man, and put him into the garden of Eden to dress it and to keep it," with man's duties clarified by the statement that before this "there was not a man to till the ground" (Gen. 1:28; 2:5, 15). Eve's concern for the

results of their "labour" of dressing and re-dressing is one of the
problems raised by the whole Creation's "wanton" tendency to be
fruitful and multiply, even to the extent of "tending to wilde."
Nature's vitality, whether in vegetation or in man and woman, is
not easy to "subdue" and keep in reasonable order.

The point has been clearly made in book 5 as Milton describes
the angel's approach to Adam's door:

> through Groves of Myrrhe,
> And flouring Odours, Cassia, Nard, and Balme;
> A Wilderness of sweets; for Nature here
> Wantond as in her prime, and plaid at will
> Her Virgin Fancies, pouring forth more sweet,
> Wilde above rule or art; enormous bliss.   [5.292–97]

Here again the words "wantond" and "wilde" give the clue to
the inherent problem: things unconfined and unrestrained tend
to become "luxurious", tend to run beyond the rule and art of
reason. Man's duty is to bring these "Virgin Fancies" of nature
under the control of reason, for fancy, we recall, can make "wilde
work". Eve is therefore completely right to show concern over the
way in which their labors seem ineffective. Adam himself has
explained to Eve the importance of their labor in book 4, as they
retire to their blissful bower:

> When *Adam* thus to *Eve:* Fair Consort, th' hour
> Of night, and all things now retir'd to rest
> Mind us of like repose, since God hath set
> Labour and rest, as day and night to men
> Successive, and the timely dew of sleep
> Now falling with soft slumbrous weight inclines
> Our eye-lids; other Creatures all day long
> Rove idle unimploid, and less need rest;
> Man hath his daily work of body or mind
> Appointed, which declares his Dignitie,
> And the regard of Heav'n on all his waies;
> While other Animals unactive range,
> And of thir doings God takes no account.   [4.610–22]

The word "account" tells us to take the divine "regard" on all
man's ways in two senses: God holds man's ways in high regard,
with affection and respect—but also, the eye of God is watching all
man's ways, and will take account of how he performs his ap-

pointed tasks. Therefore, Adam adds, at dawn "we must be ris'n /
And at our pleasant labour," which he then proceeds to describe
with exactly the conditions that are worrying Eve in book 9:

> to reform
> Yon flourie Arbors, yonder Allies green,
> Our walks at noon, with branches overgrown,
> That mock our scant manuring, and require
> More hands then ours to lop thir wanton growth . . .
>
> [4.624–29]

There again is the word "wanton", along with the witty play on the
Latin base of *manuring*—working with the hands, for such work is
surely needed: "Those Blossoms also, and those dropping
Gumms, / That lie bestrowne unsightly and unsmooth, / Ask rid-
dance, if we mean to tread with ease . . ." (4.630–32).

Thus Eve is right to be concerned over the results of their labor,
and right to consider ways of improving its effect:

> Thou therefore now advise
> Or hear what to my mind first thoughts present,
> Let us divide our labours, thou where choice
> Leads thee, or where most needs, whether to wind
> The Woodbine round this Arbour, or direct
> The clasping Ivie where to climb, while I
> In yonder Spring of Roses intermixt
> With Myrtle, find what to redress till Noon . . .   [9.212–19]

She suggests this division of labor because, she adds, when they
are together they waste too much time in looking at each other
and smiling and talking, and thus "th' hour of Supper comes
unearn'd" (9.225).

"To whom mild answer *Adam* thus return'd," maintaining some-
thing of that earlier formality of address, along with some meas-
ure of masculine condescension:

> Sole *Eve*, Associate sole, to me beyond
> Compare above all living Creatures deare,
> Well hast thou motion'd, wel thy thoughts imployd
> How we might best fulfill the work which here
> God hath assign'd us, nor of me shalt pass
> Unprais'd: for nothing lovelier can be found
> In woman, then to studie houshold good,
> And good workes in her Husband to promote.   [9.227–34]

Adam sounds here as though he had observed hundreds of wom-
en: clearly Adam is becoming Everyman. But, he adds, life in
Eden is not supposed to be so arduous. It is quite all right for us to
look and smile at each other while we work; and then he makes
man's first strategic error, for he goes on to say:

> But other doubt possesses me, least harm
> Befall thee sever'd from me; for thou knowst
> What hath bin warn'd us, what malicious Foe
> Envying our happiness, and of his own
> Despairing, seeks to work us woe and shame
> By sly assault . . .   [9.251–56]

Considering this danger, then, Adam advises,

>   leave not the faithful side
> That gave thee being, stil shades thee and protects.
> The Wife, where danger or dishonour lurks,
> Safest and seemliest by her Husband staies,
> Who guards her, or with her the worst endures.   [9.265–69]

Here again, Adam is speaking with the voice of Everyman in the
daily world, foreshadowing his decision to eat the apple and with
her the worst endure. Eve in her reply becomes Everywoman, too,
as she withdraws to her earlier mode of formal address:

> To whom the Virgin Majestie of *Eve*,
> As one who loves, and some unkindness meets,
> With sweet austeer composure thus reply'd.
> Ofspring of Heav'n and Earth, and all Earths Lord . . .
>   [9.270–73]

She goes on to say that she knows all about this enemy, for Adam
has told her about Satan, and she has overheard the warning of
the departing angel. Thus she is shocked to think that Adam
would mistrust her:

> But that thou shouldst my firmness therfore doubt
> To God or thee, because we have a foe
> May tempt it, I expected not to hear . . .
> Thoughts, which how found they harbour in thy brest,
> *Adam*, missthought of her to thee so dear?
>   To whom with healing words *Adam* reply'd.
> Daughter of God and Man, immortal *Eve* . . .
>   [9.279–81,288–91]

I do trust you, he says, I do, but—and then he flounders into a very unconvincing argument: I am only trying to prevent the dishonor that lies in the fact of being tempted. Then he tries a stronger point, which one wishes that he had tried first. I cannot get along without you, he says, I will be stronger in your presence: "I from the influence of thy looks receave / Access in every Vertue, in thy sight / More wise, more watchful, stronger . . ." (9.309–11). And now Milton tells us very plainly what he is about, for by his introductory phrasing he places the scene in our own world:

> So spake domestick *Adam* in his care
> And Matrimonial Love, but *Eve*, who thought
> Less attributed to her Faith sincere,
> Thus her reply with accent sweet renewd.
>   If this be our condition, thus to dwell
> In narrow circuit strait'nd by a Foe,
> Suttle or violent, we not endu'd
> Single with like defence, wherever met,
> How are we happie, still in fear of harm?
>
>   . . . .
>
> Fraile is our happiness, if this be so,
> And *Eden* were no *Eden* thus expos'd.   [9.318–26,340–41]

This is not what Adam has been saying: they are not confined to a narrow circuit; they can go anywhere together. And this idea that they are made, or ought to be made, to meet temptation singly— this represents, as Milton's whole poem before this has made clear, a misunderstanding of the nature of the universe, where nothing stands alone, but everything lives best in the linked universe of love, with respect for those above and care for those below. This is why Adam at last replies "fervently," exclaiming:

> O Woman, best are all things as the will
> Of God ordaind them, his creating hand
> Nothing imperfet or deficient left
> Of all that he Created . . .   [9.343–46]

The meaning of Eden, he says, has nothing to do with this idea of complete personal independence. The freedom of the will, Adam goes on to explain, exercises its power of choice within a universe of interdependent and mutual responsibility: "Not then mistrust, but tender love enjoynes, / That I should mind thee oft, and mind thou me" (9.357–58). "Mind" here does not mean simply "obey", but rather means "Pay attention to," "be mindful" of one another's best interests and advice. Then Adam goes on to make the choice very plain: "Wouldst thou approve thy constancie, approve / First thy obedience;" (9.367–68) that is, obedience to what is clearly Adam's wish and best advice. He leaves it up to her to choose, saying: "But if thou think" (and clearly he does not think so)

> trial unsought may finde
> Us both securer then thus warnd thou seemst,
> Go; for thy stay, not free, absents thee more . . .   [9.370–72]

Adam seems to be telling her that if she thinks that staying together, not seeking trial, may create a sense of false security, then it is better for her to go, since she will be staying with him against her will.

To some readers Adam has seemed weak here, but the question is highly debatable, for it may well seem that Adam is only carrying out here the view of the workings of free will that the poem has over and over again explained to us and to Adam. He has made it plain that he does not wish her to go; he has asked for her obedience to this wish. His respect for human reason makes it impossible for him to detain her by force and his love for Eve makes it impossible for him to speak more harshly. It is true that later on, after the Fall, in that unpleasant scene of domestic bickering, Eve snaps back at Adam with the bitter reproach:

> why didst not thou the Head
> Command me absolutely not to go,
> Going into such danger as thou saidst?
> Too facil then thou didst not much gainsay,
> Nay, didst permit, approve, and fair dismiss.
> Hadst thou bin firm and fixt in thy dissent,
> Neither had I transgress'd, nor thou with mee.   [9.1155–61]

But here she is angrily distorting the effect of Adam's earlier speech, where Adam seems to hope that by this evidence of his respect for her intelligence, she will come round to his point of view:

> Go in thy native innocence, relie
> On what thou hast of vertue, summon all,
> For God towards thee hath done his part, do thine.   [9.373–75]

With this meagre compliment, Adam reminds Eve that her part is to be mindful of Adam's best advice. And Adam still seems to hope that Eve will choose to take his advice.

"So spake the Patriarch of Mankinde," says Milton, but the Patriarch soon suffers the fate of his sons:

> but *Eve*
> Persisted, yet submiss, though last, repli'd.
> With thy permission then . . .   [9.376–78]

Has he really given her permission to go? It would be more accurate to say that he has given her permission to disobey his wishes if she chooses to do so, and this is exactly the permission that God himself allows the freedom of the will. God, to be sure, has laid down his commandment absolutely, but it is not, I think, valid to argue from this that Adam should have been equally absolute. Even in Milton's day, the relation between husband and wife could not have been regarded as precisely analogous to the relation between God and man. Of course we think of Milton's earlier statement in book 4:

> Hee for God only, shee for God in him:
> His fair large Front and Eye sublime declar'd
> Absolute rule . . .   [4.299–301]

But this at once is followed by the passage where he adds that Eve's "subjection" must be "requir'd with gentle sway." It is this gentle sway that Adam is attempting to exert here, but Eve, insisting on her own right to choose, makes the wrong choice. That is, the consequences prove her wrong, but neither of them can possibly know that she will fall. And we notice that Milton does not, as she departs, subject Eve to any very strong condemnation. Instead, he describes her situation and her beauty in terms that draw our strong sympathies toward her unprotected state, her utterly innocent beauty, her earnest work, her good intentions. She means no harm, and she really does have the welfare of her garden at heart. Anyhow, she is not going far—only to that rose garden over there, yonder, as she says: they can see the spot from where they are standing.

Now, as she ominously withdraws her hand from her husband's hand, Milton surrounds her with a fragrant cloud of pagan myths—all of them concerned with attractive, beneficent spirits and deities of nature:

> and like a Wood-Nymph light
> *Oread* or *Dryad*, or of *Delia's* Traine,
> Betook her to the Groves, but *Delia's* self
> In gate surpass'd and Goddess-like deport,
> Though not as shee with Bow and Quiver armd,
> But with such Gardning Tools as Art yet rude,
> Guiltless of fire had formd, or Angels brought.
> To *Pales*, or *Pomona*, thus adornd,
> Likest she seemd, *Pomona* when she fled
> *Vertumnus*, or to *Ceres* in her Prime,
> Yet Virgin of *Proserpina* from *Jove*.   [9.386–96]

Everyone has felt an ominous undercurrent here, as in the phrase "Guiltless of fire," the allusion to Pomona and her persistent wooer, Vertumnus, or the oblique reference to the sorrows of Ceres, through the loss of her daughter to the prince of Hades. But the dominant effect of all these myths is quite favorable to Eve: Delia is Diana, and by using twice the unusual name Delia, Milton reminds us of her birth, along with Apollo, on the pure and sacred island of Delos. Pales, ancient Roman goddess of flocks and herds, was a beneficent deity, worshipped by rites of purification. As for the story of Pomona, Milton has given the allusion an ominous twist by referring to the time when, he says, she "fled Vertumnus." Yet in Ovid's *Metamorphoses* this is quite an amusing and harmless story, where Pomona provides a true original for Milton's Eve:

> Gardens and fruit were all her care; no other
> Was ever more skilled or diligent. Woods and rivers
> Were nothing to her, only the fields, the branches
> Bearing the prosperous fruits. She bore no javelin,
> But the curved pruning-hook, to trim the branches,
> Check too luxuriant growth, or make incision
> For the engrafted twig to thrive and grow in.
> She would not let them thirst: the flowing waters

Poured down to the roots. This was her love, her passion.
Venus was nothing to her . . .

But all the rustic gods try to win her, especially Vertumnus, who
tries every possible disguise, every possible verbal manoeuvre, for
over a hundred lines of Ovid, with no effect at all on the cool
maiden. So at last, in desperation, he throws off his latest disguise

and stood before her
In the light of his own radiance, as the sun
Breaks through the clouds against all opposition.
Ready for force, he found no need; Pomona
Was taken by his beauty, and her passion
Answered his own. [*Met.* 14.624–34,767–71, trans. Humphries]

Such is the atmosphere of purity and harmlessness that Milton
gives to Eve.

When the poet bursts out in his own voice with his commentary,
he cannot bring himself quite to blame her, though it looks at first
as though he is going to do so: "O much deceav'd, much failing,
hapless *Eve*," he cries, but then the sentence bends over the line, in
Milton's metamorphic way and assumes a different meaning, for
it appears that the poet is saying only that she is deceived in think-
ing that she will return to Adam by noon, in time to have Adam's
lunch ready. Her failing, we see, is her failing to return to Adam
as she now promises:

And all things in best order to invite
Noontide repast, or Afternoons repose.
O much deceav'd, much failing, hapless *Eve*,
Of thy presum'd return! event perverse!
Thou never from that houre in Paradise
Foundst either sweet repast, or sound repose . . .   [9.402–07]

Notice that Milton does not say "perverse woman" but simply
"perverse event," that is to say, outcome contrary to her and
Adam's expectations. Thus the poet's sympathy and pitying admi-
ration play over the figure of Eve as she works among her roses:

them she upstaies
Gently with Mirtle band, mindless the while,
Her self,

(that is, not attentive to herself, with all her mind focused on the flowers)

> though fairest unsupported Flour
> From her best prop so farr, and storm so nigh.   [9.430–33]

Then, as we watch the serpent crawling "Among thick-wov'n Arborets and Flours . . . the hand of *Eve*," we realize that her gardening labors have already produced here an effect that, Milton says, surpasses the "feigned" gardens of Adonis, or the Gardens of King Alcinous in the *Odyssey*, or that true garden described in the Song of Solomon. Finally, to cap the climax of this mood of sympathy and admiration, Milton brings forward his greatest tribute to the beauty of the earth, as tended and inhabited now by fallen man and woman:

> As one who long in populous City pent,
> Where Houses thick and Sewers annoy the Aire,
> Forth issuing on a Summers Morn to breathe
> Among the pleasant Villages and Farmes
> Adjoynd, from each thing met conceaves delight,
> The smell of Grain, or tedded Grass, or Kine.
> Or Dairie, each rural sight, each rural sound;
> If chance with Nymphlike step fair Virgin pass,
> What pleasing seemd, for her now pleases more,
> She most, and in her looks summs all Delight.
> Such Pleasure took the Serpent to behold
> This Flourie Plat, the sweet recess of *Eve*
> Thus earlie, thus alone; her Heav'nly forme
> Angelic, but more soft, and Feminine,
> Her graceful Innocence, her every Aire
> Of gesture or lest action overawd
> His Malice, and with rapine sweet bereav'd
> His fierceness of the fierce intent it brought . . .   [9.445–62]

The effects of this great pastoral moment seem to be double. First, it throws our sympathy overwhelmingly toward Eve: so beautiful, so talented, so innocent: how unfair it seems that she should be permitted to undergo temptation by such an adversary, whose hypocrisy we know that she can never penetrate. Even Uriel, the regent of the sun, we recall, could not penetrate the disguise of that youthful cherub in book 3. At the same time the comparison suggests that Satan's design will not be wholly successful. He has not utterly destroyed God's Paradise of Delight, since the poet here still delights in these man-made scenes of farm and village, and in feminine beauty, almost as much as he delights in this imagined garden and in Eve herself.

The same kind of sympathy is thrown toward Adam before his fall, and thus much argument has raged over whether or not Adam is justified in his anguished, intuitive, passionate decision to eat the fruit and die with Eve:

> How can I live without thee, how forgoe
> Thy sweet Converse and Love so dearly joyn'd . . . [9.908–09]

Yet the poet, in his abstract assertions after the Fall, and in his picture of the painful bickering of Adam and Eve, leaves no doubt that we are supposed to condemn them both. The trouble is that Milton's sympathetic presentation makes it difficult to condemn them very firmly. As Waldock sees the problem: "the poem asks from us, at one and the same time, two incompatible responses. It requires us . . . with the full weight of our minds to believe that Adam did right, and simultaneously requires us with the full weight of our minds to believe that he did wrong. The dilemma is as critical as that, and there is no way of escape." Exactly, this is the effect of book 9, but Waldock then goes on to see this as, in some sense, a failure in Milton's total design: "*Paradise Lost* cannot take the strain at its centre, it breaks there, the theme is too much for it. . . . if the net effect of all [Milton's] labour is to justify man's ways against God's ways: well, that was one of the risks, inherent in the venture, that he did not see."[4]

But it is hard to believe that Milton, long choosing and beginning late, after a lifetime of theological study and speculation, did not understand all the risks of his venture. It seems too easy a way out to say that Milton's unconscious sympathies have led him to give a more favorable portrait of Adam and Eve than he meant to give; or that his desire to write an interesting poem led him to undermine his theological purpose; or that Milton was not really interested in the Fall so much as in portraying human nature as he knew it.

The two incompatible responses that Waldock describes result from Milton's ultimate, climactic presentation of the problems inherent in the power of choice. With Eve, vanity, ambition, and the illusions fostered by Satan lead to her disastrous choice; but such tendencies to wild are part of her perfection: she must learn by experience, since warning has not sufficed, to manage herself better, to use her reason more wisely. With Adam, passion for Eve has overcome his reason; and he too must now learn from experience to use his reason with better effect. What Milton is stressing above all is his view that there is *not a break* between the unfallen and the fallen state; there is a *continuity* implicit in the irresistible diffusion of God's goodness. God's plan was to make us as we are. Thus Eve's unruly tendencies, Adam's commotion strange, and that domestic argument where Eve chooses to go off alone—such things do not represent a couple *fallen* before the Fall, but a couple *perfectly human* before the Fall, truly the "human pair." By its constant emphasis on man's "perfection" before the Fall, the poem asks us to revise and expand our easy notions of what constituted that original innocence and perfection.[5]

Strong emotions, Milton implies, are a part of man's perfection. The tug and pull of two reasoning minds, the disagreement between two individuals who both possess the freedom of the will—this too is part of man's perfection, for how could freedom otherwise exist and how could life be of the slightest interest without that freedom? All these qualities, Milton makes clear, must of course be kept under the gentle sway of reason—but then, as Milton insists in that remarkable parenthesis of book 3, "Reason also is choice." Strange as it may seem, the problem of making the right choice, the problem of the right exercise of freedom, is shown to be as difficult before the Fall as it is afterwards. We must remember the chief point of that heavenly dialogue in book 3: that the power of choice remains essentially the same in man, whether before or after the Fall. Before the Fall, Milton's God insists, man was made "sufficient to have stood"; after the Fall, Milton's God still insists, man has "what may suffice." Man's power of choice will be renewed by grace, and the universal link of love will be made evident to man through his knowledge that the Son of God became man and died to save mankind.

Milton's view of Adam and Eve, from the moment of their creation, emphasizes the growing, kinetic, dynamic quality of their awareness. They are born in a state of perfection which involves the ability to learn from experience and instruction. Thus Eve in book 4 is led by the divine voice to leave her "watry image" and to look upon Adam, and then, as she turns to flee, she is brought back by Adam's plea to her proper place as Adam's mate. Milton's view of man's "perfection" is never static or passive: man's dignity depends upon the power of choice, which inevitably includes the right to err as well as the right to make amends for error. To Milton man's "perfection" lies in man's ability to grow, ⟵ however painfully, in wisdom and understanding.

The Winding up
of the Action

The tenth book of *Paradise Lost*, Addison remarks, "has a greater variety of Persons in it than any other in the whole Poem. The Author upon the winding up of his Action introduces all those who had any Concern in it, and shews with great Beauty the influence which it had upon each of them. It is like the last Act of a well written Tragedy, in which all who had a part in it are generally drawn up before the Audience, and represented under those Circumstances in which the determination of the Action places them."[1] Thus Milton binds his poem into unity by elements of reprise that begin with the bard's re-assertion of the power of choice in his brief prologue to book 10:

> for what can scape the Eye
> Of God All-seeing, or deceave his Heart
> Omniscient, who in all things wise and just,
> Hinder'd not *Satan* to attempt the minde
> Of Man, with strength entire, and free Will arm'd,
> Complete to have discover'd and repulst
> Whatever wiles of Foe or seeming Friend.
> For still they knew, and ought to have still remember'd
> The high Injunction not to taste that Fruit,
> Whoever tempted; which they not obeying,
> Incurr'd, what could they less, the penaltie,
> And manifold in sin, deserv'd to fall.   [10.5–16]

"What could they less?"—again, as at the outset of book 4, the
bard has entered into the center of the action, but here he checks
our human sympathy with the fall of "innocent frail man." How-
ever strong that sympathy may be, the facts of God's justice and
mercy set forth so clearly in book 3 must be remembered: man
was not "frail" except in the basic sense of being "liable to fall or
break." "With strength entire, and free Will arm'd" man's perfec-
tion held the power to make a better choice. Then follows a
heavenly conclave that overtly recalls the prophecies and doc-
trines of the similar conclave in book 3, including a memory of the
promise that the Son of God will restore man's freedom. Thus the
heavenly conclave at the outset of book 10 plays its part in what
Addison calls "the determination" or "the winding up" of the
action, while at the same time creating the effect of starting a new
action—the action of redemptive grace, counteracting chaos in
the moral realm, just as the Son of God had defeated Satan's
forces in book 6 and made way for the acts of Creation in book 7.

Milton ties all these actions of the Son together by the lines of
book 10 that recall the Son's resplendent light, as described in two
previous revelations of his triumphant glory:

> So spake the Father, and unfoulding bright
> Toward the right hand his Glorie, on the Son
> Blaz'd forth unclouded Deitie; he full
> Resplendent all his Father manifest
> Express'd, and thus divinely answer'd milde.   [10.63–67]

>   Mean while the Son
> On his great Expedition now appeer'd,
> Girt with Omnipotence, with Radiance crown'd
> Of Majestie Divine, Sapience and Love
> Immense, and all his Father in him shon.   [7.192–96]

> He said, and on his Son with Rayes direct
> Shon full, he all his Father full exprest
> Ineffably into his face receiv'd . . .   [6.719–21]

Now, as the Son begins the action of tempering justice with
mercy, he announces that he will descend without the bright "At-
tendance" and the glorious "Train" that accompanied his first two
epiphanies. He comes almost in human guise, "the mild Judge
and Intercessor both," as the language of the poem descends from

the grand style toward a biblical humility based upon the words of
Genesis and many other biblical passages. In the poem's opening
panel (which ends at line 228) there are no epic similes, no classi-
cal allusions, while latinity of diction is notably reduced in the
conversation with the fallen pair, except in Adam's words when he
repeats the satanic excuse of "necessity, the tyrant's plea," and
declares,

> strict necessitie
> Subdues me, and calamitous constraint,
> Least on my head both sin and punishment,
> However insupportable, be all
> Devolv'd . . .   [10.131–35]

Latinity of diction has its role to play in the poem's action. We may
sympathize with current efforts to diminish the number of alleged
latinisms in the poem—if by *latinisms* we mean words used only, or
primarily, in a Latin sense, or with a witty awareness of the Latin
root.[2] Still, such latinisms are the outworks of Milton's latinity:
they serve to make us aware of the various degrees of latinity
present in various parts of the poem, with significant effect. Thus
the latinity in the preceding passage, by temporarily "raising" the
style, seems to suggest an element of hollowness and pretence in
Adam's excuse, preparing for the shameful evasion that follows,
in simpler language, but still highly suspended syntax:

> This woman whom thou mad'st to be my help,
> And gav'st me as thy perfet gift, so good,
> So fit, so acceptable, so Divine,
> That from her hand I could suspect no ill,
> And what she did, whatever in it self,
> Her doing seem'd to justifie the deed;
> Shee gave me of the Tree, and I did eate.   [10.137–43]

The reminiscence of Adam's conversation with Raphael, where
Adam confessed that her beauty seemed to possess a superior
power over him, reinforces the innuendo that the fall is really
God's own fault.

The Son repeats the response that Raphael had given then with
"contracted brow", though now the voice is milder in its firm
reproach:

> Adornd
> She was indeed, and lovely to attract
> Thy Love, not thy Subjection, and her Gifts
> Were such as under Government well seem'd,
> Unseemly to beare rule, which was thy part
> And person, had'st thou known thy self aright.   [10.151–56]

Then Milton utterly turns the tables upon Adam by showing that Eve has none of this bluster and evasion, but knows her self and her guilt, which she confesses in a simple, biblical pentameter: "The Serpent me beguil'd and I did eate" (10.162).

That simple phrasing sets the tone and manner for what follows, as the Son proceeds to judgment and Milton adapts many biblical words:[3]

> then pittying how they stood
> Before him naked to the aire, that now
> Must suffer change, disdain'd not to begin
> Thenceforth the forme of servant to assume,
> As when he wash'd his servants feet, so now
> As Father of his Familie he clad
> Thir nakedness with Skins of Beasts, or slain,
> Or as the Snake with youthful Coate repaid;
> And thought not much to cloath his Enemies:
> Nor hee thir outward onely with the Skins
> Of Beasts, but inward nakedness, much more
> Opprobrious, with his Robe of righteousness,
> Araying cover'd from his Fathers sight.   [10.211–23]

The last four lines are based on Isaiah's "robe of righteousness" (61:10), while the latinate word "Opprobrious" stands forth in emphatic position as a sign of theological interpretation.

Then, after the Son has ascended to rejoin the Father, the central panel of the book opens with syntax that foretells a drastic change in style and subject:

> Meanwhile, ere thus was sin'd and judg'd on Earth,
> Within the Gates of Hell sate Sin and Death,
> In counterview within the Gates, that now
> Stood open wide, belching outrageous flame
> Farr into *Chaos*, since the Fiend pass'd through . . . [10.229–33]

The ironies and linkages are clear: the "outrageous flame"

belched into Chaos once more forms the strongest possible contrast with the perfect circle of Creation drawn by the Son of God with his golden compasses; and the implications of an Unholy Trinity are reinforced by our memory of their first appearance in book 2.

Now the epic style of the opening book reappears in a stiffened, hardened form that suggests a subtle parody of the grandeur that one has admired in the poem's beginning. The three panels of book 10 present the action of redemptive love at beginning and end, while the central panel re-enacts the fallen images and postures of the first two books. Sin and Death here bring with them a series of similes and classical allusions, presented with a gradual rise in the concentration of latinity. That rise is felt in the opening speech of Sin, as "connatural" (246) prepares the way for the strict latinism of "impassable, *impervious*" (254), where Milton cleverly stresses the inflation of the style by preceding the latinism with its definition! This leads on into the latinate pair "for intercourse / Or transmigration" (260–61) and the redundancy of the concluding "attraction and instinct" (263).

Such language leads the way toward the re-introduction of the heroic simile when Death snuffs "the smell / Of mortal change on Earth":

> As when a flock
> Of ravenous Fowl, though many a league remote,
> Against the day of Battel, to a Field,
> Where Armies lie encampt, come flying, lur'd
> With sent of living Carcasses design'd
> For death, the following day, in bloodie fight.
> So sented the grim Feature, and upturn'd
> His Nostril wide into the murkie Air,
> Sagacious of his Quarrey from so farr.   [10.272–81]

Feature is a brilliant piece of etymological wit, for the word carries backward through Middle English and Old French to the original Latin of *factura:* a formation, a thing produced; while *Sagacious* carries back to the root *sagire:* to perceive or discern quickly or acutely. Thus latinate diction supports the heroic simile on every side. Meanwhile the simile itself recalls the way in which Satan has landed on the created universe like a vulture on Imaus bred, and has sat upon the Tree of Life "like a Cormorant", in wait for the "living Carcasses" of Adam and Eve after their mortal change.

With such preparation Milton now proceeds to display another heroic work of building, traditional in epic, as in the building of Pandaemonium or Carthage; and he does so, as Tillyard long ago pointed out,[4] by suggesting a bitter parody of the account of the Creation, when

> on the watrie calme
> His brooding wings the Spirit of God outspred,
> And vital vertue infus'd, and vital warmth
> Throughout the fluid Mass, but downward purg'd
> The black tartareous cold infernal dregs
> Adverse to life . . .   [7.234–39]

Now the cold infernal dregs return from Hell to build their work, not upon a "calme", but out of raging anarchy:

> Then Both from out Hell Gates into the waste
> Wide Anarchie of *Chaos* damp and dark
> Flew divers, & with Power (thir Power was great)
> Hovering upon the Waters; what they met
> Solid or slimie, as in raging Sea
> Tost up and down, together crowded drove
> From each side shoaling towards the mouth of Hell.
>   [10.282–88]

Hovering upon the Waters: the phrase evokes not only the biblical words, "And the Spirit of God moved upon the face of the waters" (Genesis 1:2), but also Milton's adaptation of that sentence in the opening of his poem, where he prays for inspiration from the same creative power that performed the original Creation:

> Thou from the first
> Wast present, and with mighty wings outspread
> Dove-like satst brooding on the vast Abyss
> And mad'st it pregnant: What in me is dark
> Illumine, what is low raise and support . . .   [1.19–23]

For the poet himself is about to embark upon his own heroic work of building. Furthermore, the placement of the phrase *Hovering upon the Waters*, in this context, may recall a similar placement of the word *Hovering* back in the scene in Hell where Satan and Death confront each other:

> and such a frown
> Each cast at th' other, as when two black Clouds
> With Heav'ns Artillery fraught, come rattling on
> Over the *Caspian*, then stand front to front
> Hov'ring a space, till Winds the signal blow
> To joyn thir dark Encounter in midair . . .   [2.713–18]

Now in book 10 another dark encounter is accompanied with
another simile involving winds in a Russian setting, though this
time farther north, in keeping with the action of these cold infer-
nal dregs:

> As when two Polar Winds blowing adverse
> Upon the *Cronian* Sea, together drive
> Mountains of Ice, that stop th' imagin'd way
> Beyond *Petsora* Eastward, to the rich
> *Cathaian* Coast.   [10.289–93]

This structure is not only a bridge between Hell and earth, but is
also an obstruction that blocks the way toward a rich realm of
promise, whether in Heaven or in Paradise on earth.[5]

Then a heavy infiltration of latinate diction combines with in-
verted syntax and a cluster of classical allusions to give an "heroic"
grandeur to the scene:

> The aggregated Soyle
> Death with his Mace petrific, cold and dry,
> As with a Trident smote, and fix't as firm
> As *Delos* floating once; the rest his look
> Bound with *Gorgonian* rigor not to move,
> And with *Asphaltic* slime; broad as the Gate,
> Deep to the Roots of Hell the gather'd beach
> They fasten'd, and the Mole immense wraught on
> Over the foaming deep high Archt, a Bridge
> Of length prodigious joyning to the Wall
> Immoveable of this now fenceless world
> Forfeit to Death; from hence a passage broad,
> Smooth, easie, inoffensive down to Hell.   [10.293–305]

Inoffensive, like *impervious* earlier, stresses the inflation of the style,
being used in the Latin sense of *inoffensus*: without hindrance,
unobstructed; while the syntax itself seems to collapse under the
strain. The second and fourth in the heavy series of posterior
adjectives do not in fact modify their preceding nouns: *Mole im-*

mense is not in parallel with *deep high Archt*, for *high Archt* really modifies *Mole*. Likewise *length prodigious* is not in parallel with *Wall Immoveable*, for the wall of "this now fenceless world" has, alas, been removed: it is the *Bridge* (three lines before) which is now *Immoveable*. But *world* and *Forfeit* are all too exactly now allied. At the same time this subtle displacement of the adjectives creates a mimetic movement of construction from one side of the abyss to the other.

Milton then opens his next heroic simile with a phrase reminiscent of both Vergil (*Georgics* 4.176) and Ovid (*Met.* 5.416–17): "So, if great things to small may be compar'd. . . ."[6] That phrase has been used in the poem twice before. First, in book 2, as Satan stands poised on the brink of Chaos:

> Nor was his eare less peal'd
> With noises loud and ruinous (to compare
> Great things with small) then when *Bellona* storms,
> With all her battering Engines bent to rase
> Som Capital City . . .   [2.920–24]

And again in book 6 as prelude to the combat of Michael and Satan:

> from each hand with speed retir'd
> Where erst was thickest fight, th' Angelic throng,
> And left large field, unsafe within the wind
> Of such commotion, such as to set forth
> Great things by small, if Natures concord broke,
> Among the Constellations warr were sprung,
> Two planets rushing from aspect maligne
> Of fiercest opposition in mid Skie,
> Should combat, and thir jarring Sphears confound.   [6.307–15]

So here in book 10 the phrase foreshadows the destruction of Paradise and the breaking of nature's concord soon to be shown in the shifting of the planets, while the simile itself suggests Satan's effort to "yoke" man's liberty, as he voyaged from his palace of Pandaemonium:[7]

> So, if great things to small may be compar'd,
> *Xerxes*, the Libertie of *Greece* to yoke,
> From *Susa* his *Memnonian* Palace high
> Came to the Sea, and over *Hellespont*

> Bridging his way, *Europe* with *Asia* joyn'd,
> And scourg'd with many a stroak th' indignant waves.
>
> [10.306–11]

Indignant suggests a Vergilian usage, "disdaining to bear": "pontem indignatus Araxes" (*Aeneid* 8.728), along with the favorite Ovidian usage, "unable to endure": "fretaque indignantia miscent" (*Met.* 11.491). Both meanings suggest the retribution to follow.

Finally, the latinity reaches its outrageous climax in one enormous pun that derides the pretensions of every Roman pontifex:

> Now had they brought the work by wondrous Art
> Pontifical, a ridge of pendent Rock
> Over the vext Abyss, following the track
> Of *Satan*, to the self same place where hee
> First lighted from his Wing, and landed safe
> From out of *Chaos* to the outside bare
> Of this round World . . .   [10.312–18]

The pun is reinforced by the reference to "this new wondrous Pontifice" a few lines later (348). We may recall that it was at exactly this spot of Satan's landing that Milton had located his Limbo in book 3, the place where popish follies, as Milton sees them, "Fly o're the backside of the World."

It was here too, on this outer shell of the World, that Satan in book 3 had seen the juncture of the stairs let down from heaven with a "passage down to th' earth," a juncture full of beneficent overtones. But now in book 10 an ominous *trivium* has been formed by this new pontifice, this "stupendious" and "portentous" bridge, which Satan's "faire Inchanting Daughter" now hails as the result of her parent's "magnific deeds", by which God's "Quadrature" is parted from Satan's "Orbicular World," where Sin and Death, as Satan declares, will reign "Plenipotent on Earth" and "No detriment need feare" (10.351–409).

After this new work of satanic building we return with Satan to the scene of Pandaemonium, here appropriately introduced with an heroic simile combining a frozen setting with military desolation caused by warfare between barbaric armies:

> As when the *Tartar* from his *Russian* Foe
> By *Astracan* over the Snowie Plaines

Retires, or *Bactrian* Sophi from the hornes
Of *Turkish* Crescent, leaves all waste beyond
The Realme of *Aladule*, in his retreate
To *Tauris* or *Casbeen*.   [10.431–36]

It is an image of defeat that underlies the "false glitter" of Satan's
inflated account of his heroic exploit, with its old familiar pomp
again echoing the glories of heaven: "Thrones, Dominations,
Princedoms, Vertues, Powers." But he is answered by that "dismal
universal hiss" as, like Cadmus in Ovid's tale,[8]

His Visage drawn he felt to sharp and spare,
His Armes clung to his Ribs, his Leggs entwining
Each other, till supplanted down he fell
A monstrous Serpent on his Belly prone . . .   [10.511–14]

Supplanted: with sardonic memory of the Latin root, *supplantare*,
"to trip up by the heels." Meanwhile the whole assembly is trans-
formed:

dreadful was the din
Of hissing through the Hall thick swarming now
With complicated monsters, head and taile,
Scorpion and Asp, and *Amphisboena* dire,
Cerastes hornd, *Hydrus*, and *Ellops* drear,
And *Dipsas* (Not so thick swarm'd once the Soil
Bedropt with blood of *Gorgon*, or the Isle
Ophiusa) but still greatest hee the midst,
Now Dragon grown, larger then whom the Sun
Ingenderd in the *Pythian* Vale on slime,
Huge *Python*, and his Power no less he seem'd
Above the rest still to retain . . .   [10.521–32]

The memory of the change of Cadmus and Hermione seems to
have evoked the memory of other Ovidian tales: the story of Per-
seus' flight over Libya with the dripping head of the Gorgon,
the story of the Python defeated by Apollo, [9] and, with special
relevance, the story of the Cerastae, with its reference to
"Ophiusiaque arva":

Outraged by these impious sacrifices [of guests], fostering Venus
was preparing to desert her cities and her Ophiusian plains; 'but,'
she said, 'wherein have these pleasant regions, wherein have my
cities sinned? What crime is there in them? Rather let this impious

race pay the penalty by exile or by death, or by some punishment midway betwixt death and exile. And what other can that be than the penalty of a changed form?' [*Met.* 10.228–34; trans. Miller]

The whole scene of metamorphosis in book 10 evokes the earlier tale of change that Sin related in Hell, as she told of her transformation from a beauteous shape into that monstrous shape resembling Ovid's Scylla. Thus the themes of Ovidian metamorphosis tie the middle of book 10 with the ending of book 2, playing an essential part in the winding up of the action.

But the metamorphosis of Satan and his host here forecasts a sadder change, as the planets change their motions to "noxious efficacie" and "synod unbenigne" and earth begins its stormy changes:

> Now from the North
> Of *Norumbega*, and the *Samoed* shoar
> Bursting thir brazen Dungeon, armd with ice
> And snow and haile and stormie gust and flaw,
> *Boreas* and *Caecias* and *Argestes* loud
> And *Thrascias* rend the Woods and Seas upturn . . .
>
> [10.695–700]

So from discord in the winds and seasons we move on to see the beasts devouring one another, "to graze the Herb all leaving," and from there to the center of this discord, Adam, where he now lies "in a troubl'd Sea of passion tost," as Satan once lay confounded upon that burning lake.

With Adam's "complaint" (a set piece in the tradition of Ovid's *Heroides* or the tormented soliloquies of the *Metamorphoses*)[10] the third panel of the book begins, at line 720, and concludes with the scene of penitence almost 400 lines later. This panel of redemption matches the first in style and theme, but greatly exceeds it in length and in dramatic power. First we watch the workings of Adam's free will as he makes his way through all his questions and excuses toward a reasoned conclusion utterly different from that reached in Satan's soliloquy of book 4 ("Evil, be thou my Good"), for Adam's reason brings him, by relentless facing of the facts, to the conviction of his own guilt:

> Him after all Disputes
> Forc't I absolve: all my evasions vain
> And reasonings, though through Mazes, leads me still

> But to my own conviction: first and last
> On mee, mee onely, as the sourse and spring
> Of all corruption, all the blame lights due;
> So might the wrauth.   [10.828–34]

Then follows that reconciliation of Adam and Eve, so well ex-
plained by Tillyard and Summers.[11] Now Adam, unlike the Adam
at the opening of book 9, holds firm control. His power of reason
now makes the right choices, refusing Eve's suggestions that they
remain childless, or commit suicide. He chooses trust in God,
patience, and the better fortitude of using their creative powers to
offset the changed conditions of life:

> such Fire to use,
> And what may else be remedie or cure
> To evils which our own misdeeds have wrought,
> Hee will instruct us praying, and of Grace
> Beseeching him, so as we need not fear
> To pass commodiously this life, sustain'd
> By him with many comforts, till we end
> In dust, our final rest and native home.   [10.1078–85]

The relatively simple language of this ending represents the state
of "humiliation meek" that Adam and Eve have reached. The
entire final panel shows not a single epic simile, not a single overt
classical allusion. Reason, acting under grace, needs no such aids
from ancient epic. Even the element of latinity is considerably
reduced: there is plenty of the latinity normal to the writing of a
renaissance humanist, but there is none of that sense of inflated
style caused by pompous latinisms and strained inversions. The
mode of the ancient complaint is turned into a rigorous self-
examination, leading to confession of guilt, while at the very close
an elaborate expansion of the classical rhetoric of repetition is
turned into an emphasis upon the "contrite heart" of Psalm 51:[12]

> What better can we do, then to the place
> Repairing where he judg'd us, prostrate fall
> Before him reverent, and there confess
> Humbly our faults, and pardon beg, with tears
> Watering the ground, and with our sighs the Air
> Frequenting, sent from hearts contrite, in sign
> Of sorrow unfeign'd, and humiliation meek . . .
>   So spake our Father penitent, nor *Eve*
> Felt less remorse: they forthwith to the place

Repairing where he judg'd them prostrate fell
Before him reverent, and both confess'd
Humbly their faults, and pardon beg'd, with tears
Watering the ground, and with thir sighs the Air
Frequenting, sent from hearts contrite, in sign
Of sorrow unfeign'd, and humiliation meek.
                              [10.1086–92,1097–1104]

The technique of repetition may remind us of an earlier example, more intricately composed, with reversal and a rounded insistence on the word "sweet"—Eve's great love-song to Adam in book 4 (641–56). The less artful, more straightforward repetitions here may suggest a different state of mind—an awareness of a higher love without which life could not be endured.

Yet they have still much to learn. Adam's hope to pass this life "commodiously" must be qualified by the bitter scenes of misery to follow in the closing books, while his assumption that they will find their "final rest" in the dust must be altered to belief that an immortal home with God is still open to those who rightly choose.

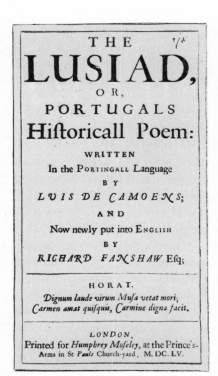

THE **LUSIAD,**
OR,
PORTUGALS
Hiftoricall Poem:

WRITTEN
In the PORTINGALL Language
BY
LUIS DE CAMOENS;
AND
Now newly put into ENGLISH
BY
RICHARD FANSHAW Efq;

HORAT.
Dignum laude virum Mufa vetat mori;
Carmen amat quifquis, Carmine digna facit.

LONDON,
Printed for *Humphrey Mofeley,* at the Prince's-
Arms in St *Pauls* Church-yard, M. DC. LV.

CHAPTER 9

"A Poem Written in Ten Books"

If we share Addison's view that book 10 represents "the winding up of the action," it seems almost inevitable that the remainder of the poem will turn to aftermath and epilogue. But I cannot agree with Prince that in reading long poems and novels we are bound to experience a flagging of interest in "the last stretch."[1] At least, the *Aeneid* and the *Lusiad* do not seem to me to end in this way, nor do *Tom Jones*, *Ulysses*, and *The Wings of the Dove*. Some better explanation or defence of Milton's ending must be found—and many have been offered, effectively explaining the theological design that underlies this ending.[2] But these explanations do not often touch upon the problem of the lowered style, so low in places that Milton seems to become almost an ordinary versifier of biblical history.

It is a gradual lowering, for there is no sudden falling-off in the grandeur and force of Milton's high style. The first half of book 11, up through the grand roll call of empires, shows Milton's poetical powers at their strongest; but gradually, with the visions and responses in the latter half of book 11, and then for most of

155

book 12, the style works downward, with occasional flashes of
power, until in the last twenty-five lines the grand style reappears
in all its sinuous complexity and power.

Like many other readers, I expressed, in *The Paradise Within*,
considerable disappointment with Milton's performance in his
finale, and I do not now wish wholly to retract that adverse view,
although the present chapter and the next will suggest several
different ways of approaching these problems. That adverse view,
contained in tempered, chastened form within the next chapter,
may at least help to clarify the reasons why so many readers have
expressed such disappointment, beginning with Dryden and Ad-
dison.[3] But, as always, it is unwise to be severe with Milton: he has
a way of defeating all his critics. It now seems likely to me that this
lowered style is designed to create a number of ironical contrasts
in the context of literary tradition. First, a contrast with the mili-
tary action in the last book of the *Aeneid*. Next, a contrast, en-
forced by an ironical parallel in structure, with the history of the
rise of Rome that Ovid presents in the closing books of the
Metamorphoses, a contrast in particular with the inflated style that
Ovid uses in his last, fifteenth book, as he praises the glories of
Augustan Rome. And thirdly, a contrast with the last, tenth book
of an epic strongly influenced by Ovid: the *Lusiad* of Camoens,
where the tenth book is devoted to delineating the past and future
glories of the Portuguese empire.

Reserving discussion of Ovid's example for a later section, I
should like to turn first to the analogies that seem to exist between
the *Lusiad* and *Paradise Lost*. These analogies may take on added
strength when we recall that Richard Fanshawe's translation, *The
Lusiad, or, Portugals Historicall Poem*, the first of many English ver-
sions, appeared in London in 1655. We may well believe that this
translation would have caught the attention of Milton, for several
reasons. It was issued by the same publisher, Humphrey Moseley,
who had published Milton's minor poems in 1645. Milton had
been for many years a strong admirer of Tasso, and Fanshawe at
the outset of his dedication stresses Tasso's admiration for the
poem: "for he was heard to say (his great *Jerusalem* being then an
Embrio) *He feared no man but Camoens*: Notwithstanding which, he
bestow'd a Sonet in his praise." And, most important, Milton was

at this very time embarking upon the sustained composition of his own epic, the fulfillment of the great work that he had been contemplating from his youth.

But the epic on the Fall of Man that appeared at last in 1667 was far different from the poem that Milton had envisioned in his early years. From many indications it is clear that Milton originally hoped to write a patriotic epic on a British theme—something to do with Britain's legendary past or Britain's dimly historical kings. In the Trinity manuscript Milton had jotted down, at about the age of thirty, no less than thirty-three different subjects from British legend or history as possible topics for tragedy or, in at least one case, for "A Heroicall Poem" on the subject of King Alfred.[4] In 1639, in his Latin poem written to Manso, Tasso's patron, Milton wrote of his hope that he might "recall in song my native kings, and Arthur setting wars in motion even beneath the earth."[5] Then a year later, in the Latin elegy upon the death of his friend Diodati, he expressed at length a similar hope, mentioning several ancient British legends and vowing that his pastoral pipe "shall be left dangling on some old pine tree far away and quite forgotten by me; or else, quite changed, you shall shrill forth a British theme to your native Muses."[6] And in 1641, in *The Reason of Church-government*, he wrote the famous passage in which he tells of all his many poetical hopes and plans—including his hopes of writing an epic on a national theme.[7]

We can see, then, why the *Lusiad* might hold a natural appeal for the young Milton. But we have no external evidence that Milton actually read the *Lusiad*, in Fanshawe's version or in any other form. All we can say is that in view of Milton's remarkable command of languages, including Latin, French, Italian, and Spanish, it seems likely that he could have made his way through the original. And in any case, long before Fanshawe's version appeared, there were available to Milton translations of the poem into Spanish, and even into Latin. As an omnivorous reader, and as a poet especially concerned with the patriotic, historical epic, Milton, I believe, could hardly have been prevented from reading this poem praised by Tasso.

We do, however, have evidence of another kind, and it lies in *Paradise Lost* itself.[8] Milton's interest in the subject of the Portuguese epic is reflected in the allusions to African places associated with Portuguese voyages and conquests, in the middle of the enormous catalogue of empires that Milton presents in book 11:

> Mombaza, and Quiloa, and Melind,
> And Sofala thought Ophir, to the Realme
> Of Congo, and Angola fardest South . . .   [11.399–401]

And then there are the two great similes referring to those who voyage round "the Cape of Hope," "Close sailing from Bengala, or the Iles / Of Ternate and Tidore" (2.636–42,4.159–65).

But by far the most interesting evidence lies in the fact that Milton first published his poem in 1667 as "A Poem Written in Ten Books." Seven years later, for the second edition, Milton gave his poem the Vergilian number of books by the simple expedient of dividing the two longest, 7 and 10, into two books apiece. This redivision was so easy to perform, and Milton's aim to emulate Vergil is so clear throughout the first two books, that we inevitably wonder why Milton ever produced his poem with ten books in the first place. Indeed, the symmetry of dividing the poem into two halves of six books apiece, after Vergil's model, leaps to the eye and is strongly enforced by Milton's prologue to the seventh book, when he says:

> Half yet remaines unsung, but narrower bound
> Within the visible Diurnal Spheare . . .   [7.21–22]

And it is approximately half the poem in number of lines and pages. Yet in 1667 Milton chose to present the second half in an asymmetrical division into four books. This deliberate violation of the obvious Vergilian expectation suggests that Milton, after all those many years of planning his epic, must have had some compelling design in mind when he offered us this poem in ten books.

Several suggestions have been made. First, that the ten books imply some kind of five-act division, according to the epic theories of the time—two books per act.[9] It is true that the first four books of Milton's poem fall very neatly into two acts of two books each. But thereafter the division becomes more and more uneven. Books 7 and 8 (1667), according to this theory, ought to form the fourth act, but in fact these books are not paired; they are clearly

Paradise loſt.

A
POEM
Written in
TEN BOOKS
By *JOHN MILTON.*

Licenſed and Entred according
to Order.

LONDON

Printed, and are to be ſold by *Peter Parker*
under *Creed* Church neer *Aldgate*; And by
Robert Boulter at the *Turks Head* in *Biſhopſgate-ſtreet*;
And *Matthias Walker*, under St. *Dunſtons* Church
in *Fleet-ſtreet*, 1667.

split off from each other by the great prologue to book 8 (1667) in which Milton says that he must change his notes to tragic and treat of

> foul distrust, and breach
> Disloyal on the part of Man, revolt,
> And disobedience: On the part of Heav'n
> Now alienated, distance and distaste,
> Anger and just rebuke, and judgement giv'n,
> That brought into this World a world of woe,
> Sinne and her shadow Death, and Miserie
> Deaths Harbinger . . .   [9.6–13]

Thus the five-act structure suggested at the outset has been dissolved, just as the latent twelve-book division has been dissolved.

Perhaps Milton's rejection of Homeric or Vergilian divisions is a way of expressing his rejection of traditional epic themes, a way of implying that his poem has an utterly different mode of inspiration and hence of organization. But why then ten books? Why not thirteen, or seventeen, or any untraditional number? But Milton could never be so untraditional. I believe that certain scholars are right in arguing that Milton saw a special significance in the number ten, which was in ancient theory regarded as the perfect number.[10] At the same time the division into ten books would serve to suggest that we are to compare this poem with certain epics of the Renaissance, Tasso's epic in twenty cantos, or the epic of Camoens in ten cantos. Indeed, the *Lusiad* is the only important epic before *Paradise Lost* that was thus divided into ten parts; hence it seems possible that the appearance of Fanshawe's translation in 1655 may have had some influence upon Milton's decision to issue his poem with a ten-book division.

In any case, it is essential to notice that in both the *Lusiad* and *Paradise Lost* (1667) the tenth book is the longest book of the poem, and in each epic this final book consists mainly of visions and descriptions of the future course of history: for Camoens the glorious history of Portuguese conquest after da Gama, for Milton, the sad history of the human race after the Fall. The ironical significance of this parallel was long ago pointed out by Bowra, when he noted the place-names that evoked the memory of Portuguese conquests in Milton's catalogue in book 11. In particular Bowra notes the echo of Camoens's line "De Quiloa, de Mombaça, e de Sofala" (*Lusiad,* 1, st.54) in Milton's line *"Mombaza,* and *Quiloa,* and *Melind"* (11.399). And he then sums up the meaning of this parallel: the world that da Gama sees

> is to be in some sense the heritage of the Portuguese; it is at least the scene of many of their glorious exploits. The world which Adam sees belongs to all mankind, and while the rolling names show how great a possession it is, they are only a preliminary to the dismal history that follows. For Milton, as for Camoens, geography has its romance, but, so far from finding satisfaction in the great world which lies before him, Adam is called to see what havoc his descendants will make of it and what a need there is for real devotion and courage.[11]

That is, for a kind of devotion and courage quite different from the qualities displayed by the great explorers and conquerors, "hitherto the onely Argument Heroic deem'd."

We should note a further detail which will reinforce the truth of Bowra's view. This prophecy by Camoens, like the final view of human history in *Paradise Lost,* is divided into two parts: one presented in narrative and the other presented in vision. In Camoens's tenth book a nymph first narrates in song the exploits of the Portuguese heroes; then the queen of the nymphs takes da Gama and his followers up to the top of a high mountain, and there, using a strange model of the universe, shows to them the vast regions of the earth that lie open for Portuguese exploration.[12] Milton has reversed the order of vision and narration, but the two-part division of this finale suggests a pointed parallel, particularly when we consider one important aspect of the *Lusiad's* final book. Perhaps the most striking aspect of Camoens's technique here lies in his sonorous, magical roll of geographical names: exotic names that evoke the mystery and lure of the East, beckoning the conqueror on with the promise of both glory and material reward. As the place-names roll forth, stanza after stanza, Camoens creates the impression of the vast, wondrous, inexhaustible variety of the earth that still remains to be won (I quote from Fanshawe's version, where the old typography gives the place-names a special prominence):

> See the *Cape* call'd of old AROMATA,
> But GUARDAFU which now the *Dwellers* call;

Where the Red-sea (so famous) doth Embay,
Dy'd with her Bottome's shade! This is the *Wall*
Or running *Boundarie*, which Asia
Divides from Affrick: And the principal
 Cities, that on the *Affrick-side* are seen,
 Are Archicho, Macua, and (chief) Suanquen. [st.97]

See *heer*, where *Nature* prodigall hath bin,
The *Kingdom* of Ulcinde; and the long
Bay of Jaquete, where the Waves flow in
With speed incredible, as fast out-throng!
Cambaya see, where this *Gulph* doth begin,
In *wealth* and *people* infinite and strong! [st.106]

Behold the City of Tavay, with which
The spatious *Empire* of Sian begins!
Tenesseri! Queda: with pepper rich
For which the praise she from all other wins!
Malacca see before, where *ye* shall pitch
Your great *Emporium*, and your *Magazins* . . . [st.123]

Through all these *Orientall* Seas behold,
Sown infinite of *Isles* that have no name!
Tidore see! Ternate, whence are roll'd
(Holding black *Night* a Torch) thick *Plumes* of *Flame*! [st.132]

Such lists of names have of course a strong precedent in Hesiod, Homer, and Vergil, and especially in Ovid; nevertheless, the placing of certain Portuguese conquests in the middle of Milton's heroic catalogue seems to evoke the glorious prediction of Camoens, along with Greek and Roman models.

His Eye might there command wherever stood
City of old or modern Fame, the Seat
Of mightiest Empire, from the destind Walls
Of *Cambalu*, seat of *Cathaian Can*
And *Samarchand* by *Oxus*, *Temirs* Throne.
To *Paquin* of *Sinoean* Kings, and thence
To *Agra* and *Lahor* of great *Mogul*
Down to the golden *Chersonese*, or where
The *Persian* in *Ecbatan* sate, or since
In *Hispahan*, or where the *Russian Ksar*
In *Mosco*, or the Sultan in *Bizance*,
Turchestan-born; nor could his eye not ken
Th' Empire of *Negus* to his utmost Port
Ercoco and the less Maritine Kings
Mombaza, and *Quiloa*, and *Melind* . . . [11.385–99]

Then, with a terrible irony, Milton spreads out before Adam, by vision and narration, the fearful story of mankind's misdeeds, beginning with the sin of Cain. Among these horrors, the exploits of the military conquerors rank high:

> Where Cattel pastur'd late, now scatterd lies
> With Carcasses and Arms th' ensanguind Field
> Deserted: Others to a Citie strong
> Lay Siege, encampt; by Batterie, Scale, and Mine,
> Assaulting; others from the Wall defend
> With Dart and Jav'lin, Stones and sulfurous Fire;
> On each hand slaughter and gigantic deeds . . .
> *Adam* was all in tears, and to his guide
> Lamenting turnd full sad; O what are these,
> Deaths Ministers, not Men, who thus deal Death
> Inhumanly to men, and multiply
> Ten thousand fould the sin of him who slew
> His Brother; for of whom such massacher
> Make they but of thir Brethren, men of men?
>
> [11.653–59,674–80]

Are these the "nobler sights" that have been promised (11.411)? But Milton has a further irony in store: the truly noble sights are those that hint of man's possible salvation even in the midst of such horrors, a possibility represented by the appearance of figures such as Enoch, Noah, Moses, and Abraham, and finally, by the narration of the birth and death of Christ. These are the nobler sights that Michael will reveal for the purpose of teaching Adam the lesson that he learns at the very close:

> Henceforth I learne, that to obey is best,
> And love with feare the onely God, to walk
> As in his presence, ever to observe
> His providence, and on him sole depend . . .   [12.561–64]

The contrast, then, between the final books of these two poems has a powerful function. For Milton seems to be saying here that all the hopes of the Renaissance as suggested by Tasso, or Camoens, or Spenser were illusory: especially the hope that a single great nation might lead the world toward true Christian greatness, the hope that Milton himself, in 1644, expressed in a famous passage of his *Areopagitica*:

Lords and Commons of England, consider what Nation it is wherof ye are, and wherof ye are the governours: a Nation not slow and dull, but of a quick, ingenious, and piercing spirit, acute to invent, suttle and sinewy to discours, not beneath the reach of any point the highest that human capacity can soar to. . . . Why else was this Nation chos'n before any other, that out of her as out of *Sion* should be proclam'd and sounded forth the first tidings and trumpet of Reformation to all *Europ*. . . . Now once again by all concurrence of signs, and by the generall instinct of holy and devout men . . . God is decreeing to begin some new and great period in his Church, ev'n to the reforming of Reformation it self: what does he then but reveal Himself to his servants, and as his manner is, first to his English-men . . .[13]

It was, presumably, upon this hope that Milton based his early plans for a national epic of England that would be "doctrinal and exemplary" to a nation of such a destiny—a poem that might do for England what Camoens had done for the history of his own small seafaring nation. But it could not be done, after the failure of the Puritan Commonwealth had broken Milton's faith in national glory and military power. Viewed in the context of Camoens's epic, Milton's tenth book in 1667 represents a bitter commentary upon his own earlier hopes and the hopes of the Renaissance. Milton's epic, and especially the last book of his epic, constitutes a fulfillment of the bitter lament of the old man at the close of Camoens's fourth canto, that lament and denunciation uttered as da Gama's fleet sets sail:

Oh, the folly of it, this craving for power, this thirsting after the vanity we call fame, this fraudulent pleasure known as honour that thrives on popular esteem! When the vapid soul succumbs to its lure, what a price it exacts, and how justly, in perils, tempests, torments, death itself! It wrecks all peace of soul and body, leads men to forsake and betray their loved ones, subtly yet undeniably consumes estates, kingdoms, empires. Men call it illustrious, and noble, when it merits instead the obloquy of infamy; they call it fame, and sovereign glory, mere names with which the common people delude themselves in their ignorance . . . O unhappy race, true heirs of that madman, whose sin and disobedience not only doomed you to gloomy exile from paradise but drove you from that other divine state of simple, tranquil innocence, the golden age, condemning you in its place to this age of iron and instruments of destruction! [4.st.95–98, trans. Atkinson][14]

Nevertheless, as this passage shows, the difference between the epic of Portuguese conquest and the epic of the Fall of Man is far from absolute. The great power of each epic lies in the fact that each can include its opposite. Thus Milton makes his Satan so attractively heroic in the first two books of *Paradise Lost* that many readers since the time of Blake have felt that Satan was the true hero of the poem;[15] and in the same complex fashion, Camoens's poem gains strength from the recognition that the achievements it sets out to celebrate may be corrupted in their very enactment.

Each poet's method is particularly clear in the seventh book of his epic, where the arrival at a land of promise is flanked on either side by warnings of possible or certain failure to make proper use of that promise. The seventh canto of the *Lusiad* relates the longed-for arrival at India, the completion of the heroic voyage and the beginning of Portugal's empire:

> And now land was close at hand, the land so many others had longed to reach, that lay between the Ganges, sprung from the earthly paradise, and the Indus. Take courage, my brave men, who have set your hearts on the victor's palm. You have arrived: the land of wealth abounding lies before you. [7.st.1; p.161]

Yet the glorious promise of the arrival has already been qualified at the very end of canto 6, as the poet warns that a special kind of hero and a special kind of virtue are required to make the proper use of this achievement:

> Their goal is such honours as their stout right arm may win them and they may justly call their own. Ever on guard, girt with tempered steel, exposed to storms and tempestuous seas . . . it is thus that there is bred in the human breast a callous, ennobling contempt for honours and wealth, the honours and wealth that come by fortune's whim and not as the reward of virtue and endurance. It is thus that, with understanding deepened and matured by experience, there are revealed to one, as from a commanding eminence, all the pettiness and futility of ordinary life. [6.st.97–99; pp.159–60]

Then stanzas 4–14 of the seventh canto itself are given over to a furious denunciation of all the other nations of Europe for fighting one another, instead of conquering the infidel. Only Portugal, through such voyages as those of da Gama, has overcome the folly of all the rest of Europe: "Madmen that you are, thirsting in your blindness for the blood of your own! But here at least, in this small land of Portugal, there will not lack those who will do and dare for Christendom" (7.st.14; p.163). One may well feel the danger that even Portugal's best may not be able to overcome the folly of other Christians.

Then, after the wonders and treacheries of Calicut have been revealed, at the very close of the seventh canto, Camoens breaks off abruptly to utter a lament on the unhappy plight of the poet himself, plagued by poverty and injustice, and showing now a full awareness of the corruption that has already beset the Portuguese empire:

> And still, O Nymphs, it was not enough that I should be hounded by such an enormity of woes. It remained for me to see my verses rewarded as they were by those whose deeds I sang. Where I had looked for leisure and laurel wreaths, they found me instead new refinements of toil and condemned me to an existence harsher than before.
>
> Reflect, Nymphs, on what a breed of stalwarts it is your Tagus nurtures, that are incapable of higher esteem than this, or other favours, for him who gives them glory through his song . . .
>
> Fear not, Muses, that I shall sing the grave and honest-seeming man who accepts office at his monarch's instance, only thereafter to rob and despoil the poor; nor the man who holds it right and just that royal decrees should be observed with all severity, yet will admit neither the fairness nor the considerateness of paying the worker for the sweat of his brow; nor him who, lacking a fund of experience, would base a claim to prudence on the ingenuity of his grounds for taxing with greedy rapacity the labours of others, from which he stands aside. [7.st.81–86; pp.176–77]

It is clear now that da Gama's band constituted a rare breed, achieving an ideal of heroic action that their successors have found difficult to maintain. And lest we misunderstand the idealized nature of the vision of empire represented in the tenth canto, the poet at the very close reveals his deep dejection and his prayer of hope that the king will, in spite of all bad auguries, achieve a further action of the honorable fame that this poem celebrates:

> And now, my Muse, let there be an end: for my lyre is no longer attuned and my voice grows hoarse, not from my song but

from seeing that those to whom I sing are become hard of hearing and hard of heart. This country of mine is made over to lusting greed, its sense of values eclipsed in an austerity of gloom and depression: there is no longer to be had from it that recognition which fans the flame of genius as nothing else can. And I know not by what turn of destiny it should have lost the sense of joyous pride and pervasive pleasure that buoys up man's spirit to face toils and travails with unfailing cheerfulness.

I appeal to you, my King, who occupy your throne in further-ance of the divine will. Look round at other peoples and reflect on the excellence of these vassals who call you their lord . . .

Prepared for any sacrifice in your service, unswerving in obedi-ence to their so distant king, receiving with a ready and unquestion-ing alacrity your every command, however harsh: with the knowl-edge that your eye is upon them they will attack in your name the very devils of hell, and I doubt not but they will make you the victor, not the vanquished, in the struggle. [10.st.145–48; p.247]

Thus the poet's voice in the *Lusiad* casts a sombre doubt upon the very exploits he has celebrated. In the same way, the poet's voice in *Paradise Lost* places the beginning of man's life amid the gloomiest of predictions. Book 7 of *Paradise Lost*, in its original version, presents Milton's account of the beauties of the new Crea-tion, including Adam and Eve, newly formed. But at the begin-ning and the end of this account of the entire Creation, Milton has placed his sombre view of his own life and the world he knows. The prologue to book 8 (1667) declares: "I now must change / Those Notes to Tragic." The prologue to book 7 is also potentially tragic in its view of the poet's personal situation, blind, sur-rounded by enemies, and living in grave danger after the fall of the Commonwealth: yet the poet can still address his Heavenly Muse, while recalling an ominous Ovidian tale:

> Standing on Earth, not rapt above the Pole,
> More safe I Sing with mortal voice, unchang'd
> To hoarce or mute, though fall'n on evil dayes,
> On evil dayes though fall'n, and evil tongues;
> In darkness, and with dangers compast round,
> And solitude; yet not alone, while thou
> Visit'st my slumbers Nightly, or when Morn
> Purples the East: still govern thou my Song,
> *Urania*, and fit audience find, though few.
> But drive farr off the barbarous dissonance

Of *Bacchus* and his Revellers, the Race
Of that wilde Rout that tore the *Thracian* Bard
In *Rhodope*, where Woods and Rocks had Eares
To rapture, till the savage clamor dround
Both Harp and Voice; nor could the Muse defend
Her Son. So fail not thou, who thee implores:
For thou art Heav'nlie, shee an empty dreame.   [7.23–39]

The voice of the bard, full of trouble and hope and personal
opinion, thus plays an essential part in the meaning and in the
success of both these epics. For in each the poet stands forth as the
representative of an ideal, spoken by a human being who has
suffered the woes of mankind and who yet believes that man can
overcome his woe.[16] Thus in the tenth canto of the *Lusiad* we hear
the poet's voice:

> And here, Calliope, in this my final labour, I invoke your aid
> again. Grant me, I beseech of you, in return for what I now seek to
> write, and seek perhaps in vain, that I may recover the joy of writ-
> ing, that is beginning to fail me. The years are closing in about me,
> and soon summer must give way to autumn. Fate's chill hand is
> descending on my muse, that I no longer boast of with pride, nor
> can even rely upon. The buffetings of fortune sweep me on towards
> the dark river of oblivion and eternal sleep. Enable me, great
> Queen of the Muses, still to accomplish my desire towards my native
> land. [10.st.8–9; p.219]

So too, in *Paradise Lost*, we hear the voice of the bard speaking at
the outset of his eighth book (1667), as he scorns the military
trappings of earlier epics:

The skill of Artifice or Office mean,
Not that which justly gives Heroic name
To Person or to Poem. Mee of these
Nor skilld nor studious, higher Argument
Remaines, sufficient of it self to raise
That name, unless an age too late, or cold
Climat, or Years damp my intended wing
Deprest, and much they may, if all be mine,
Not Hers who brings it nightly to my Ear.   [9.39–47]

In this combination of suffering and hope, anguish at man-
kind's failures and faith in his own version of heroic virtue, the
poet creates an epic in which he becomes an actor in his own poem
and himself becomes, in his own way, an example of true heroic
fortitude.

Trials
of Faith

The parallels that the preceding chapter has drawn between the
final books of *Paradise Lost* and the *Lusiad* may help us toward a
clearer understanding of the lower style that Milton has chosen to
follow in his ending. For Milton's lowered style refuses to be
heroic: the style itself scorns the distentions of empire and leads
toward the firm and quiet closing words of Adam and the angel:

> Henceforth I learne, that to obey is best,
> And love with feare the onely God, to walk
> As in his presence, ever to observe
> His providence, and on him sole depend,
> Merciful over all his works, with good
> Still overcoming evil, and by small
> Accomplishing great things, by things deemd weak
> Subverting worldly strong, and worldly wise
> By simply meek;
>
> . . . .
>
> This having learnt, thou hast attained the summe
> Of wisdom; hope no higher, though all the Starrs
> Thou knewst by name, and all th' ethereal Powers,
> All secrets of the deep, all Natures works,
> Or works of God in Heav'n, Air, Earth, or Sea,
> And all the riches of this World enjoydst,
> And all the rule, one Empire . . .   [12.561–69,575–81]

Thus the theological design should work hand in hand with the poetical, stylistic design, perhaps after the manner suggested by John Dryden in 1682, in his preface to *Religio Laici*:

> The Expressions of a Poem, design'd purely for Instruction, ought to be Plain and Natural, and yet Majestick: for here the Poet is presum'd to be a kind of Law-giver, and those three qualities which I have nam'd are proper to the Legislative style. The Florid, Elevated and Figurative way is for the Passions; for Love and Hatred, Fear and Anger, are begotten in the Soul by shewing their Objects out of their true proportion; either greater than the Life, or less; but Instruction is to be given by shewing them what they naturally are. A Man is to be cheated into Passion, but to be reason'd into Truth.[1]

What Milton has achieved in the passages just quoted seems to be something very close to what Dryden here calls "the Legislative style"—a manner that is "Plain and Natural, and yet Majestick," a style that avoids the cheats of passion and attempts to reason Adam and his descendants into truth. Elsewhere, the style at times becomes florid and elevated, when Adam is shown those scenes that stir his horror, fear, or delight; but the legislative explanations of his divine instructor always follow to reveal the cheat and show what these things naturally are, by reason and by theological truth.

The clue to the theological design[2] is given in book 11 with the opening words of "the Father, without Cloud, serene":

> I at first with two fair gifts
> Created him endowd, with Happiness
> And Immortalitie: that fondly lost,
> This other serv'd but to eternize woe;
> Till I provided Death; so Death becomes
> His final remedie, and after Life
> Tri'd in sharp tribulation, and refin'd
> By Faith and faithful works, to second Life,
> Wak't in the renovation of the just,
> Resignes him up with Heav'n and Earth renewd.   [11.57–66]

Death thus becomes a benefit, not only a penalty, since death ends all woe for the just man and "resignes him up"—that is, releases him, into a second life in the new heaven and new earth prophesied in the second epistle of Peter (3:13). But this will happen only after a life tested ("tri'd") in sharp tribulation, and purified ("refin'd") by "Faith and faithful works." Mankind is to be "justified," in the protestant sense, by faith, accompanied by works flowing from faith, works of love and gratitude.

In this mingled tone of severity and mercy, the Father then calls upon Michael to "drive out the sinful Pair" from Paradise "without remorse"—but he adds an instruction that sets forth a temperate and merciful mode of banishment:

> Yet least they faint
> At the sad Sentence rigorously urg'd,
> For I behold them soft'nd and with tears
> Bewailing thir excess, all terror hide.
> If patiently thy bidding they obey,
> Dismiss them not disconsolate; reveale
> To *Adam* what shall come in future dayes,
> As I shall thee enlighten, intermix
> My Cov'nant in the Womans seed renewd;
> So send them forth, though sorrowing, yet in peace . . .
> [11.108–17]

Certainly Adam's restored faith needs tempering, for he sees the process of salvation as lacking all bitterness and tribulation:

> *Eve*, easily may Faith admit, that all
> The good which we enjoy, from Heav'n descends
> But that from us ought should ascend to Heav'n
> So prevalent as to concerne the mind
> Of God high-blest, or to incline his will,
> Hard to belief may seem; yet this will Prayer,
> Or one short sigh of humane breath, up-borne
> Ev'n to the Seat of God. For since I saught
> By Prayer th' offended Deitie to appease,
> Kneel'd and before him humbl'd all my heart,
> Methought I saw him placable and mild,
> Bending his eare; perswasion in me grew
> That I was heard with favour; peace return'd
> Home to my brest, and to my memorie
> His promise, that thy Seed shall bruise our Foe;
> Which then not minded in dismay, yet now
> Assures me that the bitterness of death
> Is past, and we shall live. Whence Haile to thee
> *Eve* rightly call'd, Mother of all Mankind,
> Mother of all things living, since by thee
> Man is to live, and all things live for Man. [11.141–61]

The vagueness of Adam's phrasing allows a hope that perhaps the entire penalty has been annulled: that not only the "bitterness" in the process of death is past, but that the threatened death itself has been revoked, "and we shall live," perhaps forever? But the echo of the words of Agag just before his terrible death at the hands of Samuel (I Samuel 15:32–33) shows the bitter fallacy of this easy hope, while the foreshadowing of the Annunciation implies the sorrow and suffering by which man lives.

Eve too picks up the optimistic strain, saying that labor in Paradise can never be onerous:

> while here we dwell,
> What can be toilsom in these pleasant Walkes?
> Here let us live, though in fall'n state, content.   [11.178–80]

Such hopes are quickly dashed by the grim epic omens:

> The Bird of *Jove*, stoopt from his aerie tour,
> Two Birds of gayest plume before him drove:
> Down from a Hill the Beast that reigns in Woods,
> First Hunter then, pursu'd a gentle brace,
> Goodliest of all the Forrest, Hart and Hinde . . .
>   [11.185–89]

The pitying admiration of the last line here is quite appropriate to the subtle manner in which Michael and his military angels are now presented:

> A glorious Apparition, had not doubt
> And carnal fear that day dimm'd *Adams* eye.
> Not that more glorious, when the Angels met
> *Jacob* in *Mahanaim*, where he saw
> The field Pavilion'd with his Guardians bright;
> Not that which on the flaming Mount appeerd
> In *Dothan*, cover'd with a Camp of Fire,
> Against the *Syrian* King, who to surprize
> One man, Assassin-like had levied Warr,
> Warr unproclam'd.   [11.211–20]

These allusions to the beneficent presence of divine power, as experienced by Jacob and Elisha (Genesis 32:1–2; 2 Kings 6:17), foreshadow Michael's assurance of God's omnipresence, and thus serve proleptically to moderate the effect of horror with which Adam and Eve receive the word of their exile. For the two fall

from the excess of optimism into the excess of despair, Adam
being "Heart-strook with chilling gripe of sorrow," while Eve ut-
ters her piercing lament:

> O flours,
> That never will in other Climate grow,
> My early visitation, and my last
> At Eev'n, which I bred up with tender hand
> From the first op'ning bud, and gave ye Names,
> Who now shall reare ye to the Sun, or ranke
> Your Tribes, and water from th' ambrosial Fount?
> Thee lastly nuptial Bowre, by mee adornd
> With what to sight or smell was sweet; from thee
> How shall I part, and whither wander down
> Into a lower World, to this obscure
> And wilde, how shall we breath in other Aire
> Less pure, accustomd to immortal Fruits?   [11.273–85]

The passage is a tissue of ironies, for flowers will grow in that
lower world, and later Eves will breed them up from the first
opening buds, call the flowers by name, place them in rows, and
water them—though not from an ambrosial fount. And botanists
will rank their tribes in the proper species. Other nuptial bowers
will be adorned by other Eves. True, all will be "lower" in excel-
lence, but even now, outside of Paradise, the flowers and shrubs
and trees described in book 7 are awaiting the touch of mankind's
cultivation. Her thoughtless reference to "immortal Fruits" re-
minds us that it was her "mortal taste" of that forbidden fruit
which now compels her to go forth to gather mortal fruits and
flowers in the lower world.

The tone of the angel's reply to these laments is perfectly tem-
pered: he is firm, but "milde," performing his mission "with re-
gard benigne" (11.286, 334). The poem, it seems, is to end in a
delicate poise, a balance of attitudes, where the sense of loss is
subtly qualified by a sense of gain. Though the chief actors are
condemned to death, we are to sense a restoration of the world to
order, though at heavy cost.

It is such an assurance of restoration that Michael now gives, in
answer to Adam's crushed and hopeless lament for the expected
loss of God's presence:

> This most afflicts me, that departing hence,
> As from his face I shall be hid, deprivd
> His blessed count'nance; here I could frequent,
> With worship, place by place where he voutsaf'd
> Presence Divine, and to my Sons relate;
> On this Mount he appeerd, under this Tree
> Stood visible, among these Pines his voice
> I heard, here with him at this Fountain talk'd . . .
> In yonder nether World where shall I seek
> His bright appearances, or footstep trace?   [11.315–22,328–29]

As with the earlier allusions to Jacob and Elisha, the phrasing of Adam's lament itself implies the continued presence of God with the sons of Adam: Moses and Elijah will hear the voice of the Lord upon a Mount; the Lord or his angel will appear to Gideon and Zechariah under an oak or myrtle tree; and the woman of Samaria will speak with Jesus as he sits by Jacob's well. Thus Michael assures Adam, in terms of the Augustinian tradition, that the *vestigia*, the traces, the footsteps of God will be everywhere present:

> *Adam*, thou know'st Heav'n his, and all the Earth,
> Not this Rock onely; his Omnipresence fills
> Land, Sea, and Aire, and every kinde that lives,
> Fomented by his virtual power and warmd:
> All th' Earth he gave thee to possess and rule,
> No despicable gift; surmise not then
> His presence to these narrow bounds confin'd
> Of Paradise or *Eden* . . .   [11.335–42]

The power manifested in the original Creation will remain as "virtual power," inward, essential, life-giving power, for Adam and his sons to enjoy:

> Yet doubt not but in Vallie and in Plaine
> God is as here, and will be found alike
> Present, and of his presence many a signe
> Still following thee, still compassing thee round
> With goodness and paternal Love, his Face
> Express, and of his steps the track Divine.   [11.349–54]

"Which that thou mayst beleeve, and be confirmd," the angel adds—invoking the protestant doctrine of confirmation, by which a mature intelligence confirms his faith—[3]

>   know I am sent
> To shew thee what shall come in future dayes
> To thee and to thy Ofspring; good with bad
> Expect to hear, supernal Grace contending
> With sinfulness of Men, thereby to learn
> True patience, and to temper joy with fear
> And pious sorrow . . .   [11.355–62]

Such is the wholly benevolent aim of the scenes to follow.

II

    As Adam now ascends the hill to see the visions of the future, Milton skillfully brings in the means of redemption, through alluding to Christ's temptation in the wilderness and using an ambiguous syntax that for a time allows us to see the kingdoms of the world through the eyes of both the second Adam and the first:[4]

> Not higher that Hill nor wider looking round,
> Whereon for different cause the Tempter set
> Our second *Adam* in the Wilderness,
> To shew him all Earths Kingdomes and thir Glory.
> His Eye might there command wherever stood
> City of old or modern Fame, the Seat
> Of mightiest Empire . . .   [11.381–87]

And so for over twenty lines we have the gorgeous roll of names, with Milton manifesting all the power of his high style, recalling in one final burst of grandeur the epic panoply of the opening book. And all to excellent purpose here: for, as the allusion to the second Adam indicates, these are all "glories" of the fallen world, as they were in book 1, though we were then inclined to place their worth higher, despite their setting in the flames of Hell. The obvious excess of the grand roll of empires here carries the mind back through the whole poem to the building of Pandaemonium and the roll call of fallen angels, and makes a deliberate judgment of those "heroic" scenes: "but to nobler sights / *Michael* from *Adams* eyes the Filme remov'd" (11.411–12).

    We know what those nobler sights will be: sights that prove the constant presence of God in the world of men, his "goodness and paternal Love"—although Michael has also warned Adam to expect a mixture of "good with bad," as divine grace contends with man's sinfulness. Nevertheless, the first vision creates an effect of shock, in us, in Adam, and in Michael, as the scene of the murder of Abel is expanded with grim details:

> Whereat hee inlie rag'd, and as they talk'd,
> Smote him into the Midriff with a stone
> That beat out life; he fell, and deadly pale
> Groand out his Soul with gushing bloud effus'd.
> Much at that sight was *Adam* in his heart
> Dismai'd, and thus in haste to th' Angel cri'd.
>   O Teacher, some great mischief hath befall'n
> To that meek man, who well had sacrific'd;
> Is Pietie thus and pure Devotion paid?
>   T' whom *Michael* thus, hee also mov'd, repli'd.
> These two are Brethren, *Adam*, and to come
> Out of thy loyns; th' unjust the just hath slain,
> For envie that his Brothers Offering found
> From Heav'n acceptance; but the bloodie Fact
> Will be aveng'd, and th' others Faith approv'd
> Loose no reward, though here thou see him die,
> Rowling in dust and gore. To which our Sire.
>   Alas, both for the deed and for the cause!
> But have I now seen Death? Is this the way
> I must return to native dust? O sight
> Of terrour, foul and ugly to behold,
> Horrid to think, how horrible to feel!   [11.444–65]

That vision may at first seem not quite in accord with God's direction to Michael: "all terror hide," but that direction, it now appears, was meant to apply only to the demeanour of Michael and his military angels: they are not to appear in a terrifying way. But with the visions of human life a sense of terror is required, if faith is to be confirmed. Adam must now believe that the crime will be avenged, "and th' others Faith approv'd / Loose no reward," however horrible his death. For the present, however, Michael's teaching seems to have no effect in diminishing Adam's horror. Nor is Adam's equanimity restored by the grim vision that follows:

>   wherein were laid
> Numbers of all diseas'd, all maladies
> Of gastly Spasm, or racking torture, qualmes

> Of heart-sick Agonie, all feavorous kinds,
> Convulsions, Epilepsies, fierce Catarrhs,
> Intestin Stone and Ulcer, Colic pangs,
> Dropsies, and Asthma's, and Joint-racking Rheums.
>
> [11.479–85]

Such is the scene in Milton's first edition; in the revised edition of 1674 he extended the range and increased the horror by inserting these lines between the last two given above:

> Daemoniac Phrenzie, moaping Melancholie
> And Moon-struck madness, pining Atrophie,
> Marasmus, and wide-wasting Pestilence . . .

It is powerfully done; no wonder Adam weeps and cries out in anguish, asking why life should be given on these terms, and why the Image of God should be subjected to such deformities. But the appalling effectiveness of the scene receives from Michael a sharp didactic explanation that is hard to square with human experience, which tells us that many temperate men suffer the kinds of painful illness above described:

> Thir Makers Image, answerd *Michael*, then
> Forsook them, when themselves they villifi'd
> To serve ungovern'd appetite, and took
> His Image whom they serv'd, a brutish vice,
> Inductive mainly to the sin of *Eve.*
> Therefore so abject is thir punishment,
> Disfiguring not Gods likeness, but thir own,
> Or if his likeness, by themselves defac't
> While they pervert pure Natures healthful rules
> To loathsom sickness, worthily, since they
> Gods Image did not reverence in themselves.   [11.515–25]

Nevertheless Adam gives the answer proper to faith: "I yield it just, said *Adam*, and submit." He is moving through the process of his confirmation: Milton is writing a theological paradigm of the workings of faith, as his frequent repetition of the word in book 12 makes plain.[5]

Milton's following account of the gradual decline of the temperate man into old age helps to moderate Michael's didactic rigor, but as Milton proceeds into the next vision, where the grave Sons of God are seduced by the "Beavie of fair Women," Michael's tone becomes sententious, harsh, and at the close sarcastic:

> For that fair femal Troop thou sawst, that seemd
> Of Goddesses, so blithe, so smooth, so gay,
> Yet empty of all good wherein consists
> Womans domestic honour and chief praise;
> Bred onely and completed to the taste
> Of lustful appetence, to sing, to dance,
> To dress, and troule the Tongue, and roule the Eye.
> To these that sober Race of Men, whose lives
> Religious titl'd them the Sons of God,
> Shall yeild up all thir vertue, all thir fame
> Ignobly, to the traines and to the smiles
> Of these fair Atheists, and now swim in joy,
> (Erelong to swim at larg) and laugh; for which
> The world erelong a world of tears must weepe.   [11.614–27]

Meanwhile the promised consolation in the last third of book 11 resides primarily in a series of allusions to the vain attempts of the "one just Man alive" to stem the tide of evil:

> The onely righteous in a World perverse,
> And therefore hated, therefore so beset
> With Foes for daring single to be just,
> And utter odious Truth . . .   [11.701–04]

We may argue that this has been foreshadowed in the figure of Abdiel, but the parallel, undoubtedly designed with care, serves here to show how far Milton has departed from his allegory of the War in Heaven. For in this allegory of the spiritual combat, as fought from the revolt of the angels until the Day of Doom, Abdiel is indeed the only righteous in the perverse band of Satan— but he returns to join the two-thirds of the angels that have remained faithful. Milton's just man on earth has no one to join on earth, for

> all shall turn degenerate, all deprav'd,
> Justice and Temperance, Truth and Faith forgot;
> One Man except, the onely Son of light
> In a dark Age . . .   [11.806–09]

In this way life on earth is here explicitly equated with the life of Satan's host, whereas in the opening books the association of earth with evil has been developed by implication only: implication that provides the setting for a redemptive movement. The strict equation of earth with evil produces an unsettling effect in book 11, a feeling that, somehow, Milton is retreating from his earlier assertions and demonstrations that man's free will suffices to offer the possibility of recovering that paradise within.

But Milton has a careful plan, well explained by Summers when he says that we are to see "this pattern of destruction followed by a new and greater creation."[6] This aim is clearly set forth in the lines that Milton added when he divided the original book 10 into two books:

> As one who in his journey bates at Noone,
> Though bent on speed, so heer the Archangel paus'd
> Betwixt the world destroy'd and world restor'd . . .   [12.1–3]

The symbolical visions of the world of sin, we see, are only half the story: the world of consolation remains. The design is even more strongly emphasized in the Argument to book 12, written after the first edition had appeared:[7]

> *The Angel* Michael *continues from the Flood to relate what shall succeed; then, in the mention of* Abraham, *comes by degrees to explain, who that Seed of the Woman shall be, which was promised* Adam *and* Eve *in the Fall; his Incarnation, Death, Resurrection, and Ascension; the state of the Church till his second Coming.* Adam *greatly satisfied and recomforted by these Relations and Promises descends the Hill with* Michael; *wakens* Eve, *who all this while had slept, but with gentle dreams compos'd to quietness of mind and submission.* Michael *in either hand leads them out of Paradise, the fiery Sword waving behind them, and the Cherubim taking thir Stations to guard the Place.*

What happens in the poetry is something different. First of all, Milton changes the poetic method from vision to narration:

> but I perceave
> Thy mortal sight to faile; objects divine
> Must needs impaire and wearie human sense:
> Henceforth what is to com I will relate . . .   [12.8–11]

The basic reason for the change is perhaps clear enough: the process of redemption through the sacrifice of Christ involves the most complex and controversial of theological issues; to provide adequate explanation Michael must be allowed to enfold the action of history within a carefully woven network of accurate and

precise theology. Thus Milton devotes his last book primarily to a
rational account of the theology of the remnant, as developed by
the protestant reformers under the strong influence of Augus-
tine's later writings on the problem of grace. As the current theol-
ogy of the remnant begins to dominate the poem's world, its tone
and manner move farther and farther away from the poise and
tempering of attitudes promised by Michael and God at the outset
of book 11.

As a result the effects and proportions implied by the Argu-
ment to book 12 are not fulfilled. The last half of the Argument,
with its comforting and reassuring emphasis, describes what hap-
pens only in the last hundred lines of this book of 649 lines. And
the first half of the Argument, with its emphasis on the coming of
the "Seed of the Woman," is also greatly out of proportion with
what actually happens in the poem. It is not until line 360 that we
come to the birth of the Messiah, and then his whole career from
Incarnation to Ascension is dealt with in less than a hundred lines,
and these for the most part filled with theological explanation.
Milton declines to represent the gospel story in any kind of ex-
tended vision: the chief events are simply mentioned, in lines that
do not amount to more than fifteen in all, of which these are the
most detailed:

> yet at his Birth a Starr
> Unseen before in Heav'n proclaims him com,
> And guides the Eastern Sages, who enquire
> His place, to offer Incense, Myrrh, and Gold;
> His place of birth a solemn Angel tells
> To simple Shepherds, keeping watch by night;
> They gladly thither haste, and by a Quire
> Of squadrond Angels hear his Carol sung.   [12.360–67]

That Carol, we remember, has been sung in Milton's poem by the
angels before the Creation: it is not sung now.

For Milton is not here concerned with celebration or with affec-
tionate meditation: he is "expounding a doctrine," as Madsen has
very well said, and the exposition is admirably performed, in lines
that "have their own kind of intellectual energy":[8]

> The Law of God exact he shall fulfill
> Both by obedience and by love, though love

> Alone fulfill the Law . . .
> For this he shall live hated, be blasphem'd,
> Seis'd on by force, judg'd, and to death condemnd
> A shameful and accurst, naild to the Cross
> By his own Nation, slaine for bringing Life;
> But to the Cross he nailes thy Enemies,
> The Law that is against thee, and the sins
> Of all mankinde, with him there crucifi'd,
> Never to hurt them more who rightly trust
> In this his satisfaction . . .   [12.402–04,411–19]

This abstract account of salvation is set within the section of 550 lines in which Michael tells the sombre history of the world from after the Flood through the Day of Doom: it is a threefold process of corruption and renewal, each part of the process re-enacting the story of the world from the Creation to the Flood. The third cycle closes with Milton's denunciation of the corruptions and persecutions of the Church after the time of the apostles down to the bitter sufferings of the just in Milton's own day and in later ages:

> the rest, farr greater part,
> Will deem in outward Rites and specious formes
> Religion satisfi'd; Truth shall retire
> Bestuck with slandrous darts, and works of Faith
> Rarely be found: so shall the World goe on,
> To good malignant, to bad men benigne,
> Under her own waight groaning, till the day
> Appear of respiration to the just,
> And vengeance to the wicked . . .   [12.533–41]

Book 12 thus presents a twofold problem, both theological and poetical. First, the stern doctrine of the remnant seems to depart from the promise set forth by God himself in book 3, implied in the recovery of Adam and Eve in book 10, set forth again by God at the beginning of book 11, carried on by Michael's words of reassurance to Adam early in book 11, and asserted once more in the Argument to book 12. Grace is freely offered to all—but few will choose to accept that gift. Is this, then, what it means to be placed "on even ground" with Satan, sufficient to have stood, though free to fall? It is a paradox beyond any human explanation, but for Milton, his own experience seems to have proved it true:

Standing on Earth, not rapt above the Pole,
More safe I Sing with mortal voice, unchang'd
To hoarce or mute, though fall'n on evil dayes,
On evil dayes though fall'n, and evil tongues;
In darkness, and with dangers compast round,
And solitude; yet not alone, while thou
Visit'st my slumbers Nightly, or when Morn
Purples the East: still govern thou my Song,
Urania, and fit audience find, though few.   [7.23–31]

Looking back now we can see that warnings of this tragic
paradox have been given from time to time early in the poem. In
book 1, before the catalogue of devils disguised as pagan deities,
we heard how these devils wandered "ore the Earth / Through
Gods high sufferance for the tryal of man," and how

By falsities and lyes the greatest part
Of Mankind they corrupted to forsake
God their Creator, and th' invisible
Glory of him, that made them, to transform
Oft to the Image of a Brute, adorn'd
With gay Religions full of Pomp and Gold . . .   [1.365–72]

Those religions, for Milton, surely include the pomp and gold of
Roman or Laudian ceremony.[9] Thus book 1 foretells the decline
of the Church narrated in book 12. Then in book 3, just after the
promise of universal grace has been given in Heaven, we come
upon that Limbo of Vanity "to few unknown / Long after."

We have been warned—the paradox of mankind's preference
for evil over goodness has been with us from the outset of the
poem—and yet the power of Adam and Eve's recovery in book 10
is so moving that we are bound to believe that such a choice lies
open to all mankind. The resolution of this paradox is made more
difficult, not easier, by Milton's insistence upon the doctrine of the
freedom of the will as a principle that he cannot bear to renounce.
It may well seem, as it sometimes seems to Adam, that only a
faulty piece of workmanship or planning on the part of God could
have led to such an overwhelming number of wrong choices. Mil-
ton's last book forces the cruel paradox upon us.

One is left with a trial of faith.[10] We must regard the survival of
the just, few though they may be, as a fulfillment of the divine
plan of redemption. The way is open to all. If few choose to follow

that way, human beings have only themselves to blame. The
theological principle is clear: only those of little or no faith will
doubt its justice.

The starkness of the choice here is related to the lowering of
style in book 12, as evidenced in the long stretches of biblical
paraphrase, where Milton seems to have deliberately withheld his
full poetical powers, leaving the facts of biblical history to speak
for themselves, without embellishment, except for the web of
theological interpretation (as in the emphasis here on the word
"Faith"):

> I see him, but thou canst not, with what Faith
> He leaves his Gods, his Friends, and native Soile
> *Ur* of *Chaldoea*, passing now the Ford
> To *Haran*, after him a cumbrous Train
> Of Herds and Flocks, and numerous servitude;
> Not wandring poor, but trusting all his wealth
> With God, who call'd him, in a land unknown.
> *Canaan* he now attains, I see his Tents
> Pitcht about *Sechem*, and the neighbouring Plaine
> Of *Moreh*; there by promise he receaves
> Gift to his Progenie of all that Land . . .   [12.128–38]

By the plain style the plain truth will appear. Such a deliberate
humbling of the high style, bringing it gradually down to the
lowest range of the "Legislative style," would indeed be congruent
with the moral principle expressed by Adam and the angel at the
close of the world's history: "by small / Accomplishing great
things, by things deemd weak / Subverting worldly strong." To tell
of the grandest truth in a humble style may be seen as an act of
piety and devotion. The lowering of the style, then, is an act of
ascesis such as we are to see performed at length in *Paradise Re-
gain'd*. But in book 12 Milton is having some difficulty in thus
lowering his style, for there are clumsy, awkward moments:

> the like shall sing
> All Prophecie, That of the Royal Stock
> Of *David* (so I name this King) shall rise
> A Son, the Womans Seed to thee foretold,
> Foretold to *Abraham*, as in whom shall trust
> All Nations, and to Kings foretold, of Kings
> The last, for of his Reign shall be no end.   [12.324–30]

Milton has not yet learned how to handle this lower style with assurance; perhaps his long practice in the high style has made his hand unsteady here. In any case, there can be little doubt that the lowering is done as part of his total design, however the words may stumble now and then.

Milton's total design in the last book of his poem is to convey the ultimate message of the biblical prophets and of the entire New Testament: nothing abides, nothing has true value, except the spiritual bond between Jehovah and his people. The very remoteness and abstractness of Jehovah places an almost unbearable strain upon humanity. Hence the continual temptation of mankind, shown throughout books 1 and 12, to worship false gods tangibly rooted in the cults of earth. Milton's reliance on abstraction in his account of the coming joy presents us with the problem that the prophets faced: how to persuade an audience of unbelievers or half-believers that a god remote and unseeable deserves an absolute faith.[11] His "legislative" mission has, for a time, taken precedence over his full poetical powers.[12] But then, in the closing lines, that power re-emerges in all its vitality, as Milton at the close defines the heroism of those who can admit their fault, declare their faith, and go forward to face the complex life of the world we know.

CHAPTER 11

The
Solitary
Way

"In my end is my beginning," T. S. Eliot wrote in *East Coker,* "In my beginning is my end"—adapting an ancient motto said to belong to Mary, Queen of Scots. I should like, in concluding this part, to think of *Paradise Lost* from this standpoint, as a poem where the end returns to the beginning. Such an approach is implicit in the closing lines of the poem, which tell of Adam and Eve's departure from Paradise. I use the word *departure* instead of the more traditional term *expulsion*, for Milton's ending moderates the stark and threatening words of Genesis: "so he drove out the man; and he placed at the east of the garden of Eden cherubims, and a flaming sword which turned every way, to keep the way of the tree of life."

Milton's presentation also differs greatly from the usual pictorial representations of the Expulsion in renaissance or baroque art, as in the design of Milton's earliest illustrator (1688: see illustration above).[1] Here the stern-faced angel with his left hand grasps Adam firmly by the shoulder, as though partly pushing and partly steadying an Adam whose hands cover his face and

185

whose body seems about to drop to the ground with anguish.
Meanwhile, in his right hand the angel holds a sword toward
Adam's leg, threatening any effort at return. Or consider
Michelangelo's Expulsion, on the Sistine Chapel ceiling, where the
angel seems to hold the point of his sword against the back of
Adam's neck, while Adam strikes a gesture of fear and pleading,
with an expression of poignant regret and remorse, and Eve cow-
ers at his side. Or, farthest of all from Milton's conception, recall
Masaccio's fresco in the church of the Carmine at Florence, where
Eve expresses by her ragged, open mouth a cry of grief almost
beyond bearing.

But Milton, as always, does things in his own way. He has shown
the horror of the Fall throughout his last two books, with their
oppressive tale of human wickedness, which evokes Adam's cry
when he sees the murder of Abel:

> O sight
> Of terrour, foul and ugly to behold,
> Horrid to think, how horrible to feel!   [11.463–65]

Milton will not end his poem in such a mood. The angel does
not hold a sword, and he does not drive the human pair, but
rather saves them from a burning residence, as the angels in the
Book of Genesis (chapter 19) escort Lot and his family from the
doomed city of Sodom, taking them by the hand; or as Aeneas in a
different fashion escorts his son and his father from burning
Troy. Milton carefully places the guardian cherubim, with the
flaming sword "before them," at a distance from Adam and Eve,
as the procession of cherubim descends "from the other Hill:"

> High in Front advanc't,
> The brandisht Sword of God before them blaz'd
> Fierce as a Comet; which with torrid heat,
> And vapour as the *Libyan* Air adust,
> Began to parch that temperate Clime ;   [12.632–36]

"whereat," Milton continues—at the sight of the blazing sword
approaching—the angel grasps Adam by one hand and Eve by the
other, and he leads them to safety through the east gate of
Paradise and down to the plain of Eden that lies below the mount
of Paradise:

> In either hand the hastning Angel caught
> Our lingring Parents, and to th' Eastern Gate
> Led them direct, and down the Cliff as fast
> To the subjected Plaine; then disappeer'd.   [12.637–40]

This is an act of rescue, a sign of mercy, and it does not evoke horror or terror in our first parents:

> They looking back, all th' Eastern side beheld
> Of Paradise, so late thir happie seat,
> Wav'd over by that flaming Brand, the Gate
> With dreadful Faces throng'd and fierie Armes:
> Som natural tears they drop'd, but wip'd them soon;
> The World was all before them, where to choose
> Thir place of rest, and Providence thir guide:
> They hand in hand with wandring steps and slow,
> Through *Eden* took thir solitarie way.   [12.641–end]

And they will find a place of rest, as Milton has implied by a complex simile that he has placed earlier within this ending, the simile in which he compares the assembling cherubim to the evening mist that a field-laborer sees as he returns home from work in the English countryside:

> So spake our Mother *Eve*, and *Adam* heard
> Well pleas'd, but answer'd not; for now too nigh
> Th' Archangel stood, and from the other Hill
> To thir fixt Station, all in bright array
> The Cherubim descended; on the ground
> Gliding meteorous, as Ev'ning Mist
> Ris'n from a River o're the marish glides,
> And gathers ground fast at the Labourers heel
> Homeward returning.   [12.624–32]

One may feel something ominous in this glowing mist, for meteors were traditionally regarded as ominous; but there is much more in the simile than dread. There is here the sense of a fertile river valley in which the mist counteracts the effects of threatening fire and parching heat; and there is the promise of a peaceful homecoming after a hard day of labor. All this provides an implicit answer to the question: what lies ahead for Adam and Eve? The emphasis has fallen on that word *choose*, in the lines "The World was all before them, where to *choose* / Thir place of rest, and Providence thir guide." The word *choose* not only receives a special stress here by coming at the end of the line; it also seems to govern the word *Providence*. That is to say, Providence will be their guide if they choose to accept the guidance. One notices too a paradox in the word *solitarie*: they are a solitary *pair*, hand in hand, and they may if they choose also have the presence of Providence to be their guide. Furthermore, those final two words of the poem, *solitarie way*, and the word *wandring*, despite their apparent gloom and bleakness, are lighted with some hope in their full context of allusion, for these words echo Psalm 107, speaking of the Hebrew people:

> They *wandered* in the wilderness in a *solitary way*;
> They found no city to dwell in.
> Hungry and thirsty,
> Their soul fainted in them.
> Then they cried unto the Lord in their trouble,
> And he delivered them out of their distresses.
> And he led them forth by the right way,
> That they might go to a city of habitation.
> Oh that men would praise the Lord for his goodness,
> And for his wonderful works to the children of men!

The total context of that phrase *solitarie way* is thus one of hope and faith. And that sentence of the psalm, "Oh that men would praise the Lord for his goodness, And for his wonderful works to the children of men," is repeated three more times in this psalm, so that one cannot miss the meaning. It is, then, in this setting of hope and faith and love that Adam and Eve begin their life in the fallen world, while at the same time the phrases "torrid heat" and "fierie Armes," along with the imagery of meteor, blazing comet, and "*Libyan* Air adust," draw us back to the poem's opening books, as though Adam and Eve were on the verge of entering into the kind of world therein displayed.

To grasp this circular effect one needs to reconsider the double movement of the first four books: from Satan and the fallen angels in Hell upward through Chaos toward the light of Heaven and then on toward the vision of Paradise on earth. Literally, as we follow Satan's voyage, we may seem to perform a journey forward in time, moving from Hell to the new earth. Yet from another standpoint, we are performing a more significant journey

backward in time, from the fallen world of the first two books
toward the pristine, earlier world of book 4. This journey back-
ward is also a journey inward, from the fallen world of everyday
toward that center of remembrance where, as Milton's colleague,
Peter Sterry, said, the soul may experience "an awakening by
reason of the primitive Image of pure Nature raising it self by
degrees, and sparkling through the *Rubbish*, the confusions of the
present state."[2]

This effect of a journey backward and inward is created largely
by the imagistic action of the opening books, notably in that im-
mense roll call of evil that dominates the middle of the first book.
Milton's device of calling the roll of fallen angels under the names
of the later false gods has the effect of gradually dissolving our
consciousness of Hell as any special place, and instead we find
ourselves watching the operations of evil as it spreads out over the
face of the earth:

> First *Moloch*, horrid King besmear'd with blood
> Of human sacrifice, and parents tears,
> Though for the noyse of Drums and Timbrels loud
> Their childrens cries unheard, that past through fire
> To his grim Idol. Him the *Ammonite*
> Worshipt in *Rabba* and her watry Plain,
> In *Argob* and in *Basan*, to the stream
> Of utmost *Arnon* . . .
> Next *Chemos*, th' obscene dread of *Moabs* Sons,
> From *Aroer* to *Nebo*, and the wild
> Of Southmost *Abarim*; in *Hesebon*
> And *Horonaim*, *Seons* Realm, beyond
> The flowry Dale of *Sibma* clad with Vines,
> And *Eleale* to th' *Asphaltick* Pool.   [1.392–99,406–11]

Every name here has its concrete, evocative identity in the Old
Testament, including even here some promise of redemption, for
every name connotes the victory of Jehovah over some pagan
deity.[3] Yet the names create their major effect without recognition
of their specific biblical context: they locate the action in the world
of watery plains and flowery dales and vines and slimy pools.
Milton gives in this roll call a summation of human vice, depravity,
and irreligion, enacted in the landscapes of the earth.

It is the world we know, the world conveyed with equal vivid-

ness through the working of Milton's epic similes, whose subtle
inter-relations with his theme and action have been successfully
shown by many critical readings.[4] Thus in the great cluster of
comparisons (1.286–313) that comes just before the roll call of
devils, the name "*Vallombrosa*" adumbrates the valley of the
shadow of death; and "*Orion* arm'd" suggests the retributive jus-
tice of God, whose power is immediately after this displayed by
reference to the destruction of the Egyptian host in the Red Sea.
These are the tentacles of association and implication by which the
forces of evil are bound to earth; and these ties are essential in
maintaining the unity of the poem. Yet, curiously, these ties, hav-
ing performed their function, are not the matters that remain
foremost in mind after the reading: what vividly remains is the
sometimes tenuously relevant allusion to the actual world. It is not
some vague astronomer who views that moon resembling Satan's
shield: it is the famous "*Tuscan* Artist," viewing the moon "from
the top of *Fesole*, / Or in *Valdarno*." It is not simply some tall pine to
which Satan's spear is compared: it is a pine "Hewn on *Norwegian*
hills, to be the Mast / Of some great Ammiral." The fallen angels
on the lake are not simply compared with fallen autumnal leaves,
but with those leaves "that strow the Brooks / In *Vallombrosa*,
where th' *Etrurian* shades / High overarch't imbowr." These de-
tails cling to the mind long after the basis for their introduction
has been forgotten.

   The ultimate effect of all these similes is simple and sensuous:
they serve, like the roll call, to settle us within a world we know, as
in the brilliant simile that appears in book 2, just as the Satanic
parliament is adjourning:

> Thus they thir doubtful consultations dark
> Ended rejoycing in thir matchless Chief:
> As when from mountain tops the dusky clouds
> Ascending, while the North wind sleeps, o'respread
> Heavn's chearful face, the lowring Element
> Scowls ore the dark'nd lantskip Snow, or showre;
> If chance the radiant Sun with farewell sweet
> Extend his ev'ning beam, the fields revive,
> The birds thir notes renew, and bleating herds
> Attest thir joy, that hill and valley rings.   [2.486–95]

The action moves, suddenly, to the world we know; and thus the similes of the first two books come to include the varied landscapes of the earth, and all the world's activities. They include war and the literature of war, as when Satan stands before his host in pride and Milton compares this army with the "Heroic Race . . . That fought at *Theb's* and *Ilium*" and recalls everything that resounds

> In Fable or *Romance* of *Uthers* Son
> Begirt with *British* and *Armoric* Knights;
> And all who since, Baptiz'd or Infidel
> Jousted in *Aspramont* or *Montalban*,
> *Damasco*, or *Marocco*, or *Trebisond*,
> Or whom *Biserta* sent from *Afric* shore
> When *Charlemain* with all his Peerage fell
> By *Fontarabbia*.   [1.580–87]

The similes include the superstitions of the English peasant, with his moonlight elves, the barbarian hordes that overran the Roman Empire, and the great fleets that carry the world's trade.

To all these comparisons one must add the impact of those huge symbolic scenes of worldly activity: the building of the baroque palace of Pandaemonium; the council of Satan and his peers, with all the familiar political manoeuvres; and the arts and exploits displayed by the fallen angels after the council adjourns: feats of "Olympian Games," music of harp and song, philosophic reasoning "Of Providence, Foreknowledge, Will, and Fate," expeditions of discovery "O're many a Frozen, many a Fierie Alpe."[5]

These images, whether in epic simile or in literary allusion or in metaphorical tableau, succeed in creating a double action for the first four books. Literally, the action moves from Hell, through Chaos in book 2, to Heaven in book 3, and then at last to earth in book 4. But more deeply, more essentially, the action moves from the world we know toward the inward Light by which man is enabled to see a Paradise that lies within the center of the poem and within the center of the mind and memory. It is a brilliant poetical strategy. The eyes of the imagination, looking back over the first two books from the vantage point of Paradise, can see a thousand varied images of the fallen world, imbedded in a "darkness visible," licked on all sides by flame, " 'Twixt upper, nether, and surrounding Fires." Thus the literal, initial impact of these opening books becomes subtly inverted. Literally, we may say, these images from the fallen world are used to describe Hell and the fallen angels, to give them body and actuality. But essentially this whole fiery setting in Hell becomes a vast metaphor by which Milton interprets the actions of the world we know. It is from this world that Milton's bard performs a journey backward and inward, toward the Light.

Thus Milton's poem comes to assume a form that might be described in visual terms as a picture with a dark border but a bright center. The opening books and the closing books present the dark border of the world we know, in flames, in ruins: but the center holds, for at the center the voice of the bard has performed a journey backward and inward to discover the springing center of creativity described by Peter Sterry:

> as Paradise, so the *pure Image* of God in the Soul, seems to some not to be *lost* or destroyed, but *hid* beneath the ruins of the fall. Thus *Knowledge* springing in the Soul, seems to be a *remembrance*, the Life of all good, an awakening by reason of the primitive Image of pure Nature raising it self by degrees, and sparkling through the *Rubbish*, the confusions of the present state.[6]

II

Adam and Eve, as they walk through the fallen world "with wandring steps and slow," may remind us that there are in Milton's poem two other figures that move in a "solitarie way." The first of these is Satan,[7] who, after his expulsion from the Heavenly Paradise, makes what one might call a pseudo-pilgrimage from Hell to earth—and certainly in his case the word *expulsion* is appropriate:

> Him the Almighty Power
> Hurld headlong flaming from th' Ethereal Skie
> With hideous ruine and combustion down
> To bottomless perdition, there to dwell
> In Adamantine Chains and penal Fire,
> Who durst defie th' Omnipotent to Arms.   [1.44–49]

The contrast between the treatment of fallen angel and fallen
man could hardly be more pointed. Yet Satan undertakes a pil-
grimage of sorts, for Satan offers the pretense that he is making
his journey from Hell to earth in order that he may rejoice in the
wonderful works of the Lord—and this is the meaning of the
word *pilgrimage*: "a journey (usually of considerable duration)
made to some sacred place, as an act of religious devotion."[8] Such
is the motivation that Satan in book 3 offers to Uriel, the angel of
the sun, after Satan has adopted his disguise of a traveling cherub,
looking like an angel in a renaissance painting:

> Under a Coronet his flowing haire
> In curles on either cheek plaid, wings he wore
> Of many a colourd plume sprinkl'd with Gold,
> His habit fit for speed succinct, and held
> Before his decent steps a Silver wand.   [3.640–44]

It is a ludicrous and ironical scene, if we remember the enormous
size and baleful, blazing eyes of Satan in Hell. But here he has
"His habit fit for speed succinct"—his clothing is tied up or close-
fitting so that he can make all speed in his pilgrimage. And in this
neat and humble garb he addresses Uriel, in the very attitude of
Psalm 107:

> Unspeakable desire to see, and know
> All these his wondrous works, but chiefly Man,
> His chief delight and favour, him for whom
> All these his works so wondrous he ordaind
> Hath brought me from the Quires of Cherubim
> Alone thus wandring.   [3.662–67]

His way is bleakly solitary; yet he uses the language found in
Psalm 107 and in a score of other places in the psalms or other
books of the Bible where we find that phrase "wonderful works"
or "wondrous works." Uriel is taken in and replies happily, also
using the language and the lesson of the psalms:

> Faire Angel, thy desire which tends to know
> The works of God, thereby to glorifie
> The great Work-Maister, leads to no excess
> That reaches blame, but rather merits praise
> The more it seems excess, that led thee hither

> From thy Empyreal Mansion thus alone,
> To witness with thine eyes what some perhaps
> Contented with report heare onely in heav'n:
> For wonderful indeed are all his works,
> Pleasant to know, and worthiest to be all
> Had in remembrance alwayes with delight.   [3.694–704]

The last three lines contain a clear echo of Psalm 111, verse 4: "He hath made his wonderful works to be remembered." But of course Satan's pilgrimage is hardly one of love and delight, for, as we come to see, he envies the beauty of the earth and he sees "undelighted all delight" (4.286).

There is, however, another figure in this poem who walks a solitary way; he is introduced plainly at the opening of book 3, although in fact he has been with us from the very first line of the poem and he will remain until the last. He is the singer in darkness who tells this tale, and who, though blind, sees things invisible to mortal sight. Through his blindness, he says, he is now cut off from seeing the wondrous works of God, and yet with the eyes of the mind he makes his pilgrimage to paradise—revealing in his own response the delight in God's works that Satan cannot feel. It is a journey of remembrance, using all the aids that divine grace and human knowledge can provide, in accord with the principle of memory set forth by Augustine in his *De Trinitate*, as he takes pains to remove any implications of Platonic *anamnesis*. The human mind, Augustine explains,

> . . . has indeed no memory of its own blessedness; for that was once and is no longer, and the mind has totally forgotten it, so that no reminder can bring it back. It can only believe, on the faith of the Scriptures of its God, written by his prophet, the story of a happiness of paradise and the account conveyed in narrative form of man's original good and evil. But it has the memory of the Lord its God. For he ever is . . . And he is everywhere in his wholeness; so that in him the mind lives and moves and has its being, and therefore has the power to remember him. Not that it recollects having once known him in Adam, or anywhere else before this bodily life, or at its first making and planting in this body. Of none of these things has it any memory whatsoever: all of them are buried in oblivion. But it can be so reminded as to turn again unto the Lord, who is the light by which even in its turning away from him it was still somehow touched.[9]

Under the inspiration of this light a rising tide of irresistible creative power runs from the outset of book 3 on through the accounts of Paradise and Creation. The alternations here between the poet's praise and Satan's hatred create what might be called a battle between light and dark, framed between two angelic psalms in praise of Creation—psalms that foreshadow and complete the imperfect human apprehension of Paradise that lies between these two angelic poems. The first of these angelic hymns is that spoken by Uriel at the very close of book 3:

> I saw when at his Word the formless Mass,
> This worlds material mould, came to a heap:
> Confusion heard his voice, and wilde uproar
> Stood rul'd, stood vast infinitude confin'd;
> Till at his second bidding darkness fled,
> Light shon, and order from disorder sprung:
> Swift to thir several Quarters hasted then
> The cumbrous Elements, Earth, Flood, Aire, Fire,
> And this Ethereal quintessence of Heav'n
> Flew upward, spirited with various forms,
> That rowld orbicular, and turnd to Starrs
> Numberless, as thou seest, and how they move;
> Each had his place appointed, each his course,
> The rest in circuit walles this Universe.   [3.708–21]

The angel places the stress on order, rule, form, design, purpose, and thus on the wondrous power of God to control such plenitude, such rich fertility of being. Perfect beauty exists within a powerful design; the bounty of the material universe is beautiful only within an orderly and appointed plan.

Book 7 of *Paradise Lost* represents the detailed fulfillment of that vision, told by another angel, Raphael, whose long psalm of praise reveals all the richness of the six days of creation, and then concludes with these words:

> So Ev'n and Morn accomplish't the Sixt day:
> Yet not till the Creator from his work
> Desisting, though unwearied, up returnd
> Up to the Heav'n of Heav'ns his high abode,
> Thence to behold this new created World
> Th' addition of his Empire, how it shew'd
> In prospect from his Throne, how good, how faire,
> Answering his great Idea.   [7.550–57]

Milton is celebrating here the pure idea of beauty—the Platonic idea of Creation that existed in the mind of God and is now recreated here within the poet's mind and in our own minds, as we read. But this idea, in its full grandeur and power, Milton allows the two angels to tell; it is beyond human vision, except, of course, for a divinely inspired poet and prophet.

By contrast, in books 4 and 5, we watch the human singer attempting to grasp and to convey a glimpse of that divine idea of perfect beauty; we watch Adam's descendant, in his own imperfect way, attempting to fulfill the original impulse of joy and gratitude which Adam himself remembers as his earliest emotion:

> Thou Sun, said I, faire Light,
> And thou enlight'nd Earth, so fresh and gay,
> Ye Hills and Dales, ye Rivers, Woods, and Plaines
> And ye that live and move, fair Creatures, tell,
> Tell, if ye saw, how came I thus, how here?
> Not of my self; by some great Maker then,
> In goodness and in power praeeminent;
> Tell me, how may I know him, how adore,
> From whom I have that thus I move and live,
> And feel that I am happier then I know.   [8.273–82]

So every part in this portion of the poem, extending from the hymn to light at the outset of book 3 to this address to light by Adam in book 8, is held together by the voice of praise, which rises above the satanic voice of hate. This contrast is especially evident in book 4, as Adam's descendant, the modern singer, struggles to express his love and wonder at this answer to his journey of remembrance, while Satan becomes a foil to the redeemed vision of the bard, who now, overcome with delight and joy, is able to create a vision of the earthly Paradise out of his knowledge of the Bible and of human history and mythology.[10] Throughout we have a subtle distinction between Satan's point of view and that of the *human* viewer:

> Beneath him [Satan] with new wonder now he views
> To all delight of human sense expos'd
> In narrow room Natures whole wealth, yea more,
> A Heaven on Earth . . .   [4.205–08]

The wonder that Satan feels here is not the wonder of the psalms;

Satan feels amazement, astonishment, but not delight. Such delight is reserved for "human sense" in the vision of the redeemed man.[11]

But here the problem is, he goes on to say, how to deal with something that lies beyond the limits of art:

> But rather to tell how, if Art could tell,
> How from that Saphire Fount the crisped Brooks,
> Rowling on Orient Pearl and sands of Gold,
> With mazie error under pendant shades
> Ran Nectar, visiting each plant, and fed
> Flours . . .   [4.236–41]

What kind of flowers? Simply, "Flours worthy of Paradise." The poet at this point seems unable to imagine any further detail than this, and he ends his scene with a summary: "Thus was this place / A happy rural seat of various view." He has throughout proceeded by such humanizing touches: embedding this account in a specific geographical place amidst the events of human history; imaging the mount of Paradise as a sort of human organism with thirst and veins; and then, after admitting the limitations of art, coming to rest in the image of a happy English country estate—not, of course, an adequate image (nothing is), but at least it is a vestige of Paradise. It is something man has made by art out of nature—though here in Paradise is a scene that surpasses all the efforts of human imagination in gardening or architecture. The main effect is simply this: here is one of us trying to tell the story—impossible to tell.[12] "Not that fair field / Of *Enna*," nor "that sweet Grove / Of *Daphne* by *Orontes*," "nor that *Nyseian* Isle," "Nor where *Abassin* Kings thir issue Guard," none of these, says the singer, "might with this Paradise / Of *Eden* strive." The description does not matter. The very admission of the speaker's inadequacy indicates his gratitude for the gift. What matters is his love for the Creator as conveyed by his love for all created things. The expression of this love is the goal of the speaker's pilgrimage, and he conveys it all as he joins with Adam and Eve in their morning hymn in praise of the wondrous works of God:[13]

> These are thy glorious works Parent of good,
> Almightie, thine this universal Frame,

Thus wondrous fair; thy self how wondrous then!

. . . .

Joyn voices all ye living Souls, ye Birds,
That singing up to Heaven Gate ascend,
Bear on your wings and in your notes his praise;
Yee that in Waters glide, and yee that walk
The Earth, and stately tread, or lowly creep;
Witness if I be silent, Morn or Eeven,
To Hill, or Valley, Fountain, or fresh shade
Made vocal by my Song, and taught his praise.
Hail universal Lord, be bounteous still
To give us onely good; and if the night
Have gathered aught of evil or conceald,
Disperse it, as now light dispels the dark.   [5.153–55,197–208]

As long as a living poet can sing that song, the continuity between human beings, nature, and God will persist, and each human being may reach the proper goal of his solitary way—which is of course solitary only in the sense that it must be followed in accordance with each individual's deepest inner being. But Satan is truly solitary, cut off by his pride even from his followers: "this enterprize," he says as he departs from Hell upon his pilgrimage of hate, "this enterprize / None shall partake with me" (2.465–66). Milton's Hell is populated by individuals isolated by their crimes against Creation.

For humankind, in Milton's view, the way need not be solitary in this literal, single sense. The rich paradox and ambiguity of Milton's ending has nowhere been captured better than in William Blake's two great drawings of Adam and Eve leaving Paradise. In both drawings a sorrowing angel leads Adam and Eve forth gently by the hand. In both drawings Blake presents a sheet of flame behind the human pair, with terrifying effect. Hand in hand with the angel, Adam and Eve step forward toward us, their descendants. In one of Blake's drawings (see illustration here) they look upward, with considerable apprehension and uncertainty. In the other version (see frontispiece) they look downward at the serpent writhing between them on the ground, and their look is one of horror, fear, and repugnance. Will they go the way of Satan, they seem to be asking. Behind them, in both drawings, the four staring figures on horseback present no answer to that question. Their eyes are full of enigma and mystery. They look into a future that Adam and Eve must choose to make.

William Blake, "Expulsion from Paradise," Henry E. Huntington Library and Art Gallery.

PART III

Paradise Lost:
Figurations of Ovid

*In nova fert animus mutatas dicere formas
corpora; di, coeptis (nam vos mutastis et illas)
adspirate meis primaque ab origine mundi
ad mea perpetuum deducite tempora carmen!*

Metamorphoses, *1. 1–4*

CHAPTER 12

The
Anti-heroic
Epic

Milton's daughter Deborah, in her old age, recalled how she and
her sisters had read to their father the works of three favorite
authors. "Isaiah, Homer, and Ovid's metamorphoses," John Ward
reports, "were books, which they were often called to read to their
father; and at my desire she [Deborah] repeated a considerable
number of verses from the beginning of both these poets with
great readiness"—"both these poets" evidently meaning Homer
and Ovid, as distinguished from the prophet Isaiah.[1] The omis-
sion of Vergil is surprising, and it is quite possible that Deborah,
speaking many years after the event, simply failed to remember
the reading of Vergil.[2] Yet the thought comes to mind: has the
twelve-book division of *Paradise Lost* in the second edition led us
somewhat to overestimate the example of Vergil, in comparison
with Homer and Ovid? But it is enough to learn from Milton's
daughter that, during the years when Milton was composing his
epic, Ovid's *Metamorphoses* was still one of his best loved books.
With this thought in mind I should like to explore the possibility
that Ovid's example extended far beyond the many mythological

203

allusions and parallels,[3] that the presence of Ovid may be found both in minute figurations of detail and in the larger figurations of structure and form.

Over the past twenty years classical scholars have gradually recovered the view of Ovid's *Metamorphoses* which Quintilian seems to have taken as generally understood in the generation following Ovid's death: that his long poem belongs to the epic genre. Ovid's choice of hexameter verse, his frequent and overt echoes of Vergilian phrases and motifs, the vast scope of his poem, and his efforts to spin "an unbroken thread of verse" all point toward a poem of epic ambitions. Yet, if this *carmen perpetuum* is to be regarded as epic, our definition of the genre must be expanded far beyond the terms that will include the epics of Homer and Vergil. In what sense, for example, could the *Metamorphoses* be called "heroic"? It was a problem that clearly bothered Quintilian when, considering Ovid in the context of Homer, Vergil, Lucretius, Ennius, and Lucan, he found a quality that he called *lascivus*—playful, sportive, indecent, excessively ornamented—even when Ovid was writing in the heroic mode. "Ovid has a lack of seriousness even when he writes epic and is unduly enamoured of his own gifts," Quintilian said, but, he added, "portions of his work merit our praise." ("Lascivus quidem in herois quoque Ovidius et nimium amator ingenii sui, laudandus tamen in partibus.")[4] How can we account for the frequently witty episodes, the archness of tone, the showy rhetoric, and above all, how can the *Metamorphoses* be said to grow into a unity of action and theme?

Recent studies of Ovid have brought us a great way toward a solution of these problems. Brooks Otis, in his controversial, stimulating *Ovid as an Epic Poet*, finds a strong element of unity in Ovid's careful arrangement of his materials in parallel and contrasting "panels;" while Robert Coleman has stressed the subtlety of Ovid's "inset technique."[5] Charles Segal has found another element of unity in the skillfully patterned scenes of landscape, the *loci amoeni*, that occur throughout the poem.[6] And Karl Galinsky, among others, has found yet another kind of unity in the constant presence of the poet as narrator,[7] a presence culminating in the remarkable assertion of poetic immortality at the very close:

Iamque opus exegi, quid nec Iovis ira nec ignis
nec poterit ferrum nec edax abolere vetustas.
cum volet, illa dies, quae nil nisi corporis huius
ius habet, incerti spatium mihi finiat aevi:
parte tamen meliore mei super alta perennis
astra ferar, nomenque erit indelebile nostrum,
quaque patet domitis Romana potentia terris,
ore legar populi, perque omnia saecula fama,
siquid habent veri vatum praesagia, vivam.

And now my work is done, which neither the wrath of Jove, nor
fire, nor sword, nor the gnawing tooth of time shall ever be able to
undo. When it will, let that day come which has no power save over
this mortal frame, and end the span of my uncertain years. Still in
my better part I shall be borne immortal far beyond the lofty stars
and I shall have an undying name. Wherever Rome's power ex-
tends over the conquered world, I shall have mention on men's lips,
and, if the prophecies of bards have any truth, through all the ages
shall I live in fame. [15.871–end, trans. Miller]

The creative consciousness of man, Ovid seems to be saying, will
survive all his other achievements, even the achievements of em-
pire. All history, all myth, all religion will find the only hope of
immortality in the records left by the creative mind of the *vates*,
bard and prophet, who in this poem speaks the last word, *vivam*.[8]
Thus the entire immense narration of fifteen books is suffused
with the voice of the narrator, who weaves his stories together by
witty, sometimes absurdly contrived transitions, by constant repe-
tition and cross-reference, by holding story within story, by land-
scape, by chronology, by "panels," and by the continuous, over-
arching themes of love and passion: the *amor* of Venus, the *furor*
of Bacchus.[9] In order to see how the peculiar qualities of the
Metamorphoses may be reflected in *Paradise Lost*, it is essential here
to explore certain aspects of Ovid's poem.

I

One should first consider the problems raised by those "panels"
in which Ovid is clearly emulating the high heroic style of Homer
and Vergil, particularly in the narration of battles. As Otis has
shown, such episodes stand out with special emphasis, by being

flanked on either side by amatory panels which form a strong contrast in theme and manner with the heroic central panel. It may be that Otis goes too far in attempting to work out parallels and contrasts in detail, but it seems clear that significant arrangements in panels are being made, in the manner illustrated at the outset by the placing of the Phaeton episode:

Apollo-Daphne (*ab*)	Jupiter-Callisto (*b'c'*)
Phaeton Panel	
Jupiter-Io (*bc*)	Apollo-Coronis (*a'b'*)

As Otis explains, the episodes on either side of the Phaeton panel show a chiastic relation of *amores* by Jove and Apollo, an effect reinforced by cross-references within the episodes. Similarly, the epic tale of Perseus occupies a central position between two kinds of episodes:

Vengeance Episodes (Actaeon, Semele, Narcissus-Echo, Pentheus
   First Amatory Frame: Love-tales of the Minyades
      Epic Central Panel (Perseus-Andromeda-Phineus)
   Second Amatory Frame: Love-tales of the Muses (Proserpina)
Vengeance Episodes (Arachne, Niobe, Lycian Peasants, Marsyas)

Furthermore, Otis argues, the arrangements show more than simple symmetry: there is also progression: "Though the episodes after each central panel correspond to those before it, they also reveal a significant change, a change which almost insensibly prepares the reader for the next major section." In this way Ovid controls "the poem's restless variety and movement."[10]

This kind of arrangement finds a parallel in the tenth book of *Paradise Lost*, where, as I have shown in chapter 8, a long central panel of "heroic" action is set between panels with a different style and theme:

Condemnation	"Triumph" of	Reconciliation
of Adam and Eve	Sin, Death, and Satan	of Adam and Eve

That central panel contains an explicit, extended example of Ovidian metamorphosis—matching the other extended example of Ovidian metamorphosis: the transformation of Sin into a resemblance of Scylla in book 2. It seems quite possible that Milton would have sensed in the *Metamorphoses* something of the structure that Otis has discerned, for at least the placement of the heroic panels in Ovid is clear enough. But Milton's central panel here is mock-heroic, inflated, and in the end, deflated. Can Ovid's heroic panels be interpreted as similar parodies of the heroic manner?

A number of classical scholars have recently argued for this point of view.[11] The story of Phaeton (1.750–79,2.1–328), epic in its manner, hardly tells a story of heroic courage: the poor foolish boy is frightened to death. And there are elements in the Perseus panel that considerably deflate the epic pretensions of the episode.[12] For example, the heroic effect in Perseus' rescue of Andromeda is undercut by the way in which, as the monster approaches, Perseus pauses to strike a bargain with the parents! Indeed the following passage is full of phrases that detract from the heroic mode: Andromeda's parents offer wailings "befitting the occasion"—*dignos tempore fletus*: a proper introduction to a carefully negotiated bargain under stress:

> Then speaks the stranger: "There will be long time for weeping by and by; but time for helping is very short. If I sought this maid as Perseus, son of Jove and that imprisoned one whom Jove filled with his life-giving shower; if as Perseus, victor over Gorgon of the snaky locks, and as he who has dared to ride the winds of heaven on fluttering wings, surely I should be preferred to all suitors as your son-in-law. But now I shall try to add to these great gifts the gift of service, too, if only the gods will favour me. That she be mine if saved by my valour is my bargain." The parents accept the condition—for who would refuse?—and beg him to save her, promising him a kingdom as dowry in addition. [4.695–705, trans. Miller]

Quis enim dubitaret? The narrator's wry interjection stresses the absurdity of the situation, just as earlier his way of telling about Perseus' love at first sight gives a comic touch: "Smitten by the sight of her exquisite beauty, he almost forgot to move his wings in the air" (4.676–77, trans. Miller). Then Andromeda, despite her terrible situation, "bound by the arms to a rough cliff," follows the social customs for young maidens when Perseus speaks to her: "She was silent at first, for, being a maid, she did not dare address a man; she would have hidden her face modestly with her hands but that her hands were bound" (4.681–83, trans. Miller). This smacks of social comedy rather than epic. Then, after all this, the fight with the monster is presented in heroic style, full of similes and accompanied by applause from the gods above. With such a prelude, the heroic action is bound to seem a bit inflated, though still a good example of how well Ovid can imitate the heroic manner when he wishes to do so.

In book 5 the battle of Perseus with Phineus and his crowd is told in a curious way that seems to mix parody with serious epic effect. Phineus, after starting the fight, takes refuge behind the altar, while his followers die in ways that seem excessively ingenious, outdoing Homer:

> Then Phorbas of Syene, Metion's son, and Libyan Amphimedon, eager to join in the fray, slipped and fell in the blood with which all the floor was wet. As they strove to rise the sword met them, driven through the ribs of one and through the other's throat.
> But Eurytus, the son of Actor, who wielded a broad, two-edged battle-axe, Perseus did not attack with his hooked sword, but lifting high in both hands a huge mixing-bowl heavily embossed and ponderous, he hurled it crashing at the man. The red blood spouted forth as he lay dying on his back, beating the floor with his head. . . .
> Phineus did not dare to come to close combat with his enemy, but hurled his javelin. This was ill-aimed and struck Idas, who all to no purpose had kept out of the fight, taking sides with neither party. [5.74–91, trans. Miller]

Finally Perseus stands alone as "Phineus and a thousand followers close round him." Somehow this number is whittled down to two hundred, in ways that Ovid declines to explain, saying only: "It would take too long to tell the names of the rank and file who perished. Two hundred men survived the fight; two hundred saw the Gorgon and turned to stone." Then, amid the grotesque statues of his two hundred followers, the cowardly Phineus emerges begging for his life, and for an answer is allowed to decorate the house of Perseus's father-in-law: "I will make of you," says the hero, "a monument that shall endure for ages; and in the house of my father-in-law you shall always stand on view, that so my wife may find solace in the statue of her promised lord

. . . And now in marble was fixed the cowardly face, the suppliant look, the pleading hands, the whole cringing attitude" (5.157–58, 207–09,227–29,234–35, trans. Miller).

What shall one make of this mode of heroic story-telling? Is Ovid simply writing badly, because his heart is not in the heroics?[13] But it seems likely that so skillful a poet would be fully aware of his effects, and that he has deliberately composed this battle in a way that will not allow us to take it with complete solemnity. Readers sometimes speak of Ovid's addiction to cruelty, his delight in blood and brutality.[14] But is it not possible to find in these extravagant modes of death a revulsion against cruelty and brutal slaughter? No one stresses the horrors of war more fiercely than the advocates of peace.

The whole problem comes to a head in the battle of the Lapiths and the Centaurs, in book 12, where Ovid's invention of ingenious ways of slaughter goes far beyond anything in the Phineus episode and very far beyond anything in Homer or Vergil. Nestor, the narrator of this episode, is supposedly telling the tale of Caenis-Caeneus; but, with the garrulity of his old age, Nestor spends 250 lines on the battle of the Lapiths and the Centaurs before he comes at last to the role of Caeneus, whose burying under a mountain of uprooted trees forms the climax of several dozen bizarre ways of dying. These increase in ingenuity and in size of weapons used, from a mixing vat to a chandelier to a "huge altar, fire and all," "a threshold-stone, a weight for a team of oxen," an oak tree, a "rock torn from the mountain side," "a log which two yokes of cattle could scarce move" (12.260–61,281–82,341,432). Finally the Centaurs, frustrated and enraged (like Achilles) when Caeneus proves invulnerable to their spears and swords, respond to the cry: "Come then, let us heap stones and tree-trunks on him, mountains at a time! let's crush his stubborn life out with forests for our missiles!"

> saxa trabesque super totosque involvite montes
> vivacemque animam missis elidite silvis!   [12.507–08]

And so before long "Othrys was stripped of trees and Pelion had lost his shade" (513; trans. Miller).

Milton, then, could have found in Ovid considerable precedent for parodic treatment of heroic warfare, which some readers have come to see as an essential element in Milton's account of the war in Heaven.[15] As in Ovid, Milton's narration is done in a mixed style, for both poets are showing their skill in imitating Homer— while at the same time suggesting the ultimate futility of such heroic exploits. "Warr wearied hath perform'd what Warr can do," says Milton's God, as he watches the warring angels, in the climax of their fight:

> They pluckt the seated Hills with all thir load,
> Rocks, Waters, Woods, and by the shaggie tops
> Up lifting bore them in thir hands: Amaze,
> Be sure, and terrour seis'd the rebel Host,
> When coming towards them so dread they saw
> The bottom of the Mountains upward turn'd,
> Till on those cursed Engins triple-row
> They saw them whelmd, and all thir confidence
> Under the weight of Mountains buried deep . . .
> So Hills amid the Air encountered Hills
> Hurl'd to and fro with jaculation dire . . .   [6.644–52,64–65]

Milton's account of the hurling of hills is partly derived from Hesiod's account of the war against the Titans,[16] but we can hardly fail to think also of Ovid's account of the burying of Caeneus under that great mountain of uprooted trees. The difficulties that critics have had with Milton's war in Heaven are quite similar to those encountered by readers of Ovid's epic panels: is the writing simply awkward and inflated and unsure, or is it a deliberate creation of heroic parody? The taunting and jesting of Satan and Beelzebub, along with the throwing about of mountains, leads me to feel that the element of parody in Milton's war is paramount and holds the whole narration under control, as in Ovid. Consider too the strategic placing of Milton's war in Heaven: a long heroic panel set in between two episodes of pastoral: Paradise before, and the whole Creation after. Milton seems to have combined the device of the recollected narrative (modelled on the *Aeneid* and the *Odyssey*) with the Ovidian technique of placing episodes of heroic parody within contrasting panels— the structural principle followed by Milton in book 10.

Thus, throughout *Paradise Lost*, Milton has intermingled structures and motifs from what we may call the four great classical epics: the *Iliad*, the *Odyssey*, the *Aeneid*, and the *Metamorphoses*. Ovid's great poem, by its consistent transmutation of epic materials, has helped to show Milton many ways in which he might transcend the Aonian mount.

II

Milton's prologue to book 1 shows a subtle blending of motifs from the epics of Homer and Vergil, and properly so, for the first two books of *Paradise Lost* are predominantly modelled upon the heroic aspects of those three epics—along with the imitators of Homer and Vergil in the heroic mode: Claudian, Apollonius, Statius, Lucan, and others. Milton, then, begins his poem with transcendent emulation of that heroic mode. Yet echoes of Ovid, recessive at first, become more and more resonant, until, in the middle of book 2, Ovidian motifs begin openly and powerfully to mingle with the old heroic mode. Even in the opening prologue the shade of Ovid is perhaps not utterly absent, for he too, though not "first," taught "In the Beginning how the Heav'ns and Earth / Rose out of *Chaos*" (1.9–10). Ovid of course does not begin his epic *in medias res*: he begins at the beginning:

> Before the sea was, and the lands, and the sky that hangs over all, the face of Nature showed alike in her whole round, which state have men called chaos: a rough, unordered mass of things, nothing at all save lifeless bulk and warring seeds of ill-matched elements heaped in one. No sun as yet shone forth upon the world, nor did the waxing moon renew her slender horns; not yet did the earth hang poised by her own weight in the circumambient air, nor had the ocean stretched her arms along the far reaches of the lands. And, though there was both land and sea and air, no one could tread that land, or swim that sea; and the air was dark. No form of things remained the same; all objects were at odds, for within one body cold things strove with hot, and moist with dry, soft things with hard, things having weight with weightless things. [1.5–20, trans. Miller]

Milton's echoes of this passage, along with other aspects of Ovid's account of Creation, have been carefully studied by Davis Harding,[17] who shows that Milton is recalling Ovid's account in exact detail in books 2, 3, and 7 of *Paradise Lost*, especially in this passage of book 2:

> a dark
> Illimitable Ocean without bound,
> Without dimension, where length, breadth, and highth,
> And time and place are lost; where eldest Night
> And *Chaos*, Ancestors of Nature, hold
> Eternal *Anarchie*, amidst the noise
> Of endless warrs, and by confusion stand.
> For hot, cold, moist, and dry, four Champions fierce
> Strive here for Maistrie, and to Battel bring
> Thir embryon Atoms . . .
> Into this wilde Abyss,
> The Womb of nature and perhaps her Grave,
> Of neither Sea, nor Shore, nor Air, nor Fire,
> But all these in thir pregnant causes mixt
> Confus'dly, and which thus must ever fight,
> Unless th' Almighty Maker them ordain
> His dark materials to create more Worlds . . .
> [2.891–900,910–16]

One point should be added to Harding's fine analysis. As Satan flounders through this "crude consistence," Milton seems to have caught up the root meanings of *instabilis tellus*, *innabilis unda*, "earth on which one cannot stand," "wave in which one cannot swim" (*Met.* 1.16)—to create his parody of an heroic voyage, as Satan "swims or sinks, or wades, or creeps, or flyes" (2.950).

Paradise Lost moves overtly from Chaos to Creation at the juncture of books 2 and 3, as we travel with Satan through Chaos, and then, with the guidance of the bard, enter the realms of light. But we have in fact been reading a version of chaos and creation throughout book 1, as Satan and his crew at first lie "weltering," stunned, and without distinct form, in the burning lake, and Satan views his "dismal Situation waste and wilde":

> A Dungeon horrible, on all sides round
> As one great Furnace flam'd, yet from those flames
> No light, but rather darkness visible
> Serv'd only to discover sights of woe,
> Regions of sorrow, doleful shades, where peace
> And rest can never dwell, hope never comes
> That comes to all; but torture without end

> Still urges, and a fiery Deluge, fed
> With ever-burning Sulphur unconsum'd . . .   [1.60–69]

The ambiguous, shifting syntax, or melting down of syntax, seems in itself a version of chaos. "Dungeon horrible" may seem at first to be in apposition to "dismal Situation," but the phrase veers about to become the subject of the verb "flam'd"—or perhaps "flam'd" is a participle modifying "Furnace." "No light" seems to promise a firm start, but the phrase is quickly revised to "darkness visible," and both phrases then together become the implausible subject of "Serv'd only to discover." "Torture" seems at first to refer back to "comes," but then goes forward to link with "urges." This is the sort of shifting, evasive syntax that we have seen in book 10, as Sin and Death build their bridge across Chaos (10.299–304). But soon a sort of order begins to appear as Satan gradually brings his words into the form of an oration, pulls himself together to fly upward from this "abject" posture, marshalls his forces in military array, and finally builds the palace and capital of Pandaemonium. All this constitutes a process of mock-creation, factitious order arising out of chaos and assuming the illusion of a parliamentary government in Satan's "great Consult." Yet in the middle of book 2 this illusion of order gradually dissolves, ending with the revelation of a region worse than Chaos, for there is here not even the possibility of good:

> A Universe of death, which God by curse
> Created evil, for evil only good,
> Where all life dies, death lives, and nature breeds,
> Perverse, all monstrous, all prodigious things,
> Abominable, inutterable, and worse
> Then Fables yet have feign'd, or fear conceiv'd,
> *Gorgons* and *Hydra's*, and *Chimera's* dire.   [2.622–28]

Such is the close of the heroic promise delivered in the preceding portion of the first two books, an illusion delivered in terms inherited from Homer and Vergil, replete with heroic building (like that of Vergil's Carthage), heroic speeches of encouragement (such as Aeneas gave his forces after the great storm in Vergil's opening book), an heroic catalogue (of fallen angels), heroic debate of leaders, and the start of what seems to be an heroic voyage.

But now, with this breeding of monstrous things, worse than any known to Greek fables, the mode of narration undergoes a transformation into what I have called (in chapter 5) "panels of action"—a phrase that I had been using in lectures on Milton before coming upon Otis's use of the term "panels" to describe Ovid's mode of construction. This coincidence of terms may help to reinforce the validity of the analogies between Ovid and Milton that I am here proposing.

The presence of Ovid has been quite subdued in the first book and a half of Milton's poem, though sometimes emerging in collaboration with echoes of Homer and Vergil and others. Thus the reference to the myth of Typhon (1.199–200), and the following description of volcanic eruptions from mount Pelorus and mount Aetna (230–37) together evoke the memory of the stories told in Ovid about the giant Typhoeus (*Met.* 5.346–58); but Milton's description is equally indebted to Vergil's account of the rumblings of Aetna, caused by the writhings of another giant, Enceladus (*Aeneid* 3.570–82).

Another, and a more subtle blending of echoes, this time from Homer, Vergil, and Ovid, is found in Milton's account of Satan's spear:

> His Spear, to equal which the tallest Pine
> Hewn on *Norwegian* hills, to be the Mast
> Of some great Ammiral, were but a wand,
> He walkt with to support uneasie steps
> Over the burning Marle . . .   [1.292–96]

Homer describes the huge club or staff of Polyphemus, made of olive wood, and compares it with a mast (*Odyssey* 11.322); Vergil describes the Cyclops as carrying "the trunk of a pine tree to guide and support him walking" (*Aeneid* 3.659); while Ovid combines all these elements of Milton's comparison, as he speaks of "the pine tree, large enough to carry a ship's rigging, which served him as a staff" (13.782–83, trans. Innes). But these and similar allusions in book 1 of *Paradise Lost* are relatively slight, and while the change of the giant angels into less than smallest dwarfs at the close of book 1 may suggest a metamorphosis of the Ovidian kind, the only extended allusion to Ovid before the episode of Sin and Death is found near the middle of book 2:

> As when *Alcides* from *Oechalia* [18] Crown'd
> With conquest, felt th' envenom'd robe, and tore
> Through pain up by the roots *Thessalian* Pines,
> And *Lichas* from the top of *Oeta* threw
> Into th' *Euboic* Sea.   [2.542–46]

The details match closely the account of Ovid (9.136–219), thus preparing our minds for the drastic change in mode of narration marked by the strong reminiscences of Ovid that we find in the account of Sin and her transformation.

Milton turns our minds toward Ovid at the outset of the episode when he says:

> about her middle round
> A cry of Hell Hounds never ceasing bark'd
> With wide *Cerberean* mouths full loud . . .   [2.653–55]

for Ovid draws the analogy with Cerberus:

> et corpus quaerens femorum crurumque pedumque
> Cerbereos rictus pro partibus invenit illis . . .

and, feeling for her thighs, her legs, her feet, she finds in place of these only gaping dogs'-heads, such as a Cerberus might have. [14.64–65, trans. Miller]

Five lines later Milton's reference to the dogs that "Vex'd *Scylla* bathing in the sea" recalls an essential feature of Ovid's story: Scylla's habit of bathing in a certain cove, where jealous Circe caused the hideous change:

There was a little pool, curving into a deep bow, a peaceful place where Scylla loved to come . . . This pool, before the maiden's coming, the goddess befouls and tinctures with her baleful poisons. . . . Then Scylla comes and wades waist-deep into the water; when all at once she sees her loins disfigured with barking monster-shapes. [14.51–61, trans. Miller]

And the following allusion to the "Night-Hag" (662–66) recalls Circe's use of "Hecateia carmina" (14.44) while mixing her poisonous herbs. With our minds thus directed to Ovid's story, a subtle series of parallels may occur. Sin's narration of her own change reminds one of the several times Ovidian characters tell the tales of their own transformations, just as Glaucus, passionately in love with Scylla, here tells to her the story of his change from man into sea-god. Then at the close of Sin's narration her horrified efforts to flee from her fatal offspring Death may suggest Scylla's efforts to flee from the barking monsters: "And at the first, not believing that these are parts of her own body, she flees in fear and tries to drive away the boisterous, barking things. But what she flees she takes along with her" (14.61–63, trans. Miller).

> At last this odious offspring whom thou seest
> Thine own begotten, breaking violent way
> Tore through my entrails, that with fear and pain
> Distorted, all my nether shape thus grew
> Transform'd: but he my inbred enemie
> Forth issu'd, brandishing his fatal Dart
> Made to destroy: I fled, and cry'd out *Death*;
> Hell trembl'd at the hideous Name, and sigh'd
> From all her Caves, and back resounded *Death*.
> I fled, but he pursu'd . . .   [2.781–90]

The repetition is a characteristic device of Ovidian rhetoric:[19] thus at the end of the story of Narcissus and Echo we find a similar matching of words at the ends of the lines:

> indoluit, quotiensque puer miserabilis "eheu"
> dixerat, haec resonis iterabat vocibus "eheu";
> cumque suos manibus percusserat ille lacertos,
> haec quoque reddebat sonitum plangoris eundem.

and as often as the poor boy says "Alas!" again with answering utterance she cries "Alas!" and as his hands beat his shoulders she gives back the same sounds of woe. [3.495–98, trans. Miller]

The reminiscences of Ovid here are thus dominant (though they are combined with many other echoes, from Spenser, Homer, and Vergil), and they may lead us on to feel that echoes of the *Metamorphoses*, in story, in rhetoric, in structure, are helping to weave Milton's poem into a *carmen perpetuum*, interfused with echoes of other epics, ancient and modern. Ovid's voice is only one of many voices that we hear within Milton's "various style," but I believe that it deserves to be recognized as equal in importance to any other voice from Greek or Roman poetry.

So now, as Satan moves into Chaos, Ovid's account of Chaos provides the ground, *instabilis*, *innabilis*, upon which Milton inter-

weaves his many echoes of earlier heroic poems by Homer, Vergil,
Lucan, Statius, Apollonius Rhodius, and Spenser—all cohering
within a context that quite diminishes the heroic effect. For Satan
is utterly lost, as he half admits to Chaos:

> I come no Spie,
> With purpose to explore or to disturb
> The secrets of your Realm, but by constraint
> Wandring this darksome desart, as my way
> Lies through your spacious Empire up to light,
> Alone, and without guide, half-lost, I seek
> What readiest path leads where your gloomie bounds
> Confine with Heav'n . . .   [2.970–77]

And from Chaos he receives a diminishing answer: "I know thee,
stranger, who thou art" (990)—words that echo a biblical passage
in which Jesus casts out a devil who says, "I know thee who thou
art" (Luke 4:33–36): "And they were all amazed, and spake
among themselves, saying, What a word is this! for with authority
and power he commandeth the unclean spirits, and they come
out." This is the authority and power that have caused the rout
that Chaos now describes:

> I know thee, stranger, who thou art,
> That mighty leading Angel, who of late
> Made head against Heav'ns King, though overthrown.
> I saw and heard, for such a numerous host
> Fled not in silence through the frighted deep
> With ruin upon ruin, rout on rout,
> Confusion worse confounded . . .   [2.990–96]

With all these implications of Satan's weakness, the heroic
echoes turn to parody, in another example of a panel of "heroic"
style, set in between two panels of quite different mode: the al-
legorical, metamorphic panel of Satan's encounter with Sin and
Death, and the prologue to book 3, where the bard, far from
Satan's "weather-beaten" state, revisits "safe" the "holy light,"

> Escap't the *Stygian* Pool, though long detain'd
> In that obscure sojourn, which in my flight
> Through utter and through middle darkness borne
> With other notes then to th' *Orphean* Lyre
> I sung of *Chaos* and *Eternal Night* . . .   [3.14–18]

"With other notes," because the Orphean lyre represents creative power, whereas Milton's first two books, by Milton's phrasing here completely included within the realm of Chaos and Eternal Night, have presented a process of illusory creation.[20] What true creation means we are soon to learn, when we come to view the panels of Paradise.

Pastoral Love: Versions and Subversions

Thus we are prepared for a mutation from the old heroic mode into a new mode composed by one who, like Ovid, is "Not sedulous by Nature to indite / Warrs, hitherto the onely Argument / Heroic deem'd" (9.27–29). This new mutation moves on in book 4 to tell of the first human lovers; and that love-tale begins with an allusion to Ovidian myth. When Eve tells to Adam the story of her first awakening, and of her vision of herself reflected in a lake, the reminiscence of Ovid's story of Narcissus has been felt by every reader.[1] The tale in Milton is all the more Ovidian because Milton sets it in the kind of *locus amoenus* that Ovid so often presents as the scene of a metamorphosis:

> That day I oft remember, when from sleep
> I first awak't, and found my self repos'd
> Under a shade on flours, much wondring where
> And what I was, whence thither brought, and how.
> Not distant far from thence a murmuring sound
> Of waters issu'd from a Cave and spread
> Into a liquid Plain, then stood unmov'd
> Pure as th' expanse of Heav'n; I thither went
> With unexperienc't thought, and laid me downe

On the green bank, to look into the cleer
Smooth Lake, that to me seemd another Skie.
As I bent down to look, just opposite,
A Shape within the watry gleam appeerd
Bending to look on me . . .   [4.449–62]

There was a clear pool with silvery bright water, to which no
shepherds ever came, or she-goats feeding on the mountain-side, or
any other cattle; whose smooth surface neither bird nor beast nor
falling bough ever ruffled. Grass grew all around its edge, fed by
the water near, and a coppice that would never suffer the sun to
warm the spot. Here the youth, worn by the chase and the heat, lies
down, attracted thither by the appearance of the place and by the
spring. While he seeks to slake his thirst another thirst springs up,
and while he drinks he is smitten by the sight of the beautiful form
he sees. He loves an unsubstantial hope and thinks that substance
which is only shadow. [*Met.* 3.407–17, trans. Miller]

Narcissus pines away with vain desire, but Eve, with her thought
now less "unexperienc't," yields to Adam's call and touch, sees and
knows his grace and wisdom, using her reason to make a choice:
the poem's first evidence (as Burden has well said) of the human
workings of the freedom of the will.[2]

Yet how "frail" its proper workings may be is at once suggested
by a glimpse of Eve's voluptuous beauty and by an ironical allu-
sion to two deities whose jealous quarrels continually disrupt the
world of Ovidian myth:

                         half her swelling Breast
Naked met his under the flowing Gold
Of her loose tresses hid: he in delight
Both of her Beauty and submissive Charms
Smil'd with superior Love, as *Jupiter*
On *Juno* smiles, when he impregns the Clouds
That shed *May* Flowers; and press'd her Matron lip
With kisses pure . . .   [4.495–502]

It is a happy scene, but we know the escapades and impregnations
that lie behind that jovial smile.

Satan then shatters the peaceful scene with his long soliloquy of
envy, but, after the angelic guard is seen alert to aid, we return to
the peaceful scene, and Eve sings her echoing song of love, a
remarkable show-piece that concentrates in sixteen lines certain

techniques of repetition and reversal that are reminiscent of the
Ovidian style:

> Sweet is the breath of morn, her rising sweet,
> With charm of earliest Birds; pleasant the Sun
> When first on this delightful Land he spreads
> His orient Beams, on herb, tree, fruit, and flour,
> Glistring with dew; fragrant the fertil earth
> After soft showers; and sweet the coming on
> Of grateful Eevning milde, then silent Night
> With this her solemn Bird and this fair Moon,
> And these the Gemms of Heav'n, her starrie train:
> But neither breath of Morn when she ascends
> With charm of earliest Birds, nor rising Sun
> On this delightful land, nor herb, fruit, floure,
> Glistring with dew, nor fragrance after showers,
> Nor grateful Evening mild, nor silent Night
> With this her solemn Bird, nor walk by Moon,
> Or glittering Starr-light without thee is sweet.   [4.641–56]

Brief examples of this sort of repetitive technique are scattered
throughout the *Metamorphoses*.[3] One of the most striking occurs
only a few hundred lines after the tale of Narcissus, a position
especially suggestive, since the tale of Narcissus is set within the
tale of Echo; and thus a virtuoso series of echo-words and phrases
abound on either side of the Narcissus panel. Then early in book
4 Ovid tells another story of passionate love, the tale of Salmacis
and Hermaphroditus, again associated with a beautiful pool in a
typical Ovidian landscape:

> Here he saw a pool of water crystal clear to the very bottom. No
> marshy reeds grew there, no unfruitful swamp-grass, nor spiky
> rushes; it is clear water. But the edges of the pool are bordered with
> fresh grass, and herbage ever green. A nymph dwells in the pool,
> one that loves not hunting, nor is wont to bend the bow or strive
> with speed of foot. She only of the naiads follows not in swift Di-
> ana's train. Often, 'tis said, her sisters would chide her: 'Salmacis,
> take now either hunting-spear or painted quiver, and vary your
> ease with the hardships of the hunt.' But she takes no hunting-
> spear, no painted quiver, nor does she vary her ease with the hard-
> ships of the hunt; but at times she bathes her shapely limbs in her
> own pool; often combs her hair with a boxwood comb, often looks
> in the mirror-like waters to see what best becomes her. Now,

wrapped in a transparent robe, she lies down to rest on the soft grass
or the soft herbage. Often she gathers flowers; and on this occasion,
too, she chanced to be gathering flowers when she saw the boy and
longed to possess what she saw. [4.297–316, trans. Miller]

Salmacis, like Eve, uses the waters as a mirror; and like Eve she
would rather carry flowers than weapons. In this context, the
technique of negative repetition in the middle of the passage
becomes especially significant for Eve's love-song, with its turn to
"nor," "nor":

> "Salmaci, vel iaculum vel pictas sume pharetras
> et tua cum duris venatibus otia misce!"
> nec iaculum sumit nec pictas illa pharetras,
> nec sua cum duris venatibus otia miscet . . .   [4.306–09]

At the same time, we might recall the words that Vertumnus
speaks to Pomona in Ovid:

> tu primus et ultimus illi
> ardor eris, solique suos tibi devovet annos.
> adde, quod est iuvenis, quod naturale decoris
> munus habet formasque apte fingetur in omnes,
> et quod erit iussus, iubeas licet omnia, fiet.
> quid, quod amatis idem, quod, quae tibi poma coluntur,
> primus habet laetaque tenet tua munera dextra!
> sed neque iam fetus desiderat arbore demptos
> nec, quas hortus alit, cum sucis mitibus herbas
> nec quicquam nisi te . . .

You will be his first love and his last, and to you alone he will
devote his life. Consider also that he is young, blest with a native
charm, can readily assume whatever form he will, and what you bid
him, though without stint you bid, he will perform. Moreover your
tastes are similar, and the fruit which you so cherish he is the first to
have and with joyful hands he lays hold upon your gifts. But
neither the fruit of your trees, nor the sweet, succulent herbs which
your garden bears, nor anything at all does he desire save you
alone. [14.682–91, trans. Miller]

Again we have the turn near the close, with the use of "neque,"
"nec," "nec"; while the ending, *nec quicquam nisi te*—"nothing
without you"—in the context of fruit and herbs, provides a par-
ticularly close and suggestive parallel.

But the deeper roots of Eve's technique of repetition lie in the pastoral tradition, as my colleague Gordon Williams has pointed out to me. At the close of Vergil's seventh eclogue—from which Milton took the motto for his volume of 1645—we find an example of this technique along with the ancient pastoral *topos* in which the "sweetness" of herb, tree, fruit, and flower arises from or is surpassed by the beloved:

> Corydon
> Populus Alcidae gratissima, vitis Iaccho,
> formosae myrtus Veneri, sua laurea Phoebo;
> Phyllis amat corylos; illas dum Phyllis amabit,
> nec myrtus vincet corylos, nec laurea Phoebi.
> Thyrsis
> Fraxinus in silvis pulcherrima, pinus in hortis,
> populus in fluviis, abies in montibus altis;
> saepius at si me, Lycida formose, revisas,
> fraxinus in silvis cedat tibi, pinus in hortis.

> Hercules loves poplars best of all; Bacchus prefers the vine; Venus, the Queen of Beauty, loves the myrtle best; and Apollo his own bays. Phyllis is fond of hazels. As long as Phyllis likes them best, neither the myrtle nor Apollo's bays shall take a higher place than hazels.
> The ash in forests is the loveliest tree; the pine in gardens; the poplar by the river's bank; and the fir-tree on the mountain-heights. But if you, my handsome Lycidas, will spend more time with me, the ash in her own forest and the pine-tree in the garden must give place to you.   [7.61–68; trans. Rieu]

The hints of Vergilian pastoral in Eve's song, perhaps assisted by the reference to Lycidas, would not have come to Milton unmediated. Gordon Williams has also pointed out some striking parallels in Calpurnius Siculus, probably writing in Nero's reign, and in Nemesianus, of the third century A.D.—poets whose eclogues were well known in the Renaissance, and who carried on the Vergilian tradition while combining it with the intricate rhetoric of Ovid.[4] Thus in the third eclogue of Calpurnius we hear another Lycidas singing these lines as part of a long love-song for Phyllis:

> te sine, vae misero, mihi lilia nigra videntur
> nec sapiunt fontes et acescunt vina bibenti.
> at si tu venias, et candida lilia fient
> et sapient fontes et dulcia vina bibentur.

> ille ego sum Lycidas, quo te cantante solebas
> dicere felicem . . .

Without you (poor wretch that I am!), lilies seem black to me, fountains lose their taste and wine as I drink turns sour. But if you come, lilies will grow white again, fountains taste aright and wine be sweet to drink. I am that Lycidas at whose singing you used to declare your joy . . .   [3.51–56; trans. Duff][5]

Then in the second eclogue of Nemesianus we find an imitation of both Calpurnius and Vergil which strikes even nearer to the love-song of Eve:

> te sine, vae misero, mihi lilia fusca videntur
> pallentesque rosae nec dulce rubens hyacinthus,
> nullos nec myrtus nec laurus spirat odores.
> at si tu venias, et candida lilia fient
> purpureaeque rosae, et dulce rubens hyacinthus;
> tunc mihi cum myrto laurus spirabit odores.
> nam dum Pallas amat turgentes unguine bacas,
> dum Bacchus vites, Deo sata, poma Priapus,
> pascua laeta Pales, Idas te diligit unam.

Without you (poor wretch that I am!), lilies seem grey to me and roses pale, and the hyacinth has no sweet blush, nor do myrtle or laurel breathe any fragrance; but if you come, lilies will grow white once more, the roses be red, and the hyacinth regain its sweet blush; then for me will laurel with myrtle breathe fragrance forth. For while Pallas loves the olive-berries that swell with fatness, while Bacchus loves the vines, Deo her crops, Priapus his fruits and Pales the joyous pastures, Idas loves you alone.   [2.44–52; trans. Duff][6]

"Without thee"—so pastoral art lives in Milton's Paradise where the poet's vision shows the possibility of recovering the pristine love of nature, man, and God that stands as the healing center for mankind's heavy loss.

An interesting rhetorical analogy of another kind occurs in one of the best known passages in Ovid, the account of how the trees gather round at the song of Orpheus. This famous passage, like Eve's love-song, covers sixteen lines, and like Eve's song it is divided into sections of nine and seven lines, with a reversal of syntax at the tenth line:

> umbra loco venit: non Chaonis afuit arbor,
> non nemus Heliadum, non frondibus aesculus altis,

nec tiliae molles, nec fagus et innuba laurus,
et coryli fragiles et fraxinus utilis hastis
enodisque abies curvataque glandibus ilex
et platanus genialis acerque coloribus inpar
amnicolaeque simul salices et aquatica lotos
perpetuoque virens buxum tenuesque myricae
et bicolor myrtus et bacis caerula tinus.
vos quoque, flexipedes hederae, venistis et una
pampineae vites et amictae vitibus ulmi
ornique et piceae pomoque onerata rubenti
arbutus et lentae, victoris praemia, palmae
et succincta comas hirsutaque vertice pinus,
grata deum matri, siquidem Cybeleius Attis
exuit hac hominem truncoque induruit illo.   [10.90–105]

A literal translation, adapting the Loeb version, will make clear
the shift that occurs in the tenth line of this catalogue:

shade came to the place: nor was the Chaonian tree absent, nor the
grove of the Heliades, nor the oak with its deep foliage, nor the soft
linden, nor the beech and the virgin laurel, and the brittle hazel,
and the ash suitable for spear-shafts, and the smooth silver-fir, and
the ilex bending with acorns, and the pleasant plane-tree, and the
many-colored maple, and likewise the river-haunting willows, and
the lotus, lover of pools, and the ever-green boxwood, and the
slender tamarisk, and the double-colored myrtle, and the viburnum
with its dark blue berries.

"After this amazing list of 18 trees," says Anderson, "Ovid stops to
take a breath, then plunges on. He begins this second sequence
with an apostrophe to ivy and a unique epic epithet *flexipedes*":[7]

You also, pliant-footed ivy, came, and along with you tendrilled
grapes, and the elm-trees draped with vines and the mountain-ash,
and the pitch-pines, and the wild strawberry-tree loaded with ruddy
fruit, and the pliant palm, prize of victory, and the bare-trunked
pine with broad leafy top, pleasing to the mother of the gods, since
Attis, dear to Cybele, exchanged for this his human form and stif-
fened in its trunk.

The catalogue, the dimensions of the piece, and the shift in
movement at line ten all suggest a tantalizing parallel—the kind of
creative imitation that the renaissance school-boy was trained to
make, adapting the devices of Ovidian rhetoric to a quite different
subject from the original.[8] No single passage in ancient poetry,

then, lies behind the remarkable technique of Eve's love-song; it is a complex blending of many pastoral and Ovidian devices.

These Ovidian echoes serve as a reminder that a host of other echoes run throughout book 4 and the first half of book 5—the "pastoral" scenes of *Paradise Lost*. Brooks of nectar run over sands of gold (4.237–40), reminding us of Ovid's *saturnia regna* (1.111) and of his story concerning Midas and the river Pactolus (11.142–45). There are "Groves whose rich Trees wept odorous Gumms and Balme" (4.248), reminding us of the weeping tree that was Myrrha and the weeping trees that were the Heliades (*Met.* 2.340–66; 10.489–502). And the *locus amoenus* gathers up details from a dozen Ovidian settings:

> Another side, umbrageous Grots and Caves
> Of coole recess, o're which the mantling Vine
> Layes forth her purple Grape, and gently creeps
> Luxuriant; mean while murmuring waters fall
> Down the slope hills, disperst, or in a Lake,
> That to the fringed Bank with Myrtle crownd,
> Her chrystall mirror holds, unite thir streams.   [4.257–63]

Meanwhile "Universal *Pan* / Knit with the *Graces* and the *Hours* in dance / Led on th' Eternal Spring" (4.266–68), evoking the legend of Zephyrus and Chloris-Flora referred to overtly at the outset of book 5 (16)—the legend made famous by Botticelli and told by Ovid in his *Fasti* (5.195–220). The thought of eternal spring leads on to that scene in Ovid near the walls of Enna where there is a lake named Pergus—a scene of *perpetuum ver*:

> A ring of trees encircles the pool, clothing the lakeside all around, and the leaves of the trees shelter the spot from Phoebus' rays, like a screen. Their boughs afford cool shade, and the lush meadow is bright with flowers. There it is always spring. In this glade Proserpine was playing, picking violets or shining lilies. With childlike eagerness she gathered the flowers into baskets and into the folds of her gown, trying to pick more than any of her companions. Almost at one and the same time, Pluto saw her, and loved her, and bore her off—so swift is love. [5.388–96, trans. Innes]

Dis (to use Ovid's term) was there, we may recall, because the heavings of the giant Typhoeus, described by Ovid a few lines

earlier, had made him worry that his nether kingdom might be
opened to the light, and therefore he had come up above ground
to inspect the surface of Sicily. So we come to the well-known
passage in Milton:

> Not that faire field
> Of *Enna*, where *Proserpin* gathring flours
> Her self a fairer Floure by gloomie *Dis*
> Was gatherd, which cost *Ceres* all that pain
> To seek her through the world . . .   [4.268–72]

But all that pain of Ceres is not told in the *Metamorphoses*: it is told
in Ovid's other, and longer version of the story in his *Fasti*
(4.420–620). Thus both of Ovid's great treasuries of ancient myth
tend to cohere within the context of Milton's allusions, as in the
earlier reference to the legend of Chloris. This allusion to the
rape of Proserpine is the most significant mythological reference
in the entire fourth book, perhaps in the entire poem, since it
foreshadows the seduction of Eve by the Prince of the underworld
and links directly with the scene in book 9, where, shortly after the
cluster of allusions to Pomona, Ceres and Proserpine (9.393–96),
Satan in the form of the serpent spies Eve alone in a "spot more
delicious" than any *locus amoenus* ever before described:

> Veil'd in a Cloud of Fragrance, where she stood,
> Half spi'd, so thick the Roses bushing round
> About her glowd, oft stooping to support
> Each Flour of slender stalk, whose head though gay
> Carnation, Purple, Azure, or spect with Gold,
> Hung drooping unsustained, them she upstaies
> Gently with Mirtle band, mindless the while,
> Her self, though fairest unsupported Flour,
> From her best prop so farr, and storm so nigh.   [9.425–33]

In book 4, after the long imitation of the Narcissus tale and the
love-song of Eve, we come to the "blissful bower," so different
from Spenser's Bower of Bliss; a bower woven together out of
flowers and shrubs filled with a mythological redolence: the laurel
of Daphne, the myrtle of Venus, and other plants and flowers
associated with Ovidian metamorphoses: violet, crocus, and

hyacinth.[9] These associations are then reinforced and coalesced as Milton sums up the Ovidian atmosphere:

> In shadier Bower
> More sacred and sequesterd, though but feignd,
> *Pan* or *Silvanus* never slept, nor Nymph,
> Nor *Faunus* haunted. Here in close recess
> With Flowers, Garlands, and sweet-smelling Herbs
> Espoused *Eve* deckt first her Nuptial Bed . . .   [4.705–10]

Thus too the "silvan lodge" where Adam and Eve receive the angel "like *Pomona's* Arbour smil'd / With flourets deck't and fragrant smells" (5.378–79), while the reference to Pomona links with the earlier passage in book 5 where Adam and Eve hasten "to thir mornings rural work"

> Among sweet dewes and flours; where any row
> Of Fruit-trees overwoodie reachd too farr
> Thir pamperd boughes, and needed hands to check
> Fruitless imbraces: or they led the Vine
> To wed her Elm; she spous'd about him twines
> Her mariageable arms, and with her brings
> Her dowr th' adopted Clusters, to adorn
> His barren leaves.   [5.212–19]

The last five lines here adapt the passage in Ovid where Vertumnus, disguised as an old woman, attempts to win Pomona's love:

> There was an elm tree opposite, a lovely sight to see, with its bunches of shining grapes, and this the god praised, and its companion vine no less. 'But,' he said, 'if this tree trunk stood by itself, and was not wedded to the vine, it would be of no interest to anybody, except for its leaves. Moreover, the vine is supported by the elm to which it has been united, whereas if it had not been so married, it would lie trailing on the ground. And yet you are unmoved by the example of this tree! You shun marriage, and do not care to wed.' [14.661–68, trans. Innes]

The earlier part of Milton's passage echoes Ovid's preceding account of Pomona's cultivation of her fruit-trees, as with her pruning knife "she would cut away growth that was too luxurious, and prune back branches that were spreading in different directions" ("qua modo luxuriem premit et spatiantia passim / bracchia conpescit": 14.629–30, trans. Innes).

All these allusions to Ovidian myth in the pastoral scenes of *Paradise Lost* combine to warn of the imminence of change in Paradise: for Ovid himself has adapted the *locus amoenus* from the tradition of pastoral poetry, and then has used it (as Charles Segal has shown)[10] to invert, or subvert, the pastoral values of Theocritus and Vergil. In the idylls and eclogues the pastoral settings of pools, streams, fountains, caves, flowers, grass, and trees provide the cool recesses and shady bowers from which the pastoral vision can view the troubles of the world from a distance, in a purifying perspective. But in Ovid, these peaceful settings are deceptive haunts of violence; their *otium* invites the sexual ravages of self-love, rape or seduction by the gods; even Vertumnus is "ready to use force" (14.770). Pastoral *otium* creates a sense of security within the fragile peace of the pastoral moment, but Ovidian *otium* creates a sense of underlying, uncontrollable danger arising from the passionate energies that dominate the earth.

The deceptive beauty of these Ovidian scenes is summed up in the horror of Dryope's innocent plucking of the water-lotus—the plant in whose shape the nymph Lotis had found refuge "while fleeing from Priapus' vile pursuit" (9.346–48; trans. Miller). The transformation of Dryope into a tree occurs beside "a pool whose shelving banks take the form of sloping shores, the top of which a growth of myrtle crowns" ("est lacus, adclivis devexo margine formam / litoris efficiens, summum myrteta coronant": 9.334–35)—lines that Milton seems to evoke in a passage quoted earlier (4.260–63). The fatal flower is full of beautiful promise: "Near the margin of the pool a plant of the water-lotus grew full of bright blossoms, the harbingers of fruit. To please her little son the mother plucked some of these blossoms, and I was in the act to do the same [says her sister] when I saw drops of blood falling from the flowers and the branches shivering with horror" (9.340–45; trans. Miller). Thus Ovid's persistent subversion of pastoral values serves as a warning that the threat of destructive power lurks everywhere in Milton's Eden.

The illustration here reproduced was designed by Carlotta Petrina as a frontispiece for book 4 of *Paradise Lost;* but it could serve almost as well as an illustration for book 4 of Ovid's *Metamorphoses,* with its tale of Salmacis and Hermaphroditus. The artist has

caught the Ovidian implications of Milton's pastoral. The female figure making the advances could almost be the nymph Salmacis, and the passive, bemused male figure staring outward could almost be the unresponsive Hermaphroditus: "When the nymph begged and prayed for at least a sister's kiss, and was in [the] act to throw her arms round his snowy neck, he cried: 'Have done, or I must flee and leave this spot—and you'" (4.334–36). One can glimpse here also something like the mulberry tree, "full of snow-white berries," beside the "cool spring" in the tale of Pyramus and Thisbe (4.89–90), while the varied flowers (including suggestions of the water-lotus?), birds, and animals might be seen as allusions to the metamorphoses that so often overtake the mortal lovers in Ovid's myths of passion. And it is such passion—of revenge, ambition, envy, and love—that will destroy this pastoral of Paradise.

These allusions to Ovidian myth, then, are far more than decorations, or acknowledgment of an epic predecessor; they lie at the very heart of Milton's purpose: to show how this greatest of changes brought in all other forms of change and changing forms, and then to show how Ovid's sense of endless change may be converted into change that has a higher, a teleological design.

CHAPTER 14

The
Ultimate
Design

Awareness of Milton's ultimate design is maintained throughout *Paradise Lost* by the voice of the bard, the narrator, or the authorial presence, as it is sometimes called—that presence recognized in so many recent studies and frequently remarked in the preceding section of this book.[1] Such a presence, so different from the objectivity of Homer, may in part derive from Vergil's "subjective style" in the *Aeneid*. But the presence of Vergil's narrator is subtle and usually tacit, though now and then, infrequently, emerging in open exclamations of sympathy or revulsion. Ovid appears to have picked up this mode of presence from Vergil, and to have carried it several steps further in the *Metamorphoses*.[2] It may well be that Ovid's example encouraged the epic poets of the Renaissance to carry the process of authorial intervention even further, reaching a final stage in the remarkably long interventions of Camoens, Spenser, and Milton.[3] Ovid's interventions are usually quite brief, but they are persistent and pervasive in a way that may remind us of the constant presence of the narrative voice in *Paradise Lost*. A few examples from Ovid may help to suggest a general similarity in technique, while illustrating the differences in tone and attitude.

In the tale of Deucalion and Pyrrha the voice of the narrator at first emerges almost imperceptibly as Deucalion suggests that they should throw the stones:

> Coniugis augurio quamquam Titania mota est,
> spes tamen in dubio est: adeo caelestibus ambo
> diffidunt monitis; sed quid temptare nocebit?

Although Pyrrha is moved by her husband's surmise, yet hope still wavers; so distrustful are they both as to the heavenly command. But what harm will it do to try? [1.395–97, trans. Miller]

This resembles the Vergilian mode of presence, entering into the minds of the characters and expressing their inmost thoughts. Then Ovid returns to objective narration, but for only two lines:

> descendunt: velantque caput tunicasque recingunt
> et iussos lapides sua post vestigia mittunt.
> saxa (quis hoc credat, nisi sit pro teste vetustas?)
> ponere duritiem coepere suumque rigorem
> mollirique mora mollitaque ducere formam.

They go down, veil their heads, ungird their robes, and throw stones behind them just as the goddess had bidden. And the stones—who would believe it unless ancient tradition vouched for it?—began at once to lose their hardness and stiffness, to grow soft slowly, and softened to take on form. [1.398–402]

The skeptical interjection, with the appeal to tradition, is constantly recurring in the poem, sometimes in a phrase: "si modo credimus," "si credere dignum est," "prior edidit aetas," "fama est," or simply a word such as "dicitur," "fertur," "ferunt," "memorant," or "dicunt"—all meaning something like "they say"—"I don't myself vouch for it, but this is what I have heard." Such words and phrases have a great cumulative effect in creating the impression of a single controlling presence.

Then, after this strong interjection, Ovid returns to the objective manner—but again, for only two lines:

> mox ubi creverunt naturaque mitior illis
> contigit, ut quaedam, sic non manifesta videri
> forma potest hominis, sed uti de marmore coeptis
> non exacta satis rudibusque simillima signis . . .

Then, when they had grown in size and become milder in their nature, a certain likeness to the human form, indeed, could be seen, still not very clear, but such as statues just begun out of marble have, not sharply defined, and very like roughly blocked-out images. [1.403–06]

The comparison with something that the author seems to be recalling from his own observation is characteristic of Ovid's constant comparisons with everyday things.[4] This tendency is carried to the extreme in his simile of the raising of a curtain in the Roman theater (3.111–14), or his mock-hesitant comparison of the homes of the highest gods to the Palatine: "hic locus est, quem, si verbis audacia detur, / haud timeam magni dixisse Palatia caeli" (1.175–76).

Ovid concludes his account of the stones with a gesture of piety: "And in a short time, through the operation of the divine will, the stones thrown by the man's hand took on the form of men, and women were made from the stones the woman threw." Then the passage is rounded off with a characteristic *sententia*: "Hence come the hardness of our race and our endurance of toil; and we give proof from what origin we are sprung."

> inque brevi spatio superorum numine saxa
> missa viri manibus faciem traxere virorum
> et de femineo reparata est femina iactu.
> inde genus durum sumus experiensque laborum
> et documenta damus qua simus origine nati.   [1.411–15]

More dramatic examples may be found in quite a different kind of episode—the story of Tereus and Philomela, where Ovid enfolds the beginning of the fearful tale within a continuous commentary, addressing the reader in a familiar fashion, interpreting overtly every act and emotion, setting the tale within the reader's apprehension by everyday allusions (translation adapted from Miller and Innes):

> ecce venit magno dives Philomela paratu,
> divitior forma; quales audire solemus
> naidas et dryadas mediis incedere silvis,
> si modo des illis cultus similesque paratus.
> non secus exarsit conspecta virgine Tereus,

> quam si quis canis ignem supponat aristis
> aut frondem positasque cremet faenilibus herbas.

Behold, Philomela entered, attired in rich apparel, but richer still in beauty. She was like the descriptions that one often hears of the naiads and the dryads who haunt the depths of the woodlands, if only they wore ornaments and garments such as hers. The moment he saw the maiden Tereus was inflamed with love, just as if some person should set fire to ripe grain, or dry leaves, or hay stored away in the mow. [6.451–57]

The series of comparisons at the close serves to enforce the authorial interpretation of Tereus. But more open interpretation follows, at length: "Her beauty, indeed, was worth it; but in his case his own passionate nature stirred him on, and, besides, the people of his region are quick to respond to the promptings of Venus: his own fault and his nation's burnt in him."

> digna quidem facies; sed et hunc innata libido
> exstimulat, pronumque genus regionibus illis
> in Venerem est: flagrat vitio gentisque suoque.   [6.458–60]

"There was nothing which he would not do or dare, smitten by this mad passion. His heart could scarce contain the fires that burnt in it."

> et nihil est, quod non effreno captus amore
> ausit, nec capiunt inclusas pectora flammas.   [6.465–66]

Then the narrator's indignation at the shameful lies and hypocrisy of Tereus bursts out violently:

> pro superi, quantum mortalia pectora caecae
> noctis habent! ipso sceleris molimine Tereus
> creditur esse pius laudemque a crimine sumit.

O gods above, what blind night rules in the hearts of men! In the very act of pushing on his shameful plan Tereus gets credit for a kind heart and wins praise from wickedness. [6.472–74]

Milton, then, could have found in the *Metamorphoses* ample precedent for enfolding his own story within the consciousness of his own fictive presence. It is not the presence of John Milton as a person, though some of his personal attributes and experiences are there—but rather, as in Ovid, the presence of a creative, remembering, sympathizing, judging mind that holds under control materials that include and then exceed even the vast range of Ovidian mythology. For all of ancient myth must now be transcended by the new religion that was arising in Ovid's day, and was soon to offer a new faith to fill the place of the gods that were dying (while still living in affectionate memory) within the skeptical consciousness of Ovid's poem. Milton's allusions to Ovidian myth, and to the same or other myths preserved by other classical authors, combine with biblical story to create a rich remembrance of the vast world of ancient religions, some horrible, as the worship of Moloch, some beautiful, as the worship of Thammuz, some almost irresistible, as the worship of Venus and Bacchus, but all remembered and included, sometimes with reproach, sometimes with full appreciation of their beauty. Milton's poem stands as a vast memorial to the deep religious needs and purposes of mankind, fulfilled, as Milton believes, in the dynamic inclusiveness of his own faith.

II

The nature of that fulfillment is recorded in Milton's "historical" conclusion, the tenth book of the first edition, the eleventh and twelfth books of the second edition, where Milton seems to evoke an ironical memory of the closing books of Ovid's epic. In the eleventh book of the *Metamorphoses*, after the migration of Bacchus and his followers to Tmolus, the story of Midas, and the brief account of the founding of Troy, the portion of the poem devoted mainly to tales of love and passion concludes on a gentler, more beneficent note, with the story of Peleus and Thetis and the long tale of the true love of Ceyx and Alcyone. The opening of book 12 marks the movement into another theme, with the introduction of Priam, Hector, and Paris, and the thousand ships of the Greeks who sailed in vengeance. The last four books are clearly differentiated from the preceding portion of the poem; the brief account of Troy in book 11 is buried amidst Bacchic and amorous tales and cannot be taken to mark the beginning of the poem's "historical" movement—though, in Ovid's way, it foreshadows that movement. But now, in books 12–15, we turn to the story of Troy, the story of Aeneas, the story of Rome, and the glories of the Roman empire under Augustus. Up through book 11 all is myth; after that the thread of the tale is "history"—the legendary history of Troy and Rome and the actual history of Ovid's own day, interspersed, and sometimes overwhelmed, with myths—the battle of the Lapiths and Centaurs, or the love tales of Acis, Galatea, and Polyphemus, Scylla, Glaucus, and Circe, Pomona and Vertumnus.

Critics of Ovid have had much the same problems in dealing with Ovid's concluding "historical" books that critics of Milton have had in dealing with the last two books of *Paradise Lost*, where Milton turns away from the story of the Fall to recount the history of mankind. Critics have called Ovid's performance in his last four books perfunctory, "prosy," and lacking in continuity with the preceding books—except for the brilliantly told fables that constantly interrupt the "history."[5] So too critics of Milton have often viewed the last two books of *Paradise Lost* as a weak epilogue, with occasional flashes of power. But perhaps in both cases we are not catching the interplay of the poet's lowered style against the higher style that he elsewhere displays. Some classical scholars seem to be turning toward the view that Ovid's "perfunctory" account of Aeneas is an indication that Ovid will not attempt to compete with Vergil on his own ground. Ovid will recount the "history," drily and quickly, while using it to provide a "liaison" for the fables of love and passion that are his chief concern.[6] Under such circumstances the exalted praise of Julius Caesar and Augustus at the close is bound to seem inflated (though not necessarily meant to seem so by the author). Ovid's example here may have provided Milton with an opportunity to create a subtle series of ironies.

At the outset of Milton's history of the fallen world, the example of Ovid may be evoked by the grand catalogue of earth's empires that Michael shows to Adam (11.385–411). Although that catalogue is indebted to Homer, Vergil, or Camoens, still the catalogues of those poets are not usually so condensed and compact as Milton's glorious roll of proper names. For models of such compact catalogues one may turn to Ovid, since he is notorious for exactly such lists of names, places, and things.[7] We have read the catalogue of the trees that gathered around Orpheus, and to this one should add the catalogue of mountains burned during the ride of Phaeton (2.217–26), followed by the even longer catalogue of rivers (2.242–59). There is also the catalogue of Actaeon's dogs (3.206–25), the enormous list of comparisons and possessions sung by Polyphemus (13.789–820), and the heaping of place-names in the last book of the *Metamorphoses* (15.700–718), where Ovid tells of the journey of Aesculapius to Rome:

> Romethiumque legit Caulonaque Naryciamque
> evincitque fretum Siculique angusta Pelori
> Hippotadaeque domos regis Temesesque metalla
> Leucosiamque petit tepidique rosaria Paesti.
> inde legit Capreas promunturiumque Minervae
> et Surrentino generosos palmite colles
> Herculeamque urbem Stabiasque et in otia natam
> Parthenopen et ab hac Cumaeae templa Sibyllae.

[He] skirted Romethium and Caulon and Narycia; then passed the Sicilian sea and Pelorus' narrow strait, sailed by the home of Hippotades, past the copper mines of Temesa, and headed for Leucosia and mild Paestum's rose gardens. Thence he skirted Capreae, Minerva's promontory, and the hills of Surrentum rich in vines; thence sailed to Herculaneum and Stabiae and Parthenope, for soft pleasure founded, and from there to the temple of the Cumaean Sibyl (15.705–12, trans. Miller).

Such passages seem to resound within Milton's lines:

> *Mombaza*, and *Quiloa*, and *Melind*,
> And *Sofala* thought *Ophir*, to the Realme
> Of *Congo*, and *Angola* fardest South;
> Or thence from *Niger* Flood to *Atlas* Mount
> The Kingdoms of *Almansor*, *Fez* and *Sus*,
> *Marocco* and *Algiers*, and *Tremisen* . . .   [11.399–404]

Both Camoens and Milton have learned some lessons from Ovid.

Such Ovidian catalogues of course are not limited to the *Metamorphoses*: one thinks of the catalogue of places visited or viewed by Ceres in her search for Proserpine (*Fasti* 4.469–80,563–72), especially the second of these lists, with its witty, self-mocking conclusion:

> nam modo turilegos Arabas, modo despicit Indos,
> hinc Libys, hinc Meroë siccaque terra subest;

> nunc adit Hesperios Rhenum Rhodanumque Padumque
>   teque, future parens, Thybri, potentis aquae.
> quo feror?

> For now she looked down on the incense-gathering Arabs, and now
> on the Indians: beneath her lay on one side Libya, on the other side
> Meroe, and the parched land. Now she visited the western rivers,
> the Rhine, the Rhone, the Po, and thee, Tiber, future parent of a
> mighty water. Whither do I stray? [4.569–73, trans. Frazer]

"Where am I going in such a rush?" Nothing could show more
clearly that here is *Ovidius lascivus*, playing a witty game with
sound and versification, as in the earlier outrageous line
"Himeraque et Didymen Acragantaque Tauromenumque" (*Fasti*
4.475).

Milton too in his way is playing a game with his catalogue in
book 11, not the "solemn game" that Eliot once saw there,[8] but a
fierce, sardonic game by which he inflates the "glories" of empire
just before showing their crimes and follies. Then in book 12
Milton gives, by contrast, another list of places, presented in a
lower, simpler style, without rhetorical flourishes, almost clumsy
in its manner, as Michael describes to Adam the places that Ab-
raham and his seed will inhabit:

> *Canaan* he now attains, I see his Tents
> Pitcht about *Sechem*, and the neighbouring Plaine
> Of *Moreh*; there by promise he receaves
> Gift to his Progenie of all that Land;
> From *Hamath* Northward to the Desert South
> (Things by thir names I call, though yet unnam'd)
> From *Hermon* East to the great Western Sea,
> Mount *Hermon*, yonder Sea, each place behold
> In prospect, as I point them; on the shoare
> Mount *Carmel*; here the double-founted stream
> *Jordan*, true limit Eastward; but his Sons
> Shall dwell to *Senir*, that long ridge of Hills.
> This ponder, that all Nations of the Earth
> Shall in his Seed be blessed . . .   [135–48]

The Holy Land has no need of classical rhetoric to reveal its
meaning. Just as Ovid's "Aeneid" serves as "a bare narrative
framework"[9] within which delightful fables are woven, so Milton's

bare account of biblical history in book 12 serves as a framework within which high points revealing God's power are enhanced.

After his grand catalogue of empires, Milton's history of mankind falls into two parts—and so does Ovid's final book, in a way that may have suggested a two-part finale to both Camoens and Milton. The first half is given over to philosophical instruction involving the origins and primaeval years of the human race, while the second half tells of Roman myths and the glories of Roman history. King Numa "was not content with learning the rites of the Sabine race, but conceived a grander project, to inquire into the nature of the universe" (15.5–6, trans. Innes). Desiring such knowledge, he left his native town and went to Crotona, where Pythagoras was living in exile from Samos. There Numa learns the teachings of Pythagoras, whose situation, political views, and achievements are described by Ovid in a way very close to the attitudes, the hopes, and the aims of John Milton:

> There was a man here, Samian born, but he
> Had fled from Samos, for he hated tyrants
> And chose, instead, an exile's lot. His thought
> Reached far aloft, to the great gods in Heaven,
> And his imagination looked on visions
> Beyond his mortal sight. All things he studied
> With watchful eager mind, and he brought home
> What he had learned and sat among the people
> Teaching them what was worthy, and they listened
> In silence, wondering at the revelations,
> How the great world began, the primal cause,
> The nature of things, what God is, whence the snows
> Come down, where lightning breaks from, whether wind
> Or Jove speaks in the thunder from the clouds,
> The cause of earthquakes, by what law the stars
> Wheel in their courses, all the secrets hidden
> From man's imperfect knowledge. [15.60–72, trans. Humphries]

One passage in the Latin is especially evocative, when applied to Milton: "quae natura negabat / visibus humanis, oculis ea pectoris hausit"—"what nature denied to human sight he feasted upon with the eyes of the mind" (15.63–64).

Ovid then delivers the teachings of Pythagoras in the form of a four-hundred-line speech by the sage himself (15.75–478). It be-

gins with a warning against the eating of animal food, an act which led to the corruption of mankind's original innocence: "O mortals, do not pollute your bodies with a food so impious!"[10] Such a practice, he declares, was not known in the golden age, "blessed with the fruit of the trees and the herbs which the ground sends forth" (97–98). Then "all things were free from treacherous snares, fearing no guile and full of peace" (102–03). But after someone, setting a bad example, "whoever he was, envied the food of lions, and thrust down flesh as food into his greedy stomach, he opened the way for crime [fecit iter sceleri]" (104–06); then "further impiety grew out of that [longius inde nefas abiit]" (111).

> inde (fames homini vetitorum tanta ciborum est!)
> audetis vesci, genus o mortale! quod, oro,
> ne facite, et monitis animos advertite nostris!

Thence (so great is man's lust for forbidden food!) do you dare thus to feed, O race of mortals! I pray you, do not do it, but turn your minds to these my words of warning.   [138–40]

Then Pythagoras proceeds to reveal the secrets of the universe: "Great matters, never traced out by the minds of former men, things that have long been hidden, I will sing" (146–47). He tells how "our souls are deathless" (158) and live by constant transmigration into other bodies: "All things are changing; nothing dies. The spirit wanders, comes now here, now there, and occupies whatever frame it pleases. From beasts it passes into human bodies, and from our bodies into beasts, but never perishes" (165–68). That is why Pythagoras abhors the eating of flesh: "Therefore, lest your piety be overcome by appetite, I warn you as a seer, do not drive out by impious slaughter what may be kindred souls, and let not life be fed on life" (173–75).

This principle, *omnia mutantur, nihil interit* (165), operates throughout the world: "All things are in a state of flux, and everything is brought into being with a changing nature. . . . For that which once existed is no more, and that which was not has come to be; and so the whole round of motion is gone through again" (177–78, 183–85). So landscape changes, so decaying carcasses produce animal life, so great cities and empires are ever-changing:

> . . . some nations putting on new strength and others falling into weakness. So was Troy great in wealth and men, and for ten years was able to give so freely of her blood; but now, humbled to earth, she has naught to show but ancient ruins, no wealth but ancestral tombs. Sparta was at one time a famous city; great Mycenae flourished, and Cecrops' and Amphion's citadels. Sparta is now a worthless countryside, proud Mycenae has fallen; and what is the Thebes of Oedipus except a name? . . . And now fame has it that Dardanian Rome is rising, and laying deep and strong foundations by the stream of Tiber sprung from the Apennines. She therefore is changing her form by growth, and some day shall be the capital of the boundless world! [421–35]

Then he briefly recalls the prophecy that Aeneas will found a new city in a foreign land—thus recalling the whole compass of the *Aeneid*, with its celebration of the glories of *Roma Aeterna*, as in Vergil's sixth book. Ovid will go on, in the latter half of his final book, to celebrate those glories—but he will not here call that city or that empire immortal, though he has done so in the *Fasti* (3.72). Ovid's celebration of Rome is qualified by the long speech of Pythagoras, for Rome too will decay, if the lesson of Pythagoras is right.[11] Individual heroes, such as Julius Caesar and Augustus, will be transmuted into gods—but Rome itself cannot avoid the universal process of change. Only poetry will endure.

The whole speech of Pythagoras evokes analogies with the instruction of Adam by the two angels: instruction by Raphael in the secrets of the universe, in the middle books, with the stern warnings against transgressing the divine prohibition; and finally, Michael's story of the turning of man toward evil, the sad history of the crimes of the human race, down to Milton's own day and beyond.

But Milton's poem is designed to include, transcend, and contradict teachings like those of Pythagoras, for in Milton's universe eternal flux exists only in Chaos. When the elements have entered into forms created by God their circular movement plays a part in a teleological plan in which all created things prove to be

> yet regular
> Then most, when most irregular they seem:
> And in their motions harmonie Divine
> So smooths her charming tones, that Gods own ear
> Listens delighted.   [5.623–27]

Thus, although within each creature the four elements may re-
volve in their circular way, the creatures themselves are designed
in a scale that looks upward, each creature having an allegiance
toward the divine, as Raphael explains in his great organic im-
ages:

> So from the root
> Springs lighter the green stalk, from thence the leaves
> More aerie, last the bright consummate floure
> Spirits odorous breathes: flours and thir fruit
> Mans nourishment, by gradual scale sublim'd
> To vital Spirits aspire, to animal,
> To intellectual, give both life and sense,
> Fansie and understanding, whence the soule
> Reason receives, and reason is her being . . .   [5.479–87]

Raphael goes on to suggest the possibility of an even higher ascen-
sion, saying that perhaps

> Your bodies may at last turn all to Spirit,
> Improv'd by tract of time, and wingd ascend
> Ethereal, as wee, or may at choice
> Here or in Heav'nly Paradises dwell;
> If ye be found obedient . . .   [5.497–501]

Even disobedience cannot wholly interrupt that upward move-
ment: Milton's conclusion, with its sad and bitter story of the
cycles of mankind's growth and decay, nevertheless moves toward
the day when the just will receive immortal joy and time will cease.
Milton's *carmen perpetuum* records a changing movement, under
the freedom of the will, not without purpose, not without end. In
adapting the Pythagorean and Ovidian theory of change, Milton
thus invalidates its central principle, as the Jupiter who saved
Deucalion and Pyrrha from the flood is transformed into the God
of Milton:

Such grace shall one just Man find in his sight,
That he relents, not to blot out mankind,
And makes a Covenant never to destroy
The Earth again by flood, nor let the Sea
Surpass his bounds, nor Rain to drown the World
With Man therein or Beast; but when he brings
Over the Earth a Cloud, will therein set
His triple-colour'd Bow, whereon to look
And call to mind his Cov'nant: Day and Night,
Seed time and Harvest, Heat and hoary Frost
Shall hold thir course, till fire purge all things new,
Both Heav'n and Earth, wherein the just shall dwell.

[11.890–end]

PART IV

The Chosen Sons

*But when we have to do with things which we
behold with the mind, that is, with the intelli-
gence and with reason, we speak of things
which we look upon directly in the inner light
of truth which illumines the inner man and is
inwardly enjoyed.*

Augustine, **De Magistro**

Paradise Regain'd: The Interior Teacher

In the search for universals, said Augustine, "we do not listen to anyone speaking and making sounds outside ourselves. We listen to Truth which presides over our minds within us, though of course we may be bidden to listen by someone using words. Our real Teacher is he who is so listened to, who is said to dwell in the inner man, namely Christ, that is, the unchangeable power and eternal wisdom of God."[1] Milton shared this Augustinian view of "wisdom" speaking within the mind. The "prophetic function" of Christ, he said, "has two parts, one external and one internal. The first is the revelation of divine truth, the second the illumination of the mind."[2] The two roles of course cannot be separated, but it seems fair to say that *Paradise Lost,* in keeping with its epic decorum, presents the Son of God primarily in his external function, as in the revelation of his majestic power in book 6; whereas *Paradise Regain'd* shows the Son in his second, his internal function. Through a process of renunciation *Paradise Regain'd* gradually reveals the voice of Truth speaking within the illuminated mind.

A mode of renunciation is implicit in the basic style of *Paradise Regain'd*: a ground-style that Milton carefully announces in his

opening lines and maintains with strong consistency throughout
the first book:

> I who e're while the happy Garden sung,
> By one mans disobedience lost, now sing
> Recover'd Paradise to all mankind,
> By one mans firm obedience fully tri'd
> Through all temptation, and the Tempter foil'd
> In all his wiles, defeated and repuls't,
> And *Eden* rais'd in the wast Wilderness.

The allusion to *Paradise Lost* here asks us to recall that poem, and
to note how different this new poem will be in its theme and hence
in its style. We need only recall the latinate suspension and com-
pression of that first enormous sentence of *Paradise Lost* to feel the
contrast with the normal movement and scope of educated En-
glish speech in *Paradise Regain'd*. It is a simple "I" who sings this
new poem, a plain man without his bardic "robes." The voice of
the narrator now speaks in a style appropriate to a poem
prompted, not by emulation of the epic Muse, but purely by the
"Spirit who ledst this glorious Eremite / Into the Desert." Leav-
ing behind the poem that dealt with an argument

> Not less but more Heroic than the wrauth
> of stern *Achilles* on his Foe pursu'd
> Thrice Fugitive about *Troy* Wall . . .   [*PL* 9.14–16]

this poem turns "to tell of deeds / Above Heroic, though in secret
done" (*PR* 1.14–15).

"In secret"—the phrase suggests its Latin original, *in secreto:* "in
solitude, in a solitary place, in retirement," along with the English
meaning, "in private." Thus the prologue foresees the final line:
"Home to his Mothers house private return'd."

Hence the trappings of *Paradise Lost* recede from view in book 1
of *Paradise Regain'd*: as the opening lines prophesy, the syntax will
tend to display the normal, supple, easy movement of an educated
mind. Furthermore, when we recall the vast range of elaborate
epic similes in the opening book of *Paradise Lost,* it is significant to
notice that the opening book of *Paradise Regain'd* contains not a
single simile of this kind; indeed it contains no classical allusions
whatsoever, except near the close of the book, where the pagan

oracles are mentioned only in order to announce their demise, as Jesus says to Satan:

> No more shalt thou by oracling abuse
> The Gentiles; henceforth Oracles are ceast,
> And thou no more with Pomp and Sacrifice
> Shalt be enquir'd at *Delphos* or elsewhere,
> At least in vain, for they shall find thee mute.
> God hath now sent his living Oracle
> Into the World, to teach his final will,
> And sends his Spirit of Truth henceforth to dwell
> In pious Hearts, an inward Oracle
> To all truth requisite for men to know.   [1.455–64]

The firm and quiet manner of these lines, dignified, yet modest, is representative of the ground-style laid down in book 1 of *Paradise Regain'd* as a central principle of the whole poem's action. To be sure, the difference from *Paradise Lost* is not complete. The language is less obviously latinate, though there is still plenty of latinity, since this is part of the renaissance heritage. And there are still a good many of those peculiar Miltonic compressions, transcending and defying grammar. The style, in short, reminds us, at a distance, of the manner of *Paradise Lost*: but it is all deliberately muted, thoroughly absorbed into another texture of writing:

> So spake our Morning Star then in his rise,
> And looking round on every side beheld
> A pathless Desert, dusk with horrid shades;
> The way he came not having mark'd, return
> Was difficult, by humane steps untrod;
> And he still on was led, but with such thoughts
> Accompanied of things past and to come
> Lodg'd in his brest, as well might recommend
> Such Solitude before choicest Society.
> Full forty days he pass'd, whether on hill
> Sometimes, anon in shady vale, each night
> Under the covert of some ancient Oak,
> Or Cedar, to defend him from the dew,
> Or harbour'd in one Cave, is not reveal'd . . .   [1.294–307]

We can recognize the voice and the manner as Miltonic: but the language is essentially that of any educated man. This effect, both common and peculiar, suggests the phrase by which Hopkins de-

fined the language of poetry: "current language heightened"—
heightened here by a voice that belongs to a uniquely gifted indi-
vidual and yet is still the voice of a man searching inwardly in
common ways for the common bond of mankind. The muted,
chastened style[3] thus announced in the first book of *Paradise Re-
gain'd* seems appropriately chosen to pursue a work that bears
some relation to the venerable line of meditations on a Gospel
text.

From beginning to end of this poem the mind of the narrator
roams freely over the past, present, and future life of its hero. We
begin, after the brief prologue, with a memory of the scene at
Jordan during the baptism of Jesus by John: a scene that Satan
recapitulates only forty lines later when he warns his Council that
he has heard "the Sov'raign voice" at Jordan pronounce this man
"my Son." And only forty lines after this (130–67) we hear the
"Sov'raign voice" itself, addressing Gabriel in Heaven, and sum-
ming up the whole life of the Son, from the mission of Gabriel at
the Annunciation, through the coming temptation in the Wilder-
ness, where the hero will "lay down the rudiments / Of his great
warfare"—the basic principles of the warfare that will destroy the
power of Sin and Death "By Humiliation and strong Sufferance."
Thus prepared by the Father's own summation of the Son's
career, we now come to "the Son of God" himself:

> Mean while the Son of God, who yet some days
> Lodg'd in *Bethabara* where *John* baptiz'd,
> Musing and much revolving in his brest,
> How best the mighty work he might begin
> Of Saviour to mankind, and which way first
> Publish his God-like office now mature,
> One day forth walk'd alone, the Spirit leading;
> And his deep thoughts, the better to converse
> With solitude, till far from track of men,
> Thought following thought, and step by step led on,
> He entred now the bordering Desert wild,
> And with dark shades and rocks environ'd round,
> His holy Meditations thus persu'd.   [1.183–95]

The period of temptation, we see, is primarily a mental
retirement—"thought following thought"—and what follows now
(196–293) is a meditation on the entire life of Jesus, given in the

person of the hero himself, as he meditates on the meaning of his existence:

> O what a multitude of thoughts at once
> Awakn'd in me swarm, while I consider
> What from within I feel my self, and hear
> What from without comes often to my ears,
> Ill sorting with my present state compar'd.

He recalls his childhood, his visit to the Temple, his early aspirations when "victorious deeds / Flam'd in my heart, heroic acts";

> Yet held it more humane, more heavenly first
> By winning words to conquer willing hearts,
> And make perswasion do the work of fear;
> At least to try . . .

Then he recalls how his mother had "inly rejoyc'd" at his youthful thoughts, how she had informed him that he was the son of Heaven's Eternal King, how she had told him of the Annunciation and the Nativity: when

>   a glorious Quire
> Of Angels in the fields of *Bethlehem* sung
> To Shepherds watching at their folds by night,
> And told them the Messiah was now born,
> Where they might see him, and to thee they came;
> Directed to the Manger where thou lais't,
> For in the Inn was left no better room . . .

A biblical simplicity is thus interwoven with the subdued Miltonic and latinate idiom of this poem. And we learn of the Wise Men, of Simeon and Anna, and how Jesus, pondering these things, along with the Scriptures, came to realize he was the promised Messiah:

> this chiefly, that my way must lie
> Through many a hard assay even to the death,
> E're I the promis'd Kingdom can attain,
> Or work Redemption for mankind, whose sins
> Full weight must be transferr'd upon my head.

Then finally, after this glimpse of the Passion, he remembers the central scene at Jordan:

> But as I rose out of the laving stream,
> Heaven open'd her eternal doors, from whence

The Spirit descended on me like a Dove,
And last the sum of all, my Father's voice,
Audibly heard from Heav'n, pronounc'd me his,
Me his beloved Son, in whom alone
He was well pleas'd; by which I knew the time
Now full, that I no more should live obscure,
But openly begin, as best becomes
The Authority which I deriv'd from Heaven.
And now by some strong motion I am led
Into this wilderness, to what intent
I learn not yet, perhaps I need not know;
For what concerns my knowledge God reveals.

This poem, then, first of all concerns the self-discovery of the hero: what it means to be pronounced the Son of God. And indeed, as we read and re-read this poem, we are struck by the way in which that phrase "Son of God" resounds throughout the poem as the chief title by which Milton alludes to the hero. The phrase "Son of God" occurs no less than thirty-nine times; ten times in book 1 and twenty-one times in the concluding book. A few statistics may be in order here to make an important point. Milton calls his hero Jesus only six times; he calls him Savior twenty-one times, Messiah seven times—but he never once calls his hero by the name of Christ. This is not simply because he prefers to use the Hebrew equivalent, Messiah, for as I have said, this term is not used often, nor does he use the translated title "Anointed" more than once.

Why not use the term *Christ*? I think Milton avoids the term here because he is not writing only about the life of Christ, that unique being, Prophet, Priest, and King; he is writing about a composite generalized being whom he calls the Son of God in such an insistent way as to recall the opening of John's Gospel: "But as many as received him, to them gave he power to become the sons of God" (1:12); or the promise of Paul in Romans 8:14: "For as many as are led by the Spirit of God, they are the sons of God." Or, best of all, the words of John's first Epistle (3:1–3): "Behold, what manner of love the Father hath bestowed upon us, that we should be called the sons of God: therefore the world knoweth us not, because it knew him not. Beloved, now are we the sons of God, and it doth not yet appear what we shall be: but we know that, when he shall appear, we shall be like him; for we shall see him as he is. And every man that hath this hope in him purifieth himself, even as he is pure."

After tantalizing us with the phrase throughout the poem, Milton finally clarifies the issues for us at the very close, as Satan is about to make his last desperate effort: the temptation of the pinnacle. Here, with a wonderful irony, Milton matches the opening meditation of the hero by giving now Satan's own sardonic commentary on the Gospel story, Satan's version of what it means to be the Son of God:

> To whom the Fiend now swoln with rage reply'd:
> Then hear, O Son of *David*, Virgin born;
> For Son of God to me is yet in doubt,
> Of the Messiah I have heard foretold
> By all the Prophets; of thy birth at length
> Announc't by *Gabriel* with the first I knew,
> And of the Angelic Song in *Bethlehem* field,
> On thy birth-night, that sung thee Saviour born.
> From that time seldom have I ceas'd to eye
> Thy infancy, thy childhood, and thy youth,
> Thy manhood last, though yet in private bred;
> Till at the Ford of *Jordan* whither all
> Flock'd to the Baptist, I among the rest,
> Though not to be Baptiz'd, by voice from Heav'n
> Heard thee pronounc'd the Son of God belov'd.
> Thenceforth I thought thee worth my nearer view
> And narrower Scrutiny, that I might learn
> In what degree or meaning thou art call'd
> The Son of God, which bears no single sence;
> The Son of God I also am, or was,
> And if I was, I am; relation stands;
> All men are Sons of God; yet thee I thought
> In some respect far higher so declar'd.   [4.499–521]

He has not long to wait, for true relation stands: placed on the pinnacle and faced with the final temptation, the hero answers in the words of the Bible: "Tempt not the Lord thy God, he said and stood. / But Satan smitten with amazement fell." Into those brief words, "Tempt not the Lord thy God," Milton has packed a trinity of meanings: they bear no single sense.[4] First of all, in the traditional interpretation, the words give the answer that any man might give: that is, one must not ask God for unreasonable help,

one must not ask for unnecessary evidence of divine favor. But
secondly, in Milton's strategic placing of the words, they show why
Satan fell, stupefied, "strook with dread and anguish," filled with
"Ruin, and desperation, and dismay." Satan is confounded by the
revelation that he has been tempting divinity incarnate. And
thirdly, we may take the words to indicate the full self-realization
of the hero: he understands now what he has not known earlier,
or has known by glimpses only: that he is himself divine.

Certainly the critics are right who have said that this invulnera-
ble hero makes it very difficult to produce a dramatic develop-
ment in the poem.[5] Satan is "aghast" from the opening and feels
his forces shattered from the outset; his "motivation" for the
temptations seems to be the curiosity of desperation rather than
any real hope of victory. How, then, can the poem sustain our
interest? I believe the answer lies in watching the movements of
the narrating mind as it defines the nature of the Son of God. The
whole poem presents a mind that uses the "characters" to explore
the problems and besetting sins of any potential Son of God
among men: a mind that conveys the process of temptation by
creating what might be called a contest of styles. The ground of
this great warfare is laid down, stylistically, in book 1; what we feel
here, I think, is the presence of a mind engaged in an immense
effort at self-control, a mind held in leash, poised, tense, alert,
watching any tendency toward elaboration, luxury, self-
indulgence: alert to control any temptation that might lead away
from the ground that is set, ethically, theologically, and stylisti-
cally, at the end of book 1, in answer to Satan's opening man-
oeuvres:

> To whom our Saviour with unalter'd brow.
> Thy coming hither, though I know thy scope,
> I bid not or forbid; do as thou find'st
> Permission from above; thou canst not more.

Book 1 is a prelude: it draws the scene; it establishes the
ground-style; it sets the problems to be explored, and foresees
their conclusion. The action proper begins with book 2, where the
life of Jesus is considered from many different perspectives. First,
from the viewpoint of the new-born Christians who had been

baptized at Jordan—Andrew, Simon Peter, and others, whom we
meet in a pastoral setting, with a clear echo of the opening line of
Spenser's *Shepheardes Calender*—"A Shepeheards boye (no better
doe him call)":

> Then on the bank of *Jordan,* by a Creek:
> Where winds with Reeds, and Osiers whisp'ring play
> Plain Fishermen, no greater men them call,
> Close in a Cottage low together got
> Thir unexpected loss and plaints out breath'd.   [2.25–29]

From this base in pastoral diction they speak in language that
moves gracefully out of the biblical toward the latinate:

> our eyes beheld
> Messiah certainly now come, so long
> Expected of our Fathers; we have heard
> His words, his wisdom full of grace and truth,
> Now, now, for sure, deliverance is at hand,
> The Kingdom shall to *Israel* be restor'd:
> Thus we rejoyc'd, but soon our joy is turn'd
> Into perplexity and new amaze . . .   [2.31–38]

But they end with simple faith: "Soon we shall see our hope, our
joy return."

From these we turn to "Mother *Mary*" (2.60), whom we find
pondering in her heart all the major events in her son's life to this
point: the Annunciation, the Nativity—

> In such a season born when scarce a Shed
> Could be obtain'd to shelter him or me
> From the bleak air; a Stable was our warmth,
> A Manger his . . .

the flight into Egypt, his acknowledgment as Son at Jordan, the
prophecy of Simeon, and that time when Jesus visited the Temple:

> when twelve years he scarce had seen,
> I lost him, but so found, as well I saw
> He could not lose himself; but went about
> His Father's business . . .

And now as Mary "with thoughts / Meekly compos'd awaited the
fulfilling," we have a glimpse of her son, at the center of the
poem's inward action, as he,

                          tracing the Desert wild,
       Sole but with holiest Meditations fed,
       Into himself descended . . .   [2.109–11]

   After all these humble, inward scenes, so frequently marked by
a biblical simplicity of phrasing, the process of temptation now
bursts upon us in the high oratorical style of *Paradise Lost*, as we
hear Satan addressing his host of devils and consulting with them
over how to proceed in the face of such dangerous self-mastery:

       Princes, Heavens antient Sons, Aethereal Thrones,
       Demonian Spirits now, from the Element
       Each of his reign allotted, rightlier call'd,
       Powers of Fire, Air, Water, and Earth beneath . . .   [2.121–24]

That touch of the old fallen oratory leads us quickly down to the
lowest level of sensuality, as Belial moves to suggest that the Son of
God be tempted by sexual appetite. Thus Milton skillfully man-
ages to include in his poem an aspect of human weakness that
could not be associated with Jesus. Milton has Satan reject Belial's
suggestion in such a way as to remind us of lust's long history,
bringing in the first strong coloring from classical mythology that
has been allowed thus far in the poem:

       Before the Flood thou with thy lusty Crew,
       False titl'd Sons of God—

note how Milton keeps the problem ever before us: what it means
to be a Son of God—

                          roaming the Earth
       Cast wanton eyes on the daughters of men,
       And coupl'd with them, and begot a race.
       Have we not seen, or by relation heard,
       In Courts and Regal Chambers how thou lurk'st,
       In Wood or Grove by mossie Fountain side,
       In Valley or Green Meadow to way-lay
       Some beauty rare, *Calisto, Clymene,*
       Daphne, or *Semele, Antiopa,*
       Or *Amymone, Syrinx,* many more
       Too long, then lay'st thy scapes on names ador'd,
       Apollo, Neptune, Jupiter, or *Pan,*
       Satyr, or Fawn, or Silvan?   [2.178–91]

That brilliant cluster of old Ovidian myths, rejected here even by Satan, prepares us for the combat that will now develop in a long contest of styles, as the rich, sensuous coloring and the high rhetoric of the world rise up against the "frugal" ground-style set in book 1: a style which represents the way of temperance struggling against the self-indulgence of an elaborate style.

Thus the vision of the Banquet now arises (2.337–66) in an effort to obliterate the hero's self-control. It is a step upward from Belial's sensuality, but it includes a touch of Belial's suggestion in the vision of

> Nymphs of *Diana's* train, and *Naiades*
> With fruits and flowers from *Amalthea's* horn,
> And Ladies of th' *Hesperides* . . .

Its appeal to hunger of course relates back to the preliminary temptation of book 1, while the whole scene looks forward to the following temptations of wealth and regal power; for it is "A Table richly spred, in regal mode." Milton is offering a Roman banquet to all the quickened senses:

> And at a stately side-board by the wine
> That fragrant smell diffus'd, in order stood
> Tall stripling youths rich clad, of fairer hew
> Then *Ganymed* or *Hylas* . . .

The worlds of classic myth and medieval romance are ransacked for physical allurement and brought to a climax in those superbly overwrought lines of Spenserian motif and alliteration, carrying the appeal of sound to its furthest poetical extreme:

> And Ladies of th' *Hesperides,* that seem'd
> Fairer then feign'd of old, or fabl'd since
> Of Fairy Damsels met in Forest wide
> By Knights of *Logres,* or of *Lyones,*
> *Lancelot* or *Pelleas,* or *Pellenore* . . .

We return with a shock to the frugal ground-style, as Jesus rejects the offer, renouncing imagery in favor of irony—except for a brief suggestion of the communion table:

> To whom thus Jesus temperately reply'd:
> Said'st thou not that to all things I had right?

And who withholds my pow'r that right to use?
Shall I receive by gift what of my own,
When and where likes me best, I can command?
I can at will, doubt not, as soon as thou,
Command a Table in this Wilderness,
And call swift flights of Angels ministrant
Array'd in Glory on my cup to attend . . .   [2.378–86]

So the central contest, the full excitement, of the poem lies in the
movements, the fluctuations, of the narrating mind itself. It is an
inward combat created by Milton's brilliant manipulation of styles,
a contest in which the flights of poetic splendor are consistently
drawn back by the prevailing net of a frugal style to the ground of
renunciation and temperance.[6] The way in which this ground-
style represents the controlling ideal of the poem is clearly shown
now in the speech of Jesus that closes book 2, in answer to the
temptation of wealth. Here Milton gives, exactly in the center of
the poem, a definition of true Kingship, true Sonship. Jesus first
alludes to Gideon, Jephthah, and David, and then places them
beside certain men "Among the Heathen" who are also "Worthy
of Memorial": "*Quintius, Fabricius, Curius, Regulus.*" This colloca-
tion of Roman and biblical heroes of the simple life points the way
toward the association of Job with Socrates that is soon to follow in
book 3, as Jesus rejects the temptation of glory by praising higher
conquests won

By deeds of peace, by wisdom eminent,
By patience, temperance; I mention still
Him whom thy wrongs with Saintly patience born,
Made famous in a Land and times obscure;
Who names not now with honour patient *Job*?
Poor *Socrates* (who next more memorable?) . . .   [3.91–96]

Anticipating this open praise of Socrates, the great ethical
speech of the Son ending book 2 proceeds to show how the Socra-
tic reliance on the inner man (Socrates' "discovery of the soul," as
Cornford has called it)[7] leads onward into the Christian concept of
highest kingship: we note the quiet implication of the "wreath of
thorns" and the "burden" of Second Isaiah:

What if with like aversion I reject
Riches and Realms; yet not for that a Crown,

> Golden in shew, is but a wreath of thorns,
> Brings dangers, troubles, cares, and sleepless nights
> To him who wears the Regal Diadem,
> When on his shoulders each mans burden lies;
> For therein stands the office of a King,
> His Honour, Vertue, Merit and chief Praise,
> That for the Publick all this weight he bears.
> Yet he who reigns within himself, and rules
> Passions, Desires, and Fears, is more a King;
> Which every wise and vertuous man attains:
> And who attains not, ill aspires to rule
> Cities of men, or head-strong Multitudes,
> Subject himself to Anarchy within,
> Or lawless passions in him which he serves.
> But to guide Nations in the way of truth
> By saving Doctrine, and from errour lead
> To know, and knowing worship God aright,
> Is yet more Kingly, this attracts the Soul,
> Governs the inner man, the nobler part,
> That other o're the body only reigns,
> And oft by force, which to a generous mind
> So reigning can be no sincere delight.
> Besides to give a Kingdom hath been thought
> Greater and nobler done, and to lay down
> Far more magnanimous, then to assume.   [2.457–83]

"To lay down"—with his careful placing of those words at the end of a line, Milton forces us to pause and complete the phrase in the familiar words of the Gospel of John:

> As the Father knoweth me, even so know I the Father: and I lay down my life for the sheep.
> And other sheep I have, which are not of this fold: them also I must bring, and they shall hear my voice; and there shall be one fold, and one shepherd.
> Therefore doth my Father love me, because I lay down my life, that I might take it again.
> No man taketh it from me, but I lay it down of myself. I have power to lay it down, and I have power to take it again. This commandment have I received of my Father.   [John 10:15–18]
>
> Greater love hath no man than this, that a man lay down his life for his friends.   [John 15:13]

Thus the Greek virtue of magnanimity is redefined in Christian terms, as expounded by Milton in his *De Doctrina* (2.9): "High-mindedness is shown when in seeking or not seeking riches, advantages or honors, in avoiding them or accepting them, a man behaves himself as befits his own dignity, rightly understood" (trans. Carey).[8] It is important that thus, in the middle of the poem, Milton should pay tribute to classic virtue and classic thought, for the tribute helps to qualify the renunciation of Greek culture that follows in book 4.

From this steadfast center of the poem, a center defined both by concept and by style, Satan now attempts to move the hero by rhetorical and imagistic elaborations that gradually rise toward the height of Milton's grand style. The temptation of glory begins on a higher pitch of rhetorical insinuation than anything we have seen earlier, especially in contrast with the long, straightforward, temperate speech we have just heard:

> I see thou know'st what is of use to know,
> What best to say canst say, to do canst do;
> Thy actions to thy words accord, thy words
> To thy large heart give utterance due, thy heart
> Conteins of good, wise, just, the perfect shape.
> . . . wherefore deprive
> All Earth her wonder at thy acts, thy self
> The fame and glory, glory the reward
> That sole excites to high attempts the flame
> Of most erected Spirits, most temper'd pure
> Aetherial, who all pleasures else despise,
> All treasures and all gain esteem as dross,
> And dignities and powers all but the highest?   [3.7–30]

In line with such artifice and convolution the first half of the third book is devoted to abstract argument at a very high level of rhetorical elaboration and oratorical prowess.

Jesus answers this challenge with a burst of oratory that has puzzled many readers, since the harshness here seems out of line with the charity of a Savior, seems rather to voice the bitter disillusionment of John Milton himself, who had once tried to win a victory of the Just with the help of the many, and had seen the whole effort fail:

> For what is glory but the blaze of fame,
> The peoples praise, if always praise unmixt?

> And what the people but a herd confus'd,
> A miscellaneous rabble, who extol
> Things vulgar, & well weigh'd, scarce worth the praise,
> They praise and they admire they know not what;
> And know not whom, but as one leads the other;
> And what delight to be by such extoll'd,
> To live upon thir tongues and be thir talk,
> Of whom to be disprais'd were no small praise?
> His lot who dares be singularly good.
> Th' intelligent among them and the wise
> Are few, and glory scarce of few is rais'd.
> This is true glory and renown, when God
> Looking on the Earth, with approbation marks
> The just man, and divulges him through Heaven
> To all his Angels, who with true applause
> Recount his praises . . .
>
> [3.47–64]

We are right, I think, if we hear in these words the voice of the old Cromwellian, elected even in defeat. But is it a flaw in the fabric of the poem? Is it a flaw like that which Arnold Stein has seen in Milton's later description of the Parthian power, where he feels that "Milton has tampered with the perspective," so that a "narrative voice seems to have intruded without warrant"?[9] But that narrative voice has been in control of the action from the poem's outset, where we met at the first word the "I" whose thoughts enact the poem. In a pure drama, properly so called, it would indeed be a flaw if one felt another voice coming through instead of the voice appropriate to a given character in that drama. But in this inward speaking of the narrative mind, all "characters," all speeches, are enveloped within, and suffused with, the controlling voice of the narrator himself. That mind is exploring its own problems, as well as those of mankind, through the speeches of the "characters," who have indeed no separate existence, whose very function is to take upon themselves the voice of the narrator.

That is why the poem never shows any extended effort to present a drama of characters in the usual sense. Satan and the Son of God in this poem speak within the mind of one who hopes to be himself a Son of God; both these actors use the human voice that this particular possible Son of God, John Milton, possesses. So I think it is hardly valid to object that this poem does not present the Christ of the Gospels. For this is not a rehearsal of the Gospels; it is rather (as Hopkins would say) a rehearsal of the self, where the voice of the inner man discovers what a true Son of God ought to reply to such temptations.

Thus earlier we have heard Satan speak, as it might seem, "out of character," when he rebukes Belial for suggesting a temptation through female beauty:

> or should she confident,
> As sitting Queen ador'd on Beauties Throne,
> Descend with all her winning charms begirt
> To enamour, as the Zone of *Venus* once
> Wrought that effect on *Jove,* so Fables tell;
> How would one look from his Majestick brow
> Seated as on the top of Vertues hill,
> Discount'nance her despis'd, and put to rout
> All her array; her female pride deject,
> Or turn to reverent awe? for Beauty stands
> In the admiration only of weak minds
> Led captive; cease to admire, and all her Plumes
> Fall flat and shrink into a trivial toy . . .   [2.211–23]

If this strikes us as more Miltonic than Satanic,[10] it need not worry us: the "characters" of this poem exist, not for their own points of view, but as occasions, as channels, by which the narrative voice can make its way.

Now, after this brilliant battle of rhetoric has ended with the defeat of worldly glory, so, in another mode of temptation, Milton moves onward, in the second half of book 3, to show a richer, higher style arising out of the temperate ground. It is a significant touch that Milton should have the grand tableau of Parthian power, with its echoes of the grand style of *Paradise Lost*, literally rise up from a pastoral plain:

> With that (such power was giv'n him then) he took
> The Son of God up to a Mountain high.
> It was a Mountain at whose verdant feet
> A spatious plain out strech't in circuit wide
> Lay pleasant; from his side two rivers flow'd,
> Th' one winding, the other strait and left between
> Fair Champain with less rivers interveind,
> Then meeting joyn'd thir tribute to the Sea:
> Fertil of corn the glebe, of oyl and wine,

> With herds the pastures throng'd, with flocks the hills,
> Huge Cities and high towr'd, that well might seem
> The seats of mightiest Monarchs . . .   [3.251-62]

And so we come to those grandly over-wrought displays of proper
names that sum up worldly power and empire:

> *Ecbatana* her structure vast there shews,
> And *Hecatompylos* her hunderd gates,
> There *Susa* by *Choaspes*, amber stream,
> The drink of none but Kings; of later fame
> Built by *Emathian*, or by *Parthian* hands,
> The great *Seleucia, Nisibis,* and there
> *Artaxata, Teredon, Tesiphon* . . .   [3.286-92]

> From *Arachosia*, from *Candaor* East,
> And *Margiana* to the *Hyrcanian* cliffs
> Of *Caucasus*, and dark *Iberian* dales,
> From *Atropatia* and the neighbouring plains
> Of *Adiabene, Media,* and the South
> Of *Susiana* to *Balsara's* hav'n.   [3.316-21]

It is appropriate, I think, that near the close of all this splendid
panoply, Milton should bring in (at line 329) the poem's outstand-
ing example of a pompous and affected latinism: "Chariots or
Elephants *endorst* with Towers." And it is even more appropriate
that at the very end of the vision we should meet the poem's first
example of an epic comparison, one that clearly reminds us of the
allusions to chivalric romance in the opening book of *Paradise Lost*
(582-87, 763-66):

> Such forces met not, nor so wide a camp,
> When *Agrican* with all his Northern powers
> Besieg'd *Albracca,* as Romances tell;
> The City of *Gallaphrone,* from thence to win
> The fairest of her Sex *Angelica*
> His daughter, sought by many Prowest Knights,
> Both *Paynim,* and the Peers of *Charlemane*.
> Such and so numerous was thir Chivalrie . . .   [3.337-44]

This great passage on the Parthians demonstrates, as the ban-
quet scene has earlier shown, that this writer is still at the peak of
his powers. All the strength of *Paradise Lost* is still there; he can use
it when he chooses; but here the Son of God condemns the grand

vision as "argument / Of human weakness rather then of strength."

As the fourth book opens, Milton announces the imminent climax of the grand style by introducing a cluster of similes. They are not quite heroic similes; they are rather subdued echoes of the heroic mode; but they serve to prepare for the epic manner of the following tableau of Rome, where Milton bends his heroic bow still further, carrying the compressed richness of his high style to its absolute and appropriate limit:

> Thence to the gates cast round thine eye, and see
> What conflux issuing forth, or entring in,
> Pretors, Proconsuls to thir Provinces
> Hasting or on return, in robes of State;
> Lictors and rods the ensigns of thir power,
> Legions and Cohorts, turmes of horse and wings:
> Or Embassies from Regions far remote
> In various habits on the *Appian* road,
> Or on the *Aemilian,* some from farthest South,
> *Syene,* and where the shadow both way falls,
> *Meroe Nilotic* Isle, and more to West,
> The Realm of *Bocchus* to the Black-moor Sea;
> From the *Asian* Kings and *Parthian* among these,
> From *India* and the golden *Chersoness,*
> And utmost *Indian* Isle *Taprobane,*
> Dusk faces with white silken Turbants wreath'd:
> From *Gallia, Gades,* and the *Brittish* West,
> *Germans* and *Scythians,* and *Sarmatians* North
> Beyond *Danubius* to the *Tauric* Pool.   [4.61–79]

This vision of Rome is more than the climax of the high style: it is a culmination of all the many threads of temptation that have been weaving their way toward this highest "grandeur and majestic show / Of luxury," of "wealth and power, / Civility of Manners, Arts, and Arms." For the Son's answer recalls the Banquet scene of book 2:

> though thou should'st add to tell
> Thir sumptuous gluttonies, and gorgeous feasts
> On *Cittron* tables or *Atlantic* stone;
> (For I have also heard, perhaps have read)
> Their wines of *Setia, Cales,* and *Falerne,*
> *Chios* and *Creet,* and how they quaff in Gold,
> Chrystal and Myrrhine cups imboss'd with Gems

> And studs of Pearl, to me should'st tell who thirst
> And hunger still . . .   [4.113–21]

It has all been one sustained temptation,[11] from the point where
Belial first spoke of sexual appetite, up through the more refined
appetites of the banquet, and onward to this moment of final
rejection for these kingdoms of the flesh, the world, and the devil.

For this, we must note, is the end of Satan's kingdoms,[12] as
Satan himself three times says: first, in concluding his vision of
Rome:

> These having shewn thee, I have shewn thee all
> The Kingdoms of the world, and all thir glory.   [4.88–89]

Next, in his answer to the Son's rejection, where Milton concludes
the whole sequence by bringing in the ending of the second temp-
tation in Luke's account: "The Kingdoms of the world to thee I
give . . . if thou wilt fall down, / And worship me"; with the
answer: "Get thee behind me . . ." (4.163–67, 193–94). And
thirdly, by way of prologue to the next vision:

> Therefore let pass, as they are transitory,
> The Kingdoms of this world; I shall no more
> Advise thee, gain them as thou canst, or not.   [4.209–11]

But just as he had offered the sexual suggestion of Belial, before
the temptation of the Kingdoms, properly so called, here Milton
adds another temptation. What implications lie in this placing of
the final tableau of Greek culture outside of the Kingdoms of the
World? First of all, we should note, with some relief, perhaps, that
these realms of Greek culture do not lie within Satan's gift: he
does not control them, he does not offer to give them. Satan can
only urge the Son of God to use Greek culture on the wrong
terms, that is, to value Greek learning and art beyond the bounds
proper to a Son of God. Thus: shall the Son of God concede that
Athens is truly "Mother of Arts / And Eloquence," that her
Tragedians are "teachers best / Of moral prudence," "High ac-
tions, and high passions best describing"? Shall the Son of God
concede that Socrates was really "Wisest of men" and that Greek
thought is all in all because "These rules will render thee a King
Compleat / Within thy self"?

The Son has already anticipated his answer in the long speech

at the end of book 2. The Son of God can never rest within the
ideal of being "compleat / Within thy self." This, he has implied, is
a right beginning, but the Son of God must look beyond himself to
the thorns, the burden, the weight of mankind's incompleteness.

The Son's answer at first should cause us no discomfort: he does
not at first deny the value of Greek culture: he says only that it is
not necessary to the good life:

> To whom our Saviour sagely thus repli'd.
> Think not but that I know these things, or think
> I know them not; not therefore am I short
> Of knowing what I aught: he who receives
> Light from above, from the fountain of light,
> No other doctrine needs, though granted true . . .   [4.285–90]

Milton could have avoided all our modern worries over this scene
if he had only had the consideration to stop here; but, as in Satan's
scorn of sexual weakness, or in Jesus' denunciation of glory, so
here the personal involvement of the narrator runs beyond the
bounds of an easy propriety. For the Christian humanist and
platonist this is the greatest challenge: can he be brought to say
that truth resides in Greek achievements, in and by themselves?[13]
The Son of God is thus driven to make, at this point, a judgment
more drastic and more violent than that made by the rest of the
poem. For the whole poem qualifies and moderates this fierce
renunciation, while at the same time this particular episode shows
the speaker's readiness to make the ultimate sacrifice, if it should
be demanded. The tone is tense, vehement, almost savage in
places:

> But these are false, or little else but dreams,
> Conjectures, fancies, built on nothing firm.
> The first and wisest of them all profess'd
> To know this only, that he nothing knew;
> The next to fabling fell and smooth conceits . . .
> Alas what can they teach, and not mislead;
> Ignorant of themselves, of God much more,
> And how the world began, and how man fell
> Degraded by himself, on grace depending?
> Much of the Soul they talk, but all awrie,
> And in themselves seek vertue, and to themselves
> All glory arrogate, to God give none . . .   [4.291–315]

And as for learning the "secret power / Of harmony" and "moral prudence" from Greek poetry:

> All our Law and Story strew'd
> With Hymns, our Psalms with artful terms inscrib'd,
> Our Hebrew Songs and Harps in *Babylon,*
> That pleas'd so well our Victors ear, declare
> That rather *Greece* from us these Arts deriv'd;
> Ill imitated, while they loudest sing
> The vices of thir Deities, and thir own
> In Fable, Hymn, or Song, so personating
> Thir Gods ridiculous, and themselves past shame.
> Remove their swelling Epithetes thick laid
> As varnish on a Harlots cheek, the rest,
> Thin sown with aught of profit or delight,
> Will far be found unworthy to compare
> With *Sion's* songs, to all true tasts excelling,
> Where God is prais'd aright, and Godlike men,
> The Holiest of Holies, and his Saints;
> Such are from God inspir'd, not such from thee;
> Unless where moral vertue is express't
> By light of Nature not in all quite lost.   [4.334–52]

The violence of the charge, followed by the curt qualification, suggests that here is the hardest renunciation of all; but if necessary, the Son of God is prepared to lay down all. It is the same action that Milton's older contemporary, Nicholas Ferrar, performed on his deathbed, where, as the scene has come down to us, he said at last to his brother:

> When you have measured out the place for my grave, then goe and take out of my Study, those three great Hampers full of Bookes that have stood there locked up these many yeares: They were not many scores but many Hundreths in all kind of Languages, which he had in all places gotten with great search, and some cost. They were Comedies, Tragedies, Love-Hymns, Heroicall Poems, and such like. Carry (sayd he) those Hampers to the place of my grave, and upon it, see you burn them all: and this he spake with some vehemency and passion of Indignation. Goe, Let it be done, Let it be done . . .

And after the books had been burned, John Ferrar returned to his brother's bedside and "told him, all was done, as he had required." "Then he suddenly lifting up himself, sat up in his Bed,

gave God hearty thanks, and called for Pen, Inke, and Paper,"
and wrote out the following document:

> November 28th 1637. I. H. S. In the name of God, Amen.
> In as much as all the Comedyes, Tragedyes, Pastoralls etc: and all
> those they call Heroicall Poems, none excepted; and like wise all the
> Bookes of Tales, which they call Novells, and all feigned Historyes
> written in Prose, all Love Hymns, and all the like Bookes are full of
> Idolatry, and especially tend to the Overthrow of Christian Reli-
> gion, undermining the very Foundations thereof, and corrupt and
> pollute the minds of the Readers, with filthy lusts, as, woe is me, I
> have proved in my self. In this regard therefore, to shew my detes-
> tation of them to the World, and that all others may take warning, I
> have burned all of them, and most humbly have, and doe beseech
> God, to forgive me all my mispent time in them, and all the sinns
> that they have caused in me, which surely, but for his infinite Grace,
> had carryed my soule down into Hell long ere this . . . I beseech all
> that truly feare God, that love Jesus Christ, to consider these things
> well. Amen, Amen, Amen.[14]

So Milton's Son of God must also enact this final renunciation: a
stern demand, but just, in terms of the whole poem; for what has
the poem been saying if it has not said that the myths and elabora-
tions of classical literature are unnecessary, dangerous, and unre-
liable? Milton has constantly affirmed this in the ground-style of
his poem, where "swelling Epithetes" are removed, and a basic
idiom is achieved approaching the "majestic unaffected stile" that
Milton here praises in the Hebrew prophets. "So spake the Son of
God" and Satan finds himself now "Quite at a loss, for all his darts
were spent."

With those words (4.366) Milton marks the close of his long
analysis of human temptation. What remains is prophecy,
epiphany, and praise, which Milton gives in three symbolic scenes.
First Satan arouses a tremendous storm which shadows forth the
Passion and the Resurrection, as Milton makes clear by having
Satan allude to the future sufferings of Jesus immediately before
and after the storm (4.386–88, 477–83). Next comes the full reve-
lation of divine power, suggesting the Day of Judgment, as the
Son of God stands on the pinnacle, and Satan falls, accompanied
to his doom by a pair of true epic similes which drive home the
absolute finality of the defeat. And then at once the angels trans-

port the Son of God to a pastoral valley, where the "Angelic
Quires" sing their concluding hymn of praise, which Milton
phrases in a way that allows the Son of God in this poem to suggest
the restored Image of God in man, the Paradise within.

> True Image of the Father whether thron'd
> In the bosom of bliss, and light of light
> Conceiving, or remote from Heaven, enshrin'd
> In fleshly Tabernacle, and human form,
> Wandring the Wilderness, whatever place,
> Habit, or state, or motion, still expressing
> The Son of God, with Godlike force indu'd
> Against th' Attempter of thy Fathers Throne,
> And Thief of Paradise; him long of old
> Thou didst debel, and down from Heav'n cast
> With all his Army, now thou hast aveng'd
> Supplanted *Adam,* and by vanquishing
> Temptation, hast regain'd lost Paradise . . .
> For though that seat of earthly bliss be fail'd,
> A fairer Paradise is founded now
> For *Adam* and his chosen Sons, whom thou
> A Saviour art come down to re-install.
> Where they shall dwell secure, when time shall be
> Of Tempter and Temptation without fear.   [4.596–617]

For Adam and his *chosen* Sons. Milton has never before in his
poetry used the word *chosen* in quite so bare and unguarded a way.
"Some I have chosen of peculiar grace / Elect above the rest," the
voice of God has said in *Paradise Lost,* but, we are reassured, "The
rest shall hear me call, and oft be warnd / Thir sinful state," while
"offerd grace" will invite all men to repent: "for I will cleer thir
senses dark / What may suffice" (3.183–89). And the subtle analy-
sis of the doctrine of Election in his *De Doctrina* (1.4) makes it plain
that although equal grace is not offered to all, still sufficient grace
is offered to everyone. "Of one thing, then, we may be absolutely
positive," says Milton: God "excludes no man from the way of
penitence and eternal salvation, unless that man has continued to
reject and despise the offer of grace, and of grace sufficient for
salvation, until it is too late" (trans. Carey).[15] Can it be that now, at
the close of one of his latest poems, Milton is reverting to a sterner
doctrine of the chosen? Is this paradise within regained only for a
chosen few?

Perhaps such a sterner possibility may lie within the ambiguous opening of *Paradise Regain'd*:

> I who e're while the happy Garden sung,
> By one mans disobedience lost, now sing
> Recover'd Paradise to all mankind . . .

Is Paradise recovered "to all mankind," or is this poet singing to all mankind the story of a Paradise recovered—for the chosen few? Why then sing the story to all mankind? But no one can know whether he is truly one of the chosen: in the terms of traditional puritan theology, all who hear the story must search within themselves for the signs of saving faith. *Paradise Regain'd*, with its rigorous denunciation of the "people" and its stern rejection of the modes of pagan culture, may seem to lend itself to such an interpretation.

Yet the presence of *Samson Agonistes* as the "companion poem"[16] in this volume reassures us that Milton has not indeed engaged in such a Calvinistic rejection of the freedom of the will that lies at the heart of *Paradise Lost*. As Mary Ann Radzinowicz has shown in her recent admirable study,[17] *Samson Agonistes* represents the process of regeneration at work in the individual soul and demonstrates the way in which the chosen one "Elect above the rest" may lead the rest to understand the ways of God and maintain their faith in a degree that will suffice for salvation.

Paradise Regain'd has made the withdrawal to the desert, has denounced the culture of cities in a way characteristic of the biblical prophets, has declined to acknowledge an open alliance with any of the classical genres, has indeed shown a willingness to reject classical culture after the manner of the proto-puritan Father, Tertullian:

> What indeed has Athens to do with Jerusalem? What concord is there between the Academy and the Church? . . . Our instruction comes from "the porch of Solomon," who had himself taught that "the Lord should be sought in simplicity of heart." Away with all attempts to produce a mottled Christianity of Stoic, Platonic, and dialectic composition! We want no curious disputation after possessing Christ Jesus . . .[18]

But *Samson Agonistes* shows a further stage of action beyond the "private" workings of grace in the soul of man: this drama fashioned after the manner of the Greeks (with the help of the modern Italians) will show how a poet can absorb the lessons of the past and treat the ancients in the manner sanctioned by the great Alexandrian humanist, Clement:

> Thus philosophy was necessary to the Greeks for righteousness, until the coming of the Lord. . . . For God is the source of all good things; of some primarily, as of the old and new Testaments; of others by consequence, as of philosophy. But it may be, indeed, that philosophy was given to the Greeks immediately and primarily, until the Lord should call the Greeks. For philosophy was a "schoolmaster" to bring the Greek mind to Christ, as the Law brought the Hebrews. Thus philosophy was a preparation, paving the way towards perfection in Christ.[19]

Appropriately, then, Milton has chosen an ancient form, developed as part of a public religious occasion, to demonstrate the workings of free will and grace within the community of mankind. Thus, near the end of his career, Milton conveys his lifelong belief that "the holiness and wisdom in both word and deed of many of the heathens" show that "some traces of the divine image still remain in us."[20]

Samson Agonistes:
The Breath
Of Heaven

Sam. A little onward lend thy guiding hand
To these dark steps, a little further on;
For yonder bank hath choice of Sun or shade,
There I am wont to sit, when any chance
Relieves me from my task of servile toyl,
Daily in the common Prison else enjoyn'd me,
Where I a Prisoner chain'd, scarce freely draw
The air imprison'd also, close and damp,
Unwholsom draught: but here I feel amends,
The breath of Heav'n fresh-blowing, pure and sweet,
With day-spring born; here leave me to respire.

This is an opening rich with implications, for the situation suggests the opening of Sophocles' redemptive tragedy, *Oedipus at Colonus,* where the blind Oedipus is led on stage by his daughter Antigone. We know that Samson will also be accepted by the divine power, as Oedipus was at last accepted and transfigured by the divine powers at the close of that Greek play. At the same time Milton's phrasing in these opening lines contains a redemptive overtone drawn from the first chapter of the Gospel of Luke, where Zacharias prophesies the redemption of God's people: "Through the tender mercy of our God; whereby the *dayspring* from on high hath visited us, to give light *to them that sit in darkness* and in the shadow of death, *to guide our feet* into the way of peace." So the guiding hand that Samson speaks of here is a human hand, literally, and the breath of Heaven that he enjoys is a physical breeze, literally; but this opening, with Milton's characteristic mingling of classical and Christian evocations, will suggest the presence of a higher power, still to be revealed.

Samson's long prologue here displays a remarkable combination of self-control and turbulent emotional power.[1] Although he bitterly laments his captivity and his loss of sight, he refuses the temptation to blame God for his fate:

> Promise was that I
> Should *Israel* from *Philistian* yoke deliver;
> Ask for this great Deliverer now, and find him
> Eyeless in *Gaza* at the Mill with slaves,
> Himself in bonds under *Philistian* yoke;
> Yet stay, let me not rashly call in doubt
> Divine Prediction; what if all foretold
> Had been fulfilld but through mine own default,
> Whom have I to complain of but my self?   [38–46]

But as his agony swells out, the temptation returns, and is again refused:

> God, when he gave me strength, to shew withal
> How slight the gift was, hung it in my Hair.
> But peace, I must not quarrel with the will
> Of highest dispensation, which herein
> Happ'ly had ends above my reach to know:
> Suffices that to me strength is my bane,
> And proves the sourse of all my miseries;
> So many, and so huge, that each apart
> Would ask a life to wail, but chief of all,
> O loss of sight, of thee I most complain!
> Blind among enemies, O worse then chains,
> Dungeon, or beggery, or decrepit age!   [58–69]

And so on into that famous lamentation where the steady flow of the blank verse breaks under the strain and is transformed into a

lyric utterance of short and long lines, ebbing and flowing with the
speaker's almost unbearable pain:

> O dark, dark, dark, amid the blaze of noon,
> Irrecoverably dark, total Eclipse
> Without all hope of day!
> O first created Beam, and thou great Word,
> Let there be light, and light was over all;
> Why am I thus bereav'd thy prime decree?
> The Sun to me is dark
> And silent as the Moon,
> When she deserts the night
> Hid in her vacant interlunar cave.   [80–89]

How poorly the chorus understands this man, as they enter
now, judging him only by outward appearances. "Can this be
hee?" they ask, recalling the physical grandeur of his exploits:

> Can this be hee,
> That Heroic, that Renown'd,
> Irresistible *Samson*? whom unarm'd
> No strength of man, or fiercest wild beast could withstand;
> Who tore the Lion, as the Lion tears the Kid,
> Ran on embattelld Armies clad in Iron
> And weaponless himself,
> Made Arms ridiculous, useless the forgery
> Of brazen shield and spear, the hammer'd Cuirass,
> *Chalybean* temper'd steel, and frock of mail
> Adamantean Proof.   [124–34]

But more deeply, Samson's prologue has shown him to be a man
whose mind and character still retain a great potential. The func-
tion of the various episodes that we now watch is to release and
develop that deep potential.

In the first episode the "Consolation" of the chorus does not
lead Samson to blame God or lose his faith in God's justice, al-
though the "Counsel" offered by Samson's friends is full of pain-
ful queries:

> *Chor.* Tax not divine disposal, wisest Men
> Have err'd, and by bad Women been deceiv'd;
> And shall again, pretend they ne're so wise.
> Deject not then so overmuch thy self,
> Who hast of sorrow thy full load besides;

> Yet truth to say, I oft have heard men wonder
> Why thou shouldst wed *Philistian* women rather
> Then of thine own Tribe fairer, or as fair,
> At least of thy own Nation, and as noble.   [210–18]

But Samson defends his first Philistine marriage on the grounds that he "knew / From intimate impulse" that it was ordained by God for Israel's deliverance: "The work to which I was divinely call'd." And he adds that he "thought" the same was true for Dalila—though there is a tacit admission of possible error here, perhaps an error of self-deception caused by the "specious" charms of Dalila.[2]

The chorus wryly concedes Samson's ability "to provoke" the Philistines—but to what end? "Yet *Israel* still serves with all his Sons." Here, surprisingly, Samson leaps to defend both himself and God. In spite of his weaknesses, he declares, Israel had many opportunities to throw off the Philistine yoke, if they had supported him on many different occasions:

> *Sam.* That fault I take not on me, but transfer
> On *Israel's* Governours, and Heads of Tribes,
> Who seeing those great acts which God had done
> Singly by me against their Conquerours
> Acknowledg'd not, or not at all consider'd
> Deliverance offerd.   [241–46]

With the memory of his deeds and the grandeur of his language Samson convinces the chorus that the fault is indeed in the Israelites, who have before this deserted their heroes. Milton skillfully conveys the distance between such heroes and the ordinary man by a curiously deflating use of rhyme at the close of this choric response:

> *Chor.* Thy words to my remembrance bring
> How *Succoth* and the Fort of *Penuel*
> Thir great Deliverer contemn'd,
> The matchless *Gideon* in pursuit
> Of *Madian* and her vanquisht Kings:
> And how ingrateful *Ephraim*
> Had dealt with *Jephtha,* who by argument,
> Not worse then by his shield and spear
> Defended *Israel* from the *Ammonite,*

> Had not his prowess quell'd thir pride
> In that sore battel when so many dy'd
> Without Reprieve adjudg'd to death,
> For want of well pronouncing *Shibboleth*.   [277–89]

One of the astonishing things about Milton's art in this whole drama is the way in which he has, it seems, deliberately played down the choruses in the middle of the drama, refusing to give the chorus very good lines, except toward the beginning (where they are uplifted by the memory of Samson's physical prowess), and toward the end (where they are strengthened by Samson's recovery and ultimate victory). After each of the first three episodes, Milton has given the chorus words that are, for the most part, dry and commonplace, often surprisingly flat, as here at the end of the first episode:

> Yet more there be who doubt his ways not just,
> As to his own *edicts*, found contra*dicting*,
> Then give the rains to wandring thought,
> Regardless of his glories *diminution:*
> Till by thir own perplexities *involv'd*
> They ravel more, still less *resolv'd*,
> But never find self-satisfying *solution*.
> As if they would confine th' interminable,
> And tie him to his own *prescript*,
> Who made our Laws to bind us, not himself,
> And hath full right to *exempt*
> Whom so it pleases him by *choice*
> From National obstriction, without *taint*
> Of sin, or legal *debt;*
> For with his own Laws he can best *dispence*.   [300–14]

The rhymes and partial rhymes here (which I have italicized) create by their "jingling" an effect of something like triviality in the chorus; and since Milton elsewhere in the play writes so very well, we are bound to ask whether there is not some deliberate effect in thus making the chorus speak so flatly.[3] Indeed, the heavy-handed use of rhyme and partial rhyme here seems almost to mirror the contempt for rhymed verse that Milton had expressed several years earlier in the prefatory note to *Paradise Lost:*[4]

> The Measure is *English* Heroic Verse without Rime, as that of *Homer* in *Greek,* and of *Virgil* in *Latin;* Rime being no necessary

Adjunct or true Ornament of Poem or good Verse, in longer Works
especially, but the Invention of a barbarous Age, to set off wretched
matter and lame Meeter; grac't indeed since by the use of some
famous modern Poets, carried away by Custom, but much to thir
own vexation, hindrance, and constraint to express many things
otherwise, and for the most part worse then else they would have
exprest them.

Rhyme, he declares, is "a thing of it self, to all judicious eares,
triveal and of no true musical delight," which cannot be found "in
the jingling sound of like endings." The choric stanzas that I have
just quoted seem to prove the point. Is this an instance of Milton's
sardonic humor—to give the chorus stanzas of deliberate flatness?
At the very least it would appear that Milton's use of rhyme here
has the effect of lowering the tone of high seriousness and making
impossible any great dignity in this choric speech. The effect is
thus to stress, by contrast, the grandeur of Samson, the glory of
his poetry, the greatness of his mind: his difference from ordinary
men.

  This difference also appears by contrast with his father
Manoa, who now enters to begin the second episode. Manoa com-
plains bitterly to his son and seems so deeply involved in his own
grief that he cannot think about the effect that his words may have
upon Samson:

> Nay what thing good
> Pray'd for, but often proves our woe, our bane?
> I pray'd for Children, and thought barrenness
> In wedlock a reproach; I gain'd a Son,
> And such a Son as all Men hail'd me happy;
> Who would be now a Father in my stead?
>
> . . . .
> Alas methinks whom God hath chosen once
> To worthiest deeds, if he through frailty err,
> He should not so o'rewhelm, and as a thrall
> Subject him to so foul indignities,
> Be it but for honours sake of former deeds.   [350–55, 368–72]

But Samson is far from being shaken by these moans; he has faced
all this long ago; and he answers with self-control and dignity:

> Appoint not heavenly disposition, Father,
> Nothing of all these evils hath befall'n me

> But justly; I my self have brought them on,
> Sole Author I, sole cause . . .   [373–76]

And he ends, as in his great prologue, with a surge of immense
vitality, though turned against himself:

> O indignity, O blot
> To Honour and Religion! servil mind
> Rewarded well with servil punishment!
> The base degree to which I now am fall'n,
> These rags, this grinding, is not yet so base
> As was my former servitude, ignoble,
> Unmanly, ignominious, infamous,
> True slavery, and that blindness worse then this,
> That saw not how degeneratly I serv'd.   [411–19]

The distance between Samson and ordinary men is at once
emphasized by Manoa, as he proceeds to ignore the power of
Samson's self-castigation and answers at first with a querulous (and,
to the reader, half-comic) understatement: "I cannot praise thy
Marriage choises, Son, / Rather approv'd them not;" and this is
followed by obvious doubt of his son's divine inspiration in these
matters:

> but thou didst plead
> Divine impulsion prompting how thou might'st
> Find some occasion to infest our Foes.
> I state not that; this I am sure; our Foes
> Found soon occasion thereby to make thee
> Thir Captive, and thir triumph; thou the sooner
> Temptation found'st, or over-potent charms
> To violate the sacred trust of silence
> Deposited within thee.   [420–29]

Then Manoa, returning to his self-centered complaint, adds, "A
worse thing yet remains": the Philistines are today celebrating
Dagon's victory in delivering Samson into their hands (one may
hear the voice of aged self-pity):

> So *Dagon* shall be magnifi'd, and God,
> Besides whom is no God, compar'd with Idols,
> Disglorifi'd, blasphem'd, and had in scorn
> By th' Idolatrous rout amidst thir wine;
> Which to have come to pass by means of thee,

> *Samson,* of all thy sufferings think the heaviest,
> Of all reproach the most with shame that ever
> Could have befall'n thee and thy Fathers house.   [440–47]

Here again, Samson acknowledges his fault with dignity and rational power, but he goes beyond his earlier self-denunciation to assert his unbroken faith that God will triumph, even though Samson himself is now cast out from grace:

> This only hope relieves me, that the strife
> With me hath end; all the contest is now
> 'Twixt God and *Dagon; Dagon* hath presum'd,
> Me overthrown, to enter lists with God,
> His Deity comparing and preferring
> Before the God of *Abraham.* He, be sure,
> Will not connive, or linger, thus provok'd,
> But will arise and his great name assert:
> *Dagon* must stoop, and shall e're long receive
> Such a discomfit, as shall quite despoil him
> Of all these boasted Trophies won on me,
> And with confusion blank his Worshippers.   [460–71]

Manoa agrees, in a perfunctory tone, and then goes on to show that his mind is not at all on such matters, but is fixed upon his hope to ransom his son and take him home: "But for thee what shall be done?" Manoa here represents the terms of household common sense, the encouragement to believe that God somehow will perhaps relent, that things simply cannot go on being as unhappy as they are. Samson rejects all these easy consolations in one of the simplest and noblest speeches of the entire play, when Manoa suggests that he might even possibly regain his sight, if only he has patience:[5]

> All otherwise to me my thoughts portend,
> That these dark orbs no more shall treat with light,
> Nor th' other light of life continue long,
> But yield to double darkness nigh at hand:
> So much I feel my genial spirits droop,
> My hopes all flat, nature within me seems
> In all her functions weary of herself;
> My race of glory run, and race of shame,
> And I shall shortly be with them that rest.   [590–98]

The effect of his father's "consolations" has been to make Samson realize to the full his "sense of Heav'ns desertion," as he cries out in the great lyrical utterance that follows, a passage expressed, again, not in blank verse, but in undulating long and short lines which begin with a few scarcely noticed rhymes, and then utterly give up all rhymes, as the ode reaches its climax:

> I was his nursling once and choice delight,
> His destin'd from the womb,
> Promisd by Heavenly message twice descending.
> Under his special eie
> Abstemious I grew up and thriv'd amain;
> He led me on to mightiest deeds
> Above the nerve of mortal arm
> Against the uncircumcis'd, our enemies.
> But now hath cast me off as never known,
> And to those cruel enemies,
> Whom I by his appointment had provok't,
> Left me all helpless with th' irreparable loss
> Of sight, reserv'd alive to be repeated
> The subject of thir cruelty, or scorn.
> Nor am I in the list of them that hope;
> Hopeless are all my evils, all remediless;
> This one prayer yet remains, might I be heard,
> No long petition, speedy death,
> The close of all my miseries, and the balm.   [633–51]

That prayer will soon be answered; through the dark night of this despair, his thoughts are moving in the right way.

Immediately, the contrast between Samson's grandeur of despair and the commonplace musing of the chorus is enforced by some of the flattest lines and weakest rhymes that Milton ever wrote:[6]

> God of our Fathers, what is man!
> That thou towards him with hand so *various,*
> Or might I say *contrarious,*
> Temperst thy providence through his short course,
> Not evenly, as thou rul'st
> The Angelic orders and inferiour creatures *mute,*
> Irrational and *brute.*
> Nor do I name of men the common *rout,*
> That wandring loose *about*
> Grow up and perish, as the summer flie.   [667–76]

The chorus is confused and bewildered; but the chosen man is greater than the chorus can here realize, as we are soon to see.

Now, as Samson faces utterly his agonized sense of loss, the external cause of that loss sails into sight with all her streamers waving, perfumed, beautiful, seductive, weeping, penitent (she says), declaring her "conjugal affection," begging forgiveness, asking if she may take him home to her bed and board. Samson's fierceness toward Dalila is a measure of the seductive power that she still holds for him:

> My Wife, my Traytress, let her not come near me.   [725]
>
> Out, out *Hyæna*; these are thy wonted arts.   [748]

And artful she certainly is. Our opinion of Samson's character is improved here, since we see from the subtlety of her arguments and the appeal of her excuses why and how Samson fell before her earlier persuasions, as he has eloquently described her blandishments in the scene with Manoa. She uses, at first, three arguments, which may be summed up thus: (1) You say I'm weak; well, you're weak too; so let's be weak together. Forgive my weaknesses so that men may forgive your weaknesses. (2) It was love that caused it. I did it to keep you with me:

> I knew that liberty
> Would draw thee forth to perilous enterprises,
> While I at home sate full of cares and fears
> Wailing thy absence in my widow'd bed;
> Here I should still enjoy thee day and night
> Mine and Loves prisoner, not the *Philistines,*
> Whole to my self, unhazarded abroad,
> Fearless at home of partners in my love.
> These reasons in Loves law have past for good,
> Though fond and reasonless to some perhaps:
> And Love hath oft, well meaning, wrought much wo,
> Yet always pity or pardon hath obtain'd.   [803–14]

(3) I did it for my country:

> thou know'st the Magistrates
> And Princes of my countrey came in person,
> Sollicited, commanded, threatn'd, urg'd,
> Adjur'd by all the bonds of civil Duty
> And of Religion, press'd how just it was,

> How honourable, how glorious to entrap
> A common enemy, who had destroy'd
> Such numbers of our Nation.   [850–57]

Samson answers her throughout with careful, steady reasoning; he is fully in command of his mental powers, as Dalila at last realizes, when she tries to win him with a hurt and humble manner:

> In argument with men a woman ever
> Goes by the worse, whatever be her cause.   [903–04]

But he answers with strong and bitter wit:

> For want of words no doubt, or lack of breath,
> Witness when I was worried with thy peals.   [905–06]

Seeing him so resolved, she tries the last appeal: whatever is past is past; let me take care of you; let me make it up to you. We notice the insidious nature of the temptation she here offers to the blind man:

>   though sight be lost,
> Life yet hath many solaces, enjoy'd
> Where other senses want not their delights
> At home in leisure and domestic ease,
> Exempt from many a care and chance to which
> Eye-sight exposes daily men abroad.
> I to the Lords will intercede, not doubting
> Thir favourable ear, that I may fetch thee
> From forth this loathsom prison-house, to abide
> With me, where my redoubl'd love and care
> With nursing diligence, to me glad office,
> May ever tend about thee to old age
> With all things grateful chear'd, and so suppli'd,
> That what by me thou hast lost thou least shalt miss.   [914–27]

Samson himself seems almost to believe her here, for at first he responds more gently:

> No, no, of my condition take no care;
> It fits not; thou and I long since are twain.   [928–29]

But he soon moves on into the tone of more rigorous rejection:

> Nor think me so unwary or accurst
> To bring my feet again into the snare

> Where once I have been caught; I know thy trains
> Though dearly to my cost, thy ginns, and toyls;
> Thy fair enchanted cup, and warbling charms
> No more on me have power, their force is null'd,
> So much of Adders wisdom I have learn't
> To fence my ear against thy sorceries.   [930–37]

Nevertheless, the relative mildness of Samson's manner here seems to make her bolder and to urge her into one final plea: "Let me approach at least, and touch thy hand." Samson's fierce revulsion is a sign of the powerful attraction which she still holds:

> Not for thy life, lest fierce remembrance wake
> My sudden rage to tear thee joint by joint.   [952–53]

And he concludes with a tense and guarded manner, maintaining his firm self-control through bitter and fierce irony:

> At distance I forgive thee, go with that;
> Bewail thy falshood, and the pious works
> It hath brought forth to make thee memorable
> Among illustrious women, faithful wives;
> Cherish thy hast'n'd widowhood with the gold
> Of Matrimonial treason: so farewel.   [954–59]

What shall we make of Dalila here? To what extent does she mean what she says? Is it true, as Samson says, "That malice not repentance brought thee hither"? Is she, as the chorus says, "a manifest Serpent by her sting / Discover'd in the end"? Dalila remains an enigma that neither Samson, nor the chorus, nor the audience, can resolve.[7] Her speeches suggest a complex tissue of motives and impulses: curiosity, a challenge to see if she can draw him back, regret that it turned out worse than she thought it would, physical desire to have Samson back with her again, a desire to defend herself, to prove to herself perhaps that she is not as bad as it may seem. And then at the end we have the natural anger of a woman scorned, which does not necessarily prove her to be a hypocrite throughout, though Samson is surely right in thinking that she would betray him again if he went back. Whatever her nature, whatever her motives, the power of her appeal has certainly accomplished a remarkable change in Samson; she has stirred him out of his sense of loss, stung him into more positive responses.

Samson looks even stronger here if we compare this scene with
the scene in Euripides' *The Trojan Women* which it evokes: that
scene where Menelaus at last confronts his wife Helen. Menelaus
enters cursing Helen, saying that he will kill her now, or take her
home and have her killed there. His manner, however, is that of
indecisive bluster and torment; and every Greek who watched the
play knew perfectly well that Menelaus would never kill her, be-
cause in Homer's *Odyssey,* they knew, Telemachus had visited
Menelaus and Helen, and had seen them living together again,
not at all happily, after the Trojan War. So Menelaus looks weak
here in the Greek play, and Helen's cool arguments and unrepen-
tant ways, we know, will overcome his threats. Dalila is far more
impressive than the Helen of Euripides, whose brazen reliance on
her beauty shows in all her lines; and for this reason too Samson
here seems to have much greater strength of mind than
Menelaus.

Samson, we see, has now arisen beyond all temptations—and
also far beyond the denunciation of the evils of women which we
now hear presented in the chorus's inadequate commentary on
this complex and moving scene. The chorus presents its conven-
tional anti-feminist satire in what might fairly be called the
weakest rhyming of the entire play:

> It is not vertue, wisdom, valour, *wit,*
> Strength, comliness of shape, or amplest *merit*
> That womans love can win or long *inherit;*
> But what it is, hard is to *say,*
> Harder to *hit,*
> (Which way soever men refer *it*)
> Much like thy riddle, *Samson,* in one *day*
> Or seven, though one should musing *sit.*   [1010–17]

The loss of dignity in the poetry is clear; Milton, it seems, is here
drastically lowering the tone and manner of the poetry for some
particular effect.[8]

> Is it for that such outward *ornament*
> Was lavish't on thir Sex, that inward *gifts*
> Were left for hast unfinish't, judgment *scant,*
> Capacity not rais'd to appre*hend*
> Or value what is *best*

In choice, but oftest to affect the *wrong?*
Or was too much of self-love *mixt,*
Of constancy no root *infixt,*
That either they love nothing, or not *long?*
. . . .
    Therefore Gods universal *Law*
Gave to the man despotic *power*
Over his female in due *awe,*
Nor from that right to part an *hour,*
Smile she or *lowre:*
So shall he least confusion *draw*
On his whole life, not *sway'd*
By female usurpation, nor *dismay'd.*   [1025–60]

The jarring impact of the endings here should help to indicate
that this is hardly John Milton's final word of wisdom about wo-
men. We are warned against this by the weakness of the verse, by
the one-sided quality of the view, and by the exaggeration of
man's proper power over women. Authority man has—or should
have—according to Milton, but never quite a power of this grim
variety. Why, then, has Milton brought in such a choric utterance
here, weak in itself, and out of tone with the central tendency of
Samson's own self-denunciation? True, Samson blames Dalila
furiously, for showing the "arts of every woman false like thee,"
but that is far from saying that nearly every woman is false. The
chorus has picked up one aspect of the previous scene and has
driven it to the point of caricature. The effect is to relieve the
violent tension of the previous scene by a touch of satirical humor,
and thus to prepare the way for the next scene, which develops a
robustly comic tone, as Samson deflates the bragging and fastidi-
ous giant Harapha. Here is the one portion of the play in which
we have a glimpse of the old folk-hero: taunting, audacious,
primitive in his total confidence in his physical strength:

I only with an Oak'n staff will meet thee,
And raise such out-cries on thy clatter'd Iron,
Which long shall not with-hold mee from thy head,
That in a little time while breath remains thee,
Thou oft shalt wish thy self at *Gath* to boast
Again in safety what thou wouldst have done
To *Samson,* but shalt never see *Gath* more.   [1123–29]

But the glimpse of the primitive hero is brief; Milton very soon transmutes Samson into the dignified champion of God, as Samson declares (with a significant use of the word "Nativity"):

> My trust is in the living God who gave me
> At my Nativity this strength, diffus'd
> No less through all my sinews, joints and bones,
> Then thine, while I preserv'd these locks unshorn,
> The pledge of my unviolated vow.   [1140–44]

And soon Samson declares his willingness to resume the role of God's champion against Dagon, as he proceeds to accept the hope that he had earlier refused to allow:

> All these indignities, for such they are
> From thine, these evils I deserve and more,
> Acknowledge them from God inflicted on me
> Justly, yet despair not of his final pardon
> Whose ear is ever open; and his eye
> Gracious to re-admit the suppliant;
> In confidence whereof I once again
> Defie thee to the trial of mortal fight,
> By combat to decide whose god is God,
> Thine or whom I with *Israel's* Sons adore.   [1168–77]

The hero is fully restored; his great potential has now been revealed; and the play can continue rapidly towards the fulfillment of its triumphant catastrophe. But even in this ending, where the chorus is given many lines of much greater power than in the middle scenes, Milton creates the impression that these men, along with Manoa, have difficulty in grasping the true greatness of Samson's achievement. Their spirits are lifted by the scene with Harapha—to the point where their fine ode, "Oh how comely it is and how reviving," proceeds for thirty fervent lines without a single rhyme—but during the scene with Samson and the Officer, and in the scene with Manoa following Samson's departure, the chorus shows itself bewildered: "How thou wilt here come off surmounts my reach," they say in one deflating line (1380), and they agree completely with Manoa in his hopes for ransoming his son:

> Thy hopes are not ill founded nor seem vain
> Of his delivery, and thy joy thereon

> Conceiv'd, agreeable to a Fathers love,
> In both which we, as next participate.   [1504–07]

The Messenger then describes the center of Samson's great achievement in these words:

> with head a while enclin'd,
> And eyes fast fixt he stood, as one who pray'd,
> Or some great matter in his mind revolv'd.
> At last with head erect thus cryed aloud,
> Hitherto, Lords, what your commands impos'd
> I have perform'd, as reason was, obeying,
> Not without wonder or delight beheld.
> Now of my own accord such other tryal
> I mean to shew you of my strength, yet greater;
> As with amaze shall strike all who behold.   [1636–45]

We note the emphasis on mental action, on reason, and on choice: "Now of my own accord." Samson's greatness lies in his rational choice of a God-given opportunity. But here is what the chorus, in its immediate response, makes of this rational act:

> O dearly-bought revenge, yet glorious!
> Living or dying thou hast fulfill'd
> The work for which thou wast foretold
> To *Israel,* and now ly'st victorious
> Among thy slain self-kill'd
> Not willingly,[9] but tangl'd in the fold
> Of dire necessity, whose law in death conjoin'd
> Thee with thy slaughter'd foes in number more
> Then all thy life had slain before.   [1660–68]

Does the heavy rhyme, once again, help to suggest that this view is not to be taken as the whole truth? The "law" of "dire necessity" plays no part in Milton's universe:[10] by saying that Samson has died "self-kill'd / Not willingly," the chorus shows its initial failure to grasp the deeper meaning of Samson's triumph. Yet, as the chorus proceeds here, the realization of some inward act of "vertue," "illuminated" by God, breaks through:[11]

> But he though blind of sight,
> Despis'd and thought extinguish't quite,
> With inward eyes illuminated
> His fierie vertue rouz'd
> From under ashes into sudden flame . . .   [1687–91]

The latent contradiction between "necessity" and "inward eyes" is
not to be reconciled—nor need it be; it is enough to know that the
chorus at the close has glimpsed something of the essential truth.
As for Manoa, one wonders: his final thoughts are all external[12]—
on washing the "enemies blood" off Samson's body, on having a
proper funeral, on building a proper monument, where

> The Virgins also shall on feastful days
> Visit his Tomb with flowers, only bewailing
> His lot unfortunate in nuptial choice,
> From whence captivity and loss of eyes.   [1741–44]

Still harping on those foreign wives, Manoa can see no relation
between Samson's "nuptial choice" and the opportunity to
achieve, by another choice, his final victory. As Samson knows, it
was not his nuptial choice that led to his "captivity and loss of
eyes"; it was his weakness in dealing with the blandishments of his
chosen mate.

Can we, amid these circumstances, wholly believe Manoa when
he says the words that for some readers have seemed to explain
why the play is not a true tragedy?

> Nothing is here for tears, nothing to wail
> Or knock the breast, no weakness, no contempt,
> Dispraise, or blame, nothing but well and fair,
> And what may quiet us in a death so noble.   [1721–24]

Like everything else that Manoa has said in the play, this is at best
a half-truth, a partial understanding. There is much that is here
for tears, much that is not well and fair. Samson, like all tragic
heroes, has gained his victory within the self, but at terrible cost. It
is the cost of his final understanding that we must ponder, as the
chorus brings the tragedy to a quiet and conventional close. In
these final lines the chorus speaks with an effective firmness, while
the conventionality is marked by its expression in fourteen lines,
rhymed in sonnet-style:

> All is best, though we oft doubt,
> What th' unsearchable dispose
> Of highest wisdom brings about,
> And ever best found in the close.
> Oft he seems to hide his face,

> But unexpectedly returns
> And to his faithful Champion hath in place
> Bore witness gloriously; whence *Gaza* mourns
> And all that band them to resist
> His uncontroulable intent,
> His servants he with new acquist
> Of true experience from this great event
> With peace and consolation hath dismist,
> And calm of mind all passion spent.

Certainly the chorus and Manoa have been uplifted by Samson's achievement; they have received "new acquist / Of true experience" that reaffirms their faith and opens the way toward their salvation. And yet even at the close they seem not quite to grasp the complex meaning of Samson's victory.[13] They stress the "uncontroulable intent" of God, while neglecting the free intent of Samson. They stress the way in which God has borne "witness" to his "faithful Champion," rather than the way in which this faithful man has borne witness to God. The distance between the "Elect" and the "rest" has been maintained. The chorus and Manoa have missed the deep self-discovery of the hero: that he is, by his own willing choice, a chosen son of God.

Nothing could show more clearly the range and reach of Milton's poetical career than a comparison between his volumes of 1645 and 1671. The earlier book derives from a pastoral joy in the physical creation, a sense of relationship between man and nature, though shadowed in places by a growing awareness of mortality and of moral and political evil at work in the world of man. In the later book that joy in the physical creation has been rigorously restrained, and that restraint is conveyed by the rigorous control over sensuous imagery, pagan allusion, and the burgeoning language of Milton's grand style. *Paradise Regain'd,* with its desert setting, is an anti-pastoral, played in the gray country of the mind, without recourse to the fruits of earth. Or perhaps it is better called a pastoral of a kind peculiar to the Bible,[14] a retreat from the city to the wilderness and the sparse pasturing hills of Judaea, such as the Israelites and their prophets made in answer to "the voice of him that crieth in the wilderness, Prepare ye the way of the Lord, make straight in the desert a highway for our God"

PARADISE REGAIN'D,

A

POEM.

In IV BOOKS.

To which is added

SAMSON AGONISTES.

The Author

JOHN MILTON.

LONDON,

Printed by *J. M.* for *John Starkey* at the
Mitre in *Fleetstreet*, near *Temple-Bar*.
MDCLXXI.

(Isaiah 40:3). The contest of styles that is won by the Son of God in *Paradise Regain'd* finds its fulfillment in the relatively plain style of *Samson Agonistes,* where the play of sensuous imagery is severely pruned and the mode of reasoned speech prevails.[15] The result is a volume of austere greatness, a grandeur of self-abnegation that demonstrates, in both poems, the discovery of the true inner self of the chosen son.

Thus Milton's three great volumes of 1645, 1667, and 1671 might be seen as a triptych. On one side lies the green, youthful, chiefly joyous work of pastoral creation, and on the other the austere, ascetic, reasoned, rigorous work of age. In between lies the master piece, where a pastoral joy in God's Creation lives at the center of the vision, while the sombre tones of a wise and suffering maturity enfold that vision within scenes that reveal the possibilities of tragic failure and redemptive hope. Each of the three panels has an individual integrity, and can be viewed apart. Yet the measure of Milton's greatness lies in a realization of the full ensemble.

Paradise Regain'd
and the *Georgics*

"Oscillation between the heroic and the mundane is characteristic of the *Georgics*," says John Chalker: "It is easy to forget how much of the poem is epic in scope and manner, and how widely the heroic passages range." And he goes on to describe the *Georgics* as "a *montage* involving sudden shifts of subject and mood so that a pattern of comparisons and contrasts is built up which defies easy explanation."[1] The similarity between this account of the *Georgics* and my own view of the "contest of styles" in *Paradise Regain'd* has encouraged me to return to the suggestion made at the outset of the earlier versions of my essay on that poem: that *Paradise Regain'd* bears some analogy with the *Georgics*. The suggestion has not in general been welcomed,[2] perhaps because it was only a suggestion and was not explored in any detail.

The crux of the issue seems to lie in the meaning of the term "middle style," for which the *Georgics* has been taken as the model, at least since the time of Servius: "tres enim sunt characteres, humilis, medius, grandiloquus: quos omnes in hoc invenimus poeta. nam in Aeneide grandiloquum habet, in georgicis medium, in bucolicis humilem pro qualitate negotiorum et personarum."[3] Thus Addison speaks of the *Georgics* as a work written "in the middle Stile": Vergil, he says, "delivers the meanest of his Precepts with a kind of Grandeur, he breaks the Clods and tosses the Dung about with an air of gracefulness."[4]

A reading of the *Georgics* will show that the term *medius* cannot be taken to describe a style that pursues the even tenor of its way along a middle line between the *humilis* and the *grandiloquus*. *Medius* describes a style that allows for frequent oscillations upward and downward from a middle way: on the average the style lies in the middle between the humble and the grand, but it flexi-

293

bly accommodates a great deal of variation in either direction: it is
medius in the sense of being "intermediate"—"of a middle kind,
resembling each in some degree."

A middle range, however, can be found in the style, like a
thread that holds the poem under control: it is the dignified,
carefully moulded, but unpretentious style found in the poem's
opening lines:

> Quid faciat laetas segetes, quo sidere terram
> vertere, Maecenas, ulmisque adiungere vitis
> conveniat, quae cura boum, qui cultus habendo
> sit pecori, apibus quanta experientia parcis,
> hinc canere incipiam.

Dryden catches the manner to perfection:

> What makes a plenteous Harvest, when to turn
> The fruitful Soil, and when to sowe the Corn;
> The Care of Sheep, of Oxen, and of Kine;
> And how to raise on Elms the teeming Vine:
> The Birth and Genius of the frugal Bee,
> I sing, *Mecaenas,* and I sing to thee.

But then at once the style begins to modulate toward a higher
vein, moving through a series of apostrophes to various gods, and
ending with an appeal to Augustus in something close to an epic
manner:

> vos, o clarissima mundi
> lumina, labentem caelo quae ducitis annum,
> Liber et alma Ceres, vestro si munere tellus
> Chaoniam pingui glandem mutavit arista,
> poculaque inventis Acheloia miscuit uvis,
> et vos, agrestum praesentia numina, Fauni,
> (ferte simul Faunique pedem Dryadesque puellae)—
> munera vestra cano.   [1.5–12]

> Ye Deities!, who Fields and Plains protect,
> Who rule the Seasons, and the Year direct;
> *Bacchus* and fost'ring *Ceres,* Pow'rs Divine,
> Who gave us Corn for Mast, for Water Wine;
> Ye Fawns, propitious to the Rural Swains,
> Ye Nymphs that haunt the Mountains and the Plains,
> Join in my Work, and to my Numbers bring
> Your needful Succor, for your Gifts I sing. [trans. Dryden, 7–14]

tuque adeo, quem mox quae sint habitura deorum
concilia incertum est, urbesne invisere, Caesar.
terrarumque velis curam, et te maximus orbis
auctorem frugum tempestatumque potentem
accipiat cingens materna tempora myrto,
an deus immensi venias maris ac tua nautae
numina sola colant, tibi serviat ultima Thule,
teque sibi generum Tethys emat omnibus undis,
anne novum tardis sidus te mensibus addas,
qua locus Erigonen inter Chelasque sequentis
panditur (ipse tibi iam bracchia contrahit ardens
Scorpius et caeli iusta plus parte reliquit)—
quidquid eris (nam te nec sperant Tartara regem,
nec tibi regnandi veniat tam dira cupido,
quamvis Elysios miretur Graecia campos,
nec repetita sequi curet Proserpina matrem)
da facilem cursum, atque audacibus adnue coeptis,
ignarosque viae mecum miseratus agrestis
ingredere et votis iam nunc adsuesce vocari.   [1.24–42]

Dryden, caught up with the grandeur of the passage, expands Vergil's nineteen lines to thirty-four, of which I quote part, to illustrate the high tone:

And chiefly thou, whose undetermin'd State
Is yet the Business of the Gods Debate:
Whether in after Times to be declar'd
The Patron of the World, and *Rome's* peculiar Guard,
Or o're the Fruits and Seasons to preside,
And the round Circuit of the Year to guide.
Pow'rful of Blessings, which thou strew'st around,
And with thy Goddess Mother's Myrtle crown'd.
Or wilt thou, *Caesar,* chuse the watry Reign,
To smooth the Surges, and correct the Main?
Then Mariners, in Storms, to thee shall pray,
Ev'n utmost *Thule* shall thy Pow'r obey,
And *Neptune* shall resign the Fasces of the Sea. . . .
But thou, propitious *Caesar,* guide my Course,
And to my bold Endeavours add thy Force.
Pity the Poet's and the Ploughman's Cares,
Int'rest thy Greatness in our mean Affairs,
And use thy self betimes to hear our Pray'rs.   [30–42, 59–63]

When, immediately after this, the poem turns to deal with "mean

Affairs," the style abruptly and appropriately drops down to the middle range:

> Vere novo, gelidus canis cum montibus umor
> liquitur et Zephyro putris se glaeba resolvit,
> depresso incipiat iam tum mihi taurus aratro
> ingemere, et sulco attritus splendescere vomer.
> illa seges demum votis respondet avari
> agricolae, bis quae solem, bis frigora sensit;
> illius immensae ruperunt horrea messes.   [1.43–49]

Dryden's version of this passage seems to elevate the style a bit above the Latin, which here seems to be more direct and perhaps closer to the colloquial, as the translation by Day Lewis may indicate:

> Early spring, when a cold moisture sweats from the hoarhead
> Hills and the brittle clods are loosening under a west wind,
> Is the time for the bull to grunt as he pulls the plough deep-
>   driven
> And the ploughshare to take a shine, scoured clean in the furrow.
> That crop, which twice has felt the sun's heat and the frost twice,
> Will answer at last the prayers of the never-satisfied
> Farmer, and burst his barns with an overflowing harvest.

But shortly after this we find a shift upwards toward the high style, marked by the lists of names characteristic of epic: this is then followed by an equally abrupt shift downward marked by the words "ergo age"—"now let's get to work." The translation by Day Lewis seems quite faithful to the variations upward and downward exhibited by this characteristic passage:

> First you must learn the winds and changeable ways of its
>   weather,
> The land's peculiar cultivation and character,
> The different crops that different parts of it yield or yield not.
> A corn-crop here, grapes there will come to the happier issue:
> On another soil it is fruit trees, and grass of its own sweet will
> Grows green. Look you, how Tmolus gives us the saffron per-
>   fume,
> India its ivory, the unmanly Sabaeans their incense,
> The naked Chalybes iron, Pontus the rank castor,
> And Elis prize-winning mares.
> Nature imposed these laws, a covenant everlasting,
> On different parts of the earth right from the earliest days when

Deucalion cast over a tenantless world the stones
From which arose mankind, that dour race. Now, to business:
As soon as the first months of the year begin, your strong bulls
Should turn the fertile loam and leave the clods lying
For the full suns of summer to bake into a fine dust . . .
See, too, that your arable lies fallow in due rotation,
And leave the idle field alone to recoup its strength:
Or else, changing the seasons, put down to yellow spelt
A field where before you raised the bean with its rattling pods
Or the small-seeded vetch
Or the brittle stalk and rustling haulm of the bitter lupin.
For a crop of flax burns up a field, and so does an oat-crop,
And poppies drenched in oblivion burn up its energy.
Still, by rotation of crops you lighten your labour, only
Scruple not to enrich the dried-up soil with dung
And scatter filthy ashes on fields that are exhausted.[5]

[1.51–66, 71–81]

With the last few lines here we have descended very close to the
humilis, in keeping with the lowly subject:

Alternis idem tonsas cessare novalis
et segnem patiere situ durescere campum;
aut ibi flava seres mutato sidere farra,
unde prius laetum siliqua quassante legumen
aut tenuis fetus viciae tristisque lupini
sustuleris fragilis calamos silvamque sonantem.
urit enim lini campum seges, urit avenae,
urunt Lethaeo perfusa papavera sommo:
sed tamen alternis facilis labor, arida tantum
ne saturare fimo pingui pudeat sola neve
effetos cinerem immundum iactare per agros.   [1.71–81]

This technique of rising and then cutting back sharply goes on
throughout the poem, as Wilkinson and Otis have both re-
marked.[6] The effect is particularly notable after the famous pas-
sage of the second book devoted to praise of Italy in the higher
style: the translation by Bovie makes the shift clear:

Italian soil has bred a race of heroes,
Marsians, Sabines, toughened generations
From the Western Coast, and tribes of Volscians
Handy with the spear. Great Family names,
Camillus, Decius, Marius, Scipio,
And chief of all, Octavianus Caesar,

Who triumphs now on Asia's farthest shore,
And defends the hills of Rome from the timid foe.
All hail, Saturnian Land, our honored Mother!
For thee I broach these themes of ancient art
And dare disclose the sacred springs of verse,
Singing Hesiod's song through Roman towns.
    Now for the innate qualities of soils:
The color, strength, productive powers of each.
Ground that is hard to deal with, awkward hills,
Thin fields of marl, stone-cluttered undergrowths,
Welcome a grove of Pallas' long-lived olives.
Wild olives, cropping out on every side,
And fields strewn thick with berries, mark the place.
But moist and lush terrain, and fertile flatlands
Thick with grass (the sort we see below
In mountain vales where brooks slip down the rocks
And wash in fertile mud), and southern heights
That favor ferns, the bane of curving ploughs,
Will yield you hardy vineyards full of wine:
This soil is good for grapes . . .   [2.166–91][7]

And the same is true of the passage in book 3 that tells of the epic
battle of the bulls, a passage of twenty-three lines which Dryden
expands to thirty-six, bringing out the mock-heroic elements la-
tent in Vergil and stressing at the end the abrupt shift to a lower
style after the heroic simile:

Not with more Madness, rolling from afar,
The spumy Waves proclaim the watry War.
And mounting upwards, with a mighty Roar,
March onwards, and insult the rocky shoar.
They mate the middle Region with their height;
And fall no less, than with a Mountain's weight;
The Waters boil, and belching from below
Black Sands, as from a forceful Engine throw.
    Thus every Creature, and of every Kind,
The secret Joys of sweet Coition find . . .   [3.367–76]

Equally clear is the contrast set up at the outset of book 3, as
Vergil expresses his hope of ultimately dealing with epic
themes—but at present, he says, such themes are not his occupa-
tion. Then he turns to tell, in a lower style, of the problems of
breeding horses and cattle.

Meanwhile, as Dryden noted, the entire movement of the *Geor-*

gics shows, within these oscillations, a steady rise in the "Subject":
"Virgil has taken care to raise the Subject of each Georgic: In the
First, he has only dead Matter on which to work. In the second he
just steps on the World of Life, and describes that degree of it
which is to be found in Vegetables. In the third, he advances to
Animals. And in the last, singles out the Bee, which may be reck-
on'd the most sagacious of 'em, for his Subject."[8] And the rise in
subject is accompanied by an appropriate rise in the level of the
characteristic style of each book. The first book, as in *Paradise
Regain'd,* is on the whole cast in a lower style than the remaining
books, while, as Chalker says, "The most extended epic passages
are found in the fourth Book" (p. 26). There the life of the bees is
treated in a gently mock-heroic style—gently, because the bees are
held up as models for (in Dryden's words) "their prudent and
politick Administration of Affairs."[9] Addison well describes the
use of the epic techniques here when he says that Vergil

> Ennobles the Actions of so trivial a Creature, with Metaphors
> drawn from the most important Concerns of Mankind. His Verses
> are not in a greater noise and hurry in the Battels of *Aeneas* and
> *Turnus,* than in the Engagement of two Swarms. And as in his *Aeneis*
> he compares the Labours of his *Trojans* to those of Bees and Pis-
> mires, here he compares the Labours of the Bees to those of the
> *Cyclops.* In short, the last *Georgic* was a good Prelude to the *Aeneis;*
> and very well shew'd what the Poet could do in the description of
> what was really great, by his describing the Mock-grandeur of an
> Insect with so good a grace.[10]

Then at line 280, almost exactly in the middle of the fourth
book, Vergil changes his mode of narration to present the "epyll-
ion" of Aristaeus, a story which enfolds the story of Orpheus and
Eurydice in a manner that may have influenced Ovid. The parts
pertaining to Aristaeus are told in an epic, Homeric manner, as
Otis says: "The diction, periodization, metre are almost clamor-
ously epical."[11] Thus we have allusions to such "higher" matters as
the shower of Parthian arrows, invocations of the Muse, lists of
proper names, and vast geographical excursions, along with the
descent of Orpheus to the underworld—all this to relate an
aetiological myth of dying and rebirth, telling how a bee swarm is
born from the belly of an ox.

One hesitates to press the analogies here, but they seem to press themselves upon us. The fourth book of *Paradise Regain'd* is also told in two different modes of narration. The first part of the last book is given over to the visions of the glories of Rome and Greece, thus completing the long sequence of temptations that began in book 2; the sequence ends at line 364, a little more than half-way through this final book of 639 lines. After a brief transition in which Satan warns the hero that

> Sorrows, and labours, opposition, hate,
> Attends thee, scorns, reproaches, injuries,
> Violence and stripes, and lastly cruel death . . .   [4.386–88]

Milton shifts his mode of narration to tell of three symbolic actions: the storm that seems to adumbrate the Passion, the victory of the Son of God on the pinnacle of the temple, and the banquet and hymn presented to the Son of God by the angels.

Otis points out, in his fine analysis of Vergil's closing epyllion, that the story of Orpheus and Eurydice is enclosed within the story of Aristaeus in such a way as to create a tripartite structure. The Orpheus "panel" is narrated in a sympathetic way, with a concentrated dramatic impact, quite different from the more "diffuse" and objective narration found in the parts dealing directly with Aristaeus. The Orpheus panel tells "with marvellous compression" a story that deals with "the tragedy of human passion." Orpheus "cannot conquer his own impulses which destroy him in the very moment of triumph"—that is, his *furor* ruins his attempt to regain his lost Eurydice. But the Aristaeus myth, on either side of the Orpheus panel, tells a story of miraculous rebirth. Otis presses the point hard:

> What stands out and is meant to stand out is the central Orpheus panel, where the elliptical, concentrated, emotional style and above all, for once, a penetrating vignette of human feeling, come at exactly the point where we are led to expect revelation. The human meaning, the human price of passion, atonement and resurrection emerge in a blaze of light at the decisive, last instant.[12]

It may be valid to feel in this peculiar structure a distant parallel with the way in which the "panel" of Jesus' victory on the pinnacle of the temple stands out, with concentrated power, between the more diffuse narration of the storm (with its famous relaxed sentence: "Mee worse then wet thou find'st not") and the description of the pastoral banquet provided by the angels, followed by their hymn. Perhaps we have been prepared to receive this sort of parallel by the fact that the third books of both poems also display an explicit division into two approximate halves, unlike the first two books of both poems.

The chief difficulty in accepting such analogies with the *Georgics* seems to lie in a tendency to underestimate the wide-ranging implications of that poem. "It used to be thought," says Wilkinson, "that the *Georgics* consisted simply of didactic matter treated as 'poetically' as possible and relieved by set-pieces, mythological examples, similes and so forth."[13] But he points out that classical scholars, for almost fifty years before his book of 1969, had been moving toward a view that sees a high degree of unity and a deeper meaning in the poem.[14] Jackson Knight, for example, has seen the function of what used to be regarded as "digressions"—the heightened passages:

> . . . everything is coloured by contrasts, for it is all framed by a world of imagination; and accordingly nothing is entirely actual. The sheep of the farm are themselves changed, when Vergil, appealing to Pales, goddess of pastures, says that now for such a majestic subject he "must speak in deep-toned harmonics"—*magno nunc ore sonandum.* [*Georgics* 3.294][15]

"It is a serious critical error," says Charles Segal, "to read that great poem as simply a didactic treatise on farming. What it does is to present nature as a vast symbolical framework against which the eternal human themes of love, war, death, work, suffering, and loss are writ large."[16] Jacques Perret, along with Otis, has carried the possible implications of the poem even further:

> . . . through this evocation of rural life an entire philosophy is proposed to us. Virgil's laborer becomes a symbol of all human life, with the result that the poet's exhortations and vehemence produce an immediate emotional response in us . . . I myself may have no feeling for the work of the farmer; yet the images of the poet move me nonetheless: a countryside to recreate, a land to make fruitful, order to establish, a national ideal to animate, a Golden Age to give birth to . . .

It is only quite recently that it has again become possible for us to interpret the *Georgics* in this way, as a poem of human effort, of the building of a country and of the world, as a poem of God's presence in and response to human labor . . . The literary success of the *Georgics* . . . is linked much more closely than is at first apparent to a certain quality of the soul.[17]

Whether or not we agree with these interpretations (as I do), the main point of citing them is to show that Milton, if he is imitating the style and form of the *Georgics* in the renaissance manner, has chosen no unworthy model. We must remember too, that for Dryden and Addison, the *Georgics* was nothing less than Vergil's masterpiece. In the Dedication of his translation to Lord Chesterfield, Dryden speaks of the *Georgics* as "the best Poem of the best Poet," and goes on to say: "*Virgil* wrote his *Georgics* in the full strength and vigour of his Age, when his Judgment was at the height, and before his Fancy was declining." And Addison, in his essay prefaced to Dryden's translations of Vergil, declares that the poem is "the most Compleat, Elaborate, and finisht Piece of all Antiquity."

The *Aeneis* indeed is of a Nobler kind, but the *Georgic* is more perfect in its kind. The *Aeneid* has a greater variety of Beauties in it, but those of the *Georgic* are more exquisite. In short, the *Georgic* has all the perfection that can be expected in a Poem written by the greatest Poet in the Flower of his Age, when his Invention was ready, his Imagination warm, his Judgement settled, and all his Faculties in their full Vigour and Maturity.

We have no external evidence that Milton shared this remarkably high view of the poem's greatness. As with the question of the middle style, the only strong evidence lies in *Paradise Regain'd* itself. Addison's complaint that the poem has been neglected may suggest that his view was not widely held in the seventeenth century. Yet Dryden was already forty years old when *Paradise Regain'd* was published, and one might think that his views of the *Georgics* had already been established by that time.

However this may be, the evidence of analogy between these two poems is worth pursuing. It can be found by a careful comparison of the two poems, along with the studies of Wilkinson and Otis. Such a comparison may be encouraged by remembering what

Tillyard said long ago, when he remarked that *Paradise Regain'd* and the *Georgics* were poems of similar length, a little more than two thousand lines, and that they both were divided into four books.[18] Some kind of Vergilian analogy, he thought, must reside in the fact that Milton's opening line, "I who e're while the happy Garden sung," clearly echoes the lines that used to open the *Aeneid* in renaissance editions—lines, now widely regarded as authentic, which allude to Vergil's earlier work in the pastoral and georgic kinds:

> Ille ego, qui quondam gracili modulatus avena
> carmen, et egressus silvis vicina coegi
> ut quamvis avido parerent arva colono,
> gratum opus agricolis, at nunc horrentia Martis . . .

> I am that poet who in times past made the light melody of pastoral poetry. In my next poem I left the woods for the adjacent farm-lands, teaching them to obey even the most exacting tillers of the soil; and the farmers liked my work. But now I turn to the terrible strife of Mars. [trans. Knight][19]

Is Milton suggesting that his career as poet, despite his beginning with the shepherd's trade, represents a reversal of the Vergilian pattern, as Milton moves now from a subject not less but *more* heroic than that of the *Aeneid* into a poem that deals with a subject *above* heroic?

Perhaps the best and most tactful solution to the problem is that implied by Charles Dunster when, in his edition of *Paradise Regain'd* (London, 1795), he described the "species" of the poem as "the *brief,* or *didactic,* epic" (p. 2). Edward Weismiller, citing this passage in the recent volume of the *Variorum,* comments wryly on this "intertwining," this fusion, or confusion of genres:

> That the brief epic is of its nature didactic is perhaps no more self-evident than that Hesiod's *Works and Days* (for example) is in a true sense epic. And what led a particular critic, no longer living, to the intertwining of definitions ordinarily kept separate may not be discoverable. Dunster's assignment of *PR* to the 'species' he denominates so crisply may on the other hand be in part explained by a comment in his concluding note to the poem: 'Though it may be said' of *PR,* 'as Longinus has said of the *Odyssey,* that it is the *epilogue* of the preceding poem, still the

design and conduct of it is as different, as that of the *Georgics* from the *Aeneid*.'[20]

Dunster's intertwining of genres may give us a clue to an acceptable solution. What has happened, perhaps, is this: the presence of epic elements in Vergil's *Georgics* allowed Milton to fulfill his early plan for a brief epic modelled on the book of Job by merging it with the form and style of the *Georgics*. The presence of strong epic elements in the style of *Paradise Regain'd* does not in itself make the poem an epic, unless we are willing to say that for these reasons the *Georgics* too is a brief epic—with the figure of the farmer as hero. The "old Corycian swain" in Vergil's fourth book, says Chalker, "is in a sense the true heroic figure of the *Georgics*" (p. 26).

In the end it does not matter whether we call *Paradise Regain'd* a brief epic, or a georgic, as long as we recognize its analogies to the form and style of Vergil's *Georgics*. If such analogies can be accepted, then Milton's poem of renunciation does not in fact renounce the classics after all. *Samson Agonistes* is "added" to the volume of 1671, a poem of comparable length and at least equal power, as though to stress the poet's unbroken allegiance to the literary modes of Greece and Rome.

Amor and *Furor:*
Anti-heroic Themes
and the Unity of
Ovid's *Metamorphoses*

Ovid's theme of *amor* is introduced in the first tale that occurs after the world has been renewed through the piety of Deucalion and Pyrrha: the story of Phoebus and Daphne opens with the thematic word: "Primus amor Phoebi Daphne Peneia, quem non / fors ignara dedit, sed saeva Cupidinis ira" ("The first love of Phoebus was Daphne, daughter of Peneus, which was not brought about by blind chance, but by the fierce anger of Cupid": 1.452–53). For Apollo, "still exultant" over his heroic conquest of Python, had caught a glimpse of Cupid bending his bow and had said to him in scorn: "What have you to do with a warrior's arms? Weapons such as these are suited to my shoulders" (1.456–57; trans. Innes). Then, after the striking of Cupid's arrow, Apollo's cry to Daphne sets the essential motif: "amor est mihi causa sequendi!" (1.507). In the next book the power of love is pointed up by Ovid's sly remark as Jove is about to undertake the seduction of Europa: "non bene conveniunt nec in una sede morantur / maiestas et amor" ("Majesty and love do not go well together, nor tarry long in the same dwelling-place": 2.846–47; trans. Miller). So too, in book 5, the king of the underworld must submit to the power of Venus, as she sees him inspecting the volcanic region of Sicily. Embracing Cupid, she cries: "O son, both arms and hands to me, and source of all my power, take now those shafts, Cupid, with which you conquer all, and shoot your swift arrows into the heart of that god to whom the final lot of the triple kingdom fell"

(5.365–68; trans. Miller). And so occurs the rape of Proserpine in the field of Enna. Such is the "heroic" warfare of love's empire.

The whole contrast between *maiestas* and *amor* is then summed up in the weaving contest between Pallas and Arachne at the beginning of book 6. The tapestry of Pallas deals majestically with the ancient contest of the gods over the naming of Athens; but Arachne fills her tapestry with scenes depicting the *caelestia crimina* committed by the gods in their erotic escapades. So, from the opening book, on through the story of Pomona in book 14, the power of *amor* transforms the majesty of gods into animals and other earthly semblances, demonstrating an irresistible force summed up in the cry of Galatea: "pro! quanta potentia regni / est, Venus alma, tui!" ("O bountiful Venus, how powerful is your sway!": 13.758–59).

Meanwhile, in book 3, a new god is born, worshipped with new rites: Bacchus, son of Semele. As Pentheus sees and hears these wild rites, he denounces them as a threat to the old heroic code by which he lives: "Quis furor, anguigenae, proles Mavortia, vestras / attonuit mentes?" ("What madness, ye sons of the serpent's teeth, ye seed of Mars, has dulled your reason?") "Can clashing cymbals, can the pipe of crooked horn, can shallow tricks of magic, women's shrill cries, wine-heated madness, vulgar throngs and empty drums—can all these vanquish men, for whom real war, with its drawn swords, the blare of trumpets, and lines of glittering spears, had no terrors?" (3.531–37; trans. Miller). The killing of Pentheus by the Bacchantes at the end of book 3 may thus be taken to indicate the death of the old heroic order. Book 4 then opens with a sustained celebration of the new god, as the women of Thebes—all but the daughters of Minyas—gather for the festival of Bacchus, worshipping him under the many names that show his varied and widespread powers.

From here on the powers of Bacchus and Venus are intertwined, as the daughters of Minyas, scorning the rites of Bacchus, tell their many tales of love and passion, beginning with the pitiful love of Pyramus and Thisbe, and ending with the furious passion of Salmacis. This intermingling of the themes of *amor* and *furor* continues throughout the poem, reaching its climax in book 10 and the opening portion of book 11, the section of 805 lines in which the story of Orpheus himself encloses the tales of strange, violent, or perverse passion that he sings to the assembled trees, animals, and birds: Jupiter and Ganymede, Apollo and Hyacinthus, Pygmalion and the statue, the terrible passion of Myrrha for her father, Venus and Adonis, Atalanta and Hippomenes. After all these demonstrations of passion's rage, Orpheus himself is torn to pieces by the mad Ciconian women, who cry: "See, see the man who scorns us!" (11.7). Not even the bard of the rites of Bacchus (11.68, 92–93) can escape the effects of stifled love turned to *furor*. Like Pentheus, he is destroyed by frenzied women associated with the rites of the Bacchantes. By such devices of repetition and ironical reminiscence, by such persistent mingling of *amor* and *furor*—as opposed to the old heroic mode—Ovid's poem weaves itself together into a new kind of epic unity.

Notes

Reference to scholarship on Milton's minor poems and *Paradise Regain'd* is now simplified by the admirable volumes of *A Variorum Commentary on the Poems of John Milton*, vol. 1, *The Latin and Greek Poems*, ed. Douglas Bush, and *The Italian Poems*, ed. J. E. Shaw and A. Bartlett Giamatti (New York: Columbia University Press, 1970); vol. 2, parts 1, 2, and 3, *The Minor English Poems*, ed. A. S. P. Woodhouse and Douglas Bush, *With a review of Studies of Verse Form* by Edward R. Weismiller in part 3 (New York: Columbia University Press, 1972); and vol. 4 [on *Paradise Regain'd:* see below, headnote to chapter 15]; hereafter referred to as *Variorum Commentary*.

Further guidance to scholarship on all of Milton's poetry is given in the excellent introductions and annotations provided by John Carey and Alastair Fowler in their edition (really a small *variorum*) *The Poems of John Milton* (London: Longmans, 1968); hereafter referred to as "Carey and Fowler."

All quotations from Milton's poetry are taken from the text, based upon the first editions, edited by H. C. Beeching, *The Poetical Works of John Milton* (London: Oxford University Press, 1904); I have used the reprint of 1938 (normalizing line-numbers for book 11 of *Paradise Lost*).

Quotations from the Latin text of Vergil are taken from the *Opera*, edited by Frederick A. Hirtzel (Oxford: Clarendon Press, 1900); I have used the reprint of 1950.

Quotations from the Latin text of Ovid's *Metamorphoses* are taken from the volume in the Loeb Classical Library edited with a translation by Frank Justus Miller, 2nd edition, 2 vols. (London: Heinemann, 1921); I have used the reprint of 1966–68.

Quotations from Milton's prose are normally taken from *Complete Prose Works of John Milton*, Don M. Wolfe, general ed., 8 vols. (New Haven: Yale University Press, 1953–); I am especially indebted to the edition of *Christian Doctrine* in vol. 6, translated by John Carey and edited by Maurice Kelley (1973).

Throughout this work, my references to previous scholarship are of necessity highly selective: the *Variorum Commentary* and "Carey and Fowler" must be relied upon to make, by implication, many desirable acknowledgments. I have tried to single out certain books and articles for particular mention whenever they constitute a special debt or provide a parallel or divergent interpretation of some important point of discussion.

I wish to add here a general acknowledgment of the valuable articles and bibliographical aids provided by *Milton Studies, Milton Quarterly,* and *Seventeenth*

Century News. Finally, I wish to express my gratitude for the several volumes of Milton's poetry edited by Merritt Hughes, which I have used in teaching: the two editions of *Paradise Lost* (New York: Odyssey Press, 1935 and 1962); *Paradise Regained, the Minor Poems and Samson Agonistes* (Garden City: Doubleday, 1937); and *Complete Poems and Major Prose* (New York: Odyssey Press, 1957).

CHAPTER 1: The Pastoral Music: *A Maske Presented at Ludlow Castle*

The second part of this chapter is based upon materials presented in my essay "The Music of *Comus*" in *Illustrious Evidence: Approaches to English Literature of the Early Seventeenth Century,* ed. Earl Miner (Berkeley: University of California Press, 1975); "Published under the auspices of the William Andrews Clark Memorial Library." I wish to thank Louise Brown Kennedy for assistance in the preparation of the original essay for the press.

1   See Ovid's account of Chiron's teaching music to Achilles (*Fasti,* 5.379–86) and of Polyphemus' pastoral song to Galatea (*Metamorphoses,* 13.782–869). For the incident in Pholus' cave see the passage in Apollodorus' *Library,* 2.5.4 where at the banquet for Heracles the centaur Pholus opens the wine given by Dionysus to all the centaurs, and thus provokes war with the other centaurs. Anna Rist, in her illuminating commentary on Theocritus' Idyll 7, points out the undercurrent of violence and death in these allusions: "Latent seems to be a suggestion that the human cultivation which is crowned by poetry is purchased at a price." But perhaps the civilizing power of poetry is here implied. See *The Poems of Theocritus,* trans. Anna Rist (Chapel Hill: University of North Carolina Press, 1978), p. 88.

2   *Greek Pastoral Poetry,* trans. Anthony Holden (Harmondsworth: Penguin Books, 1974).

3   An extensive and illuminating study of the theme of music in Milton's early poetry is given in the opening chapter of Jon S. Lawry's *The Shadow of Heaven* (Ithaca: Cornell University Press, 1968). For surveys of musical theory see Leo Spitzer, *Classical and Christian Ideas of World Harmony* (Baltimore: Johns Hopkins Press, 1963); James Hutton, "Some English Poems in Praise of Music," *English Miscellany,* 2 (1951): 1–63; and D. P. Walker, "Orpheus the Theologian and the Renaissance Platonists," *Journal of the Warburg and Courtauld Institutes,* 16 (1953): 100–20. For the relation of Orpheus to Pythagoras see Iamblichus: "a perspicuous paradigm of the Pythagoric theology according to numbers, is in a certain respect to be found in the writings of Orpheus. Nor is it to be doubted, that Pythagoras receiving auxiliaries from Orpheus, composed his treatise Concerning the Gods." *Life of Pythagoras,* trans. Thomas Taylor (London, 1818), p. 105. For the analogy with Orpheus, see especially Angus Fletcher, *The Transcendental Masque* (Ithaca: Cornell University Press, 1971), who also treats the descriptions in lines 86–88 as indicating the "Orphic powers" of the Attendant Spirit (p. 168). See his mention of the Lady's powers as an "Orphic voice" on pp. 170

and 173 and his discussion of the Orphic voice of the poem on pp. 186–91. For the entire topic see S. K. Heninger, *Touches of Sweet Harmony: Pythagorean Cosmology and Renaissance Poetics* (San Marino: Huntington Library, 1974).

4   At the close of his speech in couplets the Genius says he cannot match the music of the spheres, "yet as we go" toward the seat of state, he adds, he will do his best to create music of praise with his "inferior hand or voice." Then in the second song he adds, "Follow me as I sing, / And touch the warbled string," as he leads the group across the lawn to where the Countess is sitting. The final song, perhaps presented as the group arrives at the seat of state, is also presumably sung by the Genius.

5   Ovid, *Metamorphoses,* trans. Mary M. Innes (Harmondsworth: Penguin Books, 1955).

6   See above, headnote, for the translation by Frank Justus Miller.

7   My appreciation of this aspect of Milton's *Maske* was greatly enriched by watching the performance of the work produced by Ars Nova (directed by John Buckingham) in London at St. John's Smith Square, September 1977. The performance was skillfully designed to approximate the original production of 1634.

8   Cf. Fletcher, *The Transcendental Masque,* p. 202.

9   See S. E. Sprott's edition, *A Maske, the Earlier Versions* (Toronto: University of Toronto Press, 1973), p. 196; also *A Maske at Ludlow,* ed. John S. Diekhoff (Cleveland: Press of Case Western Reserve University, 1968), p. [246]. This is the original reading of the Trinity MS, which is revised in accord with the printed version; both versions of the line are therefore Milton's own work.

10 See Vergil's *Eclogues*: 1.2; 6.8.

11 For a detailed discussion of this scene see Hutton, pp. 4–6, 34–38 (note 3 above). The quotations from *The Merchant of Venice* are taken from *The Riverside Shakespeare,* ed. G. Blakemore Evans (Boston: Houghton Mifflin, 1974).

12 For the analogies cf. *Romeo and Juliet,* III.ii.5, *Maske,* 553; *Macbeth,* II.i.51, *Maske,* 553; *Antony and Cleopatra,* II.ii.212–18, *Maske,* 554–59. These analogies are noted by Carey and Fowler. Cf. also *2 Henry VI,* IV.i.3–5 for analogy to *Maske,* 552–53 as noted in the *Variorum Commentary,* II, iii, 924.

13 See John Demaray, *Milton and the Masque Tradition* (Cambridge, Mass.: Harvard University Press, 1968), p. 132, on the uses of listening in *Comus*; also Raymond G. Schoen, "The Hierarchy of Senses in *A Mask,*" *Milton Quarterly,* 7 (1973): 32–37.

14 From Ficino's commentary on the *Timaeus* (*Opera Omnia,* Basel, 1561, p. 1453), as translated by D. P. Walker in *Spiritual and Demonic Magic from Ficino to Campanella* (London: Warburg Institute, 1958), p. 9.

15 "Milton's Haemony," *English Literary Renaissance,* 5 (1975): 81–95. For all quotations in this paragraph see Otten, pp. 84–88.

16 See *OED,* "rash," v^3 (with perhaps overtones of v^1).

17 John Aubrey, *Miscellanies* (London, 1696), p. 111; quoted by Otten, p. 90.

18 For a summary of the many interpretations of Haemony see the *Variorum Commentary*, II, iii, 932–38; also Otten, p. 81n; and Sacvan Bercovitch, "Milton's 'Haemony': Knowledge and Belief," *Huntington Library Quarterly*, 33 (1970): 351–59.

19 Carey and Fowler, p. 266.

20 Euripides, *Alcestis,* trans. Richard Aldington (London: Chatto, 1930), p. 39.

21 On the problem of Chiron's cave see notes in Carey and Fowler, pp. 263–64, and *The Latin Poems of John Milton,* ed. Walter MacKellar (New Haven: Yale University Press, 1930), p. 327; also *Variorum Commentary,* I, 276.

22 See also Angus Fletcher's account of the "triumph of song" in *The Transcendental Masque,* pp. 166–75.

23 See Lewis and Short, *Latin Dictionary,* "carmen."

24 Henry Lawes's autograph manuscript of the songs is on deposit in the British Library (see Coburn Gum, "Lawes Folio," *Milton Newsletter,* 3 [March, 1969], 4–5.) A second manuscript in the British Library is thought to be an eighteenth-century transcript of the autograph: see Andrew J. Sabol, *Songs and Dances for the Stuart Masque* (Providence: Brown University Press, 1959), p. 167; Sabol bases his transcription on this manuscript, which is reproduced in the Fletcher *Facsimile,* I, 340–44 (see next note). Other printed versions of Lawes's music follow the collation of the two musical manuscripts done by Hubert J. Foss for *The Mask of Comus,* ed. E. H. Visiak (Bloomsbury: The Nonesuch Press, 1937), as in Diekhoff, pp. 241–250. See *Variorum Commentary,* II, iii, 739.

25 A facsimile of the Bridgewater MS with transcription is available in *John Milton's Complete Poetical Works Reproduced in Facsimile,* ed. Harris F. Fletcher, 4 vols. (Urbana: University of Illinois Press, 1943–1948), I, 300–39. Fletcher's transcription is reprinted, with useful textual notes, in the collection edited by Diekhoff, pp. 207–40 (see note 9 above). My citations of Bridgewater are taken from Diekhoff. Sprott's *A Maske: The Earlier Versions* includes the versions of Bridgewater, Trinity, and 1637 in parallel columns.

26 This passage is taken from the Foss transcription of Lawes's songs as reprinted in Diekhoff, p. 243. Lineation and initial capitalization have been regularized and slight changes have been made in punctuation. The song version omits six lines of the longer version found at the opening of the Bridgewater MS: see Sprott, pp. 43–45; Diekhoff, p. 210.

27 Milton uses the phrase "The attendant Spirit" in the opening of the published version to refer to the figure called "A Guardian spirit or Daemon" in the Trinity and Bridgewater MSS. As the *Variorum Commentary* points out (II, iii, 853), "In English *daemon* had as one of its meanings . . . 'An attendant, ministering, or indwelling spirit' (*OED:* demon 1b)," but the word also contains specifically platonic overtones. John Arthos (*On A Mask Presented at Ludlow-Castle* [Ann Arbor: University of Michigan Press, 1954], pp. 36–41, 62–66) discusses the platonic doctrine of the demonic as being the realm of the spirit which is both intermediate and intermediary between the divine and the mortal. Sears Jayne ("The Subject of Milton's Ludlow Mask," in

Diekhoff, pp. 184–185) cites Ficino's idea of the platonic Daemon as the agent through which God governs and protects the lower world. For the intricacies of neoplatonic demonology see Frances Yates, *Giordano Bruno and the Hermetic Tradition* (London: Routledge, 1964) and Walker, *Spiritual and Demonic Magic.*

28   By "printed version" I refer to the 1645 printing as the norm: the variants in 1637 and 1673 are very few, though not negligible. The most important variants occur at lines 213, 471, 604, 607, 608, 780. See the *Variorum Commentary* and C. S. Lewis, "A Note on 'Comus,'" *Review of English Studies,* 8(1932): 170–76, reprinted in *Studies in Medieval and Renaissance Literature* (Cambridge: Cambridge University Press, 1966).

29   1645: line 890; the direction occurs in all versions, with minor variations in Trinity: see the helpful table of stage directions appended to the article by John T. Shawcross, "Certain Relationships of the Manuscripts of *Comus,*" *Papers of the Bibliographical Society of America,* 54 (1960): 38–56.

30   Eugene Haun, "An Inquiry into the Genre of *Comus,*" *Essays in Honor of Walter Clyde Curry* (Nashville: Vanderbilt University Press, 1954), p. 235.

31   But Trinity MS has the direction, "to be said" (*Facsimile,* ed. Harris Fletcher, I, 426, line 9).

32   Haun, "An Inquiry into the Genre of *Comus,*" p. 236. There has been a rather extensive and often highly technical debate about the extent to which Milton's *Maske* does, or does not, fit the conventions of the two genres, masque and opera. Gretchen Finney (*Musical Backgrounds for English Literature: 1580–1650* [New Brunswick: Rutgers University Press, 1962], pp 175–94), argues for the relation of the *Maske* to the Italian *dramma per musica,* productions in a mixed form which combined recitative and serious plot with aspects of spectacle or masque. John Hollander (*The Untuning of the Sky: Ideas of Music in English Poetry, 1500–1700* [Princeton: Princeton University Press, 1961], p. 192), and Demaray (*Milton and the Masque Tradition*), disagree with Finney and are opposed to any attempt to relate Milton's *Maske* to the development of early opera. Wilfrid Mellers (*Harmonious Meeting: A Study of the Relationship between English Music, Poetry and Theater, c. 1600–1900* [London: Dobson, 1965], pp. 166–67) argues that the *Maske* is only superficially operatic and that many of the problems of the work are attributable to the fact that it falls between the conventions of poetry and opera. Angus Fletcher (*The Transcendental Masque,* pp. 175–86) provides a summary of the technical debate. He also mentions the possibilities of English blank verse for spoken recitative and asserts that Milton is "a poet whose belief in his own verse was so strong that he could, if he wanted, write an opera without music, *opera senza musica*" (p. 184).

33   See Sprott's edition, pp. 64–65.

34   For the effect of varieties of verse form in Milton's *Maske,* see the essay by Edward Weismiller in the *Variorum Commentary,* II, iii, 1038–52, especially pp. 1049–50.

35   See Carey and Fowler, p. 188; Hollander, *The Untuning of the Sky,* p. 321;

and the *Variorum Commentary*, II, iii, 891. Another interpretation of the Lady's song is given by C. L. Barber ("*A Mask Presented at Ludlow Castle: The Masque as a Masque*," in Diekhoff, p. 200). While saying that there is no echo except in the hearing and varied responses of Comus and Thyrsis, he argues that the Lady's strength lies in her presumption that "she is in a world inhabited by 'courteous Presences.'" For an extensive discussion of various verbal echoes and musical echo-effects in the poem see Angus Fletcher, pp. 198–209. Agreeing that no echo answers the Lady, Fletcher contends that this failed response becomes, in fact, a positive sign, freeing the Lady from a narcissistic "echo chamber" to await "the true and final echo" which is heavenly.

36 *Romeo and Juliet*, III.ii.18–19.

37 See note 32 above.

38 Samuel Johnson, *Lives of the English Poets*, ed. G. B. Hill, 3 vols. (Oxford: Clarendon Press, 1905), I, 119–120.

39 For the passage from Thomas Randolph's *The Muses Looking-Glasse* frequently cited as an analogue to Comus's temptation speech, see the *Variorum Commentary*, II, iii,773–75.

40 See the essay by Philip Brockbank, "The Measure of 'Comus,'" *Essays and Studies*, 21 (1968): 46–61, for a fine discussion of three kinds of "verbal music" in Milton's masque: the "sensual music" of Comus, the "moral music" of the Elder Brother, and a third kind represented in the Lady's song: "a Miltonic song quite distinct from the sensual music and the moral music, and yet related to both: a transfigured and sublimated sensuality." For this, Brockbank finds the apt term, "Hesperian music" (pp. 55–58).

41 For an excellent treatment of the work from this standpoint, see Gale H. Carrithers, Jr., "Milton's Ludlow *Mask*: from Chaos to Community," *ELH*, 33 (1966): 23–42.

42 See the group of possible sources and analogues for Milton's *Maske* assembled by Watson Kirkconnell in *Awake the Courteous Echo: The Themes and Prosody of Comus, Lycidas, and Paradise Regained in World Literature with Translations of the Major Analogues* (Toronto: University of Toronto Press, 1973), pp. 3–75.

43 For extensive discussion of the relationship of Milton's poem to the masque tradition, and to *Tempe Restored* in particular, see Demaray, *Milton and the Masque Tradition*, pp. 59–96.

44 The terms here reflect my reading of Roy Daniell's important book, *Milton, Mannerism and Baroque* (Toronto: University of Toronto Press, 1963).

CHAPTER 2: The Rising Poet

The present chapter represents an extensive revision and expansion of materials that originally appeared in my essay, "The Rising Poet, 1645," in *The Lyric and Dramatic Milton*, ed. Joseph Summers, Selected Papers from the English Institute (New York: Columbia University Press, 1965), pp. 3–33.

1   See "Chronological Survey," *Variorum Commentary*, II, i, 11–33; and William
    Riley Parker, "Some Problems in the Chronology of Milton's Early Poems,"
    Review of English Studies, 11 (1935): 276–83; "Notes on the Chronology of
    Milton's Latin Poems," in *A Tribute to George Coffin Taylor*, ed. Arnold
    Williams (Chapel Hill: University of North Carolina Press, 1952), pp. 113–
    31.

2   *Latin Poems of John Milton*, ed. Walter MacKellar, p. 358.

3   The translation adapts the versions of Hughes and McCrea: see *John Milton:
    Complete Poems and Major Prose*, ed. Merritt Y. Hughes (New York: Odyssey
    Press, 1957), p. 146; and the translations of the Latin poems by Nelson G.
    McCrea in *The Student's Milton*, ed. Frank Allen Patterson (New York:
    Crofts, 1930), p. 109.

4   See the amusing account in David Masson's *Life of Milton*, 7 vols. (London,
    1859–94), III, 456–59; Masson sees in a passage of *Tetrachordon* a pun on
    Marshall's name. The translation of the Greek verses below is that of Mas-
    son, III, 459. On the other hand, one of my students, Nancy Pollak, has
    suggested that the engraving is meant to show Milton as he appeared in
    1645 at the age of thirty-seven: that is, the portrait represents the older poet
    looking back upon the pleasures of his youth. Perhaps Marshall (unable to
    read Latin?) misunderstood his directions and thought he was supposed to
    portray the poet of 1645. Whatever the case may be, the engraving certainly
    enforces the theme of an older man looking back upon his youth.

5   Brooks and Hardy find in this sonnet the quality "of wry humor, of an ironic
    little joke in which the poet contemplates, a little ruefully but still with a fine
    inner confidence, the place of the poet in a jostling world of men at arms
    and forays and sallies." See *Poems of Mr. John Milton: The 1645 Edition*, ed.
    Cleanth Brooks and John Edward Hardy (New York: Harcourt, 1951), p.
    157; this contains the English poems, accompanied by an important series of
    "Essays in Analysis."

6   *crescentem:* this is the preferred reading of the Oxford text; some MSS and
    editions read *nascentem.*

7   *Virgil: The Pastoral Poems*, trans. E. V. Rieu (Harmondsworth: Penguin
    Books, 1949).

8   Vergil, Eclogue 7, 12–13, trans. Rieu; cf. *Lycidas*, 86.

9   The verbal echoes are explicit, not only from the *Eclogues*, but also from the
    Georgics and the *Aeneid:* see MacKellar's admirable notes to this poem. Ralph
    Condee has now brought together his essays on Milton's Latin poetry (along
    with other essays on Milton) in *Structure in Milton's Poetry* (University Park:
    Pennsylvania State University Press, 1974); his essays on *Ad Patrem, Mansus*,
    and *Epitaphium Damonis* are particularly notable.

10 See *Latin Poems*, ed. MacKellar, p. 347.

11 For the controversy over the dating of *Elegia septima*, see *Variorum Commen-
    tary*, I, 127–29.

12 See *The Reason of Church-government*, prologue to book 2, in *Complete Prose
    Works of John Milton*, ed. Don M. Wolfe (New Haven: Yale University Press,
    1953–), I, 809.

13   See William Riley Parker, *Milton: A Biography,* 2 vols. (Oxford: Clarendon Press, 1968), I, 177; II, 828 n.45.

14   *Prose Works,* ed. Wolfe, I, 321–22. The letter is dated December 4, 1634, and Milton says he made the Greek version of the psalm "before daybreak a week ago"—that is, on or about November 27. Despite some controversy on this point, there can be no reasonable doubt that this is the poem described in the letter: see *Variorum Commentary,* I, 257.

15   For the controversy over the dating of *Ad Patrem,* see *Variorum Commentary,* I, 232–40; and Parker, *Milton,* II, 788–89.

16   See the headnote to the paraphrase of Psalm 114 in the 1645 *Poems.*

17   See *Variorum Commentary,* I, 318–19.

18   Milton's attention to chronology is emphasized in the enlarged edition of his *Poems* in 1673, where the groupings and symmetries of 1645 are blurred by the addition of early and late poems placed in positions dictated by date of composition, not by kind. It seems that Milton's concern to publish, in his last years, a complete, or nearly complete, collection of his shorter poems took precedence over his earlier concern for a well-proportioned volume. Thus *On the Death of a fair Infant,* described as written "Anno aetatis 17," is placed between the psalms written "at fifteen years old" and *The Passion,* composed at age twenty-one. According to the errata sheet of 1673 the poem on the "fair Infant" should have been followed by the lines *At a Vacation Exercise,* dated "Anno Aetatis 19." This was somehow misplaced as the second of three miscellaneous poems (the version of the fifth ode of Horace, the *Vacation Exercise,* and *On the new forcers of Conscience*) added after the expanded group of nineteen sonnets and just before *Arcades* (the sonnets usually numbered 15, 16, 17, and 22 were omitted, undoubtedly because of their risky political content). The *Mask* follows directly after *Lycidas,* without the half title of 1645, and then the English part of the 1673 volume concludes with the two late groups of versified psalms, first the set of 1653 and next the set of 1648—chronology here being discarded in favor of the biblical order.

   Among the Latin poems, *Apologus de Rustico & Hero,* a fable of uncertain date in elegiac meter, is added at the very end of the elegiac section; but it is headed with a heavy decorative bar suggesting that it is really *sui generis.* The ode to Rouse (1646) is placed as the final poem of the book, after the *Epitaphium Damonis.* The only other addition is the printing of Milton's satirical Greek verses on his portrait (part of the frontispiece in 1645) after the two Greek poems of 1645, thus observing chronological order. See the important article on chronology in the 1673 volume by John Shawcross, *Studies in English Literature,* 3 (1963): 77–84.

19   *Canzone,* 15; trans. Hughes.

20   "Ridonsi donne e giovani amorosi." Translation from Sonnet 6 by Carey; translation from the *Canzone* by Hughes.

21   For various interpretations of lines 13–14 of Sonnet 7 see *Variorum Commentary,* II, ii, 372–73.

22   See the analysis of the suspended syntax of Sonnet 10 by Alan Rudrum, *A Critical Commentary on Milton's 'Comus' and Shorter Poems* (London: Macmillan, 1967), pp. 87–88. For recent interpretations of all the sonnets (including those not published in 1645) as an integrated sequence revealing the growth toward maturity and old age, see William McCarthy, "The Continuity of Milton's Sonnets," *PMLA*, 92 (1977): 96–109; and Mary Ann Radzinowicz, *Toward Samson Agonistes* (Princeton: Princeton University Press, 1978), pp. 128–44.

23   See the essay on these poems by Don Cameron Allen, *The Harmonious Vision* (Baltimore: Johns Hopkins Press, 1954), pp. 3–23.

24   See the important brief essay by Kester Svendsen in *Explicator*, 8 (May, 1950): Item 49; here Svendsen deals with "the dynamics of the twin poem," showing "the progressive emphasis in both parts on images of sound and music." He notes how, in the finale of *Il Penseroso*, "the many references to sound and in particular to music build toward this conclusion, so that structurally it is the end of a progressive development within both poems."

25   S. Ernest Sprott, *Milton's Art of Prosody* (Oxford: Blackwell, 1953), pp. 17–18.

26   See "Studies of Verse Form in the Minor English Poems" by Edward R. Weismiller in the *Variorum Commentary*, II, iii, 1026–36. Weismiller does not stress the difference in the metric of the companion poems, but he recognizes the difference by citing Sprott's statistics and especially by quoting Carpenter's contrast between the "brisk rocking motion" of *L'Allegro* and "the smoother verse lines" of *Il Penseroso*. See Nan Cooke Carpenter, "The Place of Music in *L'Allegro* and *Il Penseroso*," *University of Toronto Quarterly*, 22 (1952–53): 354–67.

27   See *Variorum Commentary*, II, i, 281–84; and the witty, acute discussion of this controversy by Stanley E. Fish, "What it's like to read *L'Allegro* and *Il Penseroso*," in *Milton Studies*, 7 (1975): 77–99. My own interpretation, though proceeding on different critical principles, is in basic agreement with Fish's view of the differences between the two poems—that the first is delightfully relaxed in its manner and movement, while in the second "our attention is not diffused but concentrated," with an effect of "sustained mental effort" (Fish, pp. 90,94).

28   See J. B. Leishman, *Milton's Minor Poems* (London: Hutchinson, 1969), chapter 6, "*L'Allegro* and *Il Penseroso* in their relation to seventeenth-century poetry."

29   *The Republic of Plato,* trans. Francis MacDonald Cornford (New York: Oxford University Press, 1945), pp. 86–87.

30   *umbrosa Academica:* from the palinode at the end of Milton's *Elegia septima*.

31   The date is omitted in the edition of 1673.

32   See F. T. Prince, *The Italian Element in Milton's Verse* (Oxford: Clarendon Press, 1954), pp. 61–63.

33   A. S. P. Woodhouse, "Notes on Milton's Early Development," *University of Toronto Quarterly*, 13 (1943): 66–101; see p. 75; included in Woodhouse's

The Heavenly Muse: A Preface to Milton, ed. Hugh MacCallum (Toronto: University of Toronto Press, 1972), chapter 2. For others who hold similar views see *Variorum Commentary,* I, 112–15. Parker strongly dissents from this view: see the account of *Elegia sexta* in his *Milton,* I, 67–70.

34   From the translation by Charles Knapp in the Columbia edition of *The Works of John Milton* (New York: Columbia University Press, 1931–38), I, 207.

35   E. K. Rand, "Milton in Rustication," *Studies in Philology,* 19 (1922): 109–35; see pages 110, 124.

36   See *Variorum Commentary,* I, 125–26.

37   *English Madrigal Verse, 1588–1632,* ed. E. H. Fellowes, 3rd edn., revised by Frederick W. Sternfeld and David Greer (Oxford: Clarendon Press, 1967), pp. 156–57. For other analogies see Weismiller's commentary on the stanza-form of the Hymn, *Variorum Commentary,* II, iii, 1019–22.

38   *The Early English Carols,* ed. Richard Leighton Greene, 2nd edn. (Oxford: Clarendon Press, 1977), pp. 48–49. I have omitted the editor's brackets and italics.

39   For a study of the poem in the context of the genre of the literary hymn, with its *topos* of humility, see Philip Rollinson, "Milton's Nativity Poem and the Decorum of Genre," *Milton Studies,* 7 (1975): 165–88. As Rollinson points out, the *topos* of humility is discussed by Ernst Robert Curtius, *European Literature and the Latin Middle Ages,* trans. Willard R. Trask (New York: Pantheon, 1953), pp. 83–85, 407–13; the latter section, Excursus II, "Devotional Formula and Humility," is especially significant for Milton's "humble ode."

40   Lowry Nelson, Jr., *Baroque Lyric Poetry* (New Haven: Yale University Press, 1961), pp. 41–52.

CHAPTER 3: *Lycidas*: Building the Lofty Rhyme

This chapter is a revision of the essay "Who is Lycidas?" that appeared in the issue of *Yale French Studies* devoted to "Image and Symbol in the Renaissance," No. 47 (1972): 170–88. In addition to the *Variorum Commentary,* I wish to acknowledge the help of two collections: *Lycidas: the Tradition and the Poem,* ed. C. A. Patrides (New York: Holt, Rinehart and Winston, 1961); and *Milton's "Lycidas" Edited to Serve as an Introduction to Criticism,* by Scott Elledge (New York: Harper and Row, 1966).

1   See the classic analysis of the tripartite movement of these poems by Arthur Barker, "The Pattern of Milton's *Nativity Ode," University of Toronto Quarterly,* 10 (1940–41): 167–81.

2   For the many analogues see the important new study by Ellen Zetzel Lambert, *Placing Sorrow: A Study of the Pastoral Elegy Convention from Theocritus to Milton* (Chapel Hill: University of North Carolina Press, 1976); along with the anthology of precedents for and analogues with *Lycidas* collected by Watson Kirkconnell in *Awake the Courteous Echo,* pp. 79–245.

3   Idyll 7, 13–19: from *The Greek Bucolic Poets,* trans. A. S. F. Gow (Cambridge: Cambridge University Press, 1953). This translation is a revised version of that in Gow's standard edition of *Theocritus,* 2 vols. (Cambridge: Cambridge University Press, 1950), from which I have taken the line numbers.

4   Gilbert Lawall, *Theocritus' Coan Pastorals* (Washington, D.C.: Center for Hellenic Studies, 1967), pp. 80–85, 102–08.

5   The figure Lycidas appears as a gifted singer in a fragment attributed to Bion, which begins with Myrson asking, "Wilt thou sing me some sweet Sicilian song, Lycidas?" (*Greek Bucolic Poets,* trans. Gow, p. 148).

6   Cf. the study of the ninth eclogue by Michael C. J. Putnam, *Virgil's Pastoral Art* (Princeton: Princeton University Press, 1970), pp. 293–341. Putnam perhaps makes the eclogue excessively bleak, yet his view of the poem's presentation of the conflict between the world of song and the world of political power seems basically right, and his contrast with the seventh idyll of Theocritus is excellent: "*Idyl 7* is a poem about joy in song, about the beauty and variety of poetry, set in the context of a journey to a haven of particular beauty. The ninth eclogue is opposite in tone and meaning. Virgil's road leads not toward the glorious retreat of a harvest festival but out of the country in the direction of the city, through a landscape wherein song is impossible" (p. 338).

7   See James Holly Hanford, "The Pastoral Elegy and Milton's *Lycidas,*" in *John Milton, Poet and Humanist* (Cleveland: Press of Western Reserve University, 1966), pp. 149–51. Hanford assumes that Sannazaro's Phyllis met her death by drowning, but the poem gives no evidence of this. There is no doubt, however, that the latter half of the lament by Sannazaro's Lycidas contains striking analogies to the latter part of Milton's poem, especially in the lines (97–98) where Sannazaro's Lycidas calls to his Phyllis in the heavens or the "Elysian shades," saying, "Look down on us and gently come to us; you shall be ever the godhead (*numen*) of the waters, ever a happy sign to fishermen" (trans. Nash: see next note).

8   Jacopo Sannazaro, *Arcadia and Piscatorial Eclogues,* trans. Ralph Nash (Detroit: Wayne State University Press, 1966), pp. 156–65.

9   The resemblance of these lines to "a broken sonnet" echoing the Petrarchan pattern has been pointed out by Keith Rinehart, *Notes & Queries,* 198 (1953): 103. The rhymes run as follows: xabbaacdacdaxa. For detailed accounts of the rhyme and metrics of the poem see Prince, *The Italian Element in Milton's Verse,* pp. 71–88; Ants Oras, "Milton's Early Rhyme Schemes and the Structure of *Lycidas,*" *Modern Philology,* 52 (1954): 12–22; Joseph Anthony Wittreich, Jr., "Milton's 'Destin'd Urn': the Art of *Lycidas,*" *PMLA,* 84 (1969): 60–70; and Weismiller, *Variorum Commentary,* II, iii, 1057–74.

10 See David Berkeley, *Notes & Queries,* 206 (1961): 178; also *Inwrought with Figures Dim* (The Hague: Mouton, 1974), pp. 33–34.

11 *The Jerusalem Bible,* ed. Alexander Jones (Garden City: Doubleday, 1966).

12 *Webster's New International Dictionary,* 2nd edn. (Springfield, Mass.: Merriam, 1951), "welter," *v.* 2.

13 See Leishman, *Milton's Minor Poems*, pp. 324–26.

14 Barker, "The Pattern of Milton's *Nativity Ode*," pp. 171–72.

15 See the notes on "Amaryllis" and "Neaera" in *Variorum Commentary*, II, ii, 660–61.

16 See Ralph Hone, "The Pilot of the *Galilean* Lake," *Studies in Philology*, 56 (1959): 55–61. We do not need to follow Hone in seeing only the presence of Christ here; Peter is present as well.

17 For the vast and apparently endless controversy over lines 130–31 see *Variorum Commentary*, II, ii, 686–706. Perhaps the most convincing essay on this problem is that by Leon Howard, *Huntington Library Quarterly*, 15 (1952): 173–84.

18 On the consoling, soothing effect of the catalogue see Lambert, *Placing Sorrow*, pp. 172–74.

19 William Madsen (*Studies in English Literature*, 3 [1963]: 1–7) makes the interesting suggestion that Michael is himself speaking here in lines 165–81 ("Weep no more . . . And wipe the tears for ever from his eyes"). I would not go so far, but the lines do seem to be a result of the speaker's appeal, "Look homeward Angel."

20 See especially Revelation 7:17; 14:1–4; 19:6–9; 21:4; 22:1–2; *Variorum Commentary*, II, ii, 728–30.

21 See the fine interpretation of these closing lines by Isabel MacCaffrey, "*Lycidas*: the Poet in a Landscape," in *The Lyric and Dramatic Milton*, ed. Summers, pp. 89–92: "The pastoral scene is re-created; and now it is informed by the presence of the poets who first made these details into poetry, and by the redeemed imagination that has come gradually to understand their meaning."

22 See A. S. P. Woodhouse, "Milton's Pastoral Monodies," in *Studies in Honour of Gilbert Norwood*, ed. Mary E. White (Toronto: University of Toronto Press, 1952), p. 273; included in Woodhouse's *The Heavenly Muse*, chapter 3. Also Isabel MacCaffrey in the essay just cited, p. 67.

PART II: *Paradise Lost:* Poem of Exile

The *Variorum Commentary* on *Paradise Lost* is still in progress, but reference to scholarship on the epic is greatly assisted by the detailed introduction and ample annotations to *Paradise Lost* provided by Fowler in *The Poems of John Milton*, ed. John Carey and Alastair Fowler (London: Longmans, 1968); I am deeply indebted to this edition throughout parts II and III of this book.

CHAPTER 4: Princes of Exile

This chapter is based upon materials presented in the first of a series of three William Lyon Phelps Lectures delivered at Yale University in February 1967 under the general title: "*Paradise Lost:* Poem of Exile." A version of this lecture was published in *ELH,* 36 (1969): 232–49. The present chapter represents a further revision.

1   *The Works of John Milton* (New York: Columbia University Press, 1931–38), XII, 114–15; I have altered three words in the Masson translation.
2   See the important study by Robert M. Durling, *The Figure of the Poet in Renaissance Epic* (Cambridge: Harvard University Press, 1965).
3   St.-John Perse, *Exile and Other Poems,* Bilingual edition, trans. Denis Devlin, 2nd edn. (New York: Pantheon, 1949), pp. 11–15. Copyright 1940 by the Bollingen Foundation, New York.
4   See the perceptive interpretation of the prologue to book 3 by Anne Davidson Ferry, *Milton's Epic Voice* (Cambridge: Harvard University Press, 1963), pp. 25–37.
5   See Augustine, *De Trinitate,* Book 9, where he analyzes the triad: *Mens, Notitia, Amor;* see also the analysis of Augustine's trinitarian view of the Image of God by Etienne Gilson, *The Christian Philosophy of Saint Augustine* (New York: Random House, 1960), pp. 217–24.
6   *OED,* "drug," *sb.* 1.
7   See the sensitive analysis of this simile by Geoffrey Hartman, "Milton's Counterplot," *ELH,* 25 (1958): 1–12: "The ripe grain sways in the wind, so does the mind which has tended it" (p. 12). See also the quite different view in Carey and Fowler (p. 669) where, partly accepting Empson's view, Fowler says "the ploughman has to be in some sense 'like' God." Cf. William Empson, *Some Versions of Pastoral* (London: Chatto, 1935), p. 172.
8   Ovid, *Metamorphoses,* trans. Rolfe Humphries (Bloomington: Indiana University Press, 1955).
9   See T. S. Eliot's essay on Marlowe; *Selected Essays, 1917–1932* (New York: Harcourt, 1932), p. 100. The controversy over Milton's style is effectively resolved in Milton's favor by Christopher Ricks in *Milton's Grand Style* (Oxford: Clarendon Press, 1963); and by A. Bartlett Giamatti in *The Earthly Paradise and the Renaissance Epic* (Princeton: Princeton University Press, 1966), chapter 6.
10 See *Exile,* p. 35.

CHAPTER 5: The Realms of Light

This chapter stands, with minor revisions, as it appeared in *English Literary Renaissance,* 1 (1971): 71–88. That essay represented an extensive revision and expansion of the second in the series of William Lyon Phelps Lectures delivered at Yale in 1967; it incorporated passages and thoughts derived from another lecture on Milton delivered at the University of Western Ontario in February 1970.

1   Cf. Isabel G. MacCaffrey, "The Theme of *Paradise Lost,* Book III," in *New Essays on Paradise Lost,* ed. Thomas Kranidas (Berkeley: University of California Press, 1969), pp. 58–85.

2 But see the essay by Irene Samuel in *PMLA*, 72 (1957): 601–11, which argues that Milton's God here speaks in the "toneless voice of the moral law" (p. 603). See also the argument by Stanley Eugene Fish, *Surprised by Sin: The Reader in Paradise Lost* (London: Macmillan, 1967), pp. 57–91, where Fish turns the tables on the reader: "In the poem, God's speech represents the essence of Truth, and the reader's response is a judgment on him (a reflection of his 'crookednesse'), not on the dispassionate voice of the Logos" (p. 83). Fish's attractive and influential argument is valid to the extent that Milton is using a device to arouse problems in the reader's mind. The trouble is that the device is awkward and creates more problems than it should. For an extreme version of these problems see William Empson, *Milton's God*, rev. edn. (London: Chatto, 1965), chapter 3.

3 See C. A. Patrides, *Milton and the Christian Tradition* (Oxford: Clarendon Press, 1966), pp. 200–14; and Ernest Sirluck, *Paradise Lost: A Deliberate Epic*, Churchill College Overseas Fellowship Lecture No. 1 (Cambridge: Heffer, 1967), esp. pp. 19–21.

4 Cf. J. B. Broadbent, *Some Graver Subject* (London: Chatto, 1960), p. 157.

5 Cf. Ferry, *Milton's Epic Voice*, chapter 2.

6 For the use of the term "panels" by Brooks Otis in relation to Ovid's *Metamorphoses* see below, chapter 12.

7 Kenneth Burke, *Counter-Statement*, 2nd edn. (Chicago: University of Chicago Press, 1957), pp. 127–28. On Milton's assimilation of comic, satiric, pastoral, and tragic modes to the conventions of heroic poetry, see John M. Steadman, *Epic and Tragic Structure in Paradise Lost* (Chicago: University of Chicago Press, 1976), chapter 2.

8 See Steadman, *Epic and Tragic Structure*, chapters 3–5, for Aristotelian elements. In addition one might see an affinity with the Euripidean prologue of the supernatural agent in Satan's long soliloquy before the action (9.99–178). The voice of the narrator in book 9 seems in places to undertake a choric role, interpreting the series of episodes that constitute the tragedy. One can distinguish eight episodes, each carefully separated by the voice of the narrator: (1) the parting of Adam and Eve: 205–384; (2) Satan's soliloquy at sight of Eve: 473–93; (3) Satan and Eve: preliminary encounter: 532–631; (4) Satan and Eve before the Tree: Eve's Fall: 647–833; (5) Eve's return to Adam: Adam's Fall: 856–989; (6) Adam's invitation to lust: 1017–33; (7) Adam's discovery of shame: 1067–98; (8) the quarrel of Adam and Eve: 1134–86.

9 *OED*, "frail," *a*. 1,2,3.

10 For Milton's openness to highly unorthodox views see the new book by Christopher Hill, *Milton and the English Revolution* (New York: Viking, 1978).

11 Cf. Ferry, *Milton's Epic Voice*, pp. 51–56.

12 Stressed by Frank Kermode in his fine essay "Adam Unparadised," in *The Living Milton*, ed. Frank Kermode (New York: Macmillan, 1961), p. 103. The words *paradisum voluptatis* or *paradiso voluptatis* occur five times in the opening chapters of Genesis (2:8,10,15;3:23,24).

13   Cf. Ferry, *Milton's Epic Voice*, p. 52.
14   For a detailed study of this topic see John Halkett, *Milton and the Idea of Matrimony* (New Haven: Yale University Press, 1970), esp. chapter 4. Also the important essay by Peter Lindenbaum, "Lovemaking in Milton's Paradise," *Milton Studies*, 6 (1974): 277–306; and the lively, acute study by Edward LeComte, *Milton and Sex* (New York: Columbia University Press, 1978).
15   C. S. Lewis, *A Preface to Paradise Lost* (London: Oxford University Press, 1942), chapter 17.
16   The validity of this analogy has now been demonstrated in the new study by Roland Mushat Frye, *Milton's Imagery and the Visual Arts* (Princeton: Princeton University Press, 1978), pp. 227–34. See also Marjorie B. Garber, "Fallen Landscape: The Art of Milton and Poussin," *English Literary Renaissance*, 5 (1975): 96–124.

CHAPTER 6: The Diffusion of Good

About three pages in the latter part of this chapter have appeared previously, in somewhat different form, in portions of my essay in *Ventures*: see headnote to next chapter.

1   For a summary of the numerological interpretations of the poem's structure see Carey and Fowler, pp. 440–43. For the poem's numerological center see Gunnar Qvarnström, *The Enchanted Palace: Some Structural Aspects of Paradise Lost* (Stockholm: Almqvist, 1967), chapter 2; and John T. Shawcross, "The Balanced Structure of *Paradise Lost*," *Studies in Philology*, 62 (1965): 696–718. I should note that I am highly skeptical of the more detailed aspects of the numerological approach; but in discerning the larger aspects of structure the approach is helpful, as one may see in the recent study by Galbraith Miller Crump, *The Mystical Design of Paradise Lost* (Lewisburg: Bucknell University Press, 1975).
2   Cf. Carey and Fowler, note on 7.1, "Descend": "Because from this point onward the course of the poem is steadily downwards." See also Isabel Gamble MacCaffrey, *Paradise Lost as "Myth"* (Cambridge: Harvard University Press, 1959), pp. 57–59.
3   John Peter is right in his estimation of the size of Michael's army: see *A Critique of Paradise Lost* (London: Longmans, 1960), pp. 80–81; but Peter finds God "underhand and deceitful" in thus restricting the number. Empson, surprisingly, does not accept this view of the "equal" armies— apparently because it somewhat detracts from Satan's glory (see *Milton's God*, p. 41); see too the note (on 6.49) in Carey and Fowler, p. 732, where Fowler agrees with Empson in rejecting "Peter's unnecessary speculation that God only allows half of the good angels to fight."
4   For Milton's treatment of Creation see W. B. C. Watkins, *An Anatomy of Milton's Verse* (Baton Rouge: Louisiana State University Press, 1955), pp.

42–86; M. M. Mahood, *Poetry and Humanism* (New Haven: Yale University Press, 1950), chapter 6; and the impressive study by Michael Lieb, *The Dialectics of Creation: Patterns of Birth and Regeneration in Paradise Lost* (Amherst: University of Massachusetts Press, 1970), chapters 1 and 2.

5 Cf. Ricks, *Milton's Grand Style*, pp. 109–17; and Giamatti, *Earthly Paradise*, pp. 302–306.

6 E. M. W. Tillyard, *Studies in Milton* (New York: Macmillan, 1951), pp. 10–13.

7 J. M. Evans, *Paradise Lost and the Genesis Tradition* (Oxford: Clarendon Press, 1968), p. 269; see his entire chapter 10 for Milton's complex presentation of "Nature's Innocence." Barbara Lewalski has independently explored a similar point of view in her important essay "Innocence and Experience in Milton's Eden," in *New Essays on Paradise Lost,* ed. Kranidas, pp. 86–117: "primal man's nature is shown to be complex and constantly developing, not simple and stable" (p. 99). See also the summary of this "newer view of Milton's Paradise" by Lindenbaum in "Lovemaking in Milton's Paradise," pp. 298–302: "The whole emphasis on a difficult Eden and the insistence on the importance of prelapsarian sexual love . . . tend to undermine any hard and fast distinction . . . between pre- and postlapsarian life" (p. 300).

CHAPTER 7: The Power of Choice

The last two-thirds of this chapter, except for a few sentences, was published in *Ventures: Magazine of the Yale Graduate School,* 10 (1970): 37–47; this essay represented the major portion of the last lecture in the series of William Lyon Phelps Lectures delivered at Yale in 1967.

1 Milton's theme of "choice" is the basis for the illuminating explorations by Leslie Brisman in *Milton's Poetry of Choice and Its Romantic Heirs* (Ithaca: Cornell University Press, 1973). For the importance of "choice" in the poem see the careful study by Jon Lawry in *The Shadow of Heaven,* chapter 4: "'Most Reason is that Reason Overcome': Choice in *Paradise Lost.*"

2 See the similar interpretation by Arnold Stein in *The Art of Presence: The Poet and Paradise Lost* (Berkeley: University of California Press, 1977), pp. 99–101: for his subtle interpretation of the following argument between Adam and Eve see pp. 112–21.

3 See the studies by Evans and Lewalski noted above (chapter 6, n. 7). For the idea that Eve is "not sincere" in her suggestion, see Tillyard, *Studies in Milton,* p. 17.

4 A. J. A. Waldock, *Paradise Lost and Its Critics* (Cambridge: Cambridge University Press, 1947), pp. 56–57.

5 See the studies of Evans and Lewalski noted above (chapter 6, n. 7).

CHAPTER 8: The Winding up of the Action

The germ of this chapter lies in a small portion of *The Paradise Within* (New Haven: Yale University Press, 1964), pp. 135–40.

1 *The Spectator,* ed. Donald F. Bond, 5 vols. (Oxford: Clarendon Press, 1965), III, 329–30 (No. 357).

2 See Fowler's discussion in his introduction (pp. 432–33) and in many of his annotations to *Paradise Lost* in Carey and Fowler.

3 See Philippians 2:7: "and took upon him the form of a servant"; Genesis 3:21: "Unto Adam also and to his wife did the Lord God make coats of skins, and clothed them"; John 13:14–16: "If I then, your Lord and Master, have washed your feet; ye also ought to wash one another's feet . . . . The servant is not greater than his lord"; Luke 6:27–29: "Love your enemies, do good to them which hate you. . . . and him that taketh away thy cloke forbid not to take thy coat also." The curious usage of "repaid" (in the sense of "given in return"—the beasts, perhaps, were not slain, but were given new skins, "as the snake") may echo Proverbs 13:21: "to the righteous good shall be repayed."

4 In his classic essay, "The Crisis of *Paradise Lost,*" to which this chapter is deeply indebted: see his *Studies in Milton,* pp. 8–52, especially pp. 31–32.

5 See the note on 10.289–93 in Carey and Fowler, p. 940.

6 It might be noted that both in Vergil and in Ovid the phrase occurs in a less than heroic context. Cf. the similar phrase in Vergil's first eclogue (23), and the significant variation of the phrase in *Paradise Regain'd* (4.563–64): "to compare / Small things with greatest."

7 Fowler notes that "the simile gains most force from a silent allusion to the well-known story that Xerxes wept while reviewing his army, at the thought that within a century such multitudes would all be dead" (Carey and Fowler, p. 942). The simile thus forms a tacit link with Satan's tears at reviewing his army (1.620).

8 *Metamorphoses,* 4.576–603. The allusion thus links with Milton's reference to "Hermione and Cadmus" (9.503–06) cited above in chapter 4.

9 *Metamorphoses,* 4.614–20; 1.438–47.

10 I am thinking of the soliloquies of Medea (*Metamorphoses,* 7.11–72), Scylla, daughter of Nisus (8.44–80), Althaea (8.481–511), Byblis (9.474–516), and Myrrha (10.320–55). A relation to Adam's soliloquy (and also to Satan's earlier soliloquies) may be suggested by William Anderson's comment on these Ovidian passages: "The many soliloquies in the central part of the *Metamorphoses* all, to a certain extent, analyze the meaning of critical moral terms. Each speaker, aware of the moral responsibilities implicit in the word or words under discussion, tries to evade these formal obligations; and, when reason fails to justify such evasion or change, he or she then lets emotions overcome reason and morality. Knowingly, they undertake *nefas* or *scelus,* and usually they experience the consequences soon after in their moral depths" ("Multiple Change in the *Metamorphoses,*" *Transactions of the American Philological Association,* 94 (1963): 1–27: see pp. 20–21. Adam of course comes to a different conclusion, after the manner of a renaissance imitation.

11 Tillyard, *Studies in Milton,* pp. 39–42; Joseph H. Summers, *The Muse's Method: An Introduction to Paradise Lost* (London: Chatto, 1962), pp. 176–85.

12   Milton's technique here seems to be an elaborate expansion of a favorite
     Ovidian device: "date munera templis / nec timida gaudete fide! dant mun-
     era templis, / addunt et titulum: titulus breve carmen habebat" (*Metamorph-
     oses,* 9.791–93); "Dignane, cui grates ageret, cui turis honorem / ferret,
     Adoni, fui? nec grates inmemor egit, / nec mihi tura dedit." (*Met.* 10.681–
     83). See also *Heroides,* 3.5–6; 4.143–44; *Amores,* 3.5.7–8; and Milton's playful
     use of such devices in his Ovidian *Elegia quinta,* 6–7, 33, 122, 129–30. For
     further examples of this rhetorical technique, see below, chapter 13.

CHAPTER 9: "A Poem Written in Ten Books"

This chapter represents a greatly revised version of my essay "Camoens and
Milton" in *Ocidente: Revista Portuguesa de Cultura,* 35 (1972): 45–58; part of a
large special number celebrating the 400th anniversary of the publication of *Os
Lusíadas,* and including papers presented at the University of Connecticut
(Storrs) as part of a symposium honoring this anniversary.

 1   F. T. Prince, "On the Last Two Books of *Paradise Lost,*" *Essays and Studies,*
     n.s. 11 (1958): 38–52: see pp. 49–51. The difficulty, I suppose, is that the
     experience of readers and habits of reading differ too widely to make this a
     basis for critical judgment.
 2   A summation of the issues concerning books 11 and 12, with wise sugges-
     tions for their resolution, is given by Balachandra Rajan in *The Lofty Rhyme*
     (London: Routledge, 1970), chapter 6; on pp. 168–69 Rajan provides a full
     bibliography of writings on the topic, up to 1966. To this one should add:
     Stanley Fish, *Surprised by Sin* (1967), chapter 7; Dennis Burden, *The Logical
     Epic* (1967), chapter 9; Mary Ann Radzinowicz, "'Man as a Probationer of
     Immortality,'" in *Approaches to Paradise Lost,* ed. C. A. Patrides (London:
     Arnold, 1968), pp. 31–51; Jon S. Lawry, *The Shadow of Heaven,* pp. 267–88;
     Jason Rosenblatt, "Adam's Pisgah Vision," *ELH,* 39 (1972): 66–86; and
     Joseph Anthony Wittreich, Jr., "'A Poet amongst Poets': Milton and the
     Tradition of Prophecy," in *Milton and the Line of Vision,* ed. Wittreich (Madi-
     son: University of Wisconsin Press, 1975), pp. 97–142; see esp. pp. 129–42.
 3   See *Essays of John Dryden,* ed. W. P. Ker, 2 vols. (Oxford: Clarendon Press,
     1926), I, 268; II, 29; and *Spectator,* No. 369: ed. Bond, III, 386.
 4   See *Facsimile,* ed. Harris Fletcher, II, 20–23.
 5   *Mansus,* 80–81, trans. MacKellar.
 6   *Epitaphium Damonis,* 168–71; trans. Hughes.
 7   See *Prose Works,* ed. Wolfe, I, 812–14.
 8   Cf. James H. Sims, "Echoes of Camoens' *Lusiads* in Milton's *Paradise Lost*
     (I-IV)," *Revista Camoniana,* 3 (1971): 135–44; "'Delicious Paradise' in *Os
     Lusiadas* and in *Paradise Lost,*" *Ocidente,* 35 (1972): 163–72; and "Christened
     Classicism in *Paradise Lost* and *The Lusiads,*" *Comparative Literature,* 24 (1972);
     338–56.
 9   See Arthur Barker, "Structural Pattern in *Paradise Lost,*" *Philological Quar-*

terly, 28 (1949): 17–30; esp. pp. 21–23. For other views see J. R. Watson, "Divine Providence and the Structure of *Paradise Lost," Essays in Criticism,* 14 (1964), 148–55; and Wittreich's theory about the number 12, in *Milton and the Line of Vision,* ed. Wittreich, pp. 131–34. Also Crump, *The Mystical Design of Paradise Lost.*

10 [This number for the note was unplanned!] For the Pythagorean (and Augustinian) significance of the number 10 in relation to the edition of 1667 see Qvarnström, *The Enchanted Palace,* chapter 4. One may disagree with details, but there is force in the argument that Pythagorean theory is involved in Milton's grouping of his ten books into sets of 4:3:2:1, or, counting by the occurrence of the four prologues, 2:4:1:3; for the groupings bear an uncanny parallel with the "divine tetractys" of Pythagoras, in which the sum of the numbers 1234 equals 10. See the pioneer study among the numerological interpreters: James Whaler, *Counterpoint and Symbol, Anglistica,* vol. 6 (Copenhagen, 1956); and Carey and Fowler, pp. 440–43, 851–52. Also Shawcross, "The Balanced Structure of *Paradise Lost,"* pp. 708–10.

11 C. M. Bowra, *From Virgil to Milton* (London: Macmillan, 1945) pp. 238–39.

12 For an explanation of the function of this vision and a fine interpretation of the *Lusiad* see Giamatti, *The Earthly Paradise,* pp. 210–26; esp. pp. 221–23.

13 *Prose Works,* ed. Wolfe, II, 551–53.

14 This and the following prose translations are taken from *The Lusiads,* trans. William C. Atkinson (Harmondsworth: Penguin Books, 1952). Fanshawe's translation is available (with the heavy use of capital letters in 1655 reduced) in the edition by J. D. M. Ford (Cambridge, Mass.: Harvard University Press, 1940).

15 For judicious correction of the usual modern view of romantic criticism see the introduction by Joseph Anthony Wittreich, Jr., to his collection *The Romantics on Milton* (Cleveland: Press of Case Western Reserve University, 1970).

16 The role of "the voice of the bard" has been explored by Ferry, *Milton's Epic Voice* (1963); by myself, in *The Paradise Within* (1964); by William G. Riggs, *The Christian Poet in Paradise Lost* (Berkeley: University of California Press, 1972); and by Arnold Stein, *The Art of Presence* (1978), a climactic study of remarkable subtlety and depth.

CHAPTER 10: Trials of Faith

This chapter represents a drastic revision and re-thinking of the last three sections of my essay on *Paradise Lost* in *The Paradise Within* (pp. 141–67). I have been greatly helped in my revision by two friendly, but judiciously critical review-articles: Arnold Stein, "The Paradise Within and the Paradise Without," *Modern Language Quarterly,* 26 (1965): 586–600; and Isabel G. MacCaffrey, "The Meditative Paradigm," *ELH,* 32 (1965): 388–407. In Mrs. MacCaffrey's recent death the scholarly world has lost a great teacher, a deep, original mind, and a generous spirit.

1 *The Works of John Dryden,* ed. E. N. Hooker and H. T. Swedenberg, Jr., 18 vols. (Berkeley: University of California Press, 1956–), II, 109.

2 Two essays dealing with the theological design have been most helpful in my revision: one by Mary Ann Radzinowicz (see above, chapter 9, note 2), and the other by Barbara Lewalski, "Structure and the Symbolism of Vision in Michael's Prophecy," *Philological Quarterly,* 42 (1963): 25–35. The notes to books 11 and 12 in Carey and Fowler have also been particularly instructive here.

3 Cf. Carey and Fowler, note on 11.355, p. 998.

4 Cf. L. D. Lerner, "The Miltonic Simile," *Essays in Criticism,* 4 (1954): 297–308; esp. p. 307.

5 See "faith" and "faithful" in 12. 113, 128, 152, 154, 295, 306, 409, 427, 449, 462, 481, 488, 527, 529, 536, 571, 582, 599, 603.

6 Summers, *The Muse's Method,* p. 206.

7 The "Arguments" were first published in the re-issue of *Paradise Lost* in 1668, when they were printed together before the poem; in 1674 they were distributed to stand at the head of each book, the arguments for the original books 7 and 10 being broken up to head the newly divided books. The above quotation is from 1674; in 1668 the equivalent to this part of the argument is less precise in its opening portion: "thence from the Flood relates, and by degrees explains, who that Seed of the Woman shall be; his Incarnation, Death [etc.]." See *Facsimile,* ed. Harris Fletcher, II, 177–89.

8 William G. Madsen, "The Idea of Nature in Milton's Poetry," in *Three Studies in the Renaissance* (New Haven: Yale University Press, 1958), pp. 258–59.

9 Cf. Broadbent, *Some Graver Subject,* pp. 88–90.

10 This formulation is indebted to my reading of Stanley Fish's *Surprised by Sin:* see esp. his account of the last books, chapter 7.

11 My thinking here is strongly influenced by the stimulating study by Herbert N. Schneidau, *Sacred Discontent: The Bible and Western Tradition* (Berkeley: University of California Press, 1976), esp. chapters 2 and 3.

12 Cf. Addison's remark on book 12: "If *Milton's* Poem flags anywhere, it is in this Narration, where in some places the Author has been so attentive to his Divinity, that he has neglected his Poetry" (*Spectator,* No. 369: ed. Bond, III, 386).

CHAPTER 11: The Solitary Way

This chapter represents an extensive revision of the essay under this title which appeared in *The Author in His Work: Essays on a Problem in Criticism* [in honor of Maynard Mack], ed. Louis L. Martz and Aubrey Williams, with an introduction by Patricia Meyer Spacks (New Haven: Yale University Press, 1978), pp. 71–84; this essay was originally composed as a lecture, "*Paradise Lost* and the Idea of Pilgrimage," delivered at the Vermont Renaissance Symposium in April 1975. The present version incorporates the equivalent of a half-dozen pages from various portions of *The Paradise Within.*

1   The illustration is derived from Raphael: see Marcia R. Pointon, *Milton and English Art* (Manchester: Manchester University Press, 1970), p. 15; and Helen Gardner, "Milton's First Illustrator," *Essays and Studies,* n.s. 9 (1956): 27–38; see pp. 34–35. See also Merritt Y. Hughes, "Some Illustrators of Milton: The Expulsion from Paradise," *Journal of English and Germanic Philology,* 60 (1961): 670–79; Kester Svendsen, *Milton and Science* (Cambridge, Mass.: Harvard University Press, 1956), pp. 107–13; and Dick Taylor, Jr., "Milton's Treatment of the Judgment and the Expulsion in *Paradise Lost,*" *Texas Studies in English,* 10 (1960): 51–82. Pictorial representations of the Expulsion in the Middle Ages and the Renaissance have now been thoroughly explored by Roland Mushat Frye in his monumental study *Milton's Imagery and the Visual Arts* (1978), pp. 308–15, with this conclusion: "I know of nothing like [Milton's presentation] in pictorial art: when Michael takes the hands of Adam and Eve in his hands and leads them through the gate, we have a radically new version of an old and familiar scene" (pp. 312–13). The only flaw in Frye's otherwise excellent interpretation is his misreading of 12.632–34, where Frye takes "before them" (which refers to the cherubim descending from "the other Hill") to refer to Adam and Eve, and thus mistakes Milton's use of the traditional motif: "In pictorial art," Frye says, "that 'brandisht' sword always *followed* Adam and Eve, driving them before it with greater or lesser implications of immediate physical harm, whereas Milton reverses its position, and explicitly places it 'before them,' where it was 'high in front advanced'. . . . So used, the sword becomes processional, leading them forth in dignity and grace rather than driving them in terror" (p. 311). But the sword is behind them, as the Argument to book 12 says.
2   Peter Sterry, *A Discourse of the Freedom of the Will* (London: 1675), p. 99.
3   See the notes to these lines in Carey and Fowler, pp. 485–86.
4   See Ricks, *Milton's Grand Style,* chapter 4, and Christopher Grose, *Milton's Epic Process* (New Haven: Yale University Press, 1973), chapter 6, for summation and perceptive extension of critical views on the similes. For an acute study of all aspects of Milton's imagery see MacCaffrey, *Paradise Lost as "Myth",* chapter 5. Also Ferry, *Milton's Epic Voice,* chapter 3; and Hartman, "Milton's Counterplot."
5   Cf. MacCaffrey, *Paradise Lost as "Myth",* pp. 181–84; and the detailed study of Milton's Hell by Broadbent, *Some Graver Subject,* pp. 80–124.
6   See above, note 2. Milton shared in some measure this view that the Image of God in man has not been utterly destroyed, but retains some vestiges of its original creative power: see *De Doctrina,* 1.12: "it cannot be denied that some traces of the divine image still remain in us, which are not wholly extinguished by this spiritual death. . . . These traces remain in our intellect" (trans. Carey: *Prose Works,* ed. Wolfe, VI, 396). This view is the implicit basis of his treatise *Of Education* and derives from his close affiliation with Platonic thought: see Irene Samuel, *Milton and Plato* (Ithaca: Cornell University Press, 1947).
7   Cf. MacCaffrey, *Paradise Lost as "Myth",* chapter 6: "Satan's Voyage."

8   *OED,* "pilgrimage," *sb.* 1.
9   Augustine, *De Trinitate,* 14.20; *Later Works,* trans. John Burnaby, Library of
    Christian Classics, vol. 8 (London: SCM Press, 1955), pp. 118–19.
10 An excellent account of Milton's Paradise is given by John R. Knott, Jr., in
    Milton's Pastoral Vision: An Approach to Paradise Lost (Chicago: University of
    Chicago Press, 1971); Knott's footnotes provide a running bibliography of
    writings on the subject. See especially Broadbent, *Some Graver Subject,* chap-
    ter 6; Giamatti, *The Earthly Paradise,* chapter 6; Arnold Stein, *Answerable Style*
    (Minneapolis: University of Minnesota Press, 1953), pp. 52–74; Northrop
    Frye, *The Return of Eden* (Toronto: University of Toronto Press, 1965); and
    Joseph E. Duncan, *Milton's Earthly Paradise: A Historical Study of Eden* (Min-
    neapolis: University of Minnesota Press, 1972).
11 Cf. Ferry, *Milton's Epic Voice,* pp. 55–56.
12 Cf. C. S. Lewis, *A Preface to Paradise Lost,* pp. 47–50.
13 For a fine analysis of the hymn see Summers, *The Muse's Method,* chapter 3.

Coda   Many of the studies cited for particular points in the foregoing chapters
       have had, over the years, a more pervasive part in the development of the
       ideas presented in this account of *Paradise Lost.* I should like to include
       within this general acknowledgment my gratitude to a few more studies
       for which no particular mention has arisen, especially to the first on this
       list, which formed my introduction to Miltonic studies:

       E. M. W. Tillyard, *Milton* (London: Chatto, 1930).
       Maurice Kelley, *This Great Argument* (Princeton: Princeton University
          Press, 1941).
       Arthur E. Barker, *Milton and the Puritan Dilemma* (Toronto: University of
          Toronto Press, 1942).
       Douglas Bush, *Paradise Lost in Our Time* (Ithaca: Cornell University Press,
          1945).
       Thomas Greene, *The Descent from Heaven* (New Haven: Yale University
          Press, 1963); especially chapter 12.
       Michael Fixler, *Milton and the Kingdoms of God* (Evanston: Northwestern
          University Press, 1964).
       Merritt Y. Hughes, *Ten Perspectives on Milton* (New Haven: Yale Univer-
          sity Press, 1965).
       Helen Gardner, *A Reading of Paradise Lost* (Oxford: Clarendon Press,
          1965).
       Thomas Kranidas, *The Fierce Equation: A Study of Milton's Decorum* (The
          Hague: Mouton, 1965).
       Irene Samuel, *Dante and Milton* (Ithaca: Cornell University Press, 1966).
       John M. Steadman, *Milton and the Renaissance Hero* (Oxford: Clarendon
          Press, 1967), and *Milton's Epic Characters* (Chapel Hill: University of
          North Carolina Press, 1968).
       William Madsen, *From Shadowy Types to Truth* (New Haven: Yale Univer-
          sity Press, 1968).

CHAPTER 12: The Anti-heroic Epic

1   *The Life Records of John Milton,* ed. J. Milton French, 5 vols. (New Brunswick: Rutgers University Press, 1949–58), V, 110, 327.

2   Or perhaps, as one of my students, Paul Leopold, has suggested, Milton knew his Vergil by heart and had no need for a reader!

3   See Douglas Bush's indispensable chapter on Milton in *Mythology and the Renaissance Tradition in English Poetry* (Minneapolis: University of Minnesota Press, 1932), pp. 248–68. Also Jonathan H. Collett, "Milton's Use of Classical Mythology in *Paradise Lost,*" *PMLA,* 85 (1970): 88–96.

4   Quintilian, *Institutio Oratorio,* 10.1.88, trans. H. E. Butler, 4 vols., Loeb Classical Library (London: Heinemann, 1920–22), IV, 50–51.

5   Brooks Otis, *Ovid as an Epic Poet* (Cambridge: Cambridge University Press, 1966); 2nd edn., revised, 1970. The second edition is important because in it Otis has drastically changed his view of Ovid's flaws in writing heroic passages; he now sees these passages as parody; see the wholly re-written "Conclusion" to the 1970 edition. Robert Coleman, "Structure and Intention in the *Metamorphoses,*" *Classical Quarterly,* 21 (1971): 461–77.

6   Charles Paul Segal, *Landscape in Ovid's Metamorphoses, Hermes: Einzelschriften,* 23 (Wiesbaden, 1969). For the *topos* of the *locus amoenus* see Curtius, *European Literature and the Latin Middle Ages,* chapter 10.

7   G. Karl Galinsky, *Ovid's Metamorphoses* (Berkeley: University of California Press, 1975); see esp. pp. 19–25, 99. Also Otis (1970), pp. 335–38. Such views have been encouraged by the analytic catalogue of Ovid's "interventions" by Michael v. Albrecht, *Die Parenthese in Ovids Metamorphosen und ihre dichterische Funktion* (Hildesheim: Georg Olms, 1964).

8   Cf. Galinsky, pp. 24, 44–45; and Charles Segal, "Myth and Philosophy in the *Metamorphoses,*" *American Journal of Philology,* 90 (1969): 257–92; see esp. pp. 289–92.

9   In a highly illuminating article William S. Anderson finds a unifying factor in the theme of transformation by *love*—metamorphosis which consists not only in physical change, but primarily in psychological and moral changes that occur when *forma* (shape) is affected by *forma* (beauty): see "Multiple Change in the *Metamorphoses,*" *Transactions of the American Philological Association,* 94 (1963): 1–27. Otis is right, then, in saying that love "is the power that lifts the *Metamorphoses* to epic scope and unity" (1966: p. 334), while at the same time the power of love is used to deflate "divine majesty" and heroic dignity (p. 104). See Appendix 2 for a summary view of the anti-heroic action of *amor* and *furor.*

10 See Otis, *Ovid as an Epic Poet,* pp. 84–87 (pagination up to p. 306 is the same in both editions); the charts here are taken from Otis.

11 Notably Otis, in the revised "Conclusion" to his book: see his acknowledgment of the scholars who have motivated his change of mind. See also Coleman, "Structure and Intention in the *Metamorphoses,*" pp. 474–77; and

William S. Anderson's introduction to his edition of the *Metamorphoses, Books 6-10* (Norman: University of Oklahoma Press, 1972).

12   Cf. Otis (1970), pp. 346-47.

13   See Otis (1966), p. 323: "when he tried to treat heroic themes in a serious or a Virgilian way, he met an absolute check, and fell into the worst sort of bathos. His misfortune was that his epic plan and purpose could not be made to fit his peculiar abilities and deficiencies."

14   See Galinsky, *Ovid's Metamorphoses,* pp. 129-40. Coleman ("Structure and Intention," pp. 474-75) effectively takes issue with this view; in the Lapith-Centaur episode he says Ovid "is in reality pouring scorn upon the whole epic tradition of the aggrandizement of war. The epic tone here is therefore parodic" (p. 474). "What Ovid has done in fact is to deflate the whole heroic ideal, as set forth in the Homeric tradition and recently re-stated by Virgil in close and complex symbolic relation with the Augustan myth" (p. 475).

15   See Arnold Stein, *Answerable Style,* pp. 17-37; Broadbent, *Some Graver Subject,* pp. 218-28; Lieb, *Dialectics of Creation,* chapter 4; and the definitive article by Stella Revard, "Milton's Critique of Heroic Warfare in *Paradise Lost* V and VI," *Studies in English Literature,* 7 (1967): 119-39.

16   Hesiod, *Theogony,* 664-721.

17   Davis P. Harding, *Milton and the Renaissance Ovid* (Urbana: University of Illinois Press, 1946), pp. 67-79.

18   *Oechalia* is the reading of 1674; 1667 reads *Oealia,* evidently a misprint.

19   Repetition in Ovid is most frequent in small patterns, such as Anderson points to when he analyses the repetitions in *"deseruere sui nymphae* vineta Timoli, / *deseruere suas nymphae* Pactolides undas" (6.15-16), or in the "type of repetition" that he calls "peculiarly Ovidian"—the technique where "in a first clause he will use a finite verb, and the second clause will begin with the active or past participle of that verb"—as in "'a! piget, a! non est' *clamabat* 'tibia tanti.' / *clamanti* cutis est summos direpta per artus" (6.386-87); see *Metamorphoses, Books 6-10,* ed. Anderson, pp. 21-23. Nims points out a famous, longer example in the tale of Cephalus and Procris, where the word "aura" ("breeze") is skillfully repeated: "repetebam frigus et umbras / et quae de gelidis exibat vallibus *aura:* / *aura* petebatur medio mihi lenis in aestu, / *auram* exspectabam, requies erat illa labori. / '*aura*' (recordor enim), 'venias' cantare solebam. . . ." (7,809-13). Then a few lines later the repetition is compounded by a play on *aurem* ("ear"), followed by a striking repetition of words in the next line: "vocibus ambiguis deceptam praebuit *aurem* / nescio quis nomenque *aurae* tam saepe vocatum / esse putat *nymphae: nympham* mihi credit amari" (7.821-23). See the introduction by John Frederick Nims to his edition of Golding's translation of the *Metamorphoses* (New York: Macmillan, 1965), pp. xxx-xxxi.

20   Orpheus in the *Metamorphoses* pleads before Dis and Persephone in words that remind one of Milton's Hell and Chaos: "per ego haec loca plena

timoris, / per Chaos hoc ingens vastique silentia regni, / Eurydices, oro, properata retexite fata." ("I beg you, by these awful regions, by this boundless chaos, and by the silence of your vast realms, weave again Eurydice's destiny, brought too swiftly to a close." (10.29–31; trans. Innes). The music of Orpheus was successful, but his mission failed through his failure to obey divine command. Milton's bard, taught by a higher Muse, has returned "safe" to the realms of light.

CHAPTER 13: Pastoral Love: Versions and Subversions

1 Beyond the general resemblances, Thomas Newton noted that Milton "has expresly imitated some passages" from Ovid here; he calls attention to the close rhetorical imitation of *Metamorphoses*, 3.434–36,457–60: see Newton's edition of *Paradise Lost,* 2nd edn., 2 vols. (London, 1750), I, 294–95.

2 See Burden, *The Logical Epic,* pp. 83–85.

3 See above, chapter 8, n.12; chapter 12, n.19.

4 Gordon Williams, in his lecture on Vergil's fourth eclogue, has noted: "Patterned phrases, with symmetrical elements of repetition, are a characteristic feature of Theocritus' poetry." For examples he refers to the excellent summary of this Theocritean technique in *Theocritus: Select Poems,* ed. K. J. Dover (London: Macmillan, 1971), pp. xlv–xlviii. See Colloquy 7 (1973) in the series issued by The Center for Hermeneutical Studies in Hellenistic and Modern Culture, p. 16.

5 *Minor Latin Poets,* trans. J. Wight Duff and Arnold M. Duff, Loeb Classical Library, rev. edn. (London: Heinemann, 1935).

6 I have altered the opening phrases of the Loeb translation in order to stress the exact imitation of Calpurnius.

7 *Metamorphoses, Books 6–10,* ed. Anderson, p. 483 (note to 10.99).

8 See Harding, *Milton and the Renaissance Ovid,* p. 31; and Donald Lemen Clark, *John Milton at St. Paul's School* (New York: Columbia University Press, 1948), chapters 7 and 8.

9 See *Metamorphoses,* 4.256–70 (Clytie), 283 (Crocus), 10.162–219 (Hyacinthus). But, as so often in Milton, the Ovidian reminiscence here is mingled with another classical allusion: regarding the violet, crocus, and hyacinth, Newton pointed out, "Our author has taken this from Homer, who makes the same sort of flowers to spring up under Jupiter and Juno as they lay in conjugal embraces upon mount Ida, Iliad. XIV. 347." (*Paradise Lost,* ed. Newton, 2nd. edn., I, 314.) My point here, as elsewhere in this chapter, is not to argue that Ovid is the sole reminiscence, but that, when all the allusions are taken together, the presence of Ovid is dominant.

10 Segal, *Landscape in Ovid's Metamorphoses,* esp. section IV. See also Hugh Parry, "Ovid's *Metamorphoses:* Violence in a Pastoral Landscape," *Transactions of the American Philological Association,* 95 (1964): 268–82.

CHAPTER 14: The Ultimate Design

1 See above, chapter 9, n. 16.
2 See Brooks Otis, *Virgil: A Study in Civilized Poetry* (Oxford: Clarendon Press, 1964), chapter 3, "The Subjective Style"; and *Ovid as an Epic Poet* (1970), pp. 335–38.
3 Cf. Durling, *The Figure of the Poet in Renaissance Epic;* Durling deals with the narrator in Horace's *Satires* and Ovid's *Ars amatoria* and *Remedia amoris,* not with the *Metamorphoses.* But the techniques of the narrator in these elegiac poems point the way toward the voice of the narrator in Ovid's epic (see pp. 26–43). Durling goes on to deal with Chaucer, Petrarch, Boiardo, Ariosto, Tasso, and Spenser. But in this connection one should not overlook the extensive interventions of the poet found in Lucan and Statius: see Gordon Williams, *Change and Decline: Roman Literature in the Early Empire* (Berkeley: University of California Press, 1978), pp. 232–38.
4 Cf. T. F. Brunner, "The Function of the Simile in Ovid's *Metamorphoses,*" *Classical Journal,* 61 (1966): 354–63; and S. G. Owen, "Ovid's Use of the Simile," *Classical Review,* 45 (1931): 97–106.
5 See Hermann Fränkel, *Ovid, A Poet between Two Worlds* (Berkeley: University of California Press, 1945), pp. 101–11; and Otis, pp. 280, 291, 304–05, where he says "the history is not really assimilated to the myth," and speaks of "the barely disguised perfunctoriness of much of his historical liaison." Also Douglas Little, "The Speech of Pythagoras in Metamorphoses 15 and the Structure of the Metamorphoses," *Hermes,* 98 (1970): 340–60; and L. P. Wilkinson, *Ovid Recalled* (Cambridge: Cambridge University Press, 1955), pp. 221–26.
6 See Coleman, "Structure and Intention," p. 472; and Charles Segal, "Myth and Philosophy in the *Metamorphoses:* Ovid's Augustanism and the Augustan Conclusion of Book XV," *American Journal of Philology,* 90 (1969): 257–92. Also the acute older article by Frank J. Miller, "Ovid's *Aeneid* and Vergil's: A Contrast in Motivation," *Classical Journal,* 23 (1927): 33–43.
7 See Galinsky, p. 195; and Wilkinson, pp. 235–36, where he speaks of Ovid's catalogues as done "in the Hesiodic manner revived by the Alexandrians." Gordon Williams regards Ovid as virtually the "inventor" of this particular technique, which, he notes, "became a distinct stylistic feature of later epic," especially in Statius (*Change and Decline,* p. 215). The catalogue from Ovid's *Fasti* cited below is taken from the edition in the Loeb Classical Library, trans. Sir James George Frazer (London: Heinemann, 1931).
8 T. S. Eliot, "Milton" (1936), in *On Poetry and Poets* (London: Faber, 1957), p. 144.
9 Coleman, "Structure and Intention," p. 472.
10 This and all subsequent translations from Ovid's book 15 are by F. J. Miller.
11 See Segal, "Myth and Philosophy in the *Metamorphoses,*" pp. 287–88; and Kenneth J. Pratt, "Rome as Eternal," *Journal of the History of Ideas,* 26 (1965): 25–44; see esp. pp. 25–28.

CHAPTER 15: *Paradise Regain'd:* The Interior Teacher

This chapter stands substantially as it appeared in *The Paradise Within,* chapter 4, with a new conclusion and the omission of the first four pages. That chapter was itself a revision of the essay "*Paradise Regain'd:* The Meditative Combat" which appeared in *ELH,* 27 (1960): 223–47. The earlier versions of this essay opened with a suggestion that *Paradise Regain'd* bears some analogy with Vergil's *Georgics;* I have removed discussion of this possibility to an appendix, in order to explore the whole matter in some detail. Reference to scholarship on *Paradise Regain'd* is now fortunately made easy by the publication of the volume dealing with this poem in *A Variorum Commentary on the Poems of John Milton,* vol. 4, ed. Walter MacKellar, *With a Review of Studies of Style and Verse Form* by Edward R. Weismiller (New York: Columbia Univeristy Press, 1975). The problem of the poem's genre has been carefully studied by Barbara Lewalski in *Milton's Brief Epic* (Providence: Brown University Press, 1966), with two important results: we can now understand the tradition that led Milton to say that the Book of Job provided a "brief model" for an epic; and we can now see the great variety of short biblical poems before *Paradise Regain'd* that might be called "brief epics." Few of them, however, display an action that bears a significant resemblance to *Paradise Regain'd.* Consequently, her investigation seems rather to confirm the view of Northrop Frye that the structure of the poem is "a technical experiment that is practically *sui generis.*" "None of the ordinary literary categories apply to it," says Frye, "its poetic predecessors are nothing like it and it has left no descendants." He goes on to suggest that "its closest affinities are with the debate and with the dialectical colloquy of Plato and Boethius, to which most of the Book of Job also belongs." He notes, however, that "these forms usually either incorporate one argument into another dialectically or build up two different cases rhetorically; Milton's feat of constructing a double argument on the same words, each highly plausible and yet as different as light from darkness, is, so far as I know, unique in English literature" (*The Return of Eden* [Toronto: University of Toronto Press, 1965], pp. 135–36). MacKellar, after citing this passage, goes on to say: "Nor is it unique only in English literature. Among numerous Italian and French Biblical poems of the 16th and 17th centuries, I have found none which even remotely resembles *Paradise Regained.* Milton, in short, displays a singular independence of traditional literary forms" (*Variorum Commentary,* IV, 10).

The poem, paradoxically, becomes *sui generis* by reason of what Stuart Baker calls an "interplay of genres," in his persuasive essay "Sannazaro and Milton's Brief Epic," *Comparative Literature,* 20 (1968): 116–32. Baker sees Milton's poem, like Sannazaro's *De partu virginis,* as mingling epic motifs with elements drawn from "meditation, prophecy, debate, and the pastoral landscape" (p. 131)— and to these I would add elements drawn from the "didactic" genre, as described by Addison: "No rules therefore that relate to *Pastoral,* can any way affect the *Georgics,* since they fall under that class of Poetry, which consists in giving plain and direct instructions to the reader; whether they be Moral duties, as those of *Theognis* and *Pythagoras;* or Philosophical speculations, as those of *Aratus* and *Lucretius;* or Rules of practice, as those of *Hesiod* and *Virgil*" (Addison, *Miscel-*

laneous Works, ed. A. C. Guthkelch, 2 vols. [London: Bell, 1914], II, 4). Edward Weismiller *(Variorum Commentary,* IV, 297–317) has given a shrewd and fair-minded account of the various critical views that contribute to this support for finding the key to the poem in the "interplay of genres" and the "complex intermingling of styles." Stanley Fish has provided new insight into the interiority of the poem in his essay "Inaction and Silence: The Reader in *Paradise Regained,"* in the important collection: *Calm of Mind: Tercentenary Essays on Paradise Regained and Samson Agonistes in Honor of John S. Diekhoff,* ed. Joseph A. Wittreich, Jr. (Cleveland: Press of Case Western Reserve University, 1971), pp. 25–47.

1 Both this quotation and the epigraph to Part IV are taken from Augustine's *De Magistro,* 11.38; 12.40: *Augustine: Earlier Writings,* trans. John H. S. Burleigh, Library of Christian Classics, vol. 6 (London: SCM Press, 1953), pp. 95–96.

2 Milton, *De Doctrina,* 1.15: *Prose Works,* ed. Wolfe, VI, 432.

3 Cf. Tillyard, *Milton,* pp. 313–14: "the normal style of the poem is deliberately chastened or dimmed."

4 For the wide range of interpretations possible here see the study of the third temptation given by Elizabeth Marie Pope in *Paradise Regained: The Tradition and the Poem* (Baltimore: Johns Hopkins Press, 1947), chapter 7. Also the article by A. S. P. Woodhouse, "Theme and Pattern in *Paradise Regained," University of Toronto Quarterly,* 25 (1955–56): 167–82, esp. p. 181; included in Woodhouse's *The Heavenly Muse,* chapter 10.

5 See, for example, Don Cameron Allen, *The Harmonious Vision* (Baltimore: Johns Hopkins Press, 1954), pp. 110–15; and Tillyard, *Milton,* p. 307.

6 I believe that this functional view of the basic style of *Paradise Regain'd* was suggested to me by certain remarks of W. Menzies in his essay, "Milton: the Last Poems," *Essays and Studies,* 24 (1938): 80–112; see esp. pp. 109–11. A similar view is developed by Jacques Blondel in the introduction (really a sizable monograph) prefaced to his bilingual edition of *Paradise Regain'd* (Paris: Aubier, 1955); see esp. pp. 92–110 *passim.*

7 F. M. Cornford, *Before and After Socrates* (Cambridge: Cambridge University Press, 1950), chapter 2, esp. pp. 50–51.

8 Milton's *Prose Works,* ed. Wolfe, VI, 735. See MacKellar's account of the Christian reconciliation of magnanimity with humility in the *Variorum Commentary,* IV, 41–43; and Steadman's important chapter 6, "The Critique of Magnanimity," in *Milton and the Renaissance Hero.* For the essential and pervasive influence of John on Milton's poem see the significant article by Ira Clark, *"Paradise Regained* and the Gospel according to John," *Modern Philology,* 71 (1973): 1–15.

9 Arnold Stein, *Heroic Knowledge* (Minneapolis: University of Minnesota Press, 1957), p. 89. For a discussion of the ways in which Milton "intrudes" throughout the poem, see the adverse criticism by W. B. C. Watkins, *Anatomy of Milton's Verse,* pp. 113–25. For a favorable view of the narrator's role see Roger H. Sundell, "The Narrator as Interpreter in *Paradise Regained," Milton Studies,* 2 (1970): 83–101.

10   Cf. Stein, *Heroic Knowledge,* pp. 50–51, where he speaks of "the charming development of Satan rising as advocate to defend the elevated virtue of his opponent" and treating us to "a delightful piece of mythological debunking by a puritanical Satan."

11   See the excellent analysis of the sequence of the temptations according to Plato's *Republic* by Irene Samuel, *Plato and Milton,* pp. 69–129.

12   See Allan H. Gilbert, "The Temptation in *Paradise Regain'd," Journal of English and Germanic Philology,* 15 (1916): 599–611, esp. pp. 606–07. Also Pope, *Paradise Regained: the Tradition and the Poem,* p. 67.

13   For helpful discussion of the problems here see Irene Samuel, "Milton on Learning and Wisdom," *PMLA,* 64 (1949): 708–23; Lewalski, *Milton's Brief Epic,* chapter 11; and Rajan, *The Lofty Rhyme,* chapter 8.

14   *The Ferrar Papers,* ed. B. Blackstone (Cambridge: Cambridge University Press, 1938), pp. 60–63; I have expanded abbreviations and altered the punctuation slightly.

15   Milton, *Prose Works,* ed. Wolfe, VI, 194.

16   See the searching and wholly convincing study of the "companionable" nature of the two poems by Arthur Barker in "Calm Regained through Passion Spent," in *The Prison and the Pinnacle,* ed. Balachandra Rajan (Toronto: University of Toronto Press, 1973), pp. 3–48, esp. p. 35: "As the young Christ isolates himself in the wilderness of this world to engage in wholly interiorized and self-closeted meditation, so Samson, however unintelligent and uncontemplative, is forced by the wrath of his just God and the pains of enslaved defeat to withdraw into himself. As Christ meets a series of temptations by a series of cold repudiations, so Samson meets the series of his renewed temptations by a series of repudiations through which his despair is transformed into a cold anger which is the expression of the contempt for the world proper to his new spirituality . . ."

17   See headnote to next chapter.

18   Tertullian, *De Praescriptionibus Haereticorum,* chapter 7; see the translation by Peter Holmes in the *Ante-Nicene Christian Library,* ed. Alexander Roberts and James Donaldson (Edinburgh: Clark, 1870), XV, 9–10. The apostles taught in the "porch of Solomon" (Acts 3:11); the quotation about "simplicity of heart" comes from Wisdom of Solomon 1:1.

19   Clement of Alexandria, *Stromateis,* 1.5; see *Ante-Nicene Christian Library,* ed. Roberts and Donaldson, IV, 366. I have quoted the superior translation of this passage by Henry Bettenson in *Documents of the Christian Church* (London: Oxford University Press, 1947), p. 10.

20   Milton, *De Doctrina,* 1.12; trans. Carey; *Prose Works,* ed. Wolfe, VI, 396.

CHAPTER 16: *Samson Agonistes:* The Breath of Heaven

The present chapter stands substantially as it appeared in *Milton Studies,* 1 (1969): 115–34, under the title "Chorus and Character in *Samson Agonistes,*" an essay which was in turn based upon a lecture, "Tragic Transformation in *Samson Agonistes,*" delivered at the University of Pittsburgh in January 1968 as part of a series celebrating the tercentenary of *Paradise Lost*. I have here omitted the opening paragraphs and have written a new conclusion.

The volume of the *Variorum Commentary* devoted to *Samson Agonistes* has not yet appeared, but a worthy surrogate is now available in the recent book by Mary Ann Radzinowicz, *Toward Samson Agonistes: The Growth of Milton's Mind* (Princeton: Princeton University Press, 1978); along with its own illuminating commentary, this provides a thorough bibliography, detailed footnotes on points of controversy, and ample consideration of all major studies of the poem. Her view of the chorus and of Manoa is quite divergent from my own, but the strength of her objections has convinced me that my original essay tended to over-state the case, and I have therefore moderated my views in places.

1   See the analysis of this prologue by Arnold Stein, *Heroic Knowledge,* pp. 138–43.

2   Cf. Stein, pp. 145–46.

3   The question has been ably treated by John Huntley in "A Revaluation of the Chorus's Role in Milton's *Samson Agonistes*," *Modern Philology,* 64 (1966–67): 132–45; Huntley throughout presents an excellent argument for his view that the members of the chorus "are neither vicious nor saintly, but represent the vast ambivalent mass of mankind which neither knows what it feels nor feels what it knows" (p. 139). For the controversy on this point see Radzinowicz, *Toward Samson Agonistes,* pp. 62–64, 98–99; and Anthony Low, *The Blaze of Noon* (New York: Columbia University Press, 1974), pp. 118–26. Lynn Sadler suggests that the rhyming platitudes demonstrate the chorus's effort to apply legalistic Old Testament wisdom to Samson; see "Coping with Hebraic Legalism: The Chorus in *Samson Agonistes*," *Harvard Theological Review,* 66 (1973): 353–68. The problem is related to the effect of "rhythmic strangeness" in *Samson,* which Edward Weismiller has defended in his fine essay on the metrics of the play: "Again we must assume that the strangeness is intended; but we do well to recognize it as a strangeness produced in the first place by a kind of controlled metrical-rhythmical disorientation, and persisting as a strangeness of proportioning—a complex effect for which the reading of stanzaic verse, even Milton's own stanzaic verse, has hardly prepared us" (see "The 'Dry' and 'Rugged' Verse," in *The Lyric and Dramatic Milton,* ed. Summers, pp. 115–52; esp. pp. 135–36).

4   A suggestion close to this was made long ago by A. J. Wyatt: see his edition of *Samson Agonistes* in the "University Tutorial Series" (London, 1892), pp. 9–10, where he asserts that "Milton's use of rhyme here is so far in accord with his previous renunciation of it, that he intends in the rhymed passages to produce a curious effect of contempt or aversion." After listing most of the "chief passages" of rhyme, Wyatt adds that these passages were "doubtless introduced in almost every case with a purpose, probably to indicate scorn or some kindred feeling." Wyatt's suggestion is cited by W. R. Parker in his article, "The Date of *Samson Agonistes*," but rejected on the grounds that "a sympathetic application of Wyatt's theory accounts for not half of the riming passages; and Wyatt himself, in a list of 'the chief passages,' omits the

superb final chorus, the intricate rime pattern of which is reminiscent of a sonnet" (see *Philological Quarterly,* 28 (1949): 148–49). Wyatt's view is extravagant, but has some truth in it. Roberts W. French describes the choric rhymes as "superfluous decoration" which emphasizes the chorus's confidence in false convictions: see "Rhyme and the Chorus of *Samson Agonistes,*" *Laurel Review,* 10 (1970): 60–67.

5   For a contrasting view of Manoa's character, see Low, *The Blaze of Noon,* pp. 123–32; and Radzinowicz, *Toward Samson Agonistes,* pp. 337–38.

6   For strong disagreement with this point, see Low, pp. 210–14.

7   For varied opinions of Dalila see Don Cameron Allen, *The Harmonious Vision,* pp. 88–90; Thomas Kranidas, *Studies in English Literature,* 6 (1966): 125–37; and the commentaries of Low (pp. 144–58) and Radzinowicz (pp. 36–50, 99–101, 212–17).

8   Cf. *Heroic Knowledge,* p. 177, where Stein speaks of the "comic tone" and the "light verse" of this chorus. In this passage Low sees rather an expression of "near-incoherent exasperation" (p. 214).

9   Radzinowicz (p. 263), in dealing with these lines, breaks off the quotation after "Not willingly"—but the rest of the passage is essential to the meaning. Earlier (p. 107) she describes the effect of the catastrophe on the chorus in a way that seems to reveal the contradiction between the Greek view of "necessity" and the Christian view of "illumination": "As a group they accept the tragic, they do not push it away. Samson *was* 'tangl'd in the fold of dire necessity.' His enemies were 'fond'; 'insensate . . . or to sense reprobate,' they invited their own ruin. Samson's triumph lies not in their defeat but in himself: 'with inward eyes illuminated' he revived, and his virtue reflourished though his body died."

10   See Milton's *De Doctrina,* 1.3: "neither God's decree nor his foreknowledge can shackle free causes with any kind of necessity" (trans. Carey: *Prose Works,* VI, 166).

11   I now agree with Huntley's view on this point: see "Revaluation of the Chorus's Role," p. 144.

12   Franklin R. Baruch makes a similar point about the funeral rites in "Time, Body, and Spirit at the Close of *Samson Agonistes,*" *ELH,* 36 (1969), pp. 324–25. See Low's objection to this point of view, pp. 128–32.

13   Baruch seems to support this argument when he says that "the image that the Chorus offers of themselves is not the justifiable one of a group inspired to a moral choice and action by a noble example, but rather a contented, peaceful lot, well out of the active process that Milton always envisioned at the unalterable center of true Christian being" (p. 338).

14   Cf. Schneidau, *Sacred Discontent,* chapter 3.

15   Cf. Radzinowicz, pp. 22–23, 351.

APPENDIX 1: *Paradise Regain'd* and the *Georgics*

1   John Chalker, *The English Georgic* (London: Routledge, 1969), pp. 24, 209; see his whole opening chapter.

2   But see Douglas Bush, *English Literature in the Earlier Seventeenth Century,* 2nd
    edn., revised (Oxford: Clarendon Press, 1962), pp. 414–15; and, more re-
    cently, the corroborative essay, written from a thematic point of view, by
    Andrew V. Ettin, "Milton, T. S. Eliot, and the Virgilian Vision: Some Ver-
    sions of Georgic," *Genre,* 10 (1977): 233–58.

3   *Servii Grammatici Qui Feruntur in Vergilii Carmina Commentarii,* ed. G. Thilo
    and H. Hagen, 4 vols. (Leipzig, 1881–1902), III, fasc. 1, pp. 1–2.

4   See Addison's "Essay on the *Georgics*" prefixed to John Dryden's translation,
    The Works of Vergil (London, 1697): Addison, *Miscellaneous Works,* ed.
    Guthkelch, II, 9.

5   *The Eclogues and Georgics of Virgil,* trans. C. Day Lewis (Garden City:
    Doubleday-Anchor, 1964); the translation of the *Georgics* was originally
    published in 1940; copyright 1940 by Oxford University Press.

6   See Brooks Otis, *Virgil: A Study in Civilized Poetry,* pp. 164–65, 167, 186; L. P.
    Wilkinson, *The Georgics of Vergil* (Cambridge: Cambridge University Press,
    1969), pp. 71–107; esp. pp 88–89.

7   *Georgics,* trans. Smith Palmer Bovie (Chicago: University of Chicago Press,
    1956).

8   See "The Argument" at the head of Dryden's translation of the fourth book
    of the *Georgics.*

9   *Ibid.*

10 Essay prefixed to Dryden's translation; Addison, *Miscellaneous Works,* pp.
    10–11.

11 Otis, *Virgil,* p. 194.

12 Otis, *Virgil,* pp. 190–214; see esp. pp. 201, 208, 211–214.

13 Wilkinson, *The Georgics of Vergil,* p. 71.

14 Wilkinson, pp. 71–75. See also pp. 314–15 for a bibliography of studies on
    the structure of the *Georgics* since 1924.

15 W. F. Jackson Knight, *Roman Vergil* (London: Faber, 1944), p. 152.

16 Segal, *Landscape in Ovid's Metamorphoses,* p. 2.

17 Jacques Perret, "The *Georgics,*" trans. M. Brooks, in *Virgil,* ed. Steele Com-
    mager (Englewood Cliffs: Prentice-Hall, 1966), pp. 37–38, 40; from Perret's
    Virgile (Paris: Editions du Seuil, 1959).

18 Tillyard, *Milton,* p. 322.

19 *The Aeneid,* trans. W. F. Jackson Knight, rev. edn. (Harmondsworth: Penguin
    Books, 1958).

20 *Variorum Commentary,* IV, 298. For Dunster's final remark here see his edi-
    tion, p. 267. Dunster follows this with stress upon the poem's relation to the
    genre of the *Georgics:* "The *Paradise Regained* has something of the *didactic*
    character; it teaches not merely by the general moral, and by the character
    and conduct of its hero, but has also many positive precepts every where
    interspersed. It is written for the most part in a style admirably condensed,
    and with a studied reserve of ornament: it is nevertheless illuminated with
    beauties of the most captivating kind."

List of Illustrations

341

The above identifications have been aided by information in
Marcia Pointon's *Milton and English Art* (Manchester: Manchester
University Press, 1970), and in Suzanne Boorsch's study, "The
1688 *Paradise Lost* and Dr. Aldrich," *Metropolitan Museum Journal*,
6(1972): 133–50. Boorsch provides convincing evidence for at-
tributing the unsigned designs for book 2 (partly after Mantegna)
and book 12 (after Raphael) to Henry Aldrich, rather than to
Medina; but the evidence for the unsigned design for book 1 is
indeterminate.

Index

The index has been designed to serve also as a bibliographical guide; for each book or article cited, the first page-entry for the notes will provide a full reference. Modern translations are normally indexed only for the full reference. The following abbreviations have been used: *PL: Paradise Lost; PR: Paradise Regain'd; SA: Samson Agonistes.*

THEORIES OF INDUSTRIAL SOCIETY

Theories of Industrial Society

Richard J. Badham

ST. MARTIN'S PRESS
New York

Scholarly & Reference Division,
St. Martin's Press, Inc., 175 Fifth Avenue, New York, NY 10010
First published in the United States of America in 1986
Printed in Great Britain
ISBN 0-312-79640-4

Library of Congress Cataloging in Publication Data

Badham, Richard J.
  Theories of industrial society.

  Bibliography: p.
  Includes index.
  1. Industrial sociology.   2. Industry—Social
aspects.   I. Title.
HD6955.B27   1986   306'.36   86-1742
ISBN 0-312-79640-4

The author and publishers would like to thank
Sage Publications for permission to reproduce material from
Current Sociology, Vol. 32, No. 1 Spring 1984:
'Sociology of Industrial and Post-Industrial Societies'.

*To Crécy
and the end of an era*

Printed and bound in Great Britain

CONTENTS

Introduction

INTRODUCTION

In schools and universities we are presented with the powerful image of the Industrial Revolution as the 'great growling engine of change' launching the world into the modern era. Like the French Revolution, this image of the Industrial Revolution has attained enormous symbolic significance. Whereas the French Revolution became a symbol of man's capacity to shape society according to the dictates of Reason, the Industrial Revolution became a symbol of man's increasing technological power and capacity to harness the forces of nature.

In both cases, however, democratic and technological achievements were marred by widespread violence, inhumanity and suffering. The French revolution became a *locus classicus* for power abuse and rule by terror, all originating from untempered political idealism and unregulated mass action. The Industrial Revolution came to stand for the fragmentation of society and the dehumanisation of man, the poverty and ugliness of proletarian life, the spirit of disenchanted calculation and crass commercialism. Worship of the Age of Reason merged with fear of the Reign of Terror; praise of the Age of Industry went hand in hand with hatred of the 'dark satanic mills' — with an aversion to the perversity of 'Faustian man'.

This view of the Industrial Revolution is directly linked to a set of images of industrialism, industrialisation and industrial society. In the popular mind the image of an industrial Leviathan marching through history often provides a general, if only vaguely formulated, perspective on world history and contemporary societies. The 'great divide' between pre-industrial and industrial societies is commonly assumed to be *the* main bridge separating modern societies from the past, distinguishing 'developed' from 'underdeveloped' states in the present era. This image of industrial society has played a dominant role in the social sciences. In history, politics and economics, as well as in sociology, the idea of industrial society provides the background for discussions of modern history, power in contemporary societies, market economies and economic growth. Yet in recent years this image has been increasingly challenged. A number of critics have condemned the 'technocratic consciousness' and 'ideology of industrialism' associated with this perspective (Dickson 1974; Roszak 1973). In addition, the last decade witnessed a more systematic critique of the 'theory of industrial society' within the social sciences (Giddens 1982; Salaman 1981; Scott 1979). Uniting both sets of criticisms is a reaction against the cruder image of industrial society as providing both an *explanation* of the structure and change of modern societies and as an *ideal* for guiding and directing future social development.

Beyond the limited confines of academic discourse, the classical image of industrial society has played an important role in structuring contemporary social identity and political programmes. In the less affluent world, there is the widespread concern to 'industrialize'. In the more affluent world there is an uneasy combination of a desire to re-establish post-war levels of economic growth with an increasing awareness of the many 'limits of growth' and 'diseconomies of scale'. Influenced by the traditional images of industrial society, these issues are often presented in terms of 'industrialize and be damned' or 'industrialize or be damned'. There appears either a commitment to 'growth', voiced in terms of the 'need to industrialize' and the 'impossibility of turning back' or a radical critique of the inherent ills of the mechanised iron cage of an inhuman industrialism.

The image of industrial society, to the extent that it actively promotes such a view, severely restricts the social imagination. Yet the influence of the image of industrial society is even wider than its support of the more extreme technocratic and technophobic approaches to economic progress. It has continued to provide the background images and set of assumptions that underlie a wide variety of contemporary discussions of economic development and social progress — even amongst those more aware of the limitations of the traditional images of industrialism. Immense significance is still attached to unilinear industrial development as the ultimate key to all progress. In this way, we shall argue, it obscures the social structures and power relationships responsible for *selecting* the form and direction of technology and growth. Equally significantly, it prevents reflection on the need for technological and economic *choice*, and hinders widespread public debate on the criteria to be used in making such choices.

The present discussions of the 'theory of industrial society' and the 'ideology of industrialism' obtain wider significance against this general background of reaction against crude images of industry as a guide for the future. Yet the social scientific critiques of industrial society theory have generally failed to address the major issue that this raises. They have condemned the industrial perspective on modern states for its 'evolutionist', 'functionalist', 'technicist' or 'positivist' excesses. These criticisms, as we shall see, are richly deserved. They do not, however, grasp the central purpose, and hence appeal, of industrial society theory. They have left relatively unchallenged the more general assumption that it is still industrialization that crucially separates past from present. The many important variants of this general industrial society theory all share the one basic assumption: that a number of modern states are fundamentally 'industrial' societies and that social investigation and political action are, or should be, centrally concerned with understanding and attending to the implications of this fact.

Criticism can be as misleading and dangerous as the original theory that is criticized. To adapt a comment made by Marx: even in their criticisms there is mystification. To concentrate on extreme evolutionary theories of industrialism or uncritical technocratic celebrations of industrial progress is to ignore the more general industrial society theory that continues to structure our overall sense of historical time and social progress.

The concern of this book is to examine critically the pervasiveness and influence of this theory. The focus is less on the reality than on the theory of industrial society. It examines critically the implications of the initial theoretical decision to describe modern societies as fundamentally 'industrial'. The category 'industrial society' is not here taken as given, with attention accordingly concentrated on the state of research into its 'nature'.[1] The main concern, rather, is with the effect of the decision to employ this construct, together with the influence of that decision on ensuing social research. The purpose, value and problems involved in this decision have been largely ignored by previous criticisms of the theory of industrial society. Earlier critics have concentrated their attention more on the methodological weaknesses of past theories of industrial society than on the conceptual implications of the initial adoption of the industrial construct.

As has been frequently pointed out, one of the most important components of the social scientific enterprise is the explicit combination of theoretical analysis and empirical research. Only in this way can we avoid a sterile indulgence in 'grand theory' and 'abstracted empiricism'. (Mills 1975). So much is commonly accepted. All the same, there has been a relative lack of systematic theoretical analysis of many major concepts serving to direct empirical research. The interaction between fact, theory and value in structuring social investigation is easier to accept in the abstract than it is to detail in the case of any specific concept. This difficulty and neglect is particularly noticeable in the sphere of social typologies. Empirical investigations are often carried out under the heading of research into the nature of 'capitalism', 'socialism', 'democracy', 'mass society', 'industrial society', 'post-industrial society' etc. But despite the occasional exception (e.g., Giner 1976), there has been little rigorous analysis of the nature, implications and limitations of such classifications in social and political inquiry. Without this analysis, empirical studies cannot proceed with any clear understanding of what is being investigated or why it matters.

The present work aims to provide just such an analysis of the industrial society construct, and of the way in which it is linked to a specific industrial society theory. This necessarily involves a review of both the major theories of industrial society and the main empirical studies of industrial (post-capitalist, post-industrial, etc.) societies. Yet this is primarily intended neither as an exercise in the history of ideas nor as a discussion of the reliability of contemporary empirical research. It is primarily a *conceptual* analysis of 'industrial society'. This is taken as a 'category', a 'class' or 'set' of societies, which are indissolubly linked to a general social 'typology' or 'classificatory' schema. This, in turn, can be taken to reflect or presuppose a theory — in this case, 'industrial society theory'. Like all human invention, 'industrial society theory' serves a purpose. The object of the present analysis is to lay bare that purpose, to display its importance, the constraints it imposes upon further investigation, and the problems created by its use. In this way, we may see that 'abstract' conceptual analysis — burdened with typologies and theories — may have far-reaching implications, both moral and political. It brings into question, and attempts to refashion, the basic categories through which we understand, construct and reconstruct the society in which we live.

Notes

1. Previously, reviews of the literature on industrial societies have
mostly taken one of three forms: (i) a general assessment of competing
social and political theories of modern society ('Durkheimian',
'Weberian', 'Marxian', etc.); (ii) an outline of the general research into
specific areas of industrial society (the 'family in industrial society', 'class
in industrial society', 'politics in industrial society', etc.); and (iii) a
concern with the links between traditional theoretical ideas and present
empirical research ('anomie in industrial society', 'alienation in industrial
society').

PART ONE

INDUSTRIAL SOCIETY: THEORY AND RESEARCH

1 INDUSTRIAL SOCIETY: HISTORY I

The understanding of modern states as 'industrial societies' has had a definite effect on the way in which we understand and judge the modern world. Yet the term 'industrial society' is now in such widespread use that it is difficult to view it as a theoretical construct. It appears 'obvious' that much of the affluent sector of the world's population lives in 'industrial societies'. The concept of industrial society does, however, have a specific history. It has been developed, and re-established, in particular eras in an attempt to explain the nature and development of modern states *and guide it in certain directions*.

Industrial Society: A Contested Concept

When the concept first achieved popularity, with the publication by Henri de Saint-Simon of the journal *L'Industrie* in 1816, it was an extremely farsighted notion. The development of manufacturing and machine technology was only rudimentary at that time (Kumar 1978). European societies were still primarily feudal and agricultural. For Saint-Simon (1760–1825) and Auguste Comte (1798–1857), the idea was not developed in order to describe an already existing reality, but to direct political action and social reform. The future, they argued, was to be an industrial future. In order to overcome the chaos and disruption surrounding the French Revolution, the leaders of society, and the general populace, had to recognize their fate. With the aid of scientific knowledge, and the commonly accepted goal of increased production (Ionesuu 1976: 123), it was argued that an industrial society could be established that would resolve all fundamental social conflict and institutionalize political order and social change. In the work of these writers, the concept of industrial society was thus created and employed as part of a specific political programme to 'save' modern societies from chaos and to secure orderly progress.

But in order adequately to account for the fact that writers like Saint-Simon, Comte and Spencer (in the eighteenth and

9

nineteenth centuries) concerned themselves with the nature and development of 'industrial society' as *the* central issue of the modern age, we must set their work in the context of the intellectual and social ferment occurring within seventeenth- and eighteenth-century Europe. In an important sense, Saint-Simon and Comte represent both a continuation of and reaction against the ideals commonly associated with the era of the Enlightenment. In particular, they extended the eighteenth-century concern with reason and progress into a celebration of science and a worship of industry.

Enlightenment and the Unborn Age

Sociology rose to prominence through its concern with the social disruptions surrounding what have come to be known as the French and Industrial Revolutions. This does not mean, as a number of later critics have argued, that sociology is centrally concerned with the general 'problem of order' (Nisbet 1967; O'Neill 1972; Parsons 1968). This ignores sociology's preoccupation with social progress and the use of social theory in guiding society into a new and superior 'unborn age'. Sociology has traditionally been concerned with social transformation, and one transformation in particular — that defined by Saint-Simon and Comte as the transition to 'industrial society'.

There are, however, two important features of this concern that should be understood as distinct from each other. The first is the general preoccupation of social thought with improving the human condition through a general social transformation brought about with the help of informed political action. The second is the definition of this transformation in terms of the establishment of a scientifically regulated and industrially motivated 'industrial society'. What Saint-Simon and Comte inherited from the Enlightenment was a belief in the central importance and possibility, of the first enterprise. They also drew much of their inspiration for their theory of industrial society from the Enlightenment's characterization of reason and progress. It is important to recognize, however, that this radical political optimism did not necessarily culminate in the theory of industrial society. Indeed, as we shall see, this set of beliefs has continued to inspire traditions of thought directly opposed to the political project incorporated within the theory of industrial society.

What deserves initial emphasis, however, is the importance of the eighteenth-century Enlightenment in establishing the belief that social theory could play such an important role. Two main assumptions were established during that period: firstly, that human reason was capable of understanding and guiding social change; and, secondly, that the achievement of social progress was a definite possibility. The success of the Enlightenment, whatever its internal differences, in establishing these two assumptions, had a profound effect on later social thought.

It was during this period that faith in divine revelation, and the authority of the Church as interpreters of God's will, were increasingly undermined by this new confidence in the ability of human reason to provide an understanding of the world and a guide for human conduct. Similarly, the understanding of history as the chronicle of the fall of man from God's grace, with spiritual salvation only attainable in the next world, was largely replaced by a belief in human perfectibility and the increasing faith in man's power and ability to use his new-found knowledge to improve mankind's estate. The importance of these two assumptions should not be underestimated. Without the faith in reason, social theory could not be regarded as playing any important role in society. Without the belief in the possibility of progress, whatever reason's ability to understand the nature of society, social theory would not be able to fulfil any positive role in improving upon man's fate.

In this manner the Enlightenment was responsible for spreading a rational and radical optimism concerning the creation of a new 'unborn age'. However the faith in reason and progress extended even further. The Enlightenment popularized the idea that the development of reason was itself the key to social progress. Reason did not merely help to guide human action; it was, in itself, one of the main *goals* of human striving. It was Saint-Simon and Comte's specific scientistic understanding of reason that directed this belief into a call for the final ascendancy of industrial society.

Reason and the Critique of Authority

Much of the eighteenth-century confidence in the power of reason was derived from the scientific and technological achievements within the seventeenth century. The discoveries made within

Copernican astronomy, da Vinci's mechanics, and Galileo's physics, had been followed by the widely acclaimed successes of Newton. The prestige of the 'ancients' had finally been subordinated to the success of the 'moderns', not because of their innate ability but largely because the accumulation of knowledge ensured their superiority. The empiricist theory of knowledge, as the accumulation of data derived from the senses, strongly supported such a view of the progress of human knowledge. It is difficult to overstate the importance attached to the use of the scientific method and the accumulation of knowledge for the theories of progress from Bacon to Turgot and Condorcet. It was this accumulation — guaranteed by the development of writing, the invention of the printing press, the foundation of a scientific language, and the rise of commerce and industry — that provided the basis for their future optimism. The one element within society that a return to 'barbarism' could no longer remove was the progress and advance of universally advantageous knowledge.

This should not be taken to mean that the thinkers of the Enlightenment saw progress primarily in terms of the development and application of the natural sciences nor that they were all united in the belief that progress was inevitable. They were centrally interested in the development of a *society* organized on the basis of human reason and their dynamism was exemplified by their *quest* for reason, the belief that reason was a goal to be striven for rather than a fact to be accepted. It was the central importance attached to this *active* development of reason in history that transcended the difference between Cartesian rationalism and Baconian empiricism, the deism of Voltaire and the scepticism of Hume, the spiritualism of Herder and Lessing and the materialism of Condillac and Helvetius.

The appeal to reason was employed in a radical critique of existing authority. In opposition to the superstition, prejudice and established hierarchies of the theological-feudal order, the Enlightenment *philosophes* appealed to reason to justify their cause. All inequalities and structures of authority were judged unacceptable unless they were justified before the tribunal of human reason. In the words of one noted historian of the period, the Enlightenment instituted a 'conversion of philosophy into disciplined aggression against concrete problems' (Gay 1964: 183). It is this strand of critical rationalism within Enlightenment thought that has both provided an important stimulus to later thought and created an enormous degree of controversy. For radical thinkers it has provided the basis for a rational critique of existing forms of repression. The assertion that all human activities should be organized in accordance with reason challenges all forms of 'surplus repression' or 'unnecessary systematic cruelty' — which may be justified by tradition or presented as the dictates of 'reality' (Cobban 1960; Marcuse 1962). For the critics of the Enlightenment, however, it has only succeeded in undermining all necessary forms of authority and traditional belief and contributed to chaos, anarchy and the rule of terror. In addition, many commentators have pointed to the ambiguities in the concept of reason, observing that it has been variously used to refer to the use of the analytic method, appeal to the facts, the activity of self-reflection, universal *a priori* rules of human conduct, and so on.

The Enlightenment faith in reason also took the form of an identification of progress with the development of reason. This has led to the establishment of two alternative traditions of thought both of which see themselves as critics of unjustified and irrational forms of authority. Yet both traditions have been condemned by their critic for their ultimate justification of new and more repressive forms of authority, established in the name of reason itself.

Two Concepts of Reason

During the eighteenth century, the optimism of the Enlightenment was largely due to the widely held belief that human nature, embodying both self-love and benevolence, when released from the constraints imposed by ignorance and vested interest, would provide the basis for a natural harmonious organization of society, in which there would be no fundamental conflict between individuals and no inherent tension between the individual and society. The organization of society in accordance with reason therefore involved the discovery and implementation of this harmonious order. However, once this assumption of natural harmony was brought into question, the Enlightenment's optimism appeared to be more a product of its 'religious' belief in a benificent Providence rather than a consequence of its critical rationalism (Becker 1932). Yet, once the appeal to reason is separated from the assumption of natural harmony, it culminates in an unquestioned belief in the absolute value of the development of 'rationalist' or 'empiricist' knowledge. It is *this* faith in reason that a number of critics argue underlies the implicit or explicit authoritarianism of both the theory of industrial society and some of its opponents.

One strand of Enlightenment thought identified reason in terms of the experimental and deductive method of Bacon, the empirical psychology of Locke and the scepticism of Hume. The human mind was perceived as an 'empty cabinet' or a sheet of 'white paper'; knowledge was perceived to be of instrumental value in the control of nature; and reason was defined as a technical capacity which 'is and ought only to be the slave of the passions and can never pretend to any other office than to serve and obey them' (Hume, 1888: 415). This 'empiricist' conception of reason, founded on a belief in the power of the analytical method and the authority of evidence derived from the senses, supported the '*esprit systematique*' rather than the '*esprit de système*' of the seventeenth-century rationalists (Gay 1964, 1969, 1976; Horkheimer 1974).

The second strand within Enlightenment thought based its conception of reason on the rationalism of Descartes, Leibniz and Spinoza. Reason was seen as embodying a form of self-reflection or self-analysis capable of providing a rationally grounded intuitive insight into the universal and self-evident principles of human conduct. In the eighteenth century this primarily took the form of an appeal to natural law, natural religion and natural rights as a basis for challenging the existing social order. As Ernst Cassirer puts it, such a conception 'is not founded in the sphere of power and will but in the sphere of pure reason. In that which this reason conceives as "being", in that which is given in the pure nature of reason, nothing can be attained or curtailed by decree' (Cassirer 1951: 141).

This conflict, which was not resolved in the eighteenth century, has more recently been endowed with central significance. The faith in a rationalist conception of reason, it has been argued, can be used as a justification for authoritarian regimes or re-volutionary élites who claim to be acting in the interests of the people. By denegating the actual needs and wants of the population, in comparison with their true needs as revealed by reason, rationalism is defined as an inherently anti-democratic philosophy. By contrast, the adherence to an empiricist view of reason has also been condemned for its authoritarian implications.

By defining reason as a technical capacity employed by man to manipulate natural laws, empiricism celebrates a form of reason that will merely become a tool to be used by the powerful in society to manipulate the mass of the population. In addition, it encourages the subordination of society to the requirements of a purely technical good, which will, ultimately, only serve the interests of a technocratic élite or act as a legitimating cover for minority privilege.

In the work of Saint-Simon and Comte, industrial society theory was clearly grounded in the empiricist conception of reason. Like many of the Enlightenment theorists, Turgot and Condorcet in particular, Saint-Simon and Comte based their view of progress on the development of scientific and technological reason. It was science and its application that stood at the foundations of modern industrial society, not only as a result of its success in dominating and controlling nature but also through its ability to control a complex industrial society and provide a new basis for social authority and political decision.

Industrial society theory emerged, therefore, as the continuation of one strand of Enlightenment thought on reason. It was in clear opposition to the rationalist critique of theological-feudal authority embodied in appeals to such 'natural rights' as liberty, equality and freedom of conscience. Yet for some later critics it was this rationalist conception of reason that was the foundation of the Enlightenment's radicalism (Marcuse 1974, 1977). The value of the eighteenth century was attributed to its refusal to subordinate its democratic ideals to the observation of 'reality' and its courageous justification of these ideals as reason and rationality.

Like Bonald and de Maistre, Saint-Simon and Comte rejected such ideals as pure 'metaphysics', without any grounding in social reality. Unlike the French conservative theorists, however, Saint-Simon and Comte were not reacting against any attempt further to apply reason to human affairs. Their opposition to 'metaphysical' reason was its conflict with a superior type of reason — that provided by science and its industrial application. They retained the optimistic faith in the ability of human reason to ensure social progress and guide political reform, but it was scientific reason that was to provide the foundation of the new social order. They argued for the establishment of a new form of inequality, a scientific-industrial hierarchy, to replace the arbitrary and outdated authorities of the theological-military period. Their faith in scientific reason was inherently anti-democratic. From the outset, industrial society theory was opposed to the ideal of democracy and any attempts to justify the democratic system on the grounds of reason and rationality.

Two Images of Progress

Although the idea of progress has diverse origins in classical Greek thought and Christian thought as well as the Enlightenment, the eighteenth century was remarkable for its widespread belief in the possibility of progress and concern with the attainment of a superior social order. Industrial society theory was greatly influenced by the Enlightenment theories of progress. However, the eighteenth century contained two contrasting, and equally influential, models of progress: a 'dichotomous' and an 'evolutionary process' model (Gellner 1972).

Within the dichotomous model, progress is identified with the one great transition from societies based upon prejudice and vested interest to societies organized with the use of human reason and in accordance with the true nature of man and society. Influenced by Newton's view of nature as a mechanical system, the *philosophes* believed that this new natural form of organization would automatically become a balanced and stable mechanism. Whether this society took the shape of Hobbes's *Leviathan*, Rousseau's social contract, Montesquieu's system of laws and separation of powers, Adam Smith's natural economy or Helvetius's balanced set of rational laws created by a wise legislator, the underlying principle was the same: reason could establish a fixed, universal, self-equilibrating social system operating in conformity with natural laws of human conduct.

By contrast, Enlightenment theorists also put forward an evolutionary process model of history in which societies were regarded as passing through a number of stages, and progress is identified with this gradual evolutionary process rather than with one great transformation from an unnatural to a natural system. The natural state of mankind is therefore regarded as one of change and development from infancy to maturity rather than as the achievement of a self-equilibrating system of natural laws. The image of society is organic rather than mechanistic. In his *Tableau philosophique des progres succesifs de l'esprit humain*,

Turgot expresses this view when he claims that the history of mankind

> affords from age to age an ever changing spectacle. Reason, the passions and liberty ceaselessly give rise to new events: all the ages are bound up with one another by a succession of causes and effects which link the present state of the world with all those that have preceded it . . . one generation transmits to another an inheritance which is always being enlarged by the discoveries of each age. Thus the human race, considered over the period since its origin, appears to the eye of a philosopher as one vast whole, which itself, like each individual, has its infancy and its advancement (Meek 1976: 41).

The nature of this process was presented in two different ways during the eighteenth century: as stages in the development of human knowledge (Baker 1975; Manuel 1962) and stages of human subsistence — hunting, pasturage, agriculture and commerce (Meek 1973, 1976).

Industrial society theory, as developed by Saint-Simon, Comte and Spencer, continued a number of the themes of both the dichotomous and evolutionary process models of progress. In accordance with the latter model, Saint-Simon and Comte viewed the history of mankind as a process of evolution from infancy to maturity; believed that social development was a continuous and unitary process proceeding through a fixed set of stages; claimed that political regimes could only be examined in this context and that political action was forced to take into account the underlying process of social evolution and development; and held that social theory could play an important social function by using its knowledge of this evolutionary process to speed up its development and overcome the forces of ignorance and vested interest that threatened to disrupt its advance.

More specifically, however, Saint-Simon, Comte and Spencer were all influenced by the idea that progress was due to the development of scientific knowledge and the passage of mankind through different modes of subsistence culminating in the commercial or industrial stage. Yet the dichotomous image of progress was still influential in the central importance attached to the transition from the military-theological to the scientific-industrial type of society. Like the French *philosophes*, Saint-Simon and Comte regarded the new age as the final triumph of human reason and — like the Scottish classical political economists — along with Spencer they all believed that the new order would finally liberate industry from its fetters. They all agreed that they were witnessing the most fundamental transformation in history, although this was seen as the transition from one type of society to another rather than as the emergence of a 'natural' order. Not only did the course of social evolution appear as an organic process but the emerging industrial society was understood as an organic system with its own 'industrial' purposes and goals.

The reason for the convergence of the dichotomous and the evolutionary process models of progress within the work of Saint-Simon, Comte and Spencer is related to the idea of progress itself. Carl Becker has made the point that

> [r]ationally considered the idea of progress is always at war with its premises. It rests upon the notion of a universe in perpetual motion; yet the idea of progress has always carried the implication of finality, for it seems to be meaningless unless there is movement towards some fundamental objective. The formal theories of progress are vitiated by this radical inconsistency (Becker 1974: 66).

The progress *of* society is progress *towards* an ideal. In order for stages *of progress* to exist, these stages must involve the partial development of one ideal form of social organization, otherwise the stages that society passes through cannot be described as overall progress. In this sense all theories of progress ultimately imply a simple two-stage model despite any assumption of gradual accumulation or the presence of a multiplicity of stages of development.

This convergence between the two models of progress is not merely due to assumptions about the moral and social *effects* of quantitative development. The models also converge because of the necessity for examining the *preconditions* of progress. All forms of social organization will either facilitate or hinder the achievement of progress and in this sense may be examined in terms of their approximation towards two, and only two, social types. This aspect of the theory of progress has had important implications for later theories of industrial society. Although in the latter half of the twentieth century a more critical conception of industrial society has been developed, in which it is not assumed that 'industry' is the sole determinant of social change, the image of 'industrial society' retains its importance both because of the implicit value attributed to 'industry' and the focus upon the extent to which modern societies facilitate or hinder its development.

For our present purposes, the major division between the different theories of progress inherited from the Enlightenment is not therefore due to an absolute distinction between the 'dichotomous' model of eighteenth century 'rationalism' and the 'evolutionary' model associated with the Enlightenment's 'empiricism'. The most important split, as Saint-Simon and Comte frequently commented, was between, on the one hand, the Enlightenment's association of progress with autonomous and critical self-reflection within a society based upon the principles of equality, liberty and the participation of independent and rational individuals and, on the other, the identification of progress with the development of scientific technical reason and the subordination of society to the requirements of this process.

The work of the Marquis de Condorcet, through its combination of both theories of progress, provides an important illustration of this division. Condorcet's work on social mathematics, his interest in the development of scientific academies and his general theory of human perfectibility and progress through the accumulation of scientific knowledge, have frequently led critics to the assumption that his writings provide a clear bridge between the eighteenth-century *philosophes* and the scientific positivism of Saint-Simon and Comte (Manuel 1962: 95–6). Such an interpretation of Condorcet's work does not, however, accord with his persistent concern with individual liberty and equality. Despite his belief in natural inequalities and the importance of scientific organization and authority, Condorcet appeals for *universal* education and regards the inegalitarian scientific organization as a means for the furtherance of equality rather than the achievement of a rigid hierarchic system (Nisbet 1980: Chapter 6). The uneasy combination of these two themes within Condorcet's work continued the ambiguity which was present within many eighteenth-century philosophies. As Keith Baker remarked of Condorcet's work: 'The tension between scientific élitism and democratic liberalism — between rational choice and popular will — lay at the heart of the *philosophes*' theories' (Baker 1975: 94). It was the acceptance of this conflict, or at least the failure to resolve it, that distinguished the work of Condorcet and the Enlightenment *philosophes* from the later theory of industrial society developed by Saint-Simon and Comte.

It is important to stress that, as a result, there remained sharp disparities between the writings of the Enlightenment *philosophes* and the work of the early proponents of industrial society theory. Despite the important continuities outlined above, Saint-Simon and Comte were explicitly opposed to the libertarian, egalitarian and democratic strand within eighteenth-century thought. Both Saint-Simon and Comte regarded their era as a time of chaos and disorder that could only be resolved through the establishment of a new form of inequality, morality and authority. The violent disruption of society created by the French Revolution was seen as the direct consequence of Enlightenment appeals to individual reason and quest for the democratic organization of society. The establishment of industrial society was seen as the solution to the resulting chaos, in direct opposition to Enlightenment metaphysics and egalitarianism.

Industrial Society: The Solution

For Saint-Simon, Comte and Spencer, modern societies were witnessing the most fundamental transformation in human history — from a military-theological past to a scientific-industrial future. The present was represented by Saint-Simon and Comte as a 'transitional state of anarchy' (Comte 1974: 406). In the words of the Saint-Simonians, it was a 'critical' epoch lying between two major 'organic' epochs (Iggers 1972). In this context past theories of society were of little help, perhaps even detrimental, to the establishment of the new industrial order. For Saint-Simon and Comte, the metaphysics of the Enlightenment philosophers was largely responsible for the continued chaos and disruption. These 'metaphysicians', they argued, desired 'progress' without a simultaneous recognition of the requirements of 'order' (Comte 1974; Ionescu 1976; Markham 1964; Taylor 1978b). The pursuit of such ideals, Saint-Simon and Comte argued, undermined all forms of authority and, most importantly, failed to adapt its recommendations to the stage of development reached by modern civilization.

Although in many ways different to Saint-Simon and Comte,

Herbert Spencer (1896) similarly condemned all those theorists who failed to recognize the necessary course of social evolution and the requirements of industrial society. 'A fly seated on the surface of the body has about as good a conception of its internal structure as one of these schemers has of the social organization in which he is embedded' (Spencer 1896: 34). Spencer was, however, more concerned with the failure to establish an *efficient* industrial society than the inability of previous theorists to provide the intellectual foundations for an end to social anarchy. From the relative security of England,the violence of the French Revolution had less impact upon social thought.

Like Saint-Simon and Comte, Spencer believed that he had grasped the *one* necessary course of social evolution which could only be temporarily impeded by those ignorant of its laws (Rumney 1934; Spencer 1896, 1969). All three theorists adopted a form of evolutionary historicism to explain the direction of modern societies. The scientific discovery of the necessary laws of evolution was taken as the sole basis for guiding social and political action. The aim was, in Saint-Simon's words, 'simply to promote and explain a development which is inevitable' (Markham 1964: 70). The process of evolution was seen as occurring through a series of stages as the evolutionary dynamic created and then undermined successive forms of social and political organization. The modern epoch was, however, always represented as *the* great transition within history. Alternative forms of thought were condemned for either (i) failing to recognize the necessity of the process of evolution and attempting to restore a historically redundant, and now impractical, social order, or (ii) attempting to bring about a radical social change in ignorance of the laws of social development and their requirements.

A specific kind of anti-politics emerged from this approach. In contrast to comments made by many modern critics, politics *was* of central importance for Saint-Simon and Comte. But it was a specific brand of politics to do with speeding up the process of evolution, meeting its future requirements and minimizing its disruptive impact upon society. It undertook the continuous theoretical refutation of all those 'ideological' or 'utopian' theories whose lack of 'realism' threatened the stability of the new order. What they condemned was a view of politics that (i) regarded political problems as absolute rather than relative to the stage of civilization; (ii) identified politics as a universal activity of re-

flection or conflict over the human ends of society; and (iii) be-
lieved that the final source and resolution of social problems lay in
the realm of politics (Comte 1974: 414; Iggers 1972: 115).

Like nearly all philosophers of history, Saint-Simon and Comte
postulate a 'hierarchy of inevitabilities', not a total determinism,
and support particular forms of political activity which take the
overall development of society for their object, in the general
interests of society or mankind (Fletcher 1974a; Manuel 1971: 55).
This point is an important one, for most critics have condemned
this form of theory for its evolutionary determinism, its mistaken
'historicist' conception of the laws of society, and its neglect of the
role of politics (Strasser and Randal 1981; Nisbet 1969; Popper
1974). Its general influence has, however, been more subtle. It is
not so much the neglect of politics and the role of human action
that has had an enduring effect but, rather, the imposition of a
particular and definite focus for 'realistic', 'scientific' or 'non-
ideological' speculation and action. Attention is concentrated on
the *one* major issue of the age — that of ensuring the estab-
lishment and development of industrial society. All thought and
action is then directed towards, firstly, challenging those
alternative forms of thought that fail to recognize this as the
central question of the modern age and, secondly, employing the
social sciences to discover and adapt to the requirements of indus-
trial evolution.

For Saint-Simon and Comte, the Enlightenment had proved
incapable of grasping the fundamental realities of the new indus-
trial civilization. In order finally to establish an orderly and pro-
gressive industrial society, it was necessary to implement a new
scientific-industrial form of inequality, religion and social purpose.
As Saint-Simon stated bluntly in *L'Industrie*, 'a nation must of
necessity be organized with one of two ends, either to *steal* or to
produce, that is that it must be either military or industrial;
otherwise it will be nothing but a bastard association' (Ionescu
1976: 123). The evolutionary developments in science and industry
were closely intertwined. Industry, as the application of science
and the positive spirit, was to act as the source of social purpose.
Science both inspired and organized industrial activity. The de-
velopment of politics as a purely scientific 'art' was, they argued,
made both necessary and possible by scientific and industrial pro-
gress. Within a complex 'scientific-industrial' society, freed from
theological and metaphysical illusions, a science of politics was

needed to organize society, establish a new form of authority and provide the basis for a new social consensus. With the advance of science and industry, this new 'scientific politics' was provided with both the *means* and the *goal* necessary to restore society to a state of orderly progress and ensure the transition 'from the government of men to the administration of things'.

In this general form Saint-Simon and Comte established the main outlines of industrial society theory. That theory, however, is not as coherent as might appear. A number of important disparities and ambiguities exist within the work of both Saint-Simon and Comte as well as between these two theorists. In particular, there are disagreements over the nature of the central scientific- industrial dynamic and the basis for the orderly regulation of industrial society.

Both Saint-Simon and Comte, at different times, emphasize the central role of *ideas* and of *classes* (Fletcher 1974a: 80; Ionescu 1976: 98; Manuel 1956: 244; Manuel 1965: 8; Raison 1969: 31; Taylor 1978b: 30). Saint-Simon and Comte are also unclear regarding the *nature* of the ideas and classes that are allotted the central role. The authority of science refers variously to scientific methods, different scientific conclusions and a new 'terrestrial morality'. The industrial goal is ambiguously identified as both maximum production and the present material welfare of the population, hence ignoring the potential conflict between consumption and reinvestment or maximum production and humane working conditions (Comte 1974: 38, 409; Ionescu 1976; Manuel 1956: 378–9; Taylor 1978b: 41). In allocating a central role to the dynamics of class conflict, Saint-Simon and Comte are unclear whether the scientific or the industrial classes are of central significance and whether the vague term 'industrialists' refers to all those employed in production, a managerial élite, those citizens who accept industrial ideals, non- scientific leaders or non-governmental workers (Ionescu 1976: 100, 102, 107). This degree of ambiguity has had an important effect on later theories of industrial society. There remains a similar lack of consistency over the nature of the industrial dynamic, the exact nature of the goals of industry and the character of the industrial or 'technocratic' classes at the forefront of industrial organization and development.

There is a similar degree of uncertainty over the nature of politics within industrial society. Saint-Simon appears to vacillate between advocating a centralized economy run by a scientific-industrial élite and an economy in which the state is relegated to a subsidiary role as a result of its inability to understand or control a complex industrial economy (Ionescu 1976: 104; Markham 1964: 78; Taylor 1978b: 210). At times he appears to favour the establishment of a form of authoritarian technocratic state more clearly associated with August Comte while, at other times, his ideal appears closer to the non-interventionist *laissez-faire* model advocated by Herbert Spencer. This ambiguity has been retained, or at least left unresolved, in the post-war theories of the convergence of 'advanced industrial' societies towards a 'mixed economy' or a 'post-industrial' state.

Another source of continuing ambiguity and debate derives from the different emphases of Saint-Simon and Comte, on the one hand, and Herbert Spencer on the other. Saint-Simon and Comte stress the need for scientifically informed and industrially inspired *public* order to resolve social *chaos* and allocate individuals to their places within the productive system. Spencer, however, emphasizes the importance of an unregulated and *privately* motivated economic system as a basis for ensuring economic *efficiency*. Such disputes are continued in more recent discussions of the extent to which the modern 'industrial' order is capable of providing the basis of a stable meritocratic class structure and the extent to which an 'achievement-oriented' selection system provides an adequate form of industrial motivation.

Industrial society theory, in the work of these theorists, is not a complete theoretical schema. It possesses a number of internal ambiguities and allows a significant degree of conflict and dispute. This degree of variation is extended when the work of Durkheim and Weber is taken into consideration. Saint-Simon and Comte saw the development of science and industry as both the underlying cause and final solution for the chaos and disorder in eighteenth- and nineteenth-century Europe. Durkheim and Weber, however, regarded the development of a scientific and industrial ethos as part of the problem facing modern societies rather than the solution.

Industrial Society: The Problem

While both Emile Durkheim (1858–1917) and Max Weber (1846–1920) recognized that modern societies were in some sense 'industrialized', they neither concluded that 'industry' was the prime determinant of their character not that it could become a social goal capable of integrating the new social structure. For Durkheim, any discussion of the origins of modern society, its course of social development and its moral codes, had to begin with the *division of labour*, not 'industry'. Durkheim states that

> the division of labour appears to us otherwise than it does to the economists. For them, it essentially consists in greater production. For us, this greater productivity is only a necessary consequence, a repercussion of the phenomenon. If we specialize, it is not to produce more, but it is to enable us to live in new conditions of existence that have been made for us (Durkheim 1964b: 275).

The development of industry was not the 'end' of social advance but the 'effect of a cause'. If industry provides any benefits it 'only repairs the losses that it has itself caused' (Durkheim 1964b: 337). For Durkheim, it was the development of the *division of labour*, propelled by the pressures of population growth, that was 'the law of gravity of the social world' (Durkheim 1964b: 339n).

In a similar fashion, Weber regarded the development of industry as part of a more general process. But whereas Durkheim saw this process in terms of the spread of the division of labour throughout all spheres of society (not just the economic), Weber emphasized the central importance of *rationalization* as the central development within history. However, Weber does not regard the rationalization of social life as an immanent evolutionary process causing all societies to evolve according to one pre-established plan. Such an idea, he argues, 'will not work, simply because of the fact that the history of rationalism shows a development which by no means follows parallel lines in the various departments of life' (Weber 1974: 77). At different periods in history, 'rationalizations of the most varied character have existed in various departments of life and in all areas of culture'. It is thus 'necessary to know what departments are rationalized and in what direction'. For it is possible to 'rationalize life from fundamentally different basic points of view and in very different directions' (Weber 1974: 26).

In his study of modern societies, however, Weber showed the ways in which the rationalization of social life now encompassed the realms of economics, politics, public administration, law and culture. In particular, Weber focuses his attention on the rise of science and the intellectualization of life; the use of machine technology; the character of modern rational capitalism; and the development of rational law, legal-national authority and bureaucratic administration (Gerth and Mills 1948: 538–9; Weber 1961: 133,227; Weber 1974: 17,76). All these developments are represented as different and relatively autonomous forms of the general phenomenon of rationalization understood as the extension of systematic logical thought and calculation in the pursuit of conscious ends or purposes.

For Durkheim and Weber, the progress of the division of labour and the rationalization of social life created a number of social problems that could not be resolved by establishing industry as a new social purpose. The representation of industry as an answer to the anomie and alienation characteristic of modern societies was itself part of the problem. In discussing the spread of social anarchy, Durkheim argues that

> what brings about the exceptional gravity of this state, nowadays particularly, is the heretofore unknown development that economic functions have experienced for about two centuries. Whereas formerly they played only a secondary role, they are now of the first importance . . . Only the scientific functions seem to dispute their place, and even science has scarcely any prestige save to the extent that it can serve practical occupations, which are largely economic. That is why it can be said, with some justice, that society is, or tends to be, essentially industrial (Durkheim 1964b: 3).

For Durkheim, the only solution to the anomic character of modern societies lay in the establishment of a system of morality and a set of regulations that transcended industry itself. He thus explicitly condemned what he called the 'industrialist solution' to the problems besetting modern society. Both Saint-Simon and Comte, on the one hand, and Spencer and the classical economists on the other, had adopted a faulty 'principle of industrialism' as a basis for social integration. Both sets of theorists identified economic interests with social interests while failing to recognize that these interests are inherently incapable of performing such a role. This applied whether this industrialist solution was seen in terms of freeing economic interests from social control (Spencer) or providing central regulation of the economy for the pursuit of industry (Saint-Simon, Comte). In contrast, Durkheim argued, modern 'co-operative' or 'organized' societies required a new 'organic' form of solidarity based on a recognition of the need for (i) the moral regulation of all forms of co-operation, and (ii) the establishment of a system of moral authority capable of limiting and controlling the 'endless restlessness' and 'envy' resulting from the unregulated pursuit of industrial growth (Giddens 1971, 1978; Durkheim 1962). This was not, however, intended as an appeal for the resurrection of a detailed authoritarian moral code. It involved, primarily, the establishment of an extremely general system based on the 'cult of the individual' which 'only asks that we be thoughtful of our fellows and that we be just, that we fulfil our duty, that we work at the function we can best execute, and receive the just reward for our services' (Durkheim 1964b: 407). This new form of social solidarity, Durkheim believed, would emerge spontaneously from the division of labour as new rules, regulations and customs grew up with the new forms of interaction and interdependance. Durkheim's emphasis on the importance of 'equality of opportunity' and the 'corporations' was due to their role in facilitating the unproblematic development of this new system.

For Weber, the central issue was the advance of rationalization and its effect in undermining all 'substantive' rationalities and encouraging the adoption of a purely technical rationality as a final good.

> Together with the machine the bureaucratic organization is employed in building the houses of bondage of the future, in which perhaps men will one day be like peasants in the ancient Egyptian State, acquiescent and powerless, while a purely technical good, that is rational, official administration and provision becomes the sole, final value, which sovereignly decides the direction of their affairs (Weber 1974:181).

Industry was unable to provide a meaningful sense of individual and social purpose. Weber poses the central question: 'Has "progress" as such a recognizable meaning that goes beyond the technical, so that to serve it is a meaningful occupation?' (Gerth and Mills 1948: 140). Weber's pessimistic response to this question was based on his belief that the process of rationalization had undermined all other substantive goals that could give it a meaning. Scientific thought and intellectualization had extended the sphere of calculation to the critical assessment of all values. Rational capitalism had subordinated all economic ideals — whether ends of production ('useful' goods) or the means of carrying out production (the 'calling') — to the rational control of labour in the pursuit of profit. And the institution of bureaucracy involved the rejection of the Western humanist ideal of the 'cultivated' man and its replacement by an 'iron cage' of impersonal officialdom.

With the destruction of all socially effective 'substantive' rationalities,

> [t]he fate of our times is characterized by rationalization and intellectualization and, above all, by the 'disenchantment of the world'. Precisely the ultimate and most sublime values have retreated from public life either into the transcendental realm of mystic life or into the brotherliness of direct and personal human relations (Gerth and Mills 1948: 155).

Despite these reservations, Weber believed that the processes of rationalization could not be reversed and that there was no simple solution to the alienation facing modern rational societies. He predicted, and feared, that with the undermining of 'substantive' rationalities, there was emerging a public sphere characterized by a formally rational social structure shorn of its substantive rationale and subject to influence by the practical rationalist strivings of self-interested groups and individuals. It was this 'polar night of icy darkness and hardness' (Gerth and Mills 1948: 128) that any citizen had to accept if he was to act responsibly. No one could oppose the bureaucratization and intellectualization of life. Yet men could still see what they could 'oppose to this machinery in order to keep a portion of mankind free from this parcelling out of the soul' (cited in Kumar 1978: 107). Modern man could still combine 'passion and perspective' and unite an 'ethic of ultimate ends' with an 'ethic of responsibility' based on a recognition of the harsh realities of the age. (Coppens 1976; Gerth and Mills 1948: 127).

Science, Industry and Society

All of these theorists of industrial society recognized the importance of scientific reason and industrial progress as a major component of the radically new social order emerging in nineteenth-century Europe and America. Yet it is clearly not possible to see in their work the establishment of a crude form of economic determinism and technocratic optimism. In what way, then, is it valid to classify their writings as variants of a general industrial society theory?

On the one hand, as Anthony Giddens points out, Durkheim and Weber share with Saint-Simon, Comte and Spencer a number of similarities in their approach to historical development. While most of these theorists allowed for the possibility of substantial change and diversity within previous societies, this was always combined with a dichotomous image of social development. This did not mean that they discounted the significance of earlier changes. For Saint-Simon, Comte, Spencer and Durkheim, previous societies were variously classified according to the evolutionary stage they had reached. Yet their work merely hinted at, if it allowed at all, the possibility of historical jumps, reversals, stagnation or diverse paths of development. In contrast, Weber, while adopting rationalization as the focus of his studies, none the less recognized the diversity of forms in which rationalization could occur and saw that rationalization was neither inevitable nor had to continue along one fixed path. Despite such qualifications, however, all these theorists emphasized the importance of the one great transformation in history, so much so that in comparison with the crossing of this great divide all other changes appeared relatively insignificant.

It was also of crucial significance for these theories that the great transformation had begun and was in the process of completion. The future, on the other side of this great divide, was predominently seen as a period of gradual evolution in the manner of the evolutionary process model of the eighteenth century. Yet within this general view there was still room for substantial disagreement. According to the cultural lag theories produced by Saint-Simon, Comte and Durkheim, the course of social evolution had undermined the old social order and their major concern was the active creation of a new type of social and political order adapted to its requirements. For Spencer and Weber, however, it was not the previous course of social evolution or spread of rationalization that necessitated the development of industry, and neither emphasized the need for conscious political and social intervention in order to adapt society to the requirements of industrial development. Yet all of these theorists were united in their denial of any great significance to future radical political changes as a means of social reconstruction or as the foundation for a qualitatively different social organization.

It was this general view of social development that informed the unanimous rejection by these theorists of alternative conservative or utopian theories of modern society (Giddens 1972: 48; Lukes 1973: 199). The great transformation had occurred and, while there could be no turning back, it was also impossible to bring about a radical social reconstruction within or beyond the new social order. The development of science, frequently associated with this transformation, if not regarded as its fundamental component, revealed the inevitability of this transition and the necessary constraints that it imposed on human action. This shared perspective even led to mutual recrimination. Comte condemned the *laissez-faire* philosophy, such as proved central to Spencer's work, as a return to a theologically inspired optimism. In contrast, Spencer rejected Comte's work for its advocacy of a return to an outdated centralized and hierarchical militaristic form of social regulation (Spencer 1968).

Durkheim similarly condemned Comte for his advocacy of a return to a detailed authoritarian solidarity incompatible with the requirements of the new complex division of labour (Durkheim 1964b: 361). He criticized the socialists for trying to transform modern society in ignorance of its fundamental nature (Durkheim 1962: 41). In reaction to all these theorists, Weber asserted that the development of rationality, in the form of science, revealed the inability of science itself to dictate how society should develop. The attempt to use science for such a purpose was thus a regression to pre-rational forms of thought. There could be no return to the enchanted garden of earlier societies and no formally rational justification for socialist radicalism (Weber 1969: 211–18, 319–20, 337–8; Wrong 1970: 5–8, 111–12).

This theory of historical development was combined with a specific view of the structure and dynamics of the new social order. Industry had developed and become a necessary and prominent feature of modern society. Even Durkheim and Weber, who emphasized the centrality of the division of labour and rationalization rather than industry, agreed on this point (Durkheim 1964b: 272; Weber 1969: 337). Industry embodied — to an extent it ensured — the progress of one dominant principle of social organization in comparison with which all other forms of organization were either insignificant or certain to become so. The quantitative development of industry, as the expression of this one specific type of organization, was therefore of far greater significance than any stage or type of industry. As we have seen, however, for Saint-Simon, Comte and Spencer, the importance attached to industry was due to their belief that industry was the primary determinant and social goal of modern industrial societies. For Durkheim and Weber, industry was still accorded central significance, in comparison with various stages or types of industry, but this was due to its expression of the division of labour or process of rationalization rather than its autonomous impact on society. Yet all these theorists, by attributing central significance to industry or the principles of social organization that industry embodies, focus the study of industrial societies on the *structural requirements* and *dynamics* of industry rather than the impact of the various *components* of industry, *stages* of industry or *direction* of industry, or the *type of social organization* that determines the way in which industry will be developed and used. It was not the direction of science, industry, rationalization or the division of labour that was of central interest but their general development and social requirements. It is in *this* form that industrial society theory has continued to structure the 'sociological imagination'.

Discussions of social progress were, therefore, given a specific bias. Within one strand of Enlightenment thought, the advance of science and industry was directly identified with the development of reason and the achievement of moral progress. In the work of Saint-Simon, Comte and Spencer, the identification of science with reason and industry with progress was combined with the recognition that they imposed certain constraints on society. Specialization, inequality, hierarchy, secularization, and the authority of science or the constraints of industrial competition were all seen as the necessary realities of the age. Durkheim and Weber, however, not only emphasized the constraints imposed by industrial principles of organization (specialization, hierarchy and secularization in particular), but also rejected the idea that the development of science and industry was, in itself, progressive. In the discussion of the central issues facing modern society, it was the general need for a new organic solidarity or the individual's necessary acceptance of the iron cage of bureaucracy and the disenchantment of the world that preoccupied Durkheim and Weber. In comparison with these central issues, however, other changes within modern societies were given little attention or importance. Moreover, the attempt by socialist theorists to direct to a future social transformation as the central question of the age was interpreted as a reflection of their failure to come to terms with the realities of the great transition. Both theorists continued to relate the central moral questions facing all modern societies to the general development of industry and the social principles of organization that it embodies. They accepted (i) the central importance of the principles of organization expressed in industry; (ii) the inevitable development of industry within modern societies; and (iii) the lack of any fundamental conflict between industry and the organizational principles to which they attributed central significance.

Unlike the earlier Enlightenment theorists and theories of industrial society, Durkheim and Weber raised the important problems created by the continuation of anomie and alienation within modern societies. In addition, Weber, in particular, provides a social-scientific methodology and approach to comparative sociology that can encourage alternative forms of investigation and inquiry. Yet many of the general themes of their work have encouraged the continuation rather than the transcendence of industrial society theory. It is not merely, as Giddens (1975–6) suggests, that they adopt a generally similar historical model or approach to social change. Nor is it, as Kumar (1978) argues, that they finally place the economic or technical components of industry at the 'heart of their analysis' as 'carriers' of the developments they discuss. Rather it is because they continue to perceive the central issue facing modern societies as the general development, organization and social impact of science and industry. This industrial focus has directed and limited social speculation and inquiry within industrial, advanced industrial and post-industrial societies.

In the work of these authors, therefore, the theory of industrial society was established as an interpretation of modern civilization that incorporated prescriptions for political action, an interpretation of the role of social theory, and a specific understanding of the nature and problems of social progress. It is this all-embracing nature of the theory that has ensured its continuing influence. The form in which this has occurred has, in summary, five main themes: an image of industry as effecting the Great Transformation; an evolutionary view of social development after the transition; a rejection of alternative theories for their ideological or utopian failure to come to terms with the realities of industrial civilization; the centrality of 'industrial' principles of organization in structuring and transforming contemporary societies; and a view of progress that emphasizes the need to adapt society and social action to industrial development and the principles of organization embodied within industry.

2 INDUSTRIAL SOCIETY: HISTORY II

Like the social theorists of the nineteenth century, sociologists of the period after World War II were preoccupied with the fundamental social transformations affecting modern European and American societies. There was a similar concern with the course of social evolution and the reconciliation of order and progress (Aron 1967a: 19–30; Mills 1975: 11–12; Remmling 1975: 4). The scientific and comparative study of modern societies was still encouraged for both its importance in revealing the structure and dynamics of modern societies and its usefulness in challenging those ideological or utopian theories of modern society that misrepresented its character and threatened to disrupt its progress (Aron 1967a; Bell 1962). In addition, industrial development was still regarded by many as the central feature of modern advanced industrial societies and the proper object of sociological speculation. As Clark Kerr *et al.* proclaimed in a celebratory tone:

> The world is entering a new age — the age of total industrialization. Some countries are far along the road; many are just beginning the journey. But everywhere, at a faster or slower pace, the peoples of the world are on the march towards industrialism (Kerr *et al.* 1973: 29).

Sociology was accorded a prominent role in this process as a subject centrally concerned with the nature of industrial society. Consequently, it was regarded as the only discipline fully capable of informing both developed and undeveloped countries of the 'requirements of the age' (Gellner 1972).

The use of the concept of industrial society was explicitly supported by writers such as Raymond Aron and Ralf Dahrendorf as *the* main basis for an improved understanding of modern societies (Aron 1967a; Dahrendorf 1967). Although inspired by nineteenth-century theories of industrial society, an attempt was made by many of these theorists to employ the concept without reproducing the evolutionary, functionalist and positivist excesses of many of the nineteenth-century theorists. As Raymond Aron

34

put it, the concept was intended to possess a 'heuristic or critical function, not a dogmatic significance. It encourages comparative analysis and ideological debate; it does not culminate in prophecy' (Aron 1967a: 14–15). In particular, by defining industrial society in terms of the presence of industrial *technology* rather than the organization of society for the one industrial *purpose*, it was intended that more sophisticated theories of industrial society would emerge. Despite this intention, the concept *was* frequently employed in the classical manner. Our intention in this section is, therefore, not only to outline how the more extreme theories ('end of ideology', 'convergence' of industrial societies, and so on) reproduced the evolutionary and functionalist assumptions of the nineteenth-century theories of industrial society. Our aim is also to reveal how even the more critical uses of the concept of industrial society continued to adopt a similar focus of investigation and understanding of the major issues of the age. Despite their differences both the more extreme and the more critical theories of industrial society take as their central concern the realities of industrial society, stages of industrial society and types of industrial society.

Realities of Industrial Society

In its examination of the past, present and future of 'advanced industrial' societies, sociological inquiry necessarily begins by investigating the importance of industry in creating a distinctive type of society. Thus, in his work *Class and Class Conflict in Industrial Society*, Dahrendorf explicitly directs his attention to '[T]hose factors which can be shown to be generated by the structure of industrial production, and which cannot disappear, therefore, unless industry itself disappears . . .' (Dahrendorf 1967: 40). Theories of industrial society attach central importance to the very presence of industry — on the necessary assumption that the possession of industry is the major social fact limiting the options, or creating the possibilities, open to modern states.

In the ensuing discussions of the origins and requirements of 'industrial society', the post-war theories of modernization and industrialization were heavily indebted to the nineteenth century and to its evolutionary perspective. Post-War descriptions of industrial society were largely an amalgamation of concepts taken from Comte, Spencer, Tönnies, Tocqueville, Durkheim and Weber (Faunce and Form 1969; Parsons 1966). The 'image of industrialism' that they produced emphasized the decline of community; the rise of urbanism; the process of centralization, equalization and democratization; the spread of secularism, rationalism and bureaucracy; and the increase in the specialization of labour. The widespread practice was, as Kumar (1978: 53) aptly points out, one of 'bundling together all these particular versions of the industrial society into a composite stereotype of modern society: as if a good painting could be produced by pasting on to one canvas a Braque, a Matisse, and a Picasso'. In this form the transition to industrial society was represented as a total, systemic, all-inclusive transformation.

During the later 1960s and 1970s, this reinstatement of the classical model of industrialism was challenged from many quarters: by 'modernization revisionists', by Marxist theories of 'underdevelopment', by political scientists emphasizing the central importance of politics in determining the fate of pre-industrial and industrial society, and by social theorists hostile to the evolutionist enterprise (Eisenstadt 1966, 1973; Gunder-Frank 1970; Huntington 1965b, 1971; Nisbet 1969). All such critics were united in their assertion that the process of industrialization was not an inevitable evolutionary development, that it could take a number of different paths, routes or forms, and that it did not necessarily correspond to the model experienced or envisaged in the West (Faunce 1967, 1968; Gershenkron 1962; Hoselitz and Moore 1963; Landes 1969; Moore, B. 1967; Trebilcock 1981). In contrast to previous theories of industrialization as one universal all-inclusive process, it was emphasized that the industrialization of Britain (limited state intervention) had taken a different form to other European countries such as France and Germany (strong state direction); the industrialization of Europe and America (market-dominated economies) stood in strong contrast to the Russian experience (state-planned economy); Western forms of industrialization (individualist ethic) had proved inapplicable in Japan (collectivist ethic); and that nineteenth-century European industrialization (colonizers) was inadequate as a model for twentieth-century industrialization in Africa and Latin America (colonized).

As a result, there was less certainty about the exact nature of the industrialization process and the specific impact and requirements

of industry. The primary task of sociological investigation has, there-
fore, been frequently defined in terms of a renewed search for the
'core features' or 'inner structure' of industrialization. Various degrees
of emphasis have been laid on the use of large-scale complex
machinery, driven by inorganic power; on the development of science,
of commercial agriculture and of factory production; on the con-
centration of the work-force; on complex division of labour, market
production, rational calculation, capital accumulation, an entrepre-
neurial spirit, an occupationally based stratification system, and so on
(Brown and Harrison 1978; Galbraith 1974; Kemp 1978; Turner
1975). Sociology is, as has been observed, still concerned with '*de-
fining* industrialization' (Faunce and Form 1969: 3). It is still assumed
that 'some major obstacles to industrialism *must* be removed and
certain things propitious to it *must* be created before industrialization
can begin' (Gershenkron 1962: 31). It is assumed that sociology should
concern itself with discovering exactly what these prerequisites are. As
some proponents of the concept of industrial society have remarked,
unless such an assumption is made, the term 'industrial society' has no
meaning and performs no useful theoretical or social function
(Hirszowicz 1981; Kumar 1978). As suggested, this concern with the
necessary 'realities' of industrial society recurs throughout the work of
the various industrial society theorists. Displaying their awareness of
the dictates, if not the 'costs', of industrial progress, the post-war
theories of advanced industrial society have continued to stress the
effect of industry in generating *inequality*, *alienation*, and *anomie*.

The necessary fact of inequality within industrial society is lent
added significance because of the prevalence of egalitarian ideologies
and because industrial societies necessarily give rise to such ideologies.
Thus, Raymond Aron (1967a: 234) argues that '[E]very industrial
society is obliged in some fashion to invoke egalitarian ideas . . . They
spread egalitarian ideas and create hierarchical structures.' The source
of the egalitarian ideal is variously located in the critique of feudal
privilege (Bottomore 1974: 11), in the principle of equality of
opportunity (Aron 1967a: 234), and in the faith in human (scientific)
reason (Aron 1972: 25). Inequality is, however, viewed as necessary
for the motivation of the work-force (Aron 1967a: 89). It is conceived
as an inevitable consequence of both the need for authority within
industrial institutions (Dahrendorf 1967: 64) and the establishment of
an efficient meritocratic class structure (Parkin 1975: 59).

The perceived contradiction between industrial equality and indus-
trial hierarchy constitutes a major focus of investigation for theories of

industrial society. Aron (1967a: 69) claims that '[i]t is essential to scientific research to ask to what extent a particular economic and technological condition produces a distinctive type of society, egalitarian or inegalitarian and hierarchical'. Similarly, Tom Bottomore (1974: 13) focuses on the question: 'Is equality an attainable ideal in the circumstances of a complex industrial society? And conversely, what kinds and degrees of inequality are inescapable, tolerable, or even desirable in such a society.' For theories of industrial society, one of the central problems facing modern societies is the instability resulting from this conflict within societies that are 'egalitarian in inspiration and hierarchical in organization'. A serious problem of social order or political community arises as complex industrial societies need to encourage participation and social integration at the same time as they are forced to maintain an inegalitarian and hierarchical structure (Aron 1967a: 65). Hence the emergence of alternative theoretical and political orientations, Marxism being the most common of these (Aron 1967a, 1972; Bell 1962; Eldridge 1971).

A second constraint emphasized by theories of industrial society is the unavoidability of an *alienated* work-force. In direct opposition to the protests of socialists and some mass-society theorists, proponents of industrial society theory have stressed the inevitability of alienation in modern society — as one of the necessary requirements of industrial production (Harbison and Myers 1959: 48). Marx's work on alienated labour and Weber's writings on the depersonalized character of bureaucracy have been combined, and transformed, into a general theory of work in industrial society (Eldridge 1971; Salaman 1981). For example, it is claimed that '[E]very society that is technically complex is depersonalized, the individuals performing anonymous duties are, in certain respects, treated like things . . . The separation of workers from their tools, producers from their product, constitutes a structural characteristic of industrial civilization' (Aron 1972: 187). Industrial man's alienation from his work is attributed to various causes: the need to adapt to the pace and rhythms of large-scale industrial technology; the fragmentation and regulation of work routine through scientific management and the division of labour; and the rationalization of work and the centralization of authority brought about through bureaucratic forms of regulation (Kerr *et al.* 1973; Salaman 1981: Chapter 1).

In the study of work organization within industrial societies this approach to alienation has had two main effects. Firstly, the source of alienation has been located within an autonomous logic of industrialism, or the bureaucratic search for efficiency, rather than, for instance, in class conflicts or the dynamics of capitalism. Secondly, the discussion of levels of alienation has taken the form of examining the extent to which workers express 'job satisfaction' and accept the legitimacy of managerial authority. Alienation becomes defined in terms of subjective feelings of powerlessness, meaninglessness, isolation and self-estrangement. The overcoming of alienation is therefore identified with the integration of the worker within the enterprise, or community, and his acceptance of the necessity and benefits of industrial organization. In this way the critical aspect of the concept of alienation is removed (Eldridge 1971; Lukes 1978; Mennell 1974; Salaman 1981). Alienation is no longer identified with an objective lack of control over the conditions of social life. The critique of alienation is not, therefore, part of a serious attempt to increase the degree of control that the population exerts over the conditions of production and social life. Alienation is reduced to 'representing, on the personal level, the problem of lack of integration' (Salaman 1981: 96).

The problem of alienation thereby becomes transformed into a problem of anomie, the third major social 'reality' of industrial society. According to this view the development of science and industry results in the collapse of traditional forms of authority and the dissolution of all previous transcendental bases of social legitimation. It is thus argued, in the tradition of thought stemming from Saint-Simon and Comte, that industrial societies require a new social purpose in order to prevent social disorder. During the post-war period, this has been most noticeable in theories on the breakdown of the community, the disorderly state of industrial relations and the instabilities and dissatisfaction engendered within societies based on the pursuit of economic growth (Aron 1972: 167–84; Mayo 1946; Wedderburn 1974).

Stages of Industrial Society

In addition to its concern with the necessary realities of industrial society, industrial society theory also focuses its attention upon the advance of industrialism and the extent to which this results in the formation of an orderly and progressive industrial society. It is centrally concerned with *stages* of industrial development and their social consequences. The 'end of ideology' thesis, as developed in the 1950s by such theorists as S. M. Lipset (1972), Daniel Bell (1962), Edward Shils (1955) and Raymond Aron (1957), stressed the success of 'advanced' industrialism in overcoming the disorders and inefficiencies characteristic of industrial society's earlier 'immaturity' (see also Crossland 1961; Lipset 1969; MacIntyre 1971b; Rousseaus and Fargais 1963). With the advance of industrialism, it was argued, the 'fundamental political problems of the industrial revolution have been solved' (Lipset 1969: 406). All remaining political and social questions were relegated to mere technical issues. As one commentator (Aron 1967a: 164–5) remarked:

> Beyond a certain stage in its development industrial society itself seems to me to widen the range of problems referable to scientific examination and calling for the skill of the social engineer. Even forms of ownership and methods of regulation, which were the subject of doctrinal or ideological controversies during the past century seem to . . . belong to the realm of technology.

This belief in the arrival of a 'post-political' and 'post-ideological' age was accompanied in the 1960s by an explicit theory of the 'convergence' of all advanced industrial societies. Such theorists as J. K. Galbraith, Clark Kerr and Talcott Parsons continued to espouse the general themes of the 'end of ideology' thesis, while further attributing to technology the effect of totally transforming all advanced industrial societies into a similar social type — whatever the earlier differences deriving from their 'pre-industrial' context or the type of political and economic regime adopted in the earlier stages of industrialism. Within all advanced industrial societies, Kerr proclaims, '[T]he tug of industrialization — *whatever these initial differences* — is towards a greater role for the state in an eventual pluralistic rule-making system' (Kerr *et al.* 1973: 52) (emphasis added). Similarly, as Galbraith argued, in discussions of capitalist and socialist regimes, it was assumed that 'convergence between the two ostensibly different industrial systems occurs at all *fundamental* points' (Galbraith 1974: 384) (emphasis added).

In most of these theories, whether they adopt an extreme technclogical determinism or not, there is a common emphasis on the central importance of the advance of industrialism, driven by an industrial 'prime mover', 'axial principle' or 'key dynamic'. Like the nineteenth-century theories of industrial society, three major forms of this dynamic have been proposed: industrial *class*, industrial *competition* and an industrial *culture*. The development of the industrial class has referred to (i) the rise of a manageral élite within the business corporation at the expense of a 'parasitical' capitalist class (Dahrendorf 1967); (ii) the increasing role of scientists and technicians within the corporation (Galbraith 1974; Mallet 1975); (iii) the general incorporation of labour into a skilled, mobile and integrated industrial work-force (Kerr *et al.* 1973); (iv) the increasing control of the state by a scientific or technical class (Brzezinski 1977; Touraine 1974); and (v) the direction of the state by the controllers of industry.

Reflecting the influence of Marx and Weber, the development of modern industrial societies has also been attributed to the competition between different corporations and different nation-states. However, like Spencer and Durkheim, this competition is seen in terms of the establishment or pursuit of organizational or economic growth, rather than in terms of a pursuit of profits or power (Galbraith 1974; Landes 1969: 546; Mishan 1969).

Those who attributed central importance to an industrial culture have characterized this culture in a number of ways. Like Saint-Simon and Comte, central significance has been attached to (i) the commitment to economic growth (Aron 1967a); (ii) the positive attitude to science and the control of nature (Kerr *et al.* 1973); (iii) the acceptance of the legitimacy of managerial authority (Dahrendorf 1967; Harbison and Myers 1959); and (iv) the rise of a humanitarian concern with social welfare (Bell 1976). Other theorists, influenced more by Max Weber, have emphasized the central role of 'rationality'. One dominant strand of thought on industrial society has mistakenly equated Weber's concept of *rationality* with the search for *efficiency* (Salaman 1981; Skinner 1976). The development of industry has been attributed to an autonomous principle of 'economizing' (Bell 1976), to 'economic rationalism' (Dahrendorf 1967), or to a 'technocratic' world view (Reich 1974; Roszak 1970). Similarly, in the study of organizations, Salaman (1981: 159) has pointed out the influence of the 'naive interpretation of Weber's notion of rationality, whereby formal organizations' structures and processes are seen as reflecting the search for efficiency'.

This general focus on the social impact of 'advanced' stages of industrialism and the role of an industrial dynamic *cannot* be simply identified with the cruder theories of the 'end of ideology' and 'convergence'. They have continued to provide a focus of interest and investigation for even the more limited and sophisticated theories of advanced industrial society. An extreme convergence thesis, for example, may be rejected by a proponent of a more limited concept of industrialization who may readily accept that, in respect to a number of 'core' features, advanced industrial societies may be converging (Faunce and Form 1969). Thus, for example, it has been questioned whether all advanced industrial societies are increasingly characterized by a nuclear family structure, similar rankings of occupational prestige, identically high rates of social mobility, reductions in economic inequality and increasing political pluralism — even where it has been accepted that both capitalist and socialist types of industrial society tend to adopt an increasingly mixed economy and give rise to similar conflicts between organizational and bureaucratic interest groups (Dunning and Harper 1966).

As John Eldridge aptly observes, the sociology of advanced industrial societies is 'in a sense a response to the question: is there a logic of industrialism?' (Eldridge 1971: 3). It is often stated that the *extent* to which there is such a logic remains an important focus of inquiry (Hirszowicz 1981: 1; Andreski 1964b). Of course, whether a process of convergence is seen as occurring depends, to an extent, on what one is interested in (Kumar 1978: 151). Yet the decision to concentrate on whether an *industrial* form of convergence is occurring already determines the general focus of interest. Many critics emphasize that a strict technological determinism is inapplicable because the diffusion of technology passes through an autonomous 'cultural filter', that there is necessarily a 'dynamics of adjustment' to technological 'needs', and that societies are characterized by a 'looseness of fit' between their parts that makes them relatively autonomous from their technological 'core' (Lane 1976: 61; Skinner 1976: 7; Weinburg 1969). Yet rather than marking the end of the convergence thesis, such criticism often merely resurrects it in a modified form. While no longer embodying an extreme technological determinism, attention is still focused on the empirical question: 'Are industrial societies becoming more alike?' (Weinburg 1969: 1), and a study is carried out of the conflict between the dynamics of industrialism and autonomous socioeconomic, political and cultural forces. John Goldthorpe, for example, in his critique of convergence theory, reproduces rather than transcends this focus of investigations when he condemns 'the *exaggeration* of the degree of determinism which is exercised upon social structures by "material" exigencies' (Goldthorpe 1964: 117) (emphasis added). Raymond Aron (1972: 2–9) and Daniel Bell (1976: 12–13) provide a similar analysis in their focus upon the development of industry while also stressing the autonomous effectivity of contradictory political and cultural principles.

The focus on stages of industrial development and their impact on society may, therefore, be retained while rejecting the more extreme deterministic theories of industrial society. Sociological investigation may continue in an attempt to clarify the differences between the causes, consequences, components, facilitating factors and mere historical concomitants of the process of industrialization (Gershenkron 1962: 32; Scase 1977a; 9–15; Scase 1977b: 15–29). It may distinguish between those similarities within industrial societies that are attributable to the presence of industry and those which are due to other common factors (Moore, W. E. 1967: 38; Payne 1977: 11). It may separate the source of innovation and change necessarily resulting from the establishment of industry and that caused by a contingent cultural or political commitment to maximum industrialism or economic growth (Giddens 1973: 137). Investigation may separate the necessary preconditions and effects of industrial development from its most *efficient* organization (Halmos 1964: 137–8). Social enquiry may ascertain in what degree certain preconditions for the initial development or further advance of industry are required (Moore, W. E. 1967: 40). It may also provide a more sophisticated understanding of the political and cultural preconditions of industry by declining to reduce the 'core' features of industrialization to its technological and economic components (thereby avoiding implications of technological and economic determinism), and also by focusing upon those social forces and structures which will *facilitate* and *result from* the further development of industry. But while all these modifications are introduced, sociological investigation is still continuing to focus on stages of industrial development and on the constraints that such development imposes upon society, to the relative exclusion of alternative social typologies and classifications (such as those discussed in Chapter 10).

Types of Industrial Society

Although theories of industrial society stress the fundamental nature of the divide between industrial and pre-industrial societies (Aron 1967a: 42; Duvignaud 1972: 128; Kerr *et al*. 1973: 56) there is now a simultaneous awareness of the importance of different *types* of industrial society. Differences in political and economic regime and cultural form, it is argued, are quite compatible with the presence of industrial production (Bottomore 1973: 33; Aron 1967a: 4; Aron 1970: 7; Ionescu 1975: 64). To this extent the focus on industrial society and stages of industrial development does not, in any simple sense, exclude the adoption of alternative social typologies. Yet there are three main ways in which industrial society theory *has* undermined alternative classifications through its dominant concern with the establishment and development of industry.

Firstly, one of the main concerns of industrial society theory has been its condemnation of alternative typologies for their neglect of the fundamental realities of industrial civilization. Marxist critiques of capitalism, inspired by the socialist ideal, have been criticized for failing to recognize the inevitable problems of industrial inequality, alienation and anomie, and ignoring the universal problems of regulating an industrial economy — including the inherent conflict between investment and consumption (Aron 1967a). Similarly, it has been argued that the classical ideal of democracy necessarily founders upon the economic inequalities, complex bureaucratic regulations and widespread political ignorance characteristic of all industrial societies (Lipset 1969; Margolis 1979; Schumpeter 1954). Theories of mass society have been condemned for their idealization of the pre-industrial world and their neglect of many of the new forms of community, democracy and participation that emerge within industrial societies (Aron 1972; Bell 1962).

Secondly, there has been a common reaction by proponents of industrial society theory against the 'metaphysical' basis and authoritarian implications of the doctrines associated with these classifications. The socialist critique of alienation has been rejected for its mythical vision of 'socialization without repression' and its ultimately authoritarian belief in the 'objective' exploitation of a working class which does not 'subjectively' perceive this fact (Aron 1972: 196; MacIntyre 1975). In a frequent 'argument from the concentration camp', radical theories of democracy have been condemned for encouraging a return to totalitarianism through their appeal for widespread political participation, the conscious pursuit of fundamental social and political change, and the call for the implementation of 'positive' liberty (Berlin 1969; Bottomore 1975; Lukes 1978; Popper 1974). Secondly, advocates of industrial society theory have undermined alternatives though *redefining* them as types of a fundamentally industrial form of society. Socialism has become widely defined as a universal type of industrial society — more or less compatible with industrial efficiency — rather than an ideal form of society made possible by the advance of technology (Halmos 1964: 127). Marx's theory of class has become adopted but only when separated from his 'philosophical' theory of classlessness (Giddens 1973).

Similarly, discussions of democracy (which *had been* based on a critical examination of modern political institutions for their failure to live up to the highest ideals of political participation) were transformed into the study of 'pluralist' and 'non-pluralist' or 'democratic' and 'totalitarian' types of industrial society — where the central aim was to discover the kind of political regime both adapted to the requirements of industrial society and able to prevent the rise of totalitarianism. As S. M. Lipset (1969: 28) commented, 'the problem is no longer the changes needed to modify or destroy the institutions of capitalism, but the social and political conditions of a bureaucratized society'. Democracy became *defined* in terms of the pluralistic pressure group and multi-party forms of politics necessary for the attainment of a 'stable democracy' (Barry 1970; Margolis 1979).

Thirdly, the attribution of fundamental importance to the industrial – pre-industrial dichotomy assumes industry to be the central cause explaining the nature of contemporary states, and also the main criterion by which to evaluate their success (Kerr *et al.* 1973: 291). To regard industry as the major causal factor within modern states *at least* involves a dominant preoccupation with the 'hypothesis' of an industrial 'unilateral determinism' (Aron 1970: 7). Attention is focused on the limitations of theories which either underemphasize or overemphasize industry's role within modern society. In addition, to employ industry as the main criterion of significance involves assessing states in terms of the extent to which they hinder or facilitate further industrial development. An implicit ideal of a fully industrialized society is employed as a basis for assessing structural developments within existing industrial societies. Thus, for Clark Kerr,

> [I]ndustrialism is the concept of a fully industrialized society, that which the industrialization process inherently tends to create. Even the most economically advanced countries of today are to some degree and in some respects underdeveloped. They contain features derived from earlier stages of development which obscure the pure logic of the industrialization process. (Kerr *et al*. 1973: 16).

This does not necessarily imply the acceptance of an evolutionary and all-embracing logic of industrialism. What it does imply is that sociological investigation is focused on the extent to which such a logic exists. By viewing industry as both a causative factor and a criterion of significance, sociology necessarily becomes preoccupied with the industrial nature of the future. Ultimately, despite an increasing awareness of political autonomy and the dangers of authoritarian forms of government, the proponents of industrial society theory have sacrificed alternative classifications to focus on industrial society and the effects of quantitative stages of industrial development. (Gellner 1974a: 40). This is not to deny that all classifications direct and limit social inquiry. Industrial society theorists have, however, often adopted the 'industrial' category as *the* classification of modern states and presented this decision as an 'objective', 'neutral', 'realistic' or 'scientific' choice. The 'common-sense' nature of the concept of industrial society has then prevented alternatives being widely discussed. Yet, as we shall discuss in greater detail in Chapter 10, a number of important alternatives exist.

Industrial Society Theory

As Peter Laslett has remarked, '[W]e all know that . . . in England and in western Europe we live in an "advanced" industrial society'. He also emphasizes, however, what 'an exasperatingly imprecise thing it is to know' and protests that 'industrialism has been defined in almost as many ways as there have been historians and economists who have studied that elusive process' (Laslett

1975: 244). Yet the apparently common-sense nature of the concept, and the diversity of forms in which it has been used, should not be allowed to obscure the fact that the term 'industrial society' has been closely linked to a specific, if widely used, approach to modern societies. As we have seen; building upon the nineteenth-century theories of industrial society, the post-war proponents of the classification have employed the concept in a quite specific manner.

United with a 'democratic' – 'totalitarian' or 'pluralist' – monist' classification of political regimes, the 'pre-industrial' – 'industrial' typology was resurrected as part of a specific world project to prevent a revival of fascist totalitarianism, to remove the communist delusions that resulted in the rise of Stalinism, and to concentrate attention on the central realistic world issue — that of enhancing the affluence of the industrial world and providing the preconditions for affluence in the pre- industrial world.

Although often allowing for the importance of politics within social change, and recognizing the major significance of the liberal political freedoms gained in the West, this post-war world view has been predominantly opposed to any belief in the need or value of radical political change within the so-called advanced industrial societies. Given the continuation of social stability and liberal political freedoms, the fundamental reality and source of progress within modern societies, the means and the end of all fundamental social change, has been defined as the evolutionary development of science and industry. Alternative political programmes — associated with romantic theories of mass society, unrealistic theories of democracy, or ideological theories of communism — have been regarded as unrealistic in their aims and authoritarian in their implications.

In one sense this social philosophy can be praised for both revealing some of the dangers involved in radical political action and showing how importance can be attached to the development of an increasingly affluent world without necessarily desiring the full establishment of an authoritarian technocratic society. However, the dominance of this perspective, as we shall argue later, has encouraged an exaggerated complacency towards existing political structures, class relations and forms of industrial growth.

In the past the outline and critique of the theory of industrial society has been most fully elaborated by Anthony Giddens (1975,

1976, 1977b, 1978, 1979, 1982). It is closely linked, however, with John Goldthorpe's (1971) critique of 'technocratic historicism', Krishan Kumar's (1978) rejection of the 'image of industrialism, Tom Bottomore's (1960, 1973, 1975) warnings of the dangers associated with the concept of 'industrial society', David Dickson's (1974) critique of the 'ideology of industrialization', and the reaction of a number of Marxist theorists to the ideological origins and use of the concept of industrial society (Blackburn and Cockburn 1969: 176; Ross 1974: 347). Gidden's critique has also influenced a number of general works reviewing the state of empirical research on work, class and the corporation within advanced industrial societies (Salaman 1981; Scott 1979; Watson 1980).

The theory of industrial society, as outlined by Giddens, derives from the work of Henri de Saint-Simon, Emile Durkheim and Max Weber, and is continued in the writings of such theorists as Ralf Dahrendorf (1967), Clark Kerr *et al.* (1973) and Daniel Bell (1962). Yet, as Giddens is careful to emphasize, in his most recent work on the issue, the theory that he describes is only a relatively coherent theoretical construction, not a fully logical and consistent theory developed, in all its aspects, in the work of any one of these theorists.

The theory of industrial society outlined by Giddens possesses six major components. Firstly, it asserts that the fundamental change within world history is the transition from traditional agricultural to industrial mechanized societies. Secondly, it assumes that this great transition is a fundamentally progressive movement — despite the tensions, conflicts and suffering associated with the transition period. Thirdly, class conflicts are attributed to the birth pangs of the new order, a sign of industrial immaturity, rather than to structural antagonisms within modern societies. Fourthly, the rise of liberal democracy is represented as an essential part of the achievement of modernity. Fifthly, it is claimed that all industrial societies possess a fundamental unity that leads them to converge towards a common industrial type. Finally, it is argued that the modernization of the underdeveloped countries requires them to overcome their traditionalism and adopt the type of social structure present within the already industrialized societies.

After defining the general character of this theory of industrial society, Giddens and those who have adopted his definition have condemned the theory for its evolutionism, functionalism and technological determinism. The concept of industrial society is itself then brought into question through its association with this theory. As Tony Watson has stated: 'There are major objections to the concept of "industrial society" which derive from the way this term has tended to be *used* ever since its first appearance' (Watson 1980: 79) (emphasis added).

Despite its importance, this critique has a number of important limitations. Firstly, despite Gidden's apparent awareness of the problem, this theory is often understood to include under the general heading of the 'theory of industrial society' a number of different theories, many of which do not fit the specifications that he outlines. Durkheim, for example, is classified with both Saint-Simon and Comte as centrally concerned with industrial society. Yet Durkheim consistently avoided using the concept and rejected the idea that industry was either the primary determinant or a desirable social ideal of modern societies. It is also misleading, as Giddens also comments at times, to classify the work of Max Weber with the writings of such theorists, under a general heading that suggests a crude evolutionary understanding of the origins and development of modern industrial societies. In addition, few of the nineteenth-century theories of industrial society placed industrial technology at the centre of their analysis. Their classifications were variously based on stages in the development of the human mind, stages of social complexity, social differentiation and the spread of rationalization — not primarily stages of technological, or probably even economic, development. Finally, while a number of twentieth-century theorists have explicitly adopted a technological and economic industrial classification, they have often explicitly rejected any extreme form of technological determinism or simplistic theory of evolution.

These ambiguities reveal themselves in Giddens' outline of the theory. He claims, for example, that the theory of industrial society depicts the rise of the liberal democratic state as an essential aspect of modernity while also sometimes recognizing that the liberal democratic state is not a natural accompaniment to the development of industrial society. Similarly, he argues that the modernization thesis, as a component of the theory of industrial society, sometimes rejects any simple identification of modernity with Westernization. Yet Giddens, who opposes the theory of industrial society, still accepts that development can only occur through the 'adoption of modes of behaviour' found in industrialized societies. It is unclear from Giddens' writings at what stage the investigation and elaboration of such 'industrial' modes of behaviour become part of a systematic 'theory of industrial society'.

Secondly, the critics of the theory of industrial society do not clearly show how the theories they condemn are linked to the interpretation of modern states as distinctively 'industrial' societies. In most cases the problems of the theories they discuss derive from the use of a bipolar model of history, the adoption of an overly simplistic evolutionism, the employment of an extreme structural functionalism or the acceptance of a form of historicism: *not* from the fact that modern states are classified as industrial societies. This failure adequately to relate such critiques to the industrial classification is exemplified in their ambiguity over the continued value of the classification (Kumar 1978: 149–63; Bottomore 1973; Giddens 1971: xi). Surprisingly, such critics ultimately pay less attention to the implications of the concept of industrial society than they do to the methodological doctrines employed by a particular set of theories of industrial society.

Clearly these two sets of problems are interrelated. By failing to show the way in which the various theorists of industrial society share a common industrial perspective, Giddens cannot fully justify his imposition of a shared industrial schema on the work of these authors.

Industrial society theory, is broader than Giddens's *theory of industrial society*, for it is not necessarily based on the assumption of the 'convergence' of all industrial societies or on the compatibility of liberal democracy with a stage of advanced industrialism. It does, however, continue the main themes of the nineteenth-century theories of industrial society, that is, the central importance of the great transformation from pre-industrial to industrial society; the largely non-revolutionary view of social development once the great transition has occurred (little allowance is made for future discontinuities in social change, fundamental class conflicts, or active radical political change); the rejection of alternative theories for their ideological or utopian failure to recognize the realities of industrial civilization; the centrality of 'industrial' principles of organization in structuring and changing contemporary societies; and a view of progress that emphasizes the adaptation of society to industrial development and the principles of organization which industry embodies.

Industrial society theory requires neither the assumption of convergence nor the identification of industrial growth with social progress. What it does is to focus attention on the development of industry and its impact on society as the central issue of social structure and change. Progress may not be simply equated with industrial growth, but social advance is still primarily conceived in terms of industrial development and the creation of a compatible social structure free of the dangerous 'ideological' and 'romantic' delusions of Marxist critics, mass-society theorists, and so on. All the major issues of the age are related to this central question — even if, from an apparently opposing position, industrial principles of organization are directly rejected as 'inhumane' and 'alienating'. Industrial progress is still regarded as *the* reality of the age. Attention is directed away from *forms and types of technology*; the way in which these forms are *developed and used* by existing social structures and established power groups; and the purposes for which these forms *could* be employed in providing the foundations for a superior form of social order.

The connection between the industrial classification and *this* industrial society theory is not merely due to the way in which the classification has been used. There is also a more or less direct conceptual link between the two. The connection is primarily due to the focus imposed upon developments within modern states by the adoption of a pre-industrial/industrial or more industrial/less industrial classification. The central issue within modern societies is then defined in terms of the development, or lack of development, of industry, and the extent to which modern society is determined by, or adapted for, industrial progress. The classification defines the criteria to be employed in examining social persistence and social change. In this form industrial society theory provides a conceptual framework that has guided most of the research into the structure and development of contemporary societies. The main aim of the previous chapters has been to outline and examine the nature of this theoretical schema. The next two chapters examine the extent to which industrial society theory has structured research on post-war societies. Frequently described as studies of 'post-capitalist' or 'post-industrial' societies, this research has continued to accept the advance of industrialism and its impact upon society as the main focus of sociological inquiry. Industrial society theory's degree of influence upon erstwhile 'empirical' research reveals both the importance of the industrial classification and the degree of reorientation required if alternative frameworks are to be developed.

3 POST-CAPITALIST SOCIETY

Post-classical Capitalism

When the Congress for Cultural Freedom was held in 1954 it marked the beginning of a new era of speculation on the nature of 'advanced industrial' societies. In the following years, many of the prominent themes in the nineteenth-century theory of industrial society continued to dominate sociological thought and investigation. This dominance was primarily reflected in the thesis, and much criticism of the thesis, that Western industrial states were now 'post-capitalist'.

After the Second World War, both Marxists and non-Marxists were agreed that the era of 'early', 'classical', 'nineteenth-century', 'competitive', *'laissez-faire'*, 'liberal', capitalism had come to an end. Yet this was not automatically taken to imply that Western societies were now 'post-capitalist'. Advanced industrial societies came variously to be called 'late', 'modern', 'twentieth-century', 'organized', 'monopoly', 'state', 'imperialist', 'Welfare State', 'state monopoly', 'neo-', even 'bastard', capitalism. The choice of description was often significant; these different labels frequently embodied alternative assumptions about the fundamental character of the new society (Baran and Sweezy 1973; Dahrendorf 1967: 67; Dalton 1974; Giddens 1973; Habermas 1976:1; Mandel 1976: 10; *Out of Apathy*, 1964; Shonfield 1965; Sweezy 1972). Yet despite such disagreements there was widespread acceptance of the view that capitalism, at least in its traditional form, had been transformed. Moreover, a general consensus existed — even amongst a number of Marxists — on the basic features of 'advanced' industrialism that had brought about this change (Blackburn and Cockburn 1969: 72; Mandel 1976: 387). Central importance was attributed to three elements: (i) the transformation of the market situation and authority structure of the capitalist enterprise (through the rise of the large-scale corporation); (ii) the structure and role of the state (due to an increase in its size, expanded socioeconomic functions and the political participation of trade unions and social democratic parties); and (iii) the structural situation of the working class (marked by occupational differentiation and increasing access to formerly 'middle class' privileges — affluence, skilled jobs, social mobility, etc.). The extent and significance of these developments, however, was subject to dispute.

In the ensuing discussions of the structure and dynamics of advanced industrial societies, it became widely accepted (as we have seen) that advanced industrial societies represented a 'post-classical', capitalism. In addition, investigations of 'post-classical' capitalism were largely undertaken either to elaborate upon or to criticise the thesis that these states were 'post-capitalist'. In its extreme form, the 'post-capitalist' thesis combined two different arguments. Firstly, it was claimed that advanced industrial societies no longer conformed to Marx's image of capitalism. According to this argument, Marx's conception of the structure and dynamics of capitalism was based upon (i) the private ownership and control of the means of production; (ii) the economic dominance of a competitive market system in which even human labour became transformed into a commodity; and (iii) the gradual development of a structurally homogenous, politically organized and class-conscious revolutionary proletariat (Aron 1964: 80–1; Bottomore 1974: 12–13; Goldthorpe *et al.* 1971). Against this conception of capitalism, the proponents of the 'post-capitalist' thesis argued that the dominance of private ownership had declined; the market had been transcended by state intervention and corporate control; and the working class was no longer a radical social and political force.

This critique of Marx was, however, accompanied by a second claim: that the structure and dynamics of 'post-capitalist' societies could be explained in terms of the evolution of industrial society or the gradual working out of an inherent logic of industrialism. In this manner the theories of 'post-capitalism' finally replaced Marx's emphasis on the central role of capital and class (in the development of capitalism and the transition of socialism) by the dominance of politics and technology (in the evolution of 'advanced industrial' societies).

The Corporation and the State

During the 1950s and 1960s the debates over the nature of advanced industrial societies were primarily dominated by discussions of this 'post-capitalist' thesis. In this form the 'theory of industrial society' was developed in explicit opposition to Marx's theory of capitalism. Some studies of industrial society were explicitly presented as a 'Marx for the managers' or a 'non-communist manifesto' (Burnham 1941; Rostow 1971a). At the same time, the partial influence of Marx on the new theories of advanced industrial society was often openly admitted (Aron 1967a: Bell 1976: 55). A number of critics linked these theories of advanced industrial society to the work of Marx through their common emphasis on the importance of technology, evolutionary economic determinism, the business enterprise and the state (Goldthorpe 1971; Burnham 1941; Giddens 1973: 73). Not surprisingly, criticism of the 'post-capitalism' thesis is in no way confined to Marxists. It has also been undertaken by theorists who reject the evolutionary assumptions or the technological determinism associated with the theories of 'post-capitalism'. The debates over the nature of class, the corporation and the state in post-classical capitalism have not, therefore, been limited to a simple opposition between Marxism and evolutionary theories of industrial society.

One of the central features associated with the advance of industrialism has been the growth of the large-scale industrial corporation. Given the increase in production, and the growing size, complexity and expense of modern technology, the development of the modern corporation became, in the words of Berle and Means (1962: 5), 'a thoroughly logical and intelligent trend; the process could not be reversed'. For the critics of Marx, this inevitable growth of the industrial corporation has had two important effects: firstly, it has undermined the private ownership of the means of production through the divorce of ownership from control and, secondly, it has resulted in the transcendence of the market through monopolistic control, price fixing and the manipulation of consumer demand.

The decline in significance of private ownership is connected to two developments: the dispersion of share ownership and the growth of a technically specialized managerial stratum. The most extreme 'post-capitalist' theories advance four major claims: (i) that there has been a separation of legal ownership and the administration of the corporation; (ii) that this has resulted in the divorce of ownership and control; (iii) that the divorce between ownership and control has shifted the goal of the industrial enterprise away from the traditional concern with profit; and (iv) that the goals of the industrial enterprise are now economic growth and social welfare (Bell 1962; Crossland 1962; Kaysen 1957). This 'post-capitalist' thesis, therefore, assumes that managerial control is a fact, that the motives of management have changed, and that the trend is towards dispersion of share ownership and diversification of the management structure.

This interpretation of the 'managerial revolution' and the nature of 'post-capitalism' has received widespread criticism. Serious questions have been raised regarding the extent to which the separation of *legal* ownership from the *administration* of the enterprise has actually occurred. It has been argued that there are still great differences between advanced industrial societies in the degree of industrial concentration and that a large number of managers of the modern corporation are also substantial shareholders (Blackburn 1972; Westergaard 1972; Westergaard and Resler 1977; Zeitlin 1974). Serious questions have also been raised about the distinct question of divorcing *ownership* from *control*. The problem here is to do with whether the legal separation of ownership from managerial administration has actually undermined the concentrated strength of the owners and their ability to direct the corporation. It has been claimed that the dispersion of share ownership has often been exaggerated; that a disproportionate and controlling influence is frequently exerted by a small minority of large shareholders; that the board of directors commonly reflects outside ownership and banking interests; that managers are still tied to the owners through their possession of similar values, backgrounds and connections; and that, while particular operational and administrative decisions may be taken by managers, the general strategy of the firm is still dictated by the owners (O'Connor 1966; Scott 1979; Stanworth and Giddens 1974; Urry and Wakeford 1973).

Criticism has also been directed at the discussion of managerial motives. Even if long-term profit were no longer the major goal of the corporation, a number of different interpretations of the character of the new managerial class would remain. Firstly, the managerial stratum may be, and has been, portrayed as a new ruling class acting in accordance with its own vested interests, thereby creating a new form of exploitation (Burnham 1941). Secondly, the rise of the managerial stratum has been associated with the replacement of the profit motive by the pursuit of growth — in direct conflict with the social welfare of the community (Roszak

1973; Illich 1975). Thirdly, the separation of ownership and control has been regarded as a bureaucratic phenomenon which, while it encourages an increase in technical efficiency, also results in a socially regressive decline in authority or sense of enterprise (Schumpeter 1954). An extreme 'post-capitalist' thesis is that managers, at least potentially, are a socially responsible élite with an interest in the community and in long-term growth (Crossland 1962; Galbraith 1974; Bell 1976). A similar case was made by Veblen (1965a, 1965b) for the use of an engineering class.

In any such discussion of the motives of the 'managerial' class the assumptions made about the external context or setting of the industrial corporation are of crucial importance. Any discussion of managerial control must, as Nichols has observed, "be prefaced with an explicit recognition that the large corporation has in part created, and must operate within, a different economy, and a different sort of society, to that which formed the environment of the small nineteenth-century entrepreneur' (Nichols 1969: 149). The important question, of course, is the nature of this difference.

For proponents of theories of 'post-capitalism', the second major consequence of the increasing size of the 'industrial' corporation has been its effective transcendence of market competition. Through monopolistic or oligopolistic control, price fixing and the manipulation of consumer demand, the modern industrial corporation, it is argued, is no longer subordinated to the market in making decisions about future corporate behaviour. This thesis has been widely challenged on the grounds that the monopolistic or oligopolistic control of one product does not free the enterprise from competition with alternative products, that new forms of competition emerge within the limits set by price fixing, and that the ability of the corporation to manipulate consumer wants has been greatly exaggerated (Bell and Kristol 1971; Giddens 1973: Chapter 9; O'Connor 1966; Scott 1979: Chapter 6). Nor has it been shown that there has been a qualitative change in the 'monopolistic' control of production, such that 'control for the market' has been transformed into 'control of the market' (Blackburn 1972).

The State and the Economy

The expansion of the size and role of the state, like that of the corporation, is perceived as an inevitable phenomenon. It is assumed that 'in any modern industrial order, whether capitalist or socialist, the range of activities undertaken by the state necessarily grows rather than diminishes' (Giddens 1973: 126; Offe 1976). This expansion of the state can be represented in terms of an increasing proportion of the G N P and the working population taken up by the public sector; the direct intervention of the state in the economy through the nationalization of industries and public finance; the increasing state regulation of the overall economy through wage and price control and a variety of monetary and fiscal mechanisms; and the provision by the state of an increasingly complex economic infrastructure — including the financing of technological development, education, social welfare, etc. (Dalton 1974; Habermas 1976; Shonfield 1965). The interpretation of the effect of these developments has, however, varied greatly concerning the two central issues: the extent to which they result in the increasing ability of the state to control the economic system and the motivations and principles behind state activity.

In discussing the relationship between the political and economic systems, the 'post-capitalist' thesis has been based on two different themes: firstly, the separation of economic and political élites; and, secondly, the increasing role of the state in managing economic affairs. The first theme is based on the view of modern societies as 'complex' societies. It is argued that the gradual process of social differentiation has resulted in specialization both within and between institutions. As a result of this process, it is claimed, power has become 'pluralistic' as different institutions, in this case the political and economic institutions, are led by different personnel with influence and concern over separate issues (Dahl 1961; Lipset and Bendix 1967: 201–10; Margolis 1979; Parry 1969). At the same time, however, the growing complexity of the economic structure of industrial societies is seen to require a large expansion in the economic activities of the state (Kerr *et al.* 1973: 272–3). In opposition to Marx it is therefore argued not only that the owners of economic property no longer dominate the political system but that it is now the political system that is in command. In accepting both the managerialist thesis and this conception of the growing power of the state, the theories of 'post-capitalism' reject Marx's theory of class as the major determinant of economic and political development. In contrast, and this was one of the main themes of the end of ideology thesis, it is technology and politics that are now the dominant forces in society. In the words of Daniel Bell (1962: 389):

In a politico-technological world property has increasingly lost its force as a determinant of power. In almost all modern societies technical skill becomes more important than inheritance as a determinant of occupation and political power takes precedence over the economic. What then is the meaning of class?

In opposition to this aspect of the theory of 'post-capitalism' it has been argued that the process of differentiation has been exaggerated and that there is a variety of personal, cultural, educational and financial links between the holders of political office and owners of economic wealth as well as the actual participation of individuals within both spheres (Miliband 1973; Urry and Wakeford 1973). Moreover, it has been claimed that the control of the economy by the state is far less great than the optimistic theories of the mixed economy have suggested. Two arguments put forward are that the state does not have the power to constrain important vested interest groups within a complex industrial or capitalist economy, and that the state is unable adequately to control or radically to alleviate the instabilities of a complex market economy. Thus it is argued, in the face of corporate and trade union power, that the ability of the state to impose fiscal and incomes policies is severely limited (Baran and Sweezy 1973; Rowthorn 1980). Also, the attempt by the state to encourage economic growth by means of high unemployment and low inflation is said to be undermined by the instability of the international economy and by the inherent problems facing any attempt to reconcile economic growth with low inflation and high employment within a predominantly private economy (Gamble and Walton 1976; Goldthorpe and Hirsch 1978).

The second main issue facing discussions of the 'post-capitalist' state concerns the motives or purposes of the political system. For proponents of the 'post-capitalist' thesis the growth in bureaucratic and technical posts within the state has occurred in response to the 'needs' of a complex economy organized for the pursuit of economic growth (Galbraith 1974; Kerr *et al*. 1973). In addition the development of a multi-party system and the rise of pressure-group politics have been equated with the rise of a 'democratic' policy responsive to the general wishes of the citizens or the desires of all groups in society (Dahl 1961; Lipset 1969; Schumpeter 1954). The rise of a large bureaucratic pluralistic state is perceived to be both a necessary and desirable feature of complex advanced industrial societies. According to this view, the *relative autonomy* and *representation* of all groups within such societies is ensured by the dictates of a complex industrial economy — realizing equally the ideals of a liberal-democratic state. For Clark Kerr *et al.*, the rise of 'pluralistic industrialism' combines democratic representation with a neutral bureaucratic structure. While modern industrial societies 'must be administered', the 'administrators become increasingly benevolent and increasingly skilled'. In advanced industrial societies, '[t]he benevolent political bureaucracy and the benevolent economic oligarchy are matched with the more tolerant mass' (Kerr *et al*. 1973: 265).

This complacent interpretation of the purposes of the 'post-capitalist' state has been directly opposed by theories stressing either the 'late capitalist' or 'corporatist' nature of modern states. The proponents of the theory that modern states are still fundamentally capitalist base their account of the nature and purpose of the state either upon the systematic constraints imposed upon the political system by a capitalist economy (Fine and Harris 1976; O'Connor 1973; Poulantzas 1973), or upon the overrepresentation of business and wealth — direct or indirect — in party politics, administrative processes, the mass media and pressure group activities (Miliband 1973; Stanworth and Giddens 1974; Urry and Wakeford 1973). The pluralist 'group' theories of democracy are accordingly condemned for their failure adequately to reflect the state of 'imperfect competition' between different groups and classes (Miliband 1973: Chapter 6; Westergaard and Resler 1977).

In opposition to competitive 'party' theories of democracy, it is argued that there are still a number of structural constraints preventing social democratic parties from achieving any radical reforms. Some of the cases instanced relate to the moderation of party programmes; the exigencies of the capitalist economy; the conservative nature of the electorate or the party's view of it; the oligarchy of party organization and leadership; social pressures from capitalist interest groups; the limitations of parliamentary electoral politics; the demobilization of the working class when social democracy has control of government; and the brevity and precarious character of the electoral mandate (Maravall 1979). In combination, these constraining influences are regarded as a sufficient basis for qualifying the modern state as 'capitalist' rather than 'post-capitalist'. The underlying purpose of the state remains, it is argued, the defence of the capitalist system of private property, free enterprise and the pursuit of profit.

Despite their lack of precision, the most recent versions of the corporatist thesis to do with the motives and purposes of the modern state may be contrasted with theories of 'post-capitalism' and 'late capitalism' (Pahl and Winkler 1974; Panitch 1980; Schmitter 1974; Winkler 1976, 1977). Like the theories of 'post-capitalism', the corporatist thesis emphasizes the growth in the administrative structure of the state; the increasing economic role of the state within a predominantly privately owned economy; and the adoption by the state of the professed goal of economic growth and national welfare. Unlike the theories of 'post-capitalism', however, this is not associated with public control of the state, nor is it assumed that the professed aims of the corporate state will be anything other than a cover for authoritarian forms of political regulation undertaken in the interests of corporate élites (Winkler 1977: 48–9). On the other hand, in contrast to theories of 'late capitalism', the motives of this authoritarian state are not automatically identified with the pursuit of profit and the preservation of capitalism. For Pahl and Winkler, the goals of the corporate state are unity, order, nationalism and success (Winkler 1976). Yet the vague and instrumental character of these goals, as well as the imprecise nature of the general corporatist thesis, leaves the exact nature and source of the purposes of the state remarkably unclear (Westergaard 1978: 165–87).

Class in Industrial Society

For Marx, the development of capitalism, and the continued class conflict between the owners and non-owners of the means of production, would gradually result in the formation of a structurally homogenous, politically organized, class-conscious and revolutionary proletariat within a sharply polarized class structure. In direct opposition to this view, a number of theories of 'post-capitalism' have argued that the advance of industrialism results in a structurally diverse, politically institutionalized and culturally integrated industrial work-force within a fragmented or decomposed class structure. According to Marx, the working class would gradually develop from a 'class in itself' to a 'class for itself' as a result of capitalism's periodic crises, the increasing immiseration and alienation of the work-force and their concentration within large-scale capitalist enterprises. For the theories of 'post-capitalist' society, the work-force was becoming increasingly integrated and 'middle class'. Capitalist crisis was conceived to be prevented by the establishment of a regulated 'mixed economy' and rising affluence. Increasing skill and high rates of mobility were held to undermine discontent and class antagonism.

As Goldthorpe *et al.* (1971:5) have observed, this theory of advanced industrial society provided 'not only a systematic critique of Marx but also an alternative theory of the evolution of the working class . . . a theory of the progressive *integration* of the working class'. In the tradition of thought stemming from the work of Saint-Simon, Comte and Durkheim, the evolution of industrial society was associated with the emergence of a 'classless' system of stratification (Giddens 1973: 135–8) and the replacement of the anomic tendencies of modern society by an acceptance of both the cultural goals and institutional mechanisms of industrial society. This interpretation has predominated within theories of the end of ideology, convergence and the new middle class. As we have seen, theorists of the 1950s such as Daniel Bell, Edward Shils, S. M. Lipset and Raymond Aron proclaimed the end of ideology in advanced industrial societies. This involved acceptance of the desirability of economic growth and a 'mixed economy' as the best means to achieve this goal. Similarly, the proponents of the logic of industrialism agreed on the presence of a growing consensus over the values of industrial society, an acceptance of the 'web of rules' or the institutional structure of industrial society, and the formation of an increasingly affluent, mobile, skilled and committed work-force.

These overall interpretations of the nature of advanced industrial society have been connected to a variety of different theories of the 'new middle class'. According to such theories, the advance of industrialism results in an increasing percentage of the workforce being employed in occupations, or receiving financial rewards, traditionally regarded as middle class. As a result, it is claimed, this has facilitated the development of a 'new middle class' integrated into society through the adoption of traditional middle class attitudes and style of life (Goldthorpe *et al.* 1971: 14; Roberts *et al.* 1977: 37). This common theme, continuing a number of earlier speculations of the 'new middle class' (Dahrendorf 1967; Peterson 1973; Roberts *et al.* 1977), was shared by theories of the *embourgeoisement* of the 'affluent worker', the 'de-alienation' of increasingly skilled technological workers, and the 'professionalization' of the work-force through the increasing predominance of 'service' occupations (Blauner 1964; Halmos 1970; Turner 1963; Zweig 1961; Bell 1976).

In combination, the theories of the end of ideology, the logic of industrialism and the new middle class provide an image of the class structure of advanced industrial societies that directly accords with the underlying themes of the classical theories of industrial society produced by Saint-Simon, Comte and Durkheim. The critique of Marx relates not so much to the fragmentation of labour as to the formation of a new and dynamic industrial class structure. The importance of the increasingly diamond-shaped stratification system is not that it results in the formation of a complex series of different strata but that it creates a distinctive class structure. In Clark Kerr's terms, '[m]iddle incomes make for a middle class' (Kerr *et al.* 1973: 268).

In the attempts to examine the dynamics of advanced industrial society, the class structure has generally been portrayed in terms of the co-operation or institutionalized conflict between a dynamic industrial élite or managerial class and a more or less integrated industrial work-force. In the classical theories of industrial society, there was continued stress on the need for such an authority structure within industrial societies. This ultimately led to an emphasis on the importance of the industrialists (Saint-Simon), the scientists (Comte), and the heads of bureaucracy and managerial staff (Weber). Although Weber in particular emphasized the complexity of the class structure and system of authority, he argued that a typology of economic services could still be based on a twofold distinction between a directing 'managerial' agency and a 'labour' element subject to the instructions of this managerial group (Weber 1969: 219). In the more recent discussions of the class structure of advanced industrial societies, Dahrendorf has continued Weber's theme. Dahrendorf recognizes that

> bureaucratic organizations typically display continuous grada-
> tions of competence and authority and are hierarchical . . .
> Structural conflicts based on latent antagonisms of interest in
> the sense of class theory are absent from bureaucratic organiz-

ation by virtue of their hierarchical character (Dahrendorf 1967: 296).

Yet Dahrendorf, like the earlier theorists of industrial society, is centrally concerned with the dynamics of class formation and change, rather than with detailing the complex character of different strata within modern societies (Dahrendorf 1967: ix). Influenced by the earlier theory of industrial society, he emphasizes the fundamental division in all industrial societies between those who 'control the actions of others and issue commands, and others who have to allow themselves to be controlled and who have to obey' (Dahrendorf 1967: 71). Other writers have made similar observations (Bendix 1956: 13). As T. Nichols comments in his study of the general literature on managerialism, 'the "manager" in sharp contrast to the industrial worker, has been portrayed in the literature as the supreme *actor* (in the sense of the supreme decision-maker)' (Nichols 1969: 145).

For all such theories, the class structure of industrial society requires a subordinate industrial work-force and the allocation of a central role to a dominant industrial élite. In advanced industrial societies,

> The key concern of management, in its relationship to workers, is to establish, to make legitimate and to maintain its authority. The specialization of functions which industrialism demands also requires that the workforce accept tasks whose nature, time, and method of accomplishment are to be determined by management in its role as planner and order giver (Kerr *et al.* 1973: 155).

In other words, the active dynamic managerial élite within industrial society is accompanied by a 'fully committed workforce' with 'considerable formal education' and 'dedicated to hard work, a high pace of work and a keen sense of individual responsibility for the performance of assigned norms and tasks' (Kerr *et al.* 1973: 53, 180, 183).

The critique of Marx has also been undertaken by a variety of 'neo-Weberian' theorists. They have primarily emphasized the *complexity* of class structure in advanced industrial societies. In contrast to the theorists just considered, the 'neo-Weberians' do not offer an alternative theory of the dynamics of class formation.

They offer, instead, a forceful account of the fragmentation of class structure. The theoretical foundations of this account are provided by a partially reformulated Weberian conception of social stratification (Dahrendorf 1967: ix; Giddens 1973: 42–5; Lockwood 1958; Parkin 1975: 44–6). This approach has been primarily developed in the writings of such theorists as Goldthorpe *et al.* (1971) Lockwood (1958), Giddens (1973), Parkin (1974, 1975, 1979), Mann (1970, 1973) and Gallie (1979). The limitations of both Marx's model of class and that provided by the various theories of the logic of industrialism are attributed to their failure to recognize the influence upon class formation of a diversity of factors including the 'work situation', 'market situation' and 'status situation' (Lockwood 1958).

Against the 'post-capitalist' theories of the logic of industrialism and the new working class, 'neo-Weberian' theorists have argued that the admitted increase in the middle *strata* (Raynor 1971) in advanced industrial societies — due to more affluence, white collar work, skilled jobs, and service occupations — cannot be equated with the predominance of an integrated middle *class*. As regards the middle strata, important differences exist between the work situation of manual and non-manual affluent workers (Lockwood 1958), between the market strength of highly qualified and relatively unqualified white collar workers (Giddens 1973: 186–8) and between the status situation of white collar and highly skilled manual workers (Mackenzie 1973). As regards the complex question of class consciousness, great importance is attached to the attitudes that workers bring to the work-place and the important — if not central — influence of trade union organization, political parties, managerial ideologies, community life, previous occupations and cultural traditions (Bulmer 1975; Gallie 1978; Goldthorpe *et al.* 1971; Lockwood 1966; Roberts *et al.* 1977; Scase 1977b: 122–36). Thus in a rejection of Marxist theories of the immanent radicalism or historic role of the proletariat, it is argued that the diverse situations facing different sections within the working class necessarily results in an ambiguous consciousness combining 'proletarian', 'deferential' and 'pecuniary' attitudes to society and embodying elements of 'dominant', 'subordinate' and 'radical' value systems (Lockwood 1966; Mann 1970; Parkin 1975).

In opposition to monolithic interpretations of the class structure of 'capitalist', 'post-capitalist' or 'industrial' societies, neo-

Weberian theorists have emphasized the important variations in class situation and consciousness *between* different societies within this group (Kumar 1978: 154–63; Gallie 1978; Goldthorpe 1964). In addition, the complexity of the class structure *within* each society is regarded as posing unresolvable difficulties for any one-dimensional theory of working class radicalism. Evidence of working class conservatism has been accompanied by signs of middle class radicalism (Parkin 1974: 237–57; Roberts *et al.* 1977). Images of the immanent radicalism of the proletariat or the successful permeation of a 'dominant ideology' (Abercrombie and Turner 1978; Abercrombie *et al.* 1980) have been displaced by a perception of an unpredictable but potentially volatile trend towards 'instrumentalism' amongst both working and middle classes (Goldthorpe *et al.* 1971; Westergaard 1970). In short, the diverse class situations and forms of consciousness within advanced industrial societies are seen as undermining the validity of both Marx's theory of the revolutionary role of the proletariat and the 'post-capitalist' theories of the integration of the working class and the rise of a 'middle class' society. The danger is that this 'image of complexity' may not be accompanied by any wider societal perspective from which to assess the significance of the trends examined.

Industrial Society: Conflict and Consensus Models

The different perspectives on 'industrial society' are frequently portrayed in dichotomous terms as a conflict between 'radicals' (such as Tom Bottomore, Michael Harrington, George Lichtheim, Herbert Marcuse, Andre Gorz, Jurgen Habermas, Henri Lefèbvre, Serge Mallet, Alain Touraine, and Ernest Mandel) and 'conservatives' (Daniel Bell, S. M. Lipset, David Riesman, J. K. Galbraith, Raymond Aron, Anthony Crossland, Ralf Dahrendorf, and Helmut Schelsky) (Birnbaum, 1969). This conflict has been represented as one between the 'theory of industrial society' and the 'theory of capitalism' (Scott, 1979). As we have seen, such a dichotomy tends to ignore the mass of critical literature that accepts neither the existence of a strict logic of industrialism nor a logic of capitalist development.

We may, however, isolate two very different uses of the model of capitalism. The first set of theories of industrial society argue:

that the transcendence of capitalism is the inevitable byproduct of the evolutionary development of industrialism (Dahrendorf 1967: 68, 248); that the achievement of post-capitalism results in the establishment of an orderly and efficient 'advanced industrial' society (Galbraith 1974; Kerr *et al.* 1973); and that capitalism does not represent a fundamental Social type driven by its own internal dynamic but is, rather, a system of market competition and private ownership forming a transitional and unstable type of industrial society, the product of the disorganized transition to a developed industrial state. As Alvin Gouldner remarks, capitalism's flaws are seen as those of an 'underdeveloped adolescence rather than as the decrepitude of old age' (Gouldner 1979: 92).

On this account, it is the industrial irrationality of capitalism that is the source of its downfall in the later stages of industrial development. The profit motive comes into conflict with the efficient pursuit of growth; private ownership of the means of production sets limits on the formation of a meritocratic and functionally organized occupational system; market anarchy prevents the development of an orderly system of scientific-corporate regulation; and the instabilities of class conflict provide an increasingly dangerous source of social and economic disruptions hindering the planned regulation of large-scale production. The downfall of capitalism is therefore attributed to its industrial irrationality or its 'pathological' organization of industry, *not* to the inner workings of an initially self-perpetuating but finally self-destroying social system.

By contrast, the second set of theories of capitalism derive from a Marxist approach which traces all conflicts and problems in modern society to their origins in capitalist production and examines their significance in terms of their contribution to the downfall of capitalism and the transition to socialism. Such interpretations of capitalism strongly oppose the tendency to deviate from strict focus upon this. A number of critiques have consequently been directed against 'neo-Keynesian' or 'underconsumptionist' theories of the capitalist economy and writings which stress the problems of the rising surplus within monopoly capitalism or the legitimation crisis of the state (Baran 1973; Baran and Sweezy 1973; Habermas 1976) *rather than restating the centrality of Marx's law of value* (Fine and Harris 1976; Mandel 1976; Steedman 1981; Steedman *et al.* 1981). As Marx based his analysis of capitalism upon the fundamental laws of movement of the economy rooted in his labour theory of value, in his theory of exploitation and class conflict there have been a variety of criticisms directed by Marxists against critiques of capitalism grounded 'superficially' upon facts of market supply and demand or the problems facing government in its attempt to regulate the economy. Similar forms of criticism have been directed against writers who perceive the role of Marxist political theory in terms of a critique of the 'bourgeois problematics' of pluralism and man-agerialism rather than concentrating on the development of a Marxist theory of the state (Clarke 1977; Poulantzas 1973, 1975, 1979). Finally, a Marxist critique has been developed against sociologists who examine class conflict by adopting a 'neo-Weberian' focus on patterns of distribution and market arrangements and their effects rather than examining the basis of forms of inequality within the changing structure of capitalist relations of production (Binns 1975; Crompton and Gubbay 1977; Hunt 1978).

These two different models of capitalism provide clearly con-trasting accounts of development within modern societies. Yet this contrast is not the same as that between consensus and conflict models of industrial society. The consensus model of industrial society is equivalent to the extreme 'post-capitalist' thesis, repres-enting modern societies as integrated, orderly and efficient in the pursuit of industrial growth. The conflict model of industrial society accepts that modern states are in some sense 'post-capitalist', but does not represent them as orderly or efficient, recognizing the continuing tension in modern societies between their 'industrial' character and various 'countervailing processes'.

The consensus and conflict models represent important variants *within* industrial society theory. While united by a common focus on the quantitative development of industry and its impact on society, they are divided over the extent to which they regard 'advanced industrial' societies as integrated, 'mature' industrial systems. Although industry and its development remain the central 'criterion of significance' for assessing the consequences of existing social structures, proponents of the conflict model maintain that there are important and (to an extent) self-perpetuating social forces that hinder and disrupt the process of industrial advance. The conflict model takes three forms.

The first group of conflict writers is best represented by

Raymond Aron and Daniel Bell. Aron and Bell continue Saint-Simon and Comte's emphasis on the presence of destabilizing 'metaphysical' ideals within industrial societies. Saint-Simon and Comte believed that the ideals of equality and liberty would be replaced by a new scientific-industrial ethos, whereas Aron and Bell stress that the support for cultural individualism and political egalitarianism (with its attendant instability) is likely to remain a persistent feature of all advanced industrial societies (Aron 1967a: 234; 1972: 21–9; Bell 1976: 12–13). Yet, for Aron and Bell, industry still remains the central determinant and key dynamic within modern industrial and post-industrial societies.

The second set of proponents of the conflict model can be vaguely classified as 'neo-Weberian'. For these theorists, neither Marx's theory of capitalism nor the logic-of-industrialism thesis grasps the complex structure of advanced industrial societies. In contrast to the theories of 'post-capitalism', it is argued that modern states may be both disorderly and inefficient industrial societies. As John Goldthorpe remarks, 'under the weight of the empirical data, theoretical interest has been increasingly pushed towards a concern with . . . countervailing processes whereby social inequalities are in fact maintained or indeed widened' (Goldthorpe 1972: 344). In opposition to theories of late capitalism, however, it is argued either that the historic role Marx attributed to the working class is undermined or qualified by the complex conditions within modern societies (Goldthorpe 1980: 28; Mann 1973: 73) or that the changes that have occurred within capitalism render invalid any attempt to understand their further development purely in terms of the dynamics of capitalism (Gellner 1974a: 201–2; Giddens 1973: 164). Yet Gallie (1978: vii) and Goldthorpe (1964: 98; 1972: 372) praise both sets of theories for providing the necessary theoretical basis for sociological investigation.

The domination of the conflict model of industrial society within the work of these theorists is due, firstly, to their continued focus, albeit critical, on the 'post-capitalist' thesis and, secondly, to their interpretation of capitalism's persistence as primarily a 'countervailing process' hindering the establishment of an industrially rational and orderly class structure. For Frank Parkin (1975: 59), for instance, such a 'conflict between the demands for the most rational use of talent and the pressures making for class inheritance are present in all modern industrial societies'.

Influenced by Durkheim and Weber, these theorists emphasize not only the problems created by the 'anomic' and 'forced' division of labour, or the resistance of the entrepreneur to the encroachment of bureaucracy, but also the social structures which act to perpetuate such 'anti-industrial' conditions. Thus, for Parkin (1975: 59),

> [i]t would probably be a mistake to assume that the drive towards industrial efficiency will see the complete victory of meritocratic principles. This would assume that members of the dominant class have little control over events, that they are simply swept along by inexorable forces of economic progress.

For Goldthorpe (1980: 28), this situation means that significant change can only be brought about through collective class action, for

> class structures are ones highly resistant to change: those groupings who enjoy positions of superior advantage and power cannot be expected to yield them up without a struggle, but will rather typically seek to exploit the resources that they can command in order to preserve their superiority.

This general perspective has provided the focus for a number of studies of class, mobility and industrial relations in advanced industrial societies (Heath 1981; Wedderburn 1974).

A third source of the conflict model of industrial society derives from the technocratic strand within Marxist theory once the central focus on the transition to socialism is neglected. A number of technocratic themes can be found in the work of Marx in (i) the influence of the Saint-Simonian ideal of the rational scientific reorganization of society (Kumar 1978: 40); (ii) the occasional appearance of a technologically deterministic view of history with comments on the hand mill giving rise to the feudal lord, and the steam engine the industrial capitalist, as well as his statements on the most industrially developed country giving other states a vision of their own future (Shaw 1978); and (iii) the portrayal of the central conflicts within capitalist society as between the socialization of production and the system of private appropriation or the development of science and industry accompanied by the capitalist restriction of consumption (Mandel 1976: 565; Shaw

1978: 95). From this point, a number of more recent Marxist writers have provided a critique of the disorderly and inefficient character of modern 'advanced industrial' or 'complex' societies. They emphasize either the conflict between the need for forward planning and the necessary antagonism created by private ownership, *or* the instabilities created within a complex society whose economic system promises material rewards for all, but is constrained to limit the fulfillment of such promises to the few (Miliband 1973: 248; Westergaard and Resler 1977: 7).

All such theories remain within the confines of industrial society theory, for they continue, first to focus attention on the degree to which industry determines society and second, to assess the significance of independent social structures in terms of their facilitating or hindering industrial development. Despite the 'neo-Weberian' emphasis on the continuation of inequality and disorder within advanced industrial societies, there is little examination of the kind of egalitarian order that political action could establish — other than that required for an orderly industrial society. Similarly, from within the Marxist camp, John Westergaard and Ralph Miliband are remarkably lax in showing how the tensions and instabilities they record can be regarded as a force for radical change (Goldthorpe 1972: 363). This is accompanied in their work by a marked absence of any discussion of the exact nature of socialism and the type of equality that it would embody. Yet, in order to focus sociological investigation upon the possible transition from capitalism to socialism — in terms other than the gradual establishment of a more efficient industrial society — it is necessary to provide a clear model of a socialist society with its alternative 'paradigm of equality'. As Jose Maravall (1979: 268) has noted in his study of left-wing critiques of social democracy, 'a sociological political critique will not be convincing until an alternative "model of society" and an alternative "model of transition" are defined and can be used in sociological evaluations of political programmes and actions'. The emphasis on the importance of egalitarian ideals in the work of such theorists as Steven Lukes, Tom Bottomore, John Goldthorpe and Jose Maravall, may provide the basis for a focus of investigation that transcends the industrial society perspective. This can only result, however, if the focus on the creation of an egalitarian society is clearly separated from the limited form of egalitarianism associated with industrial society theory (Bottomore 1975: 143; Lukes 1978).

4 POST-INDUSTRIAL SOCIETY

Post-industrialism

During the late 1960s and early 1970s, debate over the nature of 'post-capitalism' gave way to a new concern with the rise of 'post-industrial' society. Due to the development of a number of apparently novel technological and economic trends (displayed most prominently in the United States) it was argued that advanced industrial societies were again undergoing a fundamental social transformation — one equivalent in scale and importance to the transition to industrial society. As one commentator remarked, 'what is occuring now is, in all likelihood, bigger, deeper, and more important than the industrial revolution . . . the present moment represents nothing less than the second great divide in human history' (Toffler 1975: 21).

The following are some of the 'post-industrial' trends to which great significance was attributed: the transition from a goods producing to a service economy; the increasing predominance of white collar and professional occupations; the development of electronics and the growth of automated, computer and communication technologies; the increasing role of theoretical or scientific knowledge; and, associated with the rise in widespread affluence, the growing concern with leisure and the quality of life (Kumar 1978; Bell 1976; Heilbroner 1977).

A number of new terms were coined in an attempt to understand the implications of these developments. Central importance was variously attributed to the rise of an 'active' society, a 'service' society, a 'knowledge' society, a 'technetronic' society, or a 'leisure' society (Etzioni 1968; Bell 1976; Brzezinski 1977; Dubazedier 1974). Advanced industrial societies were defined as 'post-bourgeois', 'post-modern', 'post-civilized', 'post-historic', 'post-economic' and 'post-scarcity' (Bell 1976; Bookchin 1971; Kahn 1978; Seidenberg 1950). Despite this diversity, however, one central theme was paramount: the new society was distinctively post-*industrial* — in the limited sense in which this term was used during the 1950s and 1960s.

During the post-war period, industry was widely regarded as a system of factory production based upon the use of complex machinery driven by inanimate energy. This form of production was held to be associated with the dominance of large-scale manufacture; with class structures in which the relationship between blue collar worker and industrial manager appeared as the key source of social conflict; and a cultural system based on the acceptance of the work ethic and a general consensus on the social priority of economic growth. By contrast, 'post-industrialism' was primarily defined as a system of production characterized by the dominance of the university and the increasing role of theoretical knowledge. It was associated with the rise of a service economy; with a class structure characterized by the predominance of white collar and professional occupations (the major source of conflict lying between professionals and the populace at large); and a cultural system assigning increasing priority to self-expression, equality, participation and the general 'quality of life'. Whereas the rise of industrial society was associated with the centrality of the corporation as an *economic* institution and the development of large-scale manufacturing industries producing coal, steel, cars, ships and trains, 'post-industrial' society was characterized by the rise to prominence of the university and the political system, the transformation of the corporation into a *social* institution and the development of electronics, computers and service industries.

As an interpretation of the development of modern states, the theories of 'post-industrial' society have, however, been widely condemned for both their lack of originality and their inadequate interpretation of a number of contemporary trends. In sharp contrast to the emphasis that all such theories of 'post-industrial' society place on the novelty of post-industrialism, their analyses of the new society reveal a remarkable similarity to earlier theories of industrial society. A number of direct links can be discerned between the theories of 'post-industrial' society and the end-of-ideology thesis prevalent during the 1950s, the evolutionary theories of the convergence of advanced industrial societies predominant in the 1960s, and the nineteenth-century theories of industrial society put forward by Saint-Simon, Comte, Spencer, Durkheim and Weber.

Like the end-of-ideology theories, there has been a similar emphasis on the decline of property-based class conflict, the transformation of the business corporation, the development of political pluralism, and the replacement of ideological conflict by limited 'utopias' or 'compulsive' ideas (Bell 1962; Brzezinski 1977; Chomsky 1971; Hancock 1972; Ross 1974). Many of the themes within the work of Edward Shils, S. M. Lipset, and Daniel Bell are continued in the later works of Daniel Bell, Zbigniew Brzezinski, Walt Rostow and Herman Kahn, while Marcuse's critique of the 'one-dimensional' society has, in a number of respects, been reproduced in the writings of Theodor Roszak (1970, 1973) Albert Wellmer (1974) and Charles Reich (1974). As with the theories of convergence, central significance is attached to the quantitative development of science and technology, the necessary constraints such developments impose upon society, and the extent to which they result in the formulation of a new, orderly and efficient industrial society.

The most technologically developed society — America — is again portrayed as the pinnacle of modernity and the image of Europe's future (Goldthorpe 1971; Giddens 1973). Moreover, like the nineteenth-century theories of industrial society, the novel characteristics of 'post-industrial' society are identified as the development of science (Saint-Simon), the further spread of rationality (Weber), and the extension of the division of labour within an increasingly complex, specialized and interdependent social structure (Durkheim) (Bell, 1976; Roszak, 1973; Brzezinski, 1977). These developments are equated with the increasingly important role of the scientists and technicians (Saint-Simon); the formation of large-scale bureaucratic organizations characterized by a tension between the bureaucrat and both the professional politician and the uninformed populace (Weber); and the creation of a complex society whose dedication to economic growth requires the simultaneous construction and acceptance of an authoritative moral code if it is not to degenerate into anomie and conflict (Durkheim), (Bell 1976, 1979; Illich 1975; Jones 1983).

Like a number of earlier theories of industrial society, the theories of post-industrialism have also been challenged for exaggerating both the *extent* and *significance* of the trends they describe. An important part of the first critique has been directed against the evidence produced for the increasing role of scientific or theoretical knowledge. The use of rate of expenditure on research and development is inadequate as an indicator for it ignores the change in the price of knowledge and includes expenditure on such common items as stationery and office equipment. The greater expenditure on education cannot be assumed to have resulted in increased knowledge — especially generalized knowledge. The difficulty of quantifying the contribution of science and knowledge to economic growth further undermines the reliability of the data. It is still uncertain whether the advance of knowledge is more efficiently achieved by heavily funded institutions or by small firms and research teams. It has also been observed that greater expenditure on research and development has primarily been the result of political projects rather than of necessary social trends, and has been developed for military rather than economic purposes (Kumar 1978: Chapter 6; Chomsky 1971; Heilbroner 1977: Chapter 3).

The evidence for the rise of a service society is equally suspect. Increasing employment in service occupations has often been at the expense of agriculture rather than manufacture. The declining percentage of factory workers in the work-force has often been exaggerated. Different countries show markedly different rates of occupational change. The increase of employment in the service sector is exaggerated by incorporating factors such as the commercialization of housework and community services. Much of the work in the service sector is undertaken because it is directly required by manufacture. The conditions of work within the service sector vary so greatly that to talk of a 'service' economy creating a new style of work is highly suspect — the service sector, for instance, is not necessarily small-scale or white collar (as Daniel Bell seems to suggest) and will often involve working within a rationalized and bureaucratic structure. The rising number of managerial, professional and technical occupations is of reduced significance, given long working hours, pressures of widespread unemployment, increasing bureaucratization of working conditions, and the fact that the practice of relabelling jobs has misleadingly swelled the number of occupations described as 'professional' (Kumar 1978; Giddens 1973; Heilbroner 1977; Straussman 1975).

The major problem with the post-industrialism thesis is, however, the failure to justify the significance of the trends that it describes. One of its major assumptions is that the development of theoretical knowledge, the increase in service occupations, and the rise in the number of professionals has resulted in the increasing *power* of knowledge-based classes and knowledge-based institutions and a transformation in general working conditions. This thesis suffers from three major weaknesses.

Firstly, the basis for the fundamental structural unity of the new classes (technocratic, professional, knowledge, service, counter-culture, and so on), is only vaguely defined. Both Daniel Bell and Alain Touraine, for example, recognize the divisions within these groups. For Daniel Bell, the professional or knowledge class is divided between four statuses or estates (scientific, technological, administrative and cultural) and five situses or institutional sectors (business, government, universities or research institutions, social institutions, and the military). Daniel Bell suggests that such diversity means that there is no intrinsic reason for this class, on the basis of some coherent or corporate identity, to become a new economic interest class or a new political class which would bid for power (Bell 1976: 374–5). Similarly, Alain Touraine is aware of the divisions between different sections of both the dominant 'technocratic' groups and the 'new working class' (Touraine 1974: Chapter 1). Yet he provides a fundamentally bipolar model of class formation and conflict based on differences in authority. In this respect, Touraine's appreciation of Ralf Dahrendorf's work is of some significance, for his theory of class reproduces the weaknesses of that theorist's writings (Giddens 1973: Chapter 4). Ambiguities can also be found within other theories of the 'new middle class' and the new 'service class' (Eldridge 1971; Straussman 1975). While the 'new working class' is often associated with 'dependent participant' classes in the university, government departments and science-based industries, Serge Mallet (1975) and Robert Blauner (1964) seem to apply it as a blanket term to the members of the new industries.

The second main weakness of 'post-industrialism' has been the tendency to assume that the class consciousness of such groups directly reflects their 'objective' class situation. Thus central social significance has been attributed to the service ethic of the professional class, the Promethean quest, Faustian technic, scientism, growth mania, etc., of a technocratic élite, and the increasing radicalism of the new working class. Differences resulting from variations in culture, community and other socioeconomic relations are given little, if any, attention (Gallie 1978).

Thirdly, the theorists of 'post-industrial' society not only fail to reveal the necessary unity of such classes, they also fail to justify the assumption of their increasing *power*. As a number of critics have observed, the mere fact of the increasing functional indispensability of technical classes and university or research institutions does not automatically confer power (Giddens 1973: 255–75). Rather than the state or the business corporation becoming increasingly subordinate to the needs or desires of technical élites and university establishments, the opposite relationship may hold. The new classes and research institutions may be portrayed as the servants of the military, political or corporate establishment rather than vice versa (Chomsky 1971; Dickson 1974; Ross 1974).

A second reaction against the theme of the growing power of the scientific-technological élite has also emerged from the technologically deterministic theories of post-industrialism. According to such theories the development of science and technology has now taken on its own logic and become an autonomous process (Winner 1977). A number of more limited versions of the same thesis have emerged amongst theorists more critical of the unity and power of centralized technocratic élites (Bell 1976). Both the 'servants of power' and the 'autonomous-technology' models of the new class have, therefore, brought into question its capacity to control society either as an 'enlightened élite' or 'exploitative class'.

De-industrialization and Hyper-industrialization

While in many ways projecting an image of industrialism that is already established, the theories of 'post-industrial' society have taken two markedly different forms: the one presenting 'post-industrial' society as a hyper-industrial or scientific-industrial society, the other presenting it as a form of de-industrialized society. In the former case, in the work of such theorists as Daniel Bell, Zbigniew Brzezinski and Alvin Toffler, the difference between industrial and post-industrial society is set out in terms of a contrast between a manufacturing and a service economy; between blue collar and white collar work; between the dominance of the business corporation and the dominance of the university; between an ideology of growth and an ideology of social welfare and the quality of life; between factory-based class conflict, on the one hand, and the reciprocal antagonism, on the other, of centralized technocrats (or professionals) to the general public (and to the public's political representatives). The post-industrial society is therefore seen as both 'highly technological and anti-industrial' (Toffler 1981: 24).

The second set of post-industrial society theorists largely accepts this image of post-industrialism as a description of advanced industrial society, or even, in the case of Alain Touraine, of post-industrial society. Yet for such theorists as Alain Touraine, Theodor Roszak, Ivan Illich and Krishan Kumar, this state is regarded as a further development of the principles upon which industrial society is based, rather than the formation of a truly *post*-industrial society (Kumar 1978; Roszak 1970, 1973; Touraine 1974, 1977). Industrialism, in this case, is not merely defined in terms of factory organization and the use of power-driven machinery, but as a process of centralization, bureaucratization and specialization; the identification of progress with the increasing output of large-scale institutions; and the direction of scientific or theoretical knowledge in the attempt to control nature, regulate an increasingly complex social organization and legitimate the existing social hierarchy. For such critics, the development of a truly 'post-industrial' society is associated with increasing decentralization, the 'demythologization' of science, and growing popular participation – not the reliance on science and scientific élites as suggested by Bell, Brzezinski, Toffler and others. These themes are shared in common by appeals for 'convivial' production (Illich), 'selective industrialism' (Roszak), 'intermediate technology' (Schumacher), or 'alternative technology' (Dickson).

Both sets of theories of post-industrialism emphasize the importance of the dynamic of industrialism as the central motor of change within advanced industrial societies. Similarly, they both agree that this dynamic of industrialism undermines the foundations of 'industrial' society. Their divergence over the definition of the nature of industrialism, as compared to post-industrialism, does not, therefore, mark a division between industrial society theory and its critics. To an extent these different sets of theories can be portrayed as the most recent expression of a long-standing tension between 'technocratic' and 'technophobic' forms of thought (Manuel 1965, 1971; Williams 1971: Chapters 6 and 7). They both portray the major social issues of the age in terms of the expansion or decline of technological development and the impact that this has on society, yet they take opposing value positions in their assessment of this development.

Despite the obvious applicability of this dichotomy, it does obscure two of the central elements of the recent theories of 'post-industrial' society. Firstly, the critique of the hyper-industrial theories of post-industrialism is *not* just a moral critique – it is based on the argument that the process of industrialization necessarily undermines its own foundations by giving rise to a contradictory ethos, class or set of environmental conditions. Secondly, the opposition to the vision of the hyper-industrial state does not always involve a total rejection of complex technology. It does, at times, involve an emphasis upon the importance of a 'selective industrialism' that is to say, choosing those technologies suitable for human purposes, rather than regarding technological or economic development as a goal and subordinating humans to its requirements.

Dialectic of Industrialism

In contrast to the theories of 'post-capitalism', both these strands of thought regard the transition to 'post-industrial' society as a fundamental social transformation creating a genuine social crisis. There is a greater awareness of the novel benefits and dangers accompanying the advance of industrialism. It is argued that the elimination of fundamental material scarcities has been accompanied by widespread social and ecological diseconomies (Kumar, 1978: Chapter 6 and 7); that the advance of genetic engineering, the landing of men on the moon, and the exploration of the ocean floor, have coincided with a dangerous decline in non-renewable energy sources (Toffler, 1981); that the increasing interdependence of society – brought about by the development of transport and communications technology, the complex relationships within highly complex and fast changing societies, and the increasingly widespread social effects of modern technology – has been accompanied by the continuation, if not increase, of fundamental divisions and conflicts (Brzezinksi 1977). While the development of science and technology has resulted in greater control over nature, it is argued that this development has simultaneously created an extremely complex and unstable social structure, a structure requiring a degree of social and political regulation that would appear unattainable other than by means of further development of scientific knowledge and technique (Bell 1976, 1979).

The complacent belief that 'the fundamental political problems of the industrial revolution have been solved' (Lipset 1969: 406) was replaced by a concern with 'future shock' (Toffler), 'unstable America' (Bell), and the tensions and conflicts of a society 'between two ages' (Brzezinski). The tensions of industrialization were not a thing of the past but a continuing phenomenon (Hancock 1972). The theorists of 'post-industrial society' advance a dialectic, rather than a logic, of industrialism (Kumar 1978: 305; Aron 1972: 21). Social progress after the Great Transition is not merely a gradual unfolding of the inner principles of industrialism. Although industrialism contains within itself a specific set of socio-economic and political relations, it comes into conflict with these relations as it attains new stages of development – and 'bursts them asunder'.

Rather then employ the two-stage (or dichotomous) industrial model of Herbert Spencer, the post-industrial theorists have revived, albeit in modified form, the three-stage (trichotomous) model of Henri de Saint-Simon and Auguste Comte. As indicated, this trichotomous model has taken two different forms in the shape of hyper-industrial and de-industrial theories of post-industrialism. Both of these forms, however, emphasize the *disorders* surrounding the present transition, the central role of the advance of industrialism in creating this state of crisis, and the need for an *active*, scientifically informed response to the advance of industrialism if further disorder and chaos are to be avoided. For some writers, this 'radical' approach is directly related to the trichotomous rather than the dichotomous interpretation of history (Kumar 1978: 59–60; Peel 1971: Chapter 8).

The theories of post-industrialism are, of course, more varied than this general outline suggests. There are important differences in the characterization of the central industrial dynamic (class or culture, specific technologies or the speed of technological change, level of affluence, etc.); in the structural form attributed to 'post-industrial' societies (degree of decentralization, relative priority of the ideology of growth, the role of large-scale complex technology, etc.); and in the extent to which the major technological dynamic is assumed to determine the rest of society (presence of an anti-industrial culture, continued class conflict or class incorporation, variation in political systems, etc.). Despite these variations, the main features of industrial society theory are retained. Politics is primarily portrayed as reactive, rather than as potentially innovative or revolutionary. The major source of social development is still attributed to the rise of a 'post-industrial' culture or a 'post-industrial' class. The main basis for assessing the significance of political events remains the extent to which they facilitate an orderly and efficient transition to a 'higher' level of technological development. The central focus of study continues to be the quantitative development of 'industrial' or 'post-industrial' trends, rather than the importance of political action in determining their specific *use* and *direction*.

The theorists of 'post-industrial' society, therefore, often reproduce the general structure of industrial society theory. Their major concern is with the central dynamic of industrialism and the extent to which it results in a developed 'industrial' structure – or in a directly contrasted 'de-industrialized' structure. They direct sociological investigation away from the significance of different *types* of industry, different *uses* of industry, and the balance of social forces in determining such outcomes. In opposition to earlier theories of industrial society, post-industrial theories emphasize the importance of changes *within* industrial society. Yet, as with post-capitalist theories, their dominant concern remains the orderly and efficient development of 'industrialism'.

Despite the limitations imposed by this main concern, the proponents of the theory of 'post-industrial' society have made a number of suggestive comments on the social possibilities facing modern societies. They have argued that an important new stage of development may be created by the abolition of *fundamental* material scarcities (Bottomore 1975; 53; Hancock and Sjoberg, 1972); by the creation of new, labour-saving technologies, capable of providing the *technical basis* for a meaningful 'leisure' society (Bookchin 1971; Cross *et al.* 1974; Marcuse 1974; Dubazedier 1974); by new information and communication technologies, possibly facilitating the rise of a more 'democratic' society (Margolis 1979; Williams 1974, 1983) and by greater community control over decentralized forms of production (Kumar 1978; Gershuny 1978).

The theory of 'post-industrial' society plays a useful role where it draws attention to the complex balance of social forces which facilitate or hinder the realization of new social possibilities. The theory is less useful where it continues to focus upon the deterministic impact of scientific-technological evolution and upon the 'industrial' rationality or irrationality of 'adapted' or 'disruptive' sectors of society. As this has been the dominant emphasis since the popularization of the concept by Daniel Bell, the continued usefulness of the concept is extremely doubtful. The past use of the concept, combined with its negative and vague industrially defined character, makes its further promotion of dubious value.

Conclusions

Many of the predominant themes of theories of post-capitalist and post-industrial society have been challenged over the last decade and a half. There has been growing opposition to the attachment of central significance to industry as both the means and end of significant social change. Firstly, there has been an increasing reaction against functionalist and evolutionary theories of society and an emphasis upon the importance of a multi-dimensional approach to the study of society. Secondly, there has been a greater stress upon the general importance of power relations and forms of international interdependence in affecting developments within modern states. Thirdly, a variety of empirical studies of particular sectors of modern societies have revealed the limited role of industry in determining their general structure and development. Fourthly, there has been a widespread reaction against the assumption that technological development and economic growth can be automatically equated with economic development or social progress. In particular, increasing attention has been paid to particular forms and types of industry and the social forces responsible for the choice of such forms.

In combination these criticisms provide a serious challenge to the continued dominance of an industrial society concept based upon the attachment of central significance to the quantitative development of industry and its impact on society. There has been little attempt, all the same, to develop a systematic critique of the industrial society concept or to investigate and evaluate modern societies other than in terms of industrial or non-industrial typologies. Nor has the more sophisticated understanding of the nature and context of specific technologies culminated in adequate attention being paid to their relationship to the fundamental characteristics of present societies, the structural possibilities that are available, and the power structures which will restrict the choices available. Such an approach requires a reorientation of macrosocial thought in a way that transcends industrial society theory.

The aim of Part Two is to assist in a re-orientation. It provides a closer examination of the importance of social classifications and, in particular, of the implications and limitations of industrial and non-industrial typologies. In this, the ground is prepared for an alternative approach to modern societies. In Part Three a number of examples of such an approach are provided. The intention is not, in rejecting the approach of industrial society theory, to provide *the* alternative. The aim is, rather, to show the limitations of the industrial society approach, outline some of its problems and weaknesses, and conclude by drawing attention to the nature and benefits of rethinking the fundamental features of contemporary states.

PART TWO

INDUSTRIAL SOCIETY:
CONCEPT AND CLASSIFICATION

5 IMAGES OF SOCIETY

The Industrial Imagination

During the 1950s and 1960s, the process of decolonization, the thaw in cold-war tensions and Western consensus on the benefits of the mixed economy, all contributed to a renewed interest in modern states conceived as 'industrial societies'. 'Industrial society' provided the chief conceptual framework for examination of the origin (industrialization, modernization), development (end of ideology, post-capitalism) and the future (convergence, post-industrialism) of modern states. As we have seen, the emphasis of this approach was upon the inevitability and desirability of industrial advance; the impact of such advance upon the social structure of modern societies; and the forms of social adaptation required to ensure the orderly and efficient progress of 'industry'.

For the academic social scientist, this renewed interest in the comparative study of industrial societies provided a means of avoiding the tendencies towards 'grand theory', *'liberal practicality'* or 'abstracted empiricism' so eloquently exposed by C. Wright Mills (1975). By emphasizing the importance of the comparitive investigation of industrial societies, social science could avoid falling into abstract intellectualism, the detailed study of small-scale social 'problems' or the undirected compilation of social statistics. Some social theorists regarded this form of investigation as important enough to restore sociology to the position of queen of the social sciences as a discipline of unique relevance to contemporary society. As Ernest Gellner (1972: 34) remarked:

> the heir of 'classical' political theory is now sociology. It is sociology which is concerned with the understanding of that process which is now central to validating or even conceptualizing society . . . reflection on human society in terms of which we orient ourselves . . . must spring from a substantive, well informed, systematic and sophisticated awareness of how societies in fact function and change, an awareness of the types of interdependence that exist between institutions, of the alternatives and combinations which are available and for a sense of social structure . . . we must seek our guidance in the philosophy embedded in a more adequate sociology . . . The

87

emergence of industrial society is the prime concern of sociology.

This adoption of the image of industrial society was not, however, the sole prerogative of academic social scientists. It was part of a more general image of modern societies shared by the wider population. As Maria Hirszowicz (1981:1) has commented, 'the concepts of industrialism and industrial society have become part of everyday vocabulary; they reflect the new stage of social organization in which human life is dominated by industrial production'. This assumption of the widespread prevalence of an industrial image of society is also shared by the variety of critics opposed to the ideological or deradicalizing role played by 'technocratic consciousness' (Roszak 1973; Habermas; 1976) or the 'ideology of industrialism' (Dickson 1974).

No discussion of the image of industrial society, nor of images of society in general, can be totally isolated from the wider issue of the effect that such prevailing images may have on the activities of the population (Giner 1976; Bulmer, 1975). As C. Wright Mills (1975:92) has observed:

Every society holds images of its own nature — in particular, images and slogans that justify its system of power and the ways of the powerful. The images and ideas produced by social scientists may or may not be consistent with these prevailing images, but they always carry implications for them.

Critiques of the Industrial Imagination

When, during the 1970s and 1980s, the validity and usefulness of the industrial image of society was brought into question, the implications of this critique extended beyond the boundaries of the academic establishment. The form this critique took within the social sciences was, however, initially an increasing reaction against general functionalist and evolutionary theories of society; the failure to recognize the influence of power relations and forms of international interdependence on the internal development of modern states; and the empirical inadequacy of technologically deterministic theories of the 'convergence' of advanced industrial societies (Giddens 1977b, 1982).

This critical reaction was accompanied by another important development: the growing recognition that technological development and economic growth cannot be automatically equated with economic development or social progress (Meadows *et al*. 1975; Mishan 1977; Hirsch 1977; Dickson 1974). Linked to this increasing awareness, there has been a more sophisticated attempt to understand the nature and effects of technological development, in socioeconomic, political and ideological — as well as in technical — terms (Elliott 1977; Dickson 1974; Johnston and Gummett 1979; Pacey 1983; Albury and Schwartz 1982).

In combination, these developments have brought into question the foundations of industrial society theory. Not only has it been established that the social impact of industrial technology is far less marked than often claimed, but it has also been shown that the 'core' feature of industrialization — the process of technological development itself — is strongly shaped and influenced by socioeconomic interests and power conflicts. The consequence is that doubt is cast upon the priority attached by industrial society theory to the quantitative development of industry as the major determinant and key dynamic within modern society. The value of industrial society theory as a whole is put in question where a disjunction is entertained between technological/economic growth and economic development or social progress.

Amongst the general public, technological development and economic growth are no longer accepted as the unquestioned goal of modern societies. As Arnold Pacey (1983:34) has observed:

> In the advanced societies of the world, with their market economies, open societies and democratic politics, a dominant theme appears to be spent, the theme of progress in a certain, one-dimensional sense, of linear development, of the implicit and often explicit belief in the unlimited possibilities of quantitative expansion.

Yet, while it is commonly recognized that political and economic interests guide the *form* taken by technological development and economic growth, and that it is necessary to *choose* between different types of development and growth, there has been little consideration of how such issues may be dealt with or resolved.

One of the reasons for this situation within the intellectual community has been the lack of awareness concerning the importance of general images of the modern type of society and the extent to which the image of industrial society continues to dominate social and political thought. In social thought there has been increasing concern with images of class, images of change, images of the future and images of society. It has been observed that images of society may represent societies as conflictual or co- operative (Dahrendorf 1967), as tightly integrated or loosely combined (Demerath and Peterson 1967), as imposed upon men or created by them (Dawe 1970). Images of class may include a view of class as dichotomous and conflictual or complex and co-operative (Bulmer 1975). An understanding of social change may evoke images of continuity or discontinuity, of cyclical rotation or unfolding progress (Smith 1973, 1976). Images of the future may be similarly diverse, alternating between pessimism and optimism or determinism and activism (Polack, 1961). Little attention has, however, been paid to social typologies and the image of the modern type of society which they incorporate. Yet within the social sciences, these typologies dominate the wide area of comparative study.

Social Classification and Comparative Study

Comparative study or comparative sociology ideally involves more than the mere comparison of different social actions, structures or events. Firstly, rather than being concerned with small-scale changes or events within particular societies, comparative sociology mainly focuses its attention on the nature and interrelationship of *major* social structures and processes in *different societies* (Payne 1973; Andreski 1964b: 66; Eisenstadt and Curelaru 1977: 421; Vallier 1971).

Secondly, comparison is not carried out in order to throw light upon the nature of modern societies through merely pointing out similarities to or differences from other societies. In contrast to the limited, untheoretical and unsystematic character of many general comparisons, comparative sociology is centrally concerned with the task of formulating and testing generalizations about different types of society. It is for this reason that Andreski condemns Westermarck on the grounds that he 'does not really compare but merely lists resemblances with almost complete disregard of the contexts' (Andreski 1964b: 67).

Thirdly, comparison is not undertaken in order to provide illustrations of a previously accepted theory but rather to foster historically based generalizations on the forms of persistence and change within different types of society. A variety of critiques have, therefore, been directed against those classical proponents of the 'comparative method' who only use comparison in order to illustrate their 'natural' or 'metaphysical' theories of evolution with examples drawn from 'mere' history (Nisbet 1969: Chapter 6). On Spencer's use of this 'method', Nisbet aptly comments that he did not read books about other societies, he 'mined' them (Nisbet 1969: 200). All that glitters in sociology's storehouse of comparative studies cannot be regarded as 'scientific' gold.

In contrast to limited comparisons or general comparisons that merely illuminate or illustrate similarities and differences, the value of comparative sociology is now attributed to its formulation and testing of generalizations about social persistence and change through the classification, comparison and explanation of different social types. The establishment of valid and useful societal typologies, therefore, lies at the heart of the comparative enterprise — providing the foundation for all generalization and explanation. Comparative sociology is not alone in this respect, only reflecting the more general importance of classification within the social sciences. It has often been commented (in line with this view) that, in its general method, comparative sociology is equivalent to social science itself (Durkheim 1964a: 139; Fletcher 1971: 627; Macridis and Brown 1972: v; Holt and Turner 1970; Marsh 1967).

At the most general level, no specific understanding of any singular or unique event or object can be provided without employing words or terms that have general application. This phenomenon has obvious philosophical importance as well as a linguistic and social significance (Aaron 1976; Woozley 1976; Russell 1974; Carr 1975: 63). It is important to recognize that classifications are not mere reflections of a particularized 'reality', but are theoretical and cultural constructs developed for the purpose of understanding or manipulation. Their adequacy or precision must be related to the purposes for which they are to be used. The unreflective acceptance of any classification as a simple description of reality — whether of race, class, sex, status, culture, political regime or economic structure — ignores the limited range of purposes for which the classification is valid. It is for this reason that a number of social theorists have stressed the importance of conceptual frameworks which, by dividing the world into classes and categories, specify the variables to be taken into consideration, their dimensions of variation and their general relationships (Benton 1977; Hirst 1976a: 11).

One of the central features of social classification is the link that it provides between *description* and *explanation*. In the studies of social action it is commonly recognized that there is a close connection between the description of an action as being of a certain 'type' and the explanation of that action (Bernstein 1976: 61; Outhwaite 1975: 96; Fay 1975: 72). Similarly, in the study of social systems, the description of sectors of society or social institutions involves, to a greater or lesser extent, the assumption that they have been 'motivated' in some way to fulfill certain social functions. (For an attempt to avoid such implications, see Runciman 1971, where he suggests that theorists should define the elements of society in terms of the 'means' employed. The difficulty is that one cannot select a means without some prior conception of the end or function it is to serve.)

All classifications embody hypothetical explanations or at least limit the kinds of criteria that will be considered as potential explanations. As one commentator has remarked:

> Explanations . . . presuppose a conceptual framework in terms of which to identify and classify the general types of things in the universe . . . and which specifies the general types of causal interaction which can take place between them . . . the restricting of the scope of the investigation which generated the universal law could only be rationally justified on the basis of a conceptual scheme which was the source of a hypothetical causal mechanism (or possibly several) which in turn generated criteria of relevance for the investigation' (Benton 1977: 22–3).

It is only to be expected, therefore, that societal classification plays a central role in comparative sociology. It does so in three main ways.

Firstly, social classification allows societies to be divided into different types for the purposes of comparative analysis. This is done through (i) *the possession or non-possession of a classification criterion* (for example, pre-industrial/industrial, traditional/modern, class/classless etc.); or (ii) *the possession of a classification criterion in different stages* (for example, Spencer's simple/

compound/doubly compound/trebly compound classification); or (iii) *the possession of a classification criterion in different types* (for example, Marx's distinction between slavery, feudalism and capitalism). It is the initial classification that determines the basis for contrast and comparison.

Secondly, comparative investigation is focused upon the extent to which the criterion of classification is *responsible for* a distinctive type of society. As Morris Ginsberg observed, comparative sociology does 'not consist merely in drawing comparisons, but in *explanation by means of comparison*' (Ginsberg 1961a: 196, emphasis added). This can be performed in three different ways: firstly, by contrasting societies classified as different types in order to discover their systematic differences; secondly, by examining the various societies designated as a similar type in order to disclose their universal similarities; and, thirdly, through the study of the growth or decline of specific types of social structure. In all three cases, the central aim is to examine the extent to which the classification requires or creates a distinctive type of social structure. (This is equivalent to J. S. Mill's methods of agreement, difference and concomitant variation if an attempt is also made to vary or keep constant all other relevant causal factors (see Mill 1879: Chapters 7 and 8).)

Thirdly, societal classification provides a further focus of investigation for those concerned with the overall structure and development of particular types of societies. It selects the 'facts' which are to be taken into consideration. As Comte aptly observed, the 'rational method of observation' does not consist in the general collection of facts but in the study of the 'scientific' meaning of facts — by which he meant their relevance to the overall structure and development of societies. In this sense, as Durkheim (1964: 79) argued, sociology's 'experimental method' 'tends to substitute for common sense facts . . . decisive or crucial facts'. It does so by defining — *for the purposes of investigation* — the 'fundamental' or 'essential' characteristics of different types of societies. As Louis Althusser has commented: 'This is one of the essential tasks of any theoretical attempt to produce the concept of history: to give a rigorous definition of the *historical fact*, as such . . . the *historical* fact, as opposed to all other phenomena that occur in historical existence, can be defined as a *fact which causes a mutation in the existing structural relations*' (Althusser and Balibar 1975: 102).

A fact in this sense is one which embodies or influences the social persistence or transformation of the structure of particular social types. The central concern is with what Mandelbaum has called the 'societal significance' (Gardiner 1974) of historical events. (See also the discussion of 'historical facts' in Carr 1975.)

If for example, we take the classification of societies as industrial/non-industrial, the fundamental 'facts' about modern society are defined in terms of the development or decline of industry and the development or decline of the industrial class structure, industrial institutions and industrial culture. Social investigation is then concentrated upon the extent to which this structure has developed and the extent to which the existing social structure facilitates or hinders its further development. The social classification not only provides a hypothetical *explanation* of social structure, it also provides a *focus* for investigation which defines the 'significance' or 'functional'/'dysfunctional' role of social structures or developments (Parsons 1949: 21).

In recent years it has been widely argued that modern social typologies require 'that each level or type should include a wide range of variations' (Marsh 1967: 324). Industrial societies, for instance, are less often assumed to be functionally integrated and technologically determined social configurations. It is recognized that the different national and international settings within which industrialization occurs have a substantial impact on the nature and type of industrial society that develops. But what constitutes a 'substantial impact'?

By this, the proponent of the industrial society concept may be referring to the creation of conditions which facilitate or hinder the further development of industrial society itself. Alternatively, he may conceive 'a substantial social impact' to consist in distinctly non-industrial effects, as covered by non-industrial typologies (democracy/totalitarianism, capitalism/ socialism, public/mass, etc.). Yet the recognition of 'differences' within societies of the same type does not limit the fundamental importance of social classification in suggesting explanations and focusing research. What it does is to reveal an awareness that societies are not necessarily functionally integrated social configurations organized around one determinate principle. It encourages acceptance of the fact that in order to study any particular historical society a number of classifications may be developed depending on the focus of interest and explanation. Thus, Raymond Aron (1967a: 3) has referred to the term industrial society as an 'analytical concept';

Daniel Bell (1976: Part 1) has called for a number of 'complementary' classifications of modern society; and Neil Smelser (1976: Chapter 7) has emphasized that comparative study involves an endless series of investigations which, by constantly manipulating the theoretical parameters or chosen bases for social classification, provides a systematic basis for generalization. Such variety may be required in order to approach a 'complete' understanding of any society. But in any particular instance, it is the adoption of a specific classification that defines the 'central' explanatory factors within society and the 'major' facts to be investigated. As Daniel Bell (1976: 10) remarks of his search for 'axial principles' and 'axial structures', this involves 'an effort to specify, not causation (this can only be done in a theory of empirical relationships), but centrality. Looking for the answer to the question of how a society hangs together, it seeks to specify, within a conceptual scheme, the *organizing* frame around which the other institutions are draped, or the *energizing* principle that is a primary logic for all the others.'

Reflection on the nature and importance of existing social classifications is not only needed to explain necessary social 'realities'. It is also undertaken, as Alan Blum puts it, to 'expand the possibilities inherent in ordinary looking' by 'uncovering a tacit and unformulated "possibility-for-seeing"' (Douglas 1971: 314). Comparative study in its broadest sense may, for instance, involve a comparison between existing societies and *theoretical* alternatives, which may throw a different light on the causes — and possible transformation — of existing social structures (Greenberg *et al.* 1975: Introduction). This transformed version of Weber's 'imaginative experiment' may be part of what E. H. Carr had in mind when he wrote that 'good historians, whether they think about it or not, have the future in their bones. Besides the question "Why?" the historian also asks the question "Whither?"' (Carr 1975: 108). Any assessment of the causes of social developments within past or present societies involves a *selective* focus on those which are 'significant', that is, generalizable and relevant for our present interests. Reflection on existing classifications may therefore be undertaken in an attempt to reveal the limitations that they impose upon 'future' speculation through their inbuilt conceptions of what are taken to be the 'significant' causes of modern societies.

Classifications of Industrial Society: Stages and Types

During the nineteenth century, all the major theorists of industrial society conceived it as part of a classification reflecting both stages of structural complexity and types of systemic configuration. The 'stages' approach was founded upon the isolation of a leading element within society, the quantification of its development, the formation of 'cut-off' points in this development, and the examination of the type of social structure correlated with each stage of development. This approach was therefore structural and quantitative and took the form either of stages of societal complexity (Spencer and Durkheim) or levels of scientific or technological development (Turgot, Condorcet, Saint-Simon, Comte, Mill and Hobhouse).

The systemic approach involved the study of societies as functionally integrated social units organized upon one specific principle. It involved the construction of a 'model' of society as a distinctive and efficient institutional configuration pursuing one common purpose. For Saint-Simon and Comte, this institutional configuration took the form of an 'industrial society' organized solely for the pursuit of 'industry', just as 'military societies' had been organized for the purpose of warfare. A similar distinction, between military and industrial societies, was adopted by Spencer. In contrast to Saint-Simon and Comte, Spencer related this distinction to the increasing dominance of one sector of society — and its structural principle — rather than to the emergence of a different form of organization within one sector. One of the most important points explicitly made by Spencer, however, was that this conception of the industrial type was a theoretical model — a hypothetical, institutional configuration — to be used to assess the extent to which existing societies conformed to it. In a different context, Marx made a similar point. He portrayed capitalism in *Capital* as an abstract, although essentially accurate, model, not as an historical generalization. The same systemic, teleological approach to social typology was employed by Durkheim, who viewed history as an inevitable transition from 'mechanical' to 'organic' forms of social solidarity.

These two forms of classification — according to stages of structural or technological complexity and types of institutional configuration — were not, however, separable components to be *found* within the work of the major theorists of industrial society.

These classificatory approaches were irretrievably intertwined in their conceptions of industrial society. This ocurred in three main ways.

Firstly, Comte, Spencer and Durkheim all frequently assumed that modern industrial societies were characterized both by their stage in the development of knowledge or social complexity *and* by their organization around one central 'industrial' principle of organization.

Secondly, these two characteristics of industrial society were regarded as mutually enhancing, that is to say, it was assumed that industrial organization or organic solidarity would encourage the development of social complexity or knowledge and vice versa.

Thirdly, *both* forms of classification were based upon a theory of evolution, social development or progress. The demarcation of stages of structural complexity was made on the assumption that the criterion employed was of central importance in explaining the structure and dynamics of these societies, and constituted an irreversible and, often, progressive social trend. Similarly, the classification of types of systemic configuration was made on the assumption that the industrial type had begun to emerge and would gradually come to predominate as the sole progressive basis for the organization of modern societies.

When, after the Second World War, the concept of industrial society was reinstated, its proponents frequently stressed its 'empirical', 'historical', 'heuristic', 'critical' or limited nature and condemned many of the assumptions built into it during the nineteenth century. Drawing upon, but modifying, the theory of an industrial *stage* of society, they argued that the new concept of industrial society merely offered a hypothetical explanation of the major characteristics of modern states. All industrial societies were not held to be functionally integrated social types organized exclusively for the efficient pursuit of industry. Nor were non-industrial classifications (so important for a complete under-standing of modern states) excluded. Not all industrial societies were assumed to possess a central industrial dynamic, providing an autonomous source of social development. No evolutionary assumptions, projecting the rise of industrial society as an in-evitable historical development were necessarily involved. The notion that industry was the source and definition of social pro-gress was not always accepted, industry being held to be based on the emergence of a particular form of production, rather than on production as such (Aron 1967a; Dahrendorf 1967; Giddens 1973: 259–60; Gellner 1974a).

Despite such disclaimers, acute difficulties persist. In the discussion of the new conception of industrial society as a *stage* classification, based on levels of social/technological complexity, even the more sophisticated theorists of industrial society have ambiguously fluctuated between a 'critical-heuristic' and an 'evolutionary-developmental' classification. Although the industrial/non-industrial classification is sometimes merely presented as one possibility amongst others, it is also asserted, often by the same theorists, that the industrial concept represents *the* 'essential' characteristic of modern societies, *the* 'major fact' of modern states that it provides *the* 'obvious' framework for understanding modern societies. It is not merely assumed that 'the process of modern industrialization has certain predictable institutional concomitants' (Fletcher 1971: 316) but that 'the new working methods were at once the *cause* and the *essential characteristic* of modern societies' (Aron 1967a: 16, emphasis added). Although '[t]he forces of production, the technological and economic state, should be regarded only as an analytical concept', (Aron 1967a: 14) it is claimed at the same time that, '[f]or us the *major fact* which is found in Soviet industrial societies as in Western industrial societies, is the growth in productivity' (Aron 1967a: 41). Industrial society is regarded as an 'operational' category that allows a 'multi-variable' approach to modern societies, but it is also assumed that 'it has become difficult to begin a classification of societies with any dichotomy other than industrial/pre-industrial. This distinction, so platitudinous now, did of course require clear formulation before it became *obvious*' (Budd 1964: 129; Gellner 1974a: 128, emphasis added).

Post-war theories of industrial society have also tended to confuse *stages* of industrial development with *types* of institutional configuration. Raymond Aron argues both that '[i]n any social context, industrial society is only a *means*' (Aron 1967a: 239) and that 'when a director of a firm thinks in accordance with the laws of industrial society, he asks himself how he can maximize his profits or output with the means of production at his disposal' (Aron 1967: 135). Similarly, Dahrendorf (1967:39) identifies industrial society with 'those factors which can be shown to be connected with industrial production as such, independent of its social, legal, or, economic context'. But he simultaneously explains developments within industrial society by reference to its possession of a 'goal' of industry. In Dahrendorf's words: 'the value of purposeful economic activity oriented towards the maximization of gains has never left industrial society . . . When towards the end of the nineteenth century, many countries experienced what has sometimes been called a "second industrial revolution", the value of rationality stood behind it . . . Thus the changes that led to the supersedence of capitalist society were the reflection of the values on which this type of social and economic organization was based' (Dahrendorf 1967: 68). The theories of industrial society cannot, however, have it both ways. It is not possible, on the one hand, to justify the concept of industrial society on the basis that it only refers to an industrial stage of society and then, on the other hand, to explain developments in modern states in terms of the laws or goals of a functionally integrated industrial configuration.

A number of theorists have just assumed that 'industrial' societies are dynamic industrial configurations, even if they are at present not fully developed. Thus Clark Kerr *et al.* (1973: 33) proclaimed that

[i]ndustrialism is the concept of a fully industrialized society, that which the industrialization process inherently tends to create. Even the most economically advanced countries of today are to some degree and in some respects underdeveloped. They contain features derived from earlier stages of development which obscure the pure logic of the industrialization process.

To classify a society or state as 'industrial' does of course (by definition) focus attention upon 'industry'. But to classify in terms of a stage of development does not necessarily assume that the stage indicated had historically to be reached, nor that a system reaching it must, in future, develop further in the same direction. The claim that there *is* a 'pure logic' of industrialization is based on the assumption that the dominant characteristic of industrial societies is the presence of a functionally integrated industrial configuration organized for the sole purpose of industrial development. Such an assumption cannot be derived from the presence of an industrial stage nor can it be concluded from the rise, within specific historical industrial societies, of a general commitment to industrial growth (Aron 1967a: 84).

There are thus two major weaknesses in the post-war theories of industrial society. The first stems from their classification of societies in terms of 'stages of development', without fully realizing that this approach in itself imposes a committed, non-neutral developmental perspective, one which significantly restricts the potential range of social enquiry. The second stems from the failure adequately to separate the notion of an industrial *stage* of development from that of an industrial *type* of configuration.

6 THE INDUSTRIAL COMPLEX

At the heart of industrial society theory, there lies the assumption that industry is not just *one*, but *the*, central feature of the modern world. Ever since Saint-Simon first speculated on the nature of industrial society, proponents of this theory have been almost exclusively preoccupied with the nature, preconditions and consequences of industrial advance. Ernest Gellner (1972: 37–8) remarked that political theory's 'central question — the basis of political order as opposed to anarchy — is now replaced . . . by an interest in the bases of industrial society as opposed to pre-industrial society'.

It is frequently assumed that the development of industry has a destabilizing impact on society, that it imposes conditions upon society which are unwelcome to many of its inhabitants, and that one of the responses to the impositions created by industry is a rejection of industry itself, or possibly even worse, a refusal to accept the 'costs' of industrial progress while attempting to retain its 'benefits'. Industrial society theory, on the basis of these assumptions, attaches great significance to investigating the exact requirements of industry and to popular acceptance of and adaptation to the supposed inevitability and desirability of industrial advance.

Ernest Gellner (1972:69) has put the position in the following terms:

> in this one *specific* area I believe that the Real and the Rational do happen to converge. Industrialisation is good, and industrialisation must happen. Industrialisation is good on independent grounds; but it is also good in virtue of being inevitable. To this extent, the present argument is 'historicist', it abjectly prostrates itself before what it holds to be predetermined, a cosmic or at any rate global trend. In those cases (which are rather rare) when some social — or other — development is known with adequate certainty to be inevitable, it is better to adjust oneself to it and learn to like it rather than to condemn it. This pattern of moral reasoning — the recog-

nition of necessity . . . does find application sometimes, and this is one of these times.

Yet, as we shall see, industry has been variously defined, and used to refer to a whole complex of technical, economic and social processes. The ambiguities and problems that this has created become significant because industrial society theory places such a high priority on the investigation of this industrial complex and its social requirements, as *the* major issue facing modern states. The main concerns of this and the next chapter are (i) with the ambiguity of the concept of industry, together with the effects of this ambiguity; and also (ii) with the limitations imposed upon social inquiry through the dominant focus on the 'industrial' character of modern states.

In regard to (i), it may be said that a weakness of past theories of industrial society has been the portrayal of industry, not merely as a set of technical or economic means for achieving socioeconomic goals, but as an autonomous goal inherent in modern societies. In this way, technological and economic change has often been attributed to the action of an independent industrial dynamic — ignoring other complex structural forces that determine which modern technologies are developed and how they will be used. This assumption is not merely due to the evolutionary assumptions of past theories of industrial society but can also be attributed, at least in part, to some of the ambiguity associated with the term 'industry' itself.

A related problem has been the portrayal of industrial development as an all-inclusive and unilinear process universally associated with technological and economic development — the industrial complex constituting (on this view) an integrated 'package' of interdependent processes. The inadequacy of this position can be located on three different levels. Firstly, industrialization has been taken to refer to an all-embracing social process. But the various sociopolitical and economic forms in which industrialization *can* occur have been ignored. Secondly, an attempt has been made to isolate the 'core' technological and economic features of industry as a basis for an empirical examination of their social preconditions and effects. Yet, even within this supposed 'core', there is marked variation, autonomy and substitutability of the different factors, sufficient to undermine attempts to characterize 'its' nature and effects. Thirdly, whatever the difficulties, industrial society theory is centrally concerned with defining the nature and impact of industrial development, with discovering a 'one-dimensional', central, universal process of industrial advance, of increasing technological 'efficiency' and/or economic 'output'. Technological and economic developments are ultimately, therefore, only studied from a particular perspective: the extent to which they constitute an integrated industrial package. The social significance of alternative forms or uses of modern technology are not accorded high priority.

This leads us on to (ii): the limitations imposed upon social inquiry by the adoption of an 'industrial' perspective on modern states. Industrial society theory, through its adoption of this perspective, offers a dual understanding of the fundamental 'reality' of modern civilization. Firstly, the advance of industry is taken as inevitable and/or desirable: to stop it would risk social disaster. Secondly, the social requirements of this advance are defined as the fundamental constraints which modern man has to accept.

In this form industrial society theory corresponds exactly to the positivist programme. Both positivism and industrial society theory are united by the common assumption that the growth and application of science is *the* fundamental reality of the age, and that social theory must concentrate on discovering and implementing the requirements for its further advance. As Gellner (1974a: 20) observes: there is a *'social typology which is immediately implicit in the positivist theory of knowledge and science*. The crucial question for a positivist must be — the understanding of the difference between societies in which positive knowledge can and does flourish and those in which it cannot, and a concern with the transition from the one to the other' (emphasis added).

A number of critics have argued none the less that science and industry are *not* the fundamental realities of the age, that social reality is constituted by something more than merely 'natural' or 'technological' constraints on social action, that the reality includes the power struggles between groups with vested interests in the perpetuation or transcendence of the existing order. These critics contend that industrial society theory has played, and even necessarily plays, an ideological role in justifying existing 'realities' as inevitable and preventing a critical examination and transformation of these 'realities' (Blackburn and Cockburn 1969;

Marcuse 1974). Such criticisms extend from a rejection of claims that modern technologies are the result of a 'neutral' process of technological developments (Dickson 1974) to a critique of the positivist quest for observable 'laws' of social life (Fay 1975). The central political and epistemological claims of industrial society theory about the nature and impact of the industrial complex are therefore fundamentally contentious.

The Concept of Industry

Although the image of industrialism became popular with the publication by Henri de Saint-Simon of the journal *L'Industrie* in 1816, the word 'industry' has a much longer history, reaching back at least to the fifteenth century. From the beginning, it was taken to refer to a particular human quality or attribute. From the eighteenth century, it was also taken to refer to a set of social or economic institutions (Williams 1980). Much of the present confusion over the dynamics of industrial development derives from these conflicting uses of the term.

Understood as a human attribute, industry is equivalent to the modern term 'industriousness' and represents the human ability to apply sustained effort in the execution of a task. 'Industry', therefore, indicates a capacity, one similar in many respects to those advented to by expressions like work, production, labour, toil or endeavour. It is thus opposed to sloth, idleness or play. Unlike labour or toil, however, 'industry' does not emphasize the painful or unpleasant aspects of a task. It draws attention to the useful, satisfying or creative end-product of effort and diligence. Industry refers to both a specific human capacity (perseverence, assiduousness, diligence, sustained effort) and to the specific manner in which that capacity is employed (use of talent and skill, the creation of a useful product). It cannot be understood solely in terms of either of these factors without confusing it with toil, labour or exercise (on the one hand) or a variety of forms of play or creativity (on the other).

By the eighteenth century, as indicated, 'industry' was no longer so clearly associated with work or production in general; it increasingly referred to work involving the use of particular means of production, and therefore to the complex of socioeconomic institutions embodying these means. But what these means themselves involve is not so clear. On the one hand, 'industry' has been conceived as a particular *area of production* — variably identified as non-agricultural, or as manufacture, or as any branch of large-scale, mechanized and rationalized production (including agriculture and services). This has been the source of much dispute in discussions of the differences between industrial and post-industrial society. On the other hand, 'industry' has been conceived as some *means* employed in the process of production — whether it be industrial machinery (large-scale or complex machines driven by inanimate energy) or industrial principles of organization (e.g., specialization, use of scientific 'rational' thought, etc.) plus the total *system of production* (the sum total of elements and activities involved in production).

It has often been assumed that, because a society employs 'industrial' *means* of production, or 'industrial' technology, that it is also engaged in the pursuit, perhaps exclusive pursuit, of uniquely 'industrial' *ends* or principles of organization and production. Many of the post-war theories of industrial society have tended to fall into this error. But it still does not follow, however often assumed, that those societies possessing industrial technology are necessarily driven by an 'industrial' (or industrious) spirit — variously defined as functional rationality, scientific thought, Faustian technic, technocratic ethos, rationalization, Promethean quest, growth mania, the ideology of growth, and so on. Industrial development, attributed to the presence of this industrial ethos and the social structure of modern industrial societies, is also frequently and misleadingly perceived to be the scene of conflict between the demands of industrialism and the partially non-industrial logic of an autonomous political, cultural and class structure.

'Industry', then, may be taken to signal a human attribute or capacity, that of *sustained effort*, whatever the activity. But it may equally (and distinctly) be understood as a result: the *production of useful goods*. If we confound these usages, then 'industry' *qua* sustained effort may be taken to imply an underlying motivation or desire to produce useful goods, while 'industry' *qua* result or product may be taken to include as well the human capacity of 'industriousness'.

These confusions are directly mirrored in the definition of industry as a social institution. The presence of industrial technology or *means of production* is confused with a total *system of pro-*

duction and the definition of industry as the production of a certain type of goods conflicts with the definition of industry as a set of specific means of production. In both cases the ambiguous definition of industry facilitates the making of the further assumption that the industrial system of production is centrally concerned with the development of industrial technology or that the presence of industrial technology ensures the pursuit of increased production as an economic goal.

The definition of industry as a set of means of production presents it as a technical system involving the action of 'industrial' thought in the production, control and development of 'industrial' machinery. The development of this system cannot, however, be attributed to its own internal principles of organization. The type of 'industrial' machinery that is created and the manner of its use are the product of its socioeconomic, as well as its technical, context. The use of 'rational' and 'scientific' thought in deciding how these machines are to be created does not mean that this type of thought is solely responsible for such decisions. 'Rational' thought involves the calculation of efficiency but it cannot dictate the standards according to which such calculations are made (Bauman 1976: 4). It is a socioeconomic or cultural decision to accept market prices, bureaucratic regulations, or even indicators of the control of nature as the standard criteria for such calculations. The widespread use of 'industrial' means of production and the attainment of increasingly higher levels of technological and scientific advance are not simply due to the exigencies of technology or the logic of 'rational' thought.

The type and use of 'industrial' machinery; the direction of 'rational' thought; the criteria for 'rational' calculation; the decision to allow 'industrial' machinery or 'rational' thought to be applied socially or economically; the nature of the economic relationships within which such means of production operate — all these matters cannot be solely attributed to the logic of 'industry' as a technical system. Yet, as industry is also defined as a system of production, this assumption is often implicitly, if not explicitly, made. The confusion between industry as a means of production within production and the system of production within society can result in the unsupported assumption that the dynamics of the industrial system are equivalent to the technical requirements of the developing industrial means of production. However, the industrial means of production constitute a purely technical system that cannot ensure its own development and the industrial system of production is an economic system that cannot be reduced to the principles and requirements of the technical system. The interests and motivations of workers in an industrial system of production are not necessarily in harmony with the technical requirements of an expanding industrial means of production. Even if in harmony, it is not possible to assume that the interests and motivations are industrial in inspiration as well as in effect. The confusion between 'industry' as a technical and as an economic system may attribute a dynamism to the technical system that can only be properly attributed to an economic system and a goal to the economic system that should only be defined as the principle of the technical system.

The use of the term 'industry' to refer to the human quality of industriousness as well as to industrial institutions can also create a number of difficulties. One is the frequent but false assumption that the *motivation* behind 'industrial' activity is 'industriousness' (a concern for efficiency, increased capactiy or increased production for its own sake). A second is the false assumption that criticism of 'industrialism' necessarily involves opposing production or work as such. Modern industrialization may be condemned for its failure to maximize 'useful work'; for the constraints it imposes upon the labour force; or for its ethos of technical neutrality. Yet none of these criticisms is opposed to production or work as such.

The ambiguity of the term 'industry' facilitates the assumption that modern industry not only employs industrial means of production but itself pursues the goal of increased production. This situation requires not only a more precise use of the term 'industry' but also a critical assessment of the value of its continued use. The importance of such a critical analysis is increased by the ideological role that the concept plays. This ideological role, which we shall examine in greater detail later on, has long been recognized. As Jeremy Bentham commented in 1817:

> *Labour* being necessary to the acquisition of *wealth*, and at the same time equally necessary to the preservation of *existence*, thus it is that, disguised under the name of *desire of labour*, the *desire of wealth* has been, in some measure, preserved from the reproach . . . Meantime, as to *labour* . . . considered in the character of an *end*, without any view to anything else, is a sort

of desire that seems scarcely to have place in the human breast; yet if considered in the character of a *means*, scarce a desire can be found, to the gratification of which *labour*, and therein *the desire of labour*, is not continually rendered subservient: hence again it is, that, when abstraction is made of the consideration of the *end*, there scarcely exists a desire, the name of which has been so apt to be employed for *eulogistic purposes*, and thence to contract an *eulogistic signification*, as the appelative that has been employed in bringing to view this *desire of labour*. *Industry* is this appelative: and thus it is, that, under *another* name, the *desire of wealth* has been furnished with a sort of *letter of recommendation*, which, under its *own* name, could not have been given to it. (Clayre 1977: 200–1)

Industry and Technology

There was a major attempt to clarify the nature of industry during the late 1960s and 1970s in reaction to the cruder evolutionary theories of modernization and convergence. The tendency to define industrial development as an all-embracing social process (including the decline of community; the rise of urbanism; the spread of secularism, rationalism and bureaucracy; the process of centralization, equalization and democratization; and the increase in specialization and the division of labour) was rejected in favour of a concern with the 'core' or 'inner' technological and economic structure of industrialization. This 'core' structure was associated with economic indices of *per capita* output, real income per head, value per head of working population, productivity per man hour, value of capital formation, increase in productivity, or simply output (Turner 1975; Baran 1973; Hoselitz and Moore 1963; Rostow 1971a; Galbraith 1970; Kemp 1978; Brown and Harrison 1978).

The 'inner structure' was usually said to include such elements as the use of large-scale complex machinery driven by inanimate power, the development of science, commercial agriculture, factory production and the concentration of the work-force, a complex division of labour, market production, rational calculátion, capital accumulation, an entrepreneurial spirit, an occupationally based stratification system, and so on. Theorists concerned with the fundamental nature of industrial society could, then, examine the extent to which these core features were associated with more general political, cultural and class structures. The basic problem of defining industry appeared, therefore, to be solved. Although, as one critic remarked, '[i]ndustrialism has been defined in almost as many ways as there have been historians and economists who have studied that elusive process' (Laslett 1975: 246), it was accepted that industry was now sufficiently understood to allow the identification of its central technological and economic features.

The adequacy of this conclusion is, however, in some doubt. The dividing line between the 'inner' structure of industry and its 'outer' social forms is not fully clarified through the use of a 'technological' definition. In addition, variations in the complex set of components of production make it difficult to examine the effects of industrial production *per se*. These difficulties are not, of course, insoluble. Yet they do raise the issue of how important the 'core' features of industry are and how useful it is to provide an exact analysis of their social requirements.

The attempt to define industry in technological terms has been undertaken for a number of different reasons. Firstly, it is part of a recognition of the importance of technological or technical classifications in social research. W. G. Runciman has commented that this form of classification is based on the idea that any society or social institution is most usefully classified 'in terms of the specific means peculiar to it' rather than by 'what it does' (Runciman 1971: 37, 39). Raymond Williams (1961: 13–14) stresses the significance of concepts such as 'democracy, industry, and extended communication [which] are all means rather than ends'. The advantage of technological classifications is that the ends or goals of the society are not assumed at the outset but can be investigated in the course of studying the effect of employing or extending specific means or techniques. The definition of technology, in this sense, is extremely broad and is defined by the *Encyclopaedia of the Social Sciences* as any set of 'means for accomplishing recognized purposes'. As Max Weber (1969: 161) commented:

What is concretely to be treated as a 'technology' is thus variable. The ultimate significance of any concrete act may, seen in the context of the total system of action, be of a 'technical' order; that is, it may be significant only as a means in this broader context . . . In this sense there are techniques of every conceivable type of action, techniques of prayer, of asceticism, of thought and research, of administration, of making love, of making war, of musical preferences, of sculpture and particularly, of arriving at legal decisions.

A second assumption of the technological definition of industry is the identification of industry with the *development of technology*, where technology is defined in a more restrictive sense as either (i) techniques employed in order to enhance production or (ii) a specific set of techniques employed for any purpose.

As regards conception (i), David Dickson (1974: 18) refers to those tools man employs 'as a means of changing his material environment'. Ivan Illich (1975) defines as 'tools' those institutions which produce tangible and intangible commodities. Karl Marx (1970: 392) states that '[t]echnology discloses man's mode of dealing with Nature, the process of production by which he sustains life'.

Conception (ii) of technology (specific techniques which may be employed in any sector of society) refers to either material techniques ('hardware') (Ackroyd *et al.* 1977) or to the use of a specific 'means-oriented' form of thought. The distinctive character of technology, in the latter sense, is its embodiment of science, rationalization or mechanicism. Thus, for Galbraith (1974: 31), technology is 'the systematic application of scientific or other organized knowledge to particular tasks'. For Weber, the 'lifeless machine is *petrified spirit*'. Both Weber and Ellul state that the spirit of rationalization which the machine expresses combines 'consciousness' and 'judgement' or 'rationality' and 'rationalism' — that is, conscious control and the evaluation of the consequences of specific means. For Lewis Mumford (1934: 3), the 'machine' is an expression of the 'mechanical mind'; he argues that:

Men had become mechanical before they perfected complicated machines to express their new bent and interest; and the will to order had appeared once more in the monastery and the army and the country house before it finally manifested itself in the factory.

The 'spirit of technology' referred to by these theorists may be regarded as an unequivocal indication of human progress or the source of man's increasing inhumanity, and may be applied to either the construction of material tools or to the fulfilment of social tasks. In either case, the form of thought is the same and consists of four different elements. Firstly, there is an analytical or mechanical reduction of all tasks to their constituent elements. Secondly, each element is assessed in terms of its efficiency in fulfilling a particular function within the whole. Thirdly, the fulfilment of each function is made more efficient through increasing rationalization or mechanization of work or by improving the mechanical components of machines. Fourthly, these elements are then recombined to constitute a more efficient whole. The basic assumption is that 'for practical purposes' each task can be isolated and the different means of performing this task assessed for their relative efficiency with respect to the goal or goals under consideration.

The association of industry with the development of technology may thus refer to the growth of all those means within society which contribute towards increased production; the increase in the size, amount and complexity of the material tools employed in society; or the growth of a 'mechanical' or 'technological' form of thought. The third technological definition of industry, however, limits the concept even further. In this case industry refers to a particular *type of technology* — the use of industrial means for increasing production of the employment of large-scale machinery or mechanical or technological forms of thought for industrial purposes.

The variety of meanings associated with technology helps to explain the ambiguity of 'industry'. Firstly, there is the confusion between the view of industrial technology as (i) any socioeconomic means of increasing production and (ii) the technical and economic preconditions and components of scientifically designed and power driven machinery. If the definition is strictly limited to (ii), then a number of commonly accepted and important features of 'industry' are omitted. As a result there is a tendency for theories of industrial society to extend their definition of the 'core' features beyond this minimal sphere. Yet, such an extension incorporates various sociopolitical or cultural features within the definition of 'industrial technology' (which becomes, explicitly or implicitly, defined in the former sense as any socioeconomic means for increasing production).

An occupationally based stratification system, for example, may not be required for the existence and development of power-driven machinery, yet it is clearly a form of social structure which would facilitate increased production. Such issues become important once an attempt is made to examine the options open to modern society. Future economic developments may, for example, create an increasingly leisured society or produce a degree of material affluence that undermines the importance now attached to increasing production. In this context, the stratification system may become less occupationally based. In fact, the formation of a new stratification system may be a key component of a new social order. Yet speculation on such questions is inhibited by the confusion in industrial society theory between the forms of industrial technology. An occupationally based stratification system is confused with an inevitable 'core' feature of a form of production based on power-driven machinery, and not presented as one component of industrial technology which, whatever its importance, may be replaced or go into decline as production develops.

In one sense the two definitions of industrial technology present two visions of industrial society — one defined by the 'core' features *inevitably* associated with power-driven machinery and the other characterized by the 'core' features which have acted, or are capable of acting, as *important means for increasing production*. These two visions are not the same and it is important that they be kept distinct when examining the options facing modern states.

A second point is that industrial technology may become more important in areas outside production. But can this be represented as 'industrial' development? Are its causes and consequences similar to those influencing technological development within production? Would, for example, an increased concern with the development of communications technology for cultural or democratic ends — in contrast to increased production of consumer goods — constitute a further development of 'industrial society'? This point is not of crucial significance in itself but it does reveal the extent to which visions of industrial society are limited by a view of industry that overemphasizes production (often stressing manufacturing and factory organization). The constraints of industrial society are, thereby, too readily associated with the constraints of a factory-based manufacturing society (Kumar 1978). The ambiguities within the term 'technology' have, therefore, been at least partially responsible for continuing confusion over the exact nature of industry.

Industry and Production

All theorists of industrial society, from Henri de Saint-Simon to Daniel Bell, have associated industry with the development of production. The study of the development, preconditions and consequences of industrial production has been a central focus of study for all those interested in the nature of industrial society. To take the features of industrial production as the 'core' components of industrial society then produces an image of the development of industrial society in terms of the advance of production and the establishment of the social requirements of this process.

What this perspective neglects is the extent to which production is itself composed of different elements which may develop at different rates, be subject to different influences, and have different effects. The focus on the development of production as a universal industrial 'package' ignores the relative autonomy, and choices available, between the various components of production. Both neo-classical and Marxist economists agree that the four main components of production are the producer (labour or labour power), the production resources (land or object of labour), the means of production (capital or instruments of labour) and the product (utilities or useful goods) (Shaw 1978; Samuelson 1976; Lipsey 1976). In the past, different theories have ambiguously focused on a variant of one or other of these elements of production as *the* defining characteristic of 'industry'. Various attempts have been made to define industry in terms of the character of 'industrial man', the nature of 'industrial energy' or 'industrial materials', the structure of 'industrial technology' and the number or type of 'industrial products'.

'Modern man', it has been argued, 'is uniquely industrial man' (Peterson 1973: 1). He may be seen as the source of all industrial production or its creation. In the work of Auguste Comte and Max Weber, the distinctive feature of modern 'industrial society' was its expression of the new spirit of 'scientific' and 'rational' man. Anthony Giddens (1973: 256) defends their view by claiming that 'it is a myth that industrial man was made by the machine, from its origins industrialism is the application of calculative rationality to the productive order'. Other theorists such as Clark Kerr *et al.* approach industrial man from the opposite standpoint. The question they raise is as follows: 'Given the character of science, technology and the requirements inherent in modern methods of production and distribution, what may be deduced as the necessary or the likely characteristics of workers and managers and their interrelations?' (Kerr *et al.* 1973: 43). Industrial man must be recruited, committed, advanced and maintained. In the process he becomes skilled, educated, mobile and specialized. Moreover, he comes to adhere to a set of industrial values including those of scientific and technical knowledge, education, and goods or services. Any taboos against technical change are eliminated and industrial man becomes 'dedicated to hard work, a high pace of work, and a keen sense of individual responsibility for performance of assigned norms and tasks' (Kerr *et al.* 1973: 53). He accepts a culture that upholds the desirability of economic growth and encourages a specific form of rationality (Aron 1967a: 44). The rationality that is developed is 'the adaptation of means to ends. It is the antithesis of superstition and magic. For this history, the relevant ends are production and the acquisition of material wealth' (Landes 1969: 546). Industrial man is therefore uniquely 'industrious' in his rational scientific pursuit of increased production and control over nature. Ernest Gellner (1972: 37) explicitly praises sociology for its investigation of this Industrial Man as 'subjects other than sociology have tended to let these questions go by default, either by naively treating industrial man as a kind of universal man . . . or by ignoring the relevant characteristics altogether.'

The extensive use of inanimate energy within production is also taken to be a central characteristic of modern industry. As a result a number of theories of industrial society have taken the level of energy consumption as an indicator of the level of industrialization (Inkeles 1960–61: 1–5). As W. E. Moore (1973: 41) claims: 'Industrialization means the extensive use of inanimate sources of power for economic production, and all that entails by way of organization, transportation, communication, and so on.' The importance attributed to industrial energy or materials is revealed in the frequency with which the modern period has been described as the age of steam or, more recently, the nuclear age (Richards and Hunt 1973: ix). Lewis Mumford (1934) divides history into three periods distinguished by the use of hydraulic energy (until 1750), coal (1750–1880) and electricity (from 1880).

Industrial technology may, as we have seen, be variously defined. Within economic production it can refer to both the material instruments of production and the organization involved in putting these instruments to work. As a form of 'social technology', industrial technology is represented in the differentiation and integration of production tasks within large-scale organizations. With the large increase in service industry and mass production, the nature and requirements of such large-scale organization takes on great significance. Thus, for Peter Drucker (1951: xv),

> 'Industry' once meant any organization of human work. It was only during the eighteenth and nineteenth centuries, the era of the First Industrial Revolution that the term was renamed to mean 'manufacture'. With the Second Industrial Revolution, the revolution of mass production, 'industry' again reverts to its earlier meaning.

As a form of material 'hardware', industrial technology refers to the use of complex machines driven by inanimate energy. Thus, according to Stanislav Andreski (1964b: 303–4), an industrial society is one which 'subsists on the products of big and complicated machines'. Continuing this emphasis, writers have defined the first and second industrial revolutions in terms of the replacement of, first, the human hand and, then, the human brain, by the machine (Weiner 1968). Marx also emphasized the important stages of development of the motor mechanism, the transmitting mechanism, and the tool or working machine in the spread of mechanization (Marx 1970a).

The nature or amount of industrial products has also been employed as a common definition of industrial production and used as a means for assessing levels of industrialization. For Walter Rostow the crucial factor in the development of industrial society as the rate of reinvestment, that is, the percentage of products created for the reproduction and growth of the existing level of production rather than being used for consumption or hoarded as savings (Rostow 1971a). A more common indicator of industry is taken to be the level of *per capita* income.

The definition of industrial production may refer to any of these elements of production. Such variations may frequently be found within the work of one theorist. Raymond Aron defines industrial societies by the scientific character of industrial man:

> I am taking the word 'industry' in a broad, not a narrow sense, to include any kind of collective effort transformed by the application of scientific method or the scientific spirit . . . the indispensable precondition of all the other features usually attributed to modern societies (Aron 1967: 98–9).

Industrial energy is also used by Aron as *the* defining characteristic of industrial societies:

> The energy available in societies determines the limits within which they can vary . . . Modern societies seem to belong to a completely new type, precisely because of their energy potential (Aron 1967a: 79).

At another point Aron emphasizes the centrality of industrial products:

> the major fact, which is found in Soviet industrial societies as in Western industrial societies, is the growth in productivity, the increased value produced by the whole collectivity and by each individual within it. This major fact brings us to another . . . the changes in the size of the population (Aron 1967a: 41).

Later on industrial society is defined by Aron in terms of industrial technology for

> what concerns scientific research and sociological analysis is the degree of diversity among societies which have similar technological equipment (Aron 1967a: 73).

It is not surprising therefore that Aron also defines the industrial type of society by

> a number of characteristics found in a more or less marked form in all modern societies: a predominant concern with production and productivity, a desire for growth, a changed distribution of labour, increasingly systematic application of science to technology and of technology in production, etc. (Aron 1967a: 4).

The definition of industry in terms of the development of production may refer to a variant of any or all of the different factors of production. All too often, these different factors are assumed to constitute a coherent whole, each depending upon and leading to the others. Yet not only may the development or decline of different factors occur in relative autonomy from the others, a number of critics have argued that they have done so and, moreover, come directly into conflict with each other, in a manner that is now of crucial significance for the future of modern societies.

Conclusion

In conjunction, the ambiguities in the concept of industry create a series of problems for the investigation and understanding of 'industrial' societies. The concept's conflation of a number of techno-economic factors within one broad category makes it difficult to use the concept in a discriminatory fashion while investigating the problems and contradictions within contemporary production. The lack of precision in distinguishing between the components, requirements and effects of industry often renders discussion of these 'effects' tautologous, overly deterministic, or fundamentally ambiguous. In large degree, these ambiguities are related to the complex history and shifting meanings of the concept of industry. This lack of clarity, and the tendency for the ambiguity of the concept to suggest that 'industrial' techno-economic processes have an autonomous logic of development, seriously bring into question the continued usefulness of the concept.

7 ONE-DIMENSIONAL PRODUCTION

Despite its ambiguities, the concept of industry has been widely employed to examine the social effects of increased production and economic development. This examination has assumed, however, that production can be adequately defined in terms of a unilinear process of industrial development and that the major concern of social analysis is to investigate the social consequences of this 'one-dimensional' process. These assumptions impose undesirable restrictions upon the social imagination. The aim of this chapter is to draw attention to the difficuities this creates, firstly, the existence of contradictions *within* the multifaceted processes of industrial production and their important consequences and, secondly, the significance of the political structures and cultural ideals which direct and guide these processes.

Contradictions of Industrialism

A number of critics have directly attributed the problems of modern industrialism to the fact that '[i]ndustrialism may . . . be driving itself, and the societies subject to it, into an impasse' (Kumar 1978: 299). The most obvious tendency is for the development of industrial technology and industrial products to undermine industrial men, and the supply of industrial energy and industrial materials.

The skill, health, motivation and number of industrial men is crucial for the development of industry. Yet, as Krishan Kumar (1978: 266) argues,

> the most important of the industrial society's resources — as of any kind of society — are its human ones: whether of human skills, imagination, effort, commitment or sacrifice. It is these resources however that have been most impoverished and stunted in the course of industrial development.

Human skill, autonomy, rationality and responsibility have been undermined by subservience to large-scale technology and its accompanying bureaucratic social 'machine'. The degree of autonomous responsibility and provision for human needs has declined as the industrial provision of goods and services extends into more areas of social and economic life. Human experience in the industrial work-place offers little hope for developing the individual's capacity for autonomous judgement, independent skills or even interest in the work assigned. The individual becomes, in some ways, similar to C. Wright Mills's 'cheerful robot' who 'is "with" rationality but without reason, who is increasingly self-rationalized and also increasingly uneasy.' (Mills 1975: 187) The problems of regulating large-scale organizations staffed by such employees often produce increasingly apparent 'diseconomies of scale'.

The dangerous consequences of industrial energy appear in the pollution of air, water and land from the use of fossil fuels and nuclear power (Ward 1979; Gribbin 1979). The increasing number of industrial products include advances in medicine, hygiene and food. These have helped create a larger population whose expansion has resulted in urban congestion and potential problems of food supply. Such industrial advances have themselves served to undermine health through the unknown side effects of the large-scale institutional dispensation of drugs and the environmental consequences of urban congestion. Noise, waste, crowding and pollution have all become common aspects of the modern urban environment.

The development of large-scale industrial organization has fragmented and bureaucratized working conditions, within professional as well as manual strata, and facilitated an increasingly 'instrumental' attitude to work. The absence of intrinsic motivation, accompanied by the difficulty of supervision within large-scale organizations, poses the problem of ensuring an efficient and disciplined industrial work-force. For Clark Kerr *et al.*, the problem of motivation is attributed to the conflict between the discipline required by large-scale organizations and the desire for personal autonomy encouraged by the increasing education necessitated by industrial development.

This gives rise to a central problem in industrialism: society requries more discipline to go along with the greater interdependence that the new technology brings, but the more highly educated labour force wants more freedom for spontaneous individual action, within the work environment as well as outside it (Kerr *et al.* 1973: 303).

The 'handmaiden of industrialism' then becomes its grave-digger. The motivation of industrial man is weakened by the increasingly apparent 'diseconomies' of industrial growth. As the GNP is revealed to be an inadequate indicator of social progress, the legitimacy of the industrial order declines as 'increasing rates of consumption are supposed to compensate for the frustrations experienced in other domains of social life' (Leiss 1978: 6). The various discussions of the 'diseconomies' of growth, the gross national 'disproduct' and the rising number of 'discommodities' are an indication of an increasing concern with this darker side of industrialism (Scitovsky 1976: 8; Berle 1975; Hodgson 1972).

As social crowding, congestion and environmental pollution have offset many of the advantages of economic growth, there has been an increased recognition of four sets of problems involved in the identification of economic growth with economic development or social progress.

Firstly, there is no simple equation between market price and social cost. The costs imposed upon the community by various forms of production are not necessarily incorporated in the market price, for example, unhealthy work, environmental pollution, resource depletion, and so on (Mishan 1969).

Secondly, consumer products may not be 'final' goods but, rather, 'intermediate' goods purchased for 'defensive' purposes (Mishan 1969; Scitovsky 1976; Hirsch 1977). Some goods are purchased to obtain some 'defence' from the social and economic consequences of increased production, for example, air fresheners to combat industrial smell. Also, some goods may be 'positional' in character, that is to say, the satisfaction they provide depends upon the activities and purchases of others or on the relative position that they give to the consumer. Examples of such goods may be the motor car, suburban living, tourism, education. In all these cases, increased consumption confers benefits only if other consumers do not purchase the same goods. As a result, increasing rates of growth may provide little or no positive advantage but merely represent a defensive attempt to preserve certain benefits.

Another feature of the 'defensive' character of many modern goods has been outlined by Tibor Scitovsky (1976) in his argument that mass production has been directed towards the production of standardized goods suitable for enhancing the 'comforts' of the population, that is, concentrating on the avoidance of pain and inconvenience (including the perpetuation of addictive habits and relief from status insecurities). The concern with the saving of time and effort, or the avoidance of discomfort, has therefore become dominant at the expense of the active pursuit of novelty, stimulation and positive pleasure. These advantages are probably most enhanced by skilled consumption, stimulating human inter-action, and the use of the imagination — benefits that do not easily fit in with present forms of mass production.

Thirdly, the amount and type of goods produced are often tailored to the needs of the production system in a way that undermines the benefits to the consumer. A variety of examples are cited in Vance Packard's studies of 'planned obsolescence', John Kenneth Galbraith's studies of the advance planning and market creation activities of the large industrial corporation, and Ivan Illich's critique of the 'radical monopoly' of products created by large-scale institutional organizations interested in their own self-perpetuation and expansion (Packard 1964; Galbraith 1974; Illich 1976).

Finally, the point has been made that the pursuit of increased growth has, firstly, left the consumer unable to judge the true benefits and satisfactions of the increasingly numerous and fast changing commodities with which he or she is faced, and, sec-ondly, has resulted in a neglect of the need to understand and control our own wants or 'social nature' which, ultimately, determines how satisfying our purchases will be (Leiss 1978).

As the development of industrial technology, industrial energy and industrial products may undermine the capacity and motivation of industrial man, so also the increase in industrial technology and products may undermine the resources of indus-trial energy and materials. An increasing amount of energy and materials are required to fuel the growth of industrial technology and provide the materials for its products. The exponential growth in the use of these resources, combined with the increasing cost of their extraction, is seen by a number of writers as the major problem facing modern industrial societies (Gribbin 1979). The continued viability of the 'age of steam and coal' is brought into question when the cheap supply of primary resources can no longer be assumed. Similarly, the more recent age of alloys, electricity, and nuclear energy creates its own scarcities, high costs and health hazards.

The growing recognition of such problems in industrial production provides an important illustration of the general point that the different elements of industrial production may have their own logic and effects. In order fully to discuss the growth and development of modern technologies and forms of economic growth, and their effect on society, it is necessary not merely to examine the development or decline of 'industrial production' but to study the separate development of different elements or sectors of society. One commentator made this point in a critique of theories focusing on the deterministic role of industrial development. Social stratification, she argued, is influenced by

(a) variation in the distribution of natural resources, and the position in the international division of labour that follows from this; (b) historical factors; which industries are the most established, and what technology is employed, depend in part upon the time at which a country began its industrialisation. For both these reasons, the industry mix can vary from one country to another even at similar 'levels' of development, and this has implications for the system of stratification (Platt 1964: 139).

The focus on industrial development *per se*, therefore, creates two sets of problems. Firstly it presents as the necessary consequence of industrial development what may only be the result of a particular 'industrial mix'. As a number of social scientists have pointed out, the comparative investigation of societies requires the use of classification criteria which are clearly defined, measurable and relatively persistent (Durkheim 1964a; Smelser 1976). The ambiguity and variation within industrial production greatly weakens its usefulness as a basic classification of the 'core' features of modern states. Secondly, it does not allow, what may be a crucially significant area of concern, the examination of the nature, cause and effects of particular forms or uses of components of the industrial complex. As one proponent of the industrial society model has admitted:

Making industrialization equivalent to economic development runs some risks . . . particularly for somewhat fine grained analysis of the components of economic growth. Even if the structural integration of economic systems were greater than can be empirically confirmed, the order and rate of change of one or another component in a wide range of 'economic factors' would still have significant consequences (Moore 1967: 34).

The utility of focusing on industrial production as the 'core' feature of modern societies is therefore brought into question. Yet it is not impossible for theories of industrial society to recognize the variation and conflict that obtains between the components of industrial production. However, to the extent that 'industry' remains *the* major fact and commitment within modern societies — which is the central assumption of industrial society theory — these variants and conflicts are only examined from a particular perspective, to do with the *extent* to which a process of unilinear industrial development still exists despite such variations and the *extent* to which these variants, or conflicts, undermine the further development of industrialism and the social conditions upon which it depends. This fundamental commitment to and focus upon industry, which is reflected in industrial society theory, has been directly challenged by a number of critics who have drawn attention to the ideological character of such theory.

Industry and Ideology

Over the last decade and a half there has been an increasing reaction against theories of industrial society that either exaggerate the degree to which societies are determined by the 'imperatives' of technology or accept economic growth and technological development as the unquestioned social priority or goal of modern states. Within sociology this has been expressed in critiques of 'technocratic historicism' (Goldthorpe 1971), the 'image of industrialism' (Kumar 1978), and the 'theory of industrial society' (Giddens 1977b). In more popularized works it has taken the form of critiques of 'scientism' (Roszak 1973), 'consciousness II' (Reich 1974), the 'ideology of industrialization' (Dickson 1974) and 'technocratic consciousness' (Roszak 1973).

Within social theory the critical reaction against such 'technocratic' forms of thought derives from a number of different sources — including the writings of 'neo-Weberians' and political philosophers; proponents of 'alternative technology' and exponents of the 'limits to growth'; and various forms of 'humanistic' and 'scientific' Marxism (Berlin 1967; Wolin 1961; Lukes 1978; Dickson 1974; Illich 1975; Althusser and Balibar 1975; Horkheimer 1974, 1976). Such writers have provided a sustained critique of an industrial society theory based upon such assumptions as: that the development of industry is the major fact of modern societies; and that the fundamental problems of modern societies are caused by failing to adapt to the requirements of the transition and by failing to recognize that industrial development is both the means and the end of all major future social and political transformations.

For industrial society theory, the main role of social and political theory is to discover the requirements of an orderly and efficient industrial society; to promote piecemeal institutional reforms and sectional distributional changes which enhance the efficiency of the industrial system; and to criticize those opposed theories of modern society which (inadvertantly or otherwise) threaten to undermine the stability and progress of industrial society.

Opponents of industrial society theory have rejected the idea that the development of industry is *the* major fact of modern states. The central issue facing modern societies is defined as *political action* in the pursuit of *non-technocratic* political and social ideals. The problems of modern society are not, therefore, attributed to the failure to recognize the inevitability, social requirements and desirability of industrial development. The main concern is either with those problems created by the existing *form* of industrial development or with the social problems or possibilities that are ignored or actively suppressed by a concern with industrial development and the adaptation of society to its requirements.

This opposition includes much criticism of the tendency of industrial society theory to interpret industrial development (together with its impact on society), as a unilinear process. Neo-Weberians have reacted against the evolutionary and historicist interpretation of industrial development as an autonomous and inevitable process. Anthony Giddens (1976) and John Goldthorpe (1971) have stressed the uneven character of social change, the importance of international relations in affecting 'endogenous' developments, the place of 'critical phases' of change, the 'leapfrog' character of many social developments and, in general, the role of human agency, political action and the plurality of social conditions in determining the course of change.

Proponents of 'alternative technology', and of 'limits to growth', have directly challenged the assumption that industry develops as an autonomous 'neutral' force to which society is forced to adapt. They reveal, on the contrary, the extent to which industrial development is the product of political and socioeconomic forces — which not only determine how technology is *used* but also decide the *form* that technological development takes. As David Dickson (1974: 10–11) argues, 'one can only understand the nature of the technology developed in any soceity by relating it to the patterns of production, consumption and the general social activity that maintain the interests of the politically dominant section of that society'. Although differing conceptions are offered of the 'politically dominant section', the general approach is the same. Industrial society theory is condemned, not only for justifying existing forms of domination as the 'requirements' of modern technology, but for neglecting the extent to which the form taken by industrial development is itself at least partially the product of existing socioeconomic and political relationships.

Finally, both 'humanist' and 'structuralist' forms of Marxism have condemned the ideological character of industrial society theory as obscuring the role of class relations and class conflict in both determining the form and use of industrial technology and directing the course of social change. As Richard Scase (1977b: 24) remarks, 'giving primary emphasis to the "constraints" of technology and industrialism is to detract from the consideration of more important problems . . . patterns of domination and control'.

These criticisms, however, are primarily directed at particular interpretations of industrial development and its social impact, not at the decision to focus on industrialism *per se*. Most attention is paid to interpretations of the evolution of industrial development, to the presentation of technological advance as a 'neutral' process, and to the exaggeration of industry's impact on society, and so on. Yet some critiques challenge the initial decision to assign priority to 'industry' itself as part of a supposedly objective understanding of the fundamental 'realities' of modern society. The dispute over industrial society theory then extends to a fundamental concern with the nature of social 'reality' and the role of social science, as well as with the distinctive character of modern societies.

Take the different conceptions of the fundamental 'realities' of the age.For industrial society theory, the inequality, alienation and anomie attendant upon the development of industry are the necessary price to be paid for industrial progress. Industrial societies, it is argued, are forced to adapt their structures to the requirements of industrial production. This involves, in many cases, accepting forms of social organization which are actively opposed by large numbers and from various quarters. There are metaphysical appeals for equality, liberty and freedom of thought; romantic attacks upon the depersonalization and alienation of mass society; socialist protest against capitalist exploitation. But metaphysics, romanticism and socialism are all rejected for their inability to come to terms with industrial realities or to accept the 'strain of civilization' accompanying the rise of industrialism's 'ironic cultures'. (Popper 1974; Gellner 1974b). A variety of different critics regard these claims of industrial society theory as an ideological justification of existing social realities, while its proponents suppose that it reflects a realistic awareness of the requirements of modern society.

Industrial Positivism and its Critics

This dispute between industrial society theorists and a number of their critics over the 'realities of the age' is directly related to controversies over 'positivist' definitions of social reality itself. Discussions of positivism are dogged, of course, by the ambiguity of the term. Anthony Giddens (1977b: 29) appropriately remarks that '[p]ositivism has become more a term of abuse than a technical term of philosophy'. Two recent reviews of positivism have shown, respectively, that positivism has at least four separate components that are not necessarily linked (Keat 1981) and has taken at least twelve different forms (Halfpenny 1983). But the present concern is not with the positivist tradition in its entirety. It is, more narrowly, with the scientific and industrial positivism reflected in industrial society theory. The work of the Frankfurt School provides an important, if at times ambiguous and confusing, critical approach to this form of industrial positivism.

Both proponents and critics of industrial society theory have recognized, indeed emphasized, the close conceptual links between the tradition of thought on industrial society and a general positivist belief in the power and value of scientific knowledge (Habermas 1974: 47; Gellner 1972). As Gellner (1972: 179) remarks:

Industrial society is not merely one containing 'industry', large-scale production units capable of supplying man's material needs in a way which can eliminate poverty: it is also a society in which knowledge plays a part wholly different from that which it played in earlier social forms, and which indeed possesses a quite different type of knowledge. Modern science is inconceivable outside an industrial society: but modern industrial society is equally inconceivable without modern science. Roughly, science is the mode of cognition of industrial society, and industry is the ecology of science.

This connection is, on the one hand, due to the direct link between the development of the natural sciences and its application in the form of industrial production. Industrial society theory is centrally concerned with the novelty and power of science and the social consequences of its industrial application. This is, for industrial society theory, the primary reality of the modern age. On the other hand, industrial society theory has attributed a more general social and intellectual value to scientific knowledge. Science is given priority not only as the underlying force behind industrial development but also as the only reliable and valuable source of true knowledge and as the major intellectual component in both the organization of industrial society and the protection of the social benefits that this society provides. Science provides insights into the necessary social requirements of industrial development, the forms of thought and judgement required to regulate a complex industrial society, and the 'trends' or 'laws' of industrial society which require societal adaptation. In this way, science is not just the fundamental reality of modern society — it also discloses those realities of modern society to which the population has to adapt.

Although the positivism of Saint-Simon and Comte cannot, in its developed form, be attributed to the more recent exponents of industrial society theory, there has been no abandonment of the assumption that the growth and application of science is the fundamental feature of modern societies and is practically equivalent to the development of reason (Gellner 1972; Frisby 1976; Popper 1969b).

Three common and persistent themes are to be noted. The first involves some version of Comte's Law of the Three Stages, where the fundamental development in both knowledge and society is viewed as consisting in the transition from theology (through philosophy) to science, with the result that the re-emergence of any form of metaphysical social thought is ultimately regarded as a relapse towards theology. The second common theme involves some conception of a hierarchy of the sciences, where the social sciences lag behind the natural sciences, constituting one of the major problems of modern industrial societies. The third theme involves a view of philosophy as an activity subordinate to science (science being progressive and industrially productive), but an activity none the less of fundamental political and social significance. (It reveals the advantages and requirements of science and the absurdities and dangers of alternative philosophies unable to face the 'strain of civilization' or the imperatives of 'ironic cultures'.)

In opposition to this 'positive' identification of science with reason, of industrial society with progress, there stands the alternative tradition of 'negative' philosophy. (In the work of the Frankfurt School and its followers it is referred to as 'critical' philosophy.) This strand of thought was developed most elaborately in post-seventeenth-century Germany in the form of the Hegelian and Marxian reformulations of the *Geisteswissenschaften* tradition, itself related in various ways to German romanticism, hermeneutics, historicism and expressivism (Manuel 1965, 1971; Bauman 1978; Horkheimer 1972; Taylor 1978a, 1978b). This tradition — despite internal differences — provides a conception of reason, and hence of reality and progress, which opposes that of industrial society theory. It identifies reason with a non-scientific capacity to reveal the basic nature of man, society and the material world. It identifies progress with the discovery and expression of this rational kernel rather than with the mere development of science, industry and their social consequences (Marcuse 1977).

For 'positivist' theories of industrial society, industrialism is the 'fact' of fundamental significance, representing the establishment of true knowledge and the use of that knowledge to control both nature and society. This 'true' knowledge, this 'realistic' understanding of the world, is equated with 'technical' knowledge, which alone is conceived as the vehicle of social progress, capable of enhancing our capacity to satisfy human wants and needs. For the anti-positivists, by contrast, progress cannot be identified with the advance of 'technical' knowledge. For technology has its own costs; obsession with technology imposes its own constraints; and technology may be employed by groups or societies in ways which do not genuinely improve the human condition. Scientific and technical development, while not necessarily ignored, are placed in a subordinate position to the dynamics of human self-realization, alienation and self-development — whether this takes the form of the development of Hegel's *Geist* (Hegel 1980), the overcoming of human alienation through class conflict and social transformation (as Marx and Engels (1970) suggest), or the establishment of what Illich (1975) sees as a more convivial society after the destruction of the radical monopoly of existing institutional structures.

To rely on science and technology, and make their development the primary 'fact' of modern life, is taken to neglect the fact that they are produced by humans and that their advantages depend upon the manner in which they are developed and used. The *fundamental* reality, by implication, is not science and industry, but the level of mankind's self-awareness and self-expression. This general philosophical approach underlies the more specific critiques of those theories which portray technology as 'neutral' and which take insufficient account of its ill effects. It challenges not only the exaggerated views of the importance or value of scientific-industrial development but also the basic assumption that scientific-industrial advance is the *fundamental* 'reality' of modern civilization.

Industrial society theory is burdened by the 'positivist' assumption that the main concern of social theory is to discover the necessary structure of social order and the 'laws' of change to which society must adapt. This approach takes its most extreme form in the work of Comte (1974) and Durkheim (1964a, 1964b). But the common features of this positivism still consist in the concern with (i) the constraints imposed upon human action by the necessary requirements of industrial order; (ii) the social conditions that have to be fulfilled in order to retain or further develop present advantages, most notably the advance of science, its industrial application, and, most recently, the preservation of liberal freedoms sometimes associated with this advance; and (iii) the most probable course of social development as revealed in the apparently irreversible and relatively unmodifiable trends to which some form of adaptation is required (Gellner 1972, 1974a, 1974b; Popper 1969a, 1969b, 1974; Bell 1976; Fay 1975).

This tradition of thought is also continued in the attempt to manipulate and control industrial society through the use of social laws that are constituted by observed correlations between social phenomena and then verified or falsified against further empirical data. Explanation is, thereby, identified with prediction, and social or political action with the manipulation of the conditions under which these laws operate (Fay 1975). This approach has been challenged by critics of positivism, most notably by members of the Frankfurt School, for (i) failing to locate the source of such laws in the purposes, intentions, desires and information of the actors whose actions resulted in the observed patterns of behaviour; and (ii) neglecting the fundamental or basic institutions in society which gave rise to such regularities (Horkheimer 1972).

Industrial society theory, by conceiving of these 'laws' and 'constraints' as *reality*, ultimately adopts a conservative stance towards *existing reality*. The critique of this approach by proponents of negative philosophy is not based on a denial that constraints exist, but, rather, challenges the status that is given to this 'existence'. In the case of the Frankfurt School, the fundamental 'reality' is understood in terms of a dynamic tension between the existing social reality, constructed intentionally or unintentionally by men in the pursuit of their ends, and the development of mankind's desires and potential as these come into conflict with present realities. To base an analysis of modern society on the existing 'facts' of social structure or on the present set of reified social practices (defined as 'reality') is not sufficient. The focus on the 'constraints' imposed by industry and the 'laws' of industrial life neglects to examine the source of existing forms of industry or the human intentions, desires and institutional structures that have been responsible for such 'laws'. Industrial society theory, adopting a passive attitude towards reality, is in part responsible for this 'reality': the theory plays a specifically conservative role by legitimating the existing order as the 'realm of necessity'. If the scientific study of social 'constraints' or 'laws' is defined as the *only* form of knowledge about society, or if the study of the necessary requirements of industry is characterized as *the* fundamental issue of the age, it follows that critical analysis of the dynamics of class conflict, for example, is denied major significance.

The conservatism of the positivist approach has been attributed to a number of factors including: (i) identifying the expert choice of means as a neutral decision; (ii) searching for factual con-

firmation or falsification of laws at the expense of a critical ex-
amination of the ideological function of the concepts in terms of
which these laws are expressed; (iii) tending to identify the better
theory with the one that has more, or the most, factual support;
(iv) denying the possibility of rational reflection on social and
political ends rather than means; and (v) identifying reason and
knowledge with the discovery of existing trends or laws rather than
with critical reflection upon their repression of human potential,
and the attempt to transform society in accordance with this
potential (Bauman 1976b; Benton 1977: 45; Fay 1975: 60; Marcuse
1972: 13, 15).

Such critiques of positivism have been as varied as the de-
finitions of positivism itself. However, the Frankfurt School, in
particular, is consistently united in reaction against the con-
servative nature of positivism's *denial of the status of reason to the
activity of reflection*. As Habermas (1978:7) remarked: 'That we
disavow reflection *is* positivism'. From Horkheimer to Habermas,
'traditional theory', 'positive philosophy' and the 'empirical-analy-
tic '/'historical-hermeneutic' sciences have all been condemned for
their failure to regard reflection upon the *human source and value
of existing social reality and methods of gaining knowledge about
reality* as anything other than a meaningless or irrational activity.

Within epistemological discourse positivism has been
criticized for its stress upon revealing the 'facts' of social life (to
the neglect of investigating the source of these 'facts' and critically
assessing their rationality or human value); the failure to recognize
that science is merely one form of human knowledge based on an
interest in technical control (and that an understanding of the
foundations of the scientific enterprise and an assessment of its
value requires a different form of knowledge); and the refusal to
accept that the development of knowledge can occur through
human self-reflection and self-expression in a manner that cannot
be guided by scientific methods of investigation or verified through
scientific canons of evidence (McCarthy 1978; Held 1980).

Positivism has thus been condemned for attributing central
value to the rise and application of science. Industrial society
theory has consequently been criticized as the political programme
linked to this positivist epistemology. Through the acceptance of
the inevitability and desirability of scientific and industrial pro-
gress, industrial society theory has been charged with failing to
examine the status and value of these technical developments.

Industrial society theory ultimately bases its analysis on an acceptance (rather than a critical assessment) of the 'facts' of industrial life. It informs political action through the discovery of the 'laws' and probable 'trends' within industrial society and the necessary forms of societal adaptation in order to ensure the continued orderly progress of industry (rather than aiding the process of critical self-reflection and self-expression by the populace in opposition to the constraining 'laws' of present industrial life).

Industrial society theorists may accept that industry is limited in the extent to which it determines the character of modern society, that industry is not necessarily progressive, that science cannot reveal universal 'laws' of social life, and so on. But despite these qualifications, by accepting scientific-industrial development and its social impact as *the* major reality of the modern age, industrial society theorists ultimately base the value of the social scientific enterprise on developments in external constraints that technical development imposes. In the final analysis, their primary concern is not with technological development as a human project and with the subordination of technical developments to human self-realization and self-expression. In this sense their practical understanding of the fundamental realities of the age conforms exactly to the positivist programme.

Conclusion

The focus on the industrial complex and its social impact clearly creates a number of problems for industrial society theory. It employs the term 'industry' in such a way as to imply that techno-economic development is somehow autonomous or self-propelled. It characterizes the technological and economic features of the industrial complex as the 'core' features of modern society. Yet it is unclear to what extent these features include elements of social structure. Equally disturbing, the 'core' features identified incorporate a number of relatively distinct and potentially contradictory components. Finally, the focus on the industrial complex and its social impact severely restricts sociology's approach to social reality and the fundamental realities of modern society. To the extent that the positivist approach excludes alternatives, it plays an ideological role and is unjustified in its claims to objectivity and neutrality.

It may be possible to 'save' the industrial society pigeon-hole by clarifying the concept of industry and consistently recognizing the limited and value-laden perspective that it imposes on the study of modern society. Yet such an enterprise still has a number of obstacles to overcome. Firstly, the term 'industry' is understood in the academic and in the popular mind in ways not easily altered. Secondly, industrial society theory has been part of a social philosophy of modern civilization that subordinates or excludes examination of such difficult and important issues as the structure and development of the forces that direct and shape technological advance and economic growth. In view of this, to expend yet more time and effort re-examining and re-establishing the exact nature of the industrial society category may not be worthwhile. Thirdly, in many cases the variegated interests subsumed under the industrial society concept can be expressed more precisely in terms of 'affluent', 'complex', 'scientific', 'mechanized', 'large-scale', 'manufacturing', etc., societies. To use these more precise terms has the advantage of directing attention to particular matters of immediate relevance and interest.

8 INDUSTRY AND PROGRESS

In *The Sociology of Progress*, Sklar aptly observes that 'the idea of progress and the idea of sociology were mutually reinforcing aspects of the movement in thought of the last four hundred years' (Sklar 1970:xi). Although many of the 'founding fathers' of sociology recognized some of the darker undercurrents of industrialism (Nisbet 1967: 266–70), it was widely believed that the new age would be superior to all previous ones. Faith in industry as the key component of social progress has continued into the present. As Sklar (1974: 87) comments in another context: 'The general belief that industrial development will bring happiness and an end to misery in the world, is probably the most successful form in which we currently find the ideology of innovational progress expressed.' Industrial society theory obtains much of its inspiration, and justification, from the widespread acceptance of this belief.

Yet, in recent years, the exponents of industrial society theory have often qualified the importance attached to industry by earlier theorists. In an attempt to justify a more 'critical' theory of industrial society free from the evolutionary and positivist excesses of much nineteenth-century social philosophy, Raymond Aron (1967a, 1967b), in particular, has asserted that industrial growth cannot be identified with social progress, that different industrial societies may vary according to their 'industrial mix', and that an industrial form of production is compatible with a number of alternative political and economic systems. However, such concessions to the critics of the theory of industrial society are only made at a cost — that of undermining many of the original justifications for the industrial society concept. The classification and comparative study of societies has been indissolubly linked to perspectives on social progress.

Comparative Sociology and Social Development

A brief examination of recent reviews of comparative sociology reveals the diversity of purposes for which this form of investigation

134

has been employed. It has been concerned, for instance, with change within institutions and changes of institutions, the explanation of particular historical events, and generalizations about general types of society and institutions (Ogburn and Nimkoff 1966; Fletcher 1971, 1981). To emphasize this diversity is, however, to neglect the central role that has been attached and, in many ways, continues to be attached to investigating the course of social development.

Whether or not this development is seen as part of a universal process of evolution or progress, it still involves a preoccupation with the overall structure and development of the modern type of society and, more than this, with the problematic consequences and progressive possibilities brought about by this development.

In comparative sociology, the establishment of types is undertaken to reveal the fundamental structural features, the key dynamics and the main problems and possibilities of the modern type of society. In the investigation of the social characteristics of modern societies, interest is focused, as Morris Ginsberg (1961a: 203) remarked of Hobhouse's work, on 'the light the correlations might throw on development'. It is this underlying interest that inspired the comparative investigations of such 'founding fathers' of sociology as Comte, Spencer, Marx, Durkheim and Weber. It was believed that, through an understanding of the fundamental course of development of modern societies, it would be possible to adapt to, speed up, or control its advance. Although all these writers reflected on the nature of social science, the general character of society, and the social problems and disorders resulting from what are now commonly called the French and Industrial Revolutions, it was this preoccupation with the forms of *persistence, change* and *development* of modern society that gave an overriding unity to their work (Fletcher 1971; Bottomore 1960).

While it has frequently been recognized that this concern with the overall structure and development of modern societies has been one of the main preoccupations of comparative sociology, there has been sharp dispute over its *value*. For some comparative sociology remains the primary aim and promise of sociological thought. According to C. Wright Mills (1975: 13), the first aim of the 'sociological imagination' is to ask,

What is the structure of this particular society as a whole? What are its essential components, and how are they related to one

another? How does it differ from othe varieties of social order?
Within it, what is the meaning of any particular feature for its
continuance and change.

The examination of any specific sector of society is, thereby,
concerned to ask: 'How does any particular feature we are ex-
amining affect, and how is it affected by, the historical period in
which it moves?' (Mills 1975:13)

E. H. Carr (1975: 66) similarly agrees that

Sociology if it is to become a fruitful field of study, must, like
history, concern itself with the relation between the unique and
the general . . . it must become dynamic — a study not of
society at rest (for no such society exists), but of social change
and development.

Although Raymond Aron (1967a: 22) sees this as the concern of
sociology in contrast to history, he makes the same point: that the

aim is to pick out recurrent phenomena, to interpret social
phenomena by means of general categories, and ultimately to
discover laws. Now this attempt to generalise brings us back to
the proper subject of sociology, the comparison between
societies . . .

Mills, Carr and Aron all agree on the danger of neglecting these
issues. Without constant reference to this concern, sociology risks
degenerating into a philosophy of history that imposes a 'trans-
historical straightjacket' on events; an 'elaborate and arid for-
malism' concerned solely with abstract speculation on the nature
of man and society; or a 'liberal-practicality' directed solely
towards the empirical study of small-scale structure and events.
Only by concentrating on the effects of and influences on social
change and development can social study avoid becoming 'ultra-
theoretical' or 'ultra-empirical' and leaving the 'synthetic' tasks of
sociology to philosophy while science merely concentrates on
small-scale empirical inquiries (Aron 1967a: 22).

This reaction against small-scale inquiries in favour of a
dominant concern with the overall structure and development of
types of society is based on three main arguments. Firstly, no
accumulation of small-scale studies can provide a general under-

standing of the structure and development of modern states. An attempt to explain either small-scale or large-scale developments requires the formulation of hypothetical assumptions about the *type* and *strength* of the *relationships* between different sectors of society. One consequence of this is that to 'check and reshape a broad conception, one must have detailed expositions, but the detailed expositions cannot necessarily be put together to constitute a broad conception' (Mills 1975: 77).

Secondly, a concern with piecemeal inquiries, to the neglect of the general social structure, threatens to translate social problems into 'a series of discrete technical problems of societal adjustment' (Mannheim, cited by Carr 1975: 66) and implicitly accepts the larger structure of society. As Aron (1967a: 24) remarks,

> If piecemeal investigations are developed without regard to general problems, one ends up by unconsciously accepting a particular view . . . Now, not to ask those questions . . (ownership of the firm or structure of society in discussions of industrial relations). . . is really to ask them in a specific way. In sociology as in philosophy, not to philosophise is really to do so. The desire to see the whole must not be left out of sociology if it is to remain itself.

Aron's critique of a potential sociological schizophrenia is accompanied by a third argument: that any avoidance by sociologists of general discussions of the structure and development of modern societies does *not* mean that such conceptions will not continue to exist. All individual action, as well as attempts at political change, involves a variety of assumptions about the structure and probable development of modern societies, whether these assumptions are implicit or explicit, crude or sophisticated, precise or vague. It is not a question of whether one theorizes about society or not — for such theorizing is inevitable — but the amount and type of theorizing that occurs. By avoiding such discussions, sociology fails to subject existing conceptions to critical examination or face up to the task of providing more valid alternatives. As Mills (1975: 92) remarked, and as we observed above:

> Every society holds images of its own nature — in particular, images and slogans that justify its system of power and the ways of the powerful. The images and ideas produced by social

scientists may or may not be consistent with these prevailing images, but they always carry implications for them.

To fail to discuss the overall nature of society is, therefore, to leave unchallenged the ideological justifications of existing social structures.

These arguments against attempts to limit sociology to 'piecemeal' investigations are all based on an awareness of the fact that the existing type of societal structure provides *one* of the causes of events within modern societies. In order to understand *some* developments or solve *some* problems within specific sectors of society this cause may be of central importance. For instance, a Marxist might argue that attempts at forming workers' co-operatives will prove incapable of solving the problems of alienation within capitalism — for the constraints of capitalist competition will result in the establishment of a new productive hierarchy forced to maximize profits in order to survive. Similarly, Hirsch (1977) has argued that individualistic attempts to improve accommodation or transport within modern market societies cannot be fully successful — for such attempts are met with similar efforts by others, which ultimately creates mutual frustration.

By failing to examine the influences of macro-social structures on specific sectors of society, piecemeal investigations either ignore or accept as 'reality' the effects of a particular type of social structure. To fail to reflect on this 'reality' as a modifiable, or potentially modifiable, cause is to accept the existing structure as inevitable. Yet the solution to some contemporary social problems *may* be achieved only through transformation of the underlying social structure.

The focus of comparative sociology on the overall development of modern societies has, however, been challenged by a number of critics — most notably by Karl Popper and Ronald Nisbet. In reaction against historicist attempts to predict the future develop- ment of the 'whole of society', Popper has asserted the central importance of small-scale research and 'piecemeal engineering' (Popper 1969a, 1969b, 1974). In opposition to 'compar- ative-developmental' theories of evolution, Nisbet has emphazised the need to return to the 'empirical and concrete' investigation of historical change — shorn of systematic theories of society, biological analogies, and metaphors of growth and development (Nisbet 1969). The critiques provided by these theorists have been widely influential — not least in the criticism of some of the more extreme theories of industrial society (Berlin 1959; Smith 1976; Kumar 1978).

In condemning extreme 'historicist' or 'developmental' theories, Popper and Nisbet have also challenged those classical exponents of comparative sociology who employed this method of investigation in order to study the course of social development. Thus Popper rejects J. S. Mill's interest in examining different 'states of society' through comparative 'holistic experiments' (Popper 1974: 71–3; 84–5) and Nisbet condemns those 'comparative-developmental' theories which employ comparison only '*within a presumed order of growth and development* of the types' (Nisbet 1969: 192–3).

Popper, in his somewhat ambiguous critique of historicism (Passmore 1975; Carr 1975: 91–2) puts forward three main arguments against the attempt to investigate, predict or bring about the development of 'society as a whole'. Firstly, he argues that all theories are necessarily selective and, therefore, any attempt to study society as a 'whole' is theoretically impossible. Secondly, he claims that all 'holistic' experiments, as opposed to 'piecemeal' experiments, are too complex and politically charged to provide any useful information. Thirdly, he argues that there can be no law of evolution capable of providing the basis for societal prediction because: evolution is a unique process and there is no way of testing such a law; laws are universal but conditional statements whereas the so-called laws of evolution are presented as conditionless; the search for laws of social dynamics is based on a false analogy with physical dynamics which depend, within astronomy, on recurrent events within a stationary system, not on changing events in a non-stationary system.

Nisbet, however, specifically focuses his critique upon those theories which assume that society develops *like* an organic whole and then employs this analogy as a *description* and *explanation* of concrete historical changes. Nisbet does not condemn the metaphor of growth and development as such but, rather, its application to the concrete events of historical change. The evolutionary classifications prevalent in the nineteenth century were clearly employed to illustrate a prior theory of evolutionary development. In discussing these theories, Nisbet claims that *any* attempt to discuss the overall development of society *necessarily* involves attributing to this reified entity its own internal and autonomous principles of evolutionary development:

Once we have asked ourselves the question, what has happened in time, what is now happening, and what will happen in the future to Mankind or Civilization, what alternative is there to a metaphoric answer? We begin with an abstraction that is itself metaphoric in structure and must perforce pass to metaphor when we seek to answer the question of its change in time . . . What better image of the whole process . . . than the life-cycle of the organism (Nisbet 1969: 247).

Nisbet thus condemns any attempt to describe historical change in terms of a process of growth and development or explain any developments that occur as the results of a necessary process of organic growth. By contrast, he praises the study of the 'short run' within specific areas, seeking 'generalization *from* the empirical, the concrete, and the historical . . . not generalization drawn from metaphor and analogy' (Nisbet 1969: 303–4).

The arguments put forward by Popper and Nisbet are, however, only valid as criticisms of *particular* historicist or organic theories of social development — not of the developmental enterprise itself. Firstly, the study of the overall development of the modern type of society is not equivalent to an unselective focus on the whole of society. It involves a selective focus upon the growth or decline of an aspect of social structure perceived to be of developmental significance. At one point Nisbet explicitly recognizes this (Nisbet 1969: 245).

Secondly, to discuss the development or decline of the modern type of society, it is not necessary to indulge in organic metaphors. The specification of this type of society may provide a *focus* for the investigation of the balance of forces within society. Comparative analysis may focus upon the preconditions necessary for the development of this social type, and the extent to which these preconditions are present within different societies. The structure of this type may be examined as an essential feature of both the *conditions* and *outcome* of social and political action without assuming that any development that occurs is the result of 'organic' growth. Similarly, such a focus does not imply the existence of inevitable 'laws' of social development, as Popper suggests. Popper does not always keep clear the distinction between the study of broad historical trends (plus their causes) and the attempt to identify firm laws of historical development. To identify such 'laws', of course, does not have to be the aim of development studies. Popper himself suggests the need to 'attempt to find *conditions* of progress . . . we must try to imagine *conditions under which the progress would be arrested'*. And he offers a sketch 'of the institutional conditions on whose realization scientific and industrial progress depends' (Popper 1974: 154, 156).

Thirdly, in discussing the course of historical development, many of the major social theorists of the nineteenth century were not concerned with the *whole* of society but with its *fundamental, primary* or *major* facets (Passmore 1975: 44). It was frequently stated, of course, that the primacy of these aspects was due to their causal impact on the other features of society. This again, however, does not necessarily imply the total determination of the rest of society. Interest may be focused upon the effect of these 'major facts' in creating the *'significant features'* of modern societies. The comparative investigation of the structure and development of modern types of society may, therefore, be represented in terms of a search for the *significant* characteristics' of modern societies; or for the *major* factors responsible for these characteristics; or for the evidence available on either the *likelihood* that these factors will develop or decline; or for the form(s) in which they could possibly *be made* to develop or decline. In this manner the attempt to identify persistent and widely agreed social problems, or to identify general and commonly desirable alternative social structures, lies at the heart of the comparative sociological enterprise, which continues the Enlightenment's critique of 'surplus repression' or 'unnecessary systematic cruelty' (Marcuse 1962; Cobban 1960).

One of the reasons for the continuing popularity of the 'industrial' perspective has been the claim that it is both a 'major factor' in determining the character of modern society and a 'significant criterion' for assessing developments in modern society — it is ensured that the development of industry is both a major causal influence upon social structure and an indicator of economic and social advance, of use in assessing the progressiveness of existing social structures. To a great extent controversy over the progressiveness or non-progressiveness of industry has been a key component in debates over social progress. As indicated in the previous chapter, this debate is indissolubly linked to conflicting views of reason and knowledge.

Rationality of Industrialization or Industrialization of Rationality

In the work of Auguste Comte and G. W. F. Hegel, and in the traditions of positive and negative philosophy that they established, the development of reason is identified with both the advance of knowledge and the achievement of social progress. For Comte this was achieved through the success of scientific knowledge in increasing man's control over both the natural and social world and stimulating man's intellectual and moral faculties. In more recent years, although disagreeing with Comte's positivism on many points, such theorists as Ernest Gellner and Karl Popper have continued to emphasize that the key to social progress lies in scientific-industrial advance and the intellectual and moral gains derived from the development of scientific rationality. Industrial society theory's view of progress is deeply embedded in this tradition. By defining scientific-industrial development as the core feature of social progress, and emphasizing the role of social theory in providing a scientific understanding of its nature and requirements, this theory ultimately identifies science as the core component of human reason, industry as the central feature of social progress, and the advance of industrial society as the defining characteristic of social development.

For Hegel, by contrast, social progress is associated with the development of *Vernunft*, as critical reflection upon the necessity and value of existing reality facilitates the attainment of true individual and social freedom through the increasing self-consciousness and self-expression of *Geist* (Hegel 1964, 1980). In the radical humanist 'left Hegelianism' of the Frankfurt School and among established members of the New Left (Arato and Gebhardt 1978; Connerton 1976; Schroyer 1973; Taylor 1978a), the identification of rational thought with critique, and social progress with man's increased self-consciousness and self-expression, has continued while there has been a reaction against Hegel's cosmic idealism (Horkheimer 1974; Taylor 1978b). Both positive and negative philosophies claim that they have extracted the 'rational kernel' of their main founders without reproducing their theoretical excesses or tendency to authoritarianism. On the other hand, both traditions have condemned their opponents for ultimately failing to transcend the limitations and authoritarian foundations of their founding fathers.

Both these traditions of thought base their view of progress on the development of rationality and the establishment of a society based on reason. Reason provides, in both cases, the 'criterion of significance' for examining developments in modern society. Established structures, ideologies and events are examined in terms of the extent to which they facilitate or hinder the development of reason. For industrial society theory, the advance of scientific knowledge and its industrial application remain the core feature of social development and progress — whatever qualifications are made concerning the equation between economic growth and social welfare. Once the structure and development of industrial society is adopted as the main focus for study, the justification for this enterprise ultimately relies on the assumption of the progressive character of industrial advance.

As we have seen, the adoption of developmental perspective is of central importance in the study of modern society. Once doubt is thrown on the value of the development of reason, in this case in its scientific-industrial form, social theory is left with little guidance on the nature of social development and how it can be studied. The critics of modern forms of industrialism are united in their common emphasis on the importance of forms of industrial development and on the role of political, economic and social forces in determining industry's form and use. But once the faith in scientific-industrial development is undermined, what criteria survive to distinguish between progressive and non-progressive types of technological and economic advance? Only by answering this question can social thought be restructured around a different developmental focus to that provided by industrial society theory. From Horkheimer to Habermas, the work of the Frankfurt School achieves significance as one brave attempt to find a solution (Horkheimer 1972; Habermas 1978). Once criteria are established, they can be employed as a basis for examining the extent to which progressive forms of techno-economic development are occurring, their social consequences, and the nature and strength of the social structures and forces which facilitate or hinder their further advance.

Without the explicit adoption of such criteria, and the use of these criteria for examining the overall structure and change of modern societies, specific studies of techno-economic development will operate with hidden or implicit ideological criteria, remain limited to small-scale inquiries unaware of the influence of the wider social context or the final social consequences of the developments examined, and remain incapable of providing an adequate basis for recommending or bringing about desirable reforms. In this situation there will most likely be a reversion to some form of industrial society perspective concerned with 'efficiency', 'order' and 'growth' as criteria for progressive change. These criteria may then provide ideological cover for vested interests striving for the development of self-serving forms of techoeconomic advance. These issues will be examined further in the next chapter.

PART THREE

TECHNOLOGY AND SOCIETY: NEW PERSPECTIVES

9 TECHNOCHOICE, POWER AND DEVELOPMENT

The development of new technologies is an important, if not the most important, basis for speculation and action within modern societies. The significance of technology is immediately apparent as soon as one gets away from past myths about its nature and power. In the first place technology is not merely limited to large-scale, complex, scientifically designed, pieces of material hardware — such as computers, nuclear power stations, video tapes, communications satellites, robots, and so on. 'Technology' can include the 'software' of organization and this may be extended to organizational techniques in every sphere of life from the performance of drama to the construction of a parliamentary party system. Technology, in this sense, has obviously an extremely broad and far-reaching influence upon social life.

Of course, the use of 'technology' *may* be restricted so as to cover only complex, scientifically designed pieces of material hardware, commonly recognized as vital to social change and progress in modern, affluent societies. Continuous technological innovation is a process built into the present structure of both predominantly market and predominantly planned economies. Technological change and development, in this sense, provides a significant basis for social speculation and political action. Yet, to understand and assess these issues, attention must not be limited to traditional technocratic and technophobic theories of industrial society. Even if a technological focus is adopted, technological change cannot be accepted as *the* starting point for social speculation. It is necessary to understand the economic, political, cultural and class structures which provide the context for technological change and are responsible for its development. These structures will be important in determining both the direction of technological development and the way in which technology is used.

It is also important to recognize that technology is nothing more than the sum of particular technologies and the ways in which they are produced. To talk of 'technology' having an impact on society, or of 'technology' acting or doing something, tends to reify the effects of specific technologies; it lends credence to an

147

all-embracing but misdirected theory of 'technological change'. In different societies, periods and contexts, the processes of 'technological' change will take different forms and be subject to different influences. Any modern theory focusing on technology must begin from an investigation of the causes and effects of specific, discrete technolgies. As Wilbert Moore (1972: 23–4) comments:

> The doctrine that holds technology to be the primary factor of all social causation does not need yet another post-mortem lethal blow. But some issues remain to be explored and clarified. The question is not whether technology causes social change: it does; or whether various social changes cause technology: they do. The only interesting question is: Which changes under what circumstances?

This does not merely involve an investigation of different forms of industrialization, various paths to industrial society, or different types of industrial society. If such a perspective is adopted, the central focus is still on variants of one main process. In contrast, a theory focusing on the role of modern technologies should do so from the viewpoint of their specific effect on a range of possible social alternatives. The concern is, thereby, shifted from an interest in *the* process of technological development, and its effect in creating an industrial or technological society, to a number of social alternatives and the role that specific technologies play, or may play, in bringing any of them about.

In keeping with this perspective, the focus on specific technologies, and the range of possibilities that they create, must be accompanied by an investigation of the social forces responsible for determining the specific form that these technologies have taken. The energy, machinery, material organization, and products that make up modern production may take a variety of different forms. The specific character that it finally takes is the result of a variety of political, economic and cultural, as well as scientific and technological, forces. This is not to say that processes of technological change are under complete conscious control. It is, rather, to emphasize that the kind of developments that take place are directly affected by conscious decisions and *attempts* to direct the process. Any focus on modern technologies must, therefore, take into account the phenomenon of *technochoice*.

The Idea of Technochoice

The recognition of technochoice is central for an understanding of the development and significance of technology in the modern era. To concentrate social research on technochoice does, however, involve the difficult task of accepting the importance of technology while simultaneously recognizing the *central* significance of the social relations responsible for its development and the social consequences of the form that it has taken. It is easy to fall into one of two errors: either emphasizing the importance of technology, and thereby exaggerating its impact and value or, through a desire to avoid a technological determinism or a technocratic or technophobic approach to society, neglecting the role of technology and failing to appreciate the extent of its consequences and the possibilities that it creates. A spate of books and courses have erupted over the last decade on futurology, technology and society, limits to growth, environment and technology, etc. Many of these offer an extremely crude understanding of the political and social context within which technology is developed, and frequently lapse into some form of technological determinism. Yet, traditional social science disciplines of politics, economics and sociology have often ignored the importance of modern technologies as an area of primary concern. There is little attention paid, for example, to the social implications of nuclear power, biotechnology, arms technology, new satellite and video technologies, and so on, in courses on the 'sociology of advanced industrial societies'. Sophisticated treatment of the political economy and implications of specific technologies is sadly lacking in the social sciences. Moreover, there is even less of an attempt made to relate the potential of modern technologies to visions of an improved alternative society — except from the Tofflerite, 'gee-whiz' school.

This leads us to the second main difficulty facing the technochoice approach: the formation of a set of ideals which realize the importance that technology can have in the attainment of human ambitions, while seeing technology as neither a sufficient condition for realizing such ambitions nor as the goal of human action. One of the most important reasons for industrial society theory's view of technological development as a unilinear process creating one specific type of technolgical or industrial society has been the value attached to technological progress, *not* just an exaggerated belief in its power independently to transform society. It is this faith in the value of technology that has focused social investigation on technological development and its consequences. Whether or not such development is occurring, however fast or slow the process, attention is still focused on the extent to which technological progress is being achieved and the degree to which it is creating a distinctive and desirable type of society.

This approach appeals because it provides an easy solution to the question of social progress. Social, political and economic science were all provided with a strong stimulus during the eighteenth century when it was widely believed that thought and reason had an important role to play in achieving social progress. The social sciences were seen as capable of discovering the course of social evolution, or the requirements of human nature, and designing, or at least recognizing, the kind of society best adapted to this process or requirements. When C. Wright. Mills emphasized the importance of the 'sociological imagination' in the 1950s, he was reasserting a similar theme. Although Mills did not assume any simple theory of evolution or human nature, he stressed that the significance of social thought was its capacity to relate individual 'problems' to social 'issues', and aid in the solution of these problems through fostering social reconstruction (Mills 1975). Social science is, therefore, seen as a rational discipline capable of improving the human condition — discovering and helping to remove what Herbert Marcuse called 'surplus repression' and what Alfred Cobban termed 'unnecessary systematic cruelty'.

In the attempt to follow this ideal and further social progress, social science has traditionally concentrated a substantial degree of attention on technological development. The theory of industrial society has dominated this strand of thought. The reason for this is quite easily understood. Once the potential of technology is recognized, investigation can be concentrated on the extent to which the existing social structure either facilitates or hinders its development. This avoids the dangers of positing a general theory of human nature or desires as a basis for assessing the 'progressiveness' of existing social arrangements. If it is accepted that technology provides the means necessary for enabling mankind to achieve its desires, whatever those desires may be, technological progress provides an extremely plausible standard for assessing the potential of the present order. There is the added advantage that technology, in this sense, appears to be acting for the good of all.

There is no need to offer recommendations, or propose alternatives, which are clearly based on favouring certain values or certain groups in society to the exclusion of others. The social science may therefore be presented in the guise of rationality, reasonableness and humanitarianism — in contrast to the irrationality or authoritarianism of those who place their short-term partial interests above those of humanity. Many of the more stimulating works that have emerged from the social sciences have been oriented towards social change on the basis of this general faith in the abstract development of technology and economic growth. From Saint-Simon, Comte, Durkheim, Ogburn and Veblen to Bell, Aron, Kerr, Gellner, Brzezinski, Rostow and Kahn, the emphasis has been the same. In their writings, the 'sociological imagination' has been primarily transformed into an 'industrial imagination'.

The problem with this approach to social progress is that technology is not merely a means to general human advancement which imposes no costs upon the community. *Particular* technologies impose *specific* costs upon *definite* sectors of the population. When a nuclear power station is built, for example, the workers and inhabitants nearby are those who most suffer from the dangers of radiation. In addition, particular technological developments are fostered by specific groups and act as the means for the advancement of certain sections of society. The same nuclear power station, for example, may provide great benefits for the corporations involved in their construction and for the urban electricity consumer. The form and direction that technology takes is not, therefore, neutral — nor is it necessarily humanitarian or soul-destroying — in its nature, causes, consequences or effects. As a result, abstract indicators of tehnological 'progress' cannot be taken as representing a set of universally beneficial techniques. Nor can they be made the basis of an unproblematic 'scientific' approach to society and social development. How, then, can technology be promoted out of a viable concern with social progress?

Technology and Progress

Within technocratic and technophobic forms of thought there has been a great degree of speculation on the progressive and regressive consequences of technology, technique, science, industry, mechanicism, and so on. Technology, and the form of technical thought upon which modern technology is based, has been seen as providing the foundations for either an industrial utopia of rational organization, affluence, leisure and freedom or an industrial dystopia of centralized technocratic control, a fragmented alienated citizenry, mass culture, and petrified mechanistic thought.

More interestingly, however, there has been speculation on the undesirable effects of a form of technocratic thought that is *not* the necessary consequence of technological development, but an ideology which *misrepresents* the nature and role of technology in society. Whether this form of thought is seen as part of capitalist ideology, as a distinguishing feature of Western civilization, or as a perennial human failing, it is represented as part of the present failure to place technology in its human and social context.

Now that the limitations of such traditional views on technology are recognized, and their dangers understood, the basis is provided for examining the potential of modern technologies for aiding in the establishment of desirable social alternatives. Technology can be examined as a *necessary* condition for the development of specific social arrangements and as providing the *possibility* for certain social advances to occur. It does not, however, provide *sufficient* conditions for such changes. Moreover, the technologies which are developed and used are given a form which reflects, at least in part, the interests and values of those involved in their invention and implementation. Technologies contain certain modes of thought and behaviour which, again in part, reflect the purposes for which they were designed. It must be emphasized, however, that the *effect* of technologies may be different from the original *purposes* for which these technologies were created. Technologies may have unintended effects or consequences which are not under the control of those responsible for their initial development. The examination of the effects of any specific technology involves a complex study of both the implications or constraints of the *technology itself* and the consquences of specific *uses* of the technology. On the basis of such an understanding, technologies may be employed, modified or rejected in the pursuit of desired ends. The focus of attention is not, therefore, limited to examining the extent to which technology has a determinate effect but, rather, the role that it plays in specific social contexts — and the extent to which it can be employed as part of a project of realizing various social alternatives.

Both the factors influencing the choice of alternatives and the ideals necessary to guide the future direction of technology are of crucial importance for any future discussion of social progress. Yet the examination of such questions is not easy. Social theory has tended to operate with a reified view of the nature of technology and its development — discussing issues related to technological advance in terms of such absolutes as the control of nature, the relief of human work, surveillance and manipulation of the population, the advance of communication, the accumulation and access to information, etc., rather than the specific *forms* of control over nature, the relief of particular *types* of human work, the establishment of certain *methods* of surveillance and manipulation, and the development of definite *kinds* of communication and information. One of the central issues facing modern theorists, and the general population, is that of deciding upon and justifying those forms of technological and economic development that are progressive and advantageous. Yet it is just this kind of concern that has been neglected, and hindered, by the dominance of industrial society theory in discussions of the nature and implications of modern technological and economic developments.

Technology and Social Classification

The major problem now facing the study of technology and society is building upon the advances that have been made in our understanding of the complex nature and benefits of technological development. Models of technological determinism have been replaced by an emphasis upon the complex 'interaction' between technology and the various sectors of society (Elliott and Elliott 1976). Simplistic technocratic and technophobic interpretations of the value of technology have been rejected and replaced by a critical assessment of the economic and political values embodied in the form that technologies take. Yet if the focus on social development and progress is to be restored, shorn of its 'industrial' form, the investigation of technological advance must be related anew to the type of society in which we live. The examination of communications technologies, for example, can be examined from the perspective of modern states as 'communications societies'. This should not be interpreted in narrow technological terms, but in terms of those features of modern society which inhibit or enhance communication in the family, political system, economy, between groups and classes, in the media, in education, in the culture industries, etc. The potential of a number of modern automated and communications technologies can be related to an investigation of the democratic or authoritarian character of modern institutions and class structures. In all such cases the classification or typology adopted will be of crucial importance in structuring the significance attributed to modern technologies. If studies of technology are to become part of a renewed investigation of social development, then the typologies adopted must be recognized as themselves forming a part of the sociotechnical research being undertaken.

The significance of social typologies is rarely understood. We may take Brian Chapman's (1970) investigation of the 'police state' as an example of this. After clarifying the differences between a 'traditional police state', a 'modern police state', a 'totalitarian' regime and an 'authoritarian' regime, Chapman focuses attention on: the stages of development of a police state within authoritarian regimes; distinctive police methods and the extent of their development; the internal dynamics of the police structure and psychology; and the general conditions and causes of the development and decline of the modern police state. Chapman's initial decision to focus on 'police states' thereby provides a perspective from which to examine all developments in modern society, including any study of modern technology. For example, in discussing the distinctive nature of police methods, Chapman describes these as the exercise of arbitrary power, brutality, illegal activity, and spying. As Chapman emphasizes, the presence of these methods is not an either/or situation but a question of degree in every society which possesses a police force. He states that 'those elements which we most closely identify as being properties of modern police states are, in fact, potentialities of any police system'. Technologies are thereby examined in terms of the degree to which they will hinder or enhance such potentialities. Chapman speculates on how 'modern technologies have increased the possibility of abuse' (Chapman 1970: 93).

Another example can be found in Raymond Williams's speculations on the influence of communications technologies. As Williams emphasizes, there have always been cultural means of production which have restricted 'access' and in the modern era this is due to the large-scale, capital intensive, and complex nature of communications technologies. The question of the control of these technologies therefore becomes a central social issue. Traditionally this issue has been dealt with in terms of the relative advantages of 'public' as opposed to 'private' control of the media. Williams, however, approaches the question from a different perspective. The development of a whole series of new communications technologies including cable TV, visual information systems, space satellites, video cassettes, low-cost video recording, and interactive TV has, he argues, extended the possibility of direct community input and control.

'The moment of any new technology', Williams recognizes, 'is a moment of choice' (Williams 1983: 146). The new technologies offer unique opportunities but these may not be realized. The multiplication of channels made possible by cable and satellite communications makes the programme organizers and controllers of scarce channels unnecessary. The range of channels also allows self-selecting and self-timed viewing, a development enhanced by the invention of the video recorder. In general the whole concept of an 'unviable' audience is changed as centralized network programming is supplemented by other forms of production. Yet each of the new technologies may either realize these opportunities and contribute towards a more participatory system — or be used to further the development of a 'paranational hyper-capitalism'.

Cable television may be limited by traditional television networks and controlled by these networks, showing old movies and quiz programmes, and so on, to enhance advertising revenues. They may also be limited to the more affluent urban sectors of society. On the other hand, cable television could be locally run for the service of the local community. It could become part of a whole mix of telephone signal systems, satellite domestic receivers and community relays that extend services to previously excluded rural populations and poorer urban areas and increase the range of services available to all. Satellite communications may be employed as part of an international interchange of experience and information or merely as the latest component of American cultural imperialism. Video cassettes may become part of a new set of publishing institutions and public lending libraries making possible the production and viewing of a multiplicity of different forms of community expression. Alternatively, they may merely extend the international consumer market in pornography, large-budget movies, and commercial television programmes.

Video recording may facilitate the rise of community creativity and production or become part of a privatized, low-quality, domestic 'holiday snaps' market. Interactive television may, similarly, be used as a new advertising technique or as a means for enhancing community input and information on political issues, quality of goods and services, etc.

Williams examines the new communications technologies in a way that goes beyond the traditional focus on centralized private or public control of the media. The progressive potential of the new technologies is due to their ability to encourage community production and local transmission, their possible use to strengthen voluntary organization and extend public education, their potential employment as a source of useful political and economic information, and their interactive capabilities as part of a new kind of participatory democracy.

Williams aptly points out that previous analyses of technology have been limited by the implicit 'conviction that there is nothing but the past to be won'. This is because, 'there is a determined refusal of any genuinely alternative social and cultural order' (Williams 1983: 134). Williams's alternative perspective, however, is clear. He portrays the fundamental issue thus:

> The struggle will reach into every corner of society. But that is precisely what is at stake: a new universal accessibility. Over a wide range of general television through commercial advertising to centralized information and data-processing systems, the technology that is now or is becoming available can be used to affect, to alter, and in some cases to control our whole social process. And it is ironic that the uses offer such extreme social choices. We could have inexpensive, locally based yet internationally extended television systems, making possible communication and information-sharing on a scale that not long ago would have seemed utopian. These are the contemporary tools of the long revolution towards an educated and participatory democracy, and of the recovery of effective communication in complex urban and industrial societies. But they are also the tools of what would be, in context, a short and successful counter-revolution, in which, under the cover of talk about choice and competition, a few para-national corporations, with their attendant states and agencies, could reach further into our lives, at every level from news to psycho-

drama, until individual and collective response to many different kinds of experience and problem became almost limited to choice between their programmed possibilities (Williams 1974: 151).

The central importance of technological choice in deciding alternative 'futures' for modern society is also exemplified in discussions of energy production. Lovins (1977) investigates the development of modern energy technologies in terms of whether they fit into a 'hard' or a 'soft' energy path. The 'hard path' is characterized by large-scale centralized production of high-quality energy largely in the form of electricity, the 'soft path' by decentralized locally-based forms of generation matching energy quality to end use and involving extensive use of cogeneration and conservation options. Lovins examines the economic and social benefits and costs of both options but, in arguing for the 'soft' path, stresses the high distribution costs, wastage, rigidity, vulnerability and élitist authoritarian implications of the 'hard option'.

Lovins's analysis has been very influential, but his thesis is weakened by his lack of attention to the complex political and economic factors behind the two paths and his rather facile attribution of all major problems to the one issue of scale. His analysis has, however, influenced a number of important studies of nuclear power. Falk (1982) and Camilleri (1984) have argued that nuclear power's large-scale and capital-intensive character encourages the centralization of energy production. Its scientific and technical complexity encourages the rise of a scientific energineering élite required for its construction and operation. The dangerous nature of nuclear materials further ensures that the regulation of nuclear power stations will be kept secret and the establishments well guarded. The technology therefore encourages a degree of secrecy and military preparedness. The possibility of the plutonium byproduct of nuclear reactors being used for the production of nuclear bombs fosters the rise of a small 'army' to guard the reactors and encourages the increased search for 'terrorist' organizations.

Some of the complex forces arrayed behind and against this nuclear establishment include the fact that the progress and 'costs' of the nuclear enterprise have been ensured by a 'political infrastructure' of legislation, regulation and subsidy and, secondly, that the increased opposition to nuclear power has been linked to traditions of regional autonomy and the increasing delegitimation of a central state whose 'technical' decisions appear increasingly 'political'. Falk (1982) has focused on these issues as part of an assessment of the factors affecting the potential transformation of 'late capitalist' societies.

The examples provided by Chapman, Williams and Falk all reveal the way in which the analysis of technological choice and development can be directly related to societal perspectives. In the work of Williams and Falk, the significance of the form taken by modern technologies is due to their reflection of, and impact on, the course of social development — as defined through the social dichotomies employed by these authors. The further examination, discussion and use of such models of development is a crucial feature of any future assessment of technological advance. Without the critical employment of such perspectives, the analysis of technochoice may be limited to small-scale investigations and may neglect to examine in any detail the effect of the general social structure on the form of technological development and the effects of technological changes on this structure. If such a 'macrosocial' or developmental perspective is not explicitly employed, investigations of technological advance will also tend to make implicit and unexamined assumptions concerning the overall social context in which technologies are developed — assumptions which will, most probably, lapse into some form of industrial society theory. A critical assessment of industrial society theory must be supplemented by alternative approaches to technology, society and progress, if the important concern with social development is to be retained.

Technology and Modern Politics: Crisis or Transformation

During the post-war period, industrial society theory dominated social thought on the nature and legitimating rationale for Western 'mixed economies'. Over the past decade, however, a number of changes have occurred which make the theory of industrial society appear increasingly irrelevant to the major issues of the age.

The first development is the growing scepticism over the benefits of technological development and economic growth. Of course this is nothing new. Cultural critics, intellectuals, and disadvantaged minorities have always reacted against the environmental and human costs of technological and economic development. Since the Greeks first told of the fate of Prometheus and Pandora, popular myth has warned of the dangers of technological hubris in the form of the legends of Frankenstein, Faust and Dr Jekyll or, in more recent years, the dangers of a future as portrayed in George Orwell's *1984*, Aldous Huxley's *Brave New World* or Kurt Vonnegut's *Player Piano*. From ancient Greece to the present, there have been a wide variety of romantic, humanist, Malthusian and philosophical reactions against the 'Faustian bargain', the 'dark satanic mills', the manic 'Promethean quest' and the general 'price of progress'.

Yet what is novel about the present situation is the extent to which this scepticism has spread to the general population. Caught in traffic jams, crowded in tourist resorts, aware of the depletion of natural resources, and faced with planned obsolescence, the modern populace is directly confronted with the difference between quantitative increases in GNP and a qualitative improvement in the standard of living. Nor does technological development receive unqualified support. The modern populace is no longer so strongly committed to technological 'progress', as it has become more aware of the dangers of nuclear power, the threat of nuclear armaments, the deskilling and routinization of work, the effects of automation on employment, the potential of biotechnology for the manipulation of the human embryo, and the general pollution of the environment. The ideology of growth is no longer so firmly entrenched in an era of increased recognition of natural and social 'limits to growth' and the dangerous 'externalities' of the market. The population has become increasingly aware of the importance of different forms of technological development and types of economic growth.

The second development over the past decade has been the continued increase in the size of the state and the scope of its activities. Greater attention has been paid to the growing costs of state activities and the difficulties involved in developing the necessary political capacities to fulfil its increasing functions (Brzezinski 1977; Bell 1976). One of the major consequences of this growth has been the politicization of what were previously regarded as economic or technical issues. The era of *laissez-faire*, in which major decisions on production and distribution were made within the economy, has clearly come to an end. It is now, in many cases, a question of 'politics in command' (Gellner 1974a). Although the degree of 'freedom' of the market in the *laissez-faire* period should not be exaggerated, the involvement of the modern state in economic activities has vastly increased in scale and range. This is not to say that the state is capable of *controlling* economic activity, merely that political decision has become an important component within the processes of production. With the recognition of this fact has come the increasing politicization of economic conflict. This situation is in direct contrast to what many of the 1950s end-of-ideology school saw as the 'institutionalization' of class conflict and the separation of economic and political issues (Dahrendorf 1967).

Increasing politicization of economic conflict has occurred in a number of ways. Firstly, as the state is more responsible for the regulation and stimulation of economic growth, 'economic' disputes over wages, jobs and the direction of investment have become political issues.

Secondly, the state has become more important in the process of technological development. Government is involved, in a regulative or directive capacity, in the highly technological spheres of energy production, warfare, communication, transport, and so on. The possibilities and threats posed by developments within these areas are, therefore, raised and debated within the corridors of political power.

Thirdly, the state has taken over a number of welfare activities and has established a complex network of subsidies, grants and welfare payments. This has led, unsurprisingly, to the acceptance by sectors of the population of their 'right' to certain payments. The conflicts and tensions surrounding such 'rights' is a seriously destabilizing force within late captitalist states (Bell 1979).

Fourthly, modern capitalist states face what O'Connor (1973) has called a 'fiscal crisis' as they attempt to ensure continued accumulation and growth (upon which their income finally depends) while also maintaining a belief in their fairness and legitimacy through redistributive measures, carrying out welfare functions, and limiting tax increases. Yet, with pressures for funds coming from both the 'accumulation' and 'welfare' areas of its activities, the state is tempted to borrow or print more money — a partial solution that contributes to fiscal crisis.

Finally, the increased size and scope of modern technology, and the achievement of higher levels of economic growth, has meant that these spheres of activity have further encroached upon the 'private' lives of the population. As the state is heavily involved in both technological advance and economic growth, the dividing line between 'public' and 'private' has become blurred. The citizen is increasingly affected in his or her community, family or private life by the construction of airports, roads and power stations. His or her home existence is strongly influenced by developments in video technology, cable television and communications satellites. Advances in surveillance technology, computerized data banks, medical surgery, and the manipulation of the human embryo through genetic engineering may also directly affect the 'private' citizen.

This situation might be portrayed as a crisis of industrial society requiring, as Daniel Bell suggests, the formulation by professionals of a new moral code to govern the post-industrial state. Or it might be perceived, as Jurgen Habermas argues, as initiating a profound 'legitimation crisis', one calling into question the capitalist economic order, and ultimately transforming modern societies into democratic socialist states. Without going further into the limitations of the specific analyses already mentioned, it is important to recognize, with Tom Bottomore, that

> [h]ardly anyone believes any longer that economic growth and technological innovation are self-evident goals, or that the assertion of them must put an end to all reasonable controversy. Thus the way is open for public discussion of the options which are available to men, given the stage of development of science and technology, in deciding the future form of their social life (Bottomore 1975: 193).

The modern era, Bottomore hopes, will become an 'age of intense political debate and activity' as the possibilities and problems of modern forms of technology are recognized and the need for choice is understood. In this context the continuation of industrial society theory hinders, rather than enhances, public discussion and debate. The conceptual problems and limitations of industrial society theory unite with these pressing social issues to emphasize the need for alternative frameworks for examining the relationship between technology and society. The 'industrial imagination' is no longer sufficiently relevant and unproblematic to be allowed to exhaust the 'sociological imagination'.

Social and political thought should attempt to provide a more adequate understanding of the constraints and value of modern forms of technology. It can best do this through a critical grasp of the nature of industrial society theory; of the reasons for this theory's continuing influence and popularity; and of the obstacles that face any attempt to draw up alternative frameworks for investigation. The importance of technology for political and social analysis should be recognized and made the subject of a renewed study that transcends the limitations of industrial society theory. Industrial society theory may be one of the most impressive conceptual dinosaurs in social theory, but its bulk and long history must not deflect attention from the basic flaws in its design.

10 THE INDUSTRIAL DILEMMA

Our central concern in this work has been the nature and problems of industrial society theory and the classification of modern states as 'industrial societies'. As we have seen, a variety of criticisms have been directed against the evolutionary and functionalist 'theory of industrial society'. As a theory purporting to explain the past, present and future of modern societies, and to prescribe the direction of social progress, the evolutionary and functionalist theory of industrial society has been justifiably rejected. Yet, to an extent, this variant theory of industrial society is an invention of its critics. Few modern writers would be prepared to defend it as an interpretation of modern civilization. Of wider currency, whether adopted explicitly or implicitly, is the more 'conceptual' industrial society theory discussed earlier. This theory, focusing upon modern societies and providing a perspective from which to view the development of contemporary states, is not so clearly based upon a set of specific 'testable' hypotheses, derived from a deductive system (Barry 1970).

This is not to suggest, however, that conceptual schemes possess no explanatory implications or that they do not incorporate a set of value judgements. On the contrary, such schemes limit the factors taken into consideration in explaining events and suggest a limited range of hypotheses (Benton 1977). In the case of industrial society theory, the primary focus of concern and basis for explanation relate to the effects of industry on society, and of the industrial social structure on contemporary developments. There cannot be any simple refutation of such a scheme. But the ambiguity of 'industry' does bring into question its explanatory power and its classificatory utility. A number of empirical and theoretical critiques have also been made of the exaggerated importance attached to industry and industrial development as an explanation of structure and change in modern societies. Even more significantly, recent analyses of technological and economic development have revealed the extent to which social and political factors control even the constituents of the industrial process. Any theory therefore, which accords to 'industry' a central determining role must be regarded as highly suspect.

Yet industrial society theory can always be saved from such criticisms. Industry may be defined with greater precision. The assumptions concerning the extent of industry's impact on society may be modified in line with more recent evidence. The question is whether this continuing attention to industrial society theory is worthwhile. It is at this point that the values upon which industrial society theory is based become subject to significant dispute. Is it worthwhile for the social sciences to spend further time clarifying the nature of industry and investigating its social impact and requirements? The answer is in part empirical and in part evaluative. It depends on whether industry is regarded as more *important* than the various forms, types or components of industrial technology or production. This involves judgements concerning the usefulness of 'industry', the extent of its effects, and the value of its impact — in contrast to other forms of technology and production.

In the so-called underdeveloped countries, for example, the desire to increase general economic and social welfare is often hindered by adherence to outdated models of industrialization (Hoogvelt 1976; Kemp 1978). More importantly, the general pursuit of industrial development is too vague to serve those societies faced, for example, with choices between importing large-scale, complex technologies or stimulating simpler and more labour-intensive forms of production; between encouraging agricultural production or fostering the development of manufacture; between establishing an economy regulated for the satisfaction of the primary needs of the population or creating the preconditions for a competitive economic system in which such needs are fulfilled as a byproduct of the dynamic search for profit; between diversifying the home economy or increasing the production of commodities at present in demand on the world market.

As we have seen, in the case of the so-called advanced industrial societies, there is a variety of problems and possibilities that are not adequately dealt with by a general focus on the development of industry and industrial society. A number of options are open to us. We may choose between directing scientific research and new technology into either maximizing production or reducing working hours to a minimum. We may create the economic and technical basis for a participatory economic and political system or lay the foundations for a stable and efficient form of central regulation. We may encourage military production or improve and extend the social welfare system. We may preserve and foster a pleasant natural environment or simply produce more goods. We may encourage greater production at home, or in the work-place.

The possibilities, preconditions or consequences of such choices cannot adequately be dealt with through a broad concern with 'industrial development'. Even if central importance is still attached to technological and economic development, alternative classifications may be developed by recognizing the importance of *forms of economic growth* (commodities or non-commodities, private or public goods, military weapons or consumer goods, basic consumption goods or luxury items, intermediate or final goods, positional or material goods (Hirsch 1977), investment or consumer goods); the importance of *methods of production* (wage labour or state control, participatory or authoritarian, more or less labour-intensive, polluting or non-polluting centralized or de-centralized, short or long working hours, by specialization of functions or of men, with fossil fuels or renewable fuels, as community-based or isolated from the community); and the *purposes* for which forms of growth and methods of production are developed or used (for use value or exchange value, for purposes democratic or authoritarian, egalitarian or inegalitarian, for leisure or wealth). Once such alternative bases for investigation have been identified (much less crudely than here) it becomes possible to examine their incidence, their influence, and the likely effect on their future development of existing political, economic, ideological and class structures.

The issue then becomes that of deciding the value of focusing on such areas rather than on the development and impact of 'industry'. Is, for example, the choice of nuclear as opposed to solar power more important than the general level of energy consumption? Is the increased capacity of information technology *per se* most important? Or should the design of such technologies enhance the centralized control of information? Or should it provide an interactive public information system? The use of the industrial society schema does not, of course, exclude alternative forms of investigation — because other categories and approaches may be employed as a *supplement* to the industrial focus. However, the adoption of the focus on industrial society *does* exclude alternative forms of thought in the case of a specific investigation.

When a study is made of education in industrial society, politics in industrial society, class in industrial society, the family in industrial society, leisure in industrial society, democracy in industrial society, etc., 'industrial society' is not merely a heuristic category having little effect on the investigation. It structures the basic approach to the phenomena examined. It ensures that the effect of industry and the effect on industry constitute the primary concern. *Unless* this outcome is intended there is no reason to employ 'industrial society'. The use of the concept ensures that the generalizations examined are those relevant to an 'industrial' conception of society. If the industrial category is not employed, different classes of society, forms of comparison and foci of investigation will result.

Industrial society theory has been largely successful in limiting our thought on the relationship between technology and society. In the traditional social science literature it has often been assumed that the stress on the importance of technology results in a form of technological determinism similar to that found in post-war theories of industrial society. At the same time, a vague 'industrial society' image has continued to dominate thought on the fundamental realities of modern society and the general character of social progress. As a result, a more sophisticated and critical understanding of modern technology has not been accompanied by a greatly improved understanding of its importance for the overall development of contemporary societies. A number of studies have emerged revealing the complex political, economic and social factors involved in determining the form that technology takes (Dickson 1974; Illich 1975; Albury and Schwartz 1982; Pacey 1983). Yet very few studies have gone beyond somewhat simplistic élite analyses or an anti-industrial morality in analysing and judging the political causes, consequences and value of modern forms of technology. Industrial society theory has in general discouraged a much needed display of 'sociological imagination' in the study of technological choice and development.

In this regard, the proponents of industrial society theory are faced with a central dilemma. The past value of and justification for the theory was founded upon the determining role and moral value attributed to industrial development. The more recent 'critical' theories of industrial society accept that industrial advance cannot be equated with social progress. And the more the role and value of 'industry' is denied, the less justification there is for continuing to use the construct. By contrast, there are some industrial society theorists who continue to attach great importance to 'industry', and their claims become the more dubious and ideological in the degree that they do so. Industrial society theorists, therefore, are still caught in an industrial dilemma — between the Scylla of an industrial determinism and the Charybdis of an underdetermined classification.

We do not, perhaps, 'refute' categories like 'industrial society'. But where such notions are demonstrated to be confused and unhelpful, we may do well to overleap them. To do this, we must become conscious of the variety of perspectives from which we can study modern societies, and that any perspective we choose forms part of the study we execute. This, in turn, should broaden our appreciation of the great range of choice presently available, as between distinct technologies, and between the sometimes incompatible purposes these technologies may serve. We must move more decisively from the obsession with 'industrial' determinism, to an awareness of the complexities of 'technochoice' — as discussed in Chapter 9. If this book in any way contributes to that end, it will have served its purpose.

BIBLIOGRAPHY

Aaron, R. I. (1976). *Theory of Universals*, Clarendon Press, Oxford.
Abercrombie, N., Hill, S. and Turner, B. S. (1980). *The Dominant Ideology Thesis*, George Allen and Unwin, London.
Abercrombie, N. and Turner, B. S. (1978). 'The Dominant Ideology Thesis', *British Journal of Sociology*, no. 2, pp. 1–13.
Ackroyd, A. *et al.* (1977). *The Technology of Political Control*, Penguin, Harmondsworth.
Albrow, M. (1970). *Bureaucracy*, Macmillan, London.
Albury, D. and Schwartz, J. (1982). *Partial Progress: The Politics of Science and Technology*, Pluto Press, London.
Althusser, L. (1970). *For Marx*, Vintage, New York.
—— (1971). *Lenin and Philosophy*, New Left Books, London.
—— (1972). *Politics and History*, New Left Books, London.
—— (1976). *Essays in Self Criticism*, New Left Books, London.
Althusser, L. and Balibar, E. (1975). *Reading Capital*, New Left Books, London.
Anderson, P. (1976). *Considerations on Western Marxism*, New Left Books, London.
Andreski, S. (ed.) (1964a). *The Essential Comte*, Croom Helm, London.
—— (1964b). *Elements of Comparative Sociology*, Weidenfeld and Nicolson, London.
—— (ed.) (1972). *Herbert Spencer, Structure, Function and Evolution*, Nelson, London.
Arato, A. and Gebhart, E. (eds.) (1978). *The Frankfurt School Reader*, Urzen Books, New York.
Archer, M. (1978). 'The Theoretical and Comparative Analysis of Social Structure', in Archer, M. and Giner, S. (eds.), *Contemporary Europe: Social Structure and Cultural Pattern*, Weidenfeld and Nicolson, London.
Archer, M. and Giner, S. (1971). 'Social Stratification in Europe', *Contemporary Europe: Class Status and Power*, Weidenfeld and Nicolson, London.
Aron, R. (1957). *Opium of the Intellectuals*, Secker and Warburg, London.
—— (1961). *Introduction to the Philosophy of History*, Beacon Press, Boston.
—— (1963). *World Technology and Human Destiny*, Ann Arbor, Mich.
—— (1964). *German Sociology*, Free Press, New York.
—— (1967a). *Eighteen Lectures on Industrial Society*, Weidenfeld and Nicolson, London.
—— (1967b). *The Industrial Society*, Weidenfeld and Nicolson, London.
—— (1970). *Democracy and Totalitarianism*, Weidenfeld and Nicolson, London.
—— (1972). *Progress and Disillusion: The Dialectics of Modern Society*, Penguin, Harmondsworth.
—— (1974). *Main Currents of Sociological Thought*, Penguin, Harmondsworth.
Armytage, W. H. (1965). *The Rise of the Technocrats*, Routledge and Kegan Paul, London.
Bachrach, P. and Baratz, M. (1971) 'Two Faces of Power' in Castles, Murray and Potter (1971).
Baker, K. M. (1975). *Condorcet; From Natural Philosophy to Social Mathematics*, University of Chicago Press, Chicago.
Baran, P. (1973). *The Political Economy of Growth*, Penguin, Harmondsworth.

Baran, P. and Sweezy, P. (1973). *Monopoly Capital*, Penguin, Harmondsworth.
Barry, B. (1970). *Sociologists, Economists and Democracy: Themes and Issues in Modern Sociology*, Collier/Macmillan, London.
Bauman, Z. (1973). *Culture as Praxis*, Routledge and Kegan Paul, London.
—— (1976a). *Socialism: The Active Utopia*, George Allen and Unwin, London.
—— (1976b). *Towards a Critical Sociology: An Essay on Commonsense and Emancipation*, Routledge and Kegan Paul, London.
—— (1978). *Hermeneutics and Social Science: Approaches to Understanding*, Hutchinson, London.
Becker, C. (1932). *The Heavenly City of Eighteenth Century Philosophers*, Yale University Press, New Haven.
—— (1974). 'The Idea of Progress' in Fletcher (1974b).
Beckerman, W. (1974). *In Defence of Economic Growth*, Jonathan Cape, London.
Bell, D. (1962). *The End of Ideology*, Collier, New York.
—— (1976). *The Coming of Post-industrial Society*, Penguin, Harmondsworth.
—— (1979). *The Cultural Contradictions of Capitalism*, Heinemann, London.
—— (1980). *Sociological Journeys: Essays 1960–80*, Heinemann, London.
Bell, D. and Kristol, I. (1956). *Work and Authority in Industry*, University of California Press, Berkeley.
—— (eds.((1971). *Capitalism Today*, Mentor, New York.
Benton, T. (1977). *Philosophical Foundations of the Three Sociologies*, Routledge and Kegan Paul, London.
Berg, A. van der (1980). 'Critical Theory: Is There Still Hope?', *American Journal of Sociology*, vol. 86, no. 3, pp. 435–55.
Berle, A. A. Jr (1975). 'What the G.N.P. Doesn't Tell Us', *Saturday Review*, 7 August.
Berle, A. A. Jr and Means, G. C. (1962). *The Modern Corporation and Private Property*, Macmillan, New York.
Berlin, I. (1956). *The Age of Enlightenment: The Eighteenth Century Philosophers*, Mentor Books, New York.
—— (1959). *Historical Inevitability*, Oxford University Press, London.
—— (1967). 'Does Political Theory Still Exist' in A. Quinton (1967).
—— (1969). *Four Essays on Liberty*, Oxford University Press, London.
Bernstein, R. J. (1972). *Praxis and Action*, Duckworth, London.
—— (1976). *The Restructuring of Social and Political Thought*, Basil Blackwell, Oxford.
Binns, D. (1975). *Beyond the Sociology of Conflict*, Macmillan, London.
Birnbaum, N. (1969). *The Crisis of Industrial Society*, Oxford University Press, London.
—— (ed.) (1977). *Beyond the Crisis*, Oxford University Press, New York.
Blackburn, R. (ed.) (1972). *Ideology in Social Sciences*, Fontana/Collins, London.
Blackburn, R. and Cockburn, A. (1969). *Student Power*, Penguin, Harmondsworth.
Blauner, R. (1964). *Alienation and Freedom*, University of Chicago Press, Chicago.
Bookchin, M. (1971). *Post Scarcity Anarchism*, Ramparts Press, Berkeley.
Bottomore, T. B. (1960). 'The Ideas of the Founding Fathers', *European Journal of Sociology*, vol. 1, pp. 33–49.
—— (1973). *Sociology: A Guide to the Problems and Literature*, George Allen and Unwin, London.
—— (1974). *Elites and Society*, C. A. Waits, and Co., London.
—— (1975). *Sociology as Social Criticism*, George Allen and Unwin, London.
—— (1979). *Political Sociology*, Hutchinson, London.
Brown, D. and Harrison, M. J. (1978). *A Sociology of Industrialism: An Introduction*, Macmillan, London.

Brzezinski, Z. (1977). *Between Two Ages: America's Role in the Technetronic Era*, Penguin, Harmondsworth.

Budd, S. (1964). 'A Comment on Social Stratification in Industrial Societies' in Halmos (1964).

Bulmer, M. (ed.) (1975). *Working Class Images of Society*, Routledge and Kegan Paul, London.

Burnham, J. (1941). *The Managerial Revolution*, John Day, London.

Bury, J. B. (1955). *The Idea of Progress*, Dover Publications, New York.

Camilleri, J. A. (1984). *The State and Nuclear Power*, Penguin, Harmondsworth.

Carr, E. H. (1975). *What is History?*, Penguin, Harmondsworth.

Cassirer, E. (1951). *The Philosophy of the Enlightenment*, Beacon Press, Boston.

Castles, F. G. (1976). 'Policy Innovation and Institutional Stability in Sweden', *British Journal of Political Science*, no. 6, pp. 203–16.

Castles, F. G., Murray, D. J. and Potter, D. C. (1971). *Decisions, Organization and Society*, Penguin, Harmondsworth.

Chapman, B. (1970). *Police State*, Pall Mall, London.

Charlton, D. G. (1959). *Positivist Thought in France: 1852–70*, Clarendon Press, London.

Chomsky, N. (1971). *American Power and the New Mandarins*, Penguin, Harmondsworth.

Clarke, S. (1977). 'Marxism, Sociology and Poulantzas' Theory of the State', *Capital and Class*, no. 2, pp. 1–37.

Clayre, A. (ed.) (1977). *Nature and Industrialization*, Oxford University Press/ Open University Press, Oxford.

Cobban, A. (1960). *In Search of Humanity: The Decline of Enlightenment in Modern History*, Jonathan Cape, London.

Comte, A. (1974). *The Positive Philosophy*, A.M.S. Press Inc., New York.

Connerton, P. (ed.) (1976). *Critical Sociology*, Penguin, Harmondsworth.

Coppens, P. R. de (1976). *Ideal Man in Classical Sociology*, Pennsylvania State University Press.

Coser, L. A. (1971). *Masters of Sociological Thought*, Harcourt Brace, New York.

Crompton, R. and Gubbay, J. (1977). *Economy and the Class Structure*, Macmillan, London.

Cross, N. *et al.* (1974). *Man Made Futures: Readings in Society, Technology and Design*, Hutchinson, London.

Crossland, C. A. R. (1961). 'On Economic Growth', *Encounter*, no. 16, April, pp. 65–8.

—— (1962). *The Conservative Enemy*, Jonathan Cape, London.

Dahl, R. A. (1961). *Who Governs: Democracy and Power in an American City*, Yale University Press, New Haven.

Dahrendorf, R. (1967). *Class and Class Conflict in Industrial Society*, Routledge and Kegan Paul, London.

Dalton, G. (1974). *Economic Systems and Society*, Penguin, Harmondsworth.

Davies, J. C. (1974). *Social Mobility and Political Change*, Pall Mall, London.

Dawe, A. (1971). 'The Two Sociologies' in K. Thompson and J. Tunstall, *Sociological Perspectives*, Penguin, Harmondsworth.

Demerath, N. J. and Peterson, R. A. (eds.) (1967). *System, Change and Conflict: A Reader in Contemporary Sociological Theory*, Free Press, New York.

Dickson, D. (1974). *Alternative Technology: The Politics of Technical Change*, Fontana/Collins, Glasgow.

Diggins, J. P. (1978). *The Bard of Savagery: Thorstein Veblen and Modern Social Theory*, Harvester Press, London.

Douglas, J. D. (ed.) (1971). *Understanding Social Life*, Routledge and Kegan Paul, London.

Dreitzel, H. P. (ed.) (1974). *Recent Sociology: On the Social Basis of Politics*, Collier/Macmillan, London.

Drucker, P. (1974). *The Political Uses of Ideology*, Macmillan, London.

Drucker, P. F. (1951). *The New Society: The Anatomy of the Industrial Order*, Heinemann, London.

Dubazedier, J. (1974). *Sociology of Leisure*, Elsevier, Amsterdam.

Duncan, O. D. (ed.) (1964). *On Culture and Social Change*, Phoenix, University of Chicago Press.

—— (1969). 'Social Forecasting: The State of the Art.' *The Public Interest*, no. 17, pp. 88–118.

Dunning, E. G. and Harper, E. I. (1966). 'Industrialisation and the Problem of Convergence: A Critical Note', *Sociological Review*, vol. 14, no. 2, pp. 163–86.

Durkheim, E. (1962). *Socialism*, Collier Books, New York.

—— (1964a). *Rules of Sociological Method*, Free Press, New York.

—— (1964b). *The Division of Labour in Society*, Free Press, New York.

Duvignaud, J. (1972). *The Sociology of Art*, Paladin, London.

Eisen, A. (1978). 'The Meanings and Confusion of Weber's Rationality', *British Journal of Sociology*, vol. 29, no. 1, March, pp. 57–70.

Eisenstadt, S. (1966). *Modernisation: Protest and Change*, Prentice Hall, New Jersey.

—— (1973). *Tradition, Change and Modernity*, John Wiley and Sons, New York.

Eisenstadt, S. and Curelaru, M. (1977). 'Macro-Sociology: Theory, Analysis and Comparative Study', *Current Sociology*, vol. 25, no. 2, Summer.

Eldridge, J. E. T. (1971). *Sociology and Industrial Life*, Michael Mill Joseph, London.

Elliott, D. and Elliott, R. (1976). *The Control of Technology*, John Wykeham, London.

Ellul, J. (1964). *The Technological Society*, Vintage Books, New York.

Encel, S., Marstrand, P. K. and Page, W. (eds.) (1975). *The Art of Anticipation*, Martin Robertson, London.

Etzioni, A. (1968). *The Active Society*, Free Press, New York.

Falk, J. (1982). *Global Fission: The Battle Over Nuclear Power*, Oxford University Press, Melbourne.

Faunce, W. A. (ed.) (1967). *Readings in Industrial Sociology*, Appleton Century Crofts, New York.

—— (1968). *Problems of an Industrial Society*, McGraw Hill, New York.

Faunce, W. A. and Form, W. H. (eds.) (1969). *Comparative Perspectives on Industrial Society*, Little Brown, New York.

Fay, B. (1975). *Social Theory and Political Practice*, George Allen and Unwin, London.

Fine, B. and Harris (1976). 'State Expenditure in Advanced Capitalism', *New Left Review*, no. 98, July–August, pp. 97–114.

Fletcher, R. (1971a). *The Making of Sociology*, vol. 1, *Beginnings and Foundations*, Michael Mill Joseph, London.

—— (1971b). *The Making of Sociology*, vol. 2, *Developments*, Michael Mill Joseph, London.

—— (ed.) (1974a). *The Crisis of Industrial Civilization: The Early Essays of Auguste Comte*, Heinemann, London.

—— (ed.) (1974b). *The Science of Society and the Unity of Mankind*, Heinemann, London.

—— (1981). *Sociology: The Study of Social Systems*, Batsford, London.

Frankel, C. (1951). *The Faith of Reason: The Idea of Progress in the French Enlightenment*, Beacon Press, Boston.

Frankfurt Institut for Social Research (1974). *Aspects of Sociology*, Heinemann, London.

Freund, J. (1968). *The Sociology of Max Weber*, Allen Lane, The Penguin Press, London.

Frisby, D. (1976). *The Positivist Dispute in German Sociology*, Heinemann, London.

Fromm, E. (1973). *Marx's Concept of Man*, Frederick Ungar, New York.

Gabor, D. (1964). *Inventing the Future*, Penguin, Harmondsworth.

Galbraith, J. K. (1970). *The Affluent Society*, Mentor, New York.

—— (1974). *The New Industrial State*, Penguin, Harmondsworth.

Gallie, D. (1978). *In Search of the New Working Class: Alienation and Social Integration within the Capitalist Enterprise*, Cambridge University Press, Cambridge.

—— (1979). 'Social Radicalism in the French and British Working Classes: Some Points of Comparison', *British Journal of Sociology*, vol. 30, no. 4, pp. 500–42.

Gamble, A. and Walton, P. (1976). *Capitalism in Crisis: Inflation and the State*, Macmillan, London.

Gardiner, P. (ed.) (1974). *Philosophy of History*, Oxford University Press, Oxford.

Garnsey, E. (1975). 'Occupational Stratification in Industrialised Societies: Some Notes on the Convergence Thesis in the Light of Soviet Experience', *Sociology*, vol. 9, pp. 437–58.

Gay, P. (1964). *The Enlightenment: An Interpretation, vol. 1: The Rise of Paganism*, Weidenfeld and Nicolson, London.

—— (1969). *The Party of Humanity: Studies in the Enlightenment*, Weidenfeld and Nicolson, London.

—— (1976). *The Enlightenment: An Interpretation, vol. 2: The Science of Freedom*, Weidenfeld and Nicolson, London.

Gellner, E. (1972). *Thought and Change*, Weidenfeld and Nicolson, London.

—— (1974a). *Contemporary Thought and Politics*, Routledge and Kegan Paul, London.

—— (1974b). *The Legitimation of Belief*, Cambridge University Press, Cambridge.

—— (1979). *Spectacles and Predicaments: Essays in Social Theory*, Cambridge University Press, Cambridge.

Geras, N. (1972). 'Althusser's Marxism: An Account and Assessment' *New Left Review*, no. 71, pp. 57–96.

Gerschenkron, A. (1962). *Economic Backwardness in Historical Perspective*, The Bethrop Press, Cambridge, Mass.

Gershuny, J. (1978). *After Industrial Society: The Emerging Self-Service Economy*, Macmillan, London.

Gerth, H.H. and Mills, C. Wright (eds) (1948). *From Marx to Weber: Essays in Sociology*, Oxford University Press, New York.

Giddens, A. (1971). *Capitalism and Modern Social Theory*, Cambridge University Press, London.

—— (1972). *Politics and Sociology in the Thought of Max Weber*, Macmillan London.

—— (1973) *Class Structure of Advanced Societies*, Hutchinson, London.

—— (1975–6). 'Classical Social Theory and the Origins of Sociology', *American Journal of Sociology*, vol. 18, no. 4, pp. 703–29.

—— (1976) *New Rules of Sociological Method: A Positive Critique of Interpretative Sociologies*, Hutchinson, London.

—— (ed.) (1977a). *Positivism and Sociology*, Heinemann, London.

—— (1977b). *Studies in Social and Political Theory*, Hutchinson, London.

—— (1978). *Durkheim*, Harvester Press, London.

—— (1979). *Central Problems in Sociological Theory: Action, Structure and Contradiction in Social Analysis*, Macmillan Press, London.

—— (1982). *Sociology: A Brief but Critical Introduction*, Macmillan, London.

Giner, S. (1976). *Mass Society*, Martin Robertson, London.

Ginsburg, N. (1961a) 'The Comparative Method' in N. Ginsburg, *Sociology and Social Philosophy*, vol. 3, Heinemann, London.
—— (1961b). 'The Idea of Progress' in N. Ginsburg *Sociology and Social Philosophy*, vol. 3.
—— (1961c) *Evolution and Progress*, Heinemann, London.
Godelier, M. (1972). 'Structure and Contradication in Capital' in R. Blackburn (1972).
Goldthorpe, J. (1964). 'Social Stratification in Society' in Halmos (1964).
—— (1971). 'Theories of Industrial Society: The Future of Futurology or the Recrudescence of Historicism', *European Journal of Sociology*, vol. xii, no. 2, pp. 263–88.
—— (1972) 'Class, Status and Party: Some Recent Interpretations, Marxist and Marxisant', *European Journal of Sociology*, vol. 13, no. 3, pp. 342–7.
—— (1980). *Social Mobility and Class Structure in Modern Britain*, Clarendon Press, Oxford.
Goldthorpe, J. *et al.* (1971). *The Affluent Worker in the Class Structure*, Cambridge University Press, Cambridge.
Goldthrorpe, J. and Hirsch, F. (eds) (1978). *The Political Economy of Inflation*, Martin Robertson, London.
Gorz, A. (1964). *Strategy for Labour* Beacon Press, Boston.
—— (ed.) (1976). *The Division of Labour*, Harvester Press, London.
Gough, I. (1975). 'State Expenditure in Advanced Capitalism', *New Left Review*, no. 92, pp. 53–92.
Gouldner, A. (1967). *Enter Plato: Classical Greece and the Origins of Social Theory*, Routledge and Kegan Paul, London.
—— (1971). *The Coming Crisis of Western Sociology*, Heinemann, London.
—— (1974). 'The Two Marxisms' in *For Sociology*, Penguin, Harmondsworth.
—— (1979). *The Future of the Intellectuals and the Rise of the New Class*, Macmillan, New York.
Glucksman, A. (1972). 'A Ventriloquist Structuralism', *New Left Review*, no. 72, pp. 68–92.
Glucksman, M. (1974). *Structuralist Analysis in Contemporary Thought: A Comparison of the Theories of Clause Levi-Strauss and Louis Althusser*, Routledge and Kegan Paul, London.
Greenberg, M. H., Milstead, J. W., Olander, J. D. and Warrick, P. (eds) (1975). *Social Problems Through Science Fiction*, St James Press, London.
Gribbin, J. (1979). *Future Worlds*, Abacus, London.
Gunder-Frank, A. (1970). *Sociology of Development and the Underdevelopment of Sociology*, Pluto Press, London.
Habermas, J. (1972). *Towards a Rational Society*, Heinemann, London.
—— (1974) *Theory and Practice*, Heinemann, London.
—— (1976). *Legitimation Crisis*, Heinmann, London.
—— (1978). *Knowledge and Human Interests*, Heinemann, London.
Halfpenny, P. (1983). *Positivism and Sociology*, George Allen and Unwin, London.
Halmos, P. (ed.) (1964). *The Development of Industrial Societies*, Sociological Review Monograph no. 8, Keele University.
—— (1970). *The Personal Service Society*, John Constable, London.
Hampson, N. (1976). *The Enlightenment*, Penguin, Harmondsworth.
Hancock, M. (1971). 'The United States, Europe and Post-Industrial Society', *Corporate Politics*, vol. 4, no. 1, pp. 133–47.
—— (1972). *Sweden: The Politics of Post-Industrial Change*, Dryden Press, Hinsdale, Illinois.
—— (1976). 'Elite Images and System Change in Sweden' in L. N. Lindberg (1976).
Hancock, M. and Sjoberg, G. (eds.) (1972). *Politics and the Post-Welfare State*, Columbia University Press, New York.

Hanson, D. A. (1976). *An Invitation to Critical Theory: Involvement, Criticism and Explanation*, Free Press, London.

Harbison, F. and Myers, C. A. (1959). *Management in an Industrial World*, McGraw Hill, New York.

Hawthorne, G. (1976). *Enlightenment and Despair: A History of Sociology*, Cambridge University Press, London.

Hayek, F. A. von (1955). *The Counter-Revolution of Science: Studies in the Abuse of Reason*, Free Press, Glencoe, Ill.

Hazard, P. (1965). *European Thought in the Eighteenth Century*, Penguin, Harmondsworth.

Heath, A. (1981). *Social Mobility*, Fontana, Glasgow.

Heilbroner, R. L. (1962). 'The Impact of Technology: the Western Debate' in J.T. Dunlop (ed.), *Automation and Technical Change*, Prentice Hall, New Jersey.

—— (1977). *Business Civilization in Decline*, Penguin, Harmondsworth.

Hegel, G. W. F. (1964) *Philosophy of Mind*, A.T.U., London.

—— (1980). *Lectures on the Philosophy of World History: An Introduction*, Cambridge University Press, Cambridge.

Held, D. (1980). *Introduction to Critical Theory: Horkheimer to Habermas*, Hutchinson, London.

Hindess, B. (1973). *The Use of Official Statistics in Sociology: A Critique of Positivism and Ethno-methodology*, Macmillan, London.

—— (ed.) (1976). *Economy and Society: Sociological Theories of the Economy*, Harvester Press, London.

—— (1977). *Philosophy and Methodology in the Social Sciences*, Harvester Press, London.

Hindess, B. and Hirst, P.Q. (1975). *Pre-Capitalist Modes of Production*, Routledge and Kegan Paul, London.

Hirsch, F. (1977). *The Social Limits to Growth*, Routledge and Kegan Paul, London.

Hirst, P. Q. (1975). *Durkheim, Bernard and Epistemology*, Routledge and Kegan Paul, London.

—— (1976a). *Social Evolution and Sociological Categories*, George Allen and Unwin, London.

—— (1976b) 'A Theory of Ideology', *Economy and Society*, vol.5, pp. 385–412.

Hirszowicz, M. (1981). *Industrial Sociology: An Introduction*, Martin Robertson, London.

Hodgson, H.C. (1972). *The Diseconomics of Growth*, Pan/Ballantyne, London.

Holt, R. J. and Turner, J. E. (1970). *The Methodology of Comparative Research*, Free Press, New York.

Hoogvelt, A. M. (1976). *The Sociology of Developing Societies*, Macmillan, London.

Hook, S. (1971). *From Hegel to Marx: Studies in the Intellectual Development of Karl Marx*, Ann Arbor, Michigan.

Horkheimer, M. (1972). *Critical Theory: Selected Essays*, Herder and Herder, New York.

—— (1974). *Eclipse of Reason*, Seabury Press, New York.

—— (1976). 'Traditional and Critical Theory' in Connerton (1976).

Horkheimer, M. and Adorno, T. (1972). *The Dialectic of Enlightenment*, Herder and Herder, New York.

Horowitz, I. (1974–5). 'Sociology and Futurology', *Berkeley Journal of Sociology*.

Hoselitz, B. F. and Moore, W. D. (eds) (1963). *Industrialization and Society*, UNESCO, Mauton.

Hume, D. (1888). *Treatise on Human Nature*, Oxford University Press, Oxford.

Hunt, A. (ed.) (1978). *Class and Class Structure*, Lawrence and Wishart, London.

Hunt, E. K. and Schwartz, J. G. (eds) (1972). *A Critique of Economic Theory*, Penguin, Harmondsworth.

Huntington, S. P. (1965). *Political Order in Changing Societies*, Yale University Press, New Haven.
—— (1965b). 'Political Development and Political Decay', *World Politics*, vol. 17, no. 3, pp. 386–430.
—— (1971). 'The Change to Change: Modernisation Development and Politics', *Comparative Politics*, vol. 3, no. 3, pp. 283–322.
Iggers, G. G. (ed.) (1972). *The Doctrine of Saint-Simon: An Exposition*, Schocken Books, New York.
Illich, I. D. (1971). *Deschooling Society*, Calder and Boyars, London.
—— (1974). *Energy and Equity*, Calder and Boyars, London.
—— (1975) *Tools for Conviviality*, Fontana, Glasgow.
—— (1976). *Limits to Medicine – the Medical Nemesis: Expropriation of Health*, Penguin, Harmondsworth.
—— (1977). *Celebration of Awareness*, Penguin, Harmondsworth.
Inkeles, A. (1960–1). 'Industrial Man. The Relation of Status to Experience, Perception and Values', *American Journal of Sociology*, vol. 66, no. 1, pp. 1–31.
Inkeles, A. and Geiger, K. (eds) (1961). *Soviet Society: A Book of Readings*, John Constable, London.
Ionescu, G. (1975). *Centripetal Politics: Government and the New Centres of Power*, Hart Davis MacGibbon, London.
—— (ed.) (1976). *The Political Thought of Saint-Simon*, Oxford University Press, London.
Jay, M. (1973). *The Dialectical Imagination: A History of the Frankfurt School and the Institute of Social Research. 1921–50*, Heinemann, London.
—— (1977). 'The Concept of Totality in Lukács and Adorno', *Telos*, no. 32, Summer, pp. 117–39.
Johnston, R. and Gummett R. (eds) (1979). *Directing Technology*, Croom Helm, London.
Jones, B. (1983). *Sleepers Wake!: Technology and the Future of Work*, Oxford University Press, Melbourne.
Kahn, H. (1978). *The Next Two Hundred Years*, Abacus, London.
Kahn, H. and Wiener, A. (1967). *The Year 2000*, Macmillan, New York.
Kalberg, S. (1980). 'Max Weber's Types of Rationality: Concepts for the Analysis of Rationalisation Processes in History', *American Journal of Sociology*, vol. 85, pp. 1145–78.
Kaysen, C. (1957). 'The Social Significance of the Modern Corporation', *American Economic Review*, vol. 47, no. 2, pp. 311–19.
Keane, J. (1975). 'Habermas on Work and Interaction', *New German Critique*, no. 6, Fall.
Keat, R. (1981). *The Politics of Social Theory*, Routledge and Kegan Paul, London. ·
Keat, R. and Urry, J. (1975). *Social Theory as Science*, Routledge and Kegan Paul, London.
Kemp, T. (1978). *Historical Patterns of Industrialization*, Longman, London.
Kerr, C., Dunlop, J. T., Harbison, F. H. and Meyers, C. A. (1973). *Industrialism and Industrial Man: The Problems of Labor and Management in Economic Growth*, Penguin, Harmondsworth.
Keynes, J. M. (1926). *The End of Laissez Faire*, Hogarth Press, London.
—— (1951). *Essays in Persuasion*, Rupert Hart Davis, London.
Kidron, M. (1976). *The Disintegrating West*, Penguin, Harmondsworth.
Kolakowski, L. (1971). *Marxism and Beyond: On Historical Understanding and Individual Responsibility*, Paladin, London.
—— (1978). *Main Currents of Marxism: Its Rise, Growth and Dissolution*, Clarendon Press, Oxford.
Kolegar, F. (1978). 'The Concept of Rationalization and Cultural Pessimism in Max Weber's Sociology', *Sociological Quarterly*, vol. 19, pp. 355–73.

Kolko, G. (1960). 'A Critique of Max Weber's "Philosophy of History"', *Ethics*, vol.70, pp. 21–36.

Kumar, K. (ed.) (1971a). *Revolution. The Theory and Practice of a European Idea*, Weidenfeld and Nicolson, London.

—— (1971b) 'Futurology', *The Listener*, 18 February, pp. 204–6.

—— (1978). *Prophecy and Progress: the Sociology of Industrial and Post-Industrial Societies*, Penguin, Harmondsworth.

Laclau, E. (1975). 'The Specificity of the Political: The Poulantzas–Miliband Debate' *Economy and Society*, vol. 4, pp. 89–110.

Landes, D. (1969). *The Unbound Prometheus: Technological Change and Industrial Development in the Western World from 1750 to the Present*, Cambridge University Press, Cambridge.

Lane, D. (1970). *Politics and Society in the USSR*, Weidenfeld and Nicolson, London.

—— (1976). *The Socialist Industrial State*, George Allen and Unwin, London.

Lasch, C. (1972). 'Toward a Theory of Post-Industrial Society', in Hancock and Sjoberg (1972).

Laslett, P. (1975). *The World We Have Lost*, Methuen, London.

Laslett, P. and Runciman, W. G. (eds) (1969). *Philosophy, Politics and Society*, 3rd series, Longman, London.

Leiss, W. (1978). *The Limits to Satisfaction: On Needs and Commodities*, Marion Boyars, London.

Lichtheim, G. (1966). *Marxism in Modern France*, Columbia University press, New York.

Lindberg, L. N. (ed.) (1976). *Politics and the Future of Industrial Societies: Comparative Studies of Political Life*, David MacKay, New York.

Lipset, S. M. (1969). *Political Man*, Heinemann, London.

—— (1972). 'Ideology and No End: the Controversy Till Now', *Encounter*, no. 39, July–December, pp. 17–22.

Lipset, S. M. and Bendix, R. (1959). *Social Mobility in Industrial Society*, University of California Press.

—— (eds) (1967). *Class, Status and Party: Social Stratification in Historical Perspective*, Routledge and Kegan Paul, London.

Lipsey, R. C. (1976) *An Introduction to Positive Economics*, Weidenfeld and Nicolson, London.

Lockwood, D. (1958). *The Black Coated Worker: A Study of Class Consciousness* George Allen and Unwin, London.

—— (1964). 'Social Integration and System Integration' in A. Etzioni and E. Etzioni (eds), *Social Change: Sources, Patterns and Consequences*, Basic Books, New York.

—— (1966). 'The Sources of Variation in Working Class Images of Society', *Socialist Review*, vol. 14, pp. 249–67.

Lovins, A. (1977). *Soft Energy Paths*, Penguin, Harmondsworth.

Lukács, G. (1971). *History and Class Consciousness*, Merlin Press, London.

—— (1972). 'Max Weber and German Sociology', *Economy and Society*, vol. 1, pp. 386–98.

Lukes, S. (1973a). *Emile Durkheim: His Life and Work. A Historical and Critical Study*, Allen Lane The Penguin Press, Harmondsworth.

—— (1973b). *Individualism*, Basil Blackwell, London.

—— (1975). *Power: A Radical View*, Macmillan, London.

—— (1978). *Essays in Social Theory*, Macmillan, London.

MacIntyre, A. C. (1964) Breaking the Chains of Reason' in *Out of Apathy*.

—— (1971a). *Marxism and Christianity*, Penguin, Harmondsworth.

—— (1971b). *Against the Self Images of the Age: Essays in Ideology and Philosophy*, Duckworth, London.

—— (1975). *Marcuse*, Fontana/Collins, Glasgow.

—— (1976). *A Short History of Ethics*, Routledge and Kegan Paul, London.

MacKenzie, G. (1973). *Aristocracy of Labour*, Cambridge University Press, Cambridge.

Macridis, R. C. and Brown, B. E. (eds) (1972). *Comparative Politics: Notes and Readings*, Dorsey Press, Ill.

Magee, B. (1970). *Popper*, Fontana/Collins, Glasgow.

Mallet, S. (1975). *Essays on the New Working Class*, Spokesman Books, London.

Mandel, E. (1976). *Late Capitalism*, New Left Books, London.

Mandelbaum, M. (1971). *History, Man and Reason: A Study in Nineteenth Century Thought*, John Hopkins, London.

Mann, M. (1970). 'The Social Cohesion of Liberal Democracy', *American Sociological Review*, vol. 38, no. 3, pp. 423–39.

—— (1973). *Consciousness and Action Among the Western Working Class*, Macmillan, London.

Mannheim, K. (1940). *Man and Society in an Age of Reconstruction*, Routledge and Kegan Paul, London.

—— (1972). *Ideology and Utopia: An Introduction to the Sociology of Knowledge*, Routledge and Kegan Paul, London.

Manuel, F. E. (1956). *The New World of Henri Saint-Simon*, Harvard University Press, Cambridge, Mass.

—— (1962). *Prophets of Paris*, Harvard University Press, Cambridge, Mass.

—— (ed.) (1965). *The Enlightenment*, Prentice Hall, Englewood Cliffs, N. J.

—— (ed.) (1966). *Utopias and Utopian Thought*, Souvenir Press, London.

—— (1971). *Freedom from History*, University Press, London.

Maravall, J. M. (1976). 'Subjective Conditions and Revolutionary Consciousness', *British Journal of Sociology*, vol. 27, no. 1, pp. 21–34.

—— (1979). 'The Limits of Reformism: Parliamentary Socialism and the Marxist Theory of the State', *British Journal of Sociology*, vol. 30, pp. 286–87.

Marcuse, H. (1962). *Eros and Civilisation*, Vintage Books, New York.

—— (1971). *Soviet Marxism*, Pelican Books, London.

—— (1972). *Negations: Essays in Critical Theory*, Penguin, Harmondsworth.

—— (1974). *One Dimensional Man*, Abacus, London.

—— (1977). *Reason and Revolution: Hegel and the Rise of Social Theory*, Routledge and Kegan Paul, London.

Margolis, M. (1979). *Viable Democracy*, Penguin, Harmondsworth.

Markham, F. (ed.) (1964). *Henri de Saint-Simon: Social Organisation, the Science of Man and Other Writings*, Harper and Row, New York.

Marsh, R. M. (1967). *Comparative Sociology*, Harcourt Brace and World Inc., New York

Marx, K. (1970a). *Capital*, vol. 1, Lawrence and Wishart, London.

—— (1970b). *Capital*, vol. 3, Lawrence and Wishart, London.

Marx, K. and Engels, F. (1970). *The German Ideology* Part I, Lawrence and Wishart, London.

—— (1978). *The Poverty of Philosophy – Answer to the 'Philosophy of Poverty' by M. Proudhon*, Foreign Languages Press, Peking.

Maynaud, J. (1968). *Technocracy*, Faber and Faber, London.

Mayo, E. (1946). *The Human Problems of an Industrial Civilisation*, Harvard University Press, Cambridge, Mass.

—— (1949). *The Social Problems of an Industrial Civilisation*, Routledge and Kegan Paul, London.

McCarthy, T. (1978). *The Critical Theory of J. Habermas*, Hutchinson, London.

Meadows, D. H., Meadows, D. L., Randers, J and Behrens III W. W. (1975). *The Limits to Growth*, Pan, London.

Meek, R. (1973). *Turgot on Progress, Sociology and Economics*, Cambridge University Press, Cambridge.
—— (ed.) (1976). *Social Science and the Ignoble Savage*, Cambridge University Press, Cambridge.
Mennell, S. (1974). *Sociological Theory: Uses and Unities*, Thomas Nelson, London.
Merton, R. K. (1968). *Social Theory and Social Structure*, Free Press, New York.
Mestzaros, I. (1970). *Marx's Theory of Alienation*, Merlin Press, London.
Miliband, R. (1973). *The State in Capitalist Society*, Quartet, London.
—— (1974). 'Marx on the State', *Socialist Register*, Merlin Press, London.
—— (1976). *Marxism and Politics*, Oxford University Press, Oxford.
Mill, J. S. (1879). *A System of Logic*, Longman Green, London.
Miller, S. M. (1975). 'Notes on Neo-Capitalism', *Theory and Society*, vol. 2, pp. 1–37.
Mills, C. Wright. (1951). *White Collar: The American Middle Classes*, Oxford University Press, London.
—— (1956). *The Power Elite*, Oxford University Press, New York.
—— (1975). *The Sociological Imagination*, Penguin, Harmondsworth.
Mishan, E. J. (1969). *The Cost of Economic Growth*, Penguin, Harmondsworth.
—— (1977). *The Economic Growth Debate: An Assessment*, George Allen and Unwin, London.
Montesquieu, B. (1962). *The Spirit of the Laws*, Hafner, New York.
Moore, Jr., B. (1967). *Social Origins of Dictatorship and Democracy*, Allen Lane, London.
Moore, W. E. (1963). *The Impact of Industry: Modernisation of Traditional Societies*, Prentice Hall, Englewood Cliffs, NJ.
—— (1967). *Order and Change. Essays in Comparative Sociology*, J. Wiley and Sons, New York.
—— (ed.) (1972). *Technology and Social Change*, Quadrangle, Chicago.
—— (1973). *Social Change*, Prentice Hall, Englewood Cliffs NJ.
Mueller, G. M. (1979). 'The Notion of Rationality in the Work of Max Weber', *European Journal of Sociology*, vol. 2, pp. 149–71.
Mumford, L. (1934). *Technics and Civilisation*, Routledge and Kegan Paul, London.
Nichols, T. (1960). *Ownership Control and Ideology*, George Allen and Unwin, London.
Nietzsche, F. (1968). *The Will to Power*, Vintage, New York.
Nisbet, R. (1967). *The Sociological Tradition*, Heinemann, London.
—— (1969). *Social Change and History: Aspects of the Western Theory of Development*, Oxford University Press, Oxford.
—— (1980). *History of the Idea of Progress*, Heinemann, London.
Norris, K. and Vaizey, J. (1973). *The Economics of Research and Technology*, George Allen and Unwin, London.
O'Connor, J. (1966). 'Monopoly Capital', *New Left Review*, no. 40, pp. 38–50.
—— (1973). *The Fiscal Crisis of the State*, St James's Press, London.
Offe, C. (1976). *Industry and Inequality: The Achievement Principle in Work and Social Status*, Edward Arnold, London.
Ogburn, W. F. (1964). 'The Culture Lag' in Duncan (1964).
Ogburn, W. F. and Nimkoff, M. (1966). *Sociology*, Riverside Press, Cambridge, Mass.
O'Neill, J. (1972). *Sociology as a Skin Trade: Essays Towards a Reflexive Sociology*, Heinemann, London.
Out of Apathy (1964). New Left Books, London.
Outhwaite, W. (1975). *Understanding Social Life: The Method Called Verstehen*, George Allen and Unwin, London.

Overend, T. (1978). 'Habermas' Trichotomous Conception of Science, Enquiry and Ideology', *Philosophy of the Social Sciences*, vol. 8, pp. 1–13.

Pacey, A. (1983). *The Culture of Technology*, Basil Blackwell, Oxford.

Packard, V. (1964). *The Waste Makers*, Penguin, Harmondsworth.

—— (1974). *The Hidden Persuaders*, Pocket Books, New York.

Pahl, R. E. and Winkler, J. (1974). 'The Coming Corporatism', *New Society*, 10 October.

Panitch, L. (1977). 'The Development of Corporatism in Liberal Deomocracies', *Comparative Political Studies*, vol. 10, no. 1, pp. 61–90.

—— (1980). 'Recent Theories of Corporatism', *British Journal of Sociology*, vol. 31, no. 2.

Parkin, F. (ed.) (1974). *The Social Analysis of Class Structure*, Tavistock, London.

—— (1975). *Class Inequality and Political Order*, Paladin, London.

—— (1979). *Marxism and Class Theory: A Bourgeois Critique*, Tavistock, London.

Parry, G. (1969). *Political Elites*, George Allen and Unwin, London.

Parsons, T. (1949). *Essays in Social Theory*, Free Press, New York.

—— (1964). 'Evolutionary Universals', *American Sociological Review*, vol. 29, pp. 339–57.

—— (1966). *Societies: Evolutionary and Comparative Perspectives*, Prentice Hall, Englewood Cliffs, NJ.

—— (1968). *The Structure of Social Action*, Free Press, New York.

Passmore, J. (1965) *The Perfectability of Man*, Cambridge University Press, Cambridge.

—— (1975). 'The Poverty of Historicism Revisited', *History and Theory*, vol. 14, pp. 30–47.

Pateman, C. (1971). *Participation and Democracy*, Edward Arnold, London.

Payne, G. (1973). 'Comparative Sociology: Some Problems of Theory and Method', *British Journal of Sociology*, vol. 24, pp. 13–23.

—— (1977). 'Occupational Transition in Advanced Industrial Societies', *Sociological Review*, vol. 25, no. 1.

Peel, J. Y. D. (1971). *Herbert Spencer: The Evolution of a Sociologist*, Heinemann, London.

Peterson, R. A. (1973). *The Industrial Order and Social Policy*, Prentice Hall, Englewood Cliffs, NJ.

Plamenatz, J. (1963). *Man and Society: A Critical Examination of Some Important Social and Political Theories from Machiavelli to Marx*, Longman, London.

Platt, J. A. (1964). 'A Comment on Social Stratification in Industrial Societies' in P. Habies (ed.), *The Development of Industrial Society*, Kiel University.

Polack, F. L. (1961). *The Image of the Future: Enlightening the Past, Orientating the Present, Forecasting the Future*, vol. 1: *The Promised Land: Source of Living Culture*, vol. 2: *Iconoclasses of the Images of the Future Dissolution of Culture*, Leyden, Sijthoff.

Pollard, S. (1971). *The Idea of Progress*, Penguin, Harmondsworth.

Popper, K. (1969a). *The Open Society and its Enemies*, vol. 1: *The Spell of Plato*, Routledge and Kegan Paul, London.

—— (1969b). *The Open Society and its Enemies*, vol.2: *The High Tide of Prophecy: Hegel and Marx*, Routledge and Kegan Paul, London.

—— (1974). *The Poverty of Historicism*, Routledge and Kegan Paul, London.

Poster, M. (1975). *Existentialist Marxism in Post-War France: From Sartre to Althusser*, Princeton University Press.

Poulantzas, N. (1973). *Political Power and Social Class*, New Left Books, London.

—— (1975). *Classes in Contemporary Capitalism*, New Left Books, London.

—— (1979). *State, Power and Socialism*, New Left Books, London.

Quinton, A. (ed.) (1967). *Political Philosophy*, Oxford University Press, London.

—— (1974). 'Critical Theory', *Encounter*, October.

Raison, T. (ed.) (1969) *The Founding Fathers of Social Science*, Penguin, Harmondsworth.

Raynor, J. (1971). *The Middle Class*, Longman, London.

Reich, C. (1974). *The Greening of America*, Penguin, Harmondsworth.

Remmling, G. W. (1975). *The Sociology of Karl Mannheim: with a Bibliographical Guide to the Sociology of Knowledge*, Routledge and Regan Paul, London.

Rex, J. (1972). *Discovering Sociology*, Routledge and Kegan Paul, London.

Richards, D. and Hunt, J. W. (1973). *An Illustrated History of Modern Britain: 1783–1964*, Longman, London.

Roberts, K. *et al.* (1977). *The Fragmentary Class Structure*, Heinemann, London.

Rose, G. (1978). *The Melancholy Science. An Introduction to the Thought of Theodor W. Adorno*, Macmillan, London.

Ross, G. (1974). 'The Second Coming of Daniel Bell', in *Socialist Register*, Merlin Press, London.

Rostow, W. W. (1971a). *The Stages of Economic Growth*, Cambridge University Press, Cambridge.

——(1971b). *Politics and the Stages of Growth*, Cambridge University Press, Cambridge.

Roszak, T. (1970). *The Making of a Counter-Culture*, Faber and Faber, London.

—— (1973). *Where the Wasteland Ends: Politics and Transcendence in the Post-Industrial Society*, Faber and Faber, London.

Roth, G. and Wolfgang, S. (eds) (1979). *Max Webers Vision of History: Ethics and Methods*, University of California Press.

Rousseaus, S. W. and Fargais, J. (1963). 'American Politics and the End of Ideology', *British Journal of Sociology*, no. 14.

Rowthorn, B. (1976). 'Late Capitalism', *New Left Review*, no. 98, pp. 59–84.

——(1980). 'Capitalism, Conflict and Inflation', Lawrence and Wishart, London.

Rumney, J. (1934). *Herbert Spencer*, Williams and Norgate, London.

Runciman, W. G. (1971). *Social Science and Political Theory*, Cambridge University Press, Cambridge.

—— (1972) *A Critique of Max Weber's Philosophy of Social Science*, Cambridge University Press, Cambridge.

Russell, B. (1974). *The Problems of Philosophy*, Oxford University Press, London.

——(1981). *The History of Western Philosophy*, Penguin, Harmondsworth.

Sabine, G. (1966). *A History of Political Theory*, Harrap, London.

Salaman, G. (1981). *Class and Corporation*, Fontana, Glasgow.

Samuelson, P.A. (1976). *Economics: An Introductory Analysis*, McGraw Hill, New York.

Scase, R. (1977a). *Social Democracy in Capitalist Societies: A Comparative Study of Britain and Sweden*, Croom Helm, London.

—— (ed.) (1977b). *Industrial Society: Class, Cleavage and Control*, George Allen and Unwin, London.

Schapiro, J. S. (1963). *Condorcet and the Rise of Liberalism*, Octagon Book, New York.

Schitovsky, T. (1976). *The Joyless Economy: An Inquiry Into Human Satisfaction and Consumer Dissatisfaction*, Oxford Univerisity Press, New York.

Schmitter, P. (1974). 'Still the Century of Corporatism', *Review of Politics*, vol. 36. pp. 85–131

Schon, D. (1973). *Beyond the Stable State: Public and Private Learning in a Changing Society*, Penguin, Harmondsworth.

Schroyer, T. (1973). *The Critique of Domination*, George Brazilier, New York.

—— (1978). 'The Repoliticisation of the Relations of Production', *New German Critique*, no. 5. Spring, pp. 107–29.

Schumacher, E. (1978). *Small is Beautiful: A Study of Economics As If People Really Mattered*, Abacus, London.

Schumpeter, J. A. (1954). *Capitalism, Socialism and Democracy*, George Allen and Unwin, London.

Scott, J. P. (1978). 'Critical Social Theory: An Introduction and Critique', *British Journal of Sociology*, vol. 29, no. 1, pp. 1–20.
—— (1979). *Corporations, Classes and Capitalism*, Hutchinson, London.
Seidenberg, R. (1950). *Post-Historic Man*, Chapel Hill, NC.
Shaw, W. H. (1978). *Marx's Theory of History*, Hutchinson, London.
Shils, E. Q. (1955). 'End of Ideology' *Encounter*, no. 5.
Shklar, J. (1957). *After Utopia: The Decline of Political Faith*, Princeton University Press.
Shonfield, A. (1965). *Modern Capitalism: The Changing Balance of Private and Public Power*, Cambridge University Press, Cambridge.
Simey, T. S. (1968). *Social Science and Social Purpose*, John Constable, London.
Skinner, R. J. (1976). 'Technological Determinism: A Critique of Convergence Theory', *Comparative Studies in Society and History*, vol. 18, pp. 2–27.
Sklar, L. (1970). *The Sociology of Progress*, Routledge and Kegan Paul, London.
—— (1974). 'The Idea of Progress' in R. Nisbet (ed.) *The Science of Society and the Unity of Mankind*, Heinemann, London.
Slater, P. (1977). *The Origin and Significance of the Frankfurt School: a Marxist Perspective*, Routledge and Kegan Paul, London.
Smelser, N. J. (1976). *Comparative Methods in the Social Sciences*, Prentice Hall, Englewood Cliffs, NJ.
Smelser, N. J. and Warner, R. S. (1976). *Sociological Theory: Historical and Formal*, General Lewing Press, New York.
Smith, A. D. (1973). *The Concept of Social Change. A Critique of the Evolutionary Theory of Social Change*, Routledge and Kegan Paul, London.
—— (1976). *Social Change*, Longman, London.
Spencer, H. (1896). *The Principles of Sociology*, vol. iii, Williams and Norgate, London.
—— (1968). *Reasons for Dissenting from the Philosophy of M. Comte and Other Essays*, The Glendessary Press, Berkeley.
—— (1969). *The Principles of Sociology*, Macmillan, London.
Spengler, O, (1926). *The Decline of the West*, George Allen and Unwin, London.
Stanworth, P. and Giddens, A. (eds) (1974). *Politics and Power in British Society*, Cambridge University Press, Cambridge.
Steedman, I. (1981). *Marx After Sraffa*, Verso, London.
Steedman, I. *et al* (1981). *The Value Controversy*, Verso, London.
Stockmann, N. (1978) 'Habermas, Marcuse and the Aufhebung of Science and Technology', *Philosophy of Social Science*, vol. 8, pp. 15–35.
Strasser, H. and Randall, S. C. (1981). *An Introduction to Theories of Social Charge*, Routledge and Kegan Paul, London.
Straussman, J. D. (1975). 'What Did Tomorrow's Future Look Like Yesterday?' *Comparative Politics*, vol. 8, no. 7, pp. 166–82.
Sweezy, P. M. (1946). *The Theory of Capitalist Development*, Dobson, London, reprinted 1962.
—— (1972). *Modern Capitalism and Other Essays*, Monthly Review Press, New York.
Swidler, A. (1973). 'The Concept of Rationality in the Work of Max Weber', *Sociological Inquiry*, vol. 43, pp. 35–42.
Swingewood, A. (1976). *Marx and Modern Social Theory*, Macmillan, London.
Talmon, J. L. (1952). *The Origins of Totalitarian Democracy*, Secker and Warburg, London.
Tawney, R. H. (1920). *The Acquisitive Society*, Harcourt Brace, New York.
Taylor, C. (1969). 'Neutrality in Political Science', in P. Laslett and W. G. Runciman, (1969).
—— (1978a) *Hegel*, Cambridge University Press, Cambridge.
—— (1978b) *Hegel and Modern Social Theory*, Cambridge University Press, Cambridge.

Therborn, G. (1970). 'The Frankfurt School', *New Left Reveiw*, no. 63.
—— (1971). 'Habermas: A New Eclectic', *New Left Review*, no. 67, May–June, pp. 69–84.
—— (1977). *Science, Class and Society: On the Formation of Sociology and Historical Materialism*, New Left Books, London.
Tipps, D. (1973). 'Modernisation Theory and the Comparative Study of Societies: A Critical Perspective', *Comparative Studies in Society and History*, vol. 15, no. 2, pp. 199–226.
Toffler, A. (1975). *Future Shock*, Pan, London.
—— (1981). *The Third Wave*, Pan, London.
Touraine, A. (1974). *The Post-Industrial Society*, Wildwood House, London.
—— (1977). 'Crisis of Transformation' in N. Birnbaum (1977).
Trebilcock, C. (1981). *The Industrialisation of the Continental Powers*, Longman, London.
Treiman, D. J. (1975). Industrialization and Social Stratification, *Sociological Enquiry*, no. 40, p. 70.
Turner, B. (1975). *Industrialism*, Longman, London.
Turner, G. (1963). *The Car Makers*, Eyre and Spottiswoode, London.
Turner, J. H. (1974). *The Structure of Social Theory*, Dorsey Press, Homewood. Ill.
Urry, J. and Wakeford, J. (eds) (1973). *Power in Britain*. Heinemann, London.
Vallier, I. (ed.) (1971). *Comparative Methods in Sociology*, University of California Press.
Veblen, T. (1965a). *The Theory of the Business Enterprise*, in *The Writings of Thorstein Veblen*. vol. 2, Kelley, New York.
—— (1956). *The Engineers and the Price System*, in *The Writings of Thorstein Veblen*, vol. 8.
Veltmeyer, H. (1974). 'Towards an Assessment of the Structuralist Interrogation of Marx', *Science and Society*, vol. 38, no. 4.
Vyerberg, H. (1958). *Historical Pessimism in the French Enlightenment*, Harvard University Press, Cambridge, Mass.
Walton, P. and Gamble, A. (1972). *From Alienation to Surplus Value*, Sheed and Ward, London.
Ward, B. (1979). *Progress for a Small Planet*, Penguin, Harmondsworth.
Watson, A. J. (1980). *Sociology, Work and Industry*, Routledge and Kegan Paul, London.
Weber, M. (1961). *General Economic History*, Collier, New York.
—— (1968). *Economy and Society*, vol. III, Bedminster Press, New York.
—— (1969). *The Theory of Social and Economic Organisation*, Free Press, New York.
—— (1974) *The Protestant Ethic and the Spirit of Capitalism*, George Allen and Unwin, London.
Wedderburn, D. (ed.) (1974). *Poverty, Inequality and Class Structure*, Cambridge University Press, Cambridge.
Weinberg, I. (1969). 'The Problems of the Convergence of Industrial Societies: A Critical Look at the State of a Theory' *Comparative Studies in Society and History*, vol. 3, no. 1, pp. 1–15.
Wellmer, A. (1974). *Critical Theory of Society*, Seabury Press, New York.
Westergaard, J. H. (1970). 'The Rediscovery of the Cash Nexus', *Socialist Register*, Merlin Press, London.
—— (1972). 'The Myth of Classlessness' in Blackburn (1972).
—— (1978). 'Class, Inequality and Corporatism' in Hunt (1978).
Westergaard, J. H. and Resler, H. (1977). *Class in a Capitalist Society*, Penguin, Harmondsworth.
Wiener, N. (1968). *The Human Use of Human Beings: Cybernetics and Society*, Sphere, London.

Williams Raymond. (1961) *The Long Revolution*, Penguin, Harmondsworth.
—— (1974). *Television, Technology and Cultural Form*, Fontana, Glasgow.
—— (1975). *Culture and Society 1780–1950*, Penguin, Harmondsworth.
—— (1980). *Keywords: A Vocabulary of Culture and Society*, Fontana, Glasgow.
—— (1983). *Towards 2000*, Heinemann, London.
Williams, Roger. (1971). *Politics and Technology*, Macmillan, London.
Winkler, J. (1976). 'Corporatism', *European Journal of Sociology*, vol. 17, no. 10.
—— (1977). 'Corporatism' in Scase (1977b).
Winner, L. (1977). *Autonomous Technology: Technics Out of Control as a Theme in Political Thought*, MIT Press, Cambridge, Mass.
Wolin, S. (1961). *Politics and Vision: Continuity and Innovation in Western Political Thought*, George Allen and Unwin, London.
Woodweiss, T. (1978). 'Critical Theory and the Capitalist State', *Economy and Society*, vol. 7, no. 2, May.
Woozley, A. D. (1976). *The Theory of Knowledge*, Huchinson, London.
Wrong, D. (ed.) (1970). *Max Weber*, Prentice Hall, Englewood Cliffs, NJ.
Young, M. (1965) *The Rise of the Meritocracy: An Essay on Education and Equality*, Penguin, Harmondsworth.
—— (ed.) (1968). *Forecasting and the Social Sciences*, Heinemann. London.
Zeitlin, M. (1974). 'Corporate Ownership and Control: The Large Corporation and the Capitalist Class', *American Journal of Sociology*, vol. 79, no. 5, pp. 1073–1119.
Zweig, F. (1961). *The Worker in an Affluent Society*, Heinemann, London.

INDEX